FIGHTH
EDITION

Introduction to
ECONOMIC
REASONING

WILLIAM D. ROHLF, JR.
Drury University

Addison-Wesley

Boston   Columbus   Indianapolis   New York   San Francisco   Upper Saddle River
Amsterdam   Cape Town   Dubai   London   Madrid   Milan   Munich   Paris   Montreal   Toronto
Delhi   Mexico City   Sao Paulo   Sydney   Hong Kong   Seoul   Singapore   Taipei   Tokyo

The Pearson Series in Economics

Abel/Bernanke/Croushore
Macroeconomics*

Bade/Parkin
Foundations of Economics*

Bierman/Fernandez
Game Theory with Economic Applications

Blanchard
Macroeconomics

Blau/Ferber/Winkler
The Economics of Women, Men and Work

Boardman/Greenberg/Vining/ Weimer
Cost-Benefit Analysis

Boyer
Principles of Transportation Economics

Branson
Macroeconomic Theory and Policy

Brock/Adams
The Structure of American Industry

Bruce
Public Finance and the American Economy

Carlton/Perloff
Modern Industrial Organization

Case/Fair/Oster
Principles of Economics*

Caves/Frankel/Jones
World Trade and Payments: An Introduction

Chapman
Environmental Economics: Theory, Application, and Policy

Cooter/Ulen
Law & Economics

Downs
An Economic Theory of Democracy

Ehrenberg/Smith
Modern Labor Economics

Ekelund/Ressler/Tollison
Economics*

Farnham
Economics for Managers

Folland/Goodman/Stano
The Economics of Health and Health Care

Fort
Sports Economics

Froyen
Macroeconomics

Fusfeld
The Age of the Economist

Gerber
International Economics

Gordon
Macroeconomics

Greene
Econometric Analysis

Gregory
Essentials of Economics

Gregory/Stuart
Russian and Soviet Economic Performance and Structure

Hartwick/Olewiler
The Economics of Natural Resource Use

Heilbroner/Milberg
The Making of the Economic Society

Heyne/Boettke/Prychitko
The Economic Way of Thinking

Hoffman/Averett
Women and the Economy: Family, Work, and Pay

Holt
Markets, Games and Strategic Behavior

Hubbard
Money, the Financial System, and the Economy

Hubbard/OBrien
Economics*

Hughes/Cain
American Economic History

Husted/Melvin
International Economics

Jehle/Reny
Advanced Microeconomic Theory

Johnson-Lans
A Health Economics Primer

Keat/Young
Managerial Economics

Klein
Mathematical Methods for Economics

Krugman/Obstfeld
International Economics: Theory & Policy*

Laidler
The Demand for Money

Leeds/von Allmen
The Economics of Sports

Leeds/von Allmen/Schiming
Economics*

Lipsey/Ragan/Storer
Economics*

Lynn
Economic Development: Theory and Practice for a Divided World

Melvin
International Money and Finance

Miller
Economics Today*

Understanding Modern Economics

Miller/Benjamin
The Economics of Macro Issues

Miller/Benjamin/North
The Economics of Public Issues

Mills/Hamilton
Urban Economics

Mishkin
The Economics of Money, Banking, and Financial Markets*

The Economics of Money, Banking, and Financial Markets, Business School Edition*

Murray
Econometrics: A Modern Introduction

Nafziger
The Economics of Developing Countries

O'Sullivan/Sheffrin/Perez
Economics: Principles, Applications and Tools*

Parkin
Economics*

Perloff
Microeconomics*

Microeconomics: Theory and Applications with Calculus

Perman/Common/ McGilvray/Ma
Natural Resources and Environmental Economics

Phelps
Health Economics

Pindyck/Rubinfeld
Microeconomics*

Riddell/Shackelford/Stamos/ Schneider
Economics: A Tool for Critically Understanding Society

Ritter/Silber/Udell
Principles of Money, Banking & Financial Markets*

Roberts
The Choice: A Fable of Free Trade and Protection

Rohlf
Introduction to Economic Reasoning

Ruffin/Gregory
Principles of Economics

Sargent
Rational Expectations and Inflation

Sawyer/Sprinkle
International Economics

Scherer
Industry Structure, Strategy, and Public Policy

Schiller
The Economics of Poverty and Discrimination

Sherman
Market Regulation

Silberberg
Principles of Microeconomics

Stock/Watson
Introduction to Econometrics

Introduction to Econometrics, Brief Edition

Studenmund
Using Econometrics: A Practical Guide

Tietenberg/Lewis
Environmental and Natural Resource Economics

Environmental Economics and Policy

Todaro/Smith
Economic Development

Waldman
Microeconomics

Waldman/Jensen
Industrial Organization: Theory and Practice

Weil
Economic Growth

Williamson
Macroeconomics

---

*denotes **myeconlab** titles   Log onto www.myeconlab.com to learn more

To my parents, who helped me learn the value of persistence.

Editorial Director: Sally Yagan
Editor in Chief: Donna Battista
Acquisitions Editor: Noel Kamm Seibert
Editorial Assistant: Carolyn Terbush
Executive Marketing Manager: Lori DeShazo
Senior Manufacturing Buyer: Carol Melville
Marketing Assistant: Justin Jacob
Managing Editor: Nancy H. Fenton
Senior Production Project Manager: Nancy Freihofer
Permissions Project Supervisor: Michael Joyce
Manager, Visual Research: Beth Brenzel

Photo Researcher: Rachel Lucas
Manager, Rights and Permissions: Zina Arabia
Image Permission Coordinator: Jan Marc Quisumbing
Cover Designer: Elena Sidorova
Cover Art: Caspar Benson/Getty Images
Supplements Editor: Alison Eusden
Production Coordination, Text Design, and Composition: Nesbitt Graphics, Inc.
Printer/Binder: Edwards Brothers
Cover Printer: Lehigh Phoenix
Text Font: 10/13 Palatino

We gratefully acknowledge the following for permission to use copyrighted material: p. 13: Getty Images—Photodisc-Royalty Free; p. 16: AP Photo/Paul Sakuma; p. 42: Getty Images—Photodisc-Royalty Free; p. 50: Spencer Grant/PhotoEdit Inc.; p. 134: Getty Images—Photodisc-Royalty Free; p. 157: Getty Images Royalty Free—PhotoAlto; p. 198: Photodisc/Getty Images; p. 239: Charles V. Tines/Newscom; p. 249: AP Wide World Photos; p. 264: Getty Images, Inc.—fStop; p. 299: Alamy Images Royalty Free; p. 312: AP Wide World Photos; p. 394: Roger L. Wollenberg/UPI/Landov Media; p. 399: P. Hosefros/The New York Times; p. 419: © Bettmann/CORBIS All Rights Reserved; p. 432: Michael Evans/The White House Photo Office; p. 480: Image Bank/Getty Images; p. 487: AP Wide World Photos; p. 491: Corbis RF.

Library of Congress Cataloging-in-Publication Data
Rohlf, William D.
   Introduction to economic reasoning/William D. Rohlf.—8th ed.
      p. cm.—(The Pearson series in economics)
   Includes index.
   ISBN-13: 978-0-13-136858-3
   ISBN-10: 0-13-136858-3
1. Economics. 2. United States—Economic conditions. I. Title.
   HB171.5.R73 2009
   330—dc22   2009043587

10 9 8 7 6 5 4 3 2 1

Addison-Wesley
is an imprint of

ISBN 10: 0-131-36858-3
ISBN 13: 978-0-131-36858-3

BRIEF
CONTENTS

CONTENTS

PART TWO

Microeconomics: Markets, Prices, and the Role of Competition   65

PART THREE

Macroeconomics: The Economy as a Whole   291

USE YOUR ECONOMIC REASONING NEWS ARTICLES

PREFACE

Almost one hundred years ago, Alfred Marshall defined economics as "the study of mankind in the ordinary business of life." Today, the ordinary business of life has become incredibly complex. The purpose of this textbook is to help prepare students for that life.

Introduction to Economic Reasoning is intended for students taking the one-term course in introductory economics. Many of these students, perhaps a majority, will take only one course in economics. They have a variety of interests and educational objectives. Some are enrolled in preprofessional programs; others will pursue majors in areas such as business, psychology, or the liberal arts. At a number of institutions, the one-term course also enrolls first-year students in MBA programs and other graduate business programs. Many of these students pursued nonbusiness majors as undergraduates and did not elect to take an economics course. Others desire to review economics before entering the graduate program. Although the students enrolling in the one-term course have diverse objectives and interests, they can all benefit from a course that prepares them to understand economic issues better and helps them to become better decision makers.

NEW TO THIS EDITION

For the past two years, our newspapers and TV news reports have been dominated by the financial crisis and the accompanying economic downturn. Unemployment has reached levels not seen since the early 1980s, and policymakers have been forced to become creative in an attempt to get the economy moving again. As painful as this process has been, it has provided numerous examples for teachers and students of economics. This edition is designed to take advantage of those teaching and learning opportunities. Following are some of the changes incorporated in this edition that should stimulate interest and provide opportunities for classroom discussion.

- Chapter 5 uses a current news feature to examine the connection between the "mortgage crisis" and the self-interest assumption that undergirds all economic analysis.
- The linkage between falling home prices and the overall health of the economy is discussed and illustrated in Chapter 11, including a look at how the natural instincts of consumers can serve to make the recession worse.

- The unique policy problems posed by the 2008–2009 recession are examined in Chapters 12 and 13.
- An appendix to Chapter 13 allows instructors to examine the role of bank capital requirements in explaining the financial crisis and the problems confronting Fed policymakers.
- Chapter 15 examines the potential conflict between providing short-term stimulus and fostering long-run economic growth.

Other changes to the teaching/learning tools in this edition:

- The discussion and description of foreign economic systems have been revised to reflect the ongoing changes in China, Russia, and elsewhere.
- All the economic data contained in the text have been updated based on the most recent figures available from the Bureau of Labor Statistics, the Federal Reserve, the U.S. Census Bureau, and other official sources.
- 100% of the "Use Your Economic Reasoning" articles are new to this edition, including all new discussion questions. In these articles, readers will have an opportunity to discover the relationship between cell phone usage and auto accidents, learn who is pushing for higher gasoline taxes, debate the reasons for the resurgence of Spam as a grocery staple, and explore numerous other interesting topics.

THE FOCUS OF THE BOOK

How do we prepare students to understand economic issues and help them become better decision makers? I am convinced that we cannot accomplish these objectives by focusing solely on economic issues and shortcutting a discussion of economic concepts. This approach might provide students with ready answers to existing problems, but it would do little to prepare students for coping with new social problems and little to refine their decision-making skills. To accomplish those objectives, we must teach students something about economic reasoning.

Economists are fond of saying that economics is a way of thinking, or a way of reasoning about problems. The essence of economic reasoning is the ability to use theories or models to make sense out of the real world and devise policy solutions to economic problems. If we want students to use economic reasoning, we have to help them to learn and understand the basic economic theories. Without an understanding of economic theory, a course in economics can leave the student with little more than memorized solutions to current economic problems.

THE NEED TO MAKE CHOICES

Obviously, we can't do everything in a one-term course in introductory economics. And unless we can keep the students' interest and show the relevance of economics, we can't accomplish anything. So the instructor in a one-term course (and the author of a one-term text) must make choices. He or she must decide what to include and what to exclude, how to balance theory with application, and how to motivate the students without sounding too much like a cheerleader. This textbook attempts to bridge these extremes.

Because economists use theories or models in problem solving, the core of this text is economic theory. No essential micro or macro concept is omitted. Many refinements are omitted, however, so that more time can be devoted to the careful development of the most important concepts. This is one of the distinctive features of the text: a very careful development of the core ideas in economic theory.

MAKING ECONOMICS RELEVANT

Today's student wants to know why he or she should be studying economics. What problems or issues will it help to clarify? What decisions will it help to improve? In *Introduction to Economic Reasoning*, the relevance of economics is illustrated by the use of examples in the text and through special features entitled "Use Your Economic Reasoning." These features, which are listed in a separate table of contents on pages xvi–xvii, contain current news articles that have been carefully selected to illustrate the relevance of the economic principles being discussed and to provide the student with an opportunity to test knowledge of those principles. Each article is accompanied by a set of questions to ensure that the student gains the maximum benefit from the article, and the features themselves have been designed to make them easy to locate.

WRITING STYLE

In writing this text, my overriding objective has been to make economics accessible to the average student. I have been careful to avoid unnecessarily sophisticated vocabulary and needlessly long sentences. Most important, I have worked to ensure that my explanations of economic concepts are carefully and clearly developed. Although professors may adopt a text for a wide variety of reasons, I am convinced that the most common reason for discontinuing its use is because students can't understand it. Your students will be able to read this text and understand it.

AIDS IN LEARNING

In addition to a clear writing style, the text contains a number of other learning aids:

1. Learning objectives are stated at the beginning of each chapter.
2. New terms are presented in boldface type and are always defined when they are introduced.
3. "Use Your Economic Reasoning" news article selections not only generate student interest but also give the student an opportunity to apply the concepts that have been presented and thereby reinforce learning.
4. Careful summaries highlight the contents of each chapter.
5. A glossary of new terms appears at the end of the text so that a student can easily review definitions.
6. A study guide including fill-in-the-blank and multiple-choice questions (with answers) appears at the end of each chapter. This increases the likelihood that the study guide will be used and encourages the student to review the chapter to correct deficiencies.

ADDITIONAL FEATURES

1. The demand and supply model (the core of micro theory) is more fully developed than in other one-semester texts, and the student is given numerous opportunities to test an understanding of the model.
2. The organization of the text provides for maximum flexibility in use. Instructors can choose how detailed they want to make their coverage of a given topic.
3. The importance of marginal reasoning is developed at the personal level and then extended to business decision making. Numerous illustrations make this principle come to life for the students.
4. Potentially challenging topics such as the theory of rational expectations and game theory are presented in a manner that is accessible to the beginning student.
5. International economics is presented in a streamlined manner so that the instructor will have sufficient time to introduce the rationale for free trade and the model of flexible exchange rates.

STRATEGIES FOR USING THE TEXT

Introduction to Economic Reasoning provides balanced coverage of microeconomics and macroeconomics. The book is divided into four parts. A two-chapter introduction (Part 1) examines the basic economic problem and economic systems. This is followed by seven chapters on microeconomics (Part 2), six chapters on macroeconomics (Part 3), and one chapter on international economics (Part 4).

The chapters in the text are arranged in micro-macro sequence, but an instructor could easily reverse this order by covering Chapters 1, 2, and 3 and then moving directly to Part 3. The remaining micro chapters and Part 4 could then be covered in sequence.

If an instructor desires to shorten the micro portion of the course, numerous options exist. Chapter 4, "Applications Using Demand and Supply," can be omitted with no loss of continuity. And the discussion of market models can easily be shortened by omitting Chapter 8, "Industry Structure and Public Policy." An instructor following these suggestions would be left with the core of micro theory: the model of supply and demand, the distinction between price takers and price searchers, and a discussion of market failure. Instructors desiring still briefer coverage could omit the discussion of market models (Chapters 6–8) and still expose their students to the marginal reasoning discussion contained in Chapter 5, "Costs and Decision Making."

The macro coverage can also be reduced. For instance, instructors may opt to omit Chapter 14, "The Activist–Nonactivist Debate," and/or Chapter 15, "Economic Growth: The Importance of the Long Run." The remaining macro chapters will identify measures of aggregate performance, introduce students to the aggregate demand–aggregate supply model, and discuss fiscal and monetary policies.

International economics is the last part of the book. This material has traditionally been the first to be omitted whenever an instructor found it necessary to shorten his or her coverage. By combining international trade and finance into a single chapter, I hope that I have made it easier for you to cover this material. However, if time is still too short, the discussion of exchange rates, the last half of the chapter, can easily be omitted.

SUPPLEMENTARY MATERIALS

The Online Instructor's Manual that accompanies this book is intended to make the instructor's job easier. New instructors may benefit from the teaching tips provided for each chapter. The manual also contains answers to the

"Use Your Economic Reasoning" questions and "Problems and Questions for Discussion."

The Online Test Item File contains a varied and extensive set of test questions for each chapter. The Test Item File is available in TestGen software with QuizMaster for both Windows and Macintosh computers. TestGen's friendly graphical interface enables instructors to easily view, edit, and add questions; transfer questions to tests; and print tests in a variety of fonts and forms. Filter and sort features let the instructor quickly locate questions and arrange them in a preferred order. TestGen tests can be used with or exported to well-known course management systems on the Internet. QuizMaster automatically grades exams, stores the results on disk, and allows the instructor to view or print a variety of reports over a local area network.

To facilitate classroom presentation, PowerPoint slides of all the text images are available for Macintosh and Windows.

The CourseSmart eTextbook for the text is available through www .coursesmart.com. CourseSmart goes beyond traditional expectations providing instant, online access to the textbooks and course materials you need at a lower cost to students. And, even as students save money, you can save time and hassle with a digital textbook that allows you to search the most relevant content at the very moment you need it. Whether it's evaluating textbooks or creating lecture notes to help students with difficult concepts, CourseSmart can make life a little easier. See how when you visit www.coursesmart.com/ instructors.

The Companion Website, www.pearsonhighered.com/rohlf, provides students with links to important data sites, supplemental chapters, and learning aids such as glossary flashcards and automatically graded quizzes for each chapter.

Finally, a student Workbook, written by Steven D. Mullins, is available as an additional learning aid.

ACKNOWLEDGMENTS

One author is listed on the cover of this textbook, but many people have helped in its preparation, and I owe them my thanks.

First, I would like to thank those who reviewed the eighth edition.

Phil Droke, *Highline Community College*
Marie Duggan, *Keene State College*
John S. Heywood, *University of Wisconsin–Milwaukee*
Dr. Tom Lehman, *Indiana Wesleyan University*
Ihsuan Li, *Minnesota State University–Mankato*

Their comments and suggestions have been immensely helpful to me and are reflected in the content of this revision.

As with the previous editions, I owe a particular debt of thanks to Steve Mullins, my colleague at Drury University. He was often called on to help me interpret reviewer comments and decide between conflicting opinions. His good judgment and ready assistance have made a major difference in the quality of this edition.

I would also like to thank those with whom I have worked at Pearson: Noel Seibert, Carolyn Terbush, Nancy Freihofer, Alison Eusden, and Angela Lee.

Finally, I would like to thank my wife, Bev. Without her patience and support, this edition would never have been completed.

W.D.R.
Springfield, MO

Introduction: Scarcity and the Economic System

Chapter 1 explains what the study of economics is about and how the knowledge you gain from this course may affect your thinking in many ways. Here you will be introduced to the concept of "opportunity cost"—one of the most important concepts in economics and in everyday living. You will learn about the role of economic theory in helping us make sense of the things we observe in the world around us. In Chapter 2 you will discover what an economic system is and how economic systems differ from country to country.

With that introductory material behind you, you can begin exploring economics in more detail. Part 2 of the text examines microeconomics: the study of individual markets and individual business firms. Part 3 explores macroeconomics: the study of the economy as a whole and the factors that influence the economy's overall performance. Part 4 considers international economics: the study of economic exchanges between nations.

1

The Study of Economics

1. State the fundamental economic problem and provide a definition of economics.
2. Identify the categories of economic resources.
3. Explain cost-benefit analysis and the concept of opportunity cost.
4. Draw a production possibilities curve and use it to illustrate opportunity cost, economic growth, and the benefits of trade.
5. Discuss the three fundamental economic questions.
6. Identify five common goals of economic systems and illustrate how they may conflict.
7. Define economic theories and discuss their role.
8. Explain why economists sometimes disagree.

Beginning a subject you haven't explored before is something like starting out on a blind date: You always hope for the best but anticipate the worst. This time, be reassured. No course you take in college is likely to be more relevant to your future—whatever your interests—than this one. An understanding of economic principles is valuable because so many of the questions and decisions that touch our lives have an economic aspect. This is true whether you are evaluating something as personal as your decision to attend college or attempting to grapple with one of today's fundamental social issues: the debate about how to provide adequate health care for all Americans, for example, or how to provide adequate retirement incomes for older Americans without overburdening younger Americans, or the advisability of protecting U.S. businesses and workers from foreign competition. Each of these issues has important implications for your welfare and mine, yet they are just a few of the many complex questions that confront us as consumers, workers, and citizens. To understand and evaluate what economists, politicians, and others are saying about these issues, we need a knowledge of economics. Then we can do a better job of separating the "sense" from the "nonsense" and forming intelligent opinions.

Obviously you won't learn all there is to know about economics from one short textbook. But here is your opportunity to build a solid understanding of basic economic principles and discover how economists interpret data and analyze economic problems. That is especially important because economics is as much a way of reasoning as it is a body of knowledge. Once you have learned what it means to "consider the opportunity costs," to "compare the costs and benefits," and to "think marginally," nothing will ever look quite the same again. You'll find yourself making better decisions about everything from how to use your time more effectively to whom to support in the next presidential election. Watching the TV news and reading newspapers and magazines will become more meaningful and enjoyable. You will begin to notice the economic dimension of virtually every problem confronting society—pollution, crime, health care, higher education, and so on. Your knowledge of economics will help you understand and deal better with all these problems.

THE ECONOMIC PROBLEM

The fundamental economic problem facing individuals and societies alike is the fact that our wants exceed our capacity for satisfying those wants. Consider, for example, one of your personal economic problems: how to use your limited income—your limited financial resources. With the possible exception of the very rich, none of us can afford to buy everything we'd like to have. Each of us can think of a virtually limitless number of products we want or "need": food, shelter, clothing, membership at a health club, new tires for the car, a personal computer. Economist and social critic John Kenneth Galbraith has suggested that the satisfaction of a want through the purchase of a product not only fails to reduce our wants but in fact creates new ones. Purchase an iPod, for instance, and you soon want better headphones, a docking station, car accessories, and the like.

Societies face essentially the same dilemma: The wants of their members exceed the societies' capacities for satisfying those wants. In order to satisfy human wants, societies or nations require the use of **economic resources**, the scarce inputs that are used in the process of creating a good or providing a service. Traditionally economists divide these resources into four categories: land, labor, capital, and entrepreneurship. **Land** signifies more than soil or acreage; it includes all raw materials—timber, water, minerals, and other production inputs—that are created by nature. **Labor** denotes the work—both physical and mental—that goes into the production process. **Capital** refers to physical aids to production, such as factories, machinery, and tools.[1] **Entrepreneurship** is the managerial function that combines all these economic resources in an effective way and uncovers new opportunities to earn a profit—for example, through new products or processes. Entrepreneurship is characterized by a willingness to take the risks associated with a business venture.

Every society's stock of economic resources is limited, or *scarce*, in relation to the infinite wants of its members. At any given time, even the world's richest economies have available only so much raw material, labor, equipment, and managerial talent to use in producing goods and services. Consequently, an economy's ability to produce goods and services is limited, just as an individual's ability to satisfy his or her personal wants is limited.

The inability to satisfy all our wants forces us to make choices about how we can best use our limited resources. That is what economics is all about: making wise choices about how to use scarce resources. Therefore, we define **economics** as the study of how to use our limited resources to satisfy our unlimited wants as fully as possible. When individuals, businesses, or nations try to make the most of what they have, they are "economizing."

COST-BENEFIT ANALYSIS AND OPPORTUNITY COST

In order to make wise choices, we must compare the costs and benefits associated with each alternative or option we consider. A particular decision or choice will improve our well-being only if the benefits associated with that decision exceed the costs, if what we gain is worth more to us than what we lose. Individuals, businesses, and even governments engage in **cost-benefit analysis**—a systematic comparison of costs and benefits—before deciding on a course of action.

Comparing costs and benefits probably seems like a relatively straightforward process. Sometimes that's the case, but not always. In some instances, the costs and benefits may be very subjective and hard to compare. In other instances, there may be hidden costs or benefits that are easily ignored.

One of the fundamental lessons of economics is that all our choices entail costs: There is no "free lunch." Whenever you make a decision to do or have

---

[1] Machines and tools are also known as **physical capital** or **capital goods**. This term distinguishes these physical production aids from **human capital**, the knowledge and skills possessed by workers, and **financial capital**, or money.

Use Your Economic Reasoning

British Balance Benefit vs. Cost of Latest Drugs

BY GARDINER HARRIS

When Bruce Hardy's kidney cancer spread to his lung, his doctor recommended an expensive new pill from Pfizer. But Mr. Hardy is British, and the British health authorities refused to buy the medicine. His wife has been distraught. "Everybody should be allowed to have as much life as they can," Joy Hardy said in the couple's modest home outside London.

If the Hardys lived in the United States or just about any European country other than Britain, Mr. Hardy would most likely get the drug, although he might have to pay part of the cost. A clinical trial showed that the pill, called Sutent, delays cancer progression for six months at an estimated treatment cost of $54,000. But at that price, Mr. Hardy's life is not worth prolonging, according to a British government agency, the National Institute for Health and Clinical Excellence. The institute, known as NICE, has decided that Britain, except in rare cases, can afford only 15,000 pounds, or about $22,750, to save six months of a citizen's life. British authorities, after a storm of protest, are reconsidering their decision on the cancer drug and others.

For years, Britain was almost alone in using evidence of cost-effectiveness to decide what to pay for. But skyrocketing prices for drugs and medical devices have led a growing number of countries to ask the hardest of questions: How much is life worth? For many, NICE has the answer. Top health officials in Austria, Brazil, Colombia and Thailand said in interviews that NICE now strongly influences their policies. . . . Even in the United States, rising costs have led some in Congress to propose an institute that would compare the effectiveness of new medical technologies, although the proposals so far would not allow for price considerations. . . .

The British government created NICE a decade ago to ensure that every pound spent buys as many years of good-quality life as possible, but the agency is increasingly rejecting expensive treatments. The denials have led to debate over what is to blame: company prices or the health institute's math. Dr. Michael Rawlins, chairman of NICE, blames the industry, saying that some companies raise prices "to get profits up so their executives can get better bonuses." Dr. Karol Sikora, a prominent London oncologist, said that the institute's math was flawed and that Dr. Rawlins had a "personal vendetta" against cancer treatments. . . .

Britain's National Health Service provides 95 percent of the nation's care from an annual budget, so paying for costly treatments means less money for, say, sick children. Before NICE, hospitals and clinics often came to different decisions about which drugs to buy, creating geographic disparities in care that led to outrage. (Such disparities are common in the United States, even for federal Medicare patients.) Now, any drug or device approved by the institute must be offered to patients. The institute has also written hundreds of treatment guidelines in hopes of improving, and making more consistent, basic medical care. The institute has analyzed the cost-effectiveness of surgical operations, cancer screening tests and medical devices. . . . But the decisions that get the most attention are those involving new drugs. Any drug that provides an extra six months of good-quality life for 10,000 pounds—about $15,150—or less is automatically approved, while those that give six months for $22,750 or less might get approved. More expensive medicines have been approved only rarely. The spending limits represent the health institute's best guess for how much the nation can afford. . . .

To analyze the value of the drug that Mr. Hardy, the kidney cancer patient, wanted, and the value of three other kidney cancer medicines, the British institute hired a university group that considered how many months the drugs delayed cancer's progress. . . . The academics got drug prices and calculated the costs of administering them and treating their side effects. Not one of the drugs came close to being worth their expense, the group suggested. In a preliminary ruling in August, a committee from NICE agreed. . . .

[B]ecause of the institute, Britain's National Health Service has been among the first to balk at paying such prices, which has led many companies to offer the British discounts unavailable almost anywhere else. . . . [Now] agencies like NICE are popping up across the globe. . . . The British institute has created a consulting group to advise foreign governments. . . .

But the most pressing question for the [health care] industry is what influence the British institute will have in the United States. The United States already spends more than twice as much per capita on health care as the average of other industrialized nations, while getting generally poorer health outcomes. Michael O. Leavitt, the Bush administration's secretary of health and human services, said in a September speech that, at its present growth rate, health care spending "could potentially drag our nation into a financial crisis that makes our major subprime mortgage crisis look like a warm summer rain." And while there is fierce disagreement about how and whether to control drug and device expenses as part of a broader reform of the health system, many say some cost controls are inevitable. At a September device industry conference in Washington, a seminar on the issue was standing-room only and half of the questioners mentioned NICE. . . .

USE YOUR ECONOMIC REASONING

1. Mrs. Hardy says, "Everyone should be allowed to have as much life as they can." Do you agree with that statement? What is the opportunity cost to Britain of providing Mr. Hardy with the medicine that may extend his life?

2. As the article suggests, the use of cost-benefit analysis is relatively new to the health-care arena. But in many other areas, we perform cost-benefit calculations daily, often unconsciously. To illustrate, suppose you prefer hamburgers to hot dogs if they are both available at the same price. Would you still buy the hamburger if it cost twice as much as the hot dog? Three times as much? Probably not. Why, then, is there opposition to the use of cost-benefit analysis in health care?

3. In 2009, the U.S. Congress appropriated $1.1 billion to compare the effectiveness of different treatments for the same illness. But although there is agreement about the need to compare the effectiveness of different treatments, there is opposition to considering the cost of the alternative treatments. Critics argue that if cost is taken into consideration, that information might ultimately be used (by insurers or Medicare) to deny access to expensive life-saving treatments—the situation facing Mr. Hardy in Britain—or to funnel patients into less-expensive treatments. What do you think; should Medicare (and private insurers) consider cost effectiveness in deciding what to pay for? Why is Britain considering cost effectiveness; does that justification exist in the United States?

one thing, you sacrifice the opportunity to do or have some other thing. The best, or *most valued*, alternative you must sacrifice to take a particular action is the **opportunity cost** of that action. What opportunity are you sacrificing by reading this chapter? Perhaps you could be studying for another class or watching your favorite TV show. The opportunity cost of reading this chapter is whatever you wanted to do most. When your city council or town meeting allocates tax dollars to install sidewalks, it may sacrifice books for the public library, streetlights for a residential area, or tennis courts for a local park. Whatever that body would have chosen to do if it hadn't installed sidewalks is the opportunity cost of the sidewalks.

When Congress debates the size of the defense budget, the outcome of that debate affects each of us. If a nation's resources are fully employed, an increase in the output of military goods and services requires a reduction in the output of something else. An increase in military spending may mean a cut in funding for job training, road construction, or aid to education; it may mean an increase in taxes, which, in turn, will lead to a reduction in private consumer spending and the output of consumer goods.

Either way, more military output means less civilian output because, at any given time, there is a limit to the amount of total output the economy can produce. This doesn't necessarily mean that we shouldn't spend more on military goods if there are sound reasons for doing so. It does mean that we should be aware of what that spending costs us in terms of private goods and services or other government programs. The economist's point here is that we can't make the best decisions about how to use our scarce resources unless we know the true costs and benefits of our decisions. (Attempting to weigh the benefits of drugs and medical procedures has proved to be quite controversial. To learn why, read "British Balance Benefit vs. Cost of Latest Drugs" on page 6.)

THE PRODUCTION POSSIBILITIES CURVE

We can illustrate the concept of opportunity cost with a simple graph called a production possibilities curve. (The appendix at the end of this chapter explains how graphs are constructed and interpreted.) A **production possibilities curve** shows the combinations of goods that the economy is capable of producing with its present stock of economic resources and its existing techniques of production. Because it outlines the boundaries, or limits, of the economy's ability to produce output, it is sometimes called a *production possibilities frontier.* Any point along or inside the frontier represents a combination of

EXHIBIT 1.1

The Production Possibilities Curve

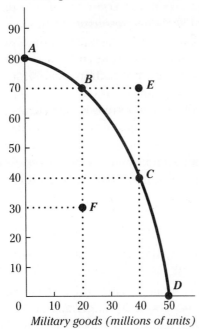

Civilian goods (millions of units)

Military goods (millions of units)

The production possibilities curve, *ABCD*, shows the combinations of civilian goods and military goods that the economy is capable of producing with its present stock of economic resources and the existing techniques of production. Any point on or below the curve is possible. Any point above the curve is ruled out (impossible).

goods that the economy can produce; any point above the curve is beyond the economy's present production capacity.

Exhibit 1.1 shows the production capabilities of a hypothetical economy. The economy's output of civilian goods is measured on the vertical axis and its output of military goods on the horizontal axis. According to this exhibit, if all the economy's resources were used to produce civilian goods, 80 million units of civilian goods could be produced each year (point *A*). On the other hand, if the economy were to use all its economic resources to produce military goods, 50 million units of military goods could be produced each year (point *D*). Between these extremes lie other production possibilities—combined outputs of military and civilian goods that the economy is capable of producing. For example, the economy might choose to produce 70 million units of civilian goods and 20 million units of military goods (point *B*). Or it might choose to produce 40 million units of civilian goods and 40 million units of military goods (point *C*). We can see, then, that the curve *ABCD* outlines the boundaries of our hypothetical economy's production abilities. Point *E*, which lies above the curve, represents a combination of products that is beyond the economy's present capacity.

Unfortunately, economies do not always live up to their production capabilities. Whenever an economy is operating at a point inside its production possibilities curve, we know that economic resources are not being fully employed. For example, at point *F* in Exhibit 1.1, our hypothetical economy is producing 30 million units of civilian goods and 20 million units of military goods each year. But according to the production possibilities curve, the economy could do much better. For example, it could increase its output of civilian goods to 70 million units a year without sacrificing any military goods (point *B*). Or it could expand its output of civilian goods to 40 million units while also expanding its production of military goods to 40 million units (point *C*). In short, when an economy has unemployed resources, it is not satisfying as many of the society's unlimited wants as it could if it used its full potential.

Opportunity Costs along the Curve

The production possibilities curve does more than outline an economy's capacity for producing output; it also illustrates opportunity cost. When an economy's resources are fully employed—that is, when an economy is operating on the production possibilities curve rather than inside it—larger amounts of one product can be obtained only by producing smaller amounts of the other product. The production possibilities curve slopes downward to the right to illustrate opportunity cost: more of one thing means less of the other thing. We can see opportunity costs changing as we move from one point on the production possibilities curve to another. For example, suppose that the society is operating at point *A* on the production possibilities curve in Exhibit 1.1, producing 80 million units of civilian goods and no military goods. If the society decides that it would prefer to operate at point *B*, the opportunity cost of acquiring the first 20 million units of military goods would be the loss of 10 million units of civilian goods. The economy can move from point *A* to point *B* only by transferring resources from the production of civilian goods to the production of military goods.

Suppose that the society would like to have even more military goods—for example, 40 million units of military goods produced each year. According to the production possibilities curve, the opportunity cost of acquiring the next 20 million units of military goods (and moving from point *B* to point *C*) would be a loss of 30 million units of civilian goods—three times what it cost the society to acquire the first 20 million units of military goods. Moving from point *C* to point *D* would be even more expensive. To acquire the last 10 million units of military goods, the society would have to sacrifice 40 million units of civilian goods.

The Law of Increasing Costs

Our hypothetical production possibilities curve illustrates an important principle known as the **law of increasing costs**: As more of a particular product is produced, its opportunity cost per unit will increase. How do we explain the law of increasing costs? Why does our hypothetical society have to sacrifice larger and larger amounts of civilian output to obtain each additional increment of military output?

The explanation is fairly simple. Not all resources are alike; some economic resources—skilled labor and specialized machinery, for instance—are better suited to the production of one product than another. In our example, some resources are better suited to the production of civilian goods and services, others to the production of military products. Consequently, when the society attempts to expand its output of military goods and services, it must eventually use resources that are not well suited to producing those military products.

To illustrate that problem, let's examine the process of transferring resources from the production of civilian products to the production of military products. Suppose that initially our hypothetical economy is not producing any military output. At first, it will not be difficult for the economy to increase its military output. Some of the existing capital resources, including factories, can be converted to the production of military products with relative ease, and many members of the labor force will have skills that are readily transferable to the production of military products. For example, it would be fairly simple to convert a clothing factory to the production of uniforms or to convert an awning factory to the production of tents. Because these conversions are relatively easy, the society will gain just about as much in military output as it will lose in civilian output.

But to continue expanding the output of military products, it will be necessary to use resources that are increasingly less suitable. For instance, consider the difficulty that might be encountered in converting an amusement park to a missile-manufacturing facility, or a toy factory to an explosives plant. Much of the equipment that was useful in producing civilian output will be of no use in producing military output. Therefore, although the conversion of these facilities will require society to give up a large quantity of civilian output (many rides at the amusement park and thousands of toys), it will not result in very many additional units of military output.

The point is that because some resources are better suited to the production of civilian goods than to the production of military products, increasing amounts of civilian goods and services will have to be sacrificed to obtain each additional increment of military output. It is this principle (the law of increasing costs) that causes the production possibilities frontier to have the curved shape depicted in Exhibits 1.1 and 1.2.

EXHIBIT 1.2

Illustrating Economic Growth

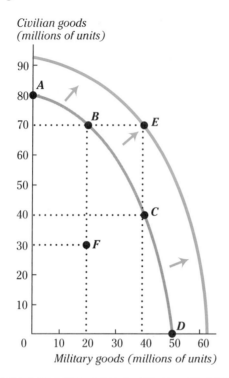

If the quantity of economic resources were to increase or better production methods were discovered, the economy's ability to produce goods and services would expand. Such economic growth can be illustrated by shifting the production possibilities curve to the right.

Economic Growth and the Benefits of Trade

As we have seen, it is important for economies to operate on, rather than inside, their production possibilities curves. But even when an economy fully employs its resources, it cannot satisfy all of a society's wants. Any point *above* the production possibilities frontier exceeds the economy's current production capabilities. For instance, point *E* in Exhibit 1.2, which combines 70 million units of civilian goods and 40 million units of military goods, is beyond the inside production possibilities curve representing the existing capacity of this hypothetical economy. Society clearly would prefer that combination of products to the combination represented by, say, point *C*, but it can't obtain it.

Of course, the economy's production capacity is not permanently fixed. If the quantity of economic resources were to increase or if better production methods were discovered, the economy could produce more goods and services. Such an increase in production capacity is usually described as *economic growth* and is illustrated by shifting the production possibilities curve to the right. The outside curve in Exhibit 1.2 represents economic growth sufficient to take point *E* within the economy's production possibilities frontier.

Trade between nations can provide benefits that are very similar to those that result from economic growth—increased amounts of goods and services. To illustrate, suppose that our hypothetical economy is operating at point *A* on the inside production possibilities curve in Exhibit 1.2, producing 80 units of civilian goods and no military goods. According to the production possibilities curve, the economy could acquire 40 million units of military goods (and move to point *C*) only if it was willing to give up 40 million units of civilian goods; the cost of acquiring each additional unit of military goods would be the sacrifice of one unit of civilian goods. But suppose that, through trade with other nations, this economy could acquire a unit of military goods by sacrificing only one-fourth of a unit of civilian goods. That would permit the economy to acquire the 40 million units of military goods it desires by giving up (trading) only 10 million units of civilian goods. The economy could move to point *E*, a point well beyond its own production capabilities.[2]

Like economic growth, free trade can increase the goods and services available for consumption.

---

[2] Unlike economic growth, trade does not shift an economy's production possibilities curve but instead merely permits a nation to consume a combination of products beyond its own production capabilities.

The ability to acquire goods at a lower opportunity cost (and thereby increase the total amount of goods and services available for consumption) is why **free trade**—trade that is not hindered by artificial restrictions or trade barriers—is generally supported by economists. Chapter 16 explores the theoretical basis for trade in much greater detail.

As you can see, the production possibilities curve is a useful tool for thinking about our economy. It shows that an economy with fully employed resources cannot produce more of one thing without sacrificing something else. Equally important, the production possibilities model can be used to illustrate the benefits of economic growth and free trade. Of course, neither economic growth nor free trade eliminates the need to make choices about how to use our scarce resources. The next section explores the nature of those choices in more detail.

THE THREE FUNDAMENTAL QUESTIONS

The choice between military goods and civilian goods is only one of the broad decisions that the United States and other nations face. The dilemma of unlimited wants and limited economic resources forces each society to make three basic choices, to answer the "three fundamental questions" of economics: (1) What goods and services will we produce and in what quantities? (2) How will these goods and services be produced? (3) For whom will these products be produced—that is, how will the output be distributed?

What to Produce

Because no society can produce everything its members desire, each society must sort through and assess its various wants and then decide which goods and services to produce in what quantities. Deciding the relative value of military products against civilian goods is only one part of the picture because each society must determine precisely which civilian and military products it will produce. For example, it must decide whether to produce clothing or to conserve its scarce resources for some other use. Next, it must decide what types of clothing to produce—how many shirts, dresses, pairs of slacks, overcoats, and so on. Finally, it must decide in what sizes to produce these items of clothing and determine the quantities of each size. Only after considering all such alternatives can a society decide which goods and services to produce.

How to Produce

After deciding which products to produce, each society must also decide what materials and methods to use in their production. In most cases, a given good or service can be produced in more than one way. For instance, a shirt can be made of cotton, wool, or acrylic fibers. It can be sewn entirely by hand, partly by hand, or entirely by machine. It can be packaged in paper, cardboard, plastic, or some combination of materials. It can be shipped by truck, train, boat, or plane. In short, the producer must choose among many options with regard to materials, production methods, and means of shipment.

For Whom to Produce

Finally, each society must decide how to distribute or divide up its limited output among those who desire to receive it. Should everyone receive equal shares of society's output? Should those who produce more receive more? What about those who don't produce at all, either because they can't work or because they don't want to work? How much of society's output should *they* receive? In deciding how to distribute output—how output will be shared—different societies are influenced by their traditions and cultural values.

Whether a society is rich or poor, simple or complex, democratic or authoritarian, it must have some *economic system* through which it addresses the three fundamental questions. Chapter 2 examines a variety of economic systems and discusses how each responds to these questions.

FIVE ECONOMIC GOALS

A given economic system's answers to the three fundamental questions are not always satisfactory to either the nation's citizens or its leaders. For example, if an economy is operating inside its production possibilities curve, it is not using all its production capabilities and is therefore not satisfying as many human wants as possible. A society with unemployed resources may want to take steps to improve the economy's performance so that it does a better job of fulfilling citizens' expectations or, in some cases, the expectations of those in power.

What should a society expect from its economic system? Before a society can attempt to improve its economic performance, it must have a set of goals, objectives, or standards by which to judge that performance. Although there is room for debate about precisely what constitutes "good performance" from an economic system, many societies recognize five essential goals:

1. *Full employment of economic resources*. If a society is to obtain maximum benefit from its scarce resources, it must utilize them fully. Whenever resources are unemployed—when factories stand idle, laborers lack work, or farmland lies untilled—the society is sacrificing the goods and services that those

resources could have produced. Therefore, it is doing a less than optimal job of satisfying the unlimited wants of its members.

2. *Efficiency*. Economic efficiency means getting the most benefit out of limited resources. This goal has two separate elements: (a) production of the goods and services that consumers desire the most and (b) realization of this production at the lowest cost in terms of scarce resources. Economic efficiency is the very essence of economics. If an economic system fully employs its resources but uses them to produce relatively unwanted products, the society cannot hope to achieve maximum satisfaction from its resources. By the same token, if an economy does not minimize the amount of resources used in producing *each* product, it will not be able to produce as many products; consequently, fewer wants will be satisfied.

3. *Economic growth*. Because most people want and expect their standard of living to improve continually, economic growth—expansion in the economy's capacity to produce goods and services—is an important objective. If population is increasing, some economic growth is necessary just to maintain the existing standard of material welfare. When a nation's population is stable or is increasing less rapidly than output, economic growth

When labor or other economic resources are unemployed, society must do without the goods and services those resources could have produced.

results in more goods and services per person, contributing to a higher standard of living.

4. *A fair distribution of income.* Distribution of income means the way income is divided among the members of a society. In modern economies the income distribution is the primary factor determining how output will be shared. (In a primitive economy, such as that of Ethiopia or Burundi, custom or tradition plays a major role in deciding how output is divided.) People with larger incomes receive larger shares of their economy's output. Is this a fair distribution of output? Some contend that it is. Others call for redistribution of income to eliminate poverty in the society. Still others argue that nothing less than an equal distribution is truly fair.

5. *A stable price level.* A major goal of most economies is a stable price level. Societies fear inflation—that is, a rise in the general level of prices. Inflation redistributes income arbitrarily: some people's incomes rise more rapidly than inflation, whereas other people find that their incomes can't keep pace. The former group emerges with a larger share of the economy's output, whereas the latter group must make do with less than before. The demoralizing effect of this redistribution can lead to social unrest.

In pursuing the five economic goals, societies strive to maintain compatibility with their noneconomic, or sociopolitical, objectives. Americans, for example, want to achieve these economic goals without harming the environment or sacrificing the rights of people to select their occupations, own property, and spend their incomes as they choose. Societies that place high value on tradition, such as Japan, may strive to pursue these economic goals without violating the customs of the past. Insofar as the cultural, political, religious, and other noneconomic values of societies differ, the relative importance of each of the five economic goals and the methods of meeting those goals will also differ.

CONFLICTS AND TRADE-OFFS

Defining economic goals is only the first step in attempting to improve our economy's performance. The next step is to decide how to achieve these goals. Often the pursuit of one goal forces us to sacrifice at least part of some other economic or noneconomic goal. That is what economists call a *trade-off*—society gets more of one thing only by giving up, or trading off, something else. This is another way of stating the problem of opportunity cost. The opportunity cost of achieving a particular goal is whatever other goal has to be sacrificed or compromised. Let's consider three problems societies face in pursuing economic goals.

Full Employment versus Stable Prices

The goal of achieving full employment may conflict with the goal of maintaining a stable price level. Experience has taught us that attempting to reduce unemployment generally results in a higher rate of inflation. By the same token, attempts to reduce the rate of inflation often lead to higher unemployment. Frequently it becomes necessary to sacrifice part of one goal in favor of the other. For instance, society may accept some unemployment to maintain a lower inflation rate. The trade-off each society makes depends partly on economic analysis but is also influenced by societal values.[3]

Economic Growth versus Environmental Protection

Conflict frequently occurs between the goals of economic growth and a clean environment. Although most Americans support these two goals, it has become apparent that expansion of the economy's output takes a toll on the environment. For instance, our attempts to expand agricultural output by using pesticides and chemical fertilizers have been partially responsible for the pollution of our rivers and streams. We make trade-offs between economic growth and environmental preservation, trade-offs that reflect prevailing national values.

Equality versus Efficiency

Consider now the potential conflict between income equality and economic efficiency. Suppose that a society decided that fair income distribution demanded greater equality of income than currently exists. Many economists would point out that efforts to achieve greater equality tend to have a negative impact on economic efficiency. Remember, efficiency means producing the most-wanted products in the least costly way. To accomplish this, the economy must be able to direct labor to the areas where it is most needed, often by making wages and salaries in these areas more attractive than those in other areas. For example, if a society needs to increase its number of computer programmers more rapidly than its number of teachers or nurses, it can encourage people to become computer programmers by making that occupation more rewarding financially than teaching or nursing.[4] If pay differentials are reduced to meet the goal of

---

[3] Most economists agree that there is a short-run trade-off between unemployment and inflation that may not exist in the long run. This issue is discussed in Chapter 11.

[4] In some economic systems these adjustments in wages and salaries would occur automatically; in others deliberate action would be required. Chapter 2 has more to say about how specific economic systems direct or allocate labor.

equality, a society will sacrifice economic efficiency because it will be more difficult to direct the flow of labor.

Choosing between Objectives

When our society's goals conflict and demand that we choose between them, it is not the function of economists to decide which is the more important. The choice between objectives such as more rapid economic growth and a cleaner environment, or between greater equality and enhanced efficiency, is not solely a matter of objective cost-benefit analysis. Rather, it involves **normative judgments**—judgments about what *should be* rather than what *is*. This is a realm in which economists have no more expertise than anyone else. Setting goals is the job of the society or its representatives. The function of the economist is to make sure that those in charge of setting goals (or devising policies to achieve goals) are aware of the alternatives available to them and the sacrifices each alternative requires—in other words, the costs and benefits of their actions.

ECONOMIC THEORY AND POLICY

Before economists can recommend policies for dealing with economic problems or achieving goals, they must understand thoroughly how the economic system operates. This is where **economic theory** comes into play.

Theories are generalizations about causal relationships between facts, or variables; they help us to understand how events are connected or what causes what in the world around us. Theories are also referred to as laws, principles, and models. When in later chapters you encounter the *law* of demand, the *principle* of comparative advantage, and the *model* of command socialism, bear in mind that each of these tools is a theory.

Theory in Everyday Life

You probably think of theory as something exotic, something you would not normally encounter or use. But nothing could be further from the truth. We each use theory in our daily life. If you don't recognize the role of theory in your life, it's because many of the theories you use were learned informally and are applied unconsciously. To illustrate, consider the following problem. You roll out of bed in the morning and crawl to the TV to turn it on. But instead of seeing your favorite morning program, all you see is a black screen—no picture, no sound, nothing. What is the *first* thing you will do to try to get the TV to work? You won't call the cable company, not at first anyway, and you won't throw the TV out the window—yet. Take some time to think about what you would do before reading further.

In response to this question, a common answer is, "I'd check to see if it's plugged in." Most people agree that that's a sensible response, but why do we agree on this sensible answer? Why don't people say, "I'd look outside to see if it's snowing," or "I'd run to my car to see if it has gas in it." They don't select these answers because we all know they have nothing to do with getting a picture on our TV. And, more important, we know that electricity *does* have something to do with getting a picture. In short, we all have theories about how TVs work, and all those theories involve electricity. Your theory may be fairly elaborate—if you've had a physics course—or it may be fairly simple, if you've learned it informally by repeated observations. Here's a simple theory of how TVs work:

$$\text{electricity} \longrightarrow \text{causes} \longrightarrow \text{pictures}.$$

Note that this theory does not fully describe the way TVs work; theories never do. Theories help us understand the real world by simplifying reality. In fact, theories or models are sometimes described as simplified pictures of the real world. By leaving out extraneous details and complexities, theories help us see the essential relationships more clearly, much as a map clarifies the shape and layout of a city by excluding unnecessary detail.

Lessons from the Production Possibilities Model

The production possibilities curve introduced earlier in the chapter is a simple model of an economy. It certainly doesn't tell us everything we would like to know about an economy; in fact, it leaves out a host of details. But it points out very clearly that every economy's production capacity is limited, so that attempts to produce more of one thing mean producing less of something else.

The production possibilities model also points out another important feature of models or theories: they are based on assumptions. The production possibilities model assumes that resources are limited and that some resources are better suited to producing one product than another.[5] Those assumptions give us a production possibilities curve that slopes downward and is concave. If we make different assumptions, we end up with a different model and different conclusions. For example, if an economy had *unlimited* resources, its production possibilities curve would slope upward because it could produce more of both products simultaneously; that is, it would not be necessary to give up some

---

[5] The production possibilities model also assumes the existing techniques of production. In other words, it assumes that technology does not change.

military products to produce more civilian products. (What would the production possibilities curve look like if resources were fixed but were equally well suited to producing either product?)[6] The objective is to start with assumptions that are sufficiently realistic so that the resulting model allows us to explain and predict the real world. Otherwise, we end up with a model of little or no practical value.

A Theory of Cigarette Consumption

Theories are absolutely essential to solving problems and making sense of the world we live in. Without a theory of how the TV works, we don't know what to do when it doesn't work; we don't know how to solve the problem. The same is true of economic problems. When you read the evening newspaper or tune in the evening news on television, you are exposed to a deluge of facts and figures about everything from housing construction to foreign trade. Without theories to help you interpret them, however, these data are of little value because you don't know what facts are relevant to the problem at hand.

In the early 1990s, researchers noted that cigarette consumption in the United States was no longer declining as rapidly as it had in the previous decade. In other words, smokers were not "kicking the habit" as readily as before. Health experts wanted to understand why the trend toward quitting smoking was slowing down. Without a theory explaining cigarette consumption, researchers wouldn't know where to begin looking for an explanation because they wouldn't know what facts were relevant.

On the other hand, suppose that over time we have developed a tentative theory, a hypothesis, that lower cigarette prices cause higher cigarette consumption. That would pinpoint certain relevant facts that might explain the increase in cigarette consumption. We could test our theory by gathering data for a number of different time periods to see if, in fact, cigarette consumption has increased and decreased consistently in accordance with changes in price.

Testing economic theories is more difficult than it might seem. For example, to determine whether cigarette consumption is, in fact, related to the price of cigarettes, economists have to be able to eliminate the impact of changes in personal income and other nonprice factors that might affect the quantity of cigarettes consumed. After all, even if the price of cigarettes is a major factor influencing the amount consumed, it is clearly not the only factor.[7] Unfortunately,

---

[6] Under these assumptions, the production possibilities curve would slope downward (because producing more of one thing would still require the sacrifice of some of the other thing), but it would be a straight line rather than curving outward.

[7] For example, it seems likely that over a given period, personal income also affects cigarette consumption. If the incomes of smokers remain constant while cigarette prices fall, cigarette consumption may well increase. But if incomes fall during the same period, offsetting the reduction in cigarette prices, cigarette consumption will probably remain the same or may even decrease.

Use Your Economic Reasoning

A Problem of the Brain, Not the Hands: Group Urges Phone Ban for Drivers

BY TARA PARKER-POPE

In half a dozen states and many cities and counties, it is illegal to use a hand-held cellphone while driving—but perfectly all right to talk on a hands-free device. The theory is that it's distracting to hold a phone and drive with just one hand. But a large body of research now shows that a hands-free phone poses no less danger than a hand-held one—that the problem is not your hands but your brain. "It's not that your hands aren't on the wheel," said David Strayer, director of the Applied Cognition Laboratory at the University of Utah and a leading researcher on cellphone safety. "It's that your mind is not on the road."

Now Dr. Strayer's research has gained a potent ally. On Monday, the National Safety Council, the nonprofit advocacy group that has pushed for seat belt laws and drunken driving awareness, called for an all-out ban on using cellphones while driving. "There is a huge misperception with the public that it's O.K. if they are using a hands-free phone," said Janet Froetscher, the council's president and chief executive. "It's the same challenge we had with seat belts and drunk driving—we've got to get people thinking the same way about cellphones."

Laboratory experiments using simulators, real-world road studies and accident statistics all tell the same story: drivers talking on a cellphone are four times as likely to have an accident as drivers who are not. That's the same level of risk posed by a driver who is legally drunk.

Why cellphone use behind the wheel is so risky isn't entirely clear, but studies suggest several factors. No matter what the device, phone conversations appear to take a significant toll on attention and visual processing skills. It may be that talking on the phone generates mental images that conflict with the spatial processing needed for safe driving. Eye-tracking studies show that while drivers continually look side to side, cellphone users tend to stare straight ahead. They may also be distracted to the point that their engaged brains no longer process much of the information that falls on their retinas, which leads to slower reaction times and other driving problems.

At the University of Utah, Dr. Strayer and his colleagues use driving simulators to study the effects of cellphone conversations. A simulator's interior looks like that of a Ford Crown Victoria, and a computer allows researchers to control driving conditions. Study participants are asked to drive under a variety of conditions: while talking on a hand-held phone or a hands-free one, while chatting with a friend in the next seat, and even after consuming enough alcohol to make them legally drunk.

economists cannot control these factors as precisely as chemists or physicists can control variables in their experiments. So economists do the next best thing; that is, they assume that other factors, such as personal incomes, remain constant. This is the assumption of **ceteris paribus**, which literally means

While in the simulator, drivers are asked to complete simple tasks, like driving for several miles along a highway and finding a particular exit, or navigating local streets where they must brake for traffic lights, change lanes and watch for pedestrians. How fast they drive, how well they stay in their lane, driving speed and eye movement are closely monitored. The Utah researchers have also placed electrodes on participants' scalps to gauge how they process information. Similar studies, using brain imaging, have been done at Carnegie Mellon.

The studies show that cellphone conversations are highly distracting compared with other speaking and listening activities in the car. One might think that listening to talk radio or an audio book would degrade driving skill; it does not. (A quiz after the driving test confirmed that the drivers were really paying attention to the programs.) Likewise, it is easy to equate talking to a friend on a cellphone with talking to a friend in the passenger seat. But a December report in the *Journal of Experimental Psychology: Applied* debunked that notion. Utah researchers put 96 drivers in a simulator, instructing them to drive several miles down the road and pull off at a rest stop. Sometimes the drivers were talking on a hands-free cellphone, and sometimes they were chatting with a friend in the next seat. Nearly every driver with a passenger found the rest stop, in part because the passenger often acted as an extra set of eyes, alerting the driver to the approaching exit. But among those talking on the cellphone, half missed the exit. "The paradox is that if the friend is sitting next to you, you drive safer," Dr. Strayer said. "When you talk to that person on a cellphone, you're much more likely to be involved in an accident."

Despite the overwhelming body of evidence that cellphone use while driving is risky, the idea of a total ban is sure to be controversial. "People understand the dangers, but they just don't want to give it up themselves," said Ms. Froetscher, of the National Safety Council. "But years ago we didn't put on seat belts, or people who might have had a drink before driving wouldn't think of it now. We have to educate people that it's a risky behavior."

USE YOUR ECONOMIC REASONING

1. In the Utah (simulator) test, researchers were able to modify the conditions facing the driver—the number of lanes of traffic and the traffic density (the number of cars in the vicinity), for instance. They were also able to regulate whether or not the driver was talking on a cellphone, listening to a radio talk show (or audio book), or conversing with a passenger. How would the researchers go about testing to determine if hands-free cellphones were safer than the handheld variety? What role does the concept of ceteris paribus play in designing this test?
2. Suppose John is driving down an empty Nevada highway at 100 mph while he listens to his radio and talks on his handheld cellphone. Joan is driving along a twisty road through the Rocky Mountains at 60 mph while she talks on her hands-free cellphone. John has an accident; Joan does not. Can we say that the handheld cellphone caused John's accident? Can we say that the hands-free cellphone is safer than the handheld cellphone? Defend your conclusions.

"other things being equal." In a sense, what economists are doing is stating the conditions under which they expect a theory to be valid. To illustrate, our theory about cigarette consumption might be restated this way: "Consumers will buy more cigarettes at lower prices than at higher prices, ceteris paribus—other things being equal or held constant." Economists then compare what actually happens to what, on the basis of theory, they expected. If the facts are not consistent with the theory, we must determine whether it is because the theory is invalid or because the assumption of ceteris paribus has been violated (that is, because something other than the price of cigarettes has changed). Of course, if the theory is found to be invalid—if its predictions are not consistent with reality—it's back to the drawing board; more work will be required to devise a better theory. (Test your understanding of ceteris paribus concept by reading "A Problem of the Brain, Not the Hands: Group Urges Phone Ban for Drivers," on page 22.)

Policies and Predictions

Once a theory has been tested and accepted, it can be used as a basis for making predictions and as a guide for formulating economic policy. On the basis of our cigarette-price theory, for example, we would predict that if cigarette prices go up, consumption will decline, and if prices fall, consumption will increase. We could also use this theory as the basis for devising policies for influencing the level of cigarette consumption. For instance, recent hikes in the excise tax on cigarettes—which result in higher cigarette prices—have been partly motivated by the desire to reduce smoking, particularly among the young who are not yet addicted.

ECONOMISTS AND CONCLUSIONS

The formulation of policies for dealing with economic problems is the most important use of economic theory and the most important function of economists. But if you listen to TV news or read the newspaper, you know that economists do not always agree on matters of economic policy. Laypersons may therefore be skeptical about the contribution that economics can make to solving society's problems. Because you are going to spend the next few months studying economics, it seems appropriate to take a few minutes now to consider the two reasons that economists disagree. Economists may disagree either because they have different views of what *should be* or because they have different views about what *is*.

We've already explained that economists possess no special expertise in choosing goals, in deciding how things ought to be. Yet like all thinking people, economists have individual values and opinions about which of society's economic goals are most important. Consider, again, the issue of smoking. Although many economists support higher cigarette taxes as a vehicle for deterring young people from smoking, others argue that such taxes impose a financial hardship on older smokers who are, on average, poorer than nonsmokers and who are unlikely to change their behavior because of the higher taxes. Here, the disagreement is about goals. Which is more important, reducing smoking by young people or protecting the living standards of older smokers? Obviously, economists with different philosophies about what the society should be attempting to achieve will have different recommendations with regard to economic policy.

Economists may also disagree about economic policies because they disagree about how things are—about how the economy works or how a particular policy would work. For example, even economists who support higher cigarette taxes to stem youth smoking may disagree about the amount of the tax hike. Here the source of disagreement is likely to be conflicting statistical evidence regarding the responsiveness of young consumers to changes in cigarette prices. For instance, one influential study shows that a 10 percent price hike will reduce youth (ages 12–17) smoking by 14 percent, while another study suggests that the same 10 percent hike will only reduce such smoking by 4 percent.[8] Because of these conflicting results, economists may make different recommendations about how much to increase cigarette taxes—recommendations that reflect their different conclusions regarding the validity of these studies and the price sensitivity of young consumers.

In summary, economists can disagree either because they have different views about what should be or because they have different views about how the economy works. Of course, these areas of dispute are more likely to be reported than areas of agreement. But the fact that economists, like all social scientists, are intensely interested in exploring and debating issues on which they disagree does not mean that they can never reach a conclusion. There are many issues and answers on which economists are in general agreement, so don't let the disagreements about particular policy questions mislead you. The study of economics has a great deal to contribute to your understanding of the world and its many social problems. Approach that study with an open mind, and it will help you to make sense out of facts and events you never before understood.

THE ORGANIZATION OF THE TEXT

Now that you have some sense of what the study of economics is about, let's take a brief look at the organization of this book. It is composed of four major parts. Part 1 forms the introduction and lays the conceptual groundwork for the rest of the text. Part 2 takes up **microeconomics**, the study of the individual units of the economy. These chapters examine how the prices of particular goods and services

---

[8] Frank J. Chaloupka and Michael Grossman, "Price, Tobacco Control Policies and Youth Smoking," Working Paper 5740 (Cambridge, MA: National Bureau of Economic Research, Inc., September 1996), pp. 3–6.

are determined and how individual consumers and businesses function. True to its name, microeconomics looks at the small units that make up the whole economy. Part 3 examines **macroeconomics**, the study of the economy's overall performance and the factors influencing that performance. These chapters address such problems as unemployment and inflation and examine the role of government in combating these economic ills. Through macroeconomics you will begin to view the economy in terms of the big picture. Part 4 turns to **international economics**, the study of international trade and finance. This section explores the reasons for trade and how transactions between nations are financed.

As you can see, economics embraces several specialized areas. Because these areas are interrelated, what you learn in Part 1 will help you understand problems taken up in Part 4. In fact, to a large extent, the chapters in this text build on one another. So please take the time to understand each one thoroughly for an easier and more rewarding trip through economic theory and practice.

SUMMARY

The fundamental economic problem facing both individuals and societies is that our wants exceed our capacity for satisfying those wants. No society has enough *economic resources* (*land*, *labor*, *capital*, and *entrepreneurship*) to satisfy its members fully. Consequently, individuals and societies must make choices about how best to use their limited resources. *Economics* is the study of how to use our limited resources to satisfy our unlimited wants as fully as possible.

Making wise choices requires *cost-benefit analysis*—a systematic comparison of costs and benefits. A decision will only improve our well-being if the benefits associated with that decision exceed the costs.

One of the principal lessons of economics is that all choices entail costs, that there is no "free lunch." Whenever you make a decision to do or have one thing, you are sacrificing the opportunity to do or have some other thing. The most valued alternative you must sacrifice to take a given action is the *opportunity cost* of that action.

A *production possibilities curve* illustrates the concept of opportunity cost by showing the combinations of goods that an economy is capable of producing with its present stock of economic resources and existing techniques of production. It shows that unless there are unemployed resources, producing more of one thing means producing less of something else.

The dilemma of unlimited wants and limited resources forces each society to make three basic choices, to answer the three fundamental questions of economics: (1) What goods and services will the society produce and in what quantities? (2) How will these goods and services be produced? (3) For whom will these products be produced?

To determine how well it is answering the three fundamental questions, a society must establish goals or objectives against which it compares its performance. Full employment, economic efficiency, economic growth, a fair distribution of income, and a stable price level are widely accepted goals. When these goals are in conflict, as they often are, the pursuit of one goal commonly requires a trade-off, some sacrifice in terms of fulfilling another goal.

Before economists can recommend policies for dealing with economic problems or achieving specific objectives, they must develop *economic theories*, generalizations about causal relationships between economic facts, or variables. Testing economic theories can be tricky because the assumption of *ceteris paribus* ("other things being equal") is often violated. This makes it difficult to determine when a theory is flawed because the results of an experiment could be biased by changes in uncontrolled factors.

Once a theory has been tested and accepted, it can be used as a basis for making predictions and as a guide to formulating economic policy. When it comes to making policy recommendations, economists do not always agree. They may disagree for one or both of two distinct reasons: because they have different views about what *should be* or because they have have different views about what *is*.

KEY TERMS

Capital	Entrepreneurship	Macroeconomics
Ceteris paribus	Free trade	Microeconomics
Cost-benefit analysis	International economics	Normative judgments
Economics	Labor	Opportunity cost
Economic resources	Land	Production possibilities curve
Economic theories	Law of increasing costs	Theories

STUDY QUESTIONS

Fill in the Blanks

1. Land, labor, and capital are examples of

   _____.

2. The dilemma of _____ wants

   and _____ resources is referred to as the economic problem.

3. _____ are combiners, innovators, and risk takers.

4. The term _____ is used by economists to describe the economic resources created by nature.

5. When we sacrifice one alternative for another, the alternative forgone is called the

   _____ of that action.

6. A(n) _____ shows the combinations of goods that an economy is capable of producing.

7. Economists use economic _____ to make sense out of the facts they observe.

8. When the pursuit of one objective forces society to sacrifice or compromise some other objective, economists say that a(n)

   _____ exists.

9. Issues involving what "should be" rather than what "is" are referred to as

   _____ issues.

10. Because economists cannot conduct controlled experiments, they often make the

    assumption of _____ to state the conditions under which they expect their theory to hold.

Multiple Choice

1. Economics is the study of how to
   a) distribute output fairly.
   b) do the best we can with what we have.
   c) reduce our unlimited wants.
   d) expand our stock of economic resources.

2. The opportunity cost of attending summer school is
   a) whatever you could have purchased with the money spent for tuition and books.
   b) negative, because you will finish college more rapidly by attending summer school.
   c) the income you could have earned over the summer.
   d) the products, income, and recreational opportunities that must be forgone.

3. The four categories of economic resources are
   a) labor, management, machinery, and money.
   b) land, labor, capital, and entrepreneurship.
   c) money, land, capital, and labor.
   d) air, soil, water, and money.

4. Producing the most-wanted products in the least costly way is
   a) full employment.
   b) economic growth.
   c) a fair income distribution.
   d) economic efficiency.

5. Economists have trouble testing their theories because
   a) people are unpredictable.

   b) the real world is too complicated to be explained.
   c) they can't hold constant the "other factors" that might influence the outcome of the experiment.
   d) the necessary economic data are almost never available.

6. Economists should not be permitted to
   a) devise policies to achieve economic goals.
   b) determine society's economic goals.
   c) explain how the economy works.
   d) explain how particular economic goals conflict.

7. Which of the following statements reflects a normative judgment?
   a) A newspaper headline that reads, "Gas prices headed up after supply disruptions."
   b) A doctor who tells you, "If you consume more calories than you burn, you will gain weight."
   c) An editorial that argues, "We are spending too many of our tax dollars on the military and too few on preventative health care."
   d) A scientist who predicts that "San Francisco will suffer a major earthquake sometime in the next 100 years."

8. Was Ted Williams the greatest hitter ever to grace a baseball diamond? An economists would say it's hard to know because

there is a "ceteris paribus" problem. In this context what does that mean?
a) Officials didn't keep the careful records needed to make a valid comparison.
b) Ted faced different pitchers and conditions than those confronting modern batters.
c) Some comparisons are normative judgments and can't be made objective.
d) All of the above

9. Of the three fundamental questions, the "distribution" question has to do with
a) who will receive the output.
b) how the output will be shipped from the place of production to the consumer.
c) how economic resources are distributed to producers.
d) what products will be produced.

10. Suppose that you have just found $10 on the street and are thinking of using it to buy a ticket to the movies. The opportunity cost of going to the show would be
a) nothing—because you found the money, you are sacrificing nothing to spend it.
b) whatever you would have bought with the money if you hadn't used it to go to the show.
c) the other activities you would have to sacrifice to attend the show.
d) b and c

11. The production possibilities curve slopes downward because
a) some resources are better suited to the production of one product than another.
b) economic resources are limited.
c) economic wants are unlimited.
d) All of the above.

Use the production possibilities curve at the end of this section to answer questions 12 through 14.

12. If the economy is operating at point C, the opportunity cost of producing an additional 10,000 automobiles will be
a) 10 million bushels of wheat.
b) 20 million bushels of wheat.
c) 30 million bushels of wheat.
d) 40 million bushels of wheat.

13. Point G on the diagram represents
a) an optimal use of the society's resources.
b) a combination of outputs beyond the economy's productive capacity.
c) a situation in which some of the economy's resources are unemployed.
d) the same output combination as point B.

14. The production possibilities curve might shift outward to include G if
a) the economy put all unemployed resources to work.
b) the economy experienced more rapid price inflation.
c) improved training increased the productivity of workers.
d) the nation's population declined.

15. Foreign trade permits an economy to
a) eliminate the problem of scarcity.
b) operate inside its production possibilities curve.
c) shift its production possibilities curve outward.
d) consume a combination of products beyond its own production possibilities.

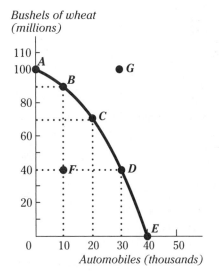

Problems and Questions for Discussion

1. List the four categories of economic resources and explain each.

2. Define *economics*. Why is economics sometimes called the "study of choice"?

3. List and explain the three fundamental choices that each society is forced to make.

4. What is meant when we say that a secretary is efficient? What about a salesclerk? Why is economic efficiency an important performance objective for an economy?

5. Airline personnel are often allowed to make a certain number of free flights each year. How would you compute the opportunity cost to the airlines of these free trips? Might this cost vary from route to route? Might the cost be different at different times of the year? Explain.

6. List and briefly explain the economic objectives recognized as worthwhile by many societies.

7. What are trade-offs? Give some examples.

8. A theory that has been around for quite some time says, "Better-educated people earn higher incomes than less-educated people, ceteris paribus." If we know a high school dropout who earns $200,000 a year, does this mean that we should discard the theory? Explain.

9. Suppose that we accept the theory given in problem 8 and decide to use it to formulate policies for reducing poverty. Apply this theory by suggesting three policies to reduce poverty.

10. Why is it important to separate the process of setting economic goals from the process of devising policies for achieving these goals? In which process is the economist more expert? Explain.

11. How would you go about using cost-benefit analysis to decide whether or not to attend college? What factors would complicate this analysis?

12. Foreign immigration into the United States normally shifts the U.S. production possibilities curve to the right. Why? If it has this impact, why do some citizens oppose immigration? Is foreign immigration a normative issue?

ANSWER KEY

Fill in the Blanks

1. economic resources
2. unlimited, limited
3. Entrepreneurs
4. land
5. opportunity cost
6. production possibilities curve
7. theories (or models)
8. trade-off
9. normative
10. ceteris paribus

Multiple Choice

1. b
2. d
3. b
4. d
5. c
6. b
7. c
8. b
9. a
10. d
11. b
12. c
13. b
14. c
15. d

WORKING WITH GRAPHS

Economists frequently use graphs to illustrate economic concepts. This appendix provides a brief review of graphing and offers some practice problems to help you become more comfortable working with graphs.

THE PURPOSE OF GRAPHS

The basic purpose of a graph is to represent the relationship between two variables. A *variable* is any quantity that can take on different numeric values. Suppose, for example, that a university has conducted a survey to determine the relationship between two variables: the number of hours its students study and their grade-point averages. The results of that hypothetical survey could be shown in table, or schedule, form, as in panel (a) of Exhibit A1.1, or they could be represented graphically, as in panel (b) of Exhibit A1.1. Notice the difference: the graph reveals the relationship between the variables at a glance; you don't have to compare data as you do when reading the table.

CONSTRUCTING A GRAPH

The first step in constructing a graph is to draw two perpendicular lines. These lines are called *axes*. In our example the vertical axis is used to measure the first variable, the grade-point average; the horizontal axis is used to measure the second variable, hours of study. The place where the two axes meet is called the *origin* because it is the starting point for measuring each of the variables; in our example the origin is zero. Once the axes are in place, we're ready to draw, or *plot*, the points that represent the relationship between the variables. Let's begin with the students who study 32 hours a week. According to the table in panel (a), these students typically earn a grade-point average of 4.0. To show this relationship graphically, we find the point on the horizontal axis that represents 32 hours of study per week. Next, we move directly upward from that point until we reach a height of 4.0 grade points. This point, which we will label *A*, represents a combination of two values; it tells us at a glance that the typical student who studies 32 hours a week will earn a 4.0 grade-point average.

The Hypothetical Relationship Between Grades and Study Time

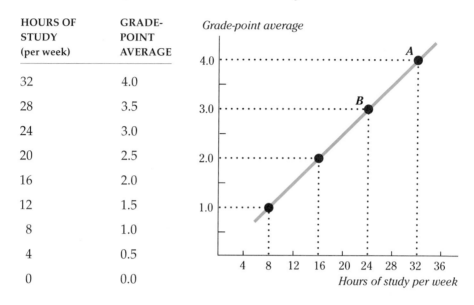

HOURS OF STUDY (per week)	GRADE-POINT AVERAGE
32	4.0
28	3.5
24	3.0
20	2.5
16	2.0
12	1.5
8	1.0
4	0.5
0	0.0

(a) Relationship with table   **(b) Relationship with graph**

Panels (a) and (b) both illustrate the relationship between hours of study and grades. Panel (a) uses a table to show this relationship; panel (b), a graph. Both illustrations show that the relationship between the two variables is direct; more hours of study tend to be associated with a higher grade-point average.

We plot the rest of the information found in panel (a) in the same way. To represent the typical, or average, grade of the student who studies 24 hours a week, all we need to do is locate the number 24 on the horizontal axis and then move up vertically from that point to a distance of 3.0 grade points (point *B*). We plot all the remaining points on the graph in the same way.

Once we've plotted all the points, we can connect them to form a curve. Economists use the term *curve* to describe any graphical relationship between two variables, so don't be surprised when you discover a straight line referred to as a curve. You can see that the resulting curve slopes upward and to the right. This indicates that there is a positive, or *direct*, relationship between the two variables—as one variable (study time) increases, the other (grade-point average) also increases. If the resulting curve had sloped downward and to the right, it would have indicated a negative, or *inverse*, relationship between the two variables—as one variable increased, the other would decrease. We'd be surprised to find an inverse relationship between these particular variables;

that would suggest the unlikely possibility that increased study time lowers the grade-point average!

PRACTICE IN GRAPHING

All graphs are basically the same, so if you understand the one we just considered, you should be able to master all the graphs in this textbook and in library sources. If you want some practice, take a few minutes to graph the three sets of data at the end of this appendix.

The first step is to draw and label the vertical and horizontal axes and mark them off in units that are convenient to work with. As you probably know, mathematicians always measure the *independent* variable (the variable that causes the other to change) along the horizontal axis and the *dependent* variable (the variable that responds to changes) along the vertical axis. Economists are less strict in deciding which variable to place on which axis, so don't be alarmed if occasionally you see the dependent variable on the horizontal axis.

Once you've decided which variable to place on which axis, the next step is to plot the information from the table as points and connect them. Then see if you can interpret your graph. What does it tell you about the relationship between the two variables? Are they directly or inversely related? (It's possible that they are not related at all. For example, there is probably no relationship between a student's weight and his or her grade-point average.) Does the relationship change somewhere along the graph? The way to become comfortable with graphs is to work with them. Try drawing these graphs to help prepare yourself for the upcoming chapters.

1. Graph the relationship between the hourly wage rate paid by the school and the number of students desiring to work in the school cafeteria. Is the relationship direct or inverse?

POINT	WAGE RATE (per hour)	NUMBER OF STUDENT WORKERS
A	$6.50	5
B	7.00	10
C	7.50	15
D	8.00	20
E	8.50	25
F	9.00	30

2. Graph the relationship between the average daily temperature and the average number of students playing tennis on the school tennis courts. How does this relationship change?

POINT	TEMPERATURE (in degrees Fahrenheit)	NUMBER OF TENNIS PLAYERS
A	60	20
B	70	30
C	80	40
D	90	30
E	100	20

3. Graph the relationship between the price of gasoline and the quantity of gasoline purchased by consumers. Is the relationship direct or inverse?

POINT	PRICE (per gallon)	QUANTITY PURCHASED (in gallons)
A	$2.00	15 million
B	2.50	12 million
C	3.00	9 million
D	3.50	6 million
E	4.00	3 million

2

Economic Systems

Every nation, from the richest to the poorest, faces the same economic dilemma: how to satisfy people's unlimited wants with its limited economic resources. Each society must decide which goods and services to produce, how to produce them, and for whom to produce them; in other words, it must establish an economic system. An **economic system** is a set of institutions and mechanisms for answering the three fundamental questions of economics—what, how, and for whom to produce.

In describing economic systems, it is helpful to ask two questions: (1) Who owns the means of production—the factories, farms, mines, and other resources used to produce goods and services? (2) Who makes the economic decisions; that is, who answers the three fundamental economic questions? The variety of real-world economic systems is probably as great as the number of world nations, but all economic systems combine elements of two divergent models. At one extreme, the means of production are privately owned, and individual buyers and sellers interacting in markets make the economic decisions. At the other extreme, the means of production are publicly owned, and a central authority makes the fundamental economic choices.

This chapter will begin by providing you with an overview of these two divergent models—the models of pure capitalism and pure command socialism. Recall from Chapter 1 that models simplify reality, making it possible to see more clearly how the parts of a system function and interact. Once we have become familiar with how "pure" capitalism and "pure" command socialism would function, we can compare the U.S. economy and other selected economies against these theoretical models to discover how these real-world economic systems conform and how they deviate from the models.

THE MODEL OF PURE CAPITALISM

The *American Heritage Dictionary* defines something as *pure* if it is "free from impurities or contaminants." So pure capitalism is a hypothetical economic system that is totally or completely capitalist, one without traces of anything else. In this section we examine the elements of such a system, diagram its operation or functioning, see how it answers the three fundamental questions, and conclude by assessing its strengths and weaknesses.

Elements of Capitalism

We define **capitalism** as an economic system in which the means of production are privately owned and fundamental economic choices are made by individual buyers and sellers interacting in markets. The model of pure capitalism is entirely consistent with our definition and contains five basic elements, which we will describe briefly.

Private Property and Freedom of Choice   One of the principal features of capitalism is private property. In a capitalist economy, private individuals and groups are the owners of the **means of production**: the raw materials, factories, farms, and other economic resources used to produce goods and services. These resource owners may sell or use their resources, including their own labor, as they see fit. Businesses are free to decide what products they will produce and to purchase the necessary economic resources from whomever they choose. Consumers, in turn, are free to spend their incomes any way they like. They can purchase whatever products they choose, and they can decide what fraction of their incomes to save and what fraction to spend.

Self-Interest

The driving force of capitalism is self-interest. In 1776 Adam Smith, the founder of economics, described a capitalist economy as one in which the primary concern of each player—of each producer, worker, and consumer—was to promote his or her own welfare.[1]

Smith introduced the **invisible hand** doctrine, which held that as individuals pursued their own interests, they would be led as if by an invisible hand to promote the good of the society as a whole. To earn the highest profits, predicted Smith, producers would generate the products consumers wanted most. Workers would offer their services where they were most needed because wages would be highest in those sectors. Consumers would favor producers who offered superior products and/or lower prices because they would seek the best value for their money. The result would be an economy that produced the goods and services desired by the society without the need for any central direction by government.

Markets and Prices

Capitalism is often described as a market system. This is because a capitalist economy contains numerous interdependent markets through which the functioning of the economy is coordinated and directed. A **market** consists of all actual or potential buyers and sellers of a particular item and can be local, regional, national, or international. For example, there are numerous local and regional markets for used automobiles, each consisting of all buyers and sellers of such vehicles in that particular area. Similar markets exist for all other goods and services and for all economic resources as well.

Market prices are determined by the interaction of buyers and sellers and serve two important functions. First, prices help to divide up, or ration, the society's limited output of goods and services among those who desire to receive it. Only those who are willing and able to pay the market price receive the product. Second, prices motivate businesses to produce more of some products and less of others. Businesses generally want to supply products that yield the highest profits, the ones with the highest prices in relation to their costs of production. These products tend to be those most desired by consumers. So, by motivating suppliers, price changes help to ensure that society's scarce resources are used to produce the goods and services most highly valued by consumers.

---

[1] Adam Smith's description of the functioning of a capitalist economy appeared in *An Inquiry into the Nature and Causes of the Wealth of Nations*, published in 1776.

Competition   Adam Smith recognized that for the invisible hand to work—for individuals seeking their own interests to promote the good of all—the pursuit of self-interest had to be guided and restrained by competition. Competition ensures that producers remain responsive to consumers and that prices remain reasonable.

Pure capitalism requires **pure competition**, a situation in which a large number of relatively small buyers and sellers interact to determine prices.[2] Under conditions of pure competition, no individual buyer or seller can set—or even significantly influence—the prevailing price of a product or resource. Prices are thus determined by market forces, not by powerful buyers or sellers, and change only when market conditions change.

Limited Government Intervention   Pure capitalism is above all a **laissez-faire economy**. (*Laissez-faire* is a French phrase that in this context means "let the people do as they choose.") The model describes no role for government in making economic decisions. Through pricing, the market makes all production and distribution decisions—what, how, and for whom to produce—and competition ensures that consumers will be charged reasonable prices. The only role of government is to provide the kind of environment in which a market economy can function well. For example, government must define and enforce the private-property rights that enable individuals to own and use property.

The Circular-Flow Model

We can represent the operation of a capitalist economy in a diagram called the circular-flow model. Exhibit 2.1 models an economy composed of only two sectors: households and businesses. You can see that these two sectors are connected through transactions, or flows, that occur continuously between them. We'll examine how each sector processes the flow it receives and returns it to the other sector.

The Household and Business Sectors   The household sector is shown at the right in Exhibit 2.1. A **household** is defined as one or more people living in the same dwelling. Whether it consists of a single person or many people, each household will have a source of income and will spend that income. The household sector is composed of all the individual households in the economy. Because households own the land, labor, capital, and entrepreneurship that businesses need to produce goods and services, this sector is the source of all economic resources in the model of pure capitalism. It is also the source of consumer spending for the goods and services produced.

---

[2] Chapter 6 describes further assumptions relating to pure competition.

The Circular Flow of Pure Capitalism

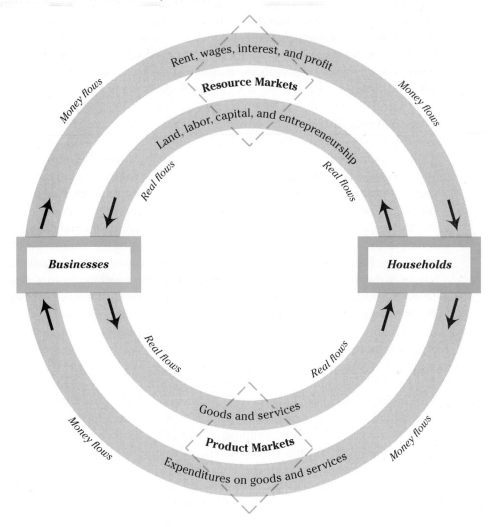

The business sector, on the left, is composed of all the businesses in the economy. The business sector purchases economic resources from households, converts those resources into products, and sells the products to the households.

Real Flows and Money Flows   You can see in the diagram that two types of flows circle in opposite directions. In the outside circle *money flows*, in the form of rent, wages, interest, and profit, go from businesses to households to pay for economic resources. These flows return to businesses as households pay for products. *Real flows* involve the physical movement of the resources and products. The inner flow in the diagram shows economic resources in the form of land, labor, capital, and entrepreneurship flowing from the household sector to the business sector, where they are used to produce goods and services. The unbroken arrows in the diagram show that these circular flows are endless.

The Resource and Product Markets   Markets are the key to the operation of a capitalist system because they hold together its decentralized economy of millions of individual buyers and sellers. The interaction of these buyers and sellers ensures that the right products (the ones desired by consumers) are produced and that economic resources flow to the right producers (the ones producing the most-wanted products at the lowest prices).

In the resource markets, depicted in the upper portion of Exhibit 2.1, the interaction of buyers and sellers determines the prices of the various economic resources. For example, in the labor market for accountants, an accountant's salary is determined by the interaction of employers seeking to hire accountants (the buyers) and accountants seeking employment (the sellers). Changes in resource prices guide and motivate resource suppliers to provide the type and quantity of resources producers need most. Using our example of labor, suppose that the number of businesses desiring accountants is expanding more rapidly than new accountants are being trained. What will happen to the salaries of accountants? They will tend to increase. As a result, we can expect more people in the household sector to invest the time and money necessary to become accountants. You can see how the price mechanism ensures that (1) the types of labor, equipment, and other resources most needed by businesses will be supplied, and (2) these resources will be supplied in the proper quantities.

In the product markets, depicted in the lower portion of Exhibit 2.1, the prices of all products—from eggs and overcoats to haircuts and airline tickets—again are determined by the interaction of buyers and sellers. Prices serve the same function here as they do in the resource market: They make it possible to divide up, or ration, the limited amount of output among all those who wish to receive it. Only those consumers who are willing and able to pay the market price can obtain the product. When prices change, this informs producers about desired changes in the amount they are producing and motivates them to supply the new quantity. For example, when consumers want more of a product than is available, they tend to bid up its price. Producers, getting a clear signal that consumers like that item, thus have an incentive to supply more of it.

How Capitalism Answers the Three Fundamental Questions

Now that we have discussed the elements of pure capitalism and have a general idea of the role of markets in such an economy, we can determine more easily how this system answers the three fundamental questions.

What to Produce   One feature of pure capitalism is **consumer sovereignty**, an economic condition in which consumers dictate which goods and services businesses will produce. Because producers are motivated by profits and because the most profitable products tend to be the ones consumers desire most, producers must be responsive to consumer preferences. To illustrate consumer sovereignty in action, let's consider how automobile manufacturers in a pure capitalist economy would respond if consumer preferences suddenly took a dramatic turn away from sport-utility vehicles (SUVs) in favor of midsized cars. If people began to buy more midsized automobiles and fewer SUVs, the price of midsize cars would rise, and they would become more profitable, whereas SUVs would decline in price and become less profitable. Therefore, automobile manufacturers would produce more midsize vehicles and fewer SUVs—just what consumers want.

Because consumers are free to spend their incomes as they choose, producers who wish to earn profits must be responsive to consumers' desires. As a result, pure capitalism might be described as a system in which the consumer is the ruler and the producer an obedient servant.

How to Produce   Automobile producers have a number of options available for manufacturing midsized cars and other vehicles that consumers desire. They can produce these automobiles through highly mechanized techniques, or they can rely primarily on skilled labor and simpler tools. They can manufacture car bodies from steel, aluminum, fiberglass, or some combination of the three. In selecting which production technique and combination of resources to use, capitalist manufacturers will minimize the cost of production; they will adopt the *least-cost* approach because lower costs contribute to higher profits.

The search for the least-cost approach is guided by the market prices of the various economic resources. Because the scarcest resources cost the most, producers use them only when they cannot substitute less-expensive resources. For example, if steel is very expensive, automobile makers will tend to use it only where other materials would be inadequate, perhaps in the frame or in other parts of the car that require great strength. And if skilled labor is expensive, as it is in Japan and the United States, robots will be used to

In a capitalist economy, highly mechanized production methods—such as those utilizing robots—may be selected if labor is expensive.

perform as many jobs as possible. Thus, the prices of resources help to ensure that resources are used to their best advantage in a capitalist economy. Abundant, cheaper resources are used when they will suffice; scarcer, more costly resources are conserved.

For Whom to Produce   Finally, we consider the task of distributing our hypothetical economy's output of automobiles. We know that only those who can afford to buy automobiles will receive them. The ability to pay, however, is only half the picture; the other half is willingness to purchase, which takes into account consumer preferences. Some of those who can afford a new car will prefer to spend their money elsewhere: remodeling their homes perhaps or sending their children to college. Some who seemingly cannot afford a new car may be able to purchase one by doing without other things—new clothes or a larger apartment, for example. Of course, consumers with low incomes will face less-attractive choices than those earning high incomes. A low-income consumer may sacrifice basic necessities to afford an automobile, whereas a wealthy consumer need choose only between the new car and some luxury item, such as a sailboat or a winter vacation. In the final analysis, those with higher incomes will always have more choices than those with lower incomes and will receive a larger share of the economy's total output.

Capitalism: Strengths and Weaknesses

Before moving on from our discussion of pure capitalism, we will describe briefly some of the strengths and weaknesses inherent in such a system. One of the major strengths of pure capitalism is *economic efficiency*. In a market economy, businesses are encouraged to produce the products that consumers want most and to produce those products at the lowest cost in terms of scarce resources. A system that accomplishes those objectives goes a long way toward ensuring that a society achieves the maximum benefit possible from its limited resources.

A second positive feature of capitalism is *economic freedom*. Under pure capitalism, consumers, workers, and producers are free to make decisions based on self-interest. To many people, this economic freedom is the overwhelming virtue of the capitalist model.

Economist Milton Friedman, a vocal advocate of competitive capitalism, noted a third strength of the system: It promotes *political freedom* by separating economic and political power. The existence of private ownership of the means of production ensures that government officials are not in a position to deny jobs or goods and services to individuals whose political views conflict with their own.[3]

Pure capitalism also has some shortcomings. First, people are not uniformly equal in ability, and some will succeed to a greater extent than others. In a capitalist system the result is the unequal distribution of income and output. This inequality tends to be perpetuated because the children of the rich usually have access to better educational opportunities and often inherit the income-producing assets of their parents. Such inequality weakens capitalism's claim that it produces the goods and services that the *society* wants the most. It is more the case that capitalism produces the products that the *consumers who have the money* want most.

A second, closely related criticism was voiced by the late Arthur Okun, chairman of the Council of Economic Advisors during the Johnson administration. In a capitalist economy, observed Okun, money can buy a great many things that are not supposed to be for sale:

Money buys legal services that can obtain preferred treatment before the law; it buys platforms that give extra weight to the owner's freedom of speech; it buys influence with elected officials and thus compromises the principle of one person,

[3]Milton Friedman, *Capitalism and Freedom* (Chicago: University of Chicago Press, 1962), p. 9.

one vote. . . . Even though money generally cannot buy extra helpings of rights directly, it can buy services that, in effect, produce more or better rights.[4]

Third, pure capitalism may be criticized for encouraging the destruction of the environment. Because air, rivers, lakes, and streams are **common-property resources** belonging to the society as a whole, they tend to be seen as free—available to be used or abused without charge or concern. The pursuit of self-interest would cause producers to dump their wastes into nearby rivers to avoid the cost of disposing of those wastes in an environmentally acceptable manner. Farmers would select pesticides according to their favorable impact on output and without regard to their undesirable effects on wildlife and water supplies. In this case, Adam Smith's invisible hand fails. The pursuit of self-interest by individuals may not promote the good of all but may instead lead to environmental destruction.[5]

THE MODEL OF PURE COMMAND SOCIALISM

The opposite of the model of pure capitalism is the model of pure command socialism. The socialist command economy described in this section represents no existing economic system. Like the model of pure capitalism, the model of pure command socialism is simply a tool to help us understand how command economies operate. Again, we will examine the basic elements of the model, diagram how the hypothetical economy operates, and see how the system decides what, how, and for whom to produce. Then we will examine the strengths and weaknesses of pure command socialism.

Elements of Command Socialism

We define **command socialism** as an economic system in which the means of production are publicly owned and the fundamental economic choices are made by a central authority. Four basic elements of command socialism support this definition.

Public Ownership   A socialist economy is characterized by state, or public, ownership of the means of production. In the model of pure command socialism,

---

[4] Arthur M. Okun, *Equality and Efficiency: The Big Tradeoff* (Washington: Brookings Institution, 1975), p. 22.

[5] It can be argued that the problem here is not capitalism, but too little capitalism. If someone were assigned the ownership of these common-property resources, that party would have both the ability and the incentive to protect those resources from abuse.

state ownership is complete. The factories, farms, mines, hospitals, and other forms of capital are all publicly owned. Even labor is publicly owned in the sense that workers and managers do not select their own employment but are assigned their jobs by the state.

Centralized Decision Making   One of the most distinctive features of command socialism is that economic choices are made by a central authority. This central authority may be either responsive to the feelings of the people (democratic socialism) or unresponsive to their wishes (authoritarian socialism or communism). In either case, this authority makes the fundamental production and distribution decisions and then takes the necessary actions to see that these decisions are carried out.

Economic Planning   In the model of command socialism, economic planning replaces the market as the method for coordinating economic decisions. The central authority, or central planning board, gathers information about existing production capacities, supplies of raw materials, and labor force capabilities. It then draws up a master plan specifying production objectives for each sector or industry in the economy. Industrywide objectives are translated into specific production targets for each factory, farm, mine, or other kind of producing unit. Central planning ensures that specific production objectives agree so that automobile manufacturers will not produce 1 million cars, for example, while tire manufacturers produce only 2 million tires.

Allocation by Command   In command socialism, resources and products are allocated by directive, or command, and the central authority uses its power to enforce these decisions. Once it determines production and distribution objectives, the central planning board dictates to each producing unit the quantity and assortment of goods the unit is to produce and the combination of resources it is to use. Commands are also issued to producers of raw materials and other production inputs to supply these inputs to the producing units that need them. Further commands direct individuals to places of employment— wherever the central planning board determines that their services are needed— and dictate distribution of the economy's output of goods and services. All the allocative functions that a capitalist economy leaves to the market and the pursuit of self-interest are accomplished in pure command socialism through planning and allocation by directive.

The Pyramid Model

Exhibit 2.2 represents a socialist command economy as a pyramid, with the central planning board at the top and the various producing and consuming

EXHIBIT 2.2

The Command Pyramid

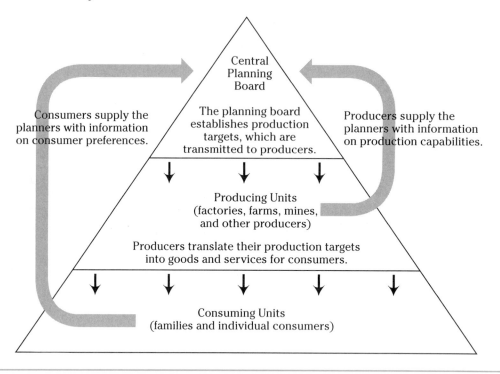

Central Planning Board

Consumers supply the planners with information on consumer preferences.

The planning board establishes production targets, which are transmitted to producers.

Producers supply the planners with information on production capabilities.

Producing Units (factories, farms, mines, and other producers)

Producers translate their production targets into goods and services for consumers.

Consuming Units (families and individual consumers)

units below it. This diagram emphasizes the primary feature of a command economy: centralization of economic decision making.

The outer arrow at the right in Exhibit 2.2 shows how information about production capacities, raw material supplies, and labor capabilities flows up from the producing units in the middle of the pyramid to the central planning board at the top. Information, if requested, about which goods and services consumers desire also flows up from the consuming units at the base of the pyramid (outer left arrow). Production objectives, or targets, are transmitted back to the individual producing units, which then supply the targeted quantity and assortment of products and produce them as specified. Finally, the output is distributed to consumers in accordance with the plan.

How Command Socialism Answers the Three Fundamental Questions

In many respects the operation of a socialist command economy is easier to understand than the functioning of a capitalist economy. The answers to the three fundamental questions are decided by the central planning board, which then uses its authority to ensure that all directives are carried out.

The central planners can select any output targets, any mix of products within the limits set by the economy's production capacity. Of course, the planners will have to gather an abundance of information before they have a good picture of the economy's capabilities. They must determine the size of the labor force and the skills it possesses, for example, as well as how many factories exist and what they are capable of producing. Until the central planners have this kind of information, they cannot establish realistic output targets. And, even then, they will face some tough decisions because, as you already know, more of one thing means less of something else. So if they decide to produce more automobiles, they won't be able to manufacture as many refrigerators and military weapons and other products.

In deciding how to produce each product, central planners must try to stretch the economy's limited resources as far as possible. This requires that each resource be used efficiently—where it makes the greatest contribution to the economy's output. If some resource is particularly scarce, planners must be careful to use it only where no other input will suffice; otherwise they won't be able to maximize the economy's output.

Even with the best planning, an economy's resources will stretch only so far. The central planning board can allocate the economy's limited output in accordance with any objective it has set. If the planning board's primary objective is equality, it can develop a method of rationing, dividing up the society's output in equal shares to each member. If it wants to promote loyalty to the government, the central authority can give supporters extra shares while penalizing dissenters. Whatever its objectives, the central planning board can use distribution as a method to further them.

Command Socialism: Strengths and Weaknesses

Like pure capitalism, the economy of pure command socialism has certain strengths and certain weaknesses. Some people argue that a major strength of command socialism is its ability to promote a high degree of equality in the distribution of income and output. Because the central planners control the distribution of goods and services, they can elect to distribute output in ways that achieve whatever degree of equality in living standard they consider appropriate. Thus, it is theoretically possible for command socialism to avoid the extremely unequal income and output distribution that characterizes pure capitalism.

Another major strength of command socialism is its potential for achieving economic objectives in a relatively short period of time. As an example, consider the power of the planners to foster more rapid economic growth. If a society wants to increase its capacity for producing goods and services, it must devote more of its resources to producing capital goods (factories and equipment) and fewer resources to producing consumer goods. In other words, society must consume less *now* to be able to produce and consume more *later*. Because the central authority has the power to dictate the fraction of the society's resources that will be devoted to capital goods production, in effect, it can force the society to make the sacrifices necessary to increase the rate of economic growth.

You probably recognize that the power to bring about rapid economic changes is not necessarily a good thing. The major shortcoming of command socialism, in fact, is the possibility that the central planning board may pursue goals that do not reflect the needs or desires of the majority. If the socialist government is not democratically elected, its goals may bear no relationship to the wants of the general population.

A second weakness in the model of command socialism is its inefficient information network. The system we have described needs more information than it can reasonably expect to acquire and process to ensure efficient use of the economy's resources. The system must not only have a substantial organizational network to acquire information about consumer preferences and production capabilities, but it must also use that network to transmit the decisions of central planners to millions of economic units. Moreover, the central planners have to be able to process all the acquired information and return it in the form of a consistent plan—a staggering task, considering that the output of one industry is often the production input required by some other industry. Finally, they must see that each product is produced efficiently. This complex and cumbersome process is bound to result in breakdowns in communication and decision making. When these occur, the wrong products may be produced or the right ones produced using the wrong combinations of resources. In either case, inefficiency means that the society does not achieve maximum benefit from its limited resources.

MIXED ECONOMIES: THE REAL-WORLD SOLUTION

No existing economic system adheres strictly to either pure capitalism or pure command socialism. All real-world economies are **mixed economies**; they represent a blending of the two models. To illustrate this point, we look next at the U.S. economy. Then we highlight the diversity of economic systems by taking a brief tour of several of the world's economies.

The U.S. Economic System

Because the U.S. economic system is marked by such a high degree of private ownership and individual decision making, American children learn early from their teachers, the news media, and others that they live in a capitalist economy. And certainly there is ample evidence to support that viewpoint. Most U.S. businesses, from industrial giants like Ford Motor Company and General Electric to small firms like your neighborhood barbershop or hair salon, are private operations, not government-owned enterprises. The U.S. economy is coordinated and directed largely by the market mechanism, the interaction of buyers and sellers in thousands of interdependent markets. Each of those buyers and sellers is guided by self-interest, which among producers takes the form of profit seeking. Fortunately for consumers, the drive for profits is usually kept in check by another feature of pure capitalism: competition. In most American industries, competition, though not pure, is adequate to keep prices reasonable and to ensure that consumers receive fair treatment.

Given these elements of pure capitalism, why do we call the United States a *mixed economy*? In part, that label stems from the degree of public ownership that exists in our economy. A second, perhaps more important, reason is the extent to which the government makes or influences the fundamental economic choices. Let's briefly consider each of these reasons.

Public Ownership of the Means of Production   Pure capitalism requires private ownership of the means of production. The U.S. economy does not fully meet that requirement. Although most American businesses are privately owned, some very important and visible producers are publicly owned enterprises. For example, the electricity on which we rely to heat and cool our homes and to run our appliances is supplied in part by municipal, state, or county power companies. The vast majority of our schoolchildren—almost 90 percent—attend public elementary and secondary schools. When we apply for admission to college, we mail those applications via the U.S. Postal Service, often to state universities. Moreover, the extent of public ownership is not a static concept. During the recent financial crisis, the federal government took partial ownership stakes in hundreds of banks in return for providing aid to these troubled institutions. There were even calls to nationalize such well-known firms as Bank of America and General Motors, rather than allowing them to fail. Although these steps were never taken, the federal government was clearly viewed as the owner of last resort.

Government Decision Making   Although government decision making is the hallmark of a socialist command economy, some government intervention is unavoidable, even in a capitalist economy. The most basic function of government is to establish a *legal framework*—the rules by which citizens must deal with one another. A capitalist economy requires rules to protect private property—from theft, damage, etc. These rules must be maintained and enforced by legal institutions—police and a court system. Without these institutions, the

A capitalist economy requires rules to protect private property.

concept of private property has little meaning, and a capitalist economy could not exist. The U.S. economy has a highly developed legal system, with well-established principles of law.

Government's role in establishing a legal framework clearly is consistent with the model of pure capitalism. But government does much more than this in the U.S. economy. Consider the following functions of government and decide for yourself which are consistent with pure capitalism and which are not.

1. *Maintaining competition.* Competition helps to channel the profit-seeking motives of producers into socially desirable outcomes. When competition is inadequate, consumers may be forced to pay higher prices or accept inferior products. In the U.S. economy, the federal government uses *antitrust laws* to discourage anticompetitive behavior and to promote competition. In one recent use of the antitrust laws, three leading flat-screen producers—LG Display of Korea, Sharp of Japan, and Chunghwa Picture Tubes of Taiwan— were prosecuted for their role in a price-fixing cartel that drove up the price of liquid-crystal display panels used in flat-screen televisions, computers, and cell phones. In essence, these firms illegally agreed among themselves to set prices rather than allowing prices to be established by competition in

the marketplace. In 2008, the three firms pled guilty and agreed to pay criminal fines totaling $585 million. The case was the result of the coordinated efforts of enforcement agencies in Europe, Asia, and the United States. Antitrust laws are discussed in greater detail in Chapter 8.

2. *Correcting for externalities*. Buyers and sellers make decisions based on costs and benefits. If an individual judges that the benefits of an action exceed the costs incurred, he or she will perform that action. If, on the other hand, the person determines the costs of the action exceed its benefits, he or she will refrain from that action. This behavior commonly leads to an efficient use of society's scarce resources. But when an action creates *externalities*—costs or benefits that spill over into third parties—the resulting decision may not be optimal for society. For instance, the managers of electricity-generating power plants may use more high-sulfur coal than is socially desirable because they ignore the damage that this variety of coal inflicts on the environment. And dog owners may opt *not* to have their pets inoculated against rabies because they ignore the benefits that this protection provides to others. The U.S. government attempts to adjust for these and other externalities by establishing laws—laws requiring rabies inoculations and limiting waste emissions, for example—and by using taxes and subsidies to alter the behavior of firms and individuals. Chapter 9 further explores the topic of externalities.

3. *Providing public goods*. Some important products cannot be profitably produced by private businesses; they must be provided by government if they are to be available. In the United States, government uses its taxing authority to pay for public goods such as national defense, flood-control dams, and tornado-warning systems. A wide variety of quasi-public goods such as fire and police protection are also financed in this manner. Public goods are discussed in more detail in Chapter 9.

4. *Redistributing income*. As we saw earlier, total reliance on the market mechanism can produce substantial income inequality. In the United States, government has assumed responsibility for reducing income inequality. This is accomplished in a variety of ways. The federal income tax is somewhat "progressive"—that is, it is intended to take a greater proportion of the incomes of the rich than the poor. Those with very low incomes qualify for an "earned income tax credit." In effect, rather than receiving taxes from them, the government pays these people. Some government programs attempt to bolster the incomes of the poor by providing them with subsidized job training. Other programs attempt to reduce poverty directly. For example, Social Security provides financial assistance to the old, the disabled, and those who are experiencing financial distress due to the death of a breadwinner. In addition, state unemployment compensation provides

financial assistance to workers who are temporarily unemployed. Despite these efforts, however, there is still substantial income inequality in the U.S. economy. The appendix to Chapter 9 covers this topic in greater detail.

5. *Stabilizing the economy.* Many economists argue that capitalist economies are inherently unstable—subject to periodic bouts of unemployment or inflation. The Employment Act of 1946 requires Congress to pursue policies aimed at achieving high employment, economic growth, and price stability. In addition, the Federal Reserve—the governmental agency that regulates the nation's money supply—attempts to guide the economy's overall performance. Later chapters will discuss the factors that influence the macroeconomic performance of our economy and examine how policymakers attempt to manage that performance.

6. *Regulating health and safety.* In addition to the preceding functions, government regulates businesses to ensure product quality and the safety of working conditions. It bans certain goods and services (fully automatic weapons, prostitution, illicit drugs, and child pornography, for example) and certain ingredients (lead in gasoline, for instance, and red dye number two). Government also mandates the purchase of certain products such as seatbelts and airbags in automobiles, smoke detectors in apartments, and lifejackets on boats. Clearly, government's role in attempting to maintain health and safety is not insignificant.

As you can see, there are many decisions that the United States does not leave to the impersonal dictates of the market. And even this relatively lengthy list is not exhaustive! Is all this government intervention a good thing? Does it allow markets to function more efficiently or more humanely? Does it succeed in making our economy more stable? This is open to debate. Succeeding chapters will examine elements of this debate further.

The Rest of the World

As we've seen, the U.S. economy does not conform to the model of pure capitalism. A number of important enterprises are publicly owned, and the visible hand of government influences many of our economic decisions. Yet the U.S. economy is probably as close to pure capitalism as any economy in existence. The rest of the world's economies represent an even more thorough blending of public and private ownership, of market and government decision making.

Consider some of the major European countries. **France** has a history of extensive state ownership of the means of production, substantial government regulation, and reliance on "indicative" planning to influence business decisions. (Under indicative planning, the planning agency collects and disseminates information but does not command that specific production targets be achieved. Instead, it uses indirect means, such as tax incentives, to influence business decisions.) In the early 1990s, France turned away from planning and began to convert some public enterprises to private enterprises. It has now fully or partially privatized many large companies, including banks, insurance companies, and such visible firms as Air France, France Telecom, and Renault, the French auto manufacturer. Despite these privatization efforts, the French government continues to maintain a strong presence in certain sectors including power production, railroads, aircraft, and defense industries. Moreover, the French economy remains highly regulated with extensive protections for workers (safety, working conditions, and hours). In addition, government tax policies and social spending are used to moderate income inequality rather than accepting the dictates of the market. As you can see, the French are clearly seeking their own middle-way between pure capitalism and command socialism.

Great Britain, prior to the long Conservative rule of Margaret Thatcher and John Major (1979–1997), was often described as a socialist economic system. This description stemmed from the size of the government's budget, the extent of publicly owned enterprises, and the nation's reliance on economic planning. The socialist label was never completely accurate, but is clearly inaccurate today. The British government has now privatized most state-owned companies—British Steel, British Coal, and British Airways, for instance—and has pursued partial privatization in the few that remain—the London Underground (subway), for instance. Economic planning, which was never practiced to the same extent as in France, has been largely abandoned. Social spending—government spending to aid the elderly, unemployed, poor, and disabled—absorbs about 21% of the U.K.'s output. That's well above the United States (16%), but substantially less than France (29%). In summary, Great Britain is clearly a mixed economy, though one with a somewhat larger role for government than the U.S. economy.

The **German** economy is the third largest in the world (behind the United States and Japan) and the largest in Europe. Privately owned enterprises dominate German industry, but the state intervenes by owning some segments of the economy—part of the banking system, for instance—by subsidizing selected industries, and by extensive rules regarding workplace safety, environmental protection, and the like. There is a state-run system of health insurance, extensive public housing for the poor, and relatively generous unemployment compensation. As a consequence, social spending in Germany accounts for about 27% of the economy's output, only slightly less than France. (In recent years, the government has attempted to cut back on some social programs largely because the high payroll taxes needed to support them have made it increasingly difficult for German firms to compete internationally.) Another distinguishing feature of the Germany economy is a government policy known as

Use Your Economic Reasoning

In Hard Times, Russia Moves in to Reclaim Private Industries

BY CLIFFORD J. LEVY

BEREZNIKI, RUSSIA—In late October, one of Vladimir V. Putin's top lieutenants abruptly summoned a billionaire mining oligarch to a private meeting. The official, Igor I. Sechin, had taken a sudden interest in a two-year-old accident at the oligarch's highly lucrative mining operations here in Russia's industrial heartland. Mr. Sechin, who is a leader of a shadowy Kremlin faction tied to the state security services, said he was ordering a new inquiry into the mishap, according to minutes of the meeting. With a deputy interior minister who investigates financial crime at his side, Mr. Sechin threatened crippling fines against the company, Uralkali. Startled, the oligarch, Dmitri E. Rybolovlev, pointed out that the government had already examined the incident thoroughly and had cleared the company of responsibility. He further sought to fend off the inquiry by saying he would pay for some of the damage to infrastructure from the accident, a mine collapse that injured no one but left a gaping sinkhole. His offer was rebuffed, and it seemed clear why: The Kremlin was maneuvering to seize Uralkali outright.

Mr. Putin, the former president and current prime minister, has long maintained that Russia made a colossal error in the 1990s by allowing its enormous reserves of oil, gas, and other natural resources to fall into private hands. He has acted uncompromisingly—most notably in the case of the Yukos Oil Company in 2003—to get them back. Now, the Kremlin seems to be capitalizing on the economic crisis, exploiting the opportunity to establish more control over financially weakened industries that it has long coveted, particularly those in natural resources. Last month, for example, the government assumed greater influence over Norilsk Nickel, the world's biggest nickel producer, whose large shareholders, two billionaire oligarchs, have ailing finances. And Mr. Putin said Thursday that he was considering other such interventions.

Yet the Uralkali affair stands out for illustrating with rare clarity the willingness of the authorities to use whatever means necessary to obtain these assets, including subjecting companies to questionable investigations that they have little chance of resisting, financial analysts here say. . . .

The Kremlin has not said when there will be a decision on Uralkali, and the company is hoping to negotiate a settlement that would

"codetermination." Codetermination means that corporations must have worker representatives on their boards of directors. In effect, this forces corporations to consider worker interest when formulating business policy. As you can see, the German economic system blends capitalism with a significant dose of government intervention intended to soften market outcomes. The Germans describe their economic system as a "social market economy."

include a fine of a few hundred million dollars. Analysts emphasized that there was still a chance that Mr. Sechin might pull back after seeing the stock market react so hostilely to the inquiry. Developments in the overall economy might also give the Kremlin pause. A growing recognition of its outsize influence over business appears to have helped sour the investment climate here and suggests in part why the Russian stock market has been among the worst performers in the world this year. . . .

With the financial crisis jolting economies around the world, Russia is hardly alone in taking ownership stakes in corporations these days. But many governments seem to view this as an uncomfortable role that has been thrust upon them. Russia's rulers, however, appear to perceive the crisis as a chance to further expand their control over the economy, concentrating ever more power and wealth in the Kremlin.

Russians undoubtedly have ambivalent feelings about oligarchs like Mr. Rybolovlev.

They tend to resent the oligarchs' wealth, believing that it was accumulated through underhanded means in the 1990s. (Mr. Rybolovlev himself was accused of orchestrating the killing of a rival back then, though he was cleared of the charges.) But they also worry that government officials want to seize these assets for their own venal purposes, and that they will end up mismanaging them, just as in Soviet times. . . .

"The Uralkali case says that the government feels it has the power to interfere in any way in these industries," said Marina Alexeenkova, a vice president at Renaissance Capital, an investment bank in Moscow. "It looks really aggressive and really risky. In general, this has been considered the most serious attack on a company since Yukos." The government imprisoned Yukos's owner—the billionaire oligarch Mikhail B. Khodorkovsky, who had angered Mr. Putin by engaging in politics—on tax charges. . . .

USE YOUR ECONOMIC REASONING

1. Many observers have suggested that Russia's poorly developed legal system with its capricious and selective enforcement of laws and regulations is a major impediment to further market reforms. Explain.
2. Russia's leaders would like more foreign investment to help develop their economy. Why do cases like the one against Uralkali reduce the willingness of outsiders to invest in Russia?
3. The article suggest that, in the wake of the worldwide financial crisis, many governments were taking ownership stakes in failing enterprises, but that many were doing so reluctantly. How would you explain the fact that nations like the United States are reluctant to take ownership stakes, whereas Russia seems to embrace the idea?

The **Swedish** economy is similar, in many respects, to the German economy. Private ownership is the norm, and markets dictate most outcomes. The state, however, goes to great lengths to maintain an egalitarian income distribution. For instance, it provides very generous benefits for retirement, medical care, education, and the like. These programs, coupled with higher taxes on those earning higher incomes, lead to a substantial redistribution of income.

This may be at least part of the reason that the income distribution in Sweden is significantly more equal than that found in the United States.

When we consider Eastern Europe and Asia, we find a number of economic systems in transition. For most of the last century, the **Soviet Union** was held up as a nearly perfect example of command socialism. Most factories, farms, and other enterprises were owned and operated by the state, and the fundamental choices about what, how, and for whom to produce were made by the State Planning Committee (GOSPLAN). When Mikhail Gorbachev became supreme leader of the Soviet Union in 1985, he was very critical of the Soviet economy, calling it rigid and inefficient. Gorbachev instituted some market reforms, but his own ambivalence about capitalism led to conflicting policy moves. The result was chaos for producers and a substantial disruption in the supplies of goods and services. As the Soviet economy disintegrated, the Communist party collapsed, and most of the Soviet republics declared their independence. Russian president Boris Yeltsin, who had advocated more rapid economic reform, moved to center stage. In December 1991, the Soviet Union was officially dissolved and replaced with the Commonwealth of Independent States, a loose federation of former Soviet republics.

In the period since the breakup, the countries of the former Soviet Union have taken very different paths. **Belarus**, **Uzbekistan**, and **Turkmenistan**, for example, have done very little to change their economic systems. On the other hand, **Russia** began introducing market reforms immediately after the breakup and is now a very different economy. Central planning has been largely abandoned, state ownership has been dramatically reduced, and free-market prices now play a much more important role in the economy. Living standards, which dropped for several years after the breakup, have been rising since 1998. The rate of poverty is falling, and there is an emerging entrepreneurial class, not too unlike that in the United States.

The Russian economy retains a certain Soviet flavor, however, and its future path is hard to predict. Although many industries have been privatized, many others remain state owned or state controlled. In fact, there has been significant expansion of government ownership since 2004, focused particularly on the oil, gas, and mining sectors. This expansion has caused some observers to wonder about a return to greater state control. Critics of the Putin/Medvedev regime argue that the selective and capricious interpretation of tax and licensing laws also seems intended to deter the emergence of private businesses and protect the power of the state. And, intentional or not, the nation's legal system clearly provides inadequate protections for private property, the foundation of capitalism. What direction is the Russian economy moving; toward freer markets or back toward more state control? We'll have to wait to see. (To learn more about Russia's recent nationalization efforts, read "In Hard Times, Russia Moves in to Reclaim Private Industries," on page 54.)

China, long considered the *other* major planned economy of the world, has taken a more gradual and cautious approach to economic reform than that pursued by Russia. The Chinese leadership began introducing modest market reforms in the late 1970s. Peasants who produced more than their production targets were allowed to sell the additional agricultural output at free-market prices, and small private businesses were allowed to develop outside the central plan. As these reforms met with success, additional modest reforms were introduced. In 1992, Deng Xiaoping, head of the Communist party, encouraged entrepreneurs to develop the nonstate sector, providing official sanctioning for this sector.[6]

Although the private sector has expanded significantly since 1992, many key industries—utilities, mining, and heavy manufacturing—remain state owned,[7] and the state continues to regulate some prices—gasoline, farm products, and cooking oil, for instance. As the private sector has grown, China's leaders have shown an increased willingness to shrink, or at least reform, state-owned enterprises (SOEs), many of which are poorly run and highly inefficient. Some SOEs have been closed or converted into private (or quasi-private) businesses. Other SOEs have been exposed to competition with foreign businesses or private businesses in an attempt to make the SOEs more efficient. One consequence of these changes has been the displacement of workers—workers who believed they had a job for life—as state enterprises shed jobs. As you might expect, this change has met with resistance. Another source of resistance has been the growing inequality in the country. Those fortunate enough to live in industrialized coastal cities (which produce products for export) have seen their incomes rise substantially, while those living in rural areas have been unaffected or even harmed. This growth in inequality has led to protests about the fairness of market reforms and the wisdom of proceeding further.

If we venture farther east, we encounter mixed economies that appear to have a strong capitalist flavor. In the **Japanese** economy, there is little public ownership, and most decisions are market driven. But Japan pursues an "industrial policy" in which state bureaucrats attempt to promote what they deem to be key sectors of the economy and phase out other, less-promising sectors. Some have described this approach as midway between planning and free markets. Similar approaches appear to characterize the economies of **South Korea and Taiwan**. In these nations, the government has routinely targeted specific industries (and specific companies) for assistance.

There are obviously many more economies in the world, but it should be clear by now that all real-world economies combine elements of both

---

[6] Robert Solomon, *The Transformation of the World Economy*, 2nd ed. (New York: St. Martin's Press, 1999), pp. 124–133.
[7] The State-Owned Assets Supervision and Administration Commission of China lists 150 SOEs, most with a number of subsidiary firms.

capitalism and socialism. The economies of the United States and **Hong Kong**, which rely heavily on markets, reserve some role for government. And markets are evident even in the most highly regulated of the world's economies—the Chinese economy, for example. But although all real-world economies combine elements of capitalism and socialism, they each blend the capitalist and socialist model in their own unique way—a blend that reflects that nation's history and traditions.

The preceding section provided some appreciation of the diversity of existing economic systems. But our primary interest is in the U.S. economy. In the remaining chapters of this text, we will examine the operation of the U.S. economy in more detail. To better understand our economy, we need to know more about how markets work and how government influences economic choices in our system. In Chapter 3 we begin to broaden our understanding of markets.

SUMMARY

An *economic system* is a set of institutions and mechanisms for answering the three fundamental questions of economics—what, how, and for whom to produce. In describing economic systems, it is helpful to ask two questions: (1) Who owns the means of production? (2) Who makes the economic decisions?

Economists commonly use theoretical models to explain the operation of economic systems. *Capitalism* describes an economic system in which the *means of production* are privately owned, and fundamental economic choices are made by individual buyers and sellers interacting in markets. The principal features of pure capitalism include private property and freedom of choice, with self-interest as the driving force (held in check by *pure competition*); price determination through markets; and a minimum of government intervention—a *laissez-faire economy*.

In a capitalist economy, *consumer sovereignty* dictates which goods and services will be produced. If consumers want more of a particular product, its price will tend to rise, encouraging profit-seeking businesses to produce more of it. To produce these products, businesses buy economic resources (e.g., labor) from *households*, thereby providing households with the money needed to purchase the output of businesses. The circular-flow model of capitalism diagrams this process by showing how the flows of money (money flows) and resources and products (real flows) circulate between the household and business sectors and operate through product and resource markets.

At the other extreme, the model of *command socialism* describes an economic system in which the means of production are owned by the public, or the state, and the fundamental economic choices are made by a central authority.

The principal features of command socialism include public ownership, centralized decision making, economic planning, and allocation by command.

In command socialism the central planning authority gathers information on production capabilities and consumer preferences (if the latter is a concern) and establishes production targets for the producing units, such as factories and farms. These units are required to produce the products dictated by the central authority in the manner specified. Output is then distributed according to the central authority's goals. Command socialism is depicted as a pyramid, with the central planning board at the top and the producing and consuming units below. The producing and consuming units supply information to the central planners, who use this information to develop production targets and decide how the limited output will be distributed among the potential customers.

No existing economic system fits neatly into either model. All real-world economic systems are *mixed economies* because they represent some blending of the two models. For example, the U.S. economy, commonly described as a capitalist system, contains some elements of a socialist economy. Public ownership is not uncommon in the United States, and government influences many of our fundamental economic choices. And markets are important even in economies like those of Russia and China, where a significant government bureaucracy guides many of the fundamental economic choices, and government ownership of the means of production remains extensive.

KEY TERMS

Capitalism	Economic system	Market
Command socialism	Household	Means of production
Common-property resources	Invisible hand	Mixed economies
Consumer sovereignty	Laissez-faire economy	Pure competition

STUDY QUESTIONS

Fill in the Blanks

1. The driving force or engine of capitalism

   is _____.

2. The functioning of a capitalist economy is coordinated and directed through

   _____ in which _____
   are determined by the interaction of buyers and sellers.

3. In the model of pure capitalism, the pursuit of self-interest by producers is kept in

   check by _____. The model

   of pure capitalism requires _____, a situation in which there are a large number of buyers and sellers of each product.

4. Because businesspeople in a capitalist economy are motivated by self-interest, they want to produce the goods and services that will allow them to earn the

   highest _____. Those products tend to be the ones that are most desired by _____.

5. According to Milton Friedman, competitive capitalism promotes

   _____ by separating economic and political power.

6. In pure command socialism, the fundamental economic decisions are made by

   the _____ and implemented

   through _____.

7. In pure command socialism, _____ replaces the market as the method of coordinating the various economic decisions.

8. It is possible to represent a socialist command economy as a(n) _____

   with the _____ at the top and producing and consuming units at the bottom.

9. One weakness of command socialism is its

   inefficient _____ network.

10. The United States and China are both

    examples of _____ economies.

Multiple Choice

1. Which of the following is *not* a characteristic of pure capitalism?
   a) Public ownership of the means of production
   b) The pursuit of self-interest
   c) Markets and prices
   d) Pure competition
   e) Limited government

2. In a market economy the scarcest resources will be used very conservatively because
   a) central planners will allocate such resources only where they are most needed.
   b) the scarcest resources will tend to have the highest prices.
   c) government officials will not permit their use.
   d) the scarcest resources will tend to have the lowest prices.

3. In a capitalist economy
   a) businesses are free to produce whatever products they choose.
   b) consumers are free to utilize their incomes as they see fit.

   c) resource owners have the freedom to sell their resources to whomever they choose.
   d) All of the above
   e) None of the above

4. Consumer sovereignty means that
   a) consumers dictate which goods and services will be produced by the way they spend their money.
   b) central planners allocate a major share of society's resources to the production of consumer goods.
   c) the role of government in the economy is very limited.
   d) all economic resources are used efficiently.

5. According to the "invisible hand" doctrine,
   a) as individuals pursue their own interests, they tend to promote the interests of society as a whole.
   b) the actions of individuals often have unanticipated and undesirable effects on society.

c) individuals should put the interests of society first.

d) when individuals attempt to promote the best interests of the entire society, they also further their own personal interests.

6. Adam Smith recognized that the "invisible hand" would function as he envisioned only if
   a) individuals unconsciously considered the welfare of others in making their decisions.
   b) government regulations forced businesses to behave in an ethical manner.
   c) a high degree of competition existed in the economy.
   d) individuals lived in accordance with the golden rule.

7. In a market economy, if consumers suddenly stop buying SUVs and start buying fuel-efficient cars,
   a) the price of SUVs will tend to fall, and more of them will be produced.
   b) the price of fuel-efficient cars will tend to rise, making them less profitable to produce and encouraging producers to supply more of them.
   c) resources will tend to be shifted from the production of SUVs to the production of fuel-efficient cars.
   d) the price of SUVs will tend to rise, making them more profitable to produce and encouraging producers to supply more of them.

8. Which of the following best describes command socialism?
   a) An economic system where the means of production are privately owned and decision making is highly centralized
   b) An economic system where the means of production are publicly owned and decision making is highly decentralized
   c) An economic system where the means of production are privately owned and decision making is highly decentralized
   d) An economic system where the means of production are publicly owned and decision making is highly centralized

9. Which of the following is correct?
   a) In command socialism, the basic economic choices are made by individuals.
   b) In pure capitalism, powerful economic units have a substantial impact on the way economic choices are made.
   c) In command socialism, producers are required to produce whatever products central planners dictate.
   d) In pure capitalism, economic planning ensures that the various production decisions will be consistent with one another.

10. In deciding what products to produce, the central planners in a socialist command economy need not consider
    a) the size of the economy's labor force.
    b) the production capabilities of the economy's factories.
    c) consumer preferences.
    d) the economy's stock of raw materials.

11. In order to get the most output from society's limited resources, the scarcest resources must be used only where no other input will suffice.
    a) In command socialism this function is performed by planners; in pure capitalism it is performed by the central government.
    b) In pure capitalism this function is performed by input prices; in command socialism it is performed by planners.
    c) In command socialism this function is performed by the producing units; in pure capitalism it is performed by planners.
    d) In pure capitalism this function is performed by government regulations; in command socialism it is performed by output targets.

12. In a comparison of command socialism and pure capitalism, which of the following is true?
    a) Prices play a larger role in command socialism than in pure capitalism.
    b) Resources are likely to be used more efficiently in command socialism than in pure capitalism.

c) Economic planning plays a larger role in pure capitalism than in command socialism.

d) Decision making is more decentralized in pure capitalism than in command socialism.

13. One function of government in the U.S. economy is to "correct for externalities." Which of the following is an example of government performing that function?
    a) Construction of a flood-control dam
    b) Paying a portion of the cost of a flu vaccination
    c) Reducing the income tax rate on citizens with low incomes
    d) Outlawing the sale of automobiles lacking seatbelts

14. One reason the United States is not an example of pure capitalism is that
    a) most producing units are publicly owned.
    b) commands are used to implement some economic decisions.
    c) the pursuit of self-interest is a powerful force.
    d) markets are used to coordinate most economic decisions.

15. Which of the following is a true statement?
    a) Codetermination is a feature of the Swedish economy.
    b) The Germans describe their economy as a "social market economy."
    c) Industrial policy is a characteristic of the British economy.
    d) Japan's leadership employs "indicative planning" in guiding its economy.

Problems and Questions for Discussion

1. What is an economic system? Why is it valid to say that no two real-world economic systems are exactly alike?

2. List the characteristics or elements of pure capitalism and explain each. Are any of these elements absent from the U.S. economy? Explain.

3. How would a socialist command economy answer the three fundamental questions? What elements of command socialism exist in the U.S. economy?

4. Explain the role of economic planning in command socialism. Who is in charge of economic planning in a capitalist economy?

5. Try to draw the circular-flow diagram without looking back at the diagram in the text. Now, label all the parts of the diagram, and indicate which flows are money flows and which are real flows. Use the diagram to explain how a capitalist economy works.

6. Draw the command pyramid and label the parts. What does the command pyramid tell us about the way a socialist economy functions?

7. Milton Friedman suggests that competitive capitalism promotes political freedom. Explain.

8. What functions does the government perform in the U.S. economy? Which of these functions is consistent with the model of pure capitalism?

9. Why can't capitalism exist without a well-developed legal system?

10. Japan, South Korea, and Taiwan all pursue an "industrial policy." Explain what is meant by an industrial policy and why this policy is inconsistent with pure capitalism.

11. How are the objectives of government intervention in Japan and Taiwan different from the objectives of government intervention in Germany and Sweden?

12. Government intervention in Sweden appears to have a single, overriding focus. Does government intervention in the U.S. economy have a single focus or objective?

13. China has introduced a number of market reforms, but continues to regulate the prices of basic agricultural commodities, cooking oil, and gasoline. Why do you believe policymakers have chosen to regulate those particular prices, rather than allowing them to be determined by market forces?

ANSWER KEY

Fill in the Blanks

1. self-interest
2. markets, prices
3. competition, pure competition
4. profits, consumers
5. political freedom
6. central authority, commands
7. economic planning
8. pyramid, planning board
9. information
10. mixed

Multiple Choice

1. a
2. b
3. d
4. a
5. a
6. c
7. c
8. d
9. c
10. c
11. b
12. d
13. b
14. b
15. b

2

Microeconomics: Markets, Prices, and the Role of Competition

In Chapter 3 we begin our study of microeconomics by investigating how prices are determined in competitive markets. You will learn the precise meanings of *supply* and *demand* and how the interaction of these forces determines prices. You will examine how prices can change and will learn the functions that price changes perform in a market economy. Chapter 4 will consider some applications of the supply and demand model. For instance, you will investigate what happens when government intervenes in the pricing process and consider why some consumers are more price sensitive than others.

Chapter 5 explores the idea that human beings are rational decision makers who are motivated by self-interest. You will find that rational decision making involves a careful comparison of costs and benefits and that the relevant costs and benefits are always "marginal." Chapter 6 examines the behavior of the purely competitive firm and explores how firms use marginal reasoning to determine the profit-maximizing output. You will discover the characteristics of a competitive industry and see why competition is beneficial for consumers. Chapter 7 examines how firms acquire pricing discretion, or market power, and how the behavior of firms that possess market power differs from that of purely competitive firms. An appendix to the chapter examines the pricing techniques actually employed by businesses and compares them with the theoretical techniques suggested by economists. Chapter 8 considers the "degrees" of competition that exist in different industry structures and explores the impact of those different industry structures on the well-being of consumers. Chapter 9 looks at some of the inherent limitations of a market economy by examining the origin of problems such as pollution.

3

Demand and Supply: Price Determination in Competitive Markets

1. Define *demand* and *supply* and represent these concepts graphically.
2. State the "laws" of demand and supply.
3. Identify the determinants of demand and supply.
4. Recognize the difference between a change in demand (supply) and a change in the quantity demanded (supplied).
5. Explain and illustrate graphically how the equilibrium price and quantity are determined.
6. Describe the rationing and motivating functions of prices.
7. Identify the factors that can cause the equilibrium price to change.
8. Use demand and supply curves to predict changes in the equilibrium price and quantity.

How do markets work? A market economy is governed by the interaction of buyers and sellers in thousands of different product and resource markets. This interaction—what you might describe as bargaining or negotiating—determines prices. The prevailing prices of goods and services tell producers which products consumers want the most. Resource prices tell producers which resources to use to produce those products profitably. Because resource prices affect consumers' incomes, they also influence the distribution of goods and services. For example, workers whose skills are particularly scarce can command higher salaries and thereby claim a larger share of the society's limited output. In short, prices play a very important role in the functioning of all mixed economies.

This chapter introduces the model of demand and supply, the model intended to illustrate how buyers and sellers interact to determine prices in competitive markets. Competitive markets are composed of many independent buyers and sellers, each too small to be able to influence the market price significantly. We'll explore the meaning of competitive markets in greater detail later in the text. For now, just remember that in competitive markets, prices are determined by the impersonal forces of demand and supply, not by manipulations of powerful buyers or sellers.

After you study this chapter, you will have a better understanding of how prices are determined and a greater appreciation of the role that prices play in a market economy. You'll understand why the price of gold fluctuates and why salaries are higher in some occupations than in others. You'll understand why antique cars often command higher prices than this year's models and why a poor wheat harvest in Canada or Ukraine can mean higher bread prices in the United States. You will also understand how prices both direct the actions of producers and determine the distribution of society's limited output of goods and services. In summary, the material in this chapter will give you a clearer comprehension of the role of markets and prices in our economy.

DEMAND

In a market economy, consumers are sovereign; that is, consumers dictate which goods and services will be produced. But it is consumer *demand* rather than consumer wants or desires that actually directs the market. We have already noted that human wants are unlimited. Wanting an item, however, and being willing and able to pay for it are two distinctly different things. If the item we want carries a price tag, we may do without it: We may lack the money to pay or we may prefer to spend that money on something else.

People who are both *willing and able* to make purchases are the consumers who determine which products a market economy will produce. When consumers lack either the willingness or the ability to spend, producers do not respond. Thus, the concept of demand includes the willingness and ability of potential buyers to purchase a product. We define **demand** as a schedule (or table) showing the quantities of a good or service that consumers are willing and able to purchase at various prices during a given time period, when all factors other than the product's price remain unchanged.

Exhibit 3.1 illustrates the concept of demand through a simple example. The schedule shows the yearly demand for jogging shoes of a given quality in the hypothetical community of Hometown, U.S.A. You can see that the number of pairs of jogging shoes that Hometown consumers are willing and able to purchase each year depends on the selling price. If jogging shoes sell for $100 a pair, Hometowners will purchase 2,000 pairs a year, assuming that other factors remain the same—their incomes, for example, and their present jogging routines.

EXHIBIT 3.1

Hometown Demand for Jogging Shoes

PRICE (per pair)	QUANTITY (pairs per year)
$100	2,000
80	4,000
60	6,000
40	8,000
20	10,000

Demand is a schedule or table showing the quantities of a good or service that consumers are willing and able to purchase at various prices.

Demand Curves

Economists usually represent schedules in the form of graphs. To graph the demand for jogging shoes, we first plot the information in Exhibit 3.1 and then connect the points to form a demand curve, as shown in Exhibit 3.2. A **demand curve** is simply a graphical representation of demand. By convention we measure price on the vertical axis and quantity on the horizontal axis. Each point on the curve represents a price and the quantity that consumers would demand per year at that price. For example, we can see in Exhibit 3.2 that at a price of $80, Hometown joggers would demand 4,000 pairs; at a price of $60, the quantity demanded would increase to 6,000 pairs.

EXHIBIT 3.2

The Demand Curve for Jogging Shoes in Hometown, U.S.A.

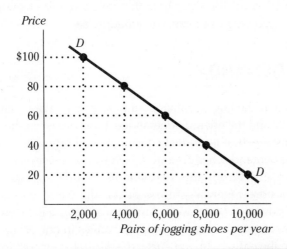

Pairs of jogging shoes per year

A demand curve is a graphical representation of demand. It demonstrates the inverse relationship between price and quantity demanded.

THE LAW OF DEMAND

Our hypothetical demand schedule and demand curve for jogging shoes demonstrate clearly what economists call the **law of demand**, which holds that the quantity demanded of a product is *negatively, or inversely, related* to its price. This simply means that consumers will purchase more of a product at lower prices than at higher prices. That's why demand curves always slope downward and to the right.

Economists believe that two factors explain the inverse relationship between price and quantity demanded:

1. When prices are lower, consumers can afford to purchase a larger quantity of the product out of any given income. Economists refer to this *ability* to purchase more as the **income effect** of a price reduction.
2. At lower prices the product becomes more attractive relative to other items serving the same function. This **substitution effect** explains the *willingness* of consumers to substitute for other products the product that has declined in price.

To illustrate the income and substitution effects, let's return to our Hometown consumers. Why will they purchase more jogging shoes at $20 than at $100? Because of the income effect, their incomes will now buy more: If the price of jogging shoes declines and other prices don't change, consumers will be able to buy more goods and services with their fixed incomes. It's almost as though each consumer had received a raise. And because of the substitution effect, consumers will buy jogging shoes instead of tennis shoes, sandals, or moccasins because jogging shoes have become a better footwear buy. Because of both the income effect and the substitution effect, we all, like these hypothetical consumers, tend to purchase more of a product at a lower price than at a higher price.

DETERMINANTS OF DEMAND

The demand curve and the law of demand emphasize the relationship between the price of a product and the quantity demanded. But price is not the only factor that determines how much of a product consumers will buy. A variety of other factors underlie the demand schedule and determine the precise position of the demand curve. These **determinants of demand** include income, tastes and preferences, expectations regarding future prices, the price of related goods, and the number of buyers in the market. Any demand curve is based on the assumption that these factors are held constant. Changes in one or more of these determinants cause the entire demand curve to shift to a new position.

Income

The most obvious determinant of demand is income. Consumers' incomes influence their *ability* to purchase goods and services. For what economists call **normal goods**, an increase in income will cause consumers to purchase more of a product than before at each possible price. For example, an increase in per capita income (income per person) will probably cause consumers to buy more steak than before at whatever price exists. We would show this by shifting the demand curve to the right, as illustrated in Exhibit 3.3.

Not all products are normal goods, however. An increase in income will cause consumers to purchase less of an **inferior good**, thus shifting the demand curve to the left. Powdered milk, generic macaroni and cheese, and cheap wine are examples of products that might be inferior goods. When consumers' incomes increase, they may choose to buy less of these products in favor of more appetizing grocery items.

Tastes and Preferences

Consumers' tastes and preferences—how well they like the product relative to other products—are also important determinants of demand. A change in tastes and preferences will affect the demand for products. For example, the

---

EXHIBIT 3.3

Income as a Determinant of Demand

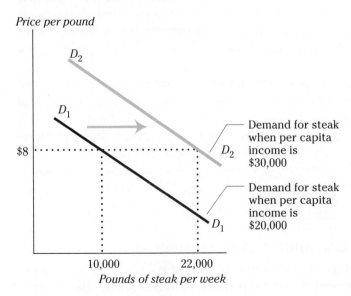

Price per pound

D_2

D_1

$8

D_2 — Demand for steak when per capita income is $30,000

D_1 — Demand for steak when per capita income is $20,000

10,000   22,000

Pounds of steak per week

An increase in per capita income will shift the demand curve for a normal good to the right. Consumers will purchase more of the product at each price.

desire to limit cholesterol intake has altered consumer tastes and preferences for various food products. Today consumers demand less red meat and fewer eggs than in times past but demand more fish and chicken. In other words, this change in tastes and preferences has caused the demand curves for red meat and eggs to shift to the left and the demand curves for fish and chicken to shift to the right.

Expectations about Prices

Expectations may also influence consumer behavior. For example, the expectation that the price of an item will rise in the future usually encourages consumers to buy it now. We would represent this by shifting the entire demand curve to the right to show that more would be demanded now at whatever price prevailed. Similarly, the expectation that a product will decline in price is a good incentive to postpone buying it; the present demand curve for the product would shift to the left.

Price of Related Goods

A somewhat-less-obvious determinant of demand is the price of related goods. Although all goods compete for a consumer's income, the price of substitutes and complements may be particularly important in explaining consumer behavior. **Substitutes** are simply products that can be used in place of other products because, to a greater or lesser extent, they satisfy the same consumer wants. Hot dogs are a typical substitute for hamburgers, and tennis shoes may substitute for jogging shoes unless one is a serious jogger. **Complements** are products normally purchased along with or in conjunction with another product. For example, pickle relish and hot dogs are complements, as are lettuce and salad dressing.

If the price of hamburgers increased and the price of hot dogs remained unchanged, consumers might be expected to buy fewer hamburgers and more hot dogs. The demand curve for hot dogs would shift to the right. By the same token, an increase in the price of lettuce is likely to have an adverse effect on the sale of salad dressing. Because people buy salad dressing as a complement to salad vegetables, anything that causes consumers to eat fewer salads causes them to demand less salad dressing. The demand curve for salad dressing would shift to the left.

The Number of Consumers in the Market

The final determinant of demand is the number of consumers in the market. The more consumers who demand a particular product, the greater the total demand for the product. When the number of consumers increases, the demand curve for the product shifts to the right to show that a greater quantity is now demanded at each price. If the number of consumers declines, the demand curve shifts to the left.

As we think about the demand for a particular product, we need to remember the five determinants we have listed and how changes in these factors will affect the demand curve. We also need to recognize that more and more U.S. firms are selling their products to consumers in Mexico, Europe, and other locations outside the United States. As a consequence, the position of the demand curve for many products is determined not solely by local or national factors but by international factors as well. For instance, rising incomes in Mexico are certain to shift the demand curve for American-made electronics, medical equipment, and computer software to the right, whereas the availability of cheap Chilean wines will probably shift the demand curve for many California wines to the left. The point is that markets are often international in scope, so we need to look beyond national boundaries to determine the level of demand.

CHANGE IN QUANTITY DEMANDED VERSUS CHANGE IN DEMAND

In analyzing the factors that cause consumers to increase or decrease their purchases of a particular product, it is helpful to distinguish between the impact of a change (1) in the price of the product and (2) in one or more of the determinants of demand.

A change in the price of the product results in a **change in quantity demanded** and is represented graphically by movement along a stationary demand curve. For example, if the price of steak declines from $8 a pound to $6 a pound, consumers will move from point A to point B on demand curve D_1 in Exhibit 3.4. Note that the consumers will now choose to purchase a greater quantity of the product because its price is lower. This is an increase in the quantity demanded. If, on the other hand, the price rises from $4 a pound to $6 a pound, the consumers will move from point C to point B on the demand curve. Here a price increase will cause a reduction in the quantity demanded.

When any determinant of demand changes, the result is a **change in demand**—an entirely new demand schedule represented graphically by a shift of the demand curve to a new position. If consumers develop a stronger preference for steak, for instance, or if the prices of substitutes for steak rise, the entire demand curve for steak will shift to the right—an increase in demand. Exhibit 3.4 depicts this shift. A leftward shift of the entire demand curve would

EXHIBIT 3.4

Distinguishing Change in Demand from Change in Quantity Demanded

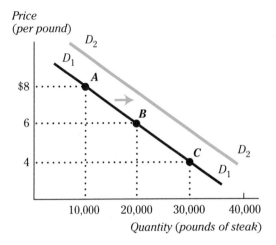

A change in the price of steak will cause a *change in the quantity demanded.* When the price of steak declines from $8 to $4 a pound, the quantity demanded increases from 10,000 to 30,000 pounds; consumers move from *A* to *C* along demand curve D_1.

A change in a determinant of demand will cause a *change in demand*: the entire curve will shift. The movement from D_1 to D_2 is an increase in demand.

denote a decrease in demand. (See "Today's Special," on page 76, to test your understanding of the difference between a change in demand and a change in the quantity demanded.)

SUPPLY

A knowledge of demand is essential to an understanding of how prices are determined, but it is only half the picture. Now we turn to the supply side of the market.

When we use the term *supply* in our everyday language, we are usually referring to a fixed quantity. That's what the owner of the local sporting-goods store means when advertising a *limited supply* of Fleet Feet tennis shoes or SuperFit swimsuits. But that's not what economists mean when they talk about supply. To economists, supply is a schedule—just as demand is. **Supply** is a schedule (or table) showing the quantities of a good or service that producers are willing and able to offer for sale at various prices during a given time period, when all factors other than the product's price remain unchanged.

Exhibit 3.5 represents the annual supply of jogging shoes in the Hometown market area. As the schedule shows, the number of pairs of jogging shoes that suppliers will make available for sale depends on the price of jogging shoes. At a price of $100 a pair, suppliers are willing to produce 10,000 pairs of jogging shoes a year; at a price of $60, they would offer only 6,000 pairs. Because supply is a schedule, we can't determine the quantity supplied unless we know the selling price.

EXHIBIT 3.5

Hometown Supply of Jogging Shoes

PRICE (per pair)	QUANTITY (pairs per year)
$100	10,000
80	8,000
60	6,000
40	4,000
20	2,000

Supply is a schedule or table showing the quantities of a good or service that producers are willing and able to offer for sale at various prices.

The Supply Curve

To transform our supply schedule into a supply curve, we follow the same procedure we used in constructing a demand curve. In Exhibit 3.6 we graph the information in Exhibit 3.5, measuring price on the vertical axis and quantity on the horizontal axis. When we've finished graphing the points from the schedule, we connect them to get a **supply curve**—a graphical representation of supply.

Interpreting a supply curve is basically the same as interpreting a demand curve. Each point on the curve represents a price and the quantity of jogging

EXHIBIT 3.6

The Supply Curve of Jogging Shoes in Hometown, U.S.A.

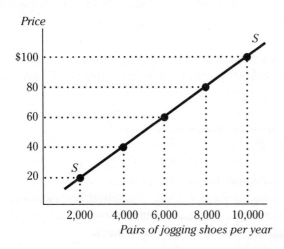

A supply curve is a graphical representation of supply. It demonstrates the direct relationship between price and quantity supplied.

Use Your Economic Reasoning

Today's Special

BY ANDREW MARTIN; CHRISTOPHER MAAG CONTRIBUTED REPORTING FROM CLEVELAND.

AUSTIN, MINN.—The economy is in tatters and, for millions of people, the future is uncertain. But for some employees at the Hormel Foods Corporation plant here, times have never been better. They are working at a furious pace and piling up all the overtime they want. The workers make Spam, perhaps the emblematic hard-times food in the American pantry. Through war and recession, Americans have turned to the glistening canned product from Hormel as a way to save money while still putting something that resembles meat on the table. Now, in a sign of the times, it is happening again, and Hormel is cranking out as much Spam as its workers can produce.

In a factory that abuts Interstate 90, two shifts of workers have been making Spam seven days a week since July, and they have been told that the relentless work schedule will continue indefinitely. Spam, a gelatinous 12-ounce rectangle of spiced ham and pork, may be among the world's most maligned

foods, dismissed as inedible by food elites and skewered by comedians who have offered smart-alecky theories on its name (one G-rated example: Something Posing As Meat).

But these days, consumers are rediscovering relatively cheap foods, Spam among them. A 12-ounce can of Spam, marketed as "Crazy Tasty," costs about $2.40. "People are realizing it's not that bad a product," said Dan Johnson, 55, who operates a 70-foot-high Spam oven. Hormel declined to cooperate with this article, but several of its workers were interviewed here recently with the help of their union, the United Food and Commercial Workers International Union Local 9. Slumped in chairs at the union hall after making 149,950 cans of Spam on the day shift, several workers said they had been through boom times before—but nothing like this. Spam "seems to do well when hard times hit," said Dan Bartel, business agent for the union local. "We'll probably see Spam lines instead of soup lines."

shoes that producers will supply at that price. You can see, for example, that producers will supply 4,000 pairs of shoes at a price of $40 per pair or 8,000 pairs at a price of $80 per pair.

THE LAW OF SUPPLY

You've probably noticed that the supply curve slopes upward and to the right. The supply curve slopes upward because the **law of supply** holds that price and quantity supplied are *positively, or directly, related*. Producers will supply a larger quantity at higher prices than at lower prices.

Even as consumers are cutting back on all sorts of goods, Spam is among a select group of thrifty grocery items that are selling steadily. Pancake mixes and instant potatoes are booming. So are vitamins, fruit and vegetable preservatives, and beer, according to data from October [2008] compiled by Information Resources, a market research firm. "We've seen a double-digit increase in the sale of rice and beans," said Teena Massingill, spokeswoman for the Safeway grocery chain, in an e-mail message. "They're real belly fillers." Kraft Foods said recently that some of its value-oriented products like macaroni and cheese, Jell-O and Kool-Aid were experiencing robust growth. . . .

Spam holds a special place in America's culinary history, both as a source of humor and of cheap protein during hard times. Invented during the Great Depression by Jay Hormel, the son of the company's founder, Spam is a combination of ham, pork, sugar, salt, water, potato starch and a "hint" of sodium nitrate "to help Spam keep its gorgeous pink color," according to Hormel's Web site for the product. Because it is vacuum-sealed in a can and does not require refrigeration, Spam can last for years. Hormel says "it's like meat with a pause button." . . .

No independent data provider compiles sales figures that include all the outlets where Spam is sold, including foreign stores, so it is not clear exactly how much sales are up. Hormel's chief executive, Jeffrey M. Ettinger, said in September that they were growing by double digits. . . . However, Hormel executives appear to be banking on the theory that Spam fits nicely into recession budgets. Workers on the Spam line in Austin—more than 40 of them work two shifts—see no signs that their work schedule will let up. . . .

USE YOUR ECONOMIC REASONING

1. The article says that Spam sales are "growing by double digits." Why are people buying more Spam; is it due to a price reduction or a change in one of the determinants of demand? Would an economist describe this as an increase in the quantity demanded or an increase in demand? How would you graph this event?
2. Spam "seems to do well when hard times hit." What label do we attach to products like Spam, rice and beans, and macaroni and cheese—products that seem to sell particularly well when average incomes are falling?
3. How would you expect Spam sales to react if the economy turned up and incomes returned to prerecession levels? How would you graph this situation?

Why would producers supply more jogging shoes at a higher price than at a lower price? The major reason is that the higher price allows them to cover the higher unit costs associated with producing the additional output. It probably costs more to produce the thousandth pair of jogging shoes than it did to produce the five hundredth pair. It's also likely that it would cost even more to produce the two thousandth pair, and so on. Producers are willing to supply a greater quantity at a higher price because the higher price enables businesses to cover the higher cost of producing the additional units—units that would not have been profitable at lower prices.

Costs per unit tend to increase with output because some of a business's resources, such as its production plant and equipment, cannot be expanded in a short period of time. Therefore, as the business increases output by hiring more labor and employing more raw materials, it eventually begins to overutilize its factory and equipment. This leads to congestion, workers waiting to use equipment, more frequent breakdowns of equipment, and production bottlenecks—situations in which one stage of the production process is slowing down the entire operation. These problems increase the cost of producing additional units. Producers will supply the additional units only if they can obtain a price high enough to justify paying the higher costs. Thus, the supply curve slopes upward because a higher price is *necessary* to call forth additional output from suppliers.

DETERMINANTS OF SUPPLY

The supply curve shows the relationship between the price of a product and the quantity supplied when other factors remain unchanged. However, price is not the only factor that influences the amount producers will offer for sale. Three major **determinants of supply** underlie the supply schedule and determine the position of the supply curve: technology, prices of the resources used in producing the product, and the number of producers in the market. Each supply curve is based on the assumption that these factors are held constant. Changes in any of the determinants will shift the entire supply curve to a new position.

Technology

Each supply curve is based on the existing technology. **Technology** is our state of knowledge about how to produce products. It influences the types of machines we use and the combinations of other resources we select to produce goods and services. A **technological advance** is the discovery of a better way to produce a product—a method that uses fewer resources to produce each unit of output or that produces more output from a given amount of resources. Because a technological advance allows producers to supply a higher quantity at any given price, it is represented by shifting the supply curve to the right, as depicted in Exhibit 3.7. As you can see, the development of a better method for producing personal computers will allow computer producers to supply a higher quantity at each price.

Resource Prices

Businesses must purchase economic resources in order to produce their products. Each supply curve assumes that the prices of resources remain unchanged.

EXHIBIT 3.7

The Impact of a Technological Advance on the Supply of Personal Computers

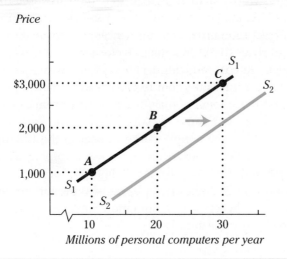

A technological advance will allow producers to supply a higher quantity at any given price.

An increase in the price of labor, materials, or some other production input will increase producers' costs and cause producers to supply less at any given price. The supply curve will shift to the left. A reduction in resource prices will have the opposite effect; the supply curve will shift to the right because producers will be able to supply a higher quantity at each price.

The Number of Producers in the Market

A third determinant of supply is the number of producers in the particular market: the more producers, the greater the supply. Each supply curve assumes that the number of producers is unchanged. If additional producers enter the market, the supply curve will shift to the right; if some producers leave, the supply curve will shift left.

Many other changes have essentially the same impact on supply as an increase or decrease in the number of producers. A severe frost destroys half the orange crop, decreasing supply; a good growing season enlarges the wheat harvest, increasing supply; trade barriers are lowered, and additional beef enters the United States, increasing supply. With each of these changes, the supply curve shifts as it would if the number of suppliers had increased or decreased.

As with demand, we need to recognize that the three determinants of supply—technology, resource prices, and the number of producers in the market—may be subject to international influences. For instance, the need to compete with foreign rivals has been a major factor spurring U.S. producers to search for and implement cost-reducing technological advances. In the furniture industry, for example, pressure from foreign producers has resulted in innovations that increase the amount of furniture produced from a given amount of wood. These innovations will cause the supply curve for furniture to shift to the right. At the same time, the supply curve of beef in the U.S. market has been shifting to the right for a very different reason. Imports of beef from Canada, Australia, New Zealand, and other foreign producers act very much like an increase the number of domestic suppliers, shifting the supply curve of beef to the right. As you can see, we cannot ignore international factors as we attempt to determine the level of supply.

CHANGE IN SUPPLY VERSUS CHANGE IN QUANTITY SUPPLIED

Earlier in this chapter you learned the difference between a change in demand and a change in *quantity* demanded. Economists make the same distinction for supply. A **change in quantity supplied** results from a change in the price of the product, with factors other than price held constant. It is represented graphically by movement along a stationary supply curve. According to Exhibit 3.8, if the price of personal computers declines from $2,000 to $1,000, the quantity supplied will decrease from 20 million units to only 10 million units a year, as suppliers move from point B to point A along supply curve S_1. But if the price of computers increases from $2,000 to $3,000, producers will move from point B to point C, and the quantity supplied will expand from 20 million to 30 million computers a year.

A **change in supply** is an increase or decrease in the amount of a product supplied at each and every price. A change in supply is caused by a change in one of the determinants of supply and is represented graphically by a shift of the entire supply curve, as depicted in Exhibit 3.8. If the supply curve shifts to the right (from S_1 to S_2), it denotes an increase in supply; a shift to the left indicates a decrease in supply. (To test your ability to distinguish between a change in supply and a change in the quantity supplied, read "Like a Lead Balloon," on page 82, and answer the questions.)

EXHIBIT 3.8

Distinguishing Change in Supply from Change in Quantity Supplied

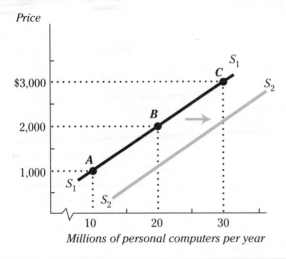

A change in the price of computers will cause a *change in the quantity supplied*. When price increases from $1,000 to $3,000, the quantity supplied increases from 10 million to 30 million computers per year; we move from A to C along supply curve S_1.

A change in a determinant of supply will cause a *change in supply*: the entire curve will shift. The movement from S_1 to S_2 is an increase in supply.

THE PROCESS OF PRICE DETERMINATION

Now that you understand the basics of demand and supply, let's put those two pieces of the puzzle together and examine how prices are determined. To do that, we'll consider again the market for jogging shoes. Exhibit 3.9 displays hypothetical demand and supply schedules for that product. As you already

EXHIBIT 3.9

The Demand and Supply of Jogging Shoes in Hometown, U.S.A.

PRICE (per pair)	QUANTITY DEMANDED (pairs per year)	QUANTITY SUPPLIED (pairs per year)
$100	2,000	10,000
80	4,000	8,000
60	6,000	6,000
40	8,000	4,000
20	10,000	2,000

Use Your Economic Reasoning

Like a Lead Balloon

BY ROB CARSON

Last summer, the world's appetite for recycled metals knew no bounds. In the Tacoma Tideflats, where most recycled metal in the Pacific Northwest winds up, the four big metal recycling firms welcomed lines of trucks piled high with car bodies, bed frames, tire chains and barbecue grills. Used metal prices were so high thieves were stripping copper wire out of light poles and prowling Park & Ride lots for catalytic converters.

Then it ended. Since September [2008], prices for used metal have dropped so precipitously the industry has essentially ground to a halt. The regular trans-Pacific shipments of scrap from Commencement Bay to China and Korea have stopped; the stream of automobile hulks heading for the Tideflats has slowed to a trickle. "This was the quickest and most violent downturn in our history, and I'm fourth generation," said Steve Glucoft, general manager of Tacoma's Calbag Metals Co., the largest nonferrous metal processor in the Northwest. "Prices are 50–60 percent of what they were 200 days ago. For us right now, it's about cash flow," Glucoft said. "It's about staying alive and keeping the doors open."

Calbag, along with Simon & Sons, Tacoma Metals and Schnitzer Steel, have been efficient and profitable forces in the international flow of metals, thanks to their easy ocean access to Asia.

The big four buy used metal products, separate them by type and crunch them into cubes or shred them. For the most part, they've been returning the scrap to China, where it has been melted down and turned into new products, many of which are shipped back to the United States through the Port of Tacoma. In September, the Asia metals market suddenly took a dive. "It hit the bottom, and everything came to a screeching halt," Glucoft said. . . .

The metals recycling industry is obviously not alone in its suffering. The worldwide financial crisis has hit virtually every sector of the economy. But the drop in scrap metal prices is also causing concern of environmentalists because of a possible side effect. Metal that isn't recycled gets tossed, which wastes resources and fills landfills. According to recycling industry figures, approximately 122,000 tons of aluminum and copper and 975,000 tons of iron were recycled in Washington last year, when the economy was flying high. Statistics collected by the Steel Recycling Institute indicate that automobiles were recycled at a rate of 110 percent in 2007. That means that, thanks in part to high metal prices, old cars were turned in for scrap faster than factories churned out new ones.

Now, however, with no financial incentive to recycle, environmentalists fear recycling

Source: The News Tribune (Tacoma, Washington), December 28, 2008, p. D1. Rob Carson © The News Tribune, (Tacoma, WA) [2008].

know, the demand schedule shows the quantities of jogging shoes that will be demanded at various prices, and the supply schedule reveals the quantities that will be supplied at those prices. But which of these possible prices will prevail in the market? And what quantity of jogging shoes will be exchanged

rates may plummet. The moral incentive of "doing the right thing" might not be enough to maintain a recycling rate that, according to the EPA, increased from 6 percent of trash in 1965 to 33 percent last year. In the South Sound, the sudden drop in recycled metal prices put an unknown number of independent junk collectors and haulers out of work. "The entrepreneurs who were out there beating the bushes for junked cars and old refrigerators won't be doing it anymore," said Jim Woods, director of public and education relations at the Steel Recycling Institute. Do-it-yourself scrap collectors, regardless of their environmental beliefs, performed an important social function, recyclers say. "They may not strap their load down properly," Glucoft said. "They may not have four perfect tires. But they're a big part of the cleanliness of this country." . . .

Ups and downs are a normal part of the recycling business, said Bruce Savage, vice president of communications at the Institute of Scrap Recycling Industries (ISRI), a trade association based in Washington, D.C. "Commodities, by their nature, are cyclical," Savage said, "but usually, when foreign demand goes down, domestic demand goes up. This time,

both domestic and foreign markets are down at the same time. It's the most precipitous and synchronous drop we've ever seen. Prices have gone down because demand has gone down," Savage said. "When consumers are not buying, companies are not manufacturing" [and they therefore don't need recycled metals to build new products.] . . .

Recyclers and junk dealers are facing cash flow problems, he said, but they're also facing a lack of space. If their strategy is to buy and hold, assuming prices eventually will come back up, they risk running out of room. "Most yards are not that big, so they can't have huge inventory building up," Savage said. "The question recycled materials brokers face becomes, 'How long do you inventory and store?'" That concern is less a factor with used metals than it is with other recycled materials, recyclers say. Paper from the Northwest that was sent to China to be turned into cardboard boxes is no longer needed there. It takes lots of room to store and deteriorates quickly. "Chances are, a lot of it (paper) will end up going into the landfill," Savage said. "Metals have much longer life. They can kind of hang around and be processed a year from now." . . .

USE YOUR ECONOMIC REASONING

1. Environmentalists fear that falling prices may lead to less recycling. How would you represent this outcome graphically? Would it be described as a reduction in supply or a reduction in the quantity supplied?
2. The author mentions the "moral incentive to do the right thing." Suppose more people became committed to recycling. How would you represent the impact of this change in behavior on the supply and demand graph for recycled paper? Would it shift the supply curve, or would it be represented as movement along the curve?
3. The price of scrap vehicles dropped from a high of $300 to about $50. Construct a supply and demand graph that represents this event. Note that you should be shifting one curve and moving along the other.

between buyers and sellers? To answer those questions, let's compare the reactions of buyers and sellers to each possible price.

What would happen in the market if jogging shoes were selling for $20 a pair? Because the $20 price would be attractive to consumers but not to producers, 10,000 pairs of jogging shoes would be demanded, but only 2,000 pairs would be supplied. At the $20 price there would be a **shortage**—an excess of quantity demanded over quantity supplied—of 8,000 pairs of jogging shoes. Therefore, some potential buyers would offer to pay a higher price to obtain the product. Competition among these buyers would tend to push the price to a higher level, and the higher price of jogging shoes would tend to reduce the quantity demanded while encouraging producers to expand the quantity supplied. In this way price increases would tend to reduce the shortage of jogging shoes.

Suppose that the price of jogging shoes rose to $40 a pair. At that price 8,000 pairs of jogging shoes would be demanded and 4,000 pairs supplied. Once again there would be a shortage, but this time it would amount to only 4,000 pairs of jogging shoes (8,000 pairs demanded minus 4,000 pairs supplied). Competition among potential buyers again would bid up the price of jogging shoes. The higher price would lead to a reduction in the quantity demanded and an increase in the quantity supplied, which would reduce the shortage still further.

You can probably see what happens as we move from lower to higher prices. Now let's reverse the process, beginning with the highest price in Exhibit 3.9. A price of $100 would tend to encourage production and discourage consumption. Producers would be willing to supply 10,000 pairs of jogging shoes a year, but consumers would demand only 2,000 pairs. The result would be a **surplus**—an excess of quantity supplied over quantity demanded—of 8,000 pairs of jogging shoes a year. How do producers react to a surplus? They begin to cut the price of the product to compete for existing customers and lure additional customers into the market. The lower price of jogging shoes tends to increase the quantity demanded and decrease the quantity supplied, thus reducing the surplus. If the price fell to $80, there would still be a surplus of 4,000 pairs of jogging shoes (8,000 pairs supplied minus the 4,000 pairs demanded). Price cutting would then continue, and the surplus would continue to shrink.

Equilibrium Price and Quantity

In our example, $60 is the market-clearing, or equilibrium, price, and 6,000 units is the equilibrium quantity. The **equilibrium price** is the price that brings about an equality between the quantity demanded and the quantity supplied. The **equilibrium quantity** is the quantity demanded and supplied at the equilibrium price. Equilibrium essentially means stability; once established, the equilibrium price will be maintained so long as the basic supply and demand conditions remain unchanged.

In a competitive market the actual, or prevailing, price will tend toward equilibrium. As you saw in Exhibit 3.9, when the price of jogging shoes is above or below equilibrium, market pressures tend to push it down or up toward the equilibrium level. Only when the existing price is at the equilibrium level will there be neither a shortage nor a surplus and no pressure for the price to change.

We use supply and demand curves to represent the process of price determination. By graphing the demand and supply schedules in Exhibit 3.9, we can construct the demand and supply curves found in Exhibit 3.10. These curves intersect at the equilibrium price ($60) and the equilibrium quantity (6,000 pairs of jogging shoes). At any price *above* equilibrium (say, $80), we can measure the amount of the surplus as the horizontal distance between the demand curve and the supply curve. For any price *below* equilibrium ($20, for example), the horizontal distance between the curves tells us the amount of the shortage. As we noted earlier, the shortage or surplus tends to shrink as price approaches the equilibrium level. The graph visually represents these shrinking amounts in the diminishing distance between the demand curve and the supply curve. When price finally achieves equilibrium, the curves intersect. At that point quantity demanded equals quantity supplied, and there is neither shortage nor surplus.

EXHIBIT 3.10

Demand and Supply Curves for Jogging Shoes in Hometown, U.S.A.

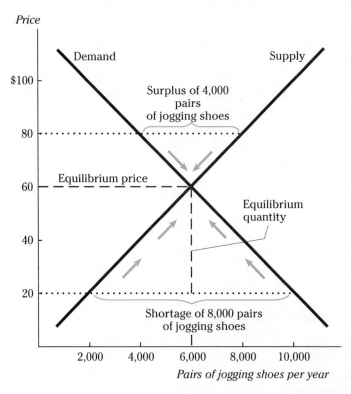

The equilibrium price is the price that equates the quantity supplied and the quantity demanded. In our example, the equilibrium price is $60. Whenever the existing price is above or below equilibrium, pressure exists to push it toward the equilibrium level. For example, at a price of $80, there would be a surplus, and price cutting would take place. At a price of $20, there would be a shortage, and the price would tend to rise to eliminate the shortage. The arrows indicate the direction of the adjustments in price and quantity.

The Rationing and Motivating Functions of Prices

In the preceding example the equilibrium price succeeds in matching up the quantity supplied and the quantity demanded because it performs two important functions. First, the equilibrium price rations jogging shoes perfectly among the various users; at a price of $60, 6,000 pairs of jogging shoes are demanded—exactly the quantity made available by producers. Second, the $60 price motivates producers to supply the correct quantity, the quantity consumers are willing to purchase at $60. Let's consider these important functions in greater detail.

You may recall from Chapter 2 that because every society faces the basic economic problem of unlimited wants and limited resources, some system must exist for **rationing**—that is, dividing up or allocating the scarce items among those who want them. In the United States and other economies that rely heavily on markets, price is the dominant rationing device. Rationing in a market economy works hand in hand with **motivating**—providing incentives to produce the desired output. Let's use Exhibit 3.10 to examine this process further, first from the perspective of the consumers demanding jogging shoes and then from the perspective of the producers supplying them.

How does the price of a product ration the supply of it among users? Prices ration because they influence our ability and willingness to purchase the product. The higher the price of jogging shoes, the more of our income it takes to buy them (which means a greater sacrifice in terms of other goods and services we must do without), and the less attractive jogging shoes become in relation to substitute products (tennis shoes, for instance).

To illustrate how price rations, let's begin with a relatively low price for jogging shoes—$20. If jogging shoes were selling for $20 (a price well below equilibrium), consumers would be willing and able to purchase a relatively high quantity—10,000 pairs. But as we learned earlier, producers are willing to supply only 2,000 pairs at that price, and so there will be a shortage, and price will tend to rise. As the price of jogging shoes rises toward its equilibrium level, the quantity demanded is reduced—fewer consumers are willing and able to pay the higher price. By discouraging consumers from purchasing the product, the higher price of jogging shoes helps to bring the quantity demanded into line with the number of jogging shoes available; it *rations* jogging shoes. By the same token, at a price initially above equilibrium—for example, $80—the quantity demanded would be too low. But price will tend to decline, and the falling price will encourage consumers to purchase more of the product. Thus, higher prices ration by reducing the quantity demanded, and lower prices ration by increasing it.

But changing prices do more than reduce or increase the quantity demanded: They also motivate producers to expand or contract production. We know from the law of supply that more will be supplied at higher prices than at lower prices. Thus, when the price of jogging shoes increases from $20 to $60, the quantity of jogging shoes supplied will increase from 2,000 pairs to 6,000 pairs. At the same time, the quantity of jogging shoes is being rationed among consumers; the quantity demanded is declining from 10,000 pairs to 6,000 pairs. This is how the rationing and motivating functions of price work together to balance the desires of consumers and producers and prevent a shortage or surplus. Every consumer who values jogging shoes enough to pay $60 will have them, and every producer that is willing to supply jogging shoes at that price will be able to sell its entire output.

CHANGES IN THE EQUILIBRIUM PRICE

You have seen that in the absence of artificial restrictions, prices in competitive markets tend toward equilibrium. Once established, the equilibrium price will hold as long as the underlying demand and supply conditions remain unchanged. Of course, such conditions don't remain unchanged forever, often not even for a short time. Anything that causes a change in either demand or supply will bring about a new equilibrium price.

The Impact of a Change in Demand

Recall from earlier in this chapter that the determinants of demand are all the factors that underlie the demand schedule and determine the precise position of the demand curve. These include consumer tastes and preferences, consumer income, the prices of substitutes and complements, expectations regarding future prices, and the number of buyers in the market. Changes in any of these factors will cause a change in demand—a shift of the entire demand curve.

The housing market provides a good example. Increased demand for new houses in your city or town could result from any of several factors: heightened desire for single-family dwellings instead of apartments, an increase in residents' incomes, rent hikes in the area, expectations of higher housing prices in the near future, or a local population expansion. Any of these changes will cause the demand curve for new homes to shift to the right, as depicted in Exhibit 3.11.

You can see that 8,000 new houses are demanded and supplied at the initial equilibrium price of $185,000. However, as demand increases from D_1 to D_2, perhaps because of an increased number of buyers in the market, there is a shortage of 4,000 houses (12,000 minus 8,000) at the $185,000 price. This shortage

EXHIBIT 3.11

The Effect of an Increase in Demand on the Equilibrium Price

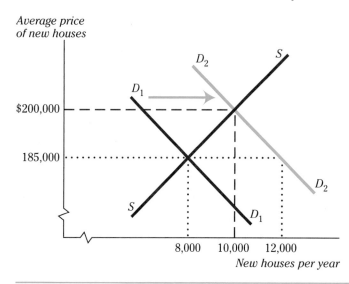

An increase in the demand for new houses will cause the equilibrium price of new homes to rise.

will lead to competition among prospective home buyers, which in turn will push the average price upward toward the new equilibrium level of $200,000. The higher price will ration new houses by reducing the quantity demanded and will motivate builders to increase the quantity supplied from 8,000 to 10,000. Note here that the increase in demand (the shift of the entire demand curve) causes an increase in the *quantity* supplied (movement along the stationary supply curve). In other words, a *shift* in one curve causes movement *along* the other curve. Thus, an increase in demand leads to a higher equilibrium in both price ($200,000) and quantity (10,000 new homes per year).

Suppose that, instead of increasing, the demand for new houses falls. What impact would that change have on the equilibrium price and quantity? As shown in Exhibit 3.12, the demand curve would shift to the left, from D_1 to D_2. As demand declines, a surplus of houses develops at the old price of $185,000 (only 4,000 homes will be demanded, but 8,000 will be supplied). This surplus will lead to price cutting as builders compete for buyers and as customers shop around for the best buys. Once again, the price change performs two functions. The falling price convinces home buyers to purchase more than 4,000 homes per year, and it motivates builders to supply fewer than 8,000 homes. Price will continue to decline until the quantity of new houses demanded is exactly equal to the quantity supplied at that price. In our example the new equilibrium price is $170,000, and the new equilibrium quantity is 6,000 new homes per year.

EXHIBIT 3.12

The Effect of a Decrease in Demand on the Equilibrium Price

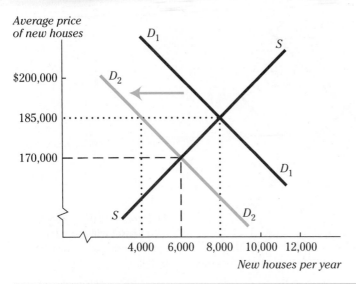

A decrease in the demand for new houses will cause the equilibrium price of new homes to fall.

The Impact of a Change in Supply

Price changes also can be initiated on the supply side. Recall the three determinants of supply: technology, prices of economic resources, and the number of suppliers in the market. Changes in any of these factors that underlie the supply schedule will cause a change in supply. In our example the supply of housing might be increased by any of the following: (1) the development of new construction methods that enable builders to produce more houses from a given amount of resources; (2) decreases in the cost of land, labor, or materials used in home construction; or (3) an increase in the number of builders, enabling the market to produce more houses than before at each possible price.

An increase in the supply of new houses is represented by shifting the supply curve to the right, as shown in Exhibit 3.13. When the supply of housing increases from S_1 to S_2, 12,000 new homes will be supplied at a price of $185,000, but only 8,000 will be demanded. As before, the surplus will lead to price cutting downward toward the new equilibrium level of $170,000. Note that here the increase in supply (the shift of the entire supply curve) causes an increase in the *quantity* demanded (movement along the stationary demand curve). As we saw earlier, a shift in one curve causes movement *along* the other. This is the process that results in the lower price and the higher equilibrium quantity. A *decrease* in the supply of housing would have the opposite effect; it would raise the equilibrium price and lower the equilibrium quantity.

EXHIBIT 3.13

Effect of an Increase in Supply on Equilibrium Price

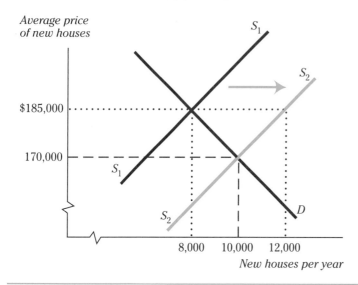

An increase in the supply of new houses will cause the equilibrium price of new homes to fall.

The Impact of Simultaneous Changes in Demand and Supply

All the price changes we have explored so far have resulted from a single cause: either a change in demand while supply remained constant or a change in supply while demand remained constant. But in many real-world situations simultaneous changes occur in demand and supply. Let's consider two examples in the housing market. In the first case we find an area undergoing a population expansion (a source of increased demand for new houses) at the same time that building-material costs are rising (causing a decrease in supply). In the second case a period of high unemployment is causing the incomes of area residents to decline (less demand for new houses), while new production methods are reducing the cost of new-home construction (increased supply).

In these two examples the forces of demand and supply are pulling in opposite directions—the demand curve is shifting one way while the supply curve is shifting the other way. Under these conditions it is relatively easy to determine what will happen to the equilibrium price. In the first example demand increases while supply decreases, so that the equilibrium price tends to rise. In the second example demand decreases while supply increases, so that the equilibrium price tends to fall. Take a minute to draw the diagrams and convince yourself of these results.

Predicting the impact of simultaneous changes in demand and supply becomes a little trickier when both the demand curve and the supply curve are shifting in the same direction. As you can see from Exhibit 3.14, when demand and supply are both increasing, we can be certain that the equilibrium quantity will also increase. But the impact on the equilibrium price is uncertain; it depends on how much demand increases relative to supply. If demand and supply increase by the same amounts, the equilibrium price will not change. If demand increases more than supply, the equilibrium price will rise. If supply increases more than demand, the equilibrium price will fall. (If demand decreases and supply increases, the equilibrium price is certain to decrease. But in this instance, the impact on equilibrium quantity will be indeterminate. See if you can predict what will happen to the equilibrium quantity if demand and supply both decrease by the same amount, if demand decreases more than supply, and if supply decreases more than demand.)

In summary the price of a product can change because of a change in demand, a change in supply, or simultaneous changes in both demand and supply. In all cases the basic principle is the same: Whenever demand increases in relation to supply, the equilibrium price will rise; whenever supply increases relative to demand, the equilibrium price will fall. By keeping that principle in

EXHIBIT 3.14

Effect of Simultaneous Increases in Demand and Supply on Equilibrium Price

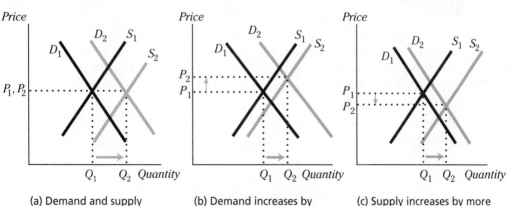

(a) Demand and supply increase by equal amounts; quantity increases, but price does not change.

(b) Demand increases by more than supply; both price and quantity increase.

(c) Supply increases by more than demand; quantity increases, but price falls.

Use Your Economic Reasoning

Don't Get Used to Cheap Oil, Analysts Say

BY JOHN PORRETTO

HOUSTON—All that money you're saving these days at the gas pump? You might want to put it in the bank. The same cheap oil that's providing relief to drivers and businesses in an awful economy is setting the stage for another price spike, perhaps as soon as next year, that will bring back painful memories of [the summer of 2008's] $4-a-gallon gas. The oil industry is scaling back on exploration and production because some projects don't make economic sense when energy prices are low. And crude is already harder to find because more nations that own oil companies are blocking outside access to their oil fields.

When the world emerges from the recession and starts to burn more fuel again, and higher demand meets lower supply, prices will almost certainly shoot higher. Some analysts say oil could eventually eclipse $150 a barrel, maybe even on its way to $200. In such a scenario, gasoline would easily cost more than the record high of $4.11 a gallon set last summer. Oil trades at about $50 today.

High prices at the pump last summer— more than $4 per gallon for gas on average— helped slash demand for oil. From November 2007 to October 2008, Americans drove 100 billion fewer miles than the year before, accord-

ing to government figures. The nation's biggest automakers lurched toward bankruptcy as sales of sport utility vehicles and trucks plummeted. "We wouldn't be bailing out the automobile industry today . . . had we not had this crazy situation with oil prices," said Daniel Yergin, chairman of Cambridge Energy Research Associates, a consulting firm, and author of "The Prize," the Pulitzer Prize–winning history of the oil industry.

Oil giants like Exxon Mobil, Chevron and ConocoPhillips have yet to announce their 2009 capital spending plans, but analysts say even the cash-rich companies are likely to shelve some projects. Already, Royal Dutch Shell has postponed a near-doubling of production in Canada's oil sands, an operation that analysts say only makes economic sense when oil is about $20 a barrel more expensive than it is now. Marathon Oil says it expects to cut capital spending by 15 percent in 2009. Brodrick said canceled or postponed oil and gas projects could contribute to a drop of 7 percent or more in global oil production this year. Smaller oil producers could cut spending by 30 percent, said Oppenheimer & Co. analyst Fadel Gheit. The majority of U.S. crude and natural gas is supplied by smaller,

Source: Associated Press, January 6, 2009. Reprinted by permission of the Associated Press. All rights reserved.

mind, we can predict what is going to happen to the price of cattle, wheat, or any other product whose price is determined in a competitive market. (Read "Don't Get Used to Cheap Oil, Analysts Say," above, and see if you can explain why the low oil prices that existed early in 2009 might have paved the way for dramatically higher prices in 2011.)

independent companies, not the Exxons and Chevrons, and smaller producers have been forced to pull back because of frozen credit markets.

All this comes as the Organization of Petroleum Exporting Countries, which controls about 40 percent of world crude supplies, embarks on its biggest single production cut ever.

It adds up to another round of price shocks for consumers that's probably inevitable, said Bruce Vincent, president of Houston-based Swift Energy Co., an independent producer. "Demand will start growing, supply will start coming down, and you'll have that intersect again where prices will take off dramatically," Vincent said. . . .

1. As the world's economies expanded in 2007–2008, the demand for crude oil increased, pushing its price from about $70 a barrel in July 2007 to a peak of almost $150 a barrel in July 2008. Draw a supply and demand graph that represents this situation. Label the axes; use hypothetical quantities.
2. The author stated that higher prices in the summer of 2008 helped "slash the demand for oil." Look at your graph. How much crude oil would have been demanded in July 2008 if the price of oil had remained at $70 a barrel (after the increase in demand)? How much less are consumers demanding because of the price hike? Does this represent a reduction in demand or a reduction in the quantity demanded? Note that economists would describe this as the "rationing effect" of the higher price.
3. Higher crude oil prices lead to higher gasoline prices because crude oil is an input used in making gasoline. Higher gasoline prices in turn tend to depress sales of SUVs and stimulate the sale of hybrid vehicles. Try to draw the graphs needed to depict what is happening in (a) the market for gasoline, (b) the market for SUVs, and (c) the market for hybrid automobiles.
4. In the second half of 2008, the price of oil plummeted, hitting about $50 a barrel when this article was written (January 2009). Gasoline prices were coming down; SUV sales were starting to pick up, but hybrid vehicles were a tough sell. Graph what was happening in these markets (gasoline, SUVs, and hybrids) and explain your graphs.
5. Each year, some oil wells go dry. As long as new wells are being drilled fast enough to replace the old ones that are drying up, the supply curve of oil is essentially stationary. But the article suggests that the lower price of oil in early 2009 ($50 a barrel and below) caused oil companies to scale back on exploration and new production. How could these decisions lead to dramatically higher oil prices "when the world emerges from the recession"? Represent this situation graphically.

ECONOMIC EFFICIENCY AND THE ROLE OF PRICES

The automatic response of price changes to changes in demand and supply conditions is an important feature of a market economy. As increasing consumer demand pushes the price of a product upward, the higher price rations some consumers out of the market and simultaneously motivates producers to expand their production of the product. Because these producers are receiving a higher price for their product, they will be able to outbid producers of less-valued items for the resources needed to expand production. In this way price changes help to ensure that businesses produce the goods and services that consumers value the most, in the quantities they desire.

Price changes also help ensure that each product is produced with as few of society's scarce resources as possible. As a particular resource becomes scarcer (because of increased demand or reduced supply), its price tends to rise. This higher cost encourages producers to economize on its use by substituting cheaper resources whenever possible. The end result is the efficient use of society's scarce resources: producers supply the most-wanted products in the least-costly way in terms of scarce resources. (Note that the fewer the resources an economy needs to produce each product, the more goods and services it can produce with its limited resource stock. Thus, an economy that is operating efficiently is producing the goods and services that consumers value the most *and* producing as many of those goods and services as possible from the society's scarce resources.) The way competitive markets promote the efficient use of resources is explored in greater detail in Chapter 6. Later chapters examine how such factors as inadequate competition and the ability of firms to ignore the "cost" of the pollution they create can interfere with the ability of markets to achieve this optimal result.

SUMMARY

In a competitive market, prices are determined by the interaction of demand and supply. *Demand* is a schedule showing the quantities of a good or service that consumers are willing and able to purchase at various prices during some given time period, when all factors other than the product's price remain unchanged. Demand may be represented graphically in a *demand curve*, which slopes downward and to the right because the *law of demand* holds that consumers will purchase more of a product at a lower price than at a higher price. *Supply* is a schedule showing the quantities of a good or service that producers are willing and able to offer for sale at various prices during a given time period, when all factors other than the product's price remain unchanged. Supply may be represented graphically as a *supply curve*. The supply curve slopes upward and to the right because the *law of supply* states that price and quantity supplied are positively related; that is, a greater quantity will be supplied at higher prices than at lower prices.

The demand curve will shift to a new position if there is a change in any of the *determinants of demand*: consumer income, tastes and preferences, expectations regarding future prices, the prices of substitute and complementary goods, and the number of consumers in the market. By the same token, the supply curve will shift if there is a change in one or more of the *determinants of supply*: technology, the prices of resources, or the number of producers in the market.

Economists are careful to distinguish between a change in the quantity demanded and a change in demand. A change in the amount purchased as a result of a change in the price of the product while other factors are held constant is a *change in quantity demanded* and is represented by movement up or down a stationary demand curve. A change in any of the determinants of demand while price is held constant will cause consumers to purchase more or less of a product at each possible price. This is described as a *change in demand* and is represented by a shift of the entire demand curve to the right (in the case of increased demand) or to the left (in the case of decreased demand).

A similar distinction is necessary on the supply side of the market. A *change in quantity supplied* results from a change in the price of the product and is represented graphically by a movement along a stationary supply curve. A *change in supply* results from a change in one of the determinants of supply and is represented by a shift of the entire supply curve to a new position.

The *equilibrium price* is the price that brings about an equality between the quantity demanded and the quantity supplied, which we call the *equilibrium quantity*. The equilibrium price can be identified by the intersection of the demand and supply curves. If the prevailing price is above equilibrium, a *surplus*—an excess of quantity supplied over quantity demanded—will occur, and sellers will be forced to reduce price to eliminate the surplus. If the prevailing price is below equilibrium, a *shortage*—an excess of quantity demanded over quantity supplied—occurs, and buyers will bid up the price as they compete for the product. Only when the existing price is at the equilibrium level will there be neither a shortage nor a surplus and no pressure for price to change.

Prices perform two important functions: They (1) *ration*, or divide, the limited amount of available output among possible buyers; and (2) *motivate* producers to supply the desired quantity. Higher prices ration by discouraging consumers from purchasing a product; they also motivate producers to increase the quantity supplied. Lower prices have the opposite effect. They encourage consumers to purchase more of the product and simultaneously motivate producers to reduce the quantity supplied. The equilibrium price succeeds in matching the quantity demanded with the quantity supplied because it balances the desires of consumers and producers. Every consumer who values the product enough to pay the equilibrium price will have it, and every producer willing to supply the product at that price will be able to sell its entire output.

In the absence of artificial restrictions, prices will rise and fall in response to changes in demand and supply. Whenever demand increases in relation to supply, the equilibrium price will tend to rise; whenever supply increases in relation to demand, the equilibrium price will fall. These price changes help to ensure that producers not only supply the goods and services consumers value the most but also use as few scarce resources as possible in the production of those goods and services.

KEY TERMS

Change in demand	Determinants of supply	Rationing
Change in quantity demanded	Equilibrium price	Shortage
	Equilibrium quantity	Substitute
Change in quantity supplied	Income effect	Substitution effect
Change in supply	Inferior good	Supply
Complement	Law of demand	Supply curve
Demand	Law of supply	Surplus
Demand curve	Motivating	Technological advance
Determinants of demand	Normal good	Technology

STUDY QUESTIONS

Fill in the Blanks

1. If the entire demand curve shifts to a new position, we describe this as a change in

   _____.

2. If a product is a normal good, an increase in income will cause the demand curve for the product to shift to the

   _____.

3. Movement along a stationary supply curve due to a change in price is called a

   change in _____.

4. The function of dividing up or allocating scarce items among those who desire to

   receive them is called _____.

5. The price that exactly clears the market is

   called _____ the price.

6. Whenever the prevailing price is above

   equilibrium, a(n)_____ will exist.

7. Prices perform two important functions: they ration scarce items among the consumers who desire to receive them, and

   they _____ producers to supply that quantity.

8. If supply rises and demand declines, we would expect the equilibrium price to

   _____.

9. If supply increases more than demand, the

   equilibrium price will _____.

10. If supply and demand both increase, we can be certain that the equilibrium

    (price/quantity) _____ will increase, but the impact on the equilibrium

    (price/quantity) _____ will be indeterminate.

Multiple Choice

1. If the price of automobiles increases and all other factors remain unchanged, it will be reasonable to expect
   a) an increase in the demand for automobiles.
   b) a decrease in the demand for automobiles.
   c) an increase in the quantity of automobiles demanded.
   d) a decrease in the quantity of automobiles demanded.

2. If the demand curve for Brock's Heavy Beer shifts to the left, this could be due to
   a) an increase in the price of Brock's Heavy Beer.
   b) an increase in consumer income.
   c) an increase in the price of other beers.
   d) a shift in tastes and preferences to light beers.

3. An increase in the price of apples is likely to cause
   a) a decrease in the demand for apples.
   b) an increase in the quantity demanded of apples.
   c) an increase in the demand for other types of fruit.
   d) an increase in the quantity demanded of other types of fruit.

4. If the price of black walnuts increases and other factors remain unchanged, it is reasonable to expect
   a) a decrease in the demand for black walnuts.
   b) an increase in the supply of black walnuts.
   c) an increase in the quantity of black walnuts supplied.
   d) a decrease in the demand for pecans and other walnut substitutes.

5. A new labor settlement that increases the cost of producing computers will probably cause
   a) a decrease in the supply of computers.
   b) a reduction in the demand for computers.
   c) a reduction in the quantity of computers supplied.
   d) the supply curve of computers to shift to the right.

6. If an excellent growing season doubles the corn harvest, the result will be
   a) an increase in the demand for corn.
   b) a lower price and an increase in the quantity of corn demanded.
   c) an increase in the quantity of corn supplied.
   d) a lower price and an increase in the demand for corn.

7. If demand increases and supply declines,
   a) the equilibrium price and quantity will both increase.
   b) the equilibrium price will rise, but the quantity will fall.
   c) the equilibrium price will fall, but the quantity will rise.
   d) the equilibrium price and quantity will both fall.
   e) the equilibrium price will rise; quantity will be indeterminate.

8. If the demand for used cars declines, the likely result will be
   a) an increase in the supply of used cars.
   b) a reduction in the equilibrium price of used cars.
   c) an increase in the equilibrium price of used cars.
   d) a temporary shortage of used cars at the old price.

9. If the price of computer chips and other component parts falls, this would lead to
   a) an increase in the supply of computers and lower computer prices.
   b) a decrease in the supply of computers and higher computer prices.
   c) an increase in the demand for computers and higher computer prices.
   d) a decrease in the demand for computers and lower computer prices.

10. When a drought destroys half of the orange crop, newspapers are likely to report a "shortage of oranges." An economist would say that
    a) a drought would lead to a surplus of oranges, not a shortage.

b) This shortage will exist until the next season, when more oranges can be produced.

c) This shortage is temporary and will be eliminated when the price of oranges rises.

d) The existing price of oranges must be above the equilibrium level.

11. Consider the market for mobile homes. If personal incomes in the United States rise, we would expect to see
   a) a decline in mobile home prices if mobile homes are a normal good.
   b) an increase in the demand for mobile homes if mobile homes are an inferior good.
   c) a decrease in mobile home prices if mobile homes are an inferior good.
   d) a decrease in the demand for mobile homes if mobile homes are a normal good.

12. If the price of coffee increases, the probable result will be
   a) a decrease in the demand for coffee.
   b) a decrease in the price of substitutes for coffee.
   c) an increase in the price of substitutes for coffee.
   d) a decrease in the supply of coffee.

13. Which of the following statements is *incorrect*?
   a) If demand increases and supply remains constant, the equilibrium price will rise.

b) If supply rises and demand remains constant, the equilibrium price will fall.

c) If demand rises and supply falls, the equilibrium price will rise.

d) If supply increases and demand decreases, the equilibrium price will rise.

14. If additional farmers enter the hog-producing industry, the result will be
   a) lower prices but a higher equilibrium quantity.
   b) higher prices but a lower equilibrium quantity.
   c) lower prices but the same equilibrium quantity.
   d) lower prices and a lower equilibrium quantity.

15. Which of the following is correct?
   a) An increase in demand results in a temporary surplus, leading to competition between consumers, which pushes up the product's price.
   b) An increase in supply results in a temporary shortage, leading to competition between consumers, which pushes up the product's price.
   c) An increase in demand results in a temporary shortage, leading to competition between consumers, which pushes up the product's price.
   d) An increase in supply results in a temporary surplus, leading to competition between suppliers, which pushes up the product's price.

Problems and Questions for Discussion

1. My eldest daughter says that she really "needs" a new sweatshirt, but she won't use her allowance to buy it. ("I don't need it *that* badly.") How can a "need" evaporate like that? What is the difference between *need* and *demand*?

2. Podunk College experienced a substantial drop in enrollment last year. What possible explanations can you, as an economist,

offer for what happened? Try to list all possibilities.

3. Why does the supply curve slope upward and to the right? In other words, why will producers supply a higher quantity at higher prices?

4. Which of the following events would cause movement along a stationary supply curve for wheat, and which would

cause the supply curve to shift? Explain each situation from the producer's point of view.
a. The price of wheat declines.
b. The cost of fertilizer rises.
c. Wheat blight destroys half the wheat crop.
d. New combines make it possible for one person to do the work of three.

5. Explain the economic reasoning behind the following newspaper headlines:
a. "Weather Slows Fishing: Seafood Prices Double"
b. "Sugar: Crisis of Plenty"
c. "Bountiful Wheat Crop Is Hurting Growers."

6. If the supply of oranges in a competitive market decreases as a result of severe weather, will there be a shortage of oranges? Why or why not? (Hint: Use graphs to help answer this question.)

7. Suppose that your local tennis courts are very crowded, and your city is considering charging a fee to ration their use. Who would like to have a fee charged? Would only wealthy individuals feel this way? Why might someone be in favor of a fee?

8. People, including news reporters, often use the terms *supply* and *demand* incorrectly. For example, you will often read "Supply exceeds demand" or "Demand exceeds supply." What is wrong with these statements? What does the writer probably mean to say?

9. Why is it important that prices in a market economy be allowed to change in response to changing demand and supply conditions? What functions do these changing prices perform?

10. Assume that consumers are buying equal numbers of hamburgers and hot dogs when these products are selling at the same price. If the supply of hamburger declines, what will happen to the price of hamburgers? What about the price of hot dogs? Graph your conclusions.

ANSWER KEY

Fill in the Blanks

1. demand
2. right
3. quantity supplied
4. rationing
5. equilibrium
6. surplus
7. motivate
8. fall
9. fall
10. quantity, price

Multiple Choice

1. d	4. c	7. e	10. c	13. d
2. d	5. a	8. b	11. c	14. a
3. c	6. b	9. a	12. c	15. c

4

Applications Using Demand and Supply

LEARNING OBJECTIVES

1. Recognize the impact of government-established maximum and minimum prices.
2. Explain what is meant by a secondary rationing device.
3. Identify the effects of government subsidies and excise taxes.
4. Define price elasticity of demand.
5. Compute and interpret the coefficient of demand elasticity.
6. Describe the degrees of price elasticity.
7. Explain the relationship between the price elasticity of demand and the total revenue received by the firm.
8. Identify the factors that influence the price elasticity of demand.
9. Explain how the impact of an excise tax is influenced by the price elasticity of demand.

In Chapter 3 we considered how demand and supply interact to determine prices, and we discovered how changes in demand or supply cause those prices to change. We also discovered that price changes perform important rationing and motivating functions—functions that help to conserve scarce resources and ensure that those resources are used to produce the goods and services most valued by consumers.

In this chapter we want to explore some applications of the supply and demand model. We begin by examining what happens when government intervenes in the pricing process. We explore the impact of price ceilings and price floors, then turn to a discussion of government subsidies and excise taxes. Considering the impact of government intervention in pricing will naturally lead us to the second topic of this chapter—the price sensitivity of consumers. In this section we will discuss why high prices may do little to deter smoking by adults, and why lower bus fares may not do much to stimulate bus ridership. We turn, first, to a consideration of government intervention in the pricing process.

GOVERNMENT INTERVENTION IN PRICING

Why might government choose to intervene in the pricing process? The short answer is "because policymakers don't like the market outcome." They believe that the market-determined price is either too high or too low. In some instances, that judgment stems from the belief that the market price is unfair because it creates hardship for producers or consumers. This is the rationale for agricultural price supports, minimum wage laws, rent controls, and interest-rate ceilings, for example. In other instances, intervention is motivated by the desire to alter consumer or producer behavior—heavily taxing cigarettes to deter consumption, for example, or subsidizing the construction of low-cost housing to encourage production. In all these instances, we can use the model of supply and demand to predict the likely impact of these policies. We begin by exploring a classic form of government intervention in pricing—price supports.

Price Supports

Government sometimes intervenes in pricing by establishing maximum or minimum prices. A **price support** is a legally established minimum price above the equilibrium price. In the 1930s, for example, the federal government initiated a program of agricultural price supports designed to raise the incomes of farmers. Under this program the government "supported" the price of the product by agreeing to purchase, at the legally established price, whatever output the farmer was unable to sell at that price.

Exhibit 4.1 shows a hypothetical situation in which the government has established a price support (or support price) for corn at $4, which is $1 above the equilibrium price of $3 per bushel. At $4 a bushel, customers are willing to purchase only 10 billion bushels a year, but producers are eager to supply 20 billion bushels. We know that in a free or unregulated market, sellers of corn would deal with the surplus of 10 billion bushels by cutting prices down to the equilibrium level of $3, at which the equilibrium quantity of 15 billion bushels would be supplied. Once the government establishes a price support of $4, however, the market remains in disequilibrium, with surpluses continuing to accumulate. The government is then required to buy the surplus corn, store it,

EXHIBIT 4.1

Price Supports and Surpluses

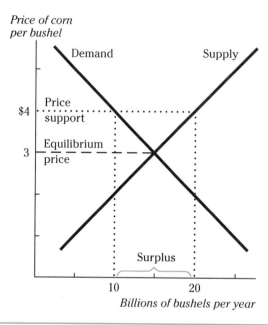

A price support will tend to produce a surplus because the price is legally fixed above the equilibrium level. In this example, a support price of $4 leads to a surplus of 10 billion bushels of corn per year.

and dispose of it (through donations to poor nations, for example), all at the expense of taxpayers.[1]

In April 1996, this expense caused Congress to pass the Freedom to Farm Act, legislation ending price supports for wheat, feed grains, cotton, and rice. To ease the transition to a free market, the bill replaced traditional price supports with fixed but declining payments every year until 2002. Although some hailed the Freedom to Farm Act as the end of government intervention in farming, that assessment has proven to be wrong. When the act expired in 2002, it was replaced by the Farm Security and Rural Investment Act (the Farm Bill of 2002), legislation providing a mixture of loans, price supports, and government

---

[1] Although Exhibit 4.1 captures the most important elements of the price support program, it is not completely accurate. Under federal price support legislation, customers would pay the market price, not the support price, as depicted in the graph. The difference is made up by the federal government in a **deficiency payment** ($1 a bushel, in this example) paid directly to the farmer. As a result, the actual surplus will be somewhat smaller than that depicted in the exhibit. Because consumers are responding to the market price, they will want to purchase 15 million bushels. On the other hand, because suppliers are responding to the support price, they will want to supply 20 million bushels. The result will be a surplus of 5 million bushels, which must be purchased by the government (at $4 a bushel).

subsidies to farmers. (The impact of subsidies will be discussed in some detail later in this chapter.) At a cost of about $190 billion over 10 years, the Farm Bill of 2002 clearly signaled a return to business as usual. In 2008, the Farm Bill's programs were extended again after a well-organized effort by the farm lobby.

When we look beyond agricultural markets, the minimum wage provides another example of a price support. By law most employers are required to pay their employees at least the federally established minimum wage ($7.25 an hour in 2009). Because the minimum wage is generally above the equilibrium wage for unskilled labor, there are more people willing to work at that wage than employers are willing to hire at that wage.[2] Of course, those who can find jobs are better off because of the minimum wage. But some unskilled workers who would have been able to find jobs at the equilibrium wage will be unemployed at the minimum wage. This occurs because employers simply do not believe that these workers will be able to contribute enough to the production process to justify that high a wage. Just as the price support for corn created a surplus of that product, the minimum wage creates a surplus of workers. To the extent that the minimum wage increases unemployment, it conflicts with our objective of raising the incomes of low-income Americans.

Price Ceilings

Government may also intervene in the pricing process when it is convinced that prevailing prices are either too high or are increasing too rapidly. In such cases the government will set **price ceilings**, maximum prices that are established below the equilibrium price. During World War II, for example, price ceilings were placed on most nonfarm prices to prevent them from being pushed to exorbitant levels by the demands of the war effort. Price ceilings (or ceiling prices) also have been used during peacetime as a technique both for combating inflation (a general rise in the level of prices) and for controlling specific prices. For instance, in 1971 President Nixon "froze" virtually all wages and prices for a period of 90 days in an attempt to slow the rate of inflation. In the same decade, the federal government used price ceilings selectively to limit the prices of beef, pork, gasoline, and natural gas, among other products.

One common example of a price ceiling is rent ceilings. **Rent ceilings** (or rent controls) are maximum rents that are established below the equilibrium level. They were first instituted in World War II to prevent transient wartime workers (who were typically well paid) from outbidding local residents for

---

[2] When established, price supports are usually above the equilibrium price. Over time, however, the equilibrium price may rise above the support level, causing the price support to be ineffective. For example, in 2006 the minimum wage (a form of price support) of $5.15 was probably below the equilibrium wage for unskilled labor in most parts of the United States.

apartments in industrial cities. After the war, these ceilings were abolished everywhere except in New York City. Then in the inflationary 1970s, rent-control laws spread to cities in Massachusetts, to much of suburban Long Island and New Jersey, to Washington, and to about half the population of California.

Although rent ceilings may seem in the best interest of consumers, they frequently create problems for prospective renters. Because the rent is fixed at an artificially low level, more people will want to rent in that city (or the rent-controlled portions of the city) than would desire to do so at the equilibrium rent. In addition, the low rent will make renting apartments less attractive to owners, who consequently will make fewer apartments available than would be provided at the equilibrium rent. The result will be a shortage of apartments and a number of unsatisfied customers.

Exhibit 4.2 represents the plight of consumers in a rent-controlled city. As you can see from the exhibit, $800 is the equilibrium rent, the rent at which the number of apartments consumers desire to rent is equal to the number that apartment owners want to make available. At the $500 rent ceiling (or ceiling rent), consumers want to rent 20,000 apartments, but owners are willing to supply only 14,000 units. There is a shortage of 6,000 apartments. We know that in unregulated markets a shortage of apartments, or any other item, will lead to a price increase, which motivates businesses to supply more of the item and

Price Ceilings and Shortages

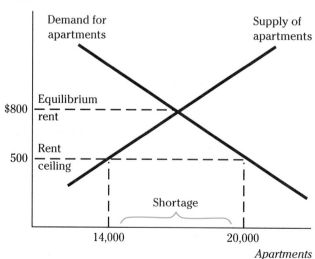

A price ceiling will tend to produce a shortage because the price is legally fixed below the equilibrium level. In this example, the rent ceiling of $500 leads to a shortage of 6,000 apartments.

which rations some consumers out of the market. A ceiling prevents the rent from rising to its equilibrium level, so that landlords are faced with more potential renters than they can satisfy. Consequently, they must use some secondary rationing device to decide which consumers will get apartments.

A **secondary rationing device** is a nonprice condition that supplements the primary rationing device, price. The prospective apartment renter in our example must not only be willing to pay the $500 rent but must also be able to satisfy some supplementary requirement imposed by landlords. Perhaps landlords will grant apartments only on the basis of first come, first served. Or perhaps they will choose to rent only to applicants without children and pets or only to those with the best jobs (and therefore the greatest likelihood of making timely rent payments). Perhaps they will rent only to retired persons or to those with verifiable references. Whether the use of a secondary, nonprice rationing device is preferable to higher rents is a matter for you to decide. It is clear, however, that rent ceilings do not eliminate the need to ration; they simply force sellers to use secondary rationing devices.

In New York City, where about 50,000 units are under strict rent control and an additional one million units are subject to more modest rent stabilization, finding an apartment is a major problem. Because rents are kept below their equilibrium level, New Yorkers face a perpetual housing shortage. To some extent, existing housing is rationed on a first-come, first-served basis, and would-be renters spend countless hours in a vain attempt to find a vacant apartment. Some frustrated searchers resort to checking obituaries in hopes of zeroing in on a newly available rental before anyone else hears of it; others make secret payments to landlords for the privilege of a new lease.

Low rents not only produce a shortage but also prevent the supply of housing from expanding. When regulations keep rents artificially low, they limit the potential return that entrepreneurs can expect from investing in that market. Profitable rental rates would provide entrepreneurs with an incentive to increase the supply of housing—by converting five-story apartment buildings into ten or twenty stories, for instance. But those investments don't make sense when rent ceilings keep apartment rents artificially low, so the shortage continues, and entrepreneurs look elsewhere for investment opportunities.

Although concern over the unintended consequences of rent ceilings has caused some cities to abolish or weaken their rent control laws, New York is not among them. In fact, in February 2009, the state legislature was considering legislation that would essentially return to regulation tens of thousands of units that had become subject to market rental rates in recent years.[3] New Yorkers will be complaining about the apartment shortage for the foreseeable future.

---

[3] Jeremy W. Peters, "Assembly Passes Rent-Regulation Revisions Opposed by Landlords," *New York Times*, February 3, 2009, p. 21.

Subsidies

While price ceilings and floors are perhaps the most obvious forms of government intervention in pricing, they are certainly not the only forms. Another relatively common form of government intervention in pricing is subsidies. A **subsidy** is a payment that government makes to private producers or consumers for each unit of output that they produce or purchase. Over the years, our federal, state, and local governments have subsidized a wide variety of products: grains (corn, wheat, and rice, for example), dairy products, housing, childhood inoculations, and education, to name just a few. The purpose of these subsidies is to encourage the production of the good or service in question. Production can be encouraged by subsidizing either producers or consumers; both approaches yield similar results. For simplicity, we will focus on subsidies paid directly to producers.

Producer subsidies have essentially the same impact as a reduction in the cost of production—they increase market supply. Subsidies have this impact because—in effect—government is paying part of the cost of producing each unit of output. To illustrate, suppose that government decides to subsidize doctors who give meningitis inoculations. Therefore, it agrees to send doctors a $20 check for each meningitis inoculation they provide. As you can see from Exhibit 4.3, the impact of this subsidy is to shift the supply curve of meningitis

---

EXHIBIT 4.3

The Impact of a Per-Unit Subsidy

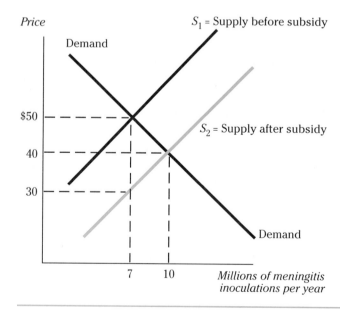

An excise subsidy of $20 per inoculation would shift the supply curve of inoculations down by $20 everywhere. The result would be a reduction in the price of meningitis inoculations and an increase in the equilibrium quantity.

inoculations down by an amount equal to the subsidy. Before the subsidy, doctors required a price of $50 to supply 7 million inoculations. After the subsidy, they would be willing to supply 7 million inoculations at a price of $30 each (because they would also be receiving $20 from government). Because the same logic applies to each point on the original supply curve, the result of the subsidy is to shift the entire inoculation supply curve down by an amount equal to the subsidy.

If you examine Exhibit 4.3 carefully, you will notice something interesting. The equilibrium price of meningitis inoculations does not decline by the amount of the subsidy. Rather than falling from $50 to $30, it falls by only $10, from $50 to $40. This outcome is simply the result of market forces. If the price of meningitis inoculations were to fall by $20, the resulting price would be too low for equilibrium, and a shortage would result. This shortage would lead to competition among consumers, which would push the price up to $40, the equilibrium or market clearing price.

Subsidies are always popular with the producers who receive them. But, like price supports and ceilings, they can have unintended consequences. For instance, government subsides to U.S. and European farmers have been blamed for depressing the world price of cotton and other agricultural commodities and intensifying poverty in developing nations.

Excise Taxes

The final form of government intervention we consider is taxation, specifically excise taxes. An **excise tax** is a tax that is levied on the sale of specific products (unlike a sales tax that is levied on everything we buy). Excise taxes are perhaps the oldest form of government intervention in pricing. In some instances the primary purpose of an excise tax is to generate revenue for government. For example, the state excise tax on gasoline is generally intended to generate revenue to help pay for road construction and repair. In other instances the purpose of the tax is to deter consumption—the most common rationale for taxing cigarettes. In either case the result of an excise tax is the same—higher prices for consumers.

When an excise tax is imposed on a good or service, it has basically the same impact as an *increase* in the cost of production—it reduces the supply of the product. To understand why it has this effect, consider the impact of the excise tax on gasoline. Gasoline sales are taxed by the states and by the federal government. State taxes vary significantly—from 8 cents a gallon in Alaska to 41.3 cents in New York. The federal tax is 18.4 cents a gallon. Let's assume that together these taxes average 50 cents a gallon. Because excise taxes are always collected from the sellers, these firms view the tax as essentially an increase in the cost of production. If they had been willing to supply 30 million gallons a day at $2.75 per gallon, they will now require $3.25 a gallon to supply the same quantity (see

Exhibit 4.4). They behave in this way because the other 50 cents goes to the government, and producers' supply decisions are only motivated by the portion of the selling price they get to keep. Because the same logic applies to each point on the supply curve, the result is to shift the entire supply curve up vertically by the amount of the excise tax. (Note that the graph depicting an excise tax is the mirror image of the graph depicting a subsidy. Although both subsidies and excise taxes shift the supply curve, they shift it in opposite directions. A subsidy tends to *increase* supply, whereas an excise tax tends to *decrease* supply.)

As you examine Exhibit 4.4, it is important to recognize that the 50-cent excise tax did not raise the equilibrium price of gasoline by 50 cents. When the 50-cent excise tax is imposed on suppliers, the equilibrium price rises by only 25 cents a gallon (from $3.00 to $3.25). In this example, suppliers absorb about half of the tax rather than passing the entire tax on to consumers. Why do they behave in this way? It's not because they love their customers; that would violate the self-interest assumption that undergirds all economic analysis. The problem is that they can't be successful in passing the entire tax on to consumers. If suppliers attempted to raise the price to $3.50, the resulting price would be above equilibrium, and there would be a surplus in the market. Of course, this surplus will lead to competition between suppliers, which would force them to lower their price to sell all their output.

The result we see here (where customers pay half the tax and producers pay half) is not the only possible outcome. In fact, this result is probably *not*

EXHIBIT 4.4

The Impact of an Excise Tax

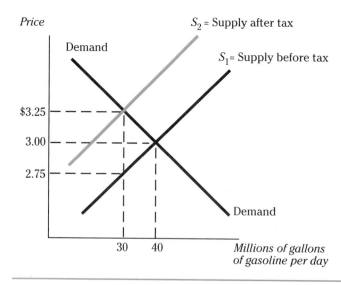

An excise tax of 50 cents per gallon would shift the supply curve of gasoline up by 50 cents everywhere. The result would be an increase in the price of gasoline and a reduction in the equilibrium quantity.

representative of the true outcome in the gasoline market. The share of the tax paid by consumers depends on how sensitive those consumers are to price changes. If they are very price sensitive—if a small price hike causes them to buy a lot less—suppliers will be unable to pass as much of the tax on to consumers and will therefore be forced to absorb a larger fraction of the tax (as lower profits). On the other hand, if consumers are *not* very price sensitive (which is probably true in the case of gasoline), a large price hike will do little to deter their purchases. Under those conditions we can expect suppliers to pass on a larger share of the tax in the form of higher prices.

As you can see, the price sensitivity of consumers has important implications for businesses and for government policymakers. We explore this important topic next.

ELASTICITY OF DEMAND

If a professional football team decides to raise the price of season tickets by $100, how many fewer tickets will fans buy? If a local health club doubles its rates, how many customers will it lose? To answer these questions, we need some knowledge of the sensitivity or responsiveness of consumers to price changes—we need to know something about the price elasticity of demand.

The **price elasticity of demand** is a measure of the responsiveness of the quantity demanded of a product to a change in its price. If the quantity demanded expands or contracts a great deal in response to a price change, demand is said to be very responsive, or *elastic*; if the quantity demanded doesn't change very much, demand is described as not very responsive, or *inelastic*.

In gauging the responsiveness of consumers, the absolute size of the changes in price and quantity means very little. To illustrate, suppose that a $5 price reduction causes consumers to demand an additional 1,000 units of some product. Should we describe the demand for this product as elastic or inelastic? We can't tell unless we know the starting point, the initial price and quantity. Suppose the firm had cut the price from $10 to $5, and this price reduction caused the quantity demanded to increase from 100,000 units to 101,000 units. Would you describe demand as elastic (very responsive to the price change) under those conditions? Probably not; a 50 percent price reduction led to only a 1 percent increase in the quantity demanded! But if the price had been reduced from $100 to $95 (the same $5 but in this case only 5 percent of the original price) and the quantity demanded had increased from 1,000 to 2,000 units (100 percent), you'd probably agree that consumers were quite responsive to the change in price; demand is elastic.

The point is that when we describe the responsiveness of consumers, we need to think in terms of percentages—the percent change in price and the percent change in the quantity demanded. This approach adjusts for the initial prices and quantities and gives us a much more meaningful comparison.

The Coefficient of Demand Elasticity

We can measure the elasticity of demand by calculating a value called the **coefficient of demand elasticity**. We compute the coefficient of elasticity by dividing the percentage change in quantity demanded by the percentage change in price:

$$\text{Coefficient of elasticity} = \frac{\dfrac{\Delta Q}{Q}}{\dfrac{\Delta P}{P}} = \frac{\text{Percentage change in quantity demanded}}{\text{Percentage change in price}}$$

In this formula for the coefficient, Q stands for quantity, P for price, and the Greek letter *delta* (Δ) for "change in." $\Delta Q/Q$ is the percentage change in quantity demanded, and $\Delta P/P$ is the percentage change in price.

Let's use this formula to calculate the elasticity of demand for Fantastic Cola. Suppose that when the price of a six-pack rises from $2.50 to $3, weekly sales decline from 1,000 six-packs to 900. What is the price elasticity of demand for Fantastic Cola? If the change in quantity demanded (ΔQ) is 100 fewer six-packs per week and the original quantity demanded (Q) is 1,000 six-packs, the percentage change in quantity demanded ($-100/1,000$) is -10 percent. And if the change in price (ΔP) is $.50 and the original price (P) is $2.50, the percentage change in price ($.50/$2.50) is 20 percent. If we divide the 10 percent reduction in quantity by the 20 percent increase in price, we arrive at an elasticity coefficient of $-.5$:[4]

$$\text{Coefficient of elasticity} = \frac{\dfrac{-100}{1,000}}{\dfrac{\$.50}{\$2.50}} = \frac{-10\%}{20\%} = -.5$$

---

[4] The simple formula we are using to compute the elasticity coefficient produces somewhat ambiguous results. If the sellers of Fantastic Cola raise the price from $2.50 to $3, the value of the elasticity coefficient is .5. But if the sellers lower their price from $3 to $2.50, the coefficient will be .67 because the initial price and quantity are different.

Economic theory does not suggest any reason that these two coefficients should be different, so we might argue that they should be the same. This can be accomplished by using the average of the two prices and the average of the two quantities as the base values for computing percentages. When this approach is used, the value of the coefficient will be the same, regardless of whether the initial price is the higher price or the lower price. In the Fantastic Cola example, the value of the elasticity coefficient would be .58. In the modified formula below, we add the two quantities Q_1 and Q_2 and divide by 2 to arrive at the average quantity. Average price is determined the same way:

$$\frac{\Delta Q / [(Q_1 + Q_2) / 2]}{\Delta P / [(P_1 + P_2) / 2]} = \frac{100 / (1,900/ 2)}{\$.50 / (\$5.50/ 2)} = \frac{100 / 950}{\$.50 / \$2.75} = \frac{10.5\%}{18.2\%} = .58$$

An elasticity coefficient of .5 means that for every 1 percent change in price, the quantity demanded will change by .5 percent. Thus, if the price of Fantastic Cola goes up by 10 percent, we would expect a 5 percent reduction in the quantity demanded. If it increases by 20 percent, we would expect a 10 percent reduction in quantity demanded. Alternatively, if the elasticity coefficient had been 2.0 instead of .5, each 1 percent change in price would cause a 2 percent change in quantity demanded. For example, a 10 percent increase in price would cause a 20 percent decrease in quantity demanded.

You will note that in our formula the elasticity coefficient ($-.5$) carries a negative sign. We know from the law of demand that changes in price normally cause the quantity demanded to change in the opposite direction. Thus, price increases cause reductions in the quantity demanded, whereas price reductions cause increases in the quantity demanded. In either case the sign is negative and is usually ignored in referring to price elasticity values.

Degrees of Elasticity

Economists use the coefficient of elasticity to define precisely the terms *elastic* and *inelastic*. Elastic demand exists when the coefficient of elasticity is greater than 1, when a given percentage change in price brings about a larger percentage change in the quantity demanded. When the elasticity coefficient is less than 1, demand is inelastic; a given percentage change in price brings about a smaller percentage change in the quantity demanded. If the coefficient is exactly 1, *unitary elasticity* prevails; a given percentage change in price results in an identical percentage change in quantity demanded. The elasticity coefficient can vary from zero to infinity, where zero represents the least elastic demand imaginable and infinity represents the most elastic demand imaginable.

If the coefficient of elasticity is zero, a change in price brings no change at all in the quantity demanded. Demand is described as *perfectly inelastic*, and the demand curve is a vertical straight line. For example, over some range of prices, the demand for lifesaving drugs, such as insulin, may be perfectly inelastic. Another example is the demand for dialysis treatment by those suffering from kidney failure.

If the coefficient of elasticity approaches infinity, a very small change in price leads to an enormous change in the quantity demanded. Demand is said to be *perfectly elastic* and is graphed as a horizontal straight line. Perfectly inelastic and perfectly elastic demand curves are depicted in Exhibit 4.5. The individual apple farmer faces a situation that illustrates perfectly elastic demand. If the market price of apples is $10 a bushel, the farmer can sell as much as desired at that price. But a farmer who attempts to charge more than $10 will sell nothing; consumers will simply buy their apples from someone else. This is the type of situation we represent with a perfectly elastic

EXHIBIT 4.5

Perfectly Inelastic and Perfectly Elastic Demand Curves

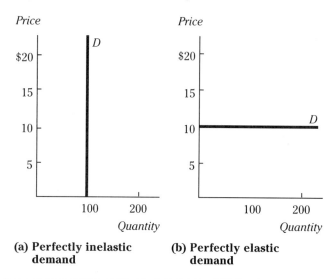

(a) Perfectly inelastic demand

(b) Perfectly elastic demand

(a) Despite an increase or decrease in price, consumers buy exactly the same quantity. The demand curve for insulin may look like this over some price range. (b) A very small increase in price would cause consumers to reduce their purchases to zero. The individual apple farmer may face a demand curve like this one.

demand curve. In Chapter 6 we will have much more to say about perfectly elastic demand curves.

Elasticity along a Straight-Line Demand Curve

In most instances demand curves do not show just one degree of elasticity; they show several. All linear, downward-sloping demand curves show unitary elasticity midway on the curve, with elastic demand above the midpoint and inelastic demand below it. Exhibit 4.6 depicts such a demand curve.

In Exhibit 4.6, note that because the demand curve is a straight line, it has a constant inclination, or *slope*. Therefore, a price change of a given size will always bring the same quantity change. In this hypothetical example each $.60 drop in price brings an increase of 60 million gallons in the quantity demanded, regardless of whether we are at the upper or the lower end of the curve. (Look, for example, at what happens to the quantity demanded when price declines from $2.40 to $1.80 or from $1.80 to $1.20; in both instances quantity increases by 60 million gallons.) That would seem to suggest that consumers are equally responsive to price changes at either end of the curve. But that's not true! We have to remember that the responsiveness, or elasticity of demand, deals with percentage changes, not with absolute quantities.

If you remember that fact, you will recognize that the responsiveness of consumers changes quite dramatically as we move along this demand curve. For instance, when price drops from $3 to $2.40 (a 20 percent decline), quantity

EXHIBIT 4.6

How Elasticity Changes along a Hypothetical Demand Curve for Gasoline

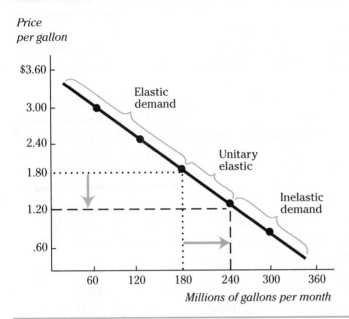

Price per gallon

Elastic demand

Unitary elastic

Inelastic demand

$3.60
3.00
2.40
1.80
1.20
.60

60   120   180   240   300   360

Millions of gallons per month

Every straight-line demand curve that is downward sloping displays unitary elasticity at its midpoint, elastic demand above it, and inelastic demand below it.

demanded increases from 60 million to 120 million gallons (a 100 percent increase). Because the percentage change in quantity is greater than the percentage change in price, demand is elastic at this upper end of the curve. At the other end the same absolute changes in price and quantity represent different percentage changes and consequently produce different elasticities. For instance, when price declines from $1.20 to $.60 (a 50 percent change), the quantity demanded increases from 240 million to 300 million gallons (a 25 percent change). The coefficient of elasticity is .5; demand is inelastic. We want to remember, then, that the slope of a demand curve is not the same as its elasticity. A linear demand curve has a constant slope, but it displays many different degrees of elasticity.

Elasticity and Total Revenue

Knowing how responsive consumers will be to price changes is of vital interest to businesses. The elasticity of demand determines what happens to a business's **total revenue**—the total receipts from the sale of its product—when it alters the price of the product it is selling. (Total revenue is equal to the price of the product multiplied by the quantity sold: $TR = P \times Q$.)

To better understand total revenue and the importance of the degree of elasticity, put yourself in the place of the seller making a pricing decision.

Suppose that you're a college president contemplating an increase in tuition from, say, $2,500 to $2,700 a semester. The basic question you face is whether the gain in revenue due to the higher tuition per student will be offset by the loss in revenue due to the smaller number of students who are willing and able to pay that higher tuition. To answer that question, you must know how responsive students will be to changes in tuition. In other words, you must have some estimate of the elasticity of demand for an education at your college.[5]

Case 1: Elastic Demand Suppose that demand is highly elastic, that is, very responsive to price changes. If tuition is increased, the college will receive more money from each student, but it will enroll considerably fewer students; the percentage *reduction* in quantity demanded will be greater than the percentage *increase* in price. As a result, the college will take in less total revenue than it did before the tuition hike. In the face of elastic demand, the logical action for the college to take—assuming there are vacant dormitory rooms and unfilled classes—would be to lower, not raise, tuition. The college will receive less from each student who enrolls, but it will enroll many more students, and total revenue will increase.

Case 2: Inelastic Demand Suppose that demand for an education at your college is inelastic, that is, not very responsive to price changes. If the college increases tuition, it will lose some students but not very many. Because the percentage increase in price will be greater than the percentage reduction in quantity demanded, the result will be an increase in the college's total revenue. If you decided to reduce tuition under these inelastic conditions, you would probably be fired. The tuition reduction wouldn't attract many new students, and all the students would pay a lower rate than before. As a result, total revenue would be lower than it was before the tuition reduction.

Case 3: Unitary Elasticity If the demand for an education at your college is of unitary elasticity, any change in price will be offset exactly by a proportional change in the quantity demanded (enrollment). If you institute a 10 percent tuition increase, 10 percent fewer students will enroll, and total revenue will be unchanged. If you put into effect a 5 percent tuition reduction, 5 percent more students will enroll, and total revenue will be unchanged. As long as

---

[5] In reality, the question faced by a college president or a businessperson would be somewhat more complicated because any pricing decision may also have an indirect impact on the firm's costs. For example, because a higher price will cause a firm to sell less of its product, the firm may also incur lower costs because it will not need to produce as much output. Before making any pricing decision, a wise entrepreneur considers its impact on costs as well as on revenues. (The nature and behavior of a firm's costs are discussed in Chapter 5.)

EXHIBIT 4.7

Elasticity and Total Revenue

DEGREE OF ELASTICITY	PRICE INCREASE	PRICE DECREASE
Case 1: Elastic demand (The coefficient of elasticity is greater than 1.)	↑ ↓ ↓ $P \times Q = TR$	↓ ↑ ↑ $P \times Q = TR$
Case 2: Inelastic demand (The coefficient of elasticity is less than 1.)	↑ ↓ ↑ $P \times Q = TR$	↓ ↑ ↓ $P \times Q = TR$
Case 3: Unitary elasticity (The coefficient of elasticity is equal to 1.)	↑ ↓ No change $P \times Q = TR$	↓ ↑ No change $P \times Q = TR$

Symbols: ↑ increase, ↓ decrease. Length of arrow indicates relative size of increase or decrease.

The elasticity of demand for a firm's product dictates what will happen to total revenue (price × quantity) when the firm alters price. When demand is elastic, a price increase results in a significantly lower quantity demanded and, therefore, in lower total revenue, whereas a price decrease leads to a significantly higher quantity demanded and, therefore, results in higher total revenue. When demand is inelastic, a price increase results in a lower quantity demanded but not much lower, so total revenue increases; a price decrease results in a higher quantity demanded but not much higher, so total revenue decreases. If demand is of unitary elasticity, any change in price will be exactly offset by the change in quantity demanded, so total revenue will not change.

demand is of unitary elasticity, total revenue is unaffected by the seller's pricing decision.

The relationship among price changes, elasticity, and total revenue (*TR*) for each of the three cases is summarized in Exhibit 4.7. Before continuing, take the time to work through the exhibit. You will see that if demand is inelastic, a price reduction will lead to a decline in total revenue, and a price increase will cause total revenue to increase. If demand is elastic, a price reduction will lead to an increase in total revenue, and a price increase will cause total revenue to decline. With unitary elasticity, a price change up or down is offset by a proportional change in quantity demanded, and total revenue remains unchanged.

The Determinants of Elasticity

As you saw in the preceding discussion, producers need to know whether the demand for their services and products is elastic or inelastic before they can make intelligent pricing decisions. But how can sellers know? Often they can gain insight into the elasticity of demand by considering two major factors that dictate the degree of elasticity: the number of good substitutes available and the importance of the product in consumers' budgets. As you examine these factors, recall our earlier discussion of the income and substitution effects that underlie the law of demand.

The Number of Available Substitutes for the Product   The primary factor in determining the price elasticity of demand is the number of good substitutes available. Recall that a substitute is a product that can be used in place of another product because, to a greater or lesser extent, it satisfies the same consumer wants. Some people consider chicken a good substitute for fish, for example; many people would acknowledge that a Dell laptop is an acceptable substitute for an HP laptop with the same features.

When a large number of good substitutes exist, demand for a product tends to be elastic because consumers have alternatives—they can buy something else if the price of the product becomes too high. But if a product has few good substitutes, demand tends to be inelastic because consumers have few options; they must buy the product even at the higher price. Movie tickets, pond-raised catfish, and women's hats have elastic demand because there are a large number of substitutes for each of these items. Cigarettes, electricity, local telephone service, and gasoline tend to have relatively inelastic demand because of the limited options available to consumers.[6]

The Importance of the Product in Consumers' Budgets   The second factor influencing the elasticity of demand for a product is the importance of the product in consumers' budgets. If consumers are spending a significant portion of their income on a particular item (rent or long-distance phone service, for example), a price hike for that item will force a vigorous search for less-expensive substitutes. Demand will tend to be elastic. But if expenditures on the product are relatively small (the average family's annual outlay for lemon juice or soy sauce, for instance), consumers are more likely to ignore the price increase. Demand will tend to be inelastic.

Some major budget items persist in having relatively inelastic demand. For example, even though many smokers spend a significant fraction of their incomes on cigarettes, statistical research shows that the demand for cigarettes by adults is quite inelastic. In this case demand is inelastic because the more

---

[6] The elasticity of demand for a product tends to increase over time. When the price of a product increases, consumers may not be aware of substitutes for that product, and so demand initially may be inelastic. But the more time that elapses after the price change, the more opportunities consumers have to discover substitutes and to develop tastes and new habits. As consumers discover more substitutes, demand tends to become more elastic.

important determinant of elasticity is the number of good substitutes. If, like cigarettes, a product has few good substitutes, the fact that it is a major expense item is generally less important to consumers. The article "Gas Price Swings Mess Up Automakers' Product Plans," on page 118, discusses why some auto executives have been supporting higher excise taxes on gasoline. Read it to test your understanding of excise taxes and the price elasticity of demand.

Looking Back: Excise Taxes and the Elasticity of Demand

Before concluding this chapter, let's go back to the excise tax example we introduced earlier and see if our new understanding of the elasticity of demand can shed any additional light on that application. As you will recall, we discovered that when an excise tax is imposed on a product, it tends to raise its price, but by less than the amount of the excise tax. Consider, for instance, Exhibit 4.8, which repeats the example we examined earlier. For now, ignore demand curve D_2 (the green demand curve) and focus only on demand curve D_1. Note that when an excise tax of 50 cents is imposed on the sale of this product, the selling price increases by only 25 cents, about half the amount of the tax. We suggested earlier that this result is not the only result that is possible, that the outcome depends on how sensitive consumers are to price changes—on the elasticity of

---

EXHIBIT 4.8

The Impact of an Excise Tax

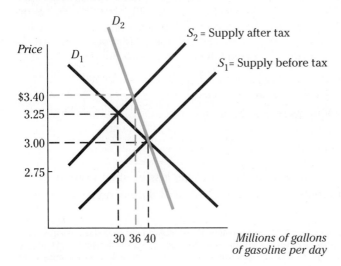

An excise tax of 50 cents per gallon would shift the supply curve of gasoline up by 50 cents everywhere. The less elastic the demand for the product, the more the price of the product will tend to rise—signifying that more of the tax has been passed on to the consumer.

Use Your Economic Reasoning

Gas Price Swings Mess Up Automakers' Product Plans

BY TOM KRISHER

Deep inside the research centers of General Motors Corp., Ford Motor Co., and Chrysler LLC, the companies are spending billions to develop plug-in electric cars at a time when gasoline has dropped below $2 per gallon. If their fears come true, gas prices will be so low when they start rolling out the cars next year that people won't buy them and all the high-priced research will have gone to waste.

At GM and Chrysler, which have nearly run out of cash and are surviving on government loans, the companies can't afford to make mistakes in spending limited research and development dollars, but they can't predict the future, either. "It's obviously a challenge when you're in a resource-constrained world," Frank Klegon, Chrysler's product development chief, said in an interview this week at the North American International Auto Show. "The market and the consumer are flexible from the perspective of what they want and what they need, and because the demand curve changes instantaneously, it appears, as good as we are, we're not that instantaneous."

In a five-month period from July to December [2008], average gas prices nationwide fell 58 percent from $4.11 per gallon to $1.74, creat-ing a huge problem for automakers to predict what vehicles to design or build to match consumer demand. The fear of producing the wrong cars has created a whisper campaign, with industry officials saying they may approach the incoming Obama administration about raising the federal gasoline tax or setting up a system that keeps the price of oil above a certain level. "It makes life very difficult if the market gyrates wildly over the course of several months, and that's exactly what we've seen happen," Ford Executive Chairman Bill Ford Jr. said in a recent interview with The Associated Press. . . .

Higher taxes or a floor would give automakers a "clearer planning horizon" because they design future models three to five years in advance, Ford said. Jim Queen, GM's global engineering head, said the Obama administration may be open to gas taxes or policies imposed by many European countries that reduce oil consumption and make it easier for manufacturers to match their products to demand. "My personal opinion is we'd be better served in the U.S. if we could somehow establish a comparable floor that you see in Europe," Queen said. "And I think with the new administration we

Source: Associated Press, January 13, 2009. Associated Press Writer David Runk contributed to this report. Reprinted by permission of the Associated Press. All rights reserved.

demand. To illustrate, suppose that demand was less elastic (more inelastic). Demand curve D_2 represents such a curve.[7] Note that if demand curve D_2 is the

[7] You can recognize that demand curve D_2 is less elastic than demand curve D_1 because any given price increase will cause a smaller reduction in the quantity demanded on demand curve D_2. For instance, a 25-cent price hike will reduce the quantity demanded by about 10 million units on D_1, but by less than 4 million units on D_2.

may have a shot under the umbrella of an energy policy to start talking about these things."

Currently federal and state gasoline taxes combined average about 40 cents per gallon in the U.S., far less than many European countries. The European Union has set a minimum gas tax of 0.38 euro per liter, or about $1.80 per gallon, and most countries tax above the minimum, said Nigel Griffiths, director of global automotive forecasting for the consulting firm IHS Global Insight in London. Raising the 18.4-cent-per-gallon federal gas tax would have benefits other than helping the automakers, because higher prices would reduce consumption and greenhouse gas emissions, said Kenneth

Medlock, an energy fellow who teaches economics at Rice University in Houston. He is against a mandated floor on oil prices because it wouldn't be a constant revenue source for government, but he favors a gas tax increase with money going for mass transit and research in alternative fuel vehicles. "That's where in my mind the role of government comes in, sort of subsidizing the uncertainty in the market," he said.

Raising taxes also is a political risk, even though it could lead to lower oil prices because it would reduce demand, Medlock said. "It's a difficult pill to swallow right now, especially given the financial hardships we've all been facing," he said. . . .

USE YOUR ECONOMIC REASONING

1. What does the auto executive mean when he says "consumer[s] are flexible . . . in what they want"? How is this related to gas prices, and why is it creating problems for automakers?
2. Suppose the United States decided to match the European Union and impose a $1.80 a gallon excise tax on gasoline. How would you represent this graphically? Would this tax raise the price of gasoline by $1.80 or by less than that?
3. In the short run, the demand for gasoline is quite inelastic; the coefficient of demand elasticity is in the neighborhood of .2. (Remember, the convention is ignore the negative sign.) Does that coefficient lead you to expect most of the tax to be passed on to consumers as higher prices, or absorbed by sellers?
4. Suppose the imposition of this tax raises the price of gasoline from $2.50 a gallon to $3.75, a 50 percent increase. If the price elasticity of demand for gasoline is .2, how much would you expect gasoline consumption to decline (in percentage terms)?
5. If consumers are given more time to adjust to price changes, they generally find more ways to adjust their behavior—finding more substitutes for the product in question. Suppose that in the long run the coefficient of demand elasticity is .5 instead of .2. How much would gasoline consumption drop in response to the 50 percent price hike?

appropriate demand curve, the 50-cent excise tax causes the equilibrium price to rise by 40 cents. In this situation, sellers are able to pass on more of the tax to consumers because those consumers are less responsive to price changes (probably because there are few substitutes for the product in question). This is probably closer to the true result for gasoline because studies show that the demand for gasoline is quite inelastic, particularly in the short run.

In summary, the more elastic the demand for the product, the less of the tax we expect consumers to pay; the less elastic the demand for the product, the more of the tax we expect consumers to pay. (The fraction of the excise tax paid by consumers also depends on the price elasticity of *supply*. Supply elasticity is discussed in the appendix to this chapter.)

SUMMARY

Government intervenes in pricing in a variety of ways, including price supports, price ceilings, subsidies, and excise taxes. *Price supports* (minimum prices above the equilibrium price) and *price ceilings* (maximum prices below the equilibrium price) prevent price from reaching its equilibrium level in the market. Because these restrictions interfere with the rationing and motivating functions of price, they tend to give rise to surpluses (supports) and shortages (ceilings). Price ceilings also create the need for *secondary rationing devices*— nonprice conditions that supplement the primary rationing device, price.

Subsidies and excise taxes also alter the selling price of products, but in a different way. A *subsidy* is a payment that government makes to private producers or consumers for each unit of output that they produce. Producer subsidies have essentially the same impact as a reduction in the cost of production—they shift the supply curve to the right, lowering the equilibrium price of the product. Excise taxes (taxes that are levied on specific products) have the opposite effect; they shift the supply curve to the left, raising the price of the product being taxed.

The precise impact of a subsidy or excise tax—how much it raises or lowers the price of the product in question—depends on the price elasticity of demand for that product. The price elasticity of demand is a measure of the responsiveness of the quantity demanded to a change in price. If a given percentage change in price brings about a larger percentage change in quantity demanded (a coefficient of elasticity greater than 1), demand is described as elastic. If a given percentage change in price brings about a smaller percentage change in quantity demanded (a coefficient less than 1), demand is said to be inelastic. If a given percentage change in price brings an equal percentage change in quantity demanded (a coefficient equal to 1), unitary elasticity prevails.

If demand is perfectly inelastic (the coefficient of elasticity is zero), a very large change in price will bring no change in the quantity demanded; the demand curve will be a vertical straight line. If demand is perfectly elastic (the coefficient approaches infinity), a very small change in price will bring an extremely large change in the quantity demanded; the demand curve will be a horizontal straight line. Most demand curves, however, do not show just one degree of elasticity; they show several. All linear, downward-sloping demand curves will show unitary elasticity in the middle, elastic demand at the upper end, and inelastic demand at the lower end.

The degree of elasticity is important to businesses because it determines what happens to *total revenue*, or total receipts from sales, when a business alters the price of its product. If demand is elastic, a price reduction will lead to an increase in total revenue, and a price increase will cause total revenue to decline. If demand is inelastic, a price reduction will lead to a decline in total revenue, and a price hike will cause total revenue to increase. With unitary elastic demand, any change in price will be offset exactly by a proportional change in the quantity demanded, and total revenue will be unchanged.

The major determinants of the elasticity of demand are the number of good substitutes that exist and the importance of the product in consumers' budgets. The greater the number of substitutes for a product and the more important the item in the budgets of consumers, the greater the elasticity of demand for the product.

KEY TERMS

Coefficient of demand
    elasticity
Deficiency payment
Excise tax

Price ceiling
Price elasticity of demand
Price support
Rent ceiling

Secondary rationing
    device
Subsidy
Total revenue

STUDY QUESTIONS

Fill in the Blanks

1. A legally established minimum price above the equilibrium price is termed a(n)

    _____.

2. A nonprice condition that supplements price as a rationing device is called a(n)

    _____ rationing device.

3. A producer subsidy tends to shift the

    (supply/demand) _____ curve of the subsidized product to the

    (right/left) _____.

4. An excise tax has essentially the same impact as (an increase/a decrease)

    _____ in the cost of production.

5. Price ceilings tend to result in

    _____, and price supports tend

    to result in _____.

6. If a decrease in the price of the product leads to a decrease in total revenue, demand must be (elastic/inelastic/unitary)

    _____.

7. If a 10 percent reduction in price leads to a 20 percent increase in quantity demanded, the coefficient of elasticity would be equal

   to _____.

8. If the coefficient of elasticity is greater

   than 1, demand is _____; if it is less than 1, demand is

   _____; if it is equal to 1, demand is _____.

9. The major determinant of the elasticity of demand for a product is the number of

   good _____ that exist for the product.

10. The greater the fraction of the family budget spent for a particular product, the

    (greater /smaller) _____ the elasticity of demand for that product.

11. A perfectly inelastic demand curve would

    be a (vertical/horizontal) _____ straight line.

12. Along a downward-sloping linear demand curve, the elasticity of demand is the greatest at the (upper/lower)

    _____ end of the curve.

Multiple Choice

1. If the U.S. government were to artificially restrict the price of beef below the equilibrium level, the result would be
   a) a shortage.
   b) a surplus.
   c) an excess of quantity supplied over quantity demanded.
   d) none of the above.

2. Which of the following is a true statement about price supports?
   a) They are established below the equilibrium price.
   b) They lead to the use of a secondary rationing device.
   c) They result in surpluses.
   d) They shift the supply curve to the left.

3. If a minimum wage is imposed above the equilibrium wage, the result will be
   a) a surplus of jobs.
   b) a reduction in the quantity of labor demanded by employers.
   c) a shortage of workers.
   d) an increase in employment.

4. When price ceilings are imposed,
   a) they shift the supply curve to the right.
   b) they lead to the use of a secondary rationing device.

   c) they result in surpluses.
   d) they shift the supply curve to the left.

5. A subsidy to wheat producers would tend to
   a) increase the demand for wheat.
   b) reduce the supply of wheat.
   c) reduce the market price of wheat.
   d) increase the cost of producing wheat.

6. An excise tax on cigarettes would tend to
   a) raise the equilibrium price and quantity.
   b) lower the equilibrium price and quantity.
   c) raise the equilibrium price but lower the equilibrium quantity.
   d) lower the equilibrium price but lower the equilibrium quantity.

7. If a seller reduces the price of a product and this leads to an increase in the quantity sold, what can be concluded?
   a) Demand is elastic.
   b) Demand is inelastic.
   c) Demand is of unitary elasticity.
   d) Nothing can be concluded about the degree of elasticity.

8. When Miracle Drug reduced the price of its Stop Smoking Pill, it sold more of its product, but its total revenue declined. We can conclude that demand for the Stop Smoking Pill must be
   a) perfectly inelastic.
   b) perfectly elastic.
   c) inelastic.
   d) elastic.

9. If a 20 percent reduction in the price of ZOLT cola brings a 40 percent increase in the quantity demanded, then the coefficient of demand elasticity is
   a) 2.0, and demand is elastic.
   b) .5, and demand is inelastic.
   c) 2.0, and demand is inelastic.
   d) 5, and demand is elastic.

10. On a downward-sloping demand curve, demand is more elastic
    a) at the upper end.
    b) at the lower end.
    c) in the middle.

11. In general, demand for a product is more elastic
    a) the fewer the substitutes and the larger the fraction of the family budget spent on that product.
    b) the greater the number of substitutes and the larger the fraction of the family budget spent on that product.
    c) the fewer the substitutes and the smaller the fraction of the family budget spent on that product.
    d) the greater the number of substitutes and the smaller the fraction of the family budget spent on that product.

12. The local transit company is contemplating an increase in bus fares to expand revenues. A local senior-citizens group, Seniors for Fair Fares (SFF), argues that a rate increase would lead to lower revenues. This disagreement suggests that
    a) the transit company does not believe that the rate increase would reduce the number of riders, but SFF believes that it would.
    b) the transit company believes that the demand for bus service is elastic, but SFF believes that it is inelastic.
    c) the transit company believes that the demand for bus service is inelastic, but SFF believes that it is elastic.

13. When an excise tax is imposed on a product,
    a) the price of that product will generally increase by the amount of the tax.
    b) the price of that product will rise by the amount of the tax if the demand for the product is perfectly elastic.
    c) the price of that product will rise by the amount of the tax if the demand for the product is perfectly inelastic.
    d) the price of that product will always rise by less than the amount of the tax.

14. When the demand for a product is very elastic,
    a) that is probably because the product has few substitutes.
    b) suppliers find it difficult to pass excise tax hikes on to consumers.
    c) the coefficient of demand elasticity is less than 1.
    d) consumers will pay a large fraction of any excise tax.

Problems and Questions for Discussion

1. Economists often oppose price ceilings and supports because they interfere with the rationing and motivating functions of prices. Explain.

2. Price ceilings tend to produce shortages, and price supports tend to produce surpluses. Show these results graphically and explain why they occur.

3. What is a "secondary rationing device," and when is such a device needed?

4. The United States and many other rich nations offer their farmers subsidies on a

wide variety of agricultural products. But the World Trade Organization (WTO) argues that these subsidies depress worldwide prices and harm farmers in poor nations. How might the subsidies provided by rich nations have this impact?

5. Imagine yourself as a state governor looking for new revenue sources. Which would raise more tax revenue, an excise tax imposed on a product with inelastic demand or an excise tax imposed on a product with elastic demand? Defend your conclusion.

6. If a college increases tuition as a method of increasing total revenue, what assumption is it making about the elasticity of demand for its service? Do you think that assumption is valid for your college? Why or why not?

7. If the price of Wrinkled jeans is reduced from $10 to $8 a pair and the quantity demanded increases from 5,000, to 10,000 pairs a month, what is the coefficient of demand elasticity?

8. According to Mark Moore, of Harvard's Kennedy School of Government, the ideal demand-side drug policy would make illegal drugs cheap for addicts and expensive for neophytes. What logic can you see for such a policy, and how would it relate to the elasticity of demand for illegal drugs?

9. Which would tend to be more elastic, the demand for automobiles or the demand for Ford automobiles? Why?

10. Suppose that the price elasticity of demand for water is 2.0 and that the government wants to reduce the quantity of water demanded by 40 percent. By how much must the price of water be raised to accomplish this objective?

11. Sales taxes are a major source of revenue for many state governments. But higher sales taxes mean higher prices, which mean lower quantities sold by merchants. If the government wants to expand its tax revenue yet inflict minimum damage on the sales of merchants, should it tax products with elastic demand or inelastic demand? Why? Can you see any drawbacks to focusing taxes on these products?

12. Suppose that when a $1.00 excise tax is imposed on a product, its price rises by 75 cents. How much of the tax are consumers paying? What happened to the rest of the tax? Is this outcome more likely when the demand for the product is highly elastic or when it is highly inelastic?

ANSWER KEY

Fill in the Blanks

1. support price	5. shortages, surpluses	9. substitutes
2. secondary	6. inelastic	10. greater
3. supply, right	7. 2.0	11. vertical
4. an increase	8. elastic, inelastic, unitary	12. upper

Multiple Choice

1. a	4. b	7. d	10. a	13. c
2. c	5. c	8. c	11. b	14. b
3. b	6. c	9. a	12. c	

THE ELASTICITY OF SUPPLY

Thus far, we have considered only how the quantity demanded responds to price changes. In this appendix, we explore the supply side of the market. The price elasticity of supply describes the responsiveness of producers to price changes. More precisely, the *price elasticity of supply* is a measure of the responsiveness of the quantity supplied of a product to a change in its price.

THE COEFFICIENT OF SUPPLY ELASTICITY

Individual producers of goods and services display varying degrees of response when the price of a product changes. Some are able to expand or contract their supply of the product significantly in a short period of time; others are able to make only minimal adjustments. The more responsive producers are to a change in price, the more elastic their supply.

We measure the elasticity of supply by calculating the *coefficient of supply elasticity*, a value that indicates the degree to which the quantity supplied will change in response to a price change. The coefficient of supply elasticity is computed by dividing the percentage change in quantity supplied by the percentage change in price:

$$\text{Coefficient of elasticity} = \frac{\dfrac{\Delta Q}{Q}}{\dfrac{\Delta P}{P}} = \frac{\text{Percentage change in quantity supplied}}{\text{Percentage change in price}}$$

Suppose that the price of coal rises from \$40 to \$50 a ton and that coal production in the United States therefore increases from 600 to 900 million tons a year. To compute the coefficient of supply elasticity, we first determine the percentage change in quantity supplied. If the change in quantity supplied (ΔQ) is 300 million tons and the original quantity supplied (Q) is 600 million tons, the percentage change in quantity supplied (300/600) is 50 percent. Next, we take the percentage change in price. If the change in price (ΔP) is \$10 and the original price is \$40, the percentage change in price (\$10/\$40) is 25 percent.

When we divide the 50 percent increase in quantity supplied by the 25 percent increase in price, we arrive at an elasticity coefficient of 2.[8]

$$\text{Coefficient of elasticity} = \frac{\dfrac{300}{600}}{\dfrac{\$10}{\$40}} = \frac{50\%}{25\%} = 2$$

Note that whereas the coefficient of demand elasticity is negative, the coefficient of supply elasticity usually is positive. Because of the law of supply, an increase in price leads to an increase in the quantity supplied.

INTERPRETING THE ELASTICITY COEFFICIENT

We interpret coefficients of supply elasticity in essentially the same way we interpret coefficients of demand elasticity. A supply elasticity of 2 means that for every 1 percent change in price, the quantity supplied will change by 2 percent. For example, a 10 percent increase in price would lead to a 20 percent increase in the quantity supplied, and a 20 percent increase in price would lead to a 40 percent increase in the quantity supplied. Of course, reductions in price will have the opposite effect. A 10 percent decrease in price would lead to a 20 percent reduction in the quantity supplied.

An elasticity coefficient greater than 1 means that supply is elastic, or very responsive to price changes; a given percentage change in price results in a larger percentage change in quantity supplied. When the elasticity coefficient is less than 1, supply is inelastic; a given percentage change in price results in a smaller percentage change in quantity supplied. If the coefficient is exactly 1, supply is of unitary elasticity; a given percentage change in price results in an identical percentage change in the quantity supplied.

USING SUPPLY ELASTICITY IN POLICY DECISIONS

An understanding of the elasticity of supply can be useful to government policymakers and others seeking solutions to economic problems. Consider, for example, the energy-policy debate that began in the late 1970s, when concerns

---

[8]As with the elasticity of demand, the more precise formula for calculating the elasticity of supply involves using the average of the two prices and the average of the two quantities as the base values for computing percentages.

about the United States' dependence on foreign oil first emerged. During this period the price of domestically produced oil was regulated; it could not rise above the government-dictated price. Imported oil was beyond government control, however, and in the mid-1970s it skyrocketed in price. To reduce dependence on foreign oil, some politicians and policymakers began to argue for the deregulation of domestic oil prices so that U.S. producers would have incentives for increased exploration and production. Deregulation began in 1978–79 and, in conjunction with consumer conservation (brought about by higher prices), helped to temporarily reduce our dependence on foreign oil.

Today, we are once again facing higher prices for imported oil. These higher prices, coupled with concerns about the volatility of the Middle East (the source of much of our imported oil), have led to new calls to increase domestic oil production. Suppose that the United States would like to increase domestic oil production by 20 percent to help reduce its dependence on foreign oil. How much would the price of domestic oil have to rise to make that possible? The answer depends on the price elasticity of supply for domestic oil. If the coefficient of supply elasticity is 2, a price hike of 10 percent would be sufficient to generate the desired 20 percent increase. (Remember, when the coefficient is 2, each 1 percent change in price brings a 2 percent change in the quantity supplied.) But if the coefficient is .5 (which is closer to the true value), a 40 percent price hike will be needed.

As you can see, the elasticity of supply allows us to determine how much price has to rise to convince suppliers to increase their output by a given amount. That kind of information is very important in making sound decisions about energy policy and addressing a host of other questions.

TIME AND THE ELASTICITY OF SUPPLY

The responsiveness of suppliers to a change in the price of their product depends on the amount of time they are given to adjust their output to the new price. As a general rule, the longer producers are given to adapt to a price change, the greater the elasticity of supply. We can see the importance of time as a determinant of elasticity by comparing the kinds of adjustments suppliers facing a price change can make in the short run with the changes they can make in the long run.

The Short Run

In economics the *short run* is defined as the period of time during which at least one of a business's inputs (usually plant and equipment) is fixed—that is, incapable of being changed. Therefore, short-run adjustments to a change in price are limited. Producers must use their existing plants and equipment more or less intensively, adding or eliminating a work shift or using a larger or smaller workforce on existing shifts.

The short-run supply curve in Exhibit A4.1 shows an increase in the price of oil from $60 to $75 a barrel ($15 equals a 25 percent increase), bringing an increase in the quantity of oil supplied from 800 to 900 million barrels (100 million barrels equals an increase of 12.5 percent). Thus, the coefficient of supply elasticity is .50 (12.5%/25%); supply is quite inelastic in the short run.

The Long Run

The *long run* is defined as the period of time during which all of a business's inputs, including plant and equipment, can be changed. The long run provides sufficient time for firms to build new production facilities and to expand or contract existing facilities. New firms can enter the industry, and existing firms can leave. These kinds of adjustments make it possible to alter output significantly in response to a price change.

Note that the long-run response to an increase in the price of oil from $60 to $75 a barrel (a 25 percent increase) is an increase in the quantity of oil supplied

---

EXHIBIT A4.1

The Effect of Time on the Elasticity of Supply

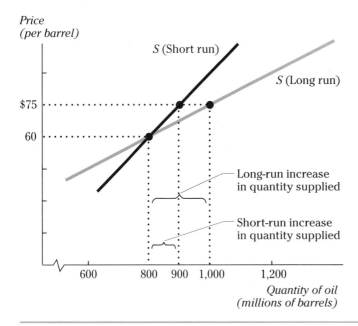

The more time a firm or industry is given to respond to a change in price, the larger the increase or decrease in the quantity supplied and the greater the elasticity of supply. Suppose, for example, that the price of oil rises from $60 to $75 a barrel. In the short run the quantity supplied can be increased from 800 million barrels per year to 900 million barrels; in the long run it is possible to increase the quantity supplied from 800 million barrels to 1 billion barrels per year.

from 800 million to 1 billion barrels (200 million barrels equals a 25 percent increase). The coefficient of supply elasticity in this case is 1.0 (25%/25%), and so supply is of unitary elasticity in the long run.

SUPPLY ELASTICITY AND THE IMPACT OF AN EXCISE TAX

As you can see from the preceding example, the elasticity of supply may vary substantially from the short run to the long run for a given product. In addition, both the short-run and the long-run elasticities of supply vary from industry to industry and even from firm to firm. One important consequence of these variations is in the impact of excise taxes.

We discovered earlier that the price elasticity of demand influences the fraction of an excise tax paid by consumers: the less elastic the demand for a product, the more of the excise tax that will be passed on to the customer in the form of a higher price. The elasticity of supply also influences the fraction of the tax passed on to consumers. As a general rule, the more elastic the supply of the product, the more of the excise tax that will be passed on to consumers; the less elastic the supply of the product, the less of the excise tax that will be passed to consumers (and the more that will be paid by the suppliers).

To illustrate, consider Exhibit A4.2. In this exhibit, government has imposed a 50-cent excise tax on each gallon of gasoline. The vertical distance between the supply curves represents that 50-cent tax. When supply is relatively inelastic (the black supply curves), the excise tax raises the market price from $3.00 to $3.25. That means that consumers pay half of the excise tax (in the form of higher prices), while producers pay the other half (in the form of lower profits). But when supply is more elastic (the green supply curves), the excise tax raises the market price by a larger amount—from $3.00 to $3.40. That means more of the tax is passed on to consumers and less comes out of the suppliers' profits.

The logic behind this result is reasonably straightforward. When an excise tax is imposed on a product, producers will search for something else to do with their resources. If they can easily switch to producing something else, they won't be willing to pay much of the excise tax (just as consumers with good alternatives—elastic demand—won't be willing to pay much of the tax). On the other hand, if their resources cannot be easily adapted to producing other things, their supply will be relatively inelastic, and they will be forced to pay more of the tax.

In summary, both the elasticity of demand and the elasticity of supply determine who pays an excise tax. When demand is highly elastic and supply is

Excise Taxes and the Elasticity of Supply

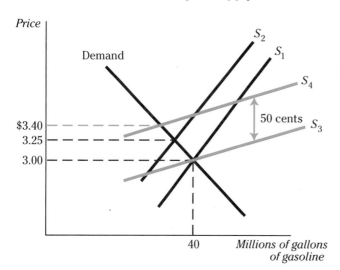

When supply is less elastic (the black supply curves), a 50-cent excise tax shifts the supply curve from S_1 to S_2 and raises the equilibrium price by 25 cents (consumers and suppliers each pay half the tax). When supply is more elastic (the green supply curves), the 50-cent tax shifts the supply curve from S_3 to S_4 and the equilibrium price rises by 40 cents (consumers pay four-fifths of the tax). Ceteris paribus, the more elastic the supply of the product, the more of the tax paid by consumers.

highly inelastic, most of the excise tax will be paid by suppliers. When demand is highly inelastic and supply is highly elastic, consumers will foot most of the bill.

CHAPTER

5

Costs and Decision Making

LEARNING OBJECTIVES

1. State the assumptions that economists make about human beings.
2. Describe how individuals and businesses use cost-benefit analysis to guide their decision making.
3. Discuss some of the pitfalls in decision making.
4. Examine the types of costs encountered by a business.
5. Explain how marginal reasoning can improve both personal and business decision making.
6. Describe how a business selects the profit-maximizing level of output.

As we learned in Chapter 1, we all use models to help us understand the world around us. The previous four chapters have introduced you to some economic models: the production possibilities model, the model of supply and demand, and the model of elasticity, for example. You will be introduced to many more theories or models in this book because, as we've already discovered, it is only through models that we can begin to explain the real world and solve real-world problems. But economics is more than a haphazard collection of theories or models with no unifying theme. Underlying all the models in economics is the assumption that human beings are motivated by self-interest and that they make rational decisions based on self-interest. We begin this chapter by examining those assumptions. We'll see that rational decision making involves a comparison of costs and benefits and that the appropriate costs and benefits for comparison are marginal costs and benefits. After examining individual decision making, we'll turn to decision making in business. We'll begin by exploring the types of costs encountered by a business and how those costs are expected to behave. The chapter concludes by examining how businesses can use the marginal principle to select the profit-maximizing level of output and make other important business decisions.

EXPLAINING HUMAN BEHAVIOR: THE ROLE OF ASSUMPTIONS

As we noted in Chapter 1, models are always based on assumptions; the more realistic the assumptions, the greater the likelihood that the resulting model will be useful in understanding the real world. In attempting to explain and predict the behavior of individuals, economists make the assumption that men and women are motivated primarily by self-interest and pursue self-interest through a rational comparison of costs and benefits.

The Pursuit of Self-Interest

Assuming that people are motivated by self-interest is clearly an oversimplification. The factors that motivate human beings are very complex and include empathy, a sense of duty or obligation, and many others. But following the lead of Adam Smith, the father of economics, economists argue that foremost among these motivations is the pursuit of self-interest.

The role of self-interest in motivating men and women may seem self-evident to you. But the fact is that we sometimes forget this fundamental characteristic of human nature. And forgetting it may cause us to make errors in judgment. Consider, for example, the automobile salesman who promises to be your friend and "give you a good deal." If self-interest is the primary factor motivating salespeople, your first response when confronted by such a pledge should be to question it. After all, a salesperson who is motivated by self-interest won't be concerned about promoting yours—at least no more than the competition demands. And when an advertisement offers "free" products or "unbelievable bargains," don't rush down to the store. Read the fine print; that's where you will generally discover the true cost.

Remembering that people are driven by self-interest will do more than help you make good decisions; it will also help you understand behavior that may seem strange if you forget this fundamental motivation. For example, why is it that college students make it a point to call their distant grandmother while they are visiting their parents but never manage a call from the pay phone in their dormitory? And why do customers eat (and waste) more food at the "All You Can Eat for $9.99" buffet than they do when they pay by the item? And how is it that some people leave large tips in restaurants they visit regularly and smaller ones when they are out of town? Economists will argue that none of this behavior is random or accidental; it simply results from the pursuit of self-interest.

Comparing Costs and Benefits

How do individuals pursue their self-interest; how do they make certain that their decisions improve their own well-being? They do so by comparing the costs and benefits of a contemplated action rather than acting impulsively. Consider, for example, the decision that confronts you in the morning when your alarm goes off. Do you get out of bed and go to class or stay in bed and get a couple more hours of sleep? Economists assume that rather than just hitting the alarm and going back to sleep (an impulsive reaction), you weigh the costs and benefits of getting up. In other words, you consider what you would learn in class and the likelihood of a quiz (the benefits of getting up) against the lost sleep (the cost of getting up) and make a decision. If the value of going to class exceeds the cost, you get up. If not, you make the rational decision and stay in bed.

There are several important things to note about this decision-making process. First, self-interest-seeking individuals consider only the costs and benefits that affect them personally. They don't consider the benefits that their presence might convey to others in the class—better class discussion, for example—or the costs that their absence might impose on others—provoking a quiz from the professor, for instance. Second, this cost-benefit comparison may be performed unconsciously—without any real deliberation. Through experience you may know that there are substantial costs associated with missing class, and so you get up automatically, without much consideration of alternatives. It's only on mornings following a particularly short night that the cost-benefit comparison really kicks in.[1] Third, this comparison is based on expected costs and benefits; you won't know the true costs and benefits until after the fact. You may jump out of bed expecting an exhilarating class period—and not get it. Or you may stay in bed expecting to miss very little, only to find out that Brad Pitt and Melanie Griffith were team-teaching class that day, or—perhaps more realistically—you missed a 20-point quiz.

THE IMPORTANCE OF MARGINAL ANALYSIS

When costs and benefits are compared, the relevant costs and benefits for comparison are the *marginal* costs and benefits. **Marginal** means extra, or additional; the marginal costs and benefits are the additional costs and benefits

---

[1] Many cost-benefit comparisons are performed instinctively or unconsciously because you've performed them many times before. For instance, do the additional benefits provided by designer jeans justify the premium prices they generally command? You probably had to reflect on that question the first few times you went shopping. But after that, the decision became much simpler. Now, all you have to hear is the price differential, and you know what you want to buy.

resulting from the decision. It may appear obvious that it's marginal costs and benefits that matter, but it's easy to confuse marginal and total values if you're not careful. And that can result in poor decision making (or in good decisions that are misunderstood).

To illustrate, consider once again that morning debate, "Do I stay in bed or get up and go to class?" Suppose that, one morning, you decide to skip class and sleep in. The next day, you tell the prof the truth—"I needed the sleep." What response might you expect from the prof? There are a number of possibilities, but one is something like this: "You mean you value sleep more than my class?" Hearing that reaction might cause you to regret missing class, but your morning's decision has actually been misrepresented. If you had to choose between sleep and, say, accounting, accounting would lose hands down. So would literature and physics and probably even the psychology of human sexuality! But that's not really the choice that most of us have to make, and it's not the choice you were trying to communicate to the prof. The choice is really not between accounting and sleep; it is between an additional or marginal hour of accounting and an additional or marginal hour of sleep. That's where decisions are always made, on the margin, between a little more of this and a little more of that.

The opportunity cost of an early morning class is the sleep you are forced to sacrifice.

As you can see, failing to recognize the difference between total and marginal values can lead to poor decisions, or it can get you into trouble for making good decisions that you can't defend. Consider the following additional examples:

1. Your boss asks you to work late to finish an important job. Your spouse calls at work to find out why you're not home. He or she asks, "Is your job more important to you than I am?"
2. You have an 85 average in accounting and a 79 average in literature. Each course requires 80 percent to earn a B grade. Final exam week finds you spending most of your time studying literature. Is literature more important to you than accounting?
3. At the family picnic, you've had three helpings of Mom's potato salad and one helping of Aunt Mildred's cole slaw. Mom sees you reach for the cole slaw and says, "Do you like the cole slaw better than my potato salad?"

In each of these instances, the failure to recognize the difference between total and marginal values is the source of the misunderstanding. Even though you value your spouse more than your job, there may be situations in which an additional evening at work is more important to you than an additional evening with him or her. And even if you love accounting and loathe literature, you still may value an additional weekend studying literature more highly than an additional weekend studying accounting. Finally, even if you prefer Mom's potato salad to Aunt Mildred's cole slaw and virtually every other food on the face of the earth, there is nothing irrational about preferring one more scoop of cole slaw, especially after already having three scoops of potato salad.

THE IMPROPER ESTIMATION OF COSTS

Even people who understand the difference between marginal and total values sometimes make bad decisions. More often than not, these poor decisions are the result of a mistaken estimate of the cost of the decision in question. Sometimes people forget to consider important costs, and sometimes they see costs where there are none. Let's consider these problems in turn.

Ignoring Implicit Costs

Economists are fond of telling us that all decisions have costs, that there is no such thing as a "free lunch." This was part of the message of Chapter 1. Any time we make a decision to do or to have one thing, we sacrifice the opportunity to do or to have some other thing. The most valued alternative we sacrifice to take an action is the opportunity cost of that action.

The opportunity-cost concept holds that costs exist whether or not money changes hands. In fact, the money you pay for a product is just a veil; the true cost of that product is the other things you could have purchased with the same money. If you spend $200 on a CD player, the real cost of the CD player is the pizzas, movie tickets, and jeans you could have bought with the same money.

Sometimes we forget that the true cost of any decision is the opportunity cost, and that can lead to poor decisions. Consider the case of Tom Sanders, a 40-year-old dentist living in College City. Tom recently decided to build a new home, and he stopped by his banker to arrange financing. When the banker asked Tom where he was planning to build, he replied that the location would be at the corner of Main and First Streets, a longtime vacant lot just across the street from State University. That seemed to the banker an expensive piece of real estate for a single-family home, so she asked Tom why he had chosen that location. Tom's response was, "Because I inherited the land and it won't cost me anything to use it." His answer illustrates a common problem in making decisions—failing to consider opportunity costs. Because Tom was not required to make an explicit dollar payment to buy the land, he assumed that it was free; he ignored the opportunity cost of using it.

In recognition of this problem, economists point out that the true cost of any action—the cost of building a new home, for instance—is the sum of the explicit and implicit costs incurred in that endeavor. **Explicit costs** are the costs that are easily recognized because they involve a monetary payment; that is, money actually changes hands. The expenditures that Tom makes for lumber and other building materials would be an example of an explicit cost, as would the wages paid to construction workers. **Implicit costs** are the nonmonetary costs associated with using your own resources. Tom's use of his own land is an implicit cost, and so is the value of his time should he decide to take part in the construction process.[2] Remembering that the true cost of your action is the sum of these two categories can prevent you from making bad decisions. For instance, had Tom recognized the true cost of using his inherited building site, he might have decided that another, less valuable site would do just as well. That would have allowed Tom to sell the inherited site for its market value and pocket the difference.

---

[2] You may be tempted to say that explicit costs are real costs, while implicit costs are opportunity costs. But that way of thinking about costs misses the point. In fact, all costs are opportunity costs. Consider the explicit monetary payment that Tom makes to hire construction labor. The reason Tom is required to pay the worker a wage is because he must draw that worker's talent away from alternative uses—the other home builders he could have worked for. The wage rate simply represents that opportunity cost of that worker's time—what he could have earned elsewhere. The distinction between explicit costs and implicit costs exists because some opportunity costs are obvious (because the decision maker is required to make a monetary payment), while others are not (because no monetary payment is required).

Failing to Ignore Fixed and Sunk Costs

Ignoring opportunity costs is not the only source of poor decision making. Another problem is mistaking fixed costs for marginal costs.

All the costs that confront us in our personal lives and in business can be categorized as either *fixed costs* or *variable costs*. **Fixed costs** are costs that do not vary with the level of the activity engaged in, whether that activity is driving a car, owning a home, or (in the case of a business) producing output. **Variable costs**, as the name implies, vary with the level of activity. They go up when you engage in more of the activity (drive more, spend more time at home, produce more output) and down when you engage in less. Fixed costs and variable costs can also be thought of as unavoidable and avoidable costs, respectively. Because fixed costs don't vary with the level of activity, they can't be avoided by doing less of the activity. Variable costs, on the other hand, are avoidable; do less of an activity and you reduce your variable costs. Consider, for example, the costs of driving a car. Some of those costs are fixed—the monthly payment, for example, and the cost of insurance. Whether you drive one mile or a thousand, the amount of your fixed costs will be unchanged. Other costs, the cost of gasoline and oil, for example, vary with the amount you drive; the more you drive, the more you spend for gas and oil.

The Flying Smiths   The distinction between fixed and variable costs is an important one for decision making. To illustrate, consider the following problem. Robin Smith and her husband, Bob, are planning a two-week ski trip. They've been given free use of a condo once they arrive, so the major expense of the ski holiday is the transportation to and from the resort. They're trying to decide whether to take a plane or drive their car. They realize that driving will use up some of their skiing time, but they think the beauty of the drive will compensate for that loss. The round-trip plane fare for the couple is $400. Robin, who is an accountant, has estimated the cost of making the trip by car as follows:

$150	gas
160	one night's motel lodging each way
200	half a month's car payment
20	half a month's car insurance
10	estimated wear on tires
$540	Total cost of transportation

Because the cost of taking the car exceeds the cost of taking the plane, the Smiths decide to take the plane. Do you agree with their decision?

As you may have noticed, the problem with Robin's estimate of the driving costs is that it fails to distinguish between fixed and variable costs. More precisely, this estimate fails to isolate the marginal cost of taking the trip.

The car payment and the monthly payment for insurance are fixed costs; those payments have to be made whether the Smiths drive or fly. The true cost of driving to Colorado is only $320—the extra or additional variable cost of operating the automobile and the added cost of lodging. If the Smiths compare that cost to the cost of airfare, driving is the clear choice.

Note that the decision-making process used to decide between taking a plane and driving a car is really no different than the cost-benefit analysis discussed earlier. The benefit of driving the car is the $400 you save by not having to take the plane. If the cost of driving the car is less than the benefit, you drive the car; otherwise, you take the plane. But if you get your estimate of costs wrong—if you include fixed costs that don't belong—you make the wrong decision and spend money needlessly.

One more note before we proceed. Even though the car payment and the insurance payment are fixed costs in this instance, they might be marginal costs under other circumstances. Suppose, for example, that you've just moved to New York City and you're trying to decide whether to buy a car or rely on mass transit to get to work and travel about the city. Under those circumstances, the car and insurance payments are marginal costs of owning an automobile. They need to be considered along with the cost of gas, parking fees, and so forth, in deciding whether it's cheaper to travel by mass transit or purchase a car. But if you decide to purchase the car and have it insured, the insurance and car payments immediately become fixed costs in determining the cost of any trip you intend to make. The point is that insurance and car payments become fixed costs only after you've made a commitment to pay them; up to that point, they are avoidable and need to be considered along with any other marginal costs and benefits.

The Travels of Bonnie and Claude

As we've seen, the irrelevance of certain costs doesn't prevent them from creeping into all kinds of decisions. Consider the trials of a young married couple, Bonnie and Claude Jones, who have been shopping for a new sofa. The couple recently found a sofa they like at a local furniture store, but it is selling for $800, somewhat more than they want to pay. A neighbor has suggested that they drive to Furnitureville—a 100-mile trip—because she's heard that the prices there are 25 percent lower. If they make the trip, Bonnie will have to miss a half day's work at a cost of about $50 in forgone income. In addition, Claude estimates that they will spend another $25 for gas. After discussion, the couple decides that the expected benefits of the trip (the $200 they anticipate saving on the sofa) justify the expense.

When they arrive, they discover that furniture prices are indeed lower than at home—but not much lower. The sofa that sold at home for $800 sells there for $775 (including delivery). Claude is very disappointed. He wants to turn around and head back home. "If we include the money we've lost because of the trip, these sofas cost $850; that's even more than the $800 they're asking back home." Bonnie isn't so sure. "I don't think we should count the cost of the trip; we've already lost that money. I think we should go ahead and buy the sofa here, since it's $25 less than back home." Who do you think is correct?

If you sided with Bonnie, you're on the right track. The cost of the trip is a **sunk cost**, a cost that has already been incurred and cannot be recovered. If the Joneses had known the sofa prices in Furnitureville before they made the trip, they would have stayed home. But once they've made the trip, they have to pay for it whether or not they buy the sofa. The correct decision is to buy the sofa in Furnitureville because the additional cost of the sofa there ($775) is less than the additional cost of the sofa back home ($800). Because the cost of the trip can't be recovered, it is irrelevant to the decision about where to buy the sofa.

Before moving on, let's consider another possible outcome from the trip to Furnitureville. Suppose that on arrival, the Joneses had discovered that the sofa they were interested in was selling for $850, $50 more than back home. Under those circumstances, the correct decision would be to buy the sofa in their hometown. But the Joneses may fall into the trap of believing that it is necessary to buy the sofa in Furnitureville to justify the cost of the trip. In other words, "We've paid for this trip, and we need to have something to show for it." But as we've already noted, the cost of the trip is sunk; it cannot be avoided. If the Joneses insist on buying the sofa in Furnitureville, all they will have to show for the trip is thinner wallets.

As the foregoing examples illustrate, there are many pitfalls in wise decision making. It's easy to ignore some relevant costs and equally easy to see costs where there are none. The key to avoiding these pitfalls is remembering to think marginally and to consider the opportunity costs. By applying these rules, you can make better personal decisions about everything from how to spend your money to what to do next Saturday night. (Bad decision making may have contributed to the financial crisis that helped propel our economy into a recession in late 2007. Read "Subprime Debacle Traps Even Very Credit-Worthy. . . ," on page 140, to explore the pitfalls that ensnared home buyers searching for suitable mortgages.)

BUSINESS DECISION MAKING AND THE PURSUIT OF PROFIT

Now that we have introduced the marginal principle and have seen how it can improve personal decision making, we shift the emphasis to business decision making. Much of this text focuses on the behavior of businesses rather than that of individuals. That's because businesses are at the center of the productive activity in our economy. They not only produce the goods and services that consumers demand, but they also provide the employment opportunities that make it possible for consumers to purchase those goods and services.

Use Your Economic Reasoning

Subprime Debacle Traps Even Very Credit-Worthy; As Housing Boomed, Industry Pushed Loans to a Broader Market

BY RICK BROOKS AND RUTH SIMON

[The recent "housing crisis" and the related "mortgage crisis" had more than one cause. One part of the story goes like this. Housing prices were rising, and homes looked like great investments—because they were appreciating in value at a rapid rate. So, people were eager to buy homes, often as much home as they could (barely) afford. If it took an unattractive "subprime" loan to make that possible, they did it. Why go for the unattractive loan? Because they believed they could always refinance into a more attractive loan a few years later. But when home prices started falling, these borrowers were trapped. Banks would not allow them to refinance their loans because they owed more than those homes were now worth. For many borrowers, this led to foreclosures and bankruptcy. This Use Your Economic Reasoning selection looks at some of the forces that led borrowers to subprime loans that they were ultimately unable to repay.]

One common assumption about the subprime mortgage crisis is that it revolves around borrowers with sketchy credit who couldn't have bought a home without paying punitively high interest rates. But it turns out that plenty of people with seemingly good credit are also caught in the subprime trap. An analysis for *The Wall Street Journal* of more than $2.5 trillion in subprime loans made since 2000 shows that as the number of subprime loans mushroomed, an increasing proportion of them went to people with credit scores high enough to often qualify for conventional loans with far better terms. . . .

The analysis also raises pointed questions about the practices of major mortgage lenders. Many borrowers whose credit scores might have qualified them for more conventional loans say they were pushed into risky subprime loans. They say lenders or brokers aggressively marketed the loans, offering easier and faster approvals—and playing down or hiding the onerous price paid over the long haul in higher interest rates or stricter repayment terms. . . . One of the biggest weapons: a compensation structure that rewarded brokers for persuading borrowers to take a loan with an interest rate higher than the borrower might have qualified for.

There isn't a hard-and-fast rule on what makes a loan subprime. But generally they are riskier than regular mortgages because lenders are more willing to bend traditional underwriting standards to accommodate borrowers. Besides having a lower credit score, borrowers might wind up with a subprime loan if the mortgage was considered risky for other reasons—such as borrowing a higher percentage of income or home value than normal, or borrowing without documenting income or assets. The resulting interest rates tend to be substantially higher than for conventional mortgages.

One key factor in determining what kind of loan a borrower gets is his credit score. Credit scores can run from 300 to 850, and many involved in the business view a credit score of 620 as a historic rough dividing line between borrowers who are unlikely to qualify for a conventional, or prime, loan, and those who may be able to. Above that score, borrowers may qualify for a conventional loan if other considerations are in their favor. Above 720, most borrowers would expect to usually qualify for conventional loans, unless they are seeking to spend more than they can afford, or don't want to have to document their income or assets—or are steered to a subprime product. . . .

In most states, mortgage brokers and loan officers aren't under any legal obligation to put borrowers in the mortgage that best suits them. . . . Tom Pool, an assistant commissioner for the California Department of Real Estate, says his office has seen a number of cases involving "totally ignorant and unsophisticated borrowers who had good credit, but were duped into loans they had no hope of repaying." But experienced borrowers with high credit scores are often too casual about the loan process. A study published last year in the *Journal of Consumer Affairs* concluded that some borrowers pay higher rates than they should because they don't shop around enough. An earlier survey by the Mortgage Bankers Association of borrowers who had bought a house within the previous 12 months found that half couldn't recall the terms of their mortgage, says the association's Mr. Duncan. . . .

USE YOUR ECONOMIC REASONING

1. Economists generally assume that we make decisions by comparing costs of benefits. But mortgage terms can be confusing, and it appears that many borrowers did not fully understand the mortgage they were signing. How would you proceed under those circumstances? Would you dedicate yourself to learning more about the alternatives? Would you seek advice from friends and others you trust? Would you rely on the lender to suggest the right product? What do you see as the limitations of each of these approaches?

2. The article suggests that the "compensation structure" for brokers was one of the reasons that many borrowers were steered toward subprime loans. Explain. Is this consistent with the model of self-interest discussed in the chapter? Why or why not?

3. According to the article, "experienced borrowers with high credit scores are often too casual about the loan process," and one reason that borrowers pay higher rates is "because they don't shop around enough." How would you explain this behavior?

4. Mortgage brokers and loan officers "aren't under any legal obligation to put borrowers in the mortgage that best suits them." Is this something that should be mandated by law? What problems can you envision in trying to accomplish this objective?

5. The Latin phrase *caveat emptor* means, in essence, "buyer beware." How would this concept guide prospective borrowers such as those described in this article? Can you see any reasons why this might fail to adequately protect these borrowers?

Business decision making is really no different than personal decision making; it involves a comparison of costs and benefits. The only real distinction between business and personal decision making is the goals involved. Economists generally assume that self-interest-seeking individuals attempt to maximize personal satisfaction, or **utility**. Businesses, on the other hand, are generally assumed to be **profit maximizers**; they are attempting to make decisions that will allow them to earn as much profit as possible.

Profit is the excess of a business firm's total revenue over its total costs. Businesses pursue profits by producing and selling products. **Total revenue** represents the total receipts of the business, that is, the amount of money it takes in from the sale of its product. Total revenue is calculated by multiplying the selling price of the product by the number of units sold. For example, if you sell five pens for $2 each, your total revenue is $10. **Total cost** refers to the sum of all the fixed and variable costs incurred by a business in producing its product and making it available for sale. As long as a business's total revenue exceeds its total costs, it is earning a profit. When total costs exceed total revenue, the business is incurring a **loss**. (*Profit* and *loss* are simple accounting terms; we'll see later why economists need special terms for different kinds of profits.)

SHORT-RUN COSTS OF PRODUCTION

How do businesses go about maximizing their profits—the difference between their costs and their revenues? As you'll soon see, they use the same cost-benefit principle that is employed by individuals. But before we begin that discussion, we need to take a closer look at a business's costs of production. We begin our examination of production costs by focusing on the short run. The **short run** is defined as a time period during which at least one of a business's inputs is incapable of being changed. In most instances, the fixed input is the business's plant and equipment—the firm's production facility. In the short run, a business does not have sufficient time to build a new factory or expand its existing factory. To expand output in the short run, a business must use its existing production facility more intensively, employing more labor and raw materials, perhaps by running two or three production shifts daily instead of a single shift. By contrast, the **long run** is defined as a time period long enough to permit all inputs to be varied. In the long run, firms have sufficient time to build new production facilities and to expand or contract existing facilities. We'll have more to say about the firm's long-run adjustments in the next chapter.

Total Costs: Fixed and Variable

Like individuals, businesses can classify their short-run costs as fixed or variable. The business's total cost (*TC*) is simply the sum of the fixed and variable costs it incurs to produce its product. To illustrate, imagine that you own a small sawmill producing pine lumber for home building. Let's examine the fixed and variable costs of this hypothetical business and explore how those costs behave or change as the firm expands or contracts the amount of lumber it produces.

Fixed Costs   Earlier, we defined fixed costs as costs that do not vary with the level of activity engaged in. For example, your monthly car payment is a fixed cost of owning a car and so is the annual payment you make to buy auto insurance. For businesses, fixed costs are those costs that do not vary or change with the level of *output*. They neither increase when the firm produces more nor decrease when the firm produces less. Fixed costs are often referred to as *overhead* and include such expenditures as insurance payments, rent on the production plant, fees for business licenses, salaries of managers, and property taxes. Exhibit 5.1 summarizes the costs of our hypothetical sawmill. As you can see from column two, the firm's total fixed costs are $200, regardless of how much output it produces.

EXHIBIT 5.1

Daily Costs of Manufacturing Pine Lumber

OUTPUT (thousands of feet of lumber)*	TOTAL FIXED COST (TFC)	TOTAL VARIABLE COST (TVC)	TOTAL COST (TC)	AVERAGE FIXED COST (AFC)	AVERAGE VARIABLE COST (AVC)	AVERAGE TOTAL COST (ATC)
0	$200	$ 0	$ 200	—	—	—
1	200	280	480	$200.00	$280.00	$480.00
2	200	500	700	100.00	250.00	350.00
3	200	680	880	66.66	226.67	293.33
4	200	880	1,080	50.00	220.00	270.00
5	200	1,100	1,300	40.00	220.00	260.00
6	200	1,360	1,560	33.33	226.67	260.00
7	200	1,660	1,860	28.57	237.14	265.71
8	200	2,010	2,210	25.00	251.25	276.25
9	200	2,420	2,620	22.22	268.89	291.11
10	200	2,890	3,090	20.00	289.00	309.00

* Large quantities of lumber are generally sold in increments of 1,000 board feet; a board foot measures 12 × 12 × 1 inches.

The distinguishing feature of fixed costs is that they have to be paid whether or not the firm is producing anything. If our hypothetical sawmill was forced to shut down because of a strike or slow business conditions, the firm would still have to pay the salaries of its managers to avoid losing them to other companies. It would still have to make interest payments on loans it had taken to purchase the production plant and equipment. It would continue making payments for damage and accident insurance, and it would still require the services of security guards. In Exhibit 5.1 this necessity is represented by the fact that total fixed costs are $200, even at an output of zero.

Variable Costs Costs that change with the level of output are termed variable costs. They tend to increase when the level of output increases and to decline when output declines. Many of a business's costs are variable costs: payments for raw materials, such as timber, iron ore, and crude oil, and the manufactured inputs transformed from such materials (lumber, sheet steel, paint); wages and salaries of production workers; payments for electricity and water; and shipping expenses. In column three of Exhibit 5.1, you can see that variable costs increase with output. For instance, total variable cost is only $500 when two units of output are produced but rises to $2,010 when eight units are produced.

In many instances a specific element of cost may be partly a fixed cost and partly a variable cost. For example, although a firm's electricity bill increases as production expands, some fraction of that bill should be considered a fixed cost because it relates to security lights, running the air conditioners in administrative offices, and other functions that are independent of the rate of output.

Average Costs: Fixed, Variable, and Total

Producers are often more interested in the average cost of producing a unit of output than they are in any of the total-cost concepts we've examined. By comparing average, or per unit, costs with those of other firms in the industry, a producer can judge how efficient (or inefficient) its own operation is. Average cost functions are of three types: average fixed cost, average variable cost, and average total cost.

Average fixed cost (AFC) is computed by dividing total fixed cost by the firm's output. For example, if the firm was producing four units of output, the AFC would be $200/4 = $50. As you can see in column five of Exhibit 5.1, average fixed cost declines as output increases.

Average fixed cost (AFC) = Total fixed cost/Output

This must be true because we are dividing a constant—total fixed cost—by larger and larger amounts of output. The decline in AFC is what a business means when it talks about "spreading its overhead" over more units of output.

Average variable cost (*AVC*) is calculated by dividing the total variable cost at a given output by the amount of output produced. For instance, if our lumber mill was producing five units of output (5,000 feet of lumber), its *AVC* would be $1,100/5 = $220. See column six in Exhibit 5.1.

Average variable cost (*AVC*) = Total variable cost/Output

As you can see from Exhibit 5.1, average variable cost declines initially and then rises as output continues to expand. The reason for this behavior will be provided a little later.

Average total cost (*ATC*) is computed by dividing the total cost at a particular level of output by the number of units of output. Using that technique, we find that the average total cost of producing four units of output is $1,080/4 = $270. Average total cost can also be calculated by summing the average fixed and average variable cost at a given output level.

Average total cost (*ATC*) = Total cost/Output
and
Average total cost (*ATC*) = Average fixed cost + Average variable cost

For instance, the average total cost of producing four units of output is equal to the average fixed cost of $50 *plus* the average variable cost of $220; that means that *ATC* is equal to $270, the same answer as before. As you can see from column seven of Exhibit 5.1, average total cost declines initially and then rises—the same general behavior as average variable cost.

Marginal Cost

Average total cost is useful in gauging a firm's efficiency in production. But, as with individuals, it is marginal cost that is really critical in decision making. As you already know, **marginal cost** (*MC*) is the additional cost of taking some action. In production decisions, marginal cost is the additional cost of producing one more unit of output. It is equal to the change in total cost from one unit of output to the next. Consider, for example, the marginal cost of the first unit of output—the first thousand feet of lumber—in Exhibit 5.2. If it costs the firm $200 to produce zero output (remember fixed costs) and $480 to produce one unit of output, the marginal cost of the first unit of lumber is $280. The *MC* of the second unit is $220, the difference between *TC* of $480 and *TC* of $700. Take a few moments to compute the marginal costs for the remaining units of output, using the total cost column in Exhibit 5.2. Then, check your answers against the marginal cost column in that exhibit.

EXHIBIT 5.2

The Marginal Cost of Manufacturing Pine Lumber

OUTPUT PER DAY	TOTAL COST	MARGINAL COST
0	$ 200	—
1	480	$280
2	700	220
3	880	180
4	1,080	200
5	1,300	220
6	1,560	260
7	1,860	300
8	2,210	350
9	2,620	410
10	3,090	470

If you examine the marginal cost column closely, you will notice that marginal cost declines initially and then increases as output expands further. Why does it behave this way? The behavior of marginal cost is related to the productivity of the economic resources used in producing the product.

When inputs are more productive, they produce more—they add more to the firm's output. This, in turn, means lower costs for the business. In small sawmills, for example, labor costs can be a major cost of doing business. The labor cost of producing an additional unit of output depends on the amount of labor time it takes to produce that unit. If our mill is paying its workers $10 an hour and it takes eight hours to produce the additional unit, the labor cost of that unit is $80. If the additional unit could be produced in only six hours, the labor cost of that unit could be reduced to $60.

The amount of labor time it takes to produce each additional unit of output is not constant. It depends on the degree of specialization of labor: the extent to which workers perform a single task rather than several. Workers who specialize tend to do their jobs better and more quickly, which means lower marginal cost.

When a firm is producing relatively little output, the labor cost of producing an additional unit tends to be high because the low volume permits little specialization. To illustrate, think about the variety of tasks you would need to perform if you wanted to run our hypothetical sawmill alone. You would be required to roll the logs onto the saws and cut them into lumber. Then, to smooth the rough surfaces of the boards, you would have to set up and operate the planer. Next, you would need to stack the lumber for drying. And, of course, you'd be the one who cleaned and serviced the equipment so that it continued to operate properly.

Many additional tasks would be required, but by now you probably get the point. If you were trying to run the mill by yourself, you would spend a great deal of time moving from one task to the next, and it's likely that you wouldn't become very proficient at any of them. As a consequence, more hours would be required to accomplish each task than would be needed if you were allowed to specialize in one job (or a few jobs) and become more skilled. This is why the marginal cost of producing the first unit of lumber is relatively high ($280).

As output expands, opportunities for specialization increase. For example, if the lumber mill needs to hire two workers to keep up with demand, one of them might do all the sawing while the other planes the boards and stacks them for drying. This greater specialization permits workers to become better at their jobs and reduces the time wasted in moving from one task to another. The result is a lower marginal cost for the second unit of output ($220) and an even lower cost for the third ($180) because the amount of labor time required to produce these additional units of output is reduced. Remember, this is a hypothetical example; the numbers are not precise but are meant only to illustrate a principle. In some businesses, specialization can result in significant reductions in marginal cost; in others, the savings may be minimal.

Marginal cost will not decline indefinitely. If the firm continues to expand output, it will eventually start to overutilize its plant and equipment, causing marginal cost to rise. In the short run, each business firm must operate with a fixed amount of plant and equipment. If the firm continues to hire additional workers to increase output, at some point it will experience congestion and workers waiting to use equipment. Of course, if workers are standing idle, they are not producing output, but they are being paid. This causes the marginal cost of producing an additional unit of output to rise, as it does in our example when the output is expanded from three to four units of lumber.

In summary, if a firm continues to expand output in the short run, it will eventually overutilize its fixed plant and equipment, causing marginal cost to rise. This principle is simply an extension of the law of increasing costs introduced in Chapter 1.

THE COST CURVES

By graphing the information found in Exhibits 5.1 and 5.2, we can construct the cost curves depicted in Exhibit 5.3. We interpret or "read" the cost curves in much the same way we read the demand and supply curves encountered in

EXHIBIT 5.3

The Cost Curves

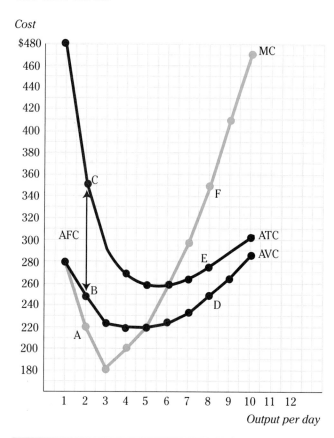

A firm's production costs can be represented graphically as cost curves. Marginal cost (*MC*), average variable cost (*AVC*), and average total cost (*ATC*) all graph as U-shaped curves; that is, they decline initially and then rise as output increases.

Chapters 3 and 4. For instance, if we are interested in knowing the marginal cost of producing the second unit of output, we find two units on the horizontal axis, move directly up from that quantity to the *MC* curve (point *A*), move across to the vertical axis, and read $220. The *MC* of producing the second unit of output is $220. To determine the *AVC* when two units are being produced, we move up to the *AVC* curve (point *B*), move across to the vertical axis, and read $250. Moving on up the graph, we find that the *ATC* of producing two units of output is $350 (point *C*). Note that the *AFC* of producing two units of output is $100, the vertical distance between the *ATC* curve and the *AVC* curves at that output level. The vertical distance between the *ATC* and *AVC* curves diminishes as output increases because *AFC* falls as output expands. (What is the marginal cost of producing the eighth unit of output? Can you determine the AVC, ATC, and AFC when eight units are produced? Try it and then see footnote 3 for the correct answers.)[3]

If you look carefully at Exhibit 5.3, you will note that marginal cost is related to average variable cost and average total cost in a very precise way; the MC curve intersects each of the curves at their lowest point, or minimum. This is not a chance intersection; it is due to the relationship between marginal and average values. A simple example will help to illustrate that relationship.

Let's assume that you want to know the average weight of the students in your class. To determine the class average, you coax each student onto the scales, add up the individual weights, and then divide by the number of students in the class. If an additional (marginal) student who weighs more than the average joins the class, the average will be pulled up. If the additional student weighs less than the previous class average, the average will be pulled down. As this example illustrates, the marginal value determines what happens to the average.

Essentially the same logic applies to the cost curves. Notice that as long as the MC curve is below the AVC curve, the AVC is falling; the marginal value is pulling down the average just as the thin student pulled down the class average. However, when MC is above AVC, AVC is rising; the marginal value is pulling the average up. When MC = AVC—that is, when MC and AVC intersect—the average will remain unchanged.

The shape of the ATC curve is also influenced by marginal cost but in a somewhat more complex manner. Recall that average total cost is the sum of average fixed cost and average variable cost. Initially, both AVC and AFC decline, and so ATC declines as well. But note that ATC continues to decline after AVC has turned upward. This occurs because AFC is continuing to decline, and for a while the downward pull of AFC outweighs the upward pull of AVC. But eventually the increase in AVC will more than offset the decrease in AFC, and ATC will begin to rise. Thus, ATC will have the same basic shape as AVC, but the minimum on the curve will occur at a somewhat higher level of output.

In summary, the marginal cost curve plays a major role in determining the shapes of both the average variable and average total cost curves. As you will see in a moment, marginal cost also plays a major role in guiding the production decisions of businesses.

---

[3] The marginal cost of producing the eighth unit of output is $350 and is represented by point F in Exhibit 5.3. When eight units are produced, the AVC (point D) is about $250, the ATC (point E) is approximately $275, and average fixed cost (the vertical distance between points D and E) is $25.

SELECTING THE PROFIT-MAXIMIZING LEVEL OF OUTPUT

The most fundamental decision that a business makes is selecting the optimal level of output, the output that will maximize its profits or minimize its losses. Managers attempt to locate that output by repeatedly asking themselves the same question: "Will the marginal benefit from producing this additional unit of output exceed the marginal cost?" As long as the answer is yes, they continue to expand production. When the answer is no, they stop; they've found the optimal level of output.

Marginal Revenue Is the Marginal Benefit

The benefit that a firm receives from producing and selling its product is the money it takes in—the revenue it receives. As we've already noted, the amount of revenue the firm generates depends on two things: the selling price of the product and the quantity of the product sold. For the sake of illustration, let's continue our sawmill example. Suppose that the prevailing price of pine lumber—the product produced by your sawmill—is $300 per thousand feet, and this price is set by market forces and is largely beyond your control. (The next chapter will examine this assumption in some detail.) Under these circumstances, what is the marginal benefit to your sawmill of selling an additional thousand feet of lumber? If you answered $300, you've got the right idea. That $300 is the price the firm receives for each unit of output (each thousand feet of lumber) it sells. It also represents the mill's marginal revenue—the additional revenue from selling one more unit of output.

If each additional unit produced and sold adds $300 to the firm's revenue, how many units should the firm produce? That depends on marginal cost. Remember the decision-making rule: Engage in an activity as long as the marginal benefit (marginal revenue) exceeds the marginal cost.

MR = MB

Using the Decision Rule: Comparing Marginal Revenue and Marginal Cost

Once we've computed marginal revenue (MR) and marginal cost (MC) at each level of output, selecting the optimal level of output is a relatively simple matter. We just apply the decision rule we've been using throughout the chapter: Continue to produce as long as the marginal benefit exceeds the marginal cost.

Exhibit 5.4 summarizes the relationship between output, marginal revenue, and marginal cost that we discovered earlier. The fourth column adds another interesting bit of information, the mill's profit (or loss) at each level of output. As we've already discovered, profit is the difference between total revenue and total cost; this column simply performs that comparison for each level of

$\Pi = TB - TC$

EXHIBIT 5.4

Selecting the Profit-Maximizing Level of Output

OUTPUT PER DAY	MARGINAL REVENUE	MARGINAL COST	PROFIT
0	—	—	$–200
1	$300	$280	–180
2	300	220	–100
3	300	180	+20
4	300	200	+120
5	300	220	+200
6	300	260	+240
7	300	300	+240
8	300	350	+190
9	300	410	+80
10	300	470	–90

output. If the $200 loss at zero output mystifies you, remember fixed costs. Even if production ceases and revenue drops to zero, some costs will remain to be paid.

Even without column four, the information contained in Exhibit 5.4 can be used to determine the optimal (profit-maximizing/loss-minimizing) level of output. As we noted earlier, production managers attempt to locate the optimal output by repeatedly asking themselves the same question: "Will the marginal revenue from producing this additional unit of output exceed the marginal cost?" As long as the answer is yes, they continue to expand production.

Let's start with the first unit of output and ask that question. As you can see from the exhibit, the marginal revenue from the sale of the first unit of output ($300) exceeds the marginal cost of producing that unit ($280). The first unit of output should be produced because it makes the mill $20 better off than it would be if it produced nothing. (Note that the mill's loss drops from $200 to $180.) What about the second unit of output; should it be produced? According to the exhibit, the answer is yes. That unit adds another $300 to the firm's revenue but only $220 to the mill's costs; it makes the business $80 better off (the mill's loss declines from $180 to $100).

How long should the mill continue expanding production? Marginal reasoning tells us to produce each unit for which MR exceeds MC but no units for which MC exceeds MR. If the mill's manager follows that logic, he or she will expand production right up to the point at which marginal revenue is equal to marginal cost, at seven units of output. Note that the mill's profit is maximized at that point. By using marginal reasoning, we have located the profit-maximizing output.

You may have noted that the mill's profit is actually maximized at either six or seven units of output. To eliminate any ambiguity, we will assume that businesses go ahead and produce the unit where $MC = MR$. As we will see in a moment, that makes it a relatively easy matter to locate the profit-maximizing output graphically. In some situations there will be no (nonfractional) level of output at which MR and MC are exactly equal. In such instances the firm should continue to produce each unit of output whose MR exceeds its MC. Our complete rule for profit maximization, then, is to expand production as long as marginal revenue is greater than or equal to marginal cost.

Graphing and Profit Maximization

Graphing the marginal revenue and marginal cost curves is an alternative method of determining the optimal level of output. This approach is represented in Exhibit 5.5. Because the mill receives an additional $300 for each and every unit of lumber it sells, its marginal revenue curve is a horizontal straight line at a height of $300. On the other hand, the mill's marginal cost curve is U-shaped; it dips and then rises. As noted earlier, this shape stems from the changing productivity of the mill's inputs. At low output levels, few opportunities for specialization lead to high marginal costs. As output expands, increased opportunities for specialization bring lower marginal costs. Ultimately, the overutilization of the mill forces workers to wait to use the equipment, driving marginal cost back up and explaining the U-shaped marginal cost curve in the exhibit.

As long as the marginal revenue curve is above the marginal cost curve, MR exceeds MC, and it makes sense for the firm to expand output. For example, the marginal revenue from the sale of the third unit of output (represented by the point labeled MR_A on the marginal revenue curve) is $300 and exceeds the $180 marginal cost of producing it (represented by point MC_A on the marginal cost curve); so the mill will be better off producing that unit. The same is true of all additional units up to the seventh. At that point the marginal revenue curve intersects the marginal cost curve, so that $MR = MC$; the additional cost of producing the unit is exactly equal to the additional revenue derived from its sale. If the mill produced more than seven units of output, the marginal cost of producing those units would exceed the marginal revenue, making the firm worse off. For example, the marginal cost of producing the eighth unit of output (represented by MC_B on the marginal cost curve) is $350, well in

---

EXHIBIT 5.5

Finding the Profit-Maximizing Output Graphically

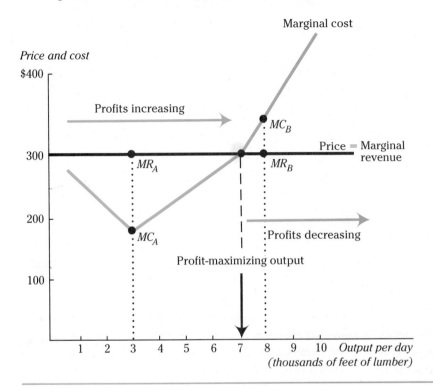

Profit is maximized at the output where marginal revenue is equal to marginal cost. As long as $MR > MC$, the firm can enlarge its profit (or reduce its loss) by expanding output. When $MC > MR$, additional units reduce the firm's profit (or increase its loss).

---

excess of the $300 marginal revenue derived from that unit (point MR_B on the marginal revenue curve). It stands to reason, then, that output should be expanded right up to the point at which marginal revenue equals marginal cost, but not beyond. That gives us a simple way of isolating the profit-maximizing rate of output graphically: Produce at the output for which the marginal cost curve intersects the marginal revenue curve (where $MR = MC$).

Wise Decisions Don't Always Lead to Profits

Even if businesses consistently apply the decision rule, they are not assured of profits. Sometimes market conditions are depressed, and the very best a firm can do is to minimize its loss. Consider, for example, a situation in which the demand for pine lumber has declined, reducing its market price from $300 to only $250. Exhibit 5.6 reveals that in this situation, there is no output level that will yield a profit. What should the mill do under these circumstances?

EXHIBIT 5.6

Selecting the Loss-Minimizing Level of Output

OUTPUT PER DAY	MARGINAL REVENUE	MARGINAL COST	PROFIT
⋮	⋮	⋮	⋮
2	$250	$220	$–200
3	250	180	–130
4	250	200	–80
5	250	220	–50
6	250	260	–60
7	250	300	–110
8	250	350	–210

It should use marginal reasoning, just as before. Look at Exhibit 5.6 and see if you can find the loss-minimizing output without using column four. (For simplicity, the table has been slightly abbreviated.)

Note that in this instance there is no output for which marginal revenue is exactly equal to marginal cost. Therefore, the mill should expand production, as long as $MR > MC$, to five units per day. Although that output will not allow the firm to earn a profit, column four confirms that five units is indeed the loss-minimizing output; once again, marginal reasoning has served us well.

There are rare but realistic circumstances in which the business will not find it desirable to expand production up to the output at which $MR = MC$. Suppose, for example, that the price of lumber became really depressed, and the mill could predict that, at the output at which $MR = MC$, it would incur a loss of, say, $250. What would it do? Under these circumstances the mill would minimize its loss by shutting down or ceasing operations until market conditions improve and it can get a better price for its product. If a mill shuts down, the loss it incurs is equal to its fixed costs—the costs that continue even at zero production. Recall that in our example the mill's fixed costs total $200 a day, substantially less than the $250 a day the business would lose by continuing to operate. The next chapter will discuss in greater detail the possibility of shutting down. For now, focus your attention on the profit-maximization rule (expand production up to the point at which $MR = MC$); it's the rule that guides business decision making in the vast majority of cases.

GAS STATIONS, FAST FOOD, AND THE ALL-NIGHT GROCERY STORE

Thus far we've concentrated on the role of marginal reasoning in helping businesses select the optimal level of output. But the role of marginal reasoning is much broader than that. It permeates every aspect of business. And knowing what it means to "think marginally" can help you understand business decisions that baffle others. Consider the following examples.

Whatever Happened to Gas Stations?

Whatever happened to gas stations? At one time there were thousands of genuine gas stations in the United States, stations that sold almost nothing but gas. And convenience stores sold quick groceries but not gas. Now, in many areas, gasoline stations are rarities, and every convenience store has gas pumps. What happened? Part of the story is the introduction of self-service gasoline; that made it possible for convenience stores to sell gas. The increase in the number of working mothers made a difference, too; that change put greater emphasis on convenience—the ability to buy a carton of milk without trudging to the grocery store. But much of the answer lies in the marginal principle, and that's what we want to discuss here.

Imagine yourself the owner of one of the few remaining genuine, honest-to-goodness gas stations in the United States. On the way home from work, you need a carton of milk and a few other groceries, so you run into a convenience store and pick them up. You notice that the price you pay is somewhat higher than what you'd pay in a grocery store, but you don't complain; the convenience is worth it. But that starts you thinking. Why can't *you* sell those items and make that money? (Notice competition rearing its head; more about that in the next chapter.) So you sit down with a pad of paper and a calculator and do some figuring. How much would it cost to rent a cooler for milk and soda pop, and a display rack for bread and snack items? Not much. What about the extra electrical cost of running the cooler? Not much. And how many extra people would you have to hire to collect money from customers buying groceries? None! Pretty soon you've cleared the junk out of your gas station, installed the cooler and display racks, and another gas station has given way to a mini convenience store; the marginal principle rides again.

Owners of early convenience stores also understood marginal reasoning, and they tended to view gasoline as a marginal item. But adding gas pumps to a convenience store probably required more thought than adding coolers to gas stations. Although the additional cost of pumping gas is minimal once the pumps are in place (and that cost is "sunk"), the cost of adding the pumps is not trivial. So, before that decision was made, the convenience store owners needed to determine whether the additional revenue that the pumps would generate would pay for the cost of the pumps, the additional electricity to run them, and the wholesale cost of the gasoline.

The answer must generally be yes because gas pumps are everywhere. The difference between gas stations and convenience stores has largely disappeared. (Note that once some convenience stores begin adding gas pumps, it puts pressure on other convenience stores in the area to do the same. If you can buy gas and groceries at Bob's Quick Mart, you won't stop at Joan's Fast Stop if it sells only groceries. So the option of not selling gasoline has now been largely eliminated for convenience store owners.)

Why Is Breakfast Everywhere?

If you want more evidence that businesses understand marginal reasoning, consider the ease with which you can find a cheap, quick breakfast. Even though lunch is clearly the main meal at McDonald's and Burger King, managers at these franchises understand that they can enlarge their profits by serving breakfast. That's because once the restaurant is in place, there is little added cost to serving the morning meal. The big expense items, rent and the cost of the franchise, are fixed costs; they have to be paid whether or not breakfast is served. So the restaurants do a quick cost-benefit analysis and compare the additional revenue they can generate by offering breakfast to the additional cost of serving breakfast (the cost of the food items, the additional labor time, the higher electric bill, etc.). On that basis, it appears that the breakfast meal must generally pay for itself. That's why there are so many places where you can grab a quick breakfast as you dash to class or to work.

Sale! Buy Below Cost!

Marginal reasoning even helps to explain those end-of-season sales. If you've ever found yourself looking through the sale merchandise, you've probably noticed that you can save quite a bit on the normal retail price. In fact, if you're patient and wait for the final reductions, those prices can be below even the wholesale prices paid by the stores. Does that make sense? Does it make sense to sell a designer sweater for $25 if it cost the store $50? Sure it does! Remember the rules: sunk costs are sunk; compare marginal costs and marginal benefits.

The amount the store paid for the sweater is irrelevant in the decision about how much to sell it for. The question is: Does the marginal benefit of selling it to you for $25 exceed the marginal cost? But what's the marginal cost of selling it to you? If the sweater hasn't sold all season, the store's next course of

What a store paid for an item is irrelevant when it comes to determining closeout prices.

action will be selling it to one of those chains that sell close-out merchandise. That may net the store only $5 or $10. If that's the case, the marginal revenue from selling that sweater to you ($25) exceeds the marginal cost (the $5 to $10 it could get elsewhere). The store's not being silly; it's using marginal reasoning.

One more thought before closing this chapter. Although marginal costs (and revenues) are the key to good decision making in the preceding examples, firms must ultimately cover all their costs—including fixed costs—to remain in business. Consider the gas station example once again. As we've seen, the station owner should ignore fixed costs such as rent and insurance in deciding whether to sell groceries and convenience items. Those costs already exist once the decision has been made to open a gas station. But if the convenience store's total operations (selling gasoline and convenience items) are unable to generate enough revenue to cover all costs, including those fixed costs, the store will eventually be forced to close its doors. After all, landlords and insurance companies expect to be paid. If they aren't, they will stop providing their services, and the convenience store will be history. We'll have much more to say about this in the next chapter. But as you can see, there is more to running a business than understanding marginal reasoning. And there's more to economics as well. In the next chapter, we will take a closer look at the behavior of business firms and explore the meaning of competitive markets.

SUMMARY

Economic models assume that people are motivated by self-interest and that they pursue self-interest through a rational comparison of costs and benefits. The relevant costs and benefits for comparison are *marginal* costs and benefits. The marginal costs and benefits are the extra or additional costs and benefits resulting from a decision. A decision will improve one's well-being only if the marginal benefits from that decision exceed the marginal costs.

Even rational people sometimes make bad decisions. Poor decisions stem from mistaking marginal and total values and from improperly estimating the costs of a decision. It is important to remember that all decisions have opportunity costs. In some instances these opportunity costs can easily be stated in monetary terms (*explicit costs*); in other instances they cannot (*implicit costs*). In either case, failure to consider all opportunity costs can lead to poor decisions. Poor decisions can also result from mistaking relevant and irrelevant costs. The only costs that are relevant for decision making are marginal costs, the additional costs that result from making a decision. Costs are irrelevant if they are unaffected by a decision. Irrelevant costs include fixed and sunk costs. *Fixed costs* are costs that do not vary with the level of activity engaged in and that cannot be avoided. *Sunk costs* are costs that have already been incurred and cannot be recovered.

Business decision making also involves a comparison of costs and benefits. The only major difference between business decision making and personal decision making is the goals involved. According to economic theory, individuals attempt to maximize personal satisfaction or *utility*, while businesses attempt to maximize profits.

Profit is the excess of a business's total revenue over its total costs. *Total revenue* represents the total receipts of a business and can be calculated by multiplying the selling price of the product by the number of units sold. *Total cost* represents the sum of all the business's costs. As long as a business's total revenue exceeds its total cost, it will earn a profit. When total costs exceed total revenue, the business will incur a loss.

In examining a business's costs of production, two time periods are relevant, the *short run* and the *long run*. In the short run, some of a business's inputs are fixed or incapable of being changed (the firm's plant and equipment), while others (raw materials and production labor, for example) can be varied. As a consequence, a firm's short-run costs of production are composed of *fixed costs* (those costs that do not vary with the level of output) and *variable costs* (those costs that do vary with the level of output). In the long run, all inputs are capable of being changed, and consequently all costs are variable.

Producers are often more interested in the average cost of producing a unit of output than they are in total cost. There are three types of average cost functions: *average fixed cost* (total fixed cost/output), *average variable cost* (total variable cost/output), and *average total cost* (total cost/output). In making production decisions, however, none of these average cost concepts is as important as *marginal cost*—the additional cost of producing one more unit of output.

The fundamental decision that a business makes is selecting the level of output that maximizes its profits or minimizes its loss. To select this output, businesses compare marginal revenue and marginal cost. Output should be expanded up to the point at which marginal revenue is equal to marginal cost ($MR = MC$) but not beyond. Graphically, the profit-maximizing output can be determined by locating the output at which the marginal revenue curve intersects the marginal cost curve. Although producing where $MR = MC$ does not ensure a profit, it generally allows the firm to do as well as possible under existing market conditions. In other words, producing the output where $MR = MC$ will generally allow the firm either to maximize its profit or to minimize its loss.

In addition to using marginal reasoning to select the profit-maximizing loss-minimizing level of output, firms use marginal reasoning in making other business decisions. For instance, fast-food restaurants use marginal reasoning when deciding whether to serve breakfast, and airlines use marginal reasoning when deciding whether to run an additional flight between two cities. Although fixed costs are irrelevant in such decisions, firms must ultimately generate enough revenue to cover all costs if they are to remain in business.

KEY TERMS

Average fixed cost	Long run	Sunk cost
Average total cost	Marginal	Total cost
Average variable cost	Marginal cost	Total revenue
Explicit cost	Profit	Utility
Fixed costs	Profit maximizer	Variable cost
Implicit cost	Short run	

STUDY QUESTIONS

Fill in the Blanks

1. Economists argue that individuals are motivated primarily by the pursuit of

    _____ .

2. Rational people make decisions by comparing _____ and

    _____ .

3. _____ costs are costs that do not vary with output and cannot be avoided.

4. Total cost is the sum of _____ cost and _____ cost.

5. _____ means extra or additional.

6. Average total cost, _____ the output for which _____

 cost, and _____ cost all is equal to _____ .
 graph as U-shaped curves.

 9. Marginal costs may initially decline as
7. Economists generally assume that output is expanded and more workers are
 individuals seek to maximize hired because higher levels of production

 _____ and that businesses seek permit greater _____ .

 to maximize _____ . 10. The statement "There's no such thing as a
 free lunch" means that every decision has
8. Economists argue that profits are generally
 maximized (or losses minimized) at a(n) _____ .

Multiple Choice

1. Economists assume that individuals
 a) are motivated primarily by concern for
 others.
 b) act impulsively.
 c) pursue their own self-interest.
 d) use their intuition to make wise
 decisions.

2. Economic models may not accurately predict the behavior of individuals if those
 individuals
 a) fail to consider the interests of
 others.
 b) act selfishly.
 c) behave in an impulsive manner.
 d) always consider the opportunity costs
 of their decisions.

3. Bob walked into the clothing store and,
 without a moment's hesitation, bought
 the first shirt he saw that was his size. His
 behavior
 a) is clearly consistent with the assumption of rationality.
 b) might be rational if he has very little
 time to shop.
 c) is clearly impulsive and is therefore inconsistent with the assumption of rationality.
 d) might be impulsive if he had previously considered the alternative shirts
 in the store and their prices.

4. Which of the following behaviors is inconsistent with the way economists assume
 individuals will act?
 a) Susie selected her car by reading reports, test-driving several models, and
 comparing their features and prices.
 b) Alex wanted to go to the concert but
 considered the likely impact on his
 calculus grade and decided to study
 instead.
 c) Fran really wanted the red dress but
 thought it was too expensive, so she
 bought the green one instead.
 d) The salesman offered to let John use the
 store phone, but because John didn't
 want to interfere with business calls,
 he used the pay phone.

5. If we use the cost-benefit model, which of
 the following high school students is most
 likely to attend college?
 a) A student with an aptitude for auto
 mechanics
 b) A student with a decent job and opportunities for advancement
 c) A student who values present income
 much more highly than future income
 d) A student who qualifies for several
 scholarships

6. Suppose that a firm's fixed cost is $100, the
 marginal cost of the first unit of output is

$20, the marginal cost of the second unit is $10, and the marginal cost of the third unit is $30. Then we can say that the total cost of producing three units of output is
a) $190.
b) $53.33.
c) $160.
d) $63.33.

7. One summer, John spent every night after work building a garage. "I did all the labor myself, so it didn't cost me anything. And I managed to save $3,000 compared to the price Ace Builders quoted me." Which of the following is true?
a) John's calculation ignores the explicit cost of his labor.
b) John must have decided that his leisure time was worth more than $3,000.
c) John must be irrational to give up that many evenings to save only $3,000.
d) John's calculation ignores the implicit cost of his labor.

8. Promise Pharmaceutical Company has invested $10 million trying to develop a cure for a rare disease. So far its efforts have been unsuccessful. Economists would describe this $10 million expenditure as a
a) sunk cost.
b) fixed cost.
c) variable cost.
d) marginal cost.

Answer questions 9–11 on the basis of the following information:

QUANTITY	TOTAL COST
0	$10
1	18
2	23
3	30

9. The firm's fixed cost is
a) $5.
b) $42.
c) $23.
d) $10.

10. The marginal cost of the third unit would be
a) $30.
b) $7.
c) $10.
d) $5.

11. If the firm produced three units, average total cost would be
a) $10.
b) $30.
c) $7.
d) None of the above

12. Profits are maximized (or losses minimized) at the output level where
a) marginal revenue exceeds marginal cost by the largest amount.
b) fixed costs are minimized.
c) marginal revenue is equal to marginal cost.
d) marginal cost is at a minimum.

13. If the marginal cost of producing an additional unit of output is $50 and the marginal revenue from selling that unit is $60,
a) the unit should not be produced because it will make the business worse off.
b) the unit should be produced because it will make the business $60 better off.
c) the unit should not be produced because the business is already maximizing its profit.
d) the unit should be produced because it will make the business $10 better off.

Use the following information in answering questions 14–16.

Use the following information in answering questions 17–21.

Data for John's Cabinet Company

OUTPUT PER WEEK	MARGINAL REVENUE	MARGINAL COST
0	—	—
1	$440	$350
2	440	325
3	440	350
4	440	375
5	440	400
6	440	450
7	440	525
8	440	625
9	440	750
10	440	900

Data for Apex Golf Cart Company

OUTPUT PER DAY	TOTAL COST
0	$ 200
1	500
2	700
3	1,000
4	1,400
5	1,900
6	2,500
7	3,300
8	4,300
9	5,500
10	7,000

14. John's Cabinet Company will maximize profit (or minimize its loss) by producing
    a) 2 cabinets a week.
    b) 5 cabinets a week.
    c) 7 cabinets a week.
    d) 10 cabinets a week.

15. If John's Cabinet Company could sell each cabinet for $525 instead of $440, the profit-maximizing level of output would be
    a) 2 cabinets a week.
    b) 5 cabinets a week.
    c) 7 cabinets a week.
    d) 10 cabinets a week.

16. John's Cabinet Company
    a) is earning a profit.
    b) is incurring a loss.
    c) cannot determine profit or loss from the information given.

17. The Apex Golf Cart Company faces fixed costs
    a) of $200 per day.
    b) of $300 per day.
    c) of $7,000 per day.
    d) that cannot be determined from the information given.

18. The marginal cost of producing the fourth golf cart each day is
    a) $1,400.
    b) $300.
    c) $400.
    d) $350.

19. If Apex can sell additional golf carts for $800 each, the profit-maximizing (loss-minimizing) level of output is
    a) 2 carts per day.
    b) 5 carts per day.
    c) 7 carts per day.
    d) 8 carts per day.

20. If the price Apex can get for its carts increases to $950, the profit-maximizing (loss-minimizing) output will be
    a) 2 carts per day.
    b) 5 carts per day.
    c) 7 carts per day.
    d) 8 carts per day.

21. Assume that the price Apex can get for its carts remains at $950 but that the company's fixed costs increase to $400 a day. Under those conditions, the profit-maximizing (loss-minimizing) output will be
    a) 2 carts per day.
    b) 5 carts per day.
    c) 7 carts per day.
    d) 8 carts per day.

Problems and Questions for Discussion

1. Bobby Goodguy volunteers for several local charities and is a member of several service organizations. Is it possible that such behavior is in his (financial) self-interest?

2. Why do individuals base their decisions on expected costs and benefits rather than true costs and benefits?

3. Studies tell us that students who have a difficult time in high school are less likely to attend college than students who find high school easy. Use the cost-benefit model to explain this finding.

4. Edith decided that her $100,000 a year job at Gord Motors wasn't fulfilling. So she invested savings of $20,000 (which had been earning 10 percent a year) in starting her own travel agency. At the end of the year, the accountants gave her the following report. After examining the report, explain why economists might criticize it and how they would be likely to amend it.

Total Revenue from customers...............$225,000

Salaries of John, Joan, and Bob...................75,000

Salary of Edith 35,000

Rent 60,000

Office supplies 10,000

Phone and utilities 15,000

Total cost.....................................195,000

Profit..$30,000

5. Susie absolutely must drive home for Christmas. She would like a rider to share the cost of the two-day trip. Her monthly car payment is $210, and car insurance costs her another $30 monthly. In addition, she estimates that gas will cost her $100. The only student who has responded to her advertisement for a rider is willing to pay $40. Should she take the rider? Defend your answer.

6. Consider your answer to question 5. Suppose that Susie could take the bus home at a cost of $120. Should she take the bus or drive? Defend your answer.

7. Complete the following:

QUANTITY	TC	TVC	TFC	MC	ATC
0	$ 50	0	$50		0
1	100	50	50	50	100
2	130	80	50	30	65
3	180	130	50	50	
4	260	210	50	80	
5	380	330	50	120	

8. (Warning: Extra tough question; try it only if you like a challenge.) Highflyer Corporation manufactures kites, which are being sold throughout the United States. It is currently producing 100,000 kites a year and operating its factory at 70 percent of capacity. At that output the average total cost of manufacturing a kite is about $2. Experience has shown that average cost drops somewhat as output is expanded beyond 100,000 units but rises again if output is increased above 125,000 units.

The Highflyer Corporation normally sells its kites for $2.50 each. It recently received an order for an additional 10,000 kites from a foreign buyer, but the buyer specified that it would pay no more than $1.50 a kite. Highflyer executives want to accept the order, but the firm's accountants estimate that at 110,000 units a year, the average cost of producing a kite would be $1.90, more than the $1.50 price being offered. Should Highflyer accept the offer?

QUANTITY	TOTAL COST
0	$ 50
1	100
2	130
3	180
4	260
5	380

9. Bill paid $50 for an old record album at an estate sale because he thought it was a rare Elvis recording. He was wrong; the album is worth only about $10. Bill won't sell at that price because he can't stand the thought of losing $40. What's wrong with his reasoning?

10. Consider the information found below. If this firm can sell as many units of its product as it chooses at $50, how many units of output should it produce? Would it earn a profit or incur a loss? How much profit or loss?

11. *(Another toughie; proceed at your own risk.)* Bonnie believes that it is possible to calculate the total cost of producing X units of output by summing (adding up) the marginal cost of producing all units of output from 1 through X. Is she correct? Why or why not?

12. The amount of money that a firm loses by shutting down and producing no output is its fixed costs. Why? Under what circumstances would it make more sense to shut down than to produce at the output at which $MR = MC$?

ANSWER KEY

Fill in the Blanks

1. self-interest
2. marginal costs; marginal benefits
3. Fixed
4. total fixed; total variable
5. Marginal
6. average variable; marginal
7. utility; profit
8. *MR*; *MC*
9. specialization
10. opportunity cost

Multiple Choice

1. c
2. c
3. b
4. d
5. d
6. c
7. d
8. a
9. d
10. b
11. a
12. c
13. d
14. b
15. c
16. c
17. a
18. c
19. c
20. c
21. c

Price Taking: The Purely Competitive Firm

1. Identify the characteristics of a purely competitive industry.
2. Explain why a purely competitive firm is described as a "price taker."
3. Describe the demand and marginal revenue curves of a price taker.
4. Describe how a price taker determines the profit-maximizing level of output.
5. Explain why the marginal cost curve is the competitive firm's supply curve.
6. Evaluate graphically the extent of a price taker's profit or loss.
7. Distinguish between an economic profit and a normal profit.
8. Explain why a firm may continue to produce output in the short run even though it is incurring a loss.
9. Explain why purely competitive firms tend to earn normal profits in the long run.
10. Discuss the distinction between production efficiency and allocative efficiency.
11. Explain how long-run price, profitability, and efficiency are related to the absence of barriers to entry.

In Chapter 3 we discussed how demand and supply interact to determine prices in competitive markets. To fully understand the operation of competitive markets, we need to step behind the scenes and examine the decision-making processes of the individual supplier, commonly known as the firm. The **firm** is the basic producing unit in a market economy. It buys economic resources—land, labor, capital, and entrepreneurship—and combines them to produce goods and services. A group of firms that produce identical or similar products is called an **industry**. ExxonMobil, ConcoPhillips, and Chevron are firms in the petroleum industry; McDonald's, KFC (Kentucky Fried Chicken), and your local pizzeria are firms in the fast-food industry.

Economists argue that the performance of firms—how effectively they serve consumers—depends on the degree of competition within the industry; the greater the competition, the better the performance.[1] This chapter examines the model of *pure* competition and explores the behavior of the individual firms that make up a purely competitive industry. We begin the chapter by examining the assumptions that underlie the model of pure competition. Then we investigate why purely competitive firms are described as *price takers* and discover how these firms determine the profit-maximizing or loss-minimizing level of production. Next, we focus on interpreting the graphs of the competitive firm and on learning to distinguish a profit from a loss. Finally, we examine the factors that cause firms to enter or leave a competitive industry, explaining why this behavior is thought to be in the best interest of consumers.

THE NATURE OF PURE COMPETITION

Since the time of Adam Smith, economists have recognized that a market economy will serve consumers well only if competition exists to protect their interests. The competition economists have in mind, however, is more than mere rivalry among a few sellers. By definition, pure competition must satisfy three basic assumptions:

1. *There must be a large number of sellers, each producing a relatively small fraction of the total industry supply.* This rules out the possibility that a single firm could affect price by altering its level of output.[2]
2. *The firms in the industry must sell identical products.* This condition excludes the possibility of any product differences, including those created through advertising, and ensures that consumers will view the products of different firms as perfect substitutes.

---

[1] As we've seen in earlier chapters, performing well in a market economy means producing the goods and services that consumers desire most and selling those goods and services at the lowest possible prices.
[2] This definition focuses on the seller's side of the industry. Pure competition can be said to exist on the buyer's side of the market when a large number of relatively small buyers ensures that each buyer is unable to significantly influence the prevailing price of the product.

3. *There can be no substantial barriers (obstacles) to entering or leaving the industry.* Examples of barriers to entry include patent restrictions, large investment requirements, and restrictive licensing regulations.

The assumptions of pure competition may sound unrealistic, but there are industries that conform reasonably well to the conditions of the model. For instance, wheat farming, cattle ranching, fish farming (aquaculture), and many other segments of agriculture are consistent with the model. In addition, the competitive model offers insights into the behavior of industries that don't meet all of the assumptions but come reasonably close. For instance, used-car retailing, the home-repair industry, and the fast-food industry are not fully consistent with the model of pure competition because the firms sell somewhat different products. But because these industries are characterized by a relatively large number of firms and modest entry barriers, the competitive model has proved very valuable in analyzing their behavior.

Although the model of pure competition has proved to be a useful tool for analyzing the behavior of existing industries, economists value it for an additional reason as well. In fact, the most important function of the competitive model is in allowing us to see how an industry would function if it conformed to the assumptions of pure competition. By using the benefits of pure competition as our standard, or yardstick, we can better understand the problems that may emerge when industries are less competitive. In later chapters we will relax these assumptions and see how the performance of industries will change when these conditions are no longer satisfied.

THE FIRM UNDER PURE COMPETITION

In a purely competitive industry, the individual firm is best described as a **price taker**; it must accept price as a given that is beyond its control. This description follows from two of the basic assumptions of our model. First, because each firm produces such a small fraction of the total industry's supply, no single firm can influence the market price by altering its level of production. Even if a firm withheld its entire output from the market, the industry supply curve would not shift significantly to the left, and the equilibrium price would be essentially unchanged. Second, because all firms sell identical products, no one firm can charge a higher price for its product without losing all its customers; consumers would simply buy cheaper identical products from other firms. As a consequence of these conditions, the firm must accept, or take, the price that is determined by the impersonal forces of supply and demand.

To illustrate how a firm operates under pure competition, we'll return to the example introduced in Chapter 5, a hypothetical producer of pine lumber. Pine lumber is an important component in the construction of new homes. It is produced by several thousand sawmills in the United States, and the lumber produced by one mill is virtually identical to the lumber produced by another. We will assume that the individual lumber producer is such a small part of the total industry that it cannot influence the market price. Whether that price means a profit or a loss, the firm can do nothing to alter it. The firm can't charge more than the prevailing price because its product is identical to that of all other producers. Withholding the firm's output from the market in an attempt to drive up prices would be fruitless because its output is just a drop in the bucket and would never be missed. (The price the firm receives for its product can change, of course, but price changes under pure competition are due to changes in industry demand and supply conditions, not to any actions the firm may take.)

Because price is a given, the demand curve facing the individual firm is a horizontal line at the equilibrium price. The horizontal demand curve in Exhibit 6.1(b) indicates that the firm can sell as much output as it wishes at the

EXHIBIT 6.1

The Firm as a Price Taker

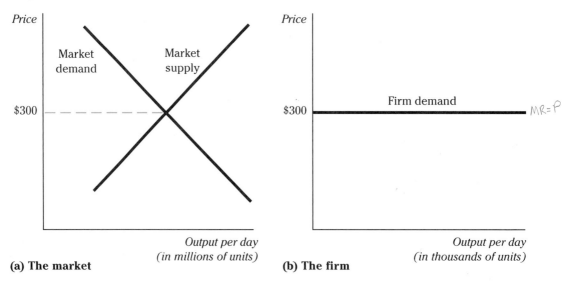

(a) The market

(b) The firm

In a purely competitive market, market forces (supply and demand) determine the equilibrium price, and the individual firm is unable to influence that price. The demand curve facing the firm is horizontal at the height of the market price because the firm can sell as much output as it desires at that price but nothing at a higher price. Note that the market output is measured in millions, whereas the firm's output is measured in thousands.

market price but no output at a higher price. You may recall from Chapter 4 that a horizontal demand curve is described as *perfectly,* or *infinitely, elastic.* Here, a very small change in price leads to an infinitely large change in the quantity demanded because our lumber mill would lose all its customers if it raised its price even slightly.

PROFIT MAXIMIZATION IN THE SHORT RUN

Because the purely competitive firm is a price taker, in effect bound to the price determined by the market, the only variable it can control to maximize its profit or minimize its loss is the level of output. In the *short run,* the purely competitive firm can produce any level of output within the capacity of its existing plant and equipment. It adjusts its output by altering the amount of variable resources (labor and raw materials, for example) that it employs in conjunction with its fixed plant and equipment. In the *long run,* of course, the firm has additional options for expanding or contracting production. We'll have more to say about those long-run adjustments later in the chapter.

Determining the Profit-Maximizing Output

How do firms go about selecting the profit-maximizing (loss-minimizing) level of output? They compare costs and benefits! In fact, the process of selecting the optimal level of output can be likened to a series of cost-benefit comparisons. Imagine a production manager repeatedly asking the same question: Does the benefit from producing one more unit of output exceed the cost? As long as the answer is yes, it is sensible for the firm to continue expanding output. When the answer is no, the firm should go no further.

For a business, the benefit from producing and selling output is the revenue it takes in. *Marginal revenue* (MR) is the additional revenue to be gained by selling one more unit of output. When firms are price takers, MR is always equal to price because the additional revenue gained by selling one more unit is exactly the market price ($MR = P$). This price must be compared with *marginal cost,* the cost of producing one more unit of output. A firm seeking the profit-maximizing output will continue to increase production as long as price or marginal revenue exceeds marginal cost. When price exceeds marginal cost ($P > MC$), each additional unit produced makes the firm better off because it adds more to the firm's revenue than to its cost.

Exhibit 6.2 illustrates this decision-making process in action. The market price in this example is $300, so each additional unit produced will add $300 to revenue. If we begin our cost-benefit comparison with the fifth unit of output,

EXHIBIT 6.2

Finding the Profit-Maximizing Output Graphically

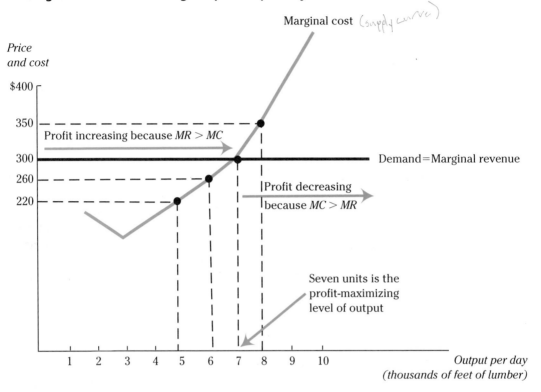

Profit is maximized at the output where marginal revenue is equal to marginal cost. As long as *MR > MC*, the firm can enlarge its profit (or reduce its loss) by expanding output. When *MC > MR*, additional units reduce the firm's profit (or increase its loss).

we can see that the $300 the firm gains from producing this unit is more than the $220 marginal cost of that unit. In short, the firm will be $80 better off for producing that unit. The firm should produce the sixth unit as well. Although marginal cost rises to $260 for that unit, it is still less than the $300 selling price, leaving the firm $40 better off. (It is important to recognize that although the sixth unit adds less to profit than the fifth unit, it continues to enlarge the firm's *total* profit, so it should be produced.)[3]

_____

[3] With the information provided thus far, we cannot determine whether this firm is earning a profit or incurring a loss. But we can say that by producing the sixth unit, the firm will either enlarge its total profit or reduce its total loss. You'll see how to determine the profit or loss in just a moment.

The seventh unit of output is a little trickier to evaluate. It brings in no more revenue ($300) than it costs to produce ($300), so the firm should be neutral or indifferent toward its production. Economists generally assume, however, that the firm will go ahead and produce that unit. As we noted in Chapter 5, this assumption provides us with a simple rule for selecting the profit-maximizing output: produce the level of output at which $MR = MC$, the output that corresponds to the point where the MR and MC curves intersect. In instances when there is no whole-number unit of output for which MR is exactly equal to MC, the firm should produce all the units for which $MR > MC$ but no unit for which $MC > MR$.

Marginal Cost and Firm Supply

Because the purely competitive firm determines the profit-maximizing output by equating price and marginal cost, any change in the prevailing market price will alter the amount of output it will choose to produce. Suppose, for example, that the existing market price was $350 instead of $300. You can see from Exhibit 6.2 that if the firm's demand curve was horizontal at that price, the firm would expand output to eight units per day (the output at which the demand curve would intersect the MC curve). Alternatively, a price of $260 would cause the firm to produce less; the demand curve would intersect the MC curve at six units. As you can see, the competitive firm always operates along its marginal cost curve, supplying whatever output is dictated by its intersection with the prevailing market price (the firm's demand curve). For that reason, the marginal cost curve can be thought of as the firm's supply curve—because it indicates how much the firm will produce or "supply" at any given price. (Actually, the firm's supply curve is only the portion of the marginal cost curve lying above the average variable cost. That's because if price falls below average variable cost, the firm won't produce any output. More about that in a moment.)

Evaluating Profit or Loss

By producing where marginal revenue is equal to marginal cost, the purely competitive firm is doing the best it can; it is either maximizing its profit or minimizing its loss. But marginal values alone won't tell us *exactly* how well the firm is doing. They won't tell us whether the firm is earning a profit or incurring a loss, and they won't tell us the amount of the profit or loss. To answer those questions, we need to calculate and compare the firm's total revenue and total cost.

You already know that total revenue is computed by multiplying the selling price of the product by the number of units sold. To compute total cost, we need the information provided by the average total cost (ATC) curve. Multiplying ATC by the number of units produced gives us the total cost of producing that

ATC·Q=TC

output level.[4] Then, by comparing total revenue with total cost, we can determine the profit or loss. Exhibit 6.3 illustrates this process step by step. Before we work through the exhibit, focus on panel one and try to use the information provided to determine the amount of the firm's profit or loss. After you've tried to find the answer on your own, read on to compare your results.

The first step in determining a firm's profit or loss is locating the profit-maximizing (or loss-minimizing) level of output and computing the firm's total revenue. As we've seen, firms should continue to produce additional units of output up to the point where $MR = MC$. As panel two reveals, this firm should expand output to seven units, the output where the MC curve intersects the MR curve. Once we've selected the optimal output, we determine the firm's total revenue by multiplying the selling price (which is equal to marginal revenue) by the number of units produced. In this example, that procedure results in a total revenue of $2,100, multiplying the $300 selling price by seven units of output. (Note that we represent total revenue graphically as an area because it is a vertical distance multiplied by a horizontal distance.)

TR= MR· Q
300 · 7

The second step in determining the firm's profit or loss is determining the firm's total cost. This is accomplished by multiplying the average total cost (at the optimal output level) by the number of units produced. Panel three shows that when seven units are produced, ATC is $270. Multiplying $270 by seven units results in a total cost of $1,890, the shaded area in the panel.

TC= ATC·Q
270 · 7

The final step in determining the profit or loss is comparing the firm's total revenue with its total cost. In this instance, the firm's total revenue ($2,100) exceeds its total cost ($1,890), so the firm is earning a profit ($210). This outcome is revealed in panel four. Note that the total revenue area (panel two) is larger than the total cost area (panel three) by the amount of the firm's profit (the area in panel four).

TR-TC

Economic Profit versus Normal Profit Thus far, we've used the term *profit* in a rather general way. But economists have different terms to describe different levels of profit. The term **normal profit** is used to describe profits that are just equal to what the owners of the firm could expect to earn elsewhere—if they invested their time and money in another industry. The term **economic profit** is reserved to describe a situation in which the firm's owners are earning more than a normal profit—more than they could expect to earn elsewhere.

In attempting to understand this distinction, it is useful to recall another distinction introduced in the last chapter, that between explicit and implicit costs. Recall that *explicit costs* involve monetary payments—the payments to

[4] Recall from Chapter 5 that average total cost is computed by performing the reverse operation: dividing total cost at a particular level of output by the number of units being produced.

EXHIBIT 6.3

Determining the Profit or Loss

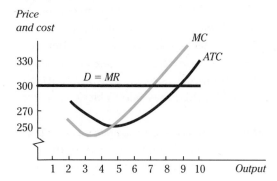

Panel One: Getting Started

Is the firm represented at the left earning a profit or incurring a loss? What is the amount of the profit or loss? Decide for yourself and then proceed to the next panel.

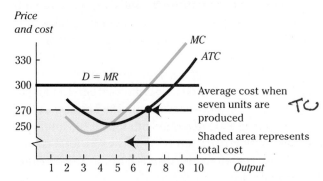

Panel Two: Finding the Best Output and the Firm's Total Revenue

The first step in determining the firm's profit or loss is locating the output where $MC = MR$. Here, that is seven units. The firm's total revenue is the selling price ($300) times the output (seven units). In this instance total revenue is $2,100.

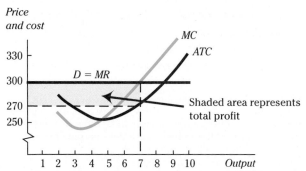

Panel Three: Finding Total Cost

If we go up from seven units to the ATC curve and then over to the vertical axis, we see that the average cost of producing seven units is $270. Thus total cost is $270 × 7 units or $1,890.

Panel Four: Finding the Profit or Loss

Because total revenue ($2,100) is greater than total cost ($1,890), we can see that this firm is earning a profit of $210. Alternatively, note that the firm is earning a profit of $30 per unit ($300 − $270), so the firm's total profit is $210 ($30 × 7 = $210).

hire labor, purchase raw materials, and buy electricity, for example. These costs are easily recognized because money changes hands. Implicit costs are less obvious because money is not exchanged. Rather, *implicit costs* represent the opportunity cost of owner-supplied resources. These are the costs that business owners incur when they use their own resources rather than selling them to others. Economists consider both explicit and implicit costs when they construct their cost curves. So in order for a firm to earn a profit—an *economic profit*—its total revenue must exceed its total cost (explicit plus implicit). If a firm's total revenue is exactly equal to its total cost, it is said to be earning zero economic profit or a *normal profit.*

$Profit_E = TR > TC_{(ex + im)}$

$TR = TC$ } normal profit

Economists consider zero economic profit a normal profit because the owners of the firm are able to earn precisely as much as they could have earned by investing their time and money elsewhere. Whatever amount they could have earned elsewhere must be the expected or normal profit. To illustrate, suppose that the owner of our sawmill had been earning $30,000 a year working for another lumber producer before he decided to buy his own mill. When he quit his job, he withdrew $20,000 from his savings account, which had been earning 10 percent interest a year, and used the money as a down payment to buy the sawmill. Because the earnings he gave up to launch this venture are his $30,000 supervisor's salary plus $2,000 interest (10 percent of $20,000), he would have to make $32,000 in his business (after subtracting all other costs) to earn a normal profit. If he made more than $32,000, he would earn an economic profit; if he earned less, he would be incurring a loss. Economists assume that a normal profit is the minimum amount required to convince a business owner to remain in a particular industry for the long run. After all, if the owner can make a normal profit elsewhere, why would he or she remain in this industry for less?[5]

Profits, Losses, and Breaking Even Exhibit 6.4 shows a purely competitive firm in the three different short-run situations described earlier. In part (a) the firm is enjoying an above-normal, or economic, profit. The amount of this profit can be determined by comparing total revenue with total cost. Total revenue is equal to $2,800 (the $350 selling price × 8 units), whereas total cost is only $2,240 (*ATC* of $280 × 8 units). Therefore, the firm is earning an economic profit of $560. Alternatively, we could determine the firm's profit by multiplying the average, or per-unit, profit by the number of units sold. Here the firm is earning a profit of $70 per unit ($350 − $280 = $70) and selling eight units; total profit is $70 × 8 = $560.

$TR > TC$

---

[5] In some circumstances an individual may be willing to remain in an industry even though he or she is earning less than could be earned elsewhere. This might be true, for instance, if the individual gained personal satisfaction from being his or her own boss. Even under these circumstances, however, some minimum income must be earned if the individual is to remain committed to this industry. The enjoyment of being your own boss won't pay the rent.

EXHIBIT 6.4

Finding the Profit or Loss

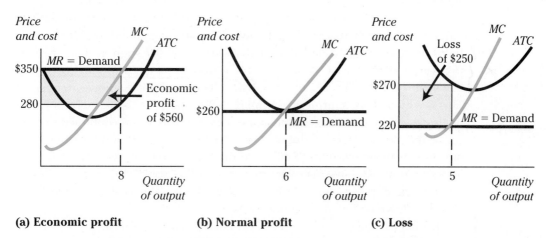

(a) Economic profit   **(b) Normal profit**   **(c) Loss**

All firms maximize their profits or minimize their losses by producing the level of output at which marginal revenue is equal to marginal cost. In some instances a firm will be able to earn an above-normal, or economic, profit. In other instances only a normal profit—zero economic profit—will be possible. In some cases a loss—less than a normal profit—will be the best the firm can do.

In part (b) the firm isn't doing as well. Its total revenue of $1,560 ($260 × 6 units) exactly matches its total cost, so that the firm is earning zero economic profit. Remember, zero economic profit is the same as normal profit, the amount the owners of the business could expect to earn if they invested their resources elsewhere. When a firm is earning a normal profit, it is sometimes described as *breaking even* because the firm's total revenue is exactly sufficient to cover its total cost.

In part (c) the firm has fallen on hard times. Price is now so low that it will no longer cover average total cost. As a result, the firm will be earning less than a normal profit and therefore facing a loss.[6] In this example the total cost is $1,350 ($270 × 5 units), whereas its total revenue is only $1,100 (*ATC* of $220 × 5 units), a loss of $250. (Note that if we multiply the per-unit loss of $50 × 5 units, we arrive at the same $250 figure for the firm's total loss.)

---

[6] In this situation, the firm is earning less than a normal profit because it is unable to cover all its explicit and implicit costs. Economists would describe this outcome as a loss, or, more precisely, as an *economic loss.* But if the firm hired an accountant to do its books, the accountant might tell the owners that the firm was earning a profit. That's because accountants don't generally consider implicit costs. Instead, their job is to focus on the explicit costs incurred by the firm. In summary, a firm can be earning an *accounting profit* even though economists describe it as incurring a loss.

Operating with a Loss Why would the company depicted in Exhibit 6.4(c) continue to produce? Why not simply **shut down** the business—temporarily stop producing output—and reopen after conditions improve? The answer has to do with fixed costs, or overhead, which must be paid whether or not any output is produced. If a firm shuts down, its loss will equal its total fixed costs. But if the price the firm can get for its product is high enough to allow the firm to cover its variable costs (costs that would not exist if the firm shut down) and pay some of its fixed costs, the firm will be better off if it continues to operate. This is why Ohio hog farmers continued to raise hogs in 2008, despite substantial losses, and why Massachusetts lobster trappers that year continued to go to sea as the global recession dragged down lobster demand and took the profit out of their business. In both cases, continuing to operate resulted in smaller losses than would have been incurred by shutting down. When price dips so low that the firm can no longer recover even the variable cost of production, it will shut down and wait for better times.

Exhibit 6.5 illustrates these two situations. In part (a) the selling price of $200 is greater than the average variable cost of $180, so each unit the firm produces (up to the point at which $MR = MC$) provides it with $20 ($200 − $180 = $20) to help pay its fixed costs. Although the firm will still incur a loss, continued

---

EXHIBIT 6.5

Minimizing a Loss

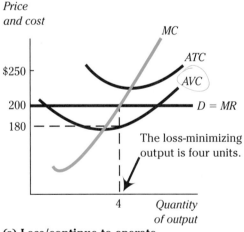

(a) Loss/continue to operate

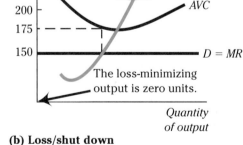

(b) Loss/shut down

Whenever price exceeds average variable cost ($P > AVC$), the firm will minimize its loss by continuing to operate. This is the situation represented in part (a), where the firm will continue to produce despite an economic loss. When price is less that average variable cost ($P < AVC$), the firm will minimize its loss by shutting down. This situation is represented in part (b).

operation will make the loss smaller than it would be if the firm shut down and paid its fixed costs. In part (b) the $150 price is less than the *AVC* of $175, so each unit the firm produces *increases* its total loss by $25. This firm would be better off to shut down, accept its fixed-cost loss, and wait for business conditions to improve. Of course, if losses continue for an extended period, eventually the firm will be forced out of business. In summary, when $P > AVC$, the firm will minimize its loss by continuing to operate; when $P < AVC$, the firm should shut down.

PROFIT MAXIMIZATION IN THE LONG RUN

In the short run the purely competitive firm must do the best it can with fixed plant and equipment, but in the long run the firm has many more options; all costs are variable in the long run. If the industry has been profitable, the firm may decide to expand the size of its production plant or otherwise increase its productive capacity. If losses have been common, it can sell out and invest in another industry, one in which the prospects for profits appear brighter. In the short run the number of firms in an industry remains constant: Time is inadequate for firms to enter or leave. But in the long run there is time for these adjustments to occur, and the industry can expand or contract. In this section we examine how firms in a purely competitive industry adjust to the presence or absence of short-run profits and how this adjustment process eventually leads to long-run equilibrium for the industry. **Long-run equilibrium** is a situation in which the size of an industry is stable: There is no incentive for additional firms to enter the industry and no pressure for existing firms to leave.

Setting the Stage: The Short-Run Picture

In Exhibit 6.6 we follow the path by which a purely competitive firm and industry arrive at long-run equilibrium. Each panel shows the demand and supply curves for the industry on the left and the diagram for a representative firm on the right. In part (a) the industry demand and supply curves establish a price of $300. The representative firm takes that price as a given and maximizes its profit by producing where $MC = MR$. Because the representative firm is earning an economic profit in the short run, additional firms will be attracted to this industry in the long run.

The Entrance of Firms: Attraction of Profits

The entrance of additional firms is made possible by one of the assumptions of the purely competitive model—the absence of significant barriers to entry. As

EXHIBIT 6.6

The Long-Run Adjustment Process

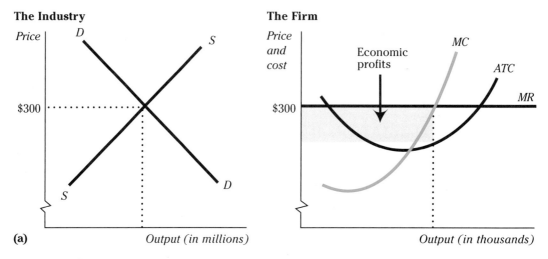

(a) At a price of $300, the firms in the industry will be able to earn an economic profit. Because above-normal profits are being earned, additional firms will be attracted to the industry. This development is reflected in (b).

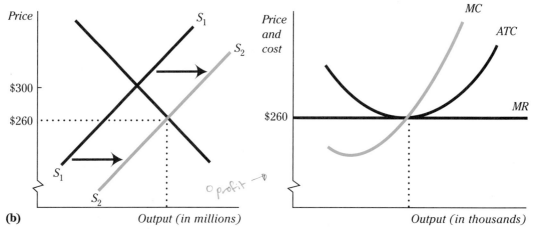

(b) The entrance of additional firms will shift the supply curve to S_2 and depress market price to $260. At that price, the firms in the industry will be able to earn only a normal profit. There will be no incentive for additional firms to enter the industry, and the industry will be in long-run equilibrium.

additional firms enter the industry, they will increase industry supply and depress the market price. The increase in industry supply occurs because the industry supply curve is the sum of all the firms' supply curves and is found by adding together those curves.[7] If additional firms enter the industry, the curves of those firms must be added, shifting the industry curve to the right. This adjustment is represented in the left-hand graph of Exhibit 6.6(b), where supply has increased to S_2 and intersects the demand curve to establish a new price of $260. Once the price of $260 is established, both the firm and the industry are in long-run equilibrium: They have achieved a state of balance, a situation in which there is no tendency for further change. The industry is in long-run equilibrium because at zero profit there is no incentive for additional firms to enter it and no incentive for established firms to leave it. The individual firms are in equilibrium because they have no incentive to alter their level of output as long as the market price remains at $260. (What does the future look like for U.S. ethanol producers? Can they expect to profit from federal government ethanol mandates, or will competition rein in any profits? Read "Ethanol Boom Is Running Out of Gas," on page 180, and decide which outcome is most likely.)

The Exit of Firms: Looking for Greener Pastures

If competitive firms experience short-run losses, a similar adjustment process is likely to result. In the long run some firms will respond to the short-run losses (less than normal profits) by leaving the industry to search for a better opportunity elsewhere. As these firms exit, industry supply decreases, and the market price rises. Firms will continue to leave the industry until the market price has risen sufficiently to afford the remaining firms exactly a normal profit. When that happens, the exodus will cease; the firms and the industry will be in long-run equilibrium.

THE BENEFITS OF PURE COMPETITION

As we noted at the beginning of this chapter, economists often use the model of pure competition as an ideal by which to judge other, less-competitive industry structures. Economists hold pure competition in such high esteem primarily because it leads to an efficient use of our scarce resources.

---

[7] Summing the supply curves of all the firms is relatively easy (remember, each firm's supply curve is its marginal cost curve above average variable cost). We simply add up the quantities that the firms will supply at each market price. For simplicity, suppose that there are only two firms in our industry. If firm A supplies five units at $300 and firm B supplies seven units at the same price, the industry supply curve would show 12 units being supplied at $300. The amount supplied by the industry at other prices would be determined in the same manner.

Use Your Economic Reasoning

Ethanol Boom Is Running Out of Gas

BY LAUREN ETTER AND ILAN BRAT

Ethanol's frenzied growth . . . is coming to a halt—at least for now. The price of ethanol has fallen by 30% over the past few months as a glut of the corn-based fuel looms, while the price of ethanol's primary component, corn, had risen. That is squeezing ethanol companies' profits and pushing some ethanol plants to the brink of bankruptcy. Financing for new ethanol plants is drying up in many areas, and plans to build are being delayed or canceled across the Midwest, as investors increasingly decide that only the most-efficient ethanol plants are worth their money. . . .

The downturn exposes the industry's reliance on political support in Washington, which has offered tax credits to refiners to blend ethanol with gasoline, as well as tariffs on imported ethanol and other measures. Some lawmakers . . . are pushing corn-based ethanol as a complement and substitute for gasoline amid tight and unpredictable global oil markets. Ethanol companies are seeking increases in pending energy legislation in the

amount of ethanol refiners are required to use. At the same time, food, cattle, poultry and other interests are quietly nudging lawmakers to pull back on subsidies that encourage ethanol production and have indirectly led to increases in food costs due to the increase in the price of corn and other grains. . . .

Fueled by government mandates and calls from President Bush that ethanol could help wean Americans off foreign sources of fuel, output of the corn-based fuel hit highs in the past year. U.S. ethanol production rose to 4.8 billion gallons last year, up from 1.7 billion gallons in 2001, according to the Renewable Fuels Association, a Washington trade group. The number of ethanol plants increased to 119, up from 56 in 2001. And there are 86 more plants under construction.

But ethanol has gotten snagged by its own success. The price of ethanol has dropped to about $1.50 a gallon, down from about $2.50 at the end of last year, according to the Oil Price Information Service. That is largely because too

Source: *Wall Street Journal*, October 1, 2007, p. A2. Reprinted by permission of the *Wall Street Journal*, Copyright © 2007 Dow Jones & Company, Inc. All Rights Reserved Worldwide. License number 2231560045787.

Production Efficiency

One of the most important features of pure competition is its tendency to promote **production efficiency**: production at the lowest possible average total cost, or minimum *ATC*. As you look at Exhibit 6.7, you'll see that the purely competitive firm is in long-run equilibrium when it is producing at the output level where its *ATC* curve is tangent to, or barely touching, its demand curve. This tangency occurs at the lowest point on the firm's *ATC* curve, showing that the firm is producing at the lowest possible average cost. In essence, this means that the product is being produced with as few scarce resources as possible.

much ethanol is being produced. Part of the problem appears to be that oil companies aren't able to blend ethanol into gasoline as quickly as ethanol is produced. By next year, U.S. ethanol capacity is expected to reach about 12 billion gallons, according to Eitan Bernstein, an energy analyst at Friedman, Billings, Ramsey Group Inc., based in Arlington, Va. Currently, demand is just less than seven billion gallons. . . .

USE YOUR ECONOMIC REASONING

1. In 2005, some ethanol plants were making about $1 a gallon in gross profit on the ethanol they produced. Assume that they were selling at a price of $2.50 a gallon and represent this situation graphically. Show both the firm and industry graphs.
2. Some estimates suggest that by 2008, profits were down to 5 cents a gallon or less. What happened? What does the article mean when it says that "ethanol has gotten snagged by its own success"? Try to represent this graphically.
3. Ethanol producers have been harmed by other factors in addition to their own success. While the price of ethanol was dropping, the price of corn—the chief input in most ethanol—was skyrocketing. Then in mid-2008, the price of gasoline started dropping—from a high of more than $4.00 a gallon, to about $1.60 a gallon by the end of the year. How would these changes affect the ethanol market?
4. By law, refiners were required to blend 10.5 billion gallons of ethanol with gasoline in 2009. Ethanol producers want an increase in that mandate. If they are successful in lobbying for an increase, what impact would you expect their efforts to have on the price of ethanol? Assuming this industry is purely competitive, would you expect the higher mandate to provide producers with long-run profits? Why or why not?
5. At present, ethanol producers receive a subsidy of about 50 cents for each gallon of ethanol they produce. For simplicity, assume that the ethanol industry was in long-run equilibrium before this subsidy was enacted. As you learned in Chapter 4, a subsidy of 50 cents will shift the market supply curve down by 50 cents, but will reduce the market price by something less than that—say 25 cents. That means ethanol producers are now earning a profit of 25 cents a gallon. Does the existence of this subsidy guarantee that ethanol producers will earn long-run profits? Why or why not?

Production efficiency is a benefit of pure competition; it allows us to spread our scarce resources across more products, and in so doing it enables us to satisfy more of society's unlimited wants.

Note also that in long-run equilibrium, consumers are able to purchase the product at a price equal to this minimum ATC. This must be true because at the tangency point in Exhibit 6.7, Price (which equals MR) = ATC. Thus, we can see that the benefits of production efficiency are passed on to consumers. They receive the lowest possible price, given the cost conditions that exist in the industry.

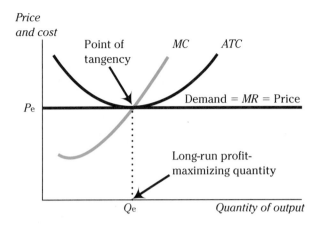

EXHIBIT 6.7

The Competitive Firm in Long-Run Equilibrium

In long-run equilibrium the competitive firm will earn only a normal profit. This is indicated in the graph by the tangency between the demand curve, or price line, and the *ATC* curve at the profit-maximizing output, where *MR* (which is Price) equals *MC*. The equality of price and minimum *ATC* indicates that the firm is achieving *production efficiency*.

Allocative Efficiency

If pure competition resulted in the efficient production of millions of buggy whips or other products not in much demand, consumers obviously would not be pleased. However, pure competition also leads to **allocative efficiency**: producers use society's scarce resources to provide consumers with the proper quantities of the goods and services they desire most. Economists argue that if pure competition prevailed throughout the economy, all our scarce resources would be allocated or distributed to produce the precise mix of products that consumers desire most.

Allocative efficiency requires that each product be produced up to the point at which the benefit its consumption provides to society (**marginal social benefit**) is exactly equal to the cost its production imposes on society (**marginal social cost**). In most instances, the benefits that a product provides to society are simply the benefits received by those who purchase the product. The value of these benefits is reflected in the price that consumers are willing to pay; the greater the benefit, the higher the price. This, in turn, can be determined from the industry demand curve. For instance, if consumers are willing to purchase 1,000 units of lumber at $300 and 1,001 units of lumber at $299, then the maximum price that consumers are willing to pay for the 1,001st unit of output must be $299 (because they were unwilling to purchase that unit at $300).[8]

---

[8] In some instances the consumption of a product conveys benefits to individuals in addition to those who purchased the product. For instance, when you purchase a flu shot, you benefit, but so do others (who will not get the flu from you). These *external benefits* are not reflected in the industry demand curve. Chapter 9 will discuss the impact of external benefits on the efficient allocation of resources.

Marginal social cost represents what society must give up to produce an additional unit of the product; in other words, it represents opportunity cost. Opportunity cost is generally reflected in the costs that the businesses incur to produce the product. In the case of pure competition, this can be determined from the industry supply curve. Because the industry supply curve is the sum of the firms' supply curves, it can be thought of as the marginal cost curve of the industry. (Remember: Under conditions of pure competition, the individual firm's supply curve is its marginal cost curve, so the industry supply curve is simply the sum of those curves.) By turning to the marginal cost curve (the industry supply curve), we can determine the sacrifice that society must make to produce an additional unit of the product in question. For instance, if the marginal cost of an additional unit of lumber is $200, that means that society must do without $200 worth of alternative goods—whatever products the same amount of raw materials, labor, and capital could have produced—to obtain this unit of lumber.[9]

As long as the marginal social benefit from an additional unit of output exceeds the marginal social cost, it is in society's interest to continue expanding production. This point is illustrated in Exhibit 6.8. Suppose the industry chose

EXHIBIT 6.8

Pure Competition and Allocative Efficiency

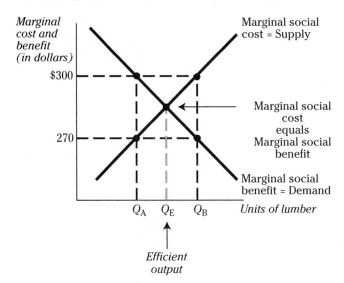

Allocative efficiency requires that each product be produced up to the point at which the marginal social benefit of the last unit produced is equal to the marginal social cost. That output is found where the demand and supply curves intersect, at Q_E in this example.

---

[9] In some instances the costs incurred by a business do not reflect all the costs associated with the production of a product. For instance, if a firm disposes of wastes by dumping them into a river to minimize its disposal costs, that action may kill fish and impose cleanup costs on other parties. These *external costs* are not reflected in the firm's cost curves. Chapter 9 will examine the impact of external costs on the allocation of scarce resources.

to produce Q_A units of output. As you can see from the diagram, the marginal social benefit of the last unit of output is $300, while the marginal social cost is only $270; clearly, output should be expanded because consumers value additional units of lumber more than the alternative products they could receive instead. If the industry chose to produce Q_B units, it would have carried production too far. The marginal social benefit of the last unit produced is equal to only $270, while the marginal social cost is equal to $300. Society would be better off if more resources were allocated to the production of other things and fewer to the production of lumber.

The optimal, or allocatively efficient, level of production occurs where the marginal social benefit and marginal social cost curves intersect, Q_E in our example. At that output the value of the benefit consumers receive from the last unit is exactly equal to the value of the alternative goods that must be sacrificed for its production. Pure competition ensures this outcome. Purely competitive industries always produce at the output level where the demand (marginal social benefit) and supply (marginal social cost) curves intersect. Therefore, pure competition ensures the efficient allocation of society's scarce resources.[10]

Let's synthesize what we have just discussed. Under conditions of pure competition, self-interest-seeking producers are guided by the presence or absence of profits to produce the right amounts of the products that consumers desire most. The forces of competition also lead to long-run equilibrium, whereby all firms in the industry operate at the lowest possible average cost (minimum *ATC*) and receive a price just equal to that cost. Thus, in the long run, consumers are able to purchase their most desired products at the lowest possible prices.

SUMMARY

The *firm* is the basic producing unit in a market economy. Firms buy economic resources and combine them to produce goods and services. *Industries* are groups of firms that produce similar or identical products. A purely competitive industry is one in which (1) a large number of sellers (firms) each produce a small fraction of the total industry supply, (2) the products offered by the different sellers are identical in the minds of consumers, and (3) no substantial barriers exist to prevent firms from entering or leaving the industry.

Firms in purely competitive industries are described as *price takers* because they must accept (or take) the price determined by market forces and are unable

---

[10] This conclusion assumes that there are no external costs or benefits associated with the production or consumption of the product. (See footnotes 8 and 9 for examples of external costs and benefits.) When externalities (external costs or benefits) exist, the industry supply and demand curves will not fully reflect social costs and benefits, and resources will not be allocated efficiently. This possibility is considered in Chapter 9.

to influence that price through their own individual actions. This description follows from two facts. First, each firm is too small to significantly influence the market price by altering its output. Second, because all firms sell identical products, no one firm can charge a higher price for its product without losing all its customers.

The model of pure competition assumes that firms are profit maximizers; that is, they are always attempting to earn the most profit possible. Because purely competitive firms are price takers, the only variable they can control to influence their profit position is the level of output. To reach its profit-maximizing level of output, each firm should continue to expand output as long as the additional revenue (*marginal revenue*) from selling another unit of output exceeds the additional cost (*marginal cost*) of producing that unit. For a price taker, marginal revenue is equal to the selling price of the product. Consequently, the profit-maximizing price taker will produce at the output level where price (P) is equal to marginal cost (MC).

By producing at the output where $MR = MC$, the competitive firm can generally ensure that it will either maximize its profit or minimize its loss. But to determine precisely how well the firm is doing—whether it is earning a profit or incurring a loss—we need to compute and compare total revenue and total cost. *Total revenue* is computed by multiplying the selling price by the number of units sold. To compute *total cost*, we need the information provided by the average total cost (ATC) curve. Multiplying ATC by the number of units of output produced gives us the total cost of producing that level of output. Then, by comparing total revenue and total cost, we can determine the profit or loss of the firm. When total revenue exceeds total cost (the sum of all explicit and implicit costs), the firm is earning an *economic profit*. When total revenue is exactly equal to total cost, the firm is earning zero economic profit or a *normal profit*. A normal profit is an amount just equal to what the owners of the firm could expect to earn by investing their time and money elsewhere—in some other industry. Economic profits represent greater profits than the owners could expect to earn elsewhere. When firms earn less than a normal profit, they are said to be incurring an *economic loss*.

Because the purely competitive firm determines the profit-maximizing (loss-minimizing) level of output by equating price (marginal revenue) with marginal cost, any change in the prevailing market price will alter the amount of output it will produce. As a result, the competitive firm's marginal cost curve can be thought of as its supply curve—because it indicates the amount that the firm will supply at any given price. More precisely, the purely competitive firm's supply curve is its marginal cost curve above average variable cost (AVC). If the market price falls below AVC, the firm will *shut down*; it will remain in the industry but produce no output.

In the long run, firms in a purely competitive industry tend to earn a normal profit. If economic profits exist in the short run, the entrance of additional firms will cause an increase in market supply and drive down the market price to the level of zero economic profits, where all firms are *breaking even* at normal profit. If losses exist, firms will exit the industry until price has risen to a level consistent with normal profits.

When long-run equilibrium is finally established, the purely competitive firm will be producing at minimum *ATC*, the point at which its *ATC* curve is tangent to its demand curve. When firms operate at minimum *ATC*, *production efficiency* exists. This is a desirable outcome because it indicates that the fewest possible scarce resources are being used to produce the product and that, therefore, more of society's unlimited wants are being met. In addition to production efficiency, pure competition leads to *allocative efficiency*: the production of the goods and services consumers want most in the quantities they desire. An efficient allocation of resources requires that each product be produced up to the point at which the *marginal social benefit* is equal to the *marginal social cost*. Pure competition ensures this outcome. Thus, we can say that pure competition achieves both production efficiency and allocative efficiency in long-run equilibrium.

KEY TERMS

Allocative efficiency
Economic profit
Firm
Industry

Long-run equilibrium
Marginal social benefit
Marginal social cost
Normal profit

Price taker
Production efficiency
Shut down

STUDY QUESTIONS

Fill in the Blanks

1. A purely competitive firm is sometimes

   described as a(n) _____ because it must accept the price dictated by
   the market.

2. The demand curve of the purely competi-

   tive firm is a(n) _____ line at
   the price determined in the market.

3. To be classified as a purely competitive industry, all firms must sell

   _____ products.

4. Patents and large investment require-

   ments are examples of _____ .

5. The purely competitive firm's supply

   curve is its _____ curve.

6. When the owners of a firm are earning as
   much as they could expect to earn elsewhere, they are earning a(n)

   _____ profit.

7. If a competitive firm wants to maximize its
   profits, it should continue to produce additional units as long as

   _____ is greater than or

   equal to _____ .

8. If economic profits exist in the short run,

   they will tend to be _____

   in the long run as firms _____
   the industry and depress market price.

9. If losses exist in the short run, firms tend

   to _____ the industry in

the long run. This will reduce market

_____ and help to push
price back up.

10. When $P = MC$, _____ effi-
    ciency exists; when a firm produces its
    product at minimum ATC,

    _____ efficiency exists.

Multiple Choice

1. Which of the following statements was
   made by a person in a purely competitive
   industry?
   a) "We can charge more than our rivals
   because our product is so much better."
   b) "I think we can count on earning those
   profits at least until our patent expires."
   c) "If we cut back on our output, we
   should be able to drive the price up
   significantly."
   d) "If we don't charge the same price as
   everyone else, we're not going to sell
   anything."

2. Is the average pizza restaurant in a large
   metropolitan area a price taker?
   a) Yes; there are a large number of sellers,
   and they all sell the same thing, so they
   must be price takers.
   b) No; there are a large number of sellers,
   but they each sell somewhat different
   products, so they can charge different
   prices.
   c) Yes; there are a large number of sellers,
   so it must be easy to enter this industry.
   d) No; we can't live without pizza, so
   these restaurants can charge any price
   they want.

3. Purely competitive firms are price takers
   because
   a) they are too small to significantly alter
   market price through their output
   decisions.
   b) they produce identical products and
   therefore cannot charge a premium for
   their product.
   c) there are no barriers to entering a
   purely competitive industry.

   d) All of the above
   e) Both a and b

4. Suppose we discover that most dry-
   cleaning establishments earn something
   approximating a normal profit. Economists would attribute this finding to the
   fact that
   a) all dry cleaners provide essentially the
   same service.
   b) it's relatively easy and inexpensive to
   start these businesses.
   c) there are a large number of these firms.
   d) All of the above

5. In pure competition, which of the following is true?
   a) The firm's demand curve is described
   as perfectly inelastic.
   b) The firm's marginal revenue is equal to
   the prevailing market price.
   c) Firms always earn an economic profit
   when they are in long-run equilibrium.
   d) All of the above
   e) Both b and c

Refer to the following diagram in answering question 6.

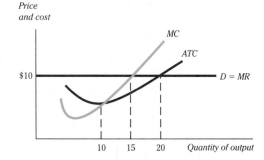

6. The firm depicted should
   a) produce 10 units and maximize its profit.
   b) produce 15 units and maximize its profit.
   c) produce 10 units and minimize its loss.
   d) produce 20 units and break even.

   Refer to the following diagram in answering question 7.

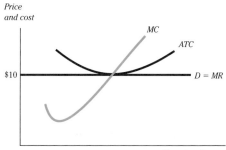

Quantity of output

7. The firm depicted is
   a) facing a loss.
   b) making an economic profit.
   c) making a normal profit.
   d) about to go out of business.

   Use the following diagram in answering questions 8–11.

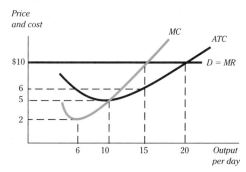

8. The firm depicted is
   a) earning an economic profit.
   b) incurring a loss.
   c) earning a normal profit.

9. The firm's profit-maximizing (loss-minimizing) output is
   a) 6 units.
   b) 10 units.

   c) 15 units.
   d) 20 units.

10. By producing the optimal output, this firm will
    a) earn a profit of $50.
    b) earn a profit of $60.
    c) earn a profit of $100.
    d) earn a normal profit.
    e) incur a loss of $50.

11. In the long run,
    a) price will be driven down to $5 by the entrance of additional firms.
    b) price will remain $10, but the firm will earn only a normal profit.
    c) firms will exit this industry until the remaining firms earn a normal profit.
    d) price will be driven down to $2 by the entrance of additional firms.

    Use the following diagram in answering questions 12–14.

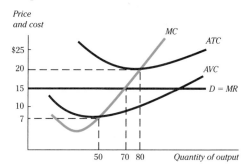

12. At the prevailing market price of $15, this firm would
    a) earn an economic profit.
    b) earn a normal profit.
    c) incur a loss but continue to operate.
    d) shut down.

13. Long-run equilibrium will be achieved when
    a) the entrance of firms reduces the market price to $7.
    b) the exit of firms reduces the market price to $7.
    c) the entrance of firms raises the market price to $20.
    d) the exit of firms raises the market price to $20.

14. Which of the following is *not* a true statement?
    a) At a price of $20, this firm would produce 80 units and earn zero economic profit.
    b) At a price of $10, this firm would produce somewhere between 50 and 70 units.
    c) At a price of $6, this firm would shut down—produce nothing.
    d) At a price of $18, this firm would produce more than 80 units.

15. The Lazy Z Ranch is a purely competitive firm producing hogs. Its owner anticipates that at the output where $MR = MC$, the firm's total costs will be $500,000, its total variable costs will be $300,000, and the firm will earn $250,000 in revenue. This firm should
    a) raise the price of its hogs.
    b) shut down to minimize its loss.
    c) continue to produce the present output to minimize its loss.
    d) expand its output.

16. If the firms in a competitive industry earn economic profits,
    a) additional firms will enter the industry, and the market supply curve will shift to the left.
    b) firms will decide to leave the industry, and the market supply curve will shift to the left.
    c) additional firms will enter the industry, and the market supply curve will shift to the right.
    d) some firms will leave the industry, and the market supply curve will shift to the right.

17. Suppose the firms in a purely competitive industry are in a long-run equilibrium when the industry experiences a reduction in demand. Which of the following will occur?
    a) In the short run, firms will earn profits and will expand output; in the long run, additional firms will enter the industry until only a normal profit is earned.

    b) In the short run, firms will incur losses but will continue to produce the same output; in the long run, firms will leave the industry until only a normal profit is earned.
    c) In the short run, firms will earn profits and will contract output; in the long run, firms will leave the industry until the remaining firms can earn an economic profit.
    d) In the short run, firms will incur losses and will contract output; in the long run, firms will leave the industry until the remaining firms can earn a normal profit.

18. If the firms in an industry are experiencing short-run losses, they should
    a) immediately leave the industry and enter a different, more profitable industry.
    b) continue to operate provided that the prevailing market price is higher than the firm's average variable cost.
    c) shut down and wait for market conditions to improve.
    d) shut down provided that the prevailing market price is less than the firm's average total cost.

19. Suppose that a firm experienced a doubling of its total fixed costs while prevailing market price did not change. Under those conditions the firm would
    a) produce less output and experience lower profits or larger losses.
    b) produce more output and experience higher profits or smaller losses.
    c) produce the same output but experience higher profits or smaller losses.
    d) produce the same output but experience lower profits or larger losses.

20. Which of the following would not cause a competitive firm to increase its output?
    a) An increase in industry demand
    b) A downward shift of the marginal cost curve
    c) An increase in the market price
    d) A wage hike that shifted the marginal cost curve upward

Problems and Questions for Discussion

1. Imagine an industry composed of a very large number of relatively small firms selling identical products. If substantial entry barriers made it difficult for *additional* firms to enter this industry, would the existing firms still be regarded as price takers?

2. Even when an industry fails to meet all the requirements for pure competition, consumers will be well served if low barriers make it easy for additional firms to enter the industry. Explain.

3. One reason for the low prices of handheld calculators and personal computers may be the fat profits earned by early producers. Explain.

4. Can you think of any undesirable aspects of pure competition? From the consumer's standpoint? From the producer's standpoint?

5. In 1997 cranberry farmers in the United States were a very happy group. Cranberry prices had soared to new highs, and farmers were enjoying record profits. But a few years later, the same group was complaining about low prices and dismal profits. Is this reversal of fortunes consistent with the competitive model? Try to represent it graphically.

6. Would it make sense for a competitive firm to advertise? What about a trade association representing the members of a competitive industry, an association of cattle ranchers or hog farmers, for example. Would advertisements make sense for such an association? Why might an individual farmer choose *not* to join this association?

7. Why would a firm continue to operate even though it is incurring a loss? When should it decide to shut down? What is the difference between *shutting down* and *leaving the industry*?

8. In agriculture, there is something known as the *cattle and hog cycle.* This cycle involves recurring instances of high prices giving way to low prices that are then replaced by high prices again in an ongoing cycle. Can the competitive model help to explain this cycle?

9. In long-run equilibrium the purely competitive firm is forced to produce where price equals minimum *ATC*. Why is this good news for consumers?

10. What is meant by allocative efficiency? Why must an industry produce at the output where supply is equal to demand for resources to be allocated efficiently?

11. Farmers are always searching for some new crop or animal that will deliver consistently high prices and profits. Catfish were once caught; now most of them come from catfish farms. Alligators were only found in the wild; now they are raised for their hides (and meat). Even animals as exotic as buffalos and emus have been bred by farmers. Alas, none of these products have proven to be the source of consistently high prices and profits. Can the competitive model shed any light on this problem?

12. In 1975 corn farmers in the United States went on a crusade to limit corn output. Leaders of the crusade went farm to farm, trying to convince fellow corn farmers to agree to plant 10 percent fewer acres of corn than in the past. But relatively few farmers went along, and the effort was largely a failure. What was the purpose of this crusade? Why did those involved want to limit corn output? Why do you think so few farmers were willing to join in this effort?

ANSWER KEY

Fill in the Blanks

1. price taker
2. horizontal
3. identical
4. barriers to entry

5. marginal cost
6. normal
7. marginal revenue; marginal cost

8. eliminated; enter
9. exit; supply
10. allocative; production

Multiple Choice

1. d	5. b	9. c	13. d	17. d
2. b	6. b	10. b	14. d	18. b
3. e	7. c	11. a	15. b	19. d
4. b	8. a	12. c	16. c	20. d

Price Searching: The Firm with Market Power

1. Define market power and discuss its sources.
2. Distinguish between a price searcher and a price taker.
3. Describe a price searcher's demand and marginal revenue curves.
4. Describe how a price searcher determines the profit-maximizing price and output.
5. Define price discrimination, and explain why some firms employ the practice, while others do not.
6. Evaluate graphically the extent of a price searcher's profit or loss.
7. Discuss the impact of barriers to entry on the long-run profitability of price searchers.
8. Explain why price searchers distort the allocation of scarce resources.
9. Explain what is meant by economies/diseconomies of scale and how they may influence the number of sellers that survive in a particular industry.

In the world of pure competition the individual firm is a price taker—it has no pricing discretion of its own because price is determined by the impersonal forces of supply and demand. The individual seller manipulates only production output, deciding how much or how little to offer for sale at the given price.

We saw in Chapter 6 that wheat farmers, cattle ranchers, and many other agricultural producers are price takers. But there are few examples of true price takers outside agriculture. In fact, most sellers in the U.S. economy possess a degree of pricing discretion or **market power**, some ability to influence the market price of their products. In this chapter we examine how firms acquire market power and how these firms select the prices they will charge for their products.

We'll explore the circumstances under which firms find it profitable to charge different prices to different customers and discuss why this practice is not universal. We'll discover why some firms with market power are able to earn long-run profits, while others are not, and we'll consider how the existence of market power can distort the allocation of scarce resources. The appendix to this chapter goes on to explore some pricing techniques employed by businesses and to evaluate the extent to which these techniques make use of economic theory.

THE ACQUISITION OF MARKET POWER

Recalling the plight of the purely competitive firm can help us understand the sources of market power. Consider the situation facing a Kansas wheat farmer. If farmer Brown wants a higher price for wheat, there is little he can do. If he attempts to charge more than the market price, he will sell nothing because his wheat is identical to that offered by other sellers. And he can't drive up wheat prices by planting less (and thereby reducing supply) because his output is only a drop in the bucket and would never be missed.

Most firms are not like Kansas wheat farmers; most firms *are* able to influence price in one or both of these ways. A firm may acquire market power (1) through **product differentiation**, distinguishing its product from similar products offered by other sellers, and/or (2) by gaining control of a significant fraction of total industry output. Sellers with either or both of these abilities can exert some influence on the market price of their product; sellers that possess neither ability are powerless to influence price.

Product Differentiation as a Source of Market Power

Product differentiation promotes market power by convincing buyers that a particular firm's product is unique or superior and therefore worth a higher price than the products offered by competitors. By claiming superiority, manufacturers of brand-name aspirin tablets manage to obtain prices that are substantially higher than those charged by sellers of generic and store-brand analgesics. By associating uniqueness with status, the makers of designer-label jeans are able to sell their product at prices much higher than nameless jeans can command.

Sellers can differentiate their products in a wide variety of ways. Some product differentiation is based on real, albeit sometimes slight, product differences; in other cases the essential differentiation is created by advertising and promotional efforts. Both types of product differentiation allow the seller to distinguish its product from the competition and thereby acquire pricing discretion that is not available to the purely competitive firm.

Control over Supply as a Source of Market Power

Firms that cannot differentiate their products successfully must turn elsewhere to acquire market power. Sellers of standardized commodities such as oil and steel can gain pricing discretion by controlling a significant share of the industry output of that product. As you already know, whenever supply is reduced, price tends to rise. When a firm produces a significant share of the total industry output, it may be able to restrict supply and thereby drive up price.

Controlling supply is a relatively easy matter when an industry is made up of a single firm, a **monopoly**. Under these circumstances, the monopolist's decision alone determines the amount of output for sale. That's the situation, for example, in the case of the cholesterol-lowering drug Lipitor, the best-selling drug in the world ($12.7 billion in sales in 2007). Pfizer's patent on atorvastatin, the active ingredient in Lipitor, gives it a monopoly on sales of atorvastatin and sole right to determine the level of output.[1] Microsoft Corporation is in a similar situation; its Windows operating system has become standard for computer users and is also protected by patents. But most products are produced by more than one firm, and that makes the task of controlling output more difficult. One firm's decision to supply less (and thereby drive up price) can be offset by another firm's decision to supply more.

Firms that are determined to restrict supply can sometimes avoid these offsetting output decisions through an arrangement known as a *cartel*. A **cartel** is a group of producers acting together to control output (supply) and the price of their product. Although cartels are illegal in the United States (and therefore must be kept secret to avoid prosecution), several international cartels exist and operate in a relatively open manner. Perhaps the best known of these is the Organization of Petroleum Exporting Countries (OPEC). This group of primarily Middle Eastern oil-producing nations attempts to control the output of its members to influence the price of oil and maximize their joint profits.[2] In the 1970s the cartel controlled a substantial fraction of the world's oil production and was able to increase prices substantially (from about $2 a barrel to more than $30) by simply cutting back on production. In the early 1980s the cartel's control over price began to slip as conservation reduced the demand for oil and

---

[1] There are cholesterol-reducing drugs in addition to Lipitor. Pfizer's monopoly is thus limited to a certain category of cholesterol-reducing drugs—those containing atorvastatin, a particular type of "statin" drug. This limited monopoly has been quite good for Pfizer. In 2007, it was estimated that Lipitor accounted for about 40 percent of Pfizer's profit—in excess of $3 billion. In 2008, generic versions of some other cholesterol drugs began to eat into Lipitor's market share. And in 2011, Lipitor's patent expires. Pfizer's monopoly is on the decline.
[2] OPEC was established in 1960 by Iran, Iraq, Kuwait, Saudi Arabia, and Venezuela. Six more countries have joined the cartel since then: Qatar, Indonesia, Libya, Algeria, Nigeria, and the United Arab Emirates.

additional supplies were discovered. This, in turn, led to a breakdown in cooperation among OPEC members, a breakdown that resulted in additional supplies of oil and still lower oil prices. Although OPEC tried to regain control of oil prices throughout the 1980s and 1990s, they were unsuccessful. But in 1998, that began to change. Improved relations between key member countries made it easier for OPEC leaders to gain the cooperation needed to reduce supply and raise oil prices. In the period since 2000, the OPEC cartel has been quite successful in maintaining high prices, aided until 2008 by expanding economies throughout the world. In 2008, a worldwide recession caused the demand for oil to plummet, and oil producers saw the price of oil fall from a high of $145 a barrel to about $32 a barrel. The article on page 196, "Oil Cartel Keeps Cuts on Track," looks at OPEC's efforts to stem the free fall in oil prices. Read it to learn more about the workings of this important cartel.[3]

Cartels are not the only method by which groups of firms attempt to limit supply and maintain high prices. In fact, when an industry is composed of just a few firms, an **oligopoly**, the mere recognition that the firms have a joint interest in limiting output may be all that is necessary to promote that behavior. (This possibility is discussed in Chapter 8.) When cartels and voluntary cooperation fail, firms can sometimes elicit government help to control the supply of a product. For instance, U.S. automakers successfully lobbied Congress for restrictions limiting the number of new foreign automobiles permitted into the United States. By limiting supply, these restrictions help domestic producers maintain high prices. Similar campaigns have been responsible for limiting the imports of shoes, peanuts, lumber, and numerous other products, all leading to higher prices for U.S. consumers.

Degrees of Market Power   It stands to reason that all firms would like to possess as much market power as possible. But some firms succeed to a greater extent than others. If your college or university is served by a single bookstore, that seller may have significant market power. Many communities are served by a single producer of electric power, or a single newspaper, or perhaps a single airline. In each of these instances, the firm is the entire industry, giving it complete control over the industry's output and significant market power.

Few firms possess the potential market power enjoyed by a monopolist utility company or the single airline serving a small community. The neighborhood

---

[3] Although OPEC is probably the best-known example of a cartel, there are others. For instance, the De Beers diamond cartel controls more than 65 percent of the world's rough (uncut) diamonds and has used that control to limit supply and maintain high diamond prices. And the Trans-Atlantic Conferences—a little-known shipping cartel—sets rates on the tens of billions of dollars of cargo transported by ships. Although these cartels have lasted for decades, they are now threatened by new suppliers and defections by their membership.

Use Your Economic Reasoning

Oil Cartel Keeps Cuts on Track

BY JAD MOUAWAD

After months of gradually closing the oil spigot, members of the OPEC cartel have managed to stop the slide in oil prices—at least for now. Showing an unusual degree of discipline, members of the Organization of the Petroleum Exporting Countries have slashed their output by more than three million barrels a day in recent months as they sought to put a floor under oil prices, which have fallen by $100 a barrel since last summer. That is about 75 percent of the production cuts pledged by members of the cartel since September. The cuts have been led by Saudi Arabia, the world's top exporter, which has trimmed its production to eight million barrels a day this month, down from nearly 10 million barrels over the summer.

In September, OPEC producers vowed to reduce their output by 4.2 million barrels a day, or about 5 percent of global production. "Compliance has been extremely high," said Kevin Norrish, an oil analyst with Barclays Capital in London. "Most OPEC countries have done most of what they'd pledged to do."

Oil lost 70 percent of its value in recent months as the global economy fizzled and oil consumption fell. In the United States, the world's biggest consumer, demand has dropped nearly 8 percent, or 1.6 million barrels a day, from a year ago. Most experts believe global oil consumption will decline in 2009 for the second straight year. But OPEC's policy seems to be catching up with the economic downturn. After hitting a peak above $145 a barrel in July, and falling to $32 a barrel by December, their lowest level since the end of 2003, oil prices have stabilized in recent weeks. As the latest OPEC cuts have influenced the markets, prices have been trading in a range from $35 to $45 a barrel.

OPEC's success has created the prospect of a rebound in prices—most oil-producing countries want prices well above $70 a barrel. But such a rebound could hobble the world economy further, making an eventual recovery more difficult. Already, retail gasoline in the United States has bottomed out and begun to

dry-cleaning establishment and the nearby pizzeria also have market power, but not very much. These establishments can charge somewhat higher prices than their competitors because they offer convenient locations and/or slightly different products, but their prices cannot be much higher because their products are very similar. In Chapter 8 we'll take a closer look at the degrees of market power that exist in different types of industries. For now, the important thing to remember is that most firms possess at least some pricing discretion; they are not price takers.

rise. It is still far below the high of $4.11 a gallon in July, but is up about 20 cents over the last month, to a national average of $1.86 a gallon. On Friday, oil prices rose $2.80 a barrel, or 6.41 percent, to settle at $46.47. While that is well below last summer's level, it remains relatively high by historical standards. . . .

The OPEC cartel's discipline reflects a more forceful stance taken by Saudi Arabia, the group's most powerful producer, which has taken the lead in aggressively cutting production in recent weeks. The country's oil minister, Ali al-Naimi, said the kingdom would go even beyond its OPEC pledges with a unilateral cut that would bring its output next month below its official target. Analysts expect the kingdom to reduce its output by an additional 300,000 barrels a day below its OPEC quota. "We are working hard to bring the market in balance," Mr. Naimi said a few days ago in New Delhi. . . .

The last time the cartel met, in December, its members pledged to reduce production by 2.2 million barrels a day. It was the group's third agreement in four months to cut its output, after pledges of 500,000 barrels a day in September and 1.5 million barrels a day in October. But not everyone believes that OPEC's actions can keep prices from falling further, especially if the global economy continues to worsen.

OPEC has announced 12 quota reductions since 1993, and 80 percent of the time the cartel succeeded in defending a floor for oil prices, according to an analysis by Deutsche Bank. The times when the cartel failed was when global economic growth was falling sharply, as in 1998 and 2001. OPEC's president, Jose Maria Botelho de Vasconcelos, has said he expected oil prices to eventually recover to around $75 a barrel this year as a result of OPEC's actions. . . .

1. The price of oil dropped from about $145 a barrel in July 2008 to about $32 a barrel in December of that year. What caused that drop? Represent it graphically.
2. How did the OPEC cartel "manage to stop the slide in oil prices"? Represent their actions on the graph you created to answer question 1. Why is the OPEC cartel able to influence price, while the competitive firm was not?
3. The article notes that "compliance [by cartel members] has been extremely high." In other words, most of the members are cutting back on oil production—are doing their share to reduce OPEC's daily output. Why is compliance important? What would happen if some members reduced output, but others refused (or increased their output)?

PRICE SEARCHING

Firms with pricing discretion are sometimes described as **price searchers**, which means that although they have some freedom in setting prices, they still must search for the profit-maximizing price. A price searcher may possess substantial market power (as does the local utility company) or very little (as does the local pizzeria), but all price searchers have one thing in common: Unlike price takers, who will lose all their customers if they raise their prices, price

When a local utility company is the sole source of a community's electricity, that firm will possess substantial market power.

searchers can charge more and still retain some customers. Conversely, although price takers can sell any quantity they desire at the market price, price searchers must reduce price to sell more.

Consider as a hypothetical example High Tech Inc., a small manufacturer of computer desks. Although a number of firms produce such furniture, we can be sure that if High Tech raises the price of its desks, it won't lose all its customers as long as it keeps its price within reason. Some customers will prefer the quality or design of the High Tech desks to those offered by other sellers. Other customers may be swayed by the firm's product warranty or by its record for prompt delivery. Still others may be influenced by the firm's policy of accepting old desks in trade or by the variety of payment plans it offers. For all these reasons and others, High Tech will still sell some desks despite the price increase. But it won't be able to sell the same quantity; it will have to choose between selling more desks at a lower price or fewer desks at a higher price. That's the fundamental dilemma faced by all price searchers.

The Price Searcher's Demand Curve

Because price searchers have to reduce their prices to sell a higher quantity, they must face downward-sloping demand curves, not the horizontal demand curves

EXHIBIT 7.1

The Price Searcher's Demand Curve

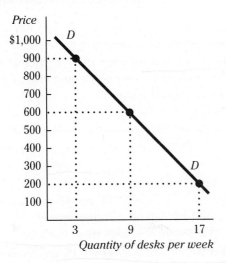

A price searcher can select any price it wants, but it must accept the quantity that results from that price. For example, High Tech can charge $900 per desk and sell three desks each week; it can charge $600 per desk and sell nine desks a week; or it can charge $200 and sell 17 desks a week.

confronting price takers. Exhibit 7.1 depicts the demand curve facing our hypo-thetical desk manufacturer. It shows that at $900 a desk, High Tech will sell only three desks each week. At $600 it will sell nine desks a week. Of course, at $200 a desk, sales will be even higher—17 desks a week. Although the price searcher can select any price it wants, it cannot choose a high price ($900 a desk) and ex-pect to sell a high quantity (such as 17 desks a week) because that combination is not a point on the demand curve. Thus, even a price searcher finds that its ac-tions are constrained by its demand curve; it cannot choose a price without be-ing locked into a quantity. The firm's task, then, is to decide which of the price-quantity combinations it prefers to maximize its profit.

THE PROFIT-MAXIMIZATION RULE

For a price searcher the profit-maximization rule is essentially the same as it is for a price taker: produce where marginal revenue equals marginal cost. The difference between a price searcher and a price taker is not in the logic used to maximize profits but in the environment confronting the seller. The price taker has no control over price, and so it uses the profit-maximization rule solely to determine the optimal level of output. The price searcher, on the other hand, uses this rule to determine both output and price.

Calculating Marginal Revenue

The first step in determining the profit-maximizing price and quantity is finding the price searcher's marginal revenue curve. Because a price searcher faces a downward-sloping demand curve, it must reduce price to sell more. Consequently, the marginal revenue that the price searcher gains by selling an additional unit of output will always be *less* than the selling price of the product (not equal to the price, as under pure competition), and the firm's marginal revenue curve will lie inside its demand curve. Because this idea is conveyed best with an example, let's consider Exhibit 7.2.

The first two columns of Exhibit 7.2 represent the demand schedule for desks that was graphed in Exhibit 7.1. You can see that at a price of $1,000, only one desk will be sold each week. At a price of $950, two desks will be sold each week, and total revenue would increase to $1,900. What will be the marginal revenue from selling a second desk? (Remember, marginal revenue is the additional revenue gained by selling one more unit.) The correct answer is $900 ($1,900 − $1,000 = $900), $50 less than the $950 selling price. This relationship—marginal revenue being less than price—holds at all price levels.[4] To understand why, we need to consider the price reduction in more detail.

When High Tech reduces the price of computer desks from $1,000 to $950, it allows the first customer—the one who would have paid $1,000—to acquire the product for $950. In return the seller manages to attract an additional customer who is willing to pay $950 but won't pay $1,000. The marginal revenue from the second desk is $900—the $950 the firm gains by selling one more unit *minus* the $50 lost by having to reduce the price on the first unit. Because marginal revenue is less than price, a price searcher's marginal revenue curve will always lie inside, or below, its demand curve (see Exhibit 7.3).

The Profit-Maximizing Price and Quantity

To maximize its profit (or minimize its loss), High Tech must produce at the output where marginal revenue is equal to marginal cost. This rule permits the firm to continue producing additional units only as long as those units add more to revenue than to costs. Exhibit 7.3 graphs High Tech's demand and marginal revenue curves along with its marginal cost curve. Note that the marginal cost curve has the U shape introduced in Chapter 5; marginal cost declines initially and then rises as output is increased.

---

[4] Note that marginal revenue will always be equal to price for the first unit of output. For all subsequent units, marginal revenue will be less than price.

EXHIBIT 7.2

Marginal Revenue for a Price Searcher

PRICE PER UNIT	QUANTITY DEMANDED	TOTAL REVENUE	MARGINAL REVENUE
$1,050	0	$ 0	
1,000	1	1,000	$1,000
950	2	1,900	900
900	3	2,700	800
850	4	3,400	700
800	5	4,000	600
750	6	4,500	500
700	7	4,900	400
650	8	5,200	300
600	9	5,400	200
550	10	5,500	100
500	11	5,500	0
450	12	5,400	−100

How many desks should High Tech produce and sell to maximize its profits? You can tell by studying the graph (or the table accompanying it) that the profit-maximizing (loss-minimizing) output is seven units per week. When output is less than seven units a week, marginal revenue exceeds marginal cost. For instance, the marginal revenue from the fifth unit of output is $600, and the marginal cost of that unit is only $300. Thus, High Tech will be $300 better off if it produces and sells that unit. The sixth unit doesn't make as great a contribution to the firm, but the marginal revenue of $500 still exceeds the marginal cost of $340, and so the unit should be produced. The seventh unit adds $400 to revenue and $400 to cost; thus, seven units represent the profit-maximizing (loss-minimizing) output: the output at which $MR = MC$. Because all subsequent units would add more to cost than to revenue, their sale would either reduce the firm's profit or increase its loss.[5]

Once the profit-maximizing output has been determined, the profit-maximizing price can be discovered by drawing a line directly up to the firm's

---

[5] In this example the firm will earn the same profit (or incur the same loss) whether it sells six or seven units of output. The firm wants to operate where $MR = MC$, not because it benefits from the last unit sold but because it benefits from each unit up to that point.

EXHIBIT 7.3

Determining the Profit-Maximizing Price

PRICE PER UNIT	QUANTITY OF DESKS	MARGINAL REVENUE	MARGINAL COST
$800	5	$600	$300
750	6	500	340
700	7	400	400
650	8	300	480
600	9	200	580

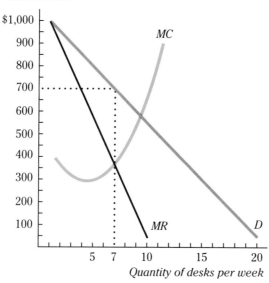

Price and cost

Quantity of desks per week

All firms maximize their profits (or minimize their losses) by producing the output at which marginal revenue is equal to marginal cost. In this example the profit-maximizing output is seven units. Once the profit-maximizing output has been determined, the profit-maximizing price can be discovered by drawing a line directly up to the firm's demand curve and over to the vertical axis. In our example the profit-maximizing price is $700 per desk.

demand curve and over to the vertical axis. Remember, the demand curve shows the amount that consumers are willing to purchase at various prices. If we know the price, we can tell how much will be purchased. Conversely, if we know the quantity (output), we can use the demand curve to determine the maximum price the firm can charge and still sell that amount of output. In our example High Tech should charge a price of $700 per desk; that's the firm's profit-maximizing price.[6]

---

[6] In many real-world situations, firms do not possess precise information about their demand and marginal cost curves, and so they find it difficult to employ the $MC = MR$ pricing rule in precisely the manner described here. The appendix to this chapter, "Pricing in Practice," examines the pricing techniques employed by these firms.

A Digression on Price Discrimination

In the preceding example we have assumed that there is a single profit-maximizing price, and we'll return to that assumption in just a moment. But in some instances there is more than one profit-maximizing price. **Price discrimination** exists when firms charge different consumers different prices for the same product.

Surgeons and lawyers and car dealers often practice "individual" price discrimination. They charge virtually every customer a different price, a price based largely on the customer's ability to pay (but limited, at least in the case of automobiles, by how much that customer has "shopped around" and become informed about the prices charged elsewhere). To illustrate, suppose that Honest John's Autos is selling the Rampage automobile. Assume also that the following represents a portion of the demand schedule for Honest John's automobiles.

PRICE	QUANTITY
$20,000	1
19,000	2
18,000	3
17,000	4
16,000	5

As you can see, only one consumer is willing to pay Honest John $20,000 for a Rampage. A second consumer won't pay $20,000 but is willing to pay $19,000. (Note that two consumers are willing to buy automobiles at a price of $19,000; one is the first consumer, who would pay $20,000.[7]) A third consumer won't pay $19,000 but will pay $18,000.

Car dealers that practice price discrimination want their sales personnel to obtain the highest price that each consumer will pay. So the salesperson would try to extract $20,000 from the first customer, $19,000 from the second, $18,000 from the third, and so on. Honest John would be willing to continue selling additional units as long as the price he could obtain was at least equal to the marginal cost of an additional vehicle. (Notice that when firms discriminate, the marginal revenue the firm receives from the sale of an additional unit is *equal* to its selling price, not less than its selling price, as it was for the nondiscriminating price searcher.) For instance, if the marginal cost of an additional Rampage is $16,500, Honest John would be willing to sell the fourth vehicle (which adds $17,000 to his revenue) but not the fifth (which contributes only $16,000).

---

[7] This assumes that each consumer buys only one automobile.

It is unlikely that the salesperson would actually be able to obtain the maximum price a consumer would be willing to pay. But effective sales personnel may come close. Sales reps who started at the sticker price on the vehicle and then haggled, giving in only when necessary, might approximate this solution. And, of course, that would mean more profit for the dealer than could be obtained by selling all four of these vehicles at a price low enough to convince the fourth buyer to participate.

Another form of price discrimination is "group" price discrimination. This is a situation in which a firm charges different prices to different *categories* of consumers. For example, movie theaters commonly charge different ticket prices to adults, students, and senior citizens. And we'd all like to order from the children's menu when we're short on cash. Even some telephone companies practice price discrimination, charging one price for long-distance service during the day (when most calls are business-related) and a lower price in the evening (when we make our personal calls).

The purpose of group price discrimination is similar to the purpose of individual price discrimination—to obtain the highest price possible from each category of consumer. Consider, for instance, the different ticket prices that airlines charge business and vacation travelers. The airlines recognize that business travelers usually *must* travel by air; they cannot afford the time involved in a lengthy automobile trip. In addition, many of these trips arise on short notice, so the business executive has no other alternative. These factors mean that the business traveler's demand curve for plane travel is less elastic—less price-sensitive—than the vacation traveler, who usually has a more flexible time schedule. By charging business travelers higher fares, the airlines maximize their profits from that group without discouraging travel by vacationers.[8]

Why doesn't everyone practice price discrimination? There are two primary reasons. First, it takes time, and time is money. Think about our car dealer again. It can take hours for the salesperson to negotiate with a customer and arrive at the price that particular customer will pay. That time expenditure makes sense in the case of big-ticket items such as cars and motor homes and boats. But it doesn't make sense for milk and clothing and most of the items we buy every day. (Even the sellers of big-ticket items may prefer to charge everyone a uniform price—if you allow them to do it. But consumers can turn the table on sellers by asking them to negotiate when they'd really prefer not to. Read "For Champions of Haggling, No Price Tag Is Sacred," on page 208, to learn more.)

A second reason firms may not practice price discrimination is that they may be unable to prevent consumers from reselling items that they can buy

---

[8] Airlines separate business and vacation travelers by requiring that the lower-priced tickets (intended for vacationers) be purchased well in advance and/or that the traveler stay over at least one Saturday night before returning. These are requirements that most business travelers are unable or unwilling to meet.

more cheaply than other customers. For instance, suppose that the Ajax TV Center was charging regular customers $300 for a TV set but allowing senior citizens to buy the same set for $250. Under these circumstances we might expect to see some seniors buying TV sets in large quantities and reselling them at a profit. That would be a nice way for those senior citizens to earn extra cash, but it would make it very difficult for Ajax to sell any television sets at the higher price. The point is that when we can't prevent a product's resale, we generally offer that product at the same price to everyone. Because most markets are characterized by uniform pricing, we will now return to our single-price model.

EVALUATING THE SHORT-RUN PROFIT OR LOSS

As we discovered in Chapter 6, producing where $MR = MC$ does not ensure a profit. It ensures only that the firm will do as well as possible in any short-run situation. Recall that we find profits by subtracting total costs from total revenue. In our present example we can't tell whether High Tech Inc. is earning a profit or incurring a loss because we've focused entirely on marginal values.

To compute High Tech's short-run profit or loss, we need to know the firm's total revenue and its total costs. Exhibit 7.4 shows our hypothetical price searcher in three different situations. In case (a) the firm is earning a profit. As in the previous chapter, the amount of the profit can be determined by comparing total revenue with total cost. Total revenue is equal to $4,900 (the $700 selling price × 7 units—the profit-maximizing output). Total cost is equal to $4,200 (the ATC of $600 × 7 units). This leaves the firm with an economic profit of $700 ($4,900 − $4,200 = $700).

Case (b) finds our price searcher earning only a normal profit. You can see in the diagram that the MC curve intersects the MR curve at an output of six desks. At that output the profit-maximizing price would be $600, so that total revenue would be $3,600 ($600 × 6 units). Because the ATC curve is tangent to the demand curve at $600, ATC must also be $600 when the firm is producing six desks. Therefore, the firm's total cost is $3,600 (the ATC of $600 × 6 units). This means that the firm is earning zero economic profit ($3,600 − $3,600 = $0), or a normal profit. Recall that a normal profit is acceptable; the owners of the business are earning as much as they could expect to earn if they invested their time and money elsewhere.

Case (c) depicts the price searcher facing a short-run economic loss (earning less than a normal profit). At the profit-maximizing (loss-minimizing) output of five desks, the firm's total cost of $3,250 ($ATC$ of $650 × 5 units) exceeds its total revenue of $2,750 (the $550 selling price × 5 units). This results in a loss

EXHIBIT 7.4

Calculating the Short-Run Profit or Loss

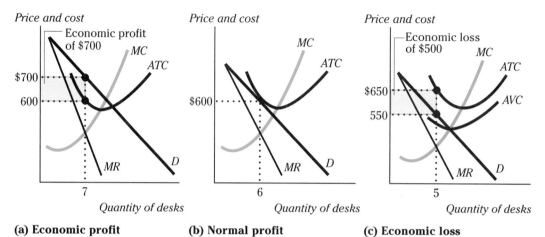

Case (a): When the profit-maximizing price is above *ATC*, the price searcher will earn an economic profit. Case (b): When the price is exactly equal to *ATC*, the price searcher will earn a zero economic profit, or a normal profit. Case (c): When the price is less than *ATC*, the firm will incur an economic loss—it will earn less than a normal profit.

of $500 ($3,250 − $2,750 = $500). Note, however, that the selling price of $550 exceeds the firm's average variable cost of approximately $500, and so the firm should continue to operate rather than shut down. Because *P* exceeds *AVC* by $50, each of the five units produced will contribute $50 toward paying the firm's fixed costs. Through continued operation, the firm reduces its loss by $250. Of course, if *AVC* exceeded price (for example, if the average variable cost curve were positioned where the *ATC* curve is located at present), the firm would minimize its loss by shutting down.

BARRIERS TO ENTRY AND LONG-RUN PROFITS

We've seen that in the short run, price searchers may gain economic profits, may earn a normal profit, or may even sustain a loss. But how do they do in the long run? Is it possible for price searchers to earn economic profits in the long run, or is a normal profit the best that can be expected? (All firms, whether price searchers or price takers, must earn at least a normal profit in the long run, or the owners will sell out and reinvest their money where a normal return is possible.)

If a price searcher is earning an economic profit in the short run, its ability to continue earning that profit in the long run depends on the extent of the barriers to entering that industry. Recall from Chapter 6 that barriers to entry are obstacles that discourage or prevent firms from entering an industry. These obstacles include patent restrictions, large investments requirements, and restrictive licensing regulations.

Some price searchers exist in industries with substantial entry barriers—prescription medicine and aircraft manufacturing, for example. Others exist in industries with very modest barriers—shoe retailing, rug cleaning, and hair styling (beauty salons) to cite a few. Because entry barriers differ from industry to industry, we can't generalize about the long-run fate of price searchers as we could about the fate of price takers. (Recall that a normal profit is the *best* that a price taker can expect in the long run. Because there are no significant barriers to entering purely competitive industries, any short-run profits will be eliminated in the long run, as additional firms enter and drive down prices.)

If price searchers are protected by substantial barriers to entry, short-run profits can turn into long-run profits. For instance, it is estimated that Hoffman–La Roche of Switzerland earned multi*billion* dollar profits from the worldwide sale of its Valium and Librium tranquilizers, drugs that were protected by patents and therefore could not be duplicated by competitors[9] Although profits of this magnitude are clearly exceptional, they indicate the impact of entry barriers. In the absence of substantial barriers, we expect economic profits to attract additional sellers into the market. This leads to price cutting and other forms of competition that have the potential to eliminate economic profits in the long run.

Thus, the fact that a price searcher earns above-normal profits in the short run is no assurance that it will be able to do so in the long run. Unless entry barriers exist, the entrance of additional firms will result in added competition for consumers' dollars and subsequent elimination of all economic profits.

PRICE SEARCHERS AND RESOURCE ALLOCATION

Consumers are obviously better off when low entry barriers ensure low prices and low profits. But the profits earned by Hoffman–La Roche and other price searchers are not the primary social concern of economists. After all, high prices harm consumers, but they benefit stockholders and others who own businesses. So we can't say that the entire society is harmed by barriers to entry. A more serious concern is the inefficient allocation of resources that results from the presence of market power.

---

[9] F. M. Scherer, *Industrial Market Structure and Economic Performance*, 2nd ed. (Chicago: Rand McNally, 1980), p. 449.

Use Your Economic Reasoning

For Champions of Haggling, No Price Tag Is Sacred

BY ALINA TUGEND

My husband and I hate haggling. In markets in Istanbul or Jerusalem or Florence, where arguing over price is a high art—and after we have given it our best shot—we always feel we have walked away paying twice as much as the seller expected. And that they are secretly, or not so secretly, laughing at us. In this country where you are expected to negotiate over cars and houses, we manage quite well, but do not find it fun or exciting. We just want it to be over. But I have friends who always seem able to strike a great deal in unexpected areas.

My friend Lou negotiates a lower price on the oil delivered to his house. On his credit card rates. On hotel rooms. At the gym. "People are afraid to ask, afraid they'll be embarrassed or afraid they won't get the right answer," he said. "Seventy-five percent of the time, I get the right answer." Lou and other successful hagglers are not worried about appearing cheap, as I am, or being turned down, because they start with a different attitude. He is not asking for a favor. Rather, he believes he deserves a good deal because he is a good customer. "I'm not just asking for a discount," he said. "I'm spending more with you than someone else, and I should be treated better or differently."

Consumer Reports reported in November [2007] that it surveyed 2,167 people and found that 90 percent of those who haggled over furniture, electronics, appliances and even medical bills had received a lower price on at least one purchase in the last three years. Most of the bargainers said they saved $50 or more, and in the case of cellphone deals and medical fees, more than a quarter saved at least $100.

Sally Greenberg, executive director of the National Consumers League, calls herself the queen of haggling and estimates that she gets a lower price 90 percent of the time. She, like most profitable deal makers, says she never acts aggressive, self-righteous or angry. "You want to be polite and say 'could you' and 'I'd be grateful,'" she said. "You have to have a fine-tuned sense of what's fair. Don't chisel people out of things if they can't afford it." Like Lou, if she is a long-term customer, she always asks for a discount. "I've spent many, many thousands at my dentist," she said. So when she needed an expensive procedure, she asked what his actual cost was versus what she was being charged—and negotiated a lower price.

Ours is one of the few countries where haggling is not generally accepted, but this was not always so, said Herb Cohen, author of the best seller *You Can Negotiate Anything*. Remember Manhattan, the Native Americans and some beads? "Americans used to have great reputations as negotiators," said Mr. Cohen, who in his career as a negotiator helped develop the F.B.I. hostage-negotiating program and was an adviser on terrorism to President Jimmy Carter. "But after World War II, we had a virtual monopoly on almost everything." So Americans no longer had to bargain. That can make it confusing to people visiting the United States.

I remember when my sister's soon-to-be father-in-law visited from Israel for her wedding. He was buying dress shoes at Nordstrom and tried to get the price down. It did not work. Our family often chuckled at that story, but the last laugh may be on us. Ms. Greenberg said that department stores are not off-limits to haggling. But a little subtlety might help. "Ask if the item is going on sale soon—or just came off sale—and whether you can have the lower price," she said. Often, the saleswoman has coupons behind the counter. "I'll ask, 'do you have a coupon for me?' and they'll pull them out," she said. "Or if you have an expired coupon, sometimes you've got to beg, and say 'C'mon, can't you honor this?' Sometimes they don't have the authority and sometimes they do." . . .

Most people I talked to said there were a few things to avoid when haggling. You can say what your budget is, but do not lie and do not plead poverty because it doesn't ring true. Even when you think the leverage is all on the other side, it may be worth a try. My friend Anne Marie once got stuck inside her son's bedroom when the original lock broke off. Her toddler was on the other side. She shouted for help from a neighbor through the window, and a locksmith came over. He wanted to charge $200. "I said, 'I won't pay that kind of money,' and got it down to around $75," she said. "It was a game of chicken."

Here are a few of Mr. Cohen's suggestions for successful negotiations: Make sure it is worth your time. Generally that means only bargain on big-ticket items. Don't fall in love with anything you're trying to buy—you should care, but not too much. Do your homework on comparable prices. Offer cash rather than a credit card. Remember—you have the power. Money talks, but money can also walk. Also, keep in mind that the more time a sales representative has invested in a sale, the more he will want to give you a bargain. Mr. Cohen gives the example of trying on three or four suits and deciding on the fifth one. "They bring in the tailor and the salesman is gleefully writing up the bill. Then I turn to the salesman and say, 'What kind of tie will you throw in for free?'" It works for free shirts, too.

USE YOUR ECONOMIC REASONING

1. Many sellers—furniture and appliance stores, electronics stores, motels, etc.—will negotiate on price, but only if asked to do so; otherwise, everyone pays the same price. Would you describe this as price discrimination? Why would sellers prefer to conceal their willingness to negotiate?
2. Imagine a furniture seller that is willing to negotiate on the price of anything in inventory. Do you think the seller will be willing to offer the same percentage discount on every item in stock? Why or why not? Will every customer be offered the same discount on a particular item? Why or why not?
3. A seller's willingness to negotiate may vary significantly depending on the state of the economy (whether unemployment is high or low, for instance), the degree of competition in the seller's particular industry, and even the season of the year (think about resorts and seasonal furniture, for example). Explain.
4. The cardinal rule in shopping is, "Don't love it until you own it." Imagine finding a used car that you really "must own." How will your emotional attachment influence your ability to negotiate? Will you still be able to walk away if you don't get an attractive deal? How can you guard against falling in love with the vehicle?

Recall from Chapter 6 that an efficient allocation of resources requires that each product be produced up to the point at which the marginal social benefit that the product provides is exactly equal to its marginal social cost. Marginal social benefit can be determined from the industry demand curve and marginal social cost from the marginal cost curve. If all production is continued up to the point at which the demand curve is intersected by the marginal cost curve, we can be assured that society's scarce resources are being used to produce the mix of products that consumers value most.[10]

When pure competition exists, production is automatically expanded to the allocatively efficient level. But that's not the case when firms possess market power. Price searchers distort the allocation of scarce resources because they do not allow production to continue up to the point at which the marginal social benefit (*MSB*) is equal to the marginal social cost (*MSC*). To do so would cause these firms to earn a smaller profit. Consider Exhibit 7.5. The profit-maximizing price searcher will produce where *MR* intersects *MC*, at seven units in this example. At that output, marginal revenue and marginal cost are equal.

EXHIBIT 7.5

Price Searchers and Resource Misallocation

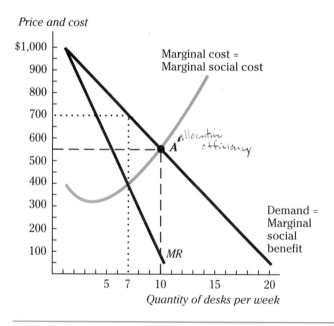

Price and cost

Marginal cost = Marginal social cost

Demand = Marginal social benefit

MR

Quantity of desks per week

Allocative efficiency requires that production take place at the output where the demand curve intersects the marginal cost curve, an output of ten units in this example. But the profit-maximizing price searcher will produce where *MR* = *MC*, an output of seven units. By restricting output, price searchers fail to provide consumers with the optimal quantity of this product and misdirect resources to the production of less-valued goods and services.

---

[10] As we noted in Chapter 6, this conclusion assumes no spillover costs or benefits associated with the production or consumption of the products in question.

But if you move upward in the exhibit from seven units of output to the demand (or marginal benefit) curve, you find that price is equal to $700. This tells us that consumers derive $700 worth of benefit from the seventh unit of output, even though its marginal cost is only $400. In short, consumers value this unit of output more highly than the alternative products that could be produced with the same resources. The same is true of the eighth and ninth units of output; marginal benefit exceeds marginal cost for each of those units.

An efficient allocation of resources would require the price searcher to produce at the output where the marginal cost curve intersects the demand (marginal benefit) curve (see point *A* in Exhibit 7.5). If our hypothetical price searcher produced ten units of output and charged a price of $550 (so that *P* = *MC*), resources would be allocated efficiently. But that won't happen because expanding output in this manner would cause the firm to earn a smaller profit. Note that for each unit beyond seven (the profit-maximizing output), marginal cost *exceeds* marginal revenue. Production of these additional units would be allocatively efficient but would lower the firm's total profit. And because it is the pursuit of profits that drives businesses (and not the goal of allocative efficiency), we can be sure that output will be expanded only to the profit-maximizing level.

In summary, price searchers distort the allocation of scarce resources by producing too little output and thereby forcing resources to be used in the production of less-valued products. In response to this resource misallocation, the government has employed a variety of means to encourage competition or correct for the negative impact of market power.

PRICE SEARCHERS AND ECONOMIES OF SCALE

Although price searchers do not achieve allocative efficiency, there may be instances in which this shortcoming is counterbalanced by lower production costs than could be achieved by price takers. This possibility exists when *economies of scale* occur in the production process.

Economies of scale are reductions in the average cost of production that occur as a firm expands its size of plant and scale of output. As you learned in Chapter 4, all inputs are variable in the long run; firms can build larger (or smaller) production facilities and can enter or leave an industry. In some instances the construction of larger production facilities can lead to lower average production cost (average total cost). When this is the case, the long-run average total cost (*LRATC*) curve of the firm slopes downward as in Exhibit 7.6. Under these circumstances "bigger is better." Larger firms, producing larger quantities of output per period, will be able to achieve lower average costs than smaller firms.

EXHIBIT 7.6

Economies of Scale

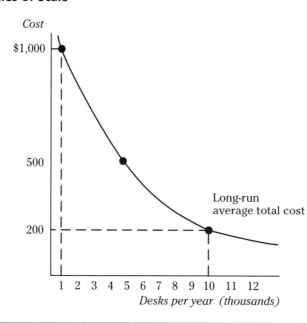

Economies of scale cause the firm's long-run average total cost curve to slope downward.

Larger firms may be able to achieve lower costs for a variety of reasons. As firms build larger facilities and expand output, they can justify specialized equipment and personnel that would not make sense for a smaller firm producing less output. For instance, large manufacturers of men's shirts can justify million-dollar pieces of equipment that do nothing but sew collars. They can justify this expense because the machine sews collars very quickly and with few errors. This saves on the labor cost of performing this operation when compared with the less-sophisticated equipment and more labor-intensive technique that would be used by a smaller firm. Of course, this saving occurs only if the machine can be kept busy so that its cost can be spread over millions of shirts. That's why only larger firms opt for this approach. Smaller firms are forced to stick with more labor-intensive processes that generally mean higher average costs. High volume also allows firms to achieve greater specialization of labor than firms producing less output. For example, our large shirt manufacturer may be able to justify employing a crew of workers whose sole job is the maintenance of equipment, and a different crew whose sole task is stocking the factory with supplies. By allowing these workers to concentrate on a single task, the firm enables them to become better at their jobs, which results in fewer errors and reduces the time necessary to perform each task. In short, more specialized equipment and greater specialization of labor may allow larger firms to produce their products at lower average costs than smaller firms, whose size makes these options uneconomical.

The importance of economies of scale varies from industry to industry. In some industries large firms have substantially lower average costs than small firms; in others the difference is insignificant. Similarly, there are industries in which the advantages of size continue indefinitely and others in which they are quickly exhausted. When the long-run average total cost curve declines indefinitely, as it does in Exhibit 7.6, it is always cheaper for a single firm (a monopolist) to serve the industry. Note that a single firm can produce an industry output of 10,000 desks at an average cost of $200, whereas if there were ten firms sharing the same market, average cost would rise to $1,000. When a market is most cheaply served by a single firm, it is described as a **natural monopoly.** This is a situation in which the benefits to society of lower production costs may outweigh the harm caused by a price searcher's tendency to restrict output below the allocatively efficient level.

If the cost curve depicted in Exhibit 7.6 were commonplace, the U.S. economy would be largely populated by monopolies. But that's not the case; monopoly is relatively rare in our economy. That's because most long-run average cost curves don't decline indefinitely; they eventually turn up. The cost curve depicted in Exhibit 7.7 displays economies of scale up to point *A* (an output of 1,000 units) and *diseconomies of scale* beyond that point. **Diseconomies of scale** are increases in the average cost of production stemming from larger plant size

EXHIBIT 7.7

Economies and Diseconomies of Scale

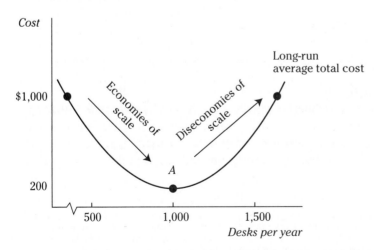

Long-run average costs decline as a result of economies of scale and increase as a result of diseconomies of scale.

and scale of output; they cause the long-run average total cost curve to turn upward, as it does to the right of point *A*. The major source of diseconomies of scale is the difficulty of managing a large enterprise. When organizations become very large, it becomes difficult to maintain the communication and information flows necessary to coordinate such enterprises. This results in long delays and inappropriate decisions, which raise the average cost of production, causing the long-run average total cost curve to turn upward.

When a firm experiences both economies and diseconomies of scale, bigger is better but only up to a point. The firm's *LRATC* curve will have the U shape depicted in Exhibit 7.7. Under these conditions the degree of competition that is likely to emerge in the industry depends on both the optimal size of the firm (the output at which the *LRATC* curve is at a minimum) and the total demand for the industry's product. In our hypothetical example, for instance, if consumers are willing to purchase 100,000 desks at $200 (a price that would provide a normal profit), this industry could support 100 optimal-sized firms (100,000/1,000 = 100), and so it would tend to be highly competitive. But if consumers were willing to purchase only 3,000 desks at that price, the industry could support only three optimal-sized firms and would be likely to develop into an oligopoly. Although more competition is generally preferred to less, under these circumstances oligopoly would probably be preferable to a more competitive industry structure because insisting on a large number of firms would require each firm to be too small to achieve significant scale economies.[11]

In summary, when firms must be relatively large to achieve economies of scale, consumers may be better off with one firm or a few large firms, even though this means an absence of competition. Under these circumstances the advantages of lower production costs (and lower prices) may more than compensate for any allocative inefficiency resulting from the limited number of competitors.

SUMMARY

In most U.S. industries, individual firms have some pricing discretion, or *market power*. A firm may acquire market power either through *product differentiation*—distinguishing its product from similar products offered by other sellers—or by gaining control of a significant fraction of total industry output. Firms with either or both of these abilities can exert some influence on the market price of their product.

---

[11] If the oligopolists enjoy substantial economies of scale, they may be able to earn economic profits and still charge a lower price than would prevail if the industry were composed of a large number of firms, each too small to achieve significant economies of scale.

Sellers with pricing discretion are described as *price searchers* because they must search for the profit-maximizing price. All price searchers face demand curves that slope downward and to the right. Unlike the price taker, which can sell as much as it desires at the market price, the price searcher has to reduce price to sell more. Therefore, the price searcher is forced to choose between selling a lower quantity at a higher price or selling a higher quantity at a lower price.

Because price must be reduced to sell more, the marginal revenue the price searcher obtains from selling an additional unit of output is always less than the unit's selling price, and the price searcher's marginal revenue curve lies inside its demand curve. The price searcher can determine the profit-maximizing (loss-minimizing) level of output by equating marginal revenue and marginal cost. The profit-maximizing price can then be discovered by drawing a line directly up from the quantity to the firm's demand curve and over to the vertical (price) axis.

Some price searchers are able to enlarge their profits by practicing price discrimination. *Price discrimination* is charging different consumers different prices for the same product. When firms engage in individual price discrimination, they attempt to charge each consumer the maximum price he or she will pay. Group price discrimination results when firms charge different prices to different categories of consumers.

Like price takers, price searchers must determine the amount of their profit or loss by comparing total revenue and total cost. If total revenue exceeds total cost, the price searcher is earning an economic profit; if total cost exceeds total revenue, the firm is incurring an economic loss. When total revenue is exactly equal to total cost, the firm is earning a normal profit.

Although a normal profit is the most a price taker can hope to earn in the long run, a price searcher may be able to do better. When price searchers are protected by substantial barriers to entry, they may continue to earn long-run economic profits.

The possibility of long-run profits is not the only outcome that distinguishes price searchers from price takers. In addition, price searchers fail to achieve allocative efficiency. Allocative efficiency requires that producers expand output up to the point at which the marginal social benefit of the last unit produced is exactly equal to its marginal social cost. Price searchers stop short of that point; that is, they produce less output than is socially desirable.

Although price searchers fail to achieve allocative efficiency, there may be instances in which this shortcoming is counterbalanced by the ability to achieve *economies of scale*. Economies of scale are reductions in the average cost of production that occur when a firm expands its plant size and the scale of its output. When economies of scale continue indefinitely, the market will always be most cheaply served by a single firm. This situation is termed a *natural monopoly*. Natural monopolies are rare. In most instances, long-run costs decline initially but eventually turn up as a result of *diseconomies of scale*.

When a production process exhibits both economies and diseconomies of scale, the firm's long-run average total cost curve will be U shaped; it will decline initially but will eventually turn upward. Under these circumstances the degree of competition that is likely to emerge in the industry depends on both the optimal size of the firm and the total demand for the industry's product. When the optimal size of the firm is relatively large, consumers may be better off with a few large firms that are able to achieve all economies of scale, even though this means less competition.

KEY TERMS

Cartel

Diseconomies of
  scale

Economies of scale

Market power

Monopoly

Natural monopoly

Oligopoly

Price discrimination

Price searcher

Product
  differentiation

STUDY QUESTIONS

Fill in the Blanks

1. Firms that possess pricing discretion are

   sometimes described as _____ .

2. _____ creates market power by convincing buyers that a particular product is unique and superior.

3. A price searcher maximizes profit by

   equating_____ and

   _____ .

4. For a price searcher, marginal revenue is

   (greater/less) _____ than price.

5. In the short run, a price searcher that is incurring a loss will continue to operate rather than shut down, provided that price

   is greater than _____ cost.

6. A price searcher will not be able to earn economic profits in the long run unless

   _____ exist.

7. A price searcher would achieve allocative efficiency if it produced at the output

   where the _____ curve intersects the marginal cost curve.

8. Price searchers will not choose to produce the allocatively efficient level of output because doing so would reduce their

   _____ .

9. A(n) _____ is a situation in which a market is most cheaply served by a single firm.

10. If the long-run average cost curve of a firm is U shaped, we know that the firm

    initially experiences _____ of scale, and ultimately experiences

    _____ of scale.

Multiple Choice

1. Safety Tire spends millions of dollars on advertisements promoting its tires as "the safest on the market." This is an example of
   a) price discrimination.
   b) market power.
   c) product differentiation.
   d) economies of scale.

2. Which of the following is false?
   a) Price searchers can raise their prices without losing all their customers.
   b) Price searchers may earn economic profits in the long run.
   c) A cartel is a firm that has substantial market power.
   d) An oligopoly is an industry composed of a few firms.

3. When a price searcher practices individual price discrimination, the marginal revenue it obtains from selling one more unit of its product is
   a) always equal to the selling price of the product.
   b) always less than the selling price of the product.
   c) always more than the selling price of the product.
   d) None of the above is true.

4. If a price searcher is operating at an output where *MR* exceeds *MC*, then
   a) the firm is producing the profit-maximizing output.
   b) the firm is producing too little output; it needs to produce more to maximize its profit.
   c) the firm is producing too much output; it needs reduce output to maximize its profit.
   d) Either b or c is true; you can't tell from the information provided.

   Use the following exhibit to answer questions 5–7.

Price and cost

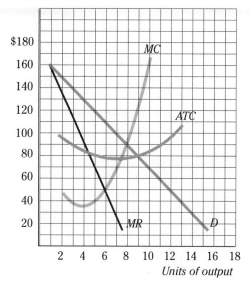

Units of output

5. To maximize its profit or minimize its loss, this price searcher should
   a) produce six units and charge a price of $50.
   b) produce six units and charge a price of $110.
   c) produce eight units and charge a price of $90.
   d) produce nine units and charge a price of $80.

6. This price searcher is
   a) incurring a loss of $180.
   b) earning a normal profit.
   c) earning a profit of $360.
   d) earning a profit of $180.

7. Allocative efficiency would require this firm to
   a) produce seven and one-half units of output and charge a price of $78.
   b) produce eight units and charge a price of $90.
   c) produce six units and charge a price of $50.
   d) None of the above

8. If a price searcher's fixed costs have increased,
   a) the firm's profit-maximizing quantity will increase.
   b) the firm's profit-maximizing quantity will not change.
   c) the firm's profit-maximizing quantity will decline.
   d) the firm will operate at a loss.

9. Sonic Waterbeds faces a traditional downward-sloping demand curve (included below), but its marginal cost curve is a horizontal straight line at a height of $600. In other words, marginal costs are constant at $600. How many units should Sonic sell, and what price should it charge to maximize profit?

PRICE (PER BED)	QUANTITY (PER DAY)
$1,000	1
900	2
800	3
700	4
600	5
500	6

   a) One unit at $1,000
   b) Two units at $900
   c) Three units at $800
   d) Four units at $700
   e) Five units at $600

10. If the waterbed retailer described in question 9 was able to practice individual price discrimination, it would sell _____ waterbeds and earn a profit of _____ dollars on the last waterbed sold.
    a) 3; 200
    b) 4; 200
    c) 5; 0
    d) 6; 0

11. When firms practice group price discrimination, they tend to charge higher prices to consumers

a) whose demand is more elastic.
b) who are more price sensitive.
c) whose demand is less elastic.
d) who do comparison shopping.

12. When a price searcher produces the output level at which marginal revenue is equal to marginal cost, it is
    a) maximizing its profit and producing the allocatively efficient level of output.
    b) maximizing its profit but producing more than the allocatively efficient level of output.
    c) maximizing its profit but producing less than the allocatively efficient level of output.
    d) producing less than the profit-maximizing output.

13. Imagine a situation in which a firm experienced diseconomies of scale immediately. The long-run average total cost curve would be
    a) U shaped.
    b) downward sloping.
    c) upward sloping.
    d) a horizontal straight line.

14. Imagine a long-run average cost curve that is U shaped and has its minimum at 5,000 units of output and an average cost of $10. Under those conditions this industry would be
    a) a natural monopoly if only 5,000 units were demanded at $10 but highly competitive if 10,000 units were demanded at that price.
    b) an oligopoly if only 5,000 units were demanded at $10 but highly competitive if 10,000 units were demanded at that price.
    c) highly competitive if 10,000 units were demanded at $10.
    d) a natural monopoly if only 5,000 units were demanded at $10 but highly competitive if 500,000 units were demanded at that price.

Problems and Questions for Discussion

1. The price searcher's price and output decisions are one and the same. Explain.

2. Explain how product differentiation conveys market power.

3. Why is marginal revenue less than price for a price searcher? Illustrate with an example.

4. From time to time, farmers have attempted to form organizations to restrict the amount of corn and other grains being planted. What is the real intent of these organizations, and why do you think they have been largely ineffective in achieving their objective?

5. Why do cartels need cooperation of their members to ensure high prices? How can cheating—selling more output than permitted, for example—undermine a cartel?

6. Why should consumers be concerned about barriers to entry?

7. Both price searchers and price takers produce at the output where $MR = MC$. Yet price takers achieve allocative efficiency, whereas price searchers do not. Explain.

8. Suppose that a price searcher finds itself incurring a short-run loss. How should it decide whether to shut down or continue to operate? What would the price searcher's graph look like if the price searcher was in a shutdown situation?

9. If the long-run average total cost curve always slopes downward, bigger is better, and the industry will probably develop into a monopoly. What do you suppose it would mean if the firm's long-run cost curve was horizontal? Would big firms be able to drive the small ones out of business? Would large firms be at a disadvantage?

10. If the firm's long-run average total cost curve is U shaped, the industry could be a monopoly or purely competitive or even an oligopoly. We can't tell from the information given. What additional information is needed, and how would we use it to determine the degree of competition in this industry?

11. The local newspaper offers the following rates for placing classified advertisements:
    $3.00 for three lines for three days (for items totaling under $100)
    $6.00 for three lines for three days (for items totaling $100–$499)
    $9.00 for three lines for five days (for items totaling $500–$3,999)
    $20.00 for three lines for eight days (for items totaling $4,000–$35,000)
    a. Is the newspaper practicing price discrimination? If so, which type of price discrimination is it practicing, individual or group?
    b. What is the logic behind the pricing scheme contained in these ad rates?

12. Suppose your college or university wanted to charge different tuition rates to different categories of students. In the following pairs, who do you think would pay the higher rates? Why?
    a. Students interested in premed or students interested in the humanities?
    b. Students who apply for early admission or those who apply later?
    c. Students who came for on-campus visits or those who did not?
    d. Entering freshmen or students beginning their senior year?

ANSWER KEY

Fill in the Blanks

1. price searchers
2. Product differentiation
3. marginal cost; marginal revenue
4. less
5. average variable
6. barriers to entry
7. demand
8. profit
9. natural monopoly
10. economies; diseconomies

Multiple Choice

1. c
2. c
3. a
4. b
5. b
6. d
7. b
8. b
9. c
10. c
11. c
12. c
13. c
14. d

PRICING IN PRACTICE

A firm's day-to-day pricing techniques may differ somewhat from the theoretically correct pricing practices that we have discussed thus far. This difference stems in part from the fact that firms are frequently guided by motives other than profit maximization. Ethical considerations, for example, may result in the pursuit of a "satisfactory" profit rather than a maximum profit. The quest for prestige is another motive that may cause the firm or its managers to maximize sales or market share, subject to some minimum profit constraint.[12] Firms pursuing objectives such as these will not select the price at which $MR = MC$. For instance, if a firm wants to maximize sales, it will choose a lower price than the one that maximizes profit to encourage additional customers to buy the product.

Even those firms motivated by the pursuit of maximum profit may find it difficult to employ the $MR = MC$ rule in precisely the manner we've described. In most real-world situations, pricing takes place in an environment beset with uncertainty. Firms seldom possess precise information about their demand and cost curves. These deficiencies force sellers to rely on other methods for determining price.

COST-PLUS PRICING

The most common technique for determining selling price is probably *cost-plus pricing* (or full-cost pricing, as it is sometimes called). In its simplest form the cost-plus method involves adding some percentage, or markup, to the cost of the goods acquired for sale. For example, a furniture store may pay $200 for a chair, mark it up 150 percent, and attempt to sell it for $500.

Firms using this method do not consider all their costs in arriving at the selling price. They assume that the markup on the *cost of goods sold* (the cost of the items they buy for resale) will be sufficient to cover all other costs—rent, utilities, wages, and salaries—and leave something for profit.

---

[12] Although firms may choose to pursue objectives other than profit maximization, they must strive to achieve at least a normal profit in the long run. Otherwise they won't be able to attract the economic resources they need to remain in business. Thus, although some firms may not choose to pursue profit *maximization*, no firm can ignore profitability entirely.

A more sophisticated version of the cost-plus technique attempts to ensure that *all* costs are recovered by building them into the price. Here the seller arrives at a price by determining first the average total cost (*ATC*) of producing the product or offering the service and then adding some margin for profit.

A Cost-Plus Example: Building a Boat

Let's assume that we have just purchased a boat-manufacturing facility for $2,000,000. It has an expected useful life of ten years and was designed with a production capacity of 1,000 boats per year. The estimated cost of materials is $1,500 per boat, and estimated direct labor cost (the cost of the labor directly involved in the manufacture of the boat) is $2,000 per boat. Besides these variable costs, we have a variety of fixed costs—everything from utility payments to the salaries of security guards—which amount to $500,000 per year. Because our factory cost $2,000,000 and has a useful life of ten years, we must also add $200,000 per year ($2,000,000/10 years) for *depreciation*—the reduction in the value of the production plant due to wear and tear and obsolescence.

Assuming that we expect to sell 1,000 boats this year, which would mean that we would be able to operate the plant at its designed capacity, we arrive at the following costs per boat:

Direct labor	$2,000
Materials	1,500
Depreciation on plant and equipment ($200,000 per year, or $200 per boat—i.e., $200,000 divided by 1,000 boats)	200
Fixed costs ($500,000 per year, or $500 per boat— i.e., $500,000 divided by 1,000 boats)	500
Total cost per boat (average total cost)	$4,200

Now that we have the average total cost of producing a boat, the final step in determining the selling price is adding on the markup that provides our profit margin. A number of factors seem to influence the size of the markup that firms strive to achieve. For instance, executives commonly mention the firm's assessment of what is a "fair" or "reasonable" profit margin.

Custom is another factor that seems to play a major role in some industries. Retailers, for example, often use a particular percentage markup simply because they have always used it or because it is the accepted, therefore "normal," markup in the industry. Obviously a markup that endures long enough to become customary must be somewhat successful in allowing firms to meet their profit objectives. In fact, it may indicate that these firms have discovered through informal means the price and output levels that would have emerged if they had applied the theoretical $MR = MC$ rule.

A final factor influencing the size of the markup is the impact of competition. Although a firm may desire high profit margins, ultimately the degree of actual and potential competition determines what margins the firm will be able to achieve. The more competitive the industry, the lower the profit margin.

Let's assume that we've considered all these factors and have decided to use a 10 percent markup on cost in determining our selling price. Our final step, then, is to add the 10 percent markup to the average total cost calculated earlier. The resulting value is the firm's selling price as determined by the cost-plus technique:

Total cost per boat (average total cost)	$4,200
Markup on cost (10 percent × $4,200)	420
Selling price	$4,620

Cost-Plus Pricing in Action

Cost-plus pricing has been criticized by economists as a naive pricing technique that ignores demand and competition and bases price solely on cost considerations. When the cost-plus technique is used in a mechanical or unthinking way, these criticisms are certainly valid. But that's seldom the case. Most businesses consider carefully the strength of demand and the degree of competition before selecting their markup or profit margin. In addition, the cost-plus price generally is viewed as a preliminary estimate, or starting point, rather than as the final price. Because demand and competition can seldom be measured precisely, the firm must be willing to adjust its price if it has misjudged market conditions. It is through these subjective adjustments that the firm gropes its way closer to the profit-maximizing price. A few examples may help to illustrate this point.

Example 1: The Department Store
A local department store receives its shipment of Nifty Popcorn Poppers just in time for the Christmas gift-buying season. It prices the item at $19.50 to earn a 30 percent markup on the popper's cost.

Two weeks later the store has sold 50 percent of the shipment, and Christmas is still six weeks away. The manager realizes that he has a "hot" selling item and that he won't be able to get any more from the manufacturer in time for Christmas. He decides to increase his markup (and consequently the product's selling price) to take advantage of the product's strong demand.

Example 2: The Car Dealer
A car dealer in a large metropolitan area has found that in the past several years she has been able to average a 15 percent profit margin on the cost of the

automobiles she sells. Her experience has taught her that it is much easier to sell a car at a high markup early in the season, when people will pay to be among the first to own the new model, than later, when the next year's model is about to be announced. So the dealer instructs her sales personnel to strive for a 20 to 25 percent markup early in the year and to settle for a 5 to 10 percent margin toward the end of the season.

Example 3: The Appliance Manufacturer

Acme Appliance manufactures refrigerators for sale to a regional market. In response to consumers' different budgets and "needs" in terms of optional features, the company offers two models: a basic model that is available only in white and a deluxe model that offers additional features and comes in a variety of colors.

In pricing its product, Acme feels that a 10 percent markup on average cost will produce the desired rate of return on its investment. Rather than use a single markup percentage, however, Acme has decided to apply a 5 percent markup to the basic model and a 15 percent markup to the deluxe model, for an average markup of 10 percent. This decision was made because previous sales experience indicated that low-income customers are substantially more sensitive to price than are intermediate- and high-income customers.

Although the cost-plus technique is essentially straightforward, its application requires management personnel to make subjective judgments about the strength of demand and the degree of competition, as these examples illustrate. Both factors are difficult to evaluate and impossible to quantify. As a consequence, pricing remains more an art than a science.

MARGINAL ANALYSIS AND MANAGERIAL DECISIONS

As the foregoing examples indicate, firms that desire to maximize profits must adjust their cost-plus prices to reflect market conditions; they cannot use the technique mechanically. Learning to "think marginally" can also lead to better decisions and greater profits.

The major limitation of the cost-plus technique is that it doesn't rely on the *marginal analysis* introduced in Chapter 5. It concentrates instead on average values, stressing the need to recover all costs plus some markup. That can lead to smaller profits (or larger losses) than necessary because (as we discovered in Chapter 5) marginal costs are the only relevant costs for many business decisions.

Although firms commonly lack the information required to use the $MR = MC$ approach to price determination, they generally have some knowledge of marginal values. For instance, even though a firm probably does not know the marginal cost of producing the 200,000th unit of output, it can usually determine the additional cost of producing some block of units—another 10,000 cars, for example. And it can probably discover the additional cost of some contemplated course of action, such as adding or discontinuing a product line. This information will allow a firm to improve the quality of its decisions.

To illustrate, suppose that you own a chain of fast-food restaurants that has traditionally opened for business at 11 a.m. What costs would you consider in deciding whether it would be profitable to open earlier to serve breakfast?

The cost-plus approach implies that the decision should be based on the full cost (or *fully allocated cost*, as it is sometimes called) of the new project—on the project's share of the firm's total costs. In other words, the breakfast meal would be expected to generate enough revenue to pay for the labor, utilities, and food used in the morning meal, plus a share of the firm's overhead costs (rent, insurance, equipment depreciation) and some profit margin. If you anticipate enough business to achieve that objective, you should open for business. Otherwise you would remain closed.

Marginal analysis yields a different conclusion. According to marginal analysis, the only costs relevant to a decision are those that are influenced by the decision. In deciding whether to open for breakfast, you should *ignore* such costs as rent and insurance because these fixed costs will have to be paid whether or not the restaurants are open for breakfast. The only true cost of serving breakfast is the marginal cost: the increase in the restaurant's total cost that results from the breakfast meal. If the marginal revenue derived from serving breakfast is expected to exceed the marginal cost, you should open earlier. If not, you should continue to serve only the noon and evening meals.

Marginal analysis can often improve the quality of managerial decisions. Many projects that don't appear to be profitable when evaluated on the basis of their fully allocated costs look quite appealing when analyzed in terms of their marginal costs and revenues. By using marginal analysis and applying judgment to cost-plus prices, firms may be able to approximate the profit levels that would be achieved by using the $MR = MC$ rule.

Test your understanding of the material contained in this appendix by answering the following questions:

1. Explain the cost-plus pricing technique.
2. Why is it often necessary to modify the result determined by the cost-plus method?
3. If a firm includes all its costs in its price by using the cost-plus method, will it ever show a loss? Explain.
4. What determines the markup used in the cost-plus pricing technique?

5. A major limitation of the cost-plus technique is that it does not utilize marginal analysis. Discuss.

6. The Springfield Bouncers, a new professional basketball team, want to rent the high school gymnasium on Sunday afternoons. How would you determine an appropriate rent? If they reject your first offer, how would you determine the *minimum* acceptable rate?

7. Bland Manufacturing Company manufactures men's suits for sale throughout the Midwest. For the past five years Bland has operated with about 20 percent unused capacity. Last month a retailer on the West Coast offered to buy as many suits as Bland could supply as long as the price did not exceed $180 per suit. This price is substantially below the price Bland charges its regular customers. Given the information presented below, should Bland accept the offer? Why or why not?

    ATC at present output level (80,000 units) = $220
    ATC at capacity output (100,000 units) = $200
    Normal markup = 40 percent on *ATC*

8 Industry Structure and Public Policy

1. Explain the meaning of "industry structure."
2. Describe how market power is related to industry structure.
3. Identify the characteristics of the four industry structures.
4. Discuss the sources of the pricing discretion enjoyed by monopolistically competitive firms, oligopolists, and monopolists and the limits of that discretion.
5. Explain why monopolists and oligopolists may be able to earn long-run profits, while monopolistically competitive and purely competitive firms cannot.
6. Define "interdependence," and explain how it influences the actions of oligopolists.
7. Describe the content and purpose of game theory.
8. Explain how monopolists and oligopolists may distort the allocation of scarce resources and alter the income distribution.
9. Identify the three major antitrust statutes and their content.
10. Explain the objectives and limitations of antitrust enforcement and industry regulation.

Nearly all the firms in our economy enjoy some pricing discretion, or market power. In Chapter 7 we saw how these firms determine their prices, and we considered the impact of market power on the allocation of scarce resources. This chapter takes a closer look at the degrees of market power that exist in different industries and considers how the makeup, or structure, of an industry influences the amount of pricing discretion enjoyed by its individual firms. This chapter also explores the impact of market power on consumer welfare and examines the role of antitrust enforcement and government regulation in limiting that power.

INDUSTRY STRUCTURE AND MARKET POWER

You have learned that a firm may acquire market power either through product differentiation—distinguishing its product from similar products offered by other sellers—or by gaining control of a significant fraction of total industry output. The degree of product differentiation and the extent to which a firm is able to control industry output are related to the structure of the industry in which the firm operates. **Industry structure** is the makeup of an industry as determined by certain factors: (1) the number of sellers and their size distribution (all sellers approximately the same size as opposed to some much larger than others); (2) the nature of the product; (3) the extent of barriers to entering or leaving the industry. Note that these factors correspond to the three assumptions of the competitive model discussed early in Chapter 6.

There are four basic industry structures: pure competition, monopolistic competition, oligopoly, and pure monopoly. Their characteristics are summarized in Exhibit 8.1. You are already familiar with pure competition, so we will use that model to open our discussion of the relationship between industry structure and market power.

PURE COMPETITION

As you learned in Chapter 6, firms that operate in a purely competitive industry are price takers and lack market power for two reasons. First, because they produce and sell identical products, no one firm can expect consumers to pay a higher price than they would pay elsewhere. Such firms must be content with the price dictated by the market. Second, because the purely competitive firm is quite small in relation to the industry, it cannot affect the total industry supply enough to alter the market price. It cannot, for instance, push up prices as do the OPEC oil cartel and the De Beers diamond cartel.

That cannot happen in wheat or corn production or any other industry that approximates pure competition. In these industries the individual seller supplies such a small fraction of total industry output that the firm is not in a position to alter the market price by reducing production. Once again, the purely competitive firm has no choice but to accept the price that is dictated by the market.

EXHIBIT 8.1
Industry Structure: A Preview

PURE COMPETITION (No pricing discretion)	MONOPOLISTIC COMPETITION (Modest pricing discretion)	OLIGOPOLY (Modest to substantial pricing discretion)	PURE MONOPOLY (Substantial pricing discretion)
1. Many sellers, each small in relation to the industry	1. Many sellers, each small in relation to the industry	1. Few sellers, large in relation to the industry	1. One firm the sole supplier
2. Identical products	2. Somewhat differentiated products	2. Identical or differentiated products	2. Unique product; no close substitutes
3. No substantial barriers to entry	3. No substantial barriers to entry	3. Substantial barriers to entry	3. Substantial barriers to entry
Examples: Wheat farming, cattle ranching, fish farming, and other agricultural industries	*Examples:* Retail trade (hair salons, restaurants, dry-cleaners) and a few manufacturing industries (women's dresses, kitchen cabinets, office furniture)	*Examples:* Steel and aluminum manufacturing (identical products); automobile and cigarette manufacturing (differentiated products)	*Examples:* Microsoft, developer of the Windows operating system; some local utility companies; the single campus bookstore

MONOPOLISTIC COMPETITION

Few industries in the U.S. economy approximate pure competition. Monopolistic competition is a much more common industry structure. Most of the retailers with which you do business regularly are firms in monopolistically competitive industries: restaurants, day-care centers, grocery stores, hair salons, and dry-cleaners, to name just a few examples. In addition, some manufacturers, such as those making women's dresses, kitchen cabinets, and office furniture, operate in monopolistically competitive industries.

Like pure competition, **monopolistic competition** is characterized by a large number of relatively small sellers and by modest barriers to entering the industry. The feature that distinguishes monopolistic competition from pure competition is product differentiation. Each monopolistically competitive firm sells a product that is slightly different from those of other firms in the industry. Firms compete on price *and* through product differentiation. Products are differentiated by style, quality, packaging, the location of the seller, advertising, the services offered by the firm (free delivery, for example), and other real or imagined characteristics.

As the term suggests, a monopolistically competitive firm is part monopolist and part competitor. It is a monopolist because it is the only firm selling its unique product; it is competitive because of the large number of firms selling products that are close substitutes. We all have a favorite pizza parlor. It is a monopolist in the limited sense that no other restaurant offers exactly the same food, service, atmosphere, and location. On the other hand, our pizza parlor is in competition with dozens, perhaps hundreds, of other restaurants that sell pizza and substitutes for pizza as well. Your neighborhood eyeglass retailer and clothing store are in a similar situation. They may have convenient locations and offer some brands that are not available elsewhere, but they face substantial competition from other sellers of similar products.

Monopolistic Competition and Market Power

Insofar as it sells a unique product, each monopolistically competitive firm has some pricing discretion. In other words, it is a price searcher rather than a price taker. If a monopolistic competitor raises the price of its product, it will lose some customers but not all of them. Some will still prefer the product because they believe it to be superior to that of competitors. We can infer, then, that the firm faces a downward-sloping demand curve, not the horizontal or perfectly elastic demand curve facing competitive firms. However, with many substitute products available, the demand for the monopolistically competitive firm's product will be quite elastic, so consumers will be very responsive to price changes. As a consequence, the market power of the firm is limited; no monopolistically competitive firm can raise its price very much without losing an injuriously large number of customers.

The low entry barriers also function as a check on market power. Additional firms can easily enter a monopolistically competitive industry to take advantage of short-run economic profits. Consider the monopolistically competitive firm represented in Exhibit 8.2. In case (a) the firm is earning a short-run profit (price exceeds ATC at the output where $MR = MC$). In the long run, however, this profit will be eliminated by the entrance of additional firms selling similar but slightly differentiated products. As the new firms enter the industry, the demand curve facing our hypothetical firm will begin to shift to the left because each firm's share of total industry demand will become smaller. If there are now 20 pizza restaurants instead of 10, the typical restaurant will have fewer customers than before. Additional firms will continue to enter the industry (and the individual firm's demand curve will continue to shift leftward) until the typical firm is earning just a normal profit.

EXHIBIT 8.2

The Long-Run Adjustment Process in Monopolistic Competition

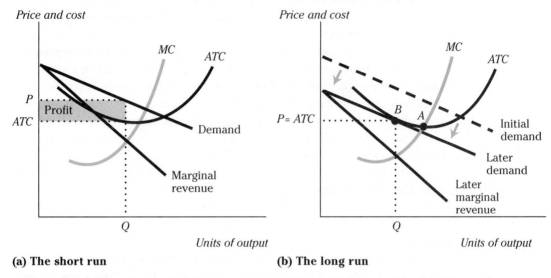

(a) The short run

(b) The long run

In the short run a monopolistically competitive firm may earn an economic profit, as represented in case (a). In the long run, however, the presence of the above-normal profit will cause additional firms to enter the industry, reducing each firm's share of the industry demand and eventually eliminating all economic profit, as in case (b). In long-run equilibrium, the typical monopolistically competitive firm will earn just a normal profit.

This situation is depicted in case (b). In long-run equilibrium, then, the monopolistically competitive firm will do no better than a purely competitive firm: It will just break even.

Evaluating Monopolistic Competition

We discovered in Chapter 6 that price searchers misallocate resources because they fail to expand output up to the point at which the marginal social benefit equals the marginal social cost. An examination of Exhibit 8.2 confirms that monopolistically competitive firms behave this way. Note that in long-run equilibrium, as shown in case (b), the firm maximizes profit at an output of Q. But at that output the price (which reflects the marginal benefit from consuming that unit) exceeds marginal cost. This tells us that society values the last unit of *this* product more highly than the other products that could be produced with the same resources. Allocative efficiency would require the firm to expand output until the marginal social benefit equals the marginal social cost, until the demand curve intersects the marginal cost curve. (Why won't the firm be willing to do that?[1]) If output must be increased to achieve allocative efficiency, we know that at present the firm must be producing less than the efficient level. In summary, monopolistically competitive firms produce less output than is socially desirable.

In addition to distorting the allocation of resources, monopolistically competitive firms are somewhat less efficient at producing their products and charge slightly higher prices than purely competitive firms with the same costs. These outcomes are at least in part the result of the overcrowding that characterizes most monopolistically competitive industries.

The crowded nature of monopolistically competitive industries is illustrated by the large number of eyeglass retailers, hair salons, convenience stores, and fast-food restaurants in your city or town. By differentiating its product, each of these firms is able to capture a small share of the market. But often so many firms share that market that it is difficult for any one of them to attract enough customers to use its facilities efficiently—to permit it to operate at minimum *ATC*.

Because the monopolistically competitive firm underutilizes its production facilities, its average cost of production will be higher than the *ATC* of a purely competitive firm with identical cost curves.[2] For example, consider the *ATC* curve in case (b) of Exhibit 8.2. In long-run equilibrium a purely competitive firm would earn zero economic profit and produce its product at minimum *ATC* (point *A*), whereas we've seen that monopolistically competitive firms will operate at a somewhat higher *ATC* (point *B*). As a consequence, the monopolistically competitive firm must charge a higher price than the purely competitive firm to earn a normal profit in the long run.

Fortunately for consumers, the difference in price is probably not substantial. Furthermore, consumers gain something for the additional dollars they pay. Remember, purely competitive firms sell products that are identical in the minds of consumers, whereas monopolistic competitors aim for product differentiation. Many of us are willing to pay a little more to obtain the product variety that monopolistic competition provides.

---

[1] The firm won't be willing to expand output because that behavior is not consistent with profit maximization; *MC* exceeds *MR* for each unit beyond *Q*. In fact, if the firm chose to produce at the output where the demand curve intersects the *MC* curve, it would incur a loss because the *ATC* curve is above the demand curve at that point.

[2] This analysis assumes that the monopolistic competitor has cost curves that are identical to those of the pure competitor. In fact, the monopolistic competitor probably has higher costs due to advertising expense and other product differentiation efforts. Thus, there are two reasons to expect its selling price to be higher: It does not operate at the minimum on its *ATC* curve (whereas a pure competitor does), *and* its *ATC* curve is higher than that of a pure competitor.

OLIGOPOLY

Millions of firms in hundreds of U.S. retail industries match the model of monopolistic competition reasonably well. However, most manufacturing industries—steel, aluminum, automobiles, and prescription drugs, for example—are more accurately described as oligopolistic. An **oligopoly** is an industry dominated by a few relatively large sellers that are protected by substantial barriers to entry. The distinguishing feature of all oligopolistic industries is the high degree of interdependence among the sellers and the very personal nature of the rivalry that results from that interdependence.

Oligopolists and Market Power

Because oligopolistic firms enjoy a large share of their market, their production decisions have a significant impact on market price. A substantial increase in production by any one of them would cause downward pressure on price; a significant decrease would tend to push price upward. Suppose, for instance, that the Aluminum Company of America (Alcoa) decided to increase production by 50 percent. Because Alcoa is a major producer, this increase in output would expand industry supply significantly and thereby depress the industry price. A substantial reduction in Alcoa's output would tend to have the opposite effect; it would push price upward.

We have seen that soybean farmers, hog producers, and others in purely competitive industries cannot influence price by manipulating industry output: They're not big enough; that is, they don't control a large enough share of the market. In addition, the large number of firms in these competitive industries makes it virtually impossible for them to coordinate their actions—to agree to limit production, for example. As a consequence, changes in the output of a competitive industry are always the unplanned result of independent actions by thousands of producers. Output in an oligopolistic industry, on the other hand, is often carefully controlled by the few large firms that dominate production. This control is one of the keys to the pricing discretion of the oligopolists.

Some oligopolists also acquire market power through product differentiation. Although producers of such commodities as aluminum ingots, steel sheet, and heating oil sell virtually identical products, many oligopolists sell differentiated products. Producers of automobiles, pet foods, video-game machines, greeting cards, cigarettes, breakfast cereals, and washers and dryers belong in this category. Oligopolistic sellers of differentiated products possess market power both because they are large in relation to the total industry *and* because their product is in some way unique.

Mutual Interdependence and Game Theory

Because oligopolistic firms have pricing discretion, they are price searchers rather than price takers. But the high degree of interdependence among oligopolists tends to restrict the pricing discretion of the individual firm and complicate its search for the profit-maximizing price.

Because there are only a few large sellers, each firm must consider the reactions of its rivals before taking any action. For instance, before altering the price of its product, Ford Motor Company must consider the reactions of Toyota, Nissan, and the other firms in the industry. And Coca-Cola must weigh the likely reactions of Pepsi-Cola and other soft-drink suppliers before contemplating any price change. In both instances, raising prices may be ill-advised unless the other firms can be counted on to match the price hike. Price reductions may be an equally poor strategy if rivals respond with matching price cuts or with deeper cuts that lead to continuing price warfare.

One tool that economists use to understand and predict the behavior of oligopolists such as Ford and Coca-Cola is *game theory*. **Game theory** is the study of the strategies employed by interdependent players involved in some form of competition, or game. The "players" can be individuals, sport teams, nations, or business firms. And the "games" involved can be true games of chance or sporting events or struggles between armies on a battlefield or business rivalries.

All games involve strategy and a payoff matrix. A strategy is simply a plan for accomplishing an objective: winning a battle or earning as much profit as possible, for example. And a payoff matrix is a grid showing the outcomes for the various combinations of strategies employed by the players. The following examples will help to illustrate these terms and will also reveal some of the important conclusions of the game theory model.

Games with Dominant Strategies   Consider the rivalry between Coca-Cola and Pepsi-Cola, the most important firms in the soft-drink industry. Let's assume that these two firms are trying to decide whether to charge $10 or $12 for each case of their soft drinks; these are the alternative strategies under consideration. In making this decision, each firm recognizes that its profit (the payoff from its strategy) depends not only on the price it selects but also on the price selected by its rival. The different possible outcomes are contained in the payoff matrix presented in Exhibit 8.3.

According to the matrix, if Coke charges $12 a case and Pepsi chooses the same price, each firm will earn a profit of $300 million (see the cell in the upper-left-hand corner of the matrix). The problem with this strategy is that neither firm can be certain that its rival will decide to charge $12. In fact, as the matrix reveals, each firm has incentive to undercut its rival. For example, if Coke selects the $12 price and Pepsi counters with a $10 price, Pepsi will earn a profit

EXHIBIT 8.3

A Game with Two Dominant Strategies

Coke's price strategies

	$12	$10
$12	Each firm earns a profit of $300 million.	Coke earns $400 million. Pepsi earns $100 million.
$10	Coke earns $100 million. Pepsi earns $400 million.	Each firm earns a profit of $200 million.

Pepsi's price strategies

The payoffs matrix shows that each firm's profits depend not only on its actions but also on the actions of its rival. For instance, if Coke charges $12, it will earn a profit of $300 million if Pepsi matches that price but only $100 million if Pepsi opts to charge $10.

In this example each firm has a *dominant strategy*, a strategy that should be pursued regardless of the strategy selected by its rival. The dominant strategy for both Coke and Pepsi is to charge $10; that strategy leads to higher profits regardless of the strategy selected by the other firm.

of $400 million (see the lower-left-hand cell), while Coke will earn only $100 million. If Pepsi charges $12 and Coke opts to charge $10, the outcome will be reversed; Coke will earn a $400 million profit, and Pepsi will earn only $100 million (see the upper-right-hand cell).

The remaining possibility is that both firms will decide to charge $10. In that case each firm will earn a profit of $200 million. Although this is not the best the firms could do, it is not the worst either because it avoids the possibility of earning a profit of only $100 million. According to game theorists, both oligopolists will see the $10 price as particularly attractive. There are two reasons for this attraction. First, if one firm decides to charge $10 and its rival opts to charge $12, the firm charging the lower ($10) price will earn a $400 million profit, the highest amount possible. Second, charging $10 eliminates the possibility that a firm will be undercut by its rival and find itself able to earn a profit of only $100 million (the lowest outcome in the matrix).

In the preceding example the decision to select the $10 price is the *dominant strategy* for both firms. A **dominant strategy** is one that should be pursued regardless of the strategy selected by the rival. In our example, for instance, Coke is better off charging the $10 price regardless of whether Pepsi opts to match that price or to charge $12 instead. The same is true for Pepsi. As a result, the equilibrium solution occurs in the lower-right-hand cell, with both firms charging $10. As long as these firms act independently, neither firm has any incentive to modify its strategy.

EXHIBIT 8.4

A Game with Only One Dominant Strategy

Coke's advertising strategies

		TV and newspaper	Newspaper only
Pepsi's advertising strategies	TV and newspaper	Coke earns $300 million. Pepsi earns $200 million.	Coke earns $200 million. Pepsi earns $300 million.
	Newspaper only	Coke earns $500 million. Pepsi earns $100 million.	Coke earns $400 million. Pepsi earns $350 million.

In this example Coke's dominant strategy is to engage in both TV and newspaper advertising. Pepsi does not have a dominant strategy; its optimal strategy depends on the strategy adopted by Coke.

Games without Dominant Strategies Not all games have dominant strategies. Others have dominant strategies for one rival but not the other. To illustrate, suppose that Coke and Pepsi are trying to decide whether to utilize both television and newspaper advertising or to limit their campaigns to newspaper advertising. As in the earlier example, the payoff for each strategy depends on the reaction of the rival. These payoffs are represented in Exhibit 8.4. Take a moment to examine the matrix before reading further. Can you determine the strategy that will be selected by each firm? Does each firm have a dominant strategy?

In this case Pepsi does *not* have a dominant strategy; its optimal strategy depends on the strategy adopted by Coke. If Coke decides to pursue both TV and newspaper advertising, Pepsi's optimal strategy is to use both TV and newspaper advertising as well (a profit of $200 million rather than $100 million). On the other hand, if Coke decides to limit its advertising to newspapers, Pepsi's best strategy is to do the same (a profit of $350 million rather than $300 million). As you can see, Pepsi does not have a dominant strategy; its best strategy depends on what Coke does.

Before Pepsi can decide on a strategy, it must predict what Coke is likely to do. In this instance that's not too difficult because Coke *does* have a dominant strategy. Here Coke's dominant strategy is to engage in both TV and newspaper advertising; that yields the most profit regardless of the strategy pursued by Pepsi.[3] Once Pepsi recognizes that Coke's dominant strategy is to advertise

---

[3]Note that if Pepsi engages in TV and newspaper advertising and Coke does the same, Coke earns a profit of $300 million rather than the $200 million it would earn if it chose only newspaper advertising. On the other hand, if Pepsi limits its campaign to newspaper advertising, Coke will earn a profit of $400 million if it matches that strategy or $500 million if it uses both media. As you can see, Coke is always better off to pursue a strategy of both TV and newspaper advertising.

in both media, it knows that its own best strategy is to follow suit. The equilibrium solution, then, is in the upper-left-hand cell, with both firms advertising in both media.[4]

One interesting point about the equilibrium solution is that neither firm earns as much profit as it could if both firms decided to avoid TV advertising. But each firm is reluctant to select this strategy for fear that the other firm *will* run TV ads. A similar problem existed in the initial example. (See Exhibit 8.3 to refresh your memory.) Even though the dominant strategy was to select the $10 price, each firm could earn more profit if both firms decided to charge $12. But, as in the advertising example, neither firm was willing to pursue that strategy for fear of being undercut by its rival. This points to the incentive that oligopolists have to cooperate (rather than compete). We turn next to the methods that they might employ to facilitate cooperation.

Tactics for Cooperating

Oligopolists may respond to their interdependence by employing tactics that allow them to cooperate and make mutually advantageous decisions. One tactic is **collusion**, agreement among sellers to fix prices, divide up the market, or in some other way limit competition. For instance, in our earlier example (see Exhibit 8.3), suppose that Pepsi and Coke secretly agreed to charge $12 (rather than $10). That action would allow each firm to earn more profit. An agreement to avoid TV advertising (see Exhibit 8.4) would have a similar impact.

Collusive agreements result in cartels, such as the OPEC oil cartel and the De Beers diamond cartel. Although collusive agreements are legal in some countries, they are illegal in the United States and are punishable by fine and imprisonment. (As a consequence, firms attempt to keep them secret.) Despite the penalties, some U.S. firms continue to engage in collusion. Dozens of violators are prosecuted each year, and many others probably go undetected. That business executives are willing to risk prison sentences to engage in collusion is testimony both to the potential financial gains and to the problems posed by interdependence.

A subtler form of cooperation (and communication) is price leadership. *Price leadership* is much like a game of follow-the-leader. One firm—perhaps the

---

[4] If both firms decide to advertise, they will have reached a **Nash equilibrium** (named for John Nash, the 1997 Nobel prize–winning economist who discovered the concept). A Nash equilibrium exists when each firm's strategy is the best it can choose, given the strategy chosen by the other firm. There is more than one way to achieve a Nash equilibrium. For example, when both firms have a dominant strategy, the result is a Nash equilibrium. But, as this example illustrates, a Nash equilibrium does not *require* that both players have dominant strategies.

biggest, the most efficient, or simply the most trusted—initiates all increases or decreases in prices. The remaining firms in the industry follow the leader. This leader–follower behavior is generally reinforced by indirect forms of communication (rather than the direct communication involved in collusion). For example, price leaders usually signal their intent to raise prices through press releases or through public speeches. This lets the follower firms know that a price increase is coming so that they will not be taken by surprise. (If the price leader hikes its price and no one follows, it will probably have to back down, creating confusion for the industry.) This tactic allows the firms in the industry to accomplish price changes legally, without collusion.

Neither collusive agreements nor price leadership may be necessary when an industry is dominated by firms that recognize their interdependence. **Conscious parallelism** occurs when, without any communication whatsoever, firms adopt similar policies. For instance, even without meeting or signaling each other, firms may come to recognize that price cutting, because it invites retaliation, leaves all firms worse off. They may therefore shun this practice as long as their rivals reciprocate. Conscious parallelism may also explain why all firms in an industry provide the same discounts to larger buyers and why they all raise prices at the same time of year.

Collusion, price leadership, and conscious parallelism all tend to result in an avoidance of price competition. Instead, oligopolists channel their competitive drive into *nonprice competition*—advertising, packaging, and new product development. This form of rivalry has two significant advantages over price competition. First, a new product or a successful advertising campaign is more difficult for a competitor to match than a price cut is, so an oligopolist may gain a more lasting advantage over its rivals. Second, rivalry through product differentiation or new product development is less likely than price competition to get out of control and severely damage the profits of all firms in the industry. Thus, nonprice competition is seen as a more promising strategy than price competition.

Factors Limiting Cooperation

Although oligopolists strive to avoid price warfare and confine their rivalry to nonprice competition, these efforts are not always successful. Collusion and price leadership often break down because of the strong temptation to cheat (price cut) to win customers. Even conscious parallelism can give way to price cutting if firms believe their actions may be undetected. To understand this temptation, look back at Exhibit 8.3 for a moment. Suppose that Coke and Pepsi have agreed, either informally or through collusion, to charge a price of $12. Each firm recognizes that if it undercuts the other firm by charging $10, it

Oligopolists often channel their competitive instincts into nonprice competition: advertising, packaging, and new product development.

can expand its profits. And if the firm is not too greedy—if the price cutting is limited to a small fraction of industry sales, for example—the practice may go undiscovered, and the rival may not retaliate.

The likelihood of cheating is greatest in markets in which prices tend to be secret (so that price cutting may go undetected) and in which long contracts may delay the impact of retaliation. Cheating also becomes more commonplace as the number of firms in the industry increases because it becomes more difficult for the firms to agree on the best price. In addition, the state of the economy clearly influences the likelihood of cheating. History shows that price cutting is particularly common in periods of weak demand, when firms have substantial excess capacity that they would like to put to work. During such periods, firms will be tempted to undercut their rivals to expand sales.

In truth, the success of oligopolists in avoiding price competition varies significantly from industry to industry. Some industries—breakfast cereal manufacturing, for instance—have demonstrated a marked ability to avoid price competition; others—steel manufacturing, for instance—experience recurring bouts of price warfare.[5] Because the behavior of oligopolists is so varied, it is difficult to generalize about the impact of oligopoly on social welfare. We will attempt some cautious observations after discussing the final industry structure, pure monopoly.

---

[5] Although cereal producers have a long history of avoiding price warfare, even their discipline can break down. In 1996 Kellogg and Philip Morris (which owns Post and Nabisco cereals) announced price cuts averaging about 20 percent. This led to price cutting by other manufacturers.

Use Your Economic Reasoning

How a Drug Maker Tries to Outwit Generics

BY JONATHAN D. ROCKOFF

President-elect Barack Obama has vowed to reduce prescription-drug costs, but the pricing moves by one pharmaceutical company show why that could be difficult. Twice this year, Cephalon Inc. has sharply raised the price of its narcolepsy drug Provigil. The drug is now 28% more expensive than it was in March [2008] and 74% more expensive than four years ago, according to DestinationRx, a pharmaceutical software and data provider. The Frazer, Pa., company has said in investor presentations that it plans to continue to raise the price.

The Provigil price increases—the drug's average wholesale price is now $8.71 a tablet—are an extreme example of a common tactic pharmaceutical companies employ in the U.S. to boost profits and steer patients away from cheaper generics. It works like this: Knowing that Provigil will face generic competition in 2012 as its patent nears expiration, Cephalon is planning to launch a longer-acting version of the drug called Nuvigil next year. To convert patients from Provigil to Nuvigil, Cephalon has suggested in investor presentations it will price Nuvigil lower than the sharply increased price of Provigil. By the time copycat versions of Provigil hit the market the company is banking that most Provigil users will have switched to the less-expensive Nuvigil, which is patent-protected until 2023. . . . "You should expect that we will likely raise Provigil prices to try to create an incentive for the reimbursers to preferentially move to Nuvigil," Chip Merritt, Cephalon's vice president of investor relations, told a Sept. 5 health-care conference, according to a transcript of the meeting. . . .

Patients with health insurance who take the drug for its officially sanctioned uses of narcolepsy, obstructive sleep apnea and shift-work sleep disorder won't likely see the price increases directly, though they are eventually passed on to them through higher health-plan premiums. Those who take the drug for other, "off label" reasons may face a direct hit since insurers often won't pay for it. Sheila Gibson, an Army retiree in Utah who has been taking Provigil for the symptoms of Parkinson's disease, says she has stopped taking the drug because she can't afford the $564.65 a monthly refill now costs. "I'm the one suffering for their greed," said Ms. Gibson, 63 years old, who has asked Cephalon and her insurer for help to no avail. Cephalon said it provides assistance to a "couple thousand patients"

MONOPOLY

Although both monopolistic competitors and oligopolists have some pricing discretion, the classic example of a firm with market power is the monopolist.

Monopoly is an industry structure in which a single firm sells a product for which there are no close substitutes. (Monopoly is sometimes called *pure*

who can't afford Provigil, but said the program reached capacity this year and it wasn't able to accept all applicants. It plans to expand the program next year.

Unlike Ms. Gibson, a large proportion of Provigil users take it as a "lifestyle drug" to help them stay awake during work or leisure activities, according to analysts who follow the company. As a result, a large proportion of Provigil's sales are off label. In September, Cephalon agreed to plead guilty to one misdemeanor count of violating the U.S. Food, Drug and Cosmetic Act and to pay $444 million to settle federal and state allegations that it promoted Provigil and two other drugs for off-label uses. Cephalon promotes Provigil as the "first in a new class" of wakefulness drugs. Provigil's global sales reached $707 million in the nine months ended Sept. 30, accounting for almost half of Cephalon's $1.43 billion in sales.

Some health plans have refused to pay for certain costly medicines altogether. Health plans are also experimenting with less punitive measures, such as imposing higher co-payments for certain drugs or asking members to try a cheaper alternative first. Some insurers require a call from a doctor before they will authorize a prescription for a pricey drug to be filled. Yet insurers say the tools at their disposal to rein in drug prices are limited, noting that many employers choose plans without tiered co-pays or other price-limiting mechanisms, that patients sometimes threaten to leave plans that restrict popular drugs, and that some drugs simply have no cheaper alternative.

Provigil's price increase over the past four years has been almost four times steeper than the 4% compound annual growth rate of the average drug price during that period, according to a DestinationRx analysis of 2,570 brand-name drugs. Some health-plan managers say it will likely be too costly for them to keep patients on Provigil once Nuvigil is introduced in 2009 because cheaper generic versions of Provigil will still be more than two years off. "It's really hard to take a higher price now for a lower price in the future when the future is very far away," said Edmund Pezalla, national medical director for Aetna Pharmacy Management. . . .

USE YOUR ECONOMIC REASONING

1. How do patents convey pricing discretion?
2. Why is Cephalon Inc. introducing Nuvigil? Isn't it basically the same as Provigil, its existing product?
3. How does the company plan to steer Provigil customers to Nuvigil?
4. In 2007, the Supreme Court made it more difficult to obtain patents on new products that combine elements of already existing inventions, like Nuvigil. If Nuvigil does basically the same thing as Provigil, but is longer lasting, should it receive 20 years of protection from copying? What do you think was the Court's rationale for making patents harder to obtain? What would society lose if we made it too hard to obtain new patents?

monopoly to emphasize that it is the industry structure farthest removed from pure competition.) A firm can become a monopolist in a variety of ways but can remain a monopolist only if barriers prevent other firms from entering the industry. One barrier to entry is exclusive control of some critical input— a basic raw material needed in the production process, for instance. A second way a firm may enjoy a monopoly is through sheer size, when larger size brings with it greater efficiency and lower production costs. Entry into the industry is effectively blocked by the large capital investment a rival would require to begin operating at competitive size. A possible third source of monopoly is government policies. For instance, the U.S. government issues patents that provide a firm with the exclusive right to control a new product for a period of 20 years. The government franchise is another example of government policies promoting monopoly. A **government franchise** is an exclusive license to provide a product or service. Government franchises account for the presence of only one restaurant chain on an interstate highway and the single boat-rental establishment in a state park. National governments can also create or preserve monopolies through their trade policies. By erecting trade barriers, governments can prevent foreign products from entering their countries, thereby reserving the market for domestic firms. (Patents are supposed to protect their holders from copying for 20 years. But drug companies are finding ways to effectively extend the lives of their patents and the monopolies they confer. Read "How a Drug Maker Tries to Outwit Generics," on page 240, to find out how.)

Monopoly and Market Power

Monopolists enjoy substantial pricing discretion because they are the sole suppliers of their products. This enables the monopolist to manipulate industry output and thereby alter the market price. The monopolist's control over output does not provide it with complete or unlimited pricing discretion, however. Complete pricing discretion would result in a vertical, perfectly inelastic demand curve, signifying the ability to increase price without losing *any* customers. This condition would represent the true opposite of the purely competitive firm, which possesses no market power and faces a horizontal, perfectly elastic demand curve.

But a monopolist does stand to lose some customers when it raises its price, because monopolists face a certain amount of competition from rivals in *other* industries. To illustrate, think about a community served by a single newspaper and a single provider of electric power. These sellers fit the description of a monopolist, but neither is without competition. If the newspaper charges a high subscription rate, residents can turn to their local TV or radio station for their news. If it charges high prices for its classified ads, residents can buy cardboard signs and post them around town. Or they can turn to the Internet and try to reach customers that way. Residents face tougher choices when it comes to dealing with the local electric company, but even here they have options. If the utility company effects a drastic rate increase for electricity, residents can begin by reducing their use of electricity. They can insulate their homes and install energy-saving appliances; ultimately, they can even purchase their own electricity generators. The point is that the availability of substitutes, however imperfect, constrains the monopolist's pricing discretion.[6]

Monopoly and Profit Maximization

Because a monopolist stands to lose some customers when it raises its price, the demand curve it faces must slope downward just as those of other price searchers do. This tells us that the monopolist must restrict output to charge a high price; conversely, it must reduce price to sell more. The monopolist will select the profit-maximizing output and price in exactly the same way other price searchers do; it will produce the output at which $MR = MC$ and find its price by going up to the demand curve. The difference between a monopolist and other price searchers is found not in the rules used to determine their price but in the competitive situation. Monopolistically competitive firms and oligopolists face some degree of competition from other firms in the industry. The monopolist *is* the industry, and so its only competition comes from firms in other industries.

Because monopolists enjoy substantial pricing discretion, it is commonly believed that they must earn economic profits. But that need not be the case. In the short run, monopolists, like other producers, may experience economic profits, normal profits, or even losses. How well a monopolist will fare depends on the demand and cost conditions that it faces. Imagine, for instance, a firm that has patented a medicine for a very rare disease—with an average diagnosis of ten cases a year. This monopolist has substantial pricing discretion with these unfortunate victims, but the demand is so limited that the product probably will be unprofitable to produce. Or consider the boat-rental concession at an isolated state park. The owner enjoys a government-granted monopoly, but if few vacationers frequent the lake, it won't be a very profitable monopoly. The point is that even a monopolist can't earn a profit if the demand for its product is very limited. High production costs can signal a similar problem. Exhibit 8.5 depicts a monopolist incurring a short-run economic loss.

When monopolists *are* able to earn short-run profits, substantial entry barriers help them to continue earning those profits in the long run. But the long run does not mean forever! Ultimately the development of new products, the introduction of new technologies, and/or the elimination of legal barriers to entry tend to undermine the monopolist's position. For example, at one time American Telephone and Telegraph (AT&T) enjoyed a monopoly

---

[6] Although most communities are still served by a single provider of electric power, technological advances and regulatory changes are undermining these monopolies. These changes may ultimately provide at least some consumers with choices about where they buy their power.

EXHIBIT 8.5

A Monopolist Incurring a Loss

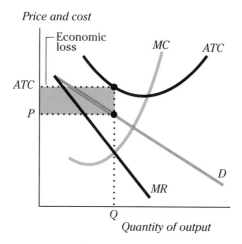

Even a monopolist can incur a loss if there is little demand for its product or if its costs are high.

in providing long-distance telephone service. But new technology ultimately destroyed its monopoly status (this will be discussed in greater detail in a moment). A similar fate seems in store for your provider of local phone service. Cell-phone companies now provide consumers with an alternative to the wired service offered by these former monopolists. Moreover, the deregulation of this industry carries the promise of additional competition for wired service as well.

Technological change is not the only thing that monopolists have to fear. When monopolists earn economic profits, the lure of those profits provides strong incentive for potential rivals to enter that market. And even patents may not be a sufficient barrier to keep them out. The profits that Burroughs Wellcome (now GlaxoSmithKline) earned on AZT, the first patented AIDS drug, helped to spur a search for alternative treatments. And the blockbuster success of Lipitor, the cholesterol-reducing drug patented by Pfizer, has clearly encouraged rivals to develop new cholesterol-reducing drugs based on compounds that do not violate Pfizer's patent.

None of this is intended to make you feel sorry for monopolists. Technological progress is hard to predict and generally occurs slowly. The development of new products is equally unpredictable; sometimes the alternatives come quickly, sometimes not. The point is that change is the norm, and eventually most monopolists find their status eroded by forces that are largely beyond their control.

THE CONSEQUENCES OF MONOPOLY OR OLIGOPOLY

The presence of monopolies can have a significant effect on consumer well-being. Monopolists tend to produce too little output and sometimes charge prices that are inflated by economic profits. These negative effects may be partially offset by lower production costs or greater innovation. Oligopoly can have a similar impact on consumer welfare, though it is much more difficult to generalize about the consequences of this industry structure.

The Problems of Misallocation of Resources and Redistribution of Income

Economists generally agree that monopolists distort the allocation of scarce resources. Like monopolistically competitive firms, monopolists fail to produce up to the point where marginal social benefit equals marginal social cost—the point at which resources would be allocated efficiently. As a consequence, too few resources are devoted to the production of the goods and services produced by monopolists, and too many resources are left over to be used in the more competitive sectors of the economy. For example, if there were only two industries in the economy, a monopolized computer industry and a purely competitive farming industry, society probably would receive too few computers and too many agricultural products.

The redistribution of income is another problem caused by monopolies. Because entrance into these industries is blocked, consumers may be required to pay higher prices than necessary, prices that include economic profits on top of the normal profits that are necessary to convince firms to continue operation. These higher prices redistribute income from consumers (who will be worse off) to monopolists (who will be better off).

Although economists are fairly confident in generalizing about the consequences of monopoly, they find it more difficult to make blanket statements regarding the impact of oligopoly. This is primarily because the behavior of oligopolists is so varied. To the extent that oligopolists cooperate and avoid price competition, the welfare effects of oligopoly probably are very similar to the effects of pure monopoly. When cooperation breaks down, consumer welfare is enhanced, and the negative effects of oligopoly are reduced. Since it is clear that oligopolists do not always succeed in avoiding price competition, the impact of oligopoly on consumer well-being probably lies somewhere between the impacts of monopoly and pure competition.

The Possible Benefits of Size

Although monopoly and oligopoly often have undesirable effects on consumer welfare, this is not always the case. Under certain conditions these structures may benefit society. For example, if a monopolist's/oligopolist's greater size leads to economies of scale (lower long-run average costs), it may be able to charge a lower price than a competitive firm even as it earns an economic profit. And because monopolists and oligopolists are often able to earn economic profits in the long run, they can afford the investment necessary to develop new products and cost-reducing production techniques. Thus, in the long run, society may receive better products and lower prices from monopolists and oligopolists than from competitive firms.

Studies of the U.S. economy provide limited support for these arguments. For example, in the refrigerator-manufacturing industry a firm needs 15 to 20 percent of the market to achieve production efficiency, or minimum *ATC*. This means that for optimal efficiency, room exists for only five or six firms in that industry. The efficient manufacture and distribution of beer requires a somewhat smaller but nevertheless substantial market share: 10 to 14 percent. But in the majority of the manufacturing industries surveyed, firms with 3 percent of the market or less were large enough to operate at minimum *ATC*. Thus, it is not generally necessary for industries to be dominated by one or a few firms to achieve efficiency in production and distribution.[7]

Evidence on business research and development is not as definitive but is modestly supportive of a similar conclusion. It appears that firms in highly competitive industries are not particularly innovative, perhaps because they are unable to earn the profits necessary to finance research and development. But firms in "tightly" oligopolistic industries (in which a very few firms are able to closely coordinate their actions to avoid competition) don't appear to be particularly innovative either. Why? One possibility is that, although these firms have the money to finance research and development efforts, they lack the incentive, which stems from competitive pressure, to invest in research and development. It may be that the most innovative firms are those in "loosely" oligopolistic industries—industries composed of several firms with no single firm being dominant. In these industries, firms often earn the economic profits necessary to support research and development efforts, and the difficulty in coordinating their actions means they face greater competitive pressure to innovate.[8]

In summary, production economies and greater innovation may sometimes compensate for the resource misallocation and income redistribution caused by monopolists and oligopolists. But the drive to lower production costs and/or

---

[7] F. M. Scherer and David Ross, *Industrial Market Structure and Economic Performance*, 3rd ed. (Boston: Houghton Mifflin, 1990), p. 140.

[8] Don E. Waldman and Elizabeth J. Jensen, *Industrial Organization: Theory and Practice*, 2nd ed. (Boston: Addison-Wesley, 2001), pp. 417–418. The authors note that, although there is some evidence of a relationship between an industry's structure and the level of innovation, it is clear that there is much more to be considered. For instance, some industries are more innovative than others simply because the nature of the industry's product offers more opportunities for innovation.

increase innovation does not explain the high degree of concentration—the dominance by a few large firms—that we see in some of our consumer-good-producing industries. Rather, it is the drive to achieve economies of scale in advertising and sales promotion that is at work. In the beer industry, for instance, Anheuser Busch is dominant in part because it can afford to promote its brews more heavily than its rivals. Any promotion cost—advertising in the Super Bowl, for instance—can be spread over its huge customer base, lowering the cost of reaching the average consumer. These advertising economies clearly benefit firms like Anheuser Busch, but their impact on consumer well-being is debatable. By increasing product differentiation, persuasive advertising tends to enlarge market power (pricing discretion) and make it more difficult for rivals or potential rivals to compete—outcomes that don't serve consumers well. In these industries, consumers would be better served if the industry structure were more, not less, competitive.

ANTITRUST AND REGULATION

Because the exercise of market power by monopolists and oligopolists can distort the allocation of scarce resources and redistribute income, the federal and state governments pursue policies designed to promote competition and restrict the actions of firms with market power. The primary weapons used in the battle against market power are antitrust laws and industry regulation. As you will see, these two approaches to the problem differ significantly in both their philosophies and the remedies they propose.

Antitrust Enforcement

Antitrust laws have as their objective the maintenance and promotion of competition. These laws (1) outlaw collusion, (2) make it illegal for a firm to attempt to achieve a monopoly, and (3) ban **mergers**, the union of two or more companies into a single firm, when such mergers are likely to result in substantially less competition.

Virtually all antitrust enforcement in the United States is based on three fundamental statutes: the Sherman Antitrust Act of 1890, the Clayton Antitrust Act of 1914, and the Federal Trade Commission Act, also passed in 1914. Exhibit 8.6 offers a brief comparison of these laws.

The Sherman Antitrust Act   The Sherman Act, the first of the big three, was a response to the monopolistic exploitation that occurred in the latter half of the nineteenth century, when trusts had become commonplace. **Trusts** are combinations of firms organized for the purpose of restraining price

EXHIBIT 8.6

The Antitrust Laws and What They Do

The Sherman Antitrust Act (1890)	Outlawed agreements to fix prices, limit output, or share the market. Also declared that monopolies and attempts to monopolize are illegal.
The Clayton Antitrust Act (1914)	Forbade competitors to merge if the impact of merger would be to lessen competition substantially. Also outlawed certain practices, such as tying contracts.
The Federal Trade Commission Act (1914)	Created the Federal Trade Commission and empowered it to initiate and decide cases involving "unfair competition." Also declared that deceptive practices and unfair methods of competition are illegal.

competition and thereby gaining economic profit. (For our purposes, a trust is the same thing as a cartel.) So many companies were merging at this time that competitors were disappearing at an alarming rate. Du Pont, for example, achieved a near monopoly in the manufacture of explosives by either merging with or acquiring some 100 rival firms between 1872 and 1912.[9] Monopolies and monopolistic practices translated into higher prices for consumers and inspired a strong political movement that led to the passage of the Sherman Antitrust Act in 1890.

The Sherman Act declared illegal all agreements between competing firms to fix prices, limit output, or otherwise restrict the forces of competition. It also declared illegal all monopolies or "attempts to monopolize any part of trade or commerce among the several states, or with foreign nations." In 1911, the law became the basis for the antitrust suit that resulted in the breakup of Standard Oil, a trust that controlled some 90 percent of the petroleum industry.

In deciding the Standard Oil case, the Supreme Court applied a principle known as the "rule of reason." According to this interpretation, possessing a monopoly is not, by itself, a violation of the law. Rather, it must be shown that the firm deliberately sought to obtain a monopoly or engaged in conduct intended to preserve its monopoly. This principle was evident on April 3, 2000, when Judge Penfield Jackson found that Microsoft had violated the Sherman Act because it had illegally protected its Windows monopoly against competitors

---

[9] F. M. Scherer, *Industrial Market Structure and Economic Performance*, 2nd ed. (Chicago: Rand McNally, 1980), p. 121.

and had attempted to monopolize the market for browsers used to navigate the World Wide Web. The judge went on to order that Microsoft be split into two companies in an attempt to reduce its monopoly power and promote competition. This remedy was later set aside in favor of milder penalties.

As a result of the limits laid down by the courts in the Standard Oil case, businesses became somewhat less aggressive in their monopolistic practices. Rather than strive for monopoly, they were content to become the dominant firms in their respective oligopolistic industries. However, many firms gained dominion not by abandoning such practices but by pursuing them in disguised and subtle ways. This led Congress in 1914 to pass two more bills aimed at curbing anticompetitive practices: the Clayton Antitrust Act and the Federal Trade Commission Act. (The Sherman Act bans price fixing. So why did the Supreme Court recently decide that it can be legal? Read "Price-Fixing Makes Comeback after Supreme Court Ruling," on page 252, to find out.)

The Clayton Antitrust Act   The Clayton Act was designed primarily to stem the tide of mergers that had already reduced competition significantly in a number of important industries, such as steel production, petroleum refining, and electrical equipment manufacture. The act prohibited mergers between competing firms if the impact of their union would be to "substantially lessen competition or to tend to create a monopoly." The act also outlawed other practices if they lessened competition. "Other practices" included **tying contracts**— agreements specifying that the purchaser would, as a condition of sale for a

Under the leadership of John D. Rockefeller, the Standard Oil trust acquired a virtual monopoly in petroleum refining.

given product, also buy some other product offered by the seller. Once again, enforcement was a problem because the courts interpreted this law in ways that permitted mergers between competing firms to continue. Finally, in 1950, the Cellar-Kefauver Act amended the Clayton Act by closing a major loophole, thus effectively eliminating the possibility of mergers involving major competitors.

During the Reagan administration, the federal government began relaxing its restrictions against mergers involving major competitors. This more consenting attitude continued, with a few exceptions, through the administration of George W. Bush. The result was a wave of merger activity beginning in the 1980s and continuing to date. Many experts believe that proposed mergers will be subject to greater scrutiny under the Obama administration. We'll have to wait and see.

The Federal Trade Commission Act The last of the three major antitrust statutes, the Federal Trade Commission Act, was also passed in 1914. Its primary purpose was to establish a special agency, the Federal Trade Commission (FTC), empowered to investigate allegations of "unfair methods of competition" and to command businesses in violation of FTC regulations to cease those practices. Although the FTC Act did not specify the precise meaning of "unfair methods of competition," the phrase has been interpreted by the commission to include practices prohibited under the Sherman and Clayton Acts—price fixing and tying contracts, for example—and any other practices that can be shown to limit competition or damage the consuming public. For instance, the FTC has deemed it unfair for a funeral home to fail to provide, in advance, an itemized price list for funeral services and merchandise or to furnish embalming without first informing customers about alternatives.

The Federal Trade Commission is one of the two federal agencies charged with the enforcement of the antitrust statutes. The other agency is the Antitrust Division of the Justice Department. The Antitrust Division is responsible for enforcing the Sherman and Clayton Acts and lesser pieces of antitrust legislation. The FTC is also charged with antitrust enforcement, including civil actions against violators of either the Sherman or Clayton Acts, but its responsibilities are somewhat broader. About half its resources are devoted to combating deception and misrepresentation: improper labeling and misleading advertisements, for example. The overlapping responsibilities of the FTC and the Antitrust Division have posed some problems of coordination, but these are at least partially offset by the likelihood that one agency's oversights may be picked up by the other.

Criticisms of Antitrust

Some economists argue that antitrust should be discarded because it is based on the outmoded perception that bigness (being large in relation to the size of the market) is bad. These economists believe that the ability of large firms to achieve economies of scale and rapid development of new products more than compensates for any reduction in competition. This is particularly true, they argue, in the era of globalization. Today, foreign rivals can put competitive pressure on even relatively large U.S. firms, reducing their market power and sometimes threatening their very existence. Think about General Motors, for instance. Once the dominant firm in the U.S. auto industry, in 2009 its very existence was in question—in part because of the strength of foreign competition.

According to these economists, U.S. antitrust laws handicap domestic producers in this competitive struggle. Consider, for example, the Japanese *keiretsu*, or "group of companies." This arrangement joins together rival producers, along with their suppliers, banks, and government agencies, to share knowledge and gain efficiency. These structures, although legal in Japan, would probably be illegal in the United States under present antitrust laws. Antitrust critics argue that by prohibiting such joint ventures, we tie the hands of our domestic producers and put them at a competitive disadvantage relative to their foreign rivals.[10]

Supporters of antitrust laws point out that while bigness is not always bad, it is not always good either. So, they argue, the correct response is not to discard antitrust enforcement but to apply it on a case-by-case basis. For example, some mergers and cooperative ventures may be in the best interest of consumers because they lower costs or create more effective competitors. But others may reduce competition without achieving offsetting efficiencies. And while competition from foreign firms has changed the economic environment for many U.S. businesses, other industries do not face significant competitive pressure from abroad. Furthermore, statistical evidence suggests that most U.S. firms are large enough to compete effectively with foreign rivals. Although there may be exceptions to this generalization—the *keiretsu* and similar foreign alliances may require that similar alliances be permitted in the United States—the existence of these exceptions does not justify abandoning our antitrust statutes.

Industry Regulation

Government regulation of industry approaches the problem of market power from a different perspective and therefore provides a different solution. The basic assumption is that certain industries cannot or should not be made competitive. Hence, the role of government is to provide a framework whereby the actions of these less-than-competitive firms can be constrained in a manner consistent with the public interest. This is accomplished by establishing regulatory agencies empowered to control the prices such firms can charge, the quality of

---

[10] Patrick M. Boarman, "Antitrust Laws in a Global Market," *Challenge*, January–February 1993, pp. 30–36.

Use Your Economic Reasoning

Price-Fixing Makes Comeback after Supreme Court Ruling

BY JOSEPH PEREIRA

Manufacturers are embracing broad new legal powers that amount to a type of price-fixing—enabling them to set minimum prices on their products and force retailers to refrain from discounting.

For the better part of a century, punishing retailers for selling at cut-rate prices was an automatic violation of antitrust law. However, a Supreme Court ruling last year [2007] involving handbag sales at a Dallas mom-and-pop store, Kay's Kloset, upended that original 1911 precedent, potentially altering the face of U.S. discount retailing.

Retailers say an array of manufacturers now require them to abide by minimum-pricing pacts, or risk having their supplies cut off. Jacob Weiss of BabyAge.com, which specializes in maternity and children's gear, says nearly 100 of his 465 suppliers now dictate minimum prices, and nearly a dozen have cut off shipments to him. "If this continues, it's going to put us out of the baby business," he says.

The new rules mean "it's becoming a nightmare operating a business," says Brian Okin, founder of WorldHomeCenter.com Inc., a home-improvement retailer. The company is suing lighting maker L. D. Kichler in New York state court alleging that L. D. Kichler's minimum-price policy caused the retailer to miss out on substantial profits. "It just makes it so difficult to compete," Mr. Okin says.

Manufacturers like the policies partly because discounts can tarnish a brand's image. "We don't want consumers to think we're the cheapest guys in the world," says Ray Minoff of L. D. Kichler, the lighting maker. Retailers also have more of an incentive to heavily market price-protected goods, manufacturers say. Critics argue the policies undermine the free market by limiting shoppers' power to decide for themselves whether to, say, buy at rock-bottom price from a no-frills outlet, or pay full price to someone offering better service or other benefits. . . .

State attorneys general are warning that minimum pricing, also known as "resale price maintenance," will feed inflation. Supreme Court Justice Stephen Breyer, in his dissent in the case, estimated that legalizing price-setting could add $300 billion to annual consumer costs. In May [2008], attorneys general from 35 states—including New York, California, Massachusetts and Pennsylvania—wrote to Congress urging passage of a law to make policies like these illegal. "As the chief antitrust enforcers in our respective States, we know all too well the harm that can be caused" by pricing pacts, the letter says.

Consumer advocates say they are seeing the impact particularly in baby goods, consumer electronics, home furnishings and pet food. Edgar Dworsky of ConsumerWorld.org, a provider of price comparisons for consumers, says retail-pricing norms have already changed significantly. "My sense is that price-fixing is becoming more common," says Mr. Dworsky, a former Massachusetts assistant attorney general who has worked on antitrust matters.

Source: Wall Street Journal, August 18, 2008, p. A1. Rachel Dodes contributed to this article. Reprinted by permission of the *Wall Street Journal,* Copyright © 2008 Dow Jones & Company, Inc. All Rights Reserved Worldwide. License number 2231561043749.

Online retailers say some policies target them specifically. Mr. Okin of WorldHome Center.com says L. D. Kichler's policy applies only to advertised prices—meaning discounting is OK as long as it isn't publicized. But online shops, by definition, publicize their prices online. "We are being punished by [the 2007 Supreme Court ruling] exactly because we're more efficient than our competitors," Mr. Okin says. Mr. Minoff of L. D. Kichler points out the policy applies to both traditional and online retailers.

It is still illegal for a group of manufacturers or retailers (or both) to band together and fix prices. That would be a violation of the Sherman Antitrust Act, which prohibits precisely that kind of anticompetitive behavior. The Supreme Court ruling at the heart of the recent changes dealt with a narrower issue: It ruled on a manufacturer's right to enforce minimum prices on its own products. In the case, Leegin Creative Leather Products Inc., a maker of women's purses and accessories, was sued by

Kay's Kloset, a Dallas retailer, after Leegin cut off shipments to Kay's. Kay's had been discounting Leegin's wears. The high court's June 2007 decision, written by Justice Anthony Kennedy, declared that minimum-pricing pacts between manufacturers and retailers could benefit customers under certain circumstances. For instance, the pacts could foster competition by giving retailers enough profit to promote a brand or offer better service, Justice Kennedy wrote. Individual price-setting agreements should be examined on a case-by-case basis, the ruling said, to be sure they're not anticompetitive. . . .

For shoppers, the reality is that there's little to be done about minimum-pricing policies, says Lino A. Graglia, a professor at the University of Texas Law School who is studying the Leegin decision. "It's going to be so difficult to prove that these resale-price-maintenance agreements are anticompetitive," he says. . . .

USE YOUR ECONOMIC REASONING

1. This article discusses minimum pricing pacts, or "resale-price-maintenance agreements." Explain how these agreements work.
2. If a manufacturer receives the same wholesale price (from the retailer it supplies), regardless of the price charged by the retailer, why does the manufacturer care what price the retailer charges?
3. Justice Kennedy's decision suggests that, under certain circumstances, pricing pacts can foster competition. Suppose that a group of retailers all must charge the same price for a given product (because of the pacts). How would they compete for customers? How is this competition different from what you would expect if the pricing pacts were illegal?
4. What do you think about the argument that shoppers ought to have the power to decide "whether to . . . buy at rock-bottom price from a no-frills outlet, or pay full price to someone offering better service or other benefits"?
5. This Supreme Court ruling allows resale-price-maintenance agreements but does not lift the ban on price-fixing agreements between rival manufacturing firms (or between rival retailers). How would you explain the Court's willingness to ban one but not the other?
6. Some economists support resale-price-maintenance agreements, some oppose them. Do you believe these agreements will "benefit customers"?

service they must provide, and the conditions under which additional firms will be allowed to enter the industry.

The reason that certain industries should not be made competitive is that they are *natural monopolies*. As we learned in the last chapter, a natural monopoly exists when a single firm can supply the entire market at a lower average cost than two or more firms could. In essence, natural monopolies are situations in which we don't want to permit competition between firms because it would interfere with our ability to achieve the lowest possible production costs. The provision of local phone service has traditionally been regarded as a natural monopoly, as has the provision of electric power. To understand why, think about your local phone company for a moment. Providing local phone service requires a very large initial investment in switching equipment, telephone poles, wires, and other hardware. These fixed costs are the major costs of doing business as a phone company; the variable cost of providing phone service is relatively low. Of course, the more customers the phone company serves, the lower the firm's average fixed cost. Because most of the phone company's costs are fixed costs, as average fixed cost falls, so does average total cost.

Because average cost declines with output, society is better off with one big firm rather than several smaller firms. At least it is if the monopolist passes on its cost savings to consumers. That's where regulation comes in. Natural monopolies like the local telephone and utility companies are generally subject to rate regulation by state regulatory commissions. The logic is straightforward. Government allows these firms to operate as monopolists to gain the benefits associated with size—low average cost. But it regulates these monopolists to ensure that some of those benefits are passed on to consumers in the form of lower prices.

Although the logic for regulating natural monopolies is straightforward, regulation has not been confined to natural monopolies. Over the years, numerous industries—including airlines, trucking, radio and television, and water carriers (ships and barges)—have been thought to be sufficiently "clothed with the public interest" to justify regulation, even though none of these would be described as natural monopolies. In the last two decades, this questionable regulation has come under increasing attack, and virtually all these industries have been deregulated. The only significant push-back from this laissez-faire trend has been the call for greater regulation of the banking sector following the financial meltdown of 2008–2009. Although the objectives of banking regulation are quite different from the industry regulation described here, this philosophical shift may affect other forms of economic regulation in the future.[11]

---

[11]Regulation designed to deal with the problems posed by market power—the primary thrust of this section of the textbook—is sometimes described as "price and entry regulation." That is distinct from two other forms of regulation in our economy: "health, safety, and regulation," which is intended to protect the physical well-being of workers and consumers, and "financial regulation," which is intended to protect depositors and ensure the stability of the banking system.

SUMMARY

In the U.S. economy, most firms have some market power, or pricing discretion. Market power is exercised through product differentiation or by altering total industry output. The extent of the firm's market power depends on the structure, or makeup, of the industry in which it operates. The definitive characteristics of *industry structure* are the number of sellers in the industry and their size distribution, the nature of the product, and the extent of barriers to entry. The four basic industry structures are pure competition, monopolistic competition, oligopoly, and pure monopoly.

At one end of the spectrum lie purely competitive firms, which are totally without market power. Because the competitive industry is characterized by a large number of relatively small firms selling undifferentiated products, each firm is powerless to influence price. The absence of significant barriers to entry prevents purely competitive firms from earning economic profits in the long run.

Monopolistic competition is the market structure most closely resembling pure competition; the difference is that monopolistically competitive firms sell differentiated products. The ability to differentiate its product allows the monopolistically competitive firm some pricing discretion, although that discretion is limited by the availability of close substitutes offered by competing firms. Monopolistically competitive firms misallocate resources because they fail to produce up to the point at which marginal social benefits equal marginal social costs. They also are somewhat less efficient at producing their products than are purely competitive firms with identical cost curves. These disadvantages are at least partially offset by the product variety offered by these sellers.

The third market structure, *oligopoly*, is characterized by a small number of relatively large firms that are protected by significant barriers to entry. Although these firms may enjoy substantial pricing discretion, their market power is constrained by the high degree of interdependence that exists among oligopolistic firms. *Game theory* is one of the tools used to understand and predict the behavior of these interdependent rivals.

Oligopolists sometime use *collusion,* secret agreements to fix prices, and *price leadership*, informal agreements to follow the price changes of one firm, as tactics to reduce competition. Even in the absence of collusion or price leadership, oligopolists may choose to avoid price competition because it tends to invite retaliation. Instead these firms tend to channel their competitive instincts into *nonprice competition*—advertising, packaging, and new-product development.

The market structure farthest removed from pure competition is monopoly, or *pure monopoly*. The monopolist enjoys substantial pricing discretion and dictates the level of output. The monopoly *is* the industry because it is the sole seller of a product for which there are no close substitutes. Unlike that of the purely competitive firm, the monopolist's position is protected by substantial barriers to entry, which may enable monopolistic firms to earn economic profits in the long run.

Like monopolistically competitive firms, monopolists tend to distort the allocation of resources by halting production short of the point at which marginal social benefit equals marginal social cost. Monopolists may charge higher prices than necessary—prices that include economic profits. These higher prices redistribute income from consumers to the monopolists. Oligopoly can have a similar impact on consumer welfare, but it is more difficult to generalize about the consequences of that market structure. In some industries the negative consequences of monopoly or oligopoly may be offset by the lower production costs that result from their greater size or by greater innovation due to their ability to invest economic profits in research and development.

Because monopolists and oligopolists may misallocate resources and redistribute income, the U.S. Congress has passed antitrust laws and created regulatory agencies. Enacted in response to the formation of *trusts* (combinations of firms organized to restrain competition), *antitrust laws* prohibit certain kinds of behavior: price fixing, *tying contracts*, and *mergers* entered into for the purpose of limiting competition. The major antitrust statutes are the Sherman Antitrust Act of 1890, the Clayton Antitrust Act of 1914, and the Federal Trade Commission Act, also passed in 1914.

Critics of antitrust argue that it should be discarded because it is based on the misperception that bigness is bad. According to this view, the ability of large firms to achieve economies of scale and more rapid new-product development more than compensates for any reduction in competition. Moreover, in an era of increased foreign competition, even relatively large U.S. firms may be small in comparison with the world market. In fact, cooperative ventures between U.S. firms may be necessary to compete effectively with foreign rivals.

Supporters of antitrust respond by pointing out that size does not always confer advantages such as economies of scale or more rapid new product development. In addition, available evidence suggests that most U.S. firms are large enough to compete effectively with their foreign rivals.

Industry regulation, the other approach to dealing with potentially exploitive market power, is designed to establish and police rules of behavior for *natural monopolies,* industries in which competition cannot or should not develop because of technical or cost considerations. In addition, regulation was once extended to some industries where there is little evidence of natural monopoly status—transportation, for example. Today, virtually all this questionable regulation has been eliminated, and technological changes are undermining some longstanding natural monopolies.

KEY TERMS

Antitrust laws	Government franchise	Nash equilibrium
Collusion	Industry structure	Oligopoly
Conscious parallelism	Mergers	Price leadership
Dominant strategy	Monopolistic competition	Trusts
Game theory	Monopoly	Tying contract

STUDY QUESTIONS

Fill in the Blanks

1. Firms that can influence the price of their product are said to possess _____.

2. An industry dominated by a few relatively large sellers is a(n) _____.

3. The closest market structure to pure competition is _____.

4. In long-run equilibrium, purely competitive firms and _____ firms can earn only a normal profit.

5. The distinguishing feature of oligopoly is the high degree of _____ that exists among sellers.

6. A(n) _____ is the sole seller of a product for which there are no good substitutes.

7. _____ is agreement between sellers to fix prices or limit competition.

8. Monopolists distort the allocation of scarce resources because they produce (more/less) _____ of their product than is socially desirable.

9. The first major antitrust law, the _____ Act, was passed in 1890.

10. Both oligopolists and monopolists may earn economic profits in the long run because they are protected by substantial _____.

11. The study of the strategies used by interdependent firms is known as _____.

12. _____ refers to oligopolists adopting similar policies without any communication whatsoever.

Multiple Choice

1. Which of the following is *not* an element of industry structure?
   a) The number of sellers in the industry
   b) The extent of barriers to entry
   c) The existence of economic profits
   d) The size distribution of sellers

2. Which of the following statements about unregulated monopolists is *false*?
   a) They may incur an economic loss in the short run.
   b) They maximize their profit (or minimize their loss) by producing the output at which *MR* equals *MC*.

c) They sell their product at a price equal to marginal cost.

d) They face competition from rivals in other industries.

3. Which of the following is *not* a characteristic of monopolistic competition?
   a) Substantial barriers to entry
   b) Differentiated products
   c) A large number of sellers
   d) Small firms

4. In a large city, a doughnut shop is probably an example of
   a) a purely competitive firm.
   b) a monopolistically competitive firm.
   c) an oligopolist.
   d) a monopolist.

5. American Airlines will not raise prices without first considering how United will behave. This is probably evidence of their
   a) cutthroat competition.
   b) collusion.
   c) interdependence.
   d) price fixing.

6. Which of the following is usually *not* a characteristic of oligopolistic industries?
   a) Mutual interdependence
   b) Substantial barriers to entry
   c) Relatively large sellers
   d) Fierce price competition

7. Which of the following do monopolistically competitive firms, oligopolists, and monopolists have in common?
   a) All are relatively large.
   b) All have some market power.
   c) All are protected by substantial barriers to entry.

d) All are concerned about the reactions of rivals to any actions they take.

8. Which of the following statutes outlawed "attempts to monopolize"?
   a) The Sherman Act
   b) The Clayton Act
   c) The Cellar-Kefauver Act
   d) The Federal Trade Commission Act

9. What is the primary difference between antitrust enforcement and industry regulation?
   a) Antitrust enforcement attempts to promote competition; industry regulation does not.
   b) Antitrust enforcement has some critics; industry regulation does not.
   c) Antitrust enforcement is concerned about the public interest; industry regulation attempts to protect the regulated firms.
   d) Industry regulation deals only with natural monopolies; antitrust does not.

10. The concept of conscious parallelism suggests that oligopolists
    a) will always collude.
    b) can adopt similar policies without any communication.
    c) use price leadership to coordinate their pricing policies.
    d) prefer price competition to nonprice competition.

Use the payoff matrix at the bottom of this page in answering questions 11 and 12.

11. Which of the following is true?
    a) X's dominant strategy is to charge $15; Y doesn't have a dominant strategy.
    b) The dominant strategy for both X and Y is to charge $15.

Firm X's price strategies

		$15	$20
Firm Y's price strategies	$15	Each firm earns a $20,000 profit.	X earns $10,000. Y earns $40,000.
	$20	X earns $40,000. Y earns $10,000.	Each firm earns a $30,000 profit.

c) Y's dominant strategy is to charge $20; X doesn't have a dominant strategy.

d) The dominant strategy for both X and Y is to charge $20.

12. If both firms charge $15,
    a) each firm will earn a profit of $30,000.
    b) there will be incentive to collude and raise the price to $20.
    c) firm X will earn $40,000.
    d) firm Y will earn $40,000.

13. Cheating on collusive agreements is more likely when
    a) there are very few firms in the industry.
    b) the economy is weak and firms have excess capacity.
    c) each firm's prices are readily known.
    d) cheaters can expect swift retaliation.

14. Which of the following is a true statement about industry regulation in the United States?
    a) It is intended to create more competition in the regulated industry.
    b) It has been applied only to natural monopolies.
    c) It has largely replaced antitrust as a method of controlling market power.
    d) It is playing a smaller role as technological advances undermine natural monopolies.

15. Firms that are monopolists
    a) always earn economic profits in the short run.
    b) always earn economic profits in the long run.
    c) can see their monopoly status eroded by technological progress.
    d) All of the above

16. When a monopolistically competitive firm is in long-run equilibrium,
    a) price equals marginal cost.
    b) the demand curve is tangent to the marginal cost curve.
    c) price equals average total cost.
    d) the firm earns an economic profit.

17. If the firms in a monopolistically competitive industry are earning economic profits,
    a) additional firms will enter the industry, shifting each firm's demand curve to the right.
    b) firms will tend to leave the industry until a normal profit is earned.
    c) firms will enter the industry, reducing the demand for each firm's product.
    d) firms will enter the industry until each firm's demand curve is tangent to its marginal cost curve.

Use the payoff matrix below in answering questions 18–20.

18. Which of the following is true?
    a) A's dominant strategy is to advertise.
    b) B's dominant strategy is not to advertise.
    c) A does not have a dominant strategy.
    d) B's dominant strategy is to advertise.

19. If A decides not to advertise, B's best strategy is
    a) not to advertise, in which case it will earn $40,000.
    b) to advertise, in which case it will earn $40,000.
    c) not to advertise, in which case it will earn $80,000.

Firm A's advertising strategies

		Don't advertise	Advertise
Firm B's advertising strategies	Don't advertise	A earns $100,000. B earns $80,000.	A earns $150,000. B earns $0 profit.
	Advertise	A earns $0 profit. B earns $60,000.	A earns $60,000. B earns $40,000.

   d) to advertise, in which case it will earn
      $80,000.

20. Because B knows that A's dominant strat-
    egy is
    a) to advertise, B's best strategy is to ad-
       vertise also.

   b) not to advertise, B will also opt not to
      advertise.
   c) to advertise, B's best strategy is not to
      advertise.
   d) not to advertise, B's best strategy is to
      advertise.

Problems and Questions for Discussion

1. What constrains a monopolist's pricing
   discretion?

2. What problems might be associated with
   monopolistic or oligopolistic market structures? That is, how might they harm consumer well-being?

3. How do firms acquire market power?
   What impact do barriers to entry have on
   a firm's market power?

4. Why would we expect prices to be somewhat higher under monopolistic competition than under pure competition?

5. Suppose that there is only one grocery store
   in your neighborhood. What limits its market power? If your neighborhood were
   more isolated, would that increase or decrease the grocery store's market power?

6. In some communities, grocery stores may
   act as oligopolists, whereas in other communities, they may act as monopolistically
   competitive firms. How is this possible?
   How would you distinguish the first situation from the second?

7. Under what circumstances might consumers be better off with monopoly or oligopoly than with a competitive structure?

8. What is meant by a *natural monopoly*, and
   how can its existence justify regulation?

9. Some economists argue that antitrust is an
   outmoded policy that should be discarded.
   Discuss the basis for this conclusion, and
   summarize the opposing view.

10. Explain what is meant by a dominant
    strategy.

ANSWER KEY

Fill in the Blanks

1. market power
2. oligopoly
3. monopolistic competition
4. monopolistically
   competitive

5. interdependence
6. monopoly
7. Collusion
8. less

9. Sherman
10. barriers to entry
11. game theory
12. Conscious parallelism

Multiple Choice

1. c	5. c	9. a	13. b	17. c
2. c	6. d	10. b	14. d	18. a
3. a	7. b	11. b	15. c	19. c
4. b	8. a	12. b	16. c	20. a

CHAPTER

9

Market Failure

1. Define market failure and identify its sources.
2. Distinguish between internal and external costs (and benefits).
3. Describe how externalities distort the allocation of scarce resources.
4. Examine the three basic approaches for dealing with externalities.
5. Explain pollution as the result of poorly defined property rights.
6. Discuss why pollution taxes are superior to uniform regulation.
7. Distinguish between private and public goods.
8. Explain the free-rider problem and its consequences.
9. Discuss the views of public-choice economists and the concept of government failure.

One of the major strengths of market economies is their ability to use resources to produce the goods and services that consumers value most highly. But sometimes markets produce too much or too little of certain products and thus fail to make the most efficient use of society's limited resources. This, as you might expect, is referred to as **market failure**.

We've already discussed one source of market failure, the existence of market power. As you discovered in Chapters 7 and 8, firms with market power tend to restrict output to force up prices. As a consequence, too few of society's resources are allocated to the goods and services they produce. Instead, these resources will flow to the production of products that consumers value less. Markets are "failing" in the sense that they are not allocating resources in the most efficient way, that is, to the production of the goods and services that consumers value most highly. Because market power has already been discussed extensively in preceding chapters, this chapter will focus on the two remaining sources of market failure, externalities and public goods. We turn first to the discussion of externalities.

EXTERNALITIES AS A SOURCE OF MARKET FAILURE

To understand the concept of externalities and why they represent a source of market failure, we need to recall how decisions are made. We learned in Chapter 5 that rational decision makers make decisions by comparing costs and benefits. But what costs and benefits? The answer, of course, is the costs and benefits that affect them!

When business owners and managers are deciding what production techniques to use and what resources to purchase, they consider only **private costs** or **internal costs**—the costs actually borne by the firm. They do not take into account any external costs that are borne by (or spill over onto) other parties. Consumers behave in a similar manner: They tend to consider only **private benefits** or **internal benefits**—the benefits that accrue to the person or persons purchasing the product—and ignore any external benefits that might be received by others.

If businesses and consumers are permitted to ignore these external costs and benefits, or **externalities**, the result will be an inefficient use of our scarce resources. We will produce too much of some items because we do not consider the full costs; we will produce too little of others because we do not consider the full benefits.

Externalities: The Case of External Costs

It's not difficult to think of personal situations in which external costs have come into play. Perhaps you've planned to savor a quiet dinner at your favorite restaurant, only to have a shrieking baby seated with its harried parents at the next table. Think about the movie you might have enjoyed if that rambunctious five-year-old hadn't been using the back of your seat as a bongo drum. Why do parents bring young children to these places, knowing that they will probably disturb the people around them? According to the teachings of Adam Smith, they are pursuing their own self-interest—in this case by minimizing the monetary cost of an evening's entertainment. But their actions are imposing different kinds of costs on everyone around them. The

frazzled nerves, poorly digested meals, and generally spoiled evenings experienced by you and your fellow diners or moviegoers are examples of
external costs: the costs created by one party or group and imposed on, or
spilled over onto, some other (nonconsenting) party or group.

The classic example of external costs (or **negative externalities**, as they
are also known) is pollution: the contamination of our land, air, and water
caused by the litter that lines our streets and highways, the noxious fumes
emitted into our atmosphere, and the wastes dumped into our rivers, lakes,
and streams. Why does pollution exist? The answer is really quite obvious.
It's less expensive for a manufacturer to dispose of its wastes in a nearby river,
for example, than to haul that material to a so-called safe area. But it is a low-
cost method of disposal only in terms of the private costs borne by the manufacturing firm. If we consider the social cost, there may well be a cheaper
method of disposal.

Social cost refers to the full cost to society of producing a product. It represents the sum of private costs plus external costs. In situations where there
are no external costs, private costs and social costs will be the same. But when
external costs are present, social costs will be higher than private costs. That's

Dumping wastes into a river may minimize private costs, but it can create substantial
external costs.

the case in our example of the polluting manufacturing firm. The private cost of manufacturing the firm's product includes the payments made for materials, labor, rent, and everything else it takes to run a business. But it does not include a payment for the damage done when the river is used for waste disposal. Because the firm is able to ignore this cost, it is described as an external cost; it is external to the firm's decision making.

To understand why pollution is a cost, think of the damage it does. Polluted water means fewer fish and fewer people enjoying water sports. It also means less income for people who rent boats and cottages and sell fishing bait, for example. It further affects the people living downstream, who need water for drinking and bathing; they will have to pay—through taxes—to purify the water. Finally, it may have a deadly effect on the birds and animals that live off the fish and other creatures in the water. Thus, water pollution may create numerous costs for society, costs that are ignored by polluters.

External Costs and Resource Misallocation

When the act of producing or consuming a product creates external costs, an exclusive reliance on private markets and the pursuit of self-interest will result in a misallocation of society's resources. We can illustrate why this is so by investigating a single, hypothetical industry.

For the purpose of our investigation, let's assume that the paint industry is purely competitive. Under those circumstances, the equilibrium price and quantity will be determined by the interaction of the industry demand and supply curves. In Exhibit 9.1, demand curve D shows the quantity of paint that would be demanded at each possible price. Recall from Chapter 6 that the demand curve is a product's marginal benefit curve because it tells us the value that consumers place on an additional unit of the product. For example, the 100,000th can of paint provides benefits worth $10, and the 120,000th can of paint provides benefits worth $8.

The other important element in the diagram is the supply curve. As you already know, when an industry is purely competitive, the supply curve can be thought of as the marginal cost curve for the industry because it is found by summing the marginal cost curves of the firms in the industry. The first supply curve, S_1, shows the quantity of paint the industry would supply if each firm in the industry considered only its private costs and disposed of its wastes by dumping them into local rivers. As you can see, under these conditions the demand and supply curves reveal an equilibrium price of $8 per can of paint and an equilibrium quantity of 120,000 cans per year.

The equilibrium output of 120,000 cans is labeled the "market output" because that is the output that will be produced in the absence of government intervention. Remember, businesses respond only to private costs; they tend to ignore external costs unless they are required to take them into consideration.

EXHIBIT 9.1

The Impact of External Costs

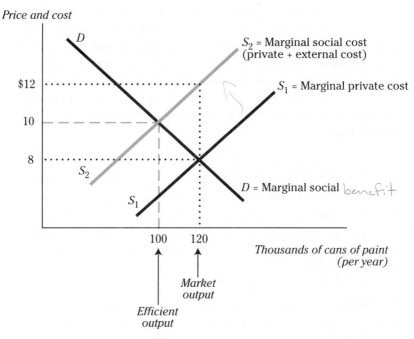

Because paint producers consider only private costs, they produce 120,000 units, more than the optimal, or allocatively efficient, output of 100,000 units.

Suppose that we find a way to require the firms in the industry to consider the external costs they have been ignoring. Under those conditions the supply curve would shift to S_2, the curve reflecting the full social cost of production. (Recall that whenever there is an increase in resource prices or anything else that increases the cost of production, the supply curve will shift left, or upward.) As you can see from the diagram, the result of this reduction in supply is an increase in the price of paint to $10 a can and a reduction in the equilibrium quantity to 100,000 cans. Note that 100,000 cans is the allocatively efficient level of output, the output for which the marginal social benefit equals the marginal social cost. Consumers receive $10 worth of benefits from the 100,000th can of paint, exactly enough to justify the $10 marginal cost of producing that can.

If 100,000 units is the optimal or efficient level of output, 120,000 must have been too much! So long as paint producers were allowed to shift some of their production costs to society as a whole (or to some portion of society), the price of paint was artificially low; that is, it did not reflect the true social cost of producing paint. Consumers responded to this low price by purchasing an artificially high quantity of paint—more than they would have purchased if the price reflected the true social cost of production. As a consequence, more of society's scarce resources were allocated to the production of paint than was socially optimal. (Note that consumers receive marginal benefits worth $8 from the 120,000th can of paint, but the marginal social cost of producing that unit is $12; production has been carried too far.) In summary, when businesses fail to consider external costs, they produce too much of their product from society's point of view.

Correcting for External Costs   How can individuals and businesses be encouraged to consider all the costs of their actions, to treat external costs as if they were private or internal costs? There are three basic approaches to internalizing external costs: private bargaining, regulating the activity that gives rise to the external cost, and using taxes to discourage the externality-creating activity.

Private Bargaining   In many instances, disputes involving externalities can be resolved through private bargaining and negotiation. To illustrate, suppose that your neighbor regularly uses his noisy woodworking machinery at night, disturbing your relaxation and even your sleep. If you bring this problem to his attention (so that he becomes aware of this externality), you may be able to reach an agreement that confines his woodworking fun to the early evening, where the disruption is more easily tolerated. If that solution is inadequate, you might offer to pay to soundproof his workshop or ask him to pay to soundproof your bedroom. Other solutions are undoubtedly possible, but these alternatives illustrate the principle: Bargaining and negotiation can be used to resolve many disputes involving negative externalities.

The issue of who pays to resolve this dispute may trouble you. You may feel that you are entitled to a good night's sleep and that your noisy neighbor should pay you to soundproof your bedroom. Your neighbor, on the other hand, may be convinced that your need for quiet is unreasonably interfering with his hobby, particularly if you like turning in before the sun goes down. Here the real issue is poorly defined property rights. **Property rights** are the legal rights to use goods, services, or resources. For example, you have the right to use your car and lawnmower and barbecue grill; your neighbor does not. But who owns the right to solitude in your neighborhood? That issue is not so clear-cut, and that lack of clarity may hinder your ability to reach an agreement.

In our society many cases involving externalities are resolved by negotiation after the courts have clarified property rights.[1] For instance, if you complained to the court about your noisy neighbor and the court sided with you, your neighbor would then be in a position to consider alternative ways of preserving your quiet. If the judge sided with your neighbor, you would need to consider compensating your neighbor and the other alternatives discussed earlier. Either way, the issue could be resolved through negotiation.[2]

As you might imagine, this bargaining solution works only in situations in which the transactions costs—the costs of striking a bargain between the parties—are relatively low and in which the number of people involved is relatively small. When bargaining and negotiation do not work, another method must be sought to solve the problem.

Government Regulation When private bargaining is ineffective or impractical, another common method for dealing with negative externalities is government regulation, the *command and control* approach. Government regulations are commonplace in our economy. For instance, many communities attempt to prevent or limit the potential noise problems presented by the cabinet-making neighbor by using zoning ordinances to prohibit certain types of activities in residential neighborhoods and by ordinances that specifically prohibit "noise disturbances." Regulation has also been the primary method used to limit pollution. The emissions standards imposed on automobile manufacturers are an example of such government regulations, as are the leaf-burning ordinances in your local community.

Under a command and control system, firms and individuals are told how much pollution they will be allowed to emit into the environment, and they are often told what specific technique they must use to meet the standard. As firms take steps to reduce their emissions to the mandated level, their cost of production tends to increase. This, in turn, leads to higher product prices. When consumers are required to pay a price that more fully reflects the true cost of production, they purchase fewer units of the formerly underpriced items. Therefore resources can be reallocated to the production of other items whose prices more accurately reflect the full social cost of production.

---

[1] For instance, New York City agreed to pay neighboring Catskill communities and farms approximately $700 million to follow practices that will preserve the water quality of the Catskill Mountain region—the region from which the city obtains its drinking water (Duane Chapman, *Environmental Economics: Theory, Application, and Policy,* Addison-Wesley, 2000, p. 75).

[2] The idea of solving externality problems by assigning property rights and encouraging negotiation is based on the work of Ronald Coase. Coase demonstrated that when property rights are clearly defined, resources will be used efficiently, regardless of who is assigned their ownership. So, for instance, if your sleep is more valuable than your neighbor's woodworking, your sleep will be preserved (essentially because you are willing to pay more to preserve it than your neighbor is willing to pay to preserve his hobby).

Although pollution standards have helped to reduce pollution, they have been criticized as needlessly expensive. There are two reasons for this criticism. First, because government often specifies precisely how the environmental standard is to be met, businesses have no incentive to seek out less-expensive methods of reducing their pollution. Second, this approach requires that all firms meet the same environmental standard, even though some firms find it much more expensive to meet that standard than others. Although this approach may appear to be "fair," it increases the total cost to society of achieving any given level of environmental quality.

Levying Taxes   Because regulation is often quite costly and private bargaining sometimes impractical, the most effective way of addressing negative externalities often involves the use of taxes. As you discovered in Chapter 4, excise taxes (and subsidies) can be used to alter behavior. If an excise tax is imposed on a product, the product's supply curve will shift left, raise the item's price, and discourage its consumption. By that reasoning, taxing products whose consumption creates external costs will allow policymakers to bring consumption more in line with the efficient level. For example, the excise taxes on cigarettes and gasoline have been justified, in part, by the desire to reduce the consumption of these externality-creating products.

Pollution Taxes   When the *production* of a product creates pollution as a by-product, economists have suggested an even more direct approach—tax the pollution itself. Under a system of *pollution taxes*, firms could discharge as much waste into the environment as they choose, but they would have to pay a specified levy—say, $50—for each unit emitted. Ideally, this tax would bring the desired reduction in pollution. If not, it would be raised to whatever dollar amount would convince firms to reduce pollution to acceptable levels.

A major advantage of a pollution tax is that it would allow the firms themselves to decide which ones could cut back on emissions (the discharges of wastes) at the lowest cost. For example, given a fee of $50 for each ton of wastes emitted into the environment, those firms that could reduce their emissions for less than $50 per ton would do so; other firms would continue to pollute and pay the tax. As a result, pollution would be reduced by the firms that could do so most easily and at the lowest cost. Society would then have achieved a given level of environmental quality at the lowest cost in terms of its scarce resources.

A simple example may help to illustrate why the pollution tax is a less expensive approach. Assume that the economy is made up of firms A and B and that each firm is discharging 4 tons of waste a year. Assume also that it costs firm A $30 per ton to reduce emissions and firm B $160 per ton.

Suppose that society wants to reduce the discharge of wastes by 4 tons a year. An emissions standard that required each firm to limit its emissions to 2 tons a year would cost society $380 ($60 for firm A and $320 for firm B). A pollution tax of $50 a ton would accomplish the same objective at a cost of $120 because it would cause firm A to reduce its emissions from 4 tons to zero. (Firm A would opt to reduce its emissions because this approach is less costly than paying the pollution tax. If the firm pays the pollution tax, it will be billed $50 × 4 tons = $200. But it can reduce emissions at a cost of $30 × 4 tons = $120. Thus, it would prefer to reduce its emissions rather than pay the pollution tax.) Note that firm B will prefer to pay the tax; thus, government will receive $200 in pollution tax revenue. This $200 should not be considered a cost of reducing pollution since it can be used to build roads or schools or be spent in any other way society chooses.

Tradable Emission Permits The Clean Air Act of 1990 contains provisions that, like pollution taxes, encourage businesses to reduce pollution in the least costly way. First, firms are given more flexibility in meeting pollution standards; the technique is not strictly mandated. Second, firms that exceed the standard—that reduce their pollution below the permitted amount—may sell the residual to other firms. In effect, these firms are selling their unused rights to pollute. These rights are known as *tradable emission permits* (or credits); they are the marketable right to discharge a specified amount of a pollutant.

Who would want to buy emissions permits? The buyers will be other businesses that find it very costly to reduce their own emissions. By giving firms the option of either buying permits or reducing their own emissions, the act aims to achieve its air-quality standards at the lowest possible cost.

Emissions trading has allowed the United States to sharply reduce sulfur dioxide (SO_2) emissions from power plants and has done so at a lower cost than originally anticipated. Our success in using emissions trading has encouraged other nations to try this approach. For example, the European Union (EU) has established a similar system for reducing carbon dioxide (CO_2), in an effort to combat global warming. The EU's "cap-and-trade system" established overall limits for carbon-dioxide emissions in each of the EU's 27-member countries and then distributed permits to the businesses within those countries. Companies that exceed their emissions allocations need to buy additional permits. Over time, the plan is to lower the emissions caps, increasing the cost of polluting and achieving the desired reductions in CO_2. (The Obama administration is pushing the cap-and-trade approach to regulating carbon emissions in the United States. But many economists argue that a carbon tax would be a better approach. Read "Greenhouse Gases; What to Do about CO_2," on page 270, to learn why.)

The Optimal Level of Negative Externalities Reducing pollution and other negative externalities is a good thing. But it is possible to have too much of a good thing. Economists support reducing pollution only so long as the benefits of added pollution controls exceed their costs. It doesn't make sense to force firms to pay an additional $30 million to reduce pollution if the added

Use Your Economic Reasoning

Greenhouse Gases; What to Do about CO_2; Some Are Touting the Benefits of a Carbon Tax over a Cap-and-Trade System for Regulating Harmful Emissions

BY TOM FOWLER

Attacking climate change through a complex greenhouse gas trading system is a centerpiece of the incoming Obama administration's energy policy. But economists and energy analysts of all ideological stripes are saying a better approach to getting a cleaner atmosphere might involve a political dirty word—tax.

A cap-and-trade system for carbon dioxide, already operating in Europe and contained in some proposed U.S. energy legislation, would aim to reduce greenhouse gases by setting a cap on carbon dioxide emissions, issuing emissions permits and allowing companies to trade them in an open market. Over time, the number of permits would drop, forcing companies to lower emissions. A tax, on the other hand, would simply impose a fee for every ton of CO_2 produced by users of fossil fuels, like power plants and refineries. Over time the tax would increase, again encouraging companies to find alternatives. Both options give companies incentives to lower emissions, and both would result in higher energy prices for consumers.

But proponents of a tax on CO_2 emissions say it would be less complicated and less expensive to administer and monitor. And the cost would be more predictable to businesses and consumers than a trading system, in which prices can fluctuate greatly. Gregory Mankiw, the former head of the Bush administration's Council of Economic Advisers, and the Congressional Budget Office, among others, have touted a CO_2 tax as a better path. . . . "There seems to be a pretty good consensus among economists in support of a tax, which is sur-

prising given the admiration most have for the strength of markets," said Amy Myers Jaffe, an energy fellow at Rice University's Baker Institute for Public Policy.

But getting a new tax passed could be a long shot, despite growing public support for climate change legislation and a Democratic administration and Congress that are more inclined to support taxes on industry than Republican predecessors. "So even if a tax is better, can a tax actually get passed by Congress?" asked Francisco Padua, a trader at Amerex Brokers in Sugar Land, which is active in existing emissions markets. "Why even talk about it?" . . .

Cap-and-trade programs enjoy strong support for many reasons. Such a program has been used for more than a decade to cut acid rain in the U.S. by reducing the amount of sulfur dioxide power plants produce. The program assigned a cap on emissions from coal-fired power plants and then created a trading system for allowances that lets companies decide whether it's more cost effective to reduce emissions or buy allowances to pollute. Over time, the number of available allowances was lowered. This made it more expensive to buy emission allowances than to install cleaner technologies at the power plants—so plants installed more equipment to clean emissions.

The acid rain program cut sulfur dioxide emissions more than 30 percent below 1990 levels, according to the Environmental Protection Agency, in a way that was predictable and cost-effective to businesses. A similar program aimed at reducing nitrogen oxides, a key component of

Source: Houston Chronicle, January 18, 2009, p. 1. Reprinted by permission of the Houston Chronicle Publishing Company. All rights reserved.

smog, helped cut those emissions 74 percent below 1990 levels in 20 Eastern states. . . .

How much CO_2 might decline under a U.S. cap-and-trade program would depend upon how it was structured, what caps were set and other factors. But success with sulfur dioxide and nitrogen oxides trading won't necessarily translate to CO_2. Those trading schemes were applied only to a segment of one industry—certain coal-fired power plants. CO_2 trading would apply to all power plants and many other industries, so it would be more complex and require more oversight. Power plants also have several relatively easy options for sulfur dioxide and nitrogen oxides reductions, such as switching the type of fuels burned or adding smokestack scrubbers. For CO_2, there are currently few easy options, highlighting a need for new methods.

And the early results for Europe's CO_2 cap-and-trade system—which is many times larger than the U.S. sulfur dioxide and nitrogen oxides programs—are seen by some as less than stellar. The first round of emission credits were free, allowing some emitters to sell permits at big profits without actually lowering their CO_2 output. And too many credits were issued, leading to a steep crash in carbon credit prices in 2006. . . .

Brice Lalonde, France's special ambassador in charge of climate change, defends the European Union's trading scheme, saying early problems will resolve themselves as the market develops. "I don't see that many missteps," Lalonde said. "We had an experimental phase to start with, and we are trying to learn by doing. The main outcome is that the cap-and-trade system works." . . .

The Baker Institute's Jaffe has misgivings because a cap-and-trade system creates a large commodity market designed by the U.S. Congress under the influence of competing special interests. . . . And just like any large commodity market, CO_2 prices could be highly volatile, said Craig Pirrong, a finance professor at the University of Houston who is co-teaching a graduate-level carbon trading class this semester. "Banks like the volatility and complexity, because the more volatile and complex, the more money they could make," Pirrong said. "But volatility may make companies put off investing in cleaner technology because they can't get an accurate estimate on the costs." . . .

Still, some leading environmental groups prefer cap-and-trade. The Environmental Defense Fund has favored trading, in part because it sets limits on carbon emissions and a tax sets only a price. And many are skeptical that the government would make good use of tax proceeds. Various proposals call for the money to go directly back to consumers or to pay for research in low-carbon energy technology, but some worry that the money could just be used for other, un-related projects. "The private sector would do a better job using that value," Amerex's Padua said. . . .

USE YOUR ECONOMIC REASONING

1. Proponents of a tax on CO_2 (also called a "carbon tax") argue that it would be less expensive to administer and its cost would be more predictable for the affected businesses than the cap-and-trade alternative. Explain this argument.
2. Why does the Environmental Defense Fund favor the cap-and-trade system?
3. Suppose two firms—A and B—can reduce their CO_2 emissions for $100 per ton and $400 per ton, respectively. What would you expect each firm to do if it had to pay a $250 per ton tax on its emissions? Do you think the two firms would respond the same under a permit system where the price each must pay for a permit equals $250?
4. The article says that "both options . . . would result in higher energy prices for consumers." Why, then, do politicians favor the cap-and-trade system and distance themselves from the carbon tax?

benefits to society amount to only $10 million. For that reason, any rational system of pollution control—whether based on regulation or pollution taxes—will permit some pollution. Unfortunately, because it is difficult to measure the costs and benefits of pollution control in an exact manner, it is also difficult to determine whether efforts to control pollution have been carried too far or not far enough.

Externalities: The Case of External Benefits

Not all externalities are harmful. Sometimes the actions of individuals or businesses create **external benefits**—benefits that are paid for by one party but spill over to other parties. One example is the flowers your neighbors plant in their yard each year. You can enjoy their beauty without contributing to the cost of their planting and upkeep. Another example is flu shots. You pay for them, and they help protect you from the flu. But they also help protect everyone else; if you don't come down with the flu, you can't pass it on to others.

Businesses also can create external benefits. For example, most firms put their workers—particularly their young and/or inexperienced workers—through some sort of training program. Of course, the sponsoring firm gains a more productive, more valuable employee. But most people do not stay with one employer for their entire working careers; when trained employees decide to move on, their other employers will benefit from the training they have received.

External Benefits and Resource Allocation   In a pure market economy, individuals would tend to demand too small a quantity of those products that generate external benefits. To understand why this is so, consider your own consumption decisions for a moment. When you are deciding whether to purchase a product (or how much of a product to purchase), you compare the product's benefits with its price. If you value a unit of the product more than the other items you could purchase with the same money, you buy it. If not, you spend your money on the product you value more highly. In effect, you are deciding which product delivers the most benefits for the money. But whose benefits are you considering? Your own, of course! In other words, you respond to private rather than external benefits. Most consumption decisions are made this way. As a result, consumers purchase too small a quantity of the products that create external benefits, and our scarce resources are misallocated. That is to say, fewer resources are devoted to producing these products than are justified by their **social benefits**—the sum of the private benefits received by those who purchase the product and the external benefits received by others.

To illustrate the underproduction of products that carry external benefits, let's examine what would happen if elementary education were left to the discretion of the private market. Reading, writing, and arithmetic are basic skills that have obvious benefits for the individual, but they also benefit society as a whole. In his prize-winning book *Capitalism and Freedom*, economist Milton Friedman made the case as follows:

> A stable and democratic society is impossible without a minimum amount of literacy and knowledge on the part of most citizens and without widespread acceptance of some common set of values. Education can contribute to both. In consequence, the gain from the education of a child accrues not only to the child or to his parents but also to other members of the society. . . .[3]

For the sake of our example, let's suppose that all elementary education in the United States is provided through private schools on a voluntary basis. In such a situation the number of children enrolled in these schools would be determined by the forces of demand and supply. As shown in Exhibit 9.2, the market would establish a price of $3,000 per student, and at that price 3 million students would attend elementary school each year. The market demand curve (D_1) provides an incomplete picture, however. It considers marginal private benefits—the benefits received by the students and their parents—but ignores external benefits. If we include the external benefits of education, society would want even more children educated. Demand curve D_2 shows that society would choose to educate 5 million students a year if it considered the full social benefits (private plus external benefits) of education, leading to an equilibrium price of $4,200 per student.

As you can see from Exhibit 9.2, individuals pursuing their own self-interest would choose to purchase less education than is justified on the basis of the full social benefits. (To confirm this conclusion, note that the marginal *social* benefit derived from the education of the 3 millionth student is $6,000, well in excess of the $3,000 marginal social cost of providing that education. Too few students are being educated, from society's point of view.)

Adjusting for External Benefits When external benefits exist, how can they be incorporated into the decision making of the parties involved? As with external costs, there are three basic approaches: government regulation, subsidies, and private bargaining.

Government Regulation One method of capturing external benefits is through regulation. For example, most cities require that dogs be inoculated

---

[3] Milton Friedman, *Capitalism and Freedom* (Chicago: University of Chicago Press, 1962), p. 86.

EXHIBIT 9.2

The Impact of External Benefits

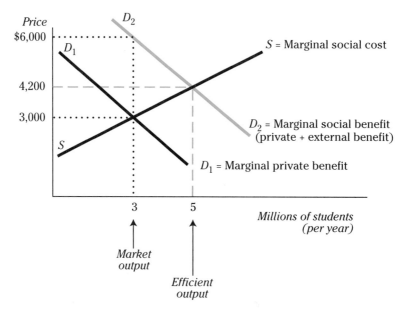

When individuals consider only the private benefits of education, they choose to educate only 3 million students per year, less than the optimal, or allocatively efficient, level of 5 million students per year.

against rabies. While this regulation helps to protect the animals, its real intention is protecting bystanders—reaping the external benefits. Similarly, most states require that children receive inoculations against childhood diseases—measles, chickenpox, etc.—before beginning school. To the extent that the vaccines are effective, the children are protected and so are those around them.

If this simple regulatory approach were extended to basic education, each child would be required to attend school for some minimum number of years, allowing the child's parents to select the school and find the money to pay for it. As you know, the United States has taken a different approach. Most elementary and secondary schools are operated by local governments and financed through taxes rather than through fees charged to parents. This spreads the financial burden for education among all taxpayers rather than just the parents of school-age children. The rationale for this approach is clear-cut. Because all taxpayers share in the benefits of education (the external benefits, at least), they should share in the costs as well. We'll have more to say about this approach in a moment.

Subsidies   A second approach to encouraging the consumption of products yielding external benefits is government subsidies. Consider the flu shots we noted earlier. Many people opt to pay for flu shots each year, but many others weigh the costs and benefits and decide against the expense. If we want more people to get flu shots (but we don't want to pass a law requiring such shots), we could have the government subsidize all or part of the cost. The lower the price of flu shots, the more people who will agree to get them.

There is no reason that subsidized flu shots would have to be provided by government doctors; the government could simply agree to pay private doctors for each flu shot administered. It is precisely this approach that Milton Friedman would like to see implemented in education. Rather than continuing to subsidize public schools, Friedman would prefer a system that permitted students to select their own privately run schools:

> Government could require a minimum level of schooling financed by giving parents vouchers redeemable for a specified maximum sum per child per year if spent on "approved educational services." Parents would then be free to spend this sum and any additional sum they themselves provided on purchasing educational services from an "approved institution of their own choice" . . . The role of government would be limited to insuring that the schools met certain minimum standards.[4]

Whether or not you agree with Friedman's particular approach to education, it illustrates how subsidies can be useful in correcting for market failure. It also shows how regulation and subsidies can be combined to achieve the desired result (requiring X years of school but using subsidies to reduce the cost). This combined approach is actually commonplace. For instance, most communities require childhood inoculations, but also offer them for "free" at the public health office. (Of course, there is no free lunch. These vaccinations are free only if you consider a four-hour wait amids screaming children to be "free.")

Private Bargaining   Because the external benefits associated with a basic education are widely diffused, private bargaining is unlikely to be an effective method of incorporating them into decision making. But other situations are more promising. Return to your high-school days and imagine that your older brother has hired a math tutor to help him survive trigonometry. The tutor's primary concern is helping your brother, but during the lulls in trigonometry tutoring she also helps you to fight your way through your geometry homework. By agreeing to pay a portion of the tutor's hourly wage, you can probably help to extend the tutor's hours in a way that reflects the external benefits of her

---

[4] Milton Friedman, *Capitalism and Freedom* (Chicago, University of Chicago Press, 1962), p. 86.

tutoring. As a second example, consider a downtown restaurant that triples its business whenever a nearby hotel advertises its "weekend getaway" rates. The restaurant may be able to encourage more weekend specials by agreeing to share a portion of its added profits with the hotel or by helping to defray the marketing costs of these special events. As these examples illustrate, private bargaining has a role to play in internalizing external benefits as well as external costs.

MARKET FAILURE AND THE PROVISION OF PUBLIC GOODS

Market power and the existence of externalities are not the only sources of market failure. Markets may also fail to produce optimal results because some products are simply not well suited to sale by private firms. These products must be provided by government or they will not be provided at all.

Private Goods versus Public Goods

To understand this problem, we must think first about the types of goods and services our economy produces. Those goods and services fall into three categories: pure private goods, private goods that yield external benefits, and public goods.

Pure private goods are products that convey their benefits only to the purchaser.[5] The hamburger you had for lunch falls in that category, as does the jacket you wore to class. Most of the products we purchase in the marketplace are pure private goods.

Some products convey most of their benefits to the person making the purchase but also create substantial external benefits for others. These are **private goods that yield significant external benefits**. We have talked about education and flu shots, but there are numerous other examples—fire protection, police protection, and driver's training, to name just a few.

The third category, **public goods**, consists of products that convey their benefits equally to paying and nonpaying members of society. National defense is probably the best example of a public good. If a business attempted to sell "units" of national defense through the marketplace, what problems would arise? The major problem would be that nonpayers would receive virtually the same protection from foreign invasion as those who paid for the protection.

---

[5] Note that although pure private goods convey their benefits only to the purchaser, the purchaser may *choose* to share those benefits with others. For instance, you may decide to share your hamburger with another person or allow someone else to wear your jacket. But if others share in the benefits of a pure private good, it is because the purchaser allows them to share those benefits, not because the benefits automatically spilled over onto them.

There's no way to protect your house from foreign invasion without simultaneously protecting your neighbor's. The inability to exclude nonpayers from receiving the same benefits as those who have paid for the product is what economists call the *free-rider problem*.

The Free-Rider Problem

Why does the inability to exclude certain individuals from receiving benefits constitute a problem? Think about national defense for just a moment. How would you feel if you were paying for national defense and your neighbor received exactly the same protection for nothing? Very likely, you would decide to become a free rider yourself, as would many other people. Products such as national defense, flood-control dams, and tornado warning systems cannot be offered so as to restrict their benefits to payers alone. Therefore, no private business can expect to earn a profit by offering such goods and services, and private markets cannot be relied on to produce these products, no matter how important they are for the well-being of the society. Unless the government intervenes, they simply will not be provided at all.

Of course, we're not willing to let that happen. That's why a substantial amount of our tax money pays for national defense and other public goods. (Not all publicly *provided* goods are public goods. Our tax dollars are used to pay for education and public swimming pools and a host of other goods and services that do not meet the characteristics of public goods.) As we have emphasized, the ultimate objective of government intervention is to improve the allocation of society's scarce resources so that the economy will do a better job of satisfying our unlimited wants. To the extent that government intervention contributes to that result, it succeeds in correcting for market failure and in improving our social welfare.

GOVERNMENT FAILURE: THE THEORY OF PUBLIC CHOICE — ⋂o —

The existence of market failures suggests that market economies do not always use resources efficiently. But whether government can be relied on to improve the allocation of scarce resources is open to debate. In fact, public-choice economists point out that **government failure**—the enactment of government policies that produce inefficient or inequitable results, or both—is also a possibility.

Public choice is the study of how government makes economic decisions. This area of economics was developed by James Buchanan, a professor at George Mason University and the 1986 recipient of the Nobel Prize in economics.

Although many of us would like to think of government as an altruistic body concerned with the public interest, public-choice economists advise us to think of government as a collection of individuals each pursuing his or her self-interest. Just as business executives are interested in maximizing profits, politicians are interested in maximizing their ability to get votes. And government bureaucrats are interested in maximizing their income, power, and longevity. As you can see, public-choice economists apply economic principles to explain behavior in the political sphere. They caution us to remember that individuals remain rational and self-interested, even when they act as voters, politicians, and government bureaucrats. Next, we explore the implications of that observation.

Voters and Rational Ignorance

Self-interested voters want to support the politicians who will do the most for them—who will provide them with the greatest benefits and impose the fewest costs. Unfortunately, individuals may be less well informed as voters than they are as consumers.

When consumers are searching for a new automobile or a new ski boat, they are likely to spend a significant amount of time researching their purchase and thinking about the decision. They know that this is their decision and they want to make the correct one. Voters, on the other hand, know that their individual ballot is unlikely to determine the outcome of the election so they have little incentive to become well informed about the candidates or the issues. Public-choice economists describe this as the **rational ignorance effect**—voters choose to remain uninformed because the costs of becoming informed outweigh the likely benefits.

Even if a politician believes that her policies will be best for her constituents, she has to get elected and stay in office to pursue her goals. To do that, politicians have to be focused vote-getters. Attracting the attention of rationally ignorant voters requires effort. To do that, politicians hire consultants in an attempt to determine which issues matter most to voters, and they spend money—lots of money—trying to keep their name in front of the public and trying to craft an image that is easily conveyed in the short "sound bites" that these voters are likely to recall.

Special-Interest Groups

Recognizing that most voters are rationally ignorant and that politicians are merely "vote maximizers" can help us to understand why special-interest groups exert a disproportionate influence on political outcomes. Consider, for example, the efforts of farmers to maintain price supports, land set-asides (payments to farmers for not raising crops on certain acreage), and other forms of aid to agriculture. If this aid is eliminated, each of these individuals will be significantly harmed. So farm lobbyists make it clear that their primary interest in selecting a senator or representative is his or her position on this one issue. And they reward those who support their position with significant financial contributions. The rewards for opposing these agricultural subsidies are likely to be nonexistent! Because the cost of farm subsidies to any one consumer is relatively small, few voters are likely to choose their next senator or representative on the basis of how they voted on this issue. In fact, the rational ignorance effect predicts that few voters are even likely to know how their representative voted! As a consequence, public-choice theory predicts that the members of Congress will vote in favor of agricultural subsidies even though they lead to an overproduction of agricultural products (are inefficient) and benefit people with incomes greater than the national average (are inequitable).

A related problem stems from the logrolling efforts that are commonplace in Congress. **Logrolling** is trading votes to gain support for a proposal; politicians agree to vote for a project they oppose in order to gain votes for a project they support. For example, a senator from Missouri might agree to vote in favor of a bill that would expand the federal highway system in Florida in return for a Florida senator's favorable vote on a bill appropriating more money for Missouri's military bases. In many instances, logrolling can lead to efficient outcome. But in others, it can lead to the approval of projects or programs whose costs exceed their benefits.

The Limits of Majority Voting

It is not just special-interest groups that can distort the spending decisions of government. The voting mechanism itself may lead to inefficient outcomes, even in cases where the voters are accurately informed about the costs and benefits of the proposed action. Consider, for example, a vote regarding the building of a flood-control dam. Even if the benefits of the dam vastly outweigh the costs, majority voting may prevent its construction. Although voters living near the dam stand to benefit in a major way from its construction, most voters will see little reason to help pay for it. As a consequence, the project is likely to be rejected even though it represents an efficient use of society's resources. The problem here is that there is no way for voters to reflect the strength of their preferences. They can vote in favor of an issue, or against it, but they cannot indicate the strength of their favor or opposition.

Bureaucrats and Inefficiency

In addition to the problems posed by special-interest groups and the voting process itself, public-choice economists point to the problems posed by government bureaucrats. Many of the spending decisions that are made by our local, state, and federal governments are not made by elected officials; they are made by the bureaucrats who run our various government agencies. Public-choice economists argue that these individuals, like the rest of us, pursue their own self-interest. In other words, they seek to increase their salaries, their longevity, and their influence. Rather than attempting to run lean, efficient agencies, their goal is to expand their power and resist all efforts to restrict their agencies' growth or influence. As a consequence, these agencies may become unjustifiably larger and require tax support in excess of the benefits they provide to citizens.

Final Thoughts on Public-Choice Theory

As you can see, public-choice economists are not optimistic that government will make decisions that improve either efficiency or equity. Instead, they see politicians and bureaucrats making decisions intended largely to benefit themselves. How accurate are these observations? While public-choice economists make important points, they may overstate their case. Over the past two decades, significant strides have been made in reducing trade barriers, despite howls of protest from those adversely affected. The trend toward deregulation has eliminated or drastically reduced the regulatory powers of several regulatory agencies, even though the bureaucrats running those agencies would probably have preferred otherwise. These reforms indicate that government action can lead to a more efficient use of society's scarce resources. In addition, although majority voting can lead to inefficient results, it can also lead to outcomes that are more efficient than those produced by private markets. This is likely to be true, for example, in the case of public goods, where markets may fail to provide the product at all.

The real message of public-choice economists is not that government action always leads to inefficiency or inequity. Rather, it is that we need to be just as alert to the possibility of government failure as we are to the possibility of market failure.

– n0 –

SUMMARY

Market failure occurs when a market economy produces too much or too little of certain products and thus fails to make the most efficient use of society's limited resources.

There are three major sources of market failure: market power, externalities, and public goods. The exercise of market power can lead to a misuse of society's resources because firms with market power tend to restrict output to force up prices. Consequently, too few of society's resources will be allocated to the production of the goods and services provided by firms with market power.

Another source of market failure is the market's inability to reflect all costs and benefits. In some instances the act of producing or consuming a product creates *externalities*—costs or benefits that are not borne by either buyers or sellers but that spill over onto third parties. When this happens, the market has no way of taking those costs and benefits into account and adjusting production and consumption decisions accordingly. As a consequence, the market fails to give us optimal results; our resources are not used as well as they could be. We produce too much of some things because we do not consider all costs; we produce too little of other things because we do not consider all benefits. There are three basic approaches to correcting these problems: private bargaining, government regulation, and using taxes or subsidies to discourage or encourage the externality-creating activity.

Markets may also fail to produce optimal results simply because some products are not well suited to sale by private firms. Public goods fall into that category. Public goods are products that convey their benefits equally to all members of society, whether or not the members have paid for those products. National defense is probably the best example. It is virtually impossible to sell national defense through markets because there is no way to exclude nonpayers from receiving the same benefits as payers. Because there is no way for a private businessperson to earn a profit by selling such products, private markets cannot be relied on to produce these goods or services, no matter how important they are to the well-being of the society.

Although market economies may fail to use resources efficiently, public-choice economists are not convinced that government can be counted on to improve the outcome. *Public choice* is the study of how government makes economic decisions. According to public-choice economists, government is a collection of individuals each pursuing his or her own interest. Because politicians and bureaucrats make decisions largely to benefit themselves, we cannot count on them to pursue policies that further the public interest. In fact, *government failure*—the enactment of government policies that produce inefficient or inequitable results, or both—is also a possible consequence.

KEY TERMS

External benefits
External costs
Externalities
Government failure
Internal benefits
Internal costs
Internalize costs

Logrolling
Market failure
Negative externalities
Private benefits
Private costs
Private goods that yield significant external benefits

Property rights
Public choice
Public goods
Pure private goods
Rational ignorance effect
Social benefit
Social cost

STUDY QUESTIONS

Fill in the Blanks

1. _Market failure_ are instances in which a market economy fails to make the most efficient use of society's limited resources.

2. The term _externalities_ is used to describe costs borne or benefits received by parties other than those involved in the transaction.

3. Social costs are the sum of _private costs_ and _external costs_.

4. One way to encourage the consumption of products with external benefits would be to _subsidize_ their purchase.

5. _Pure Private_ are products that convey their benefits only to the buyer.

6. National defense is an example of a(n) _public good_.

7. Another word for private costs and benefits is _internal_ costs and benefits.

8. _external benefits_ are benefits that are paid for by one party but that spill over to other parties.

9. The major reason our rivers and streams have been used as disposal sites is that this approach minimized the firm's _internal_ costs of production.

10. If an action creates no external costs or benefits, private costs will equal _social_ costs.

11. _____ is the study of how government makes economic decisions.

12. When politicians trade votes to gain support for a proposal, they are engaging in

_____.

Multiple Choice

1. The three approaches for resolving disputes involving negative externalities are
   a) government regulation, taxation, and private bargaining.
   b) command and control, taxation, and government regulation.
   c) private bargaining, government regulation, and subsidies.
   d) direct control, taxation, and government regulation.

2. Private bargaining is most likely to be effective in resolving externality-related disputes when
   a) the dispute involves a large number of parties.
   b) property rights are poorly defined.
   c) the dispute involves very few parties and property rights are well defined.

   d) it is very costly for the parties to negotiate a settlement.

3. Which of the following is most likely to produce external costs?
   a) Liquor
   b) A steak
   c) A flower garden
   d) A storm warning system

4. Suppose that chicken-processing plants create external costs. Then, in the absence of government intervention, it is likely that
   a) too few chickens will be processed, from a social point of view, and the price of a processed chicken will be artificially low.
   b) too many chickens will be processed, from a social point of view, and the price of a processed chicken will be artificially high.

c) too few chickens will be processed, from a social point of view, and the price of a processed chicken will be artificially high.

d) too many chickens will be processed, from a social point of view, and the price of a processed chicken will be artificially low.

5. If the firms in an industry have been creating pollution and are forced to find a method of waste disposal that does not damage the environment, the result will probably be
   a) a lower price for the product offered by the firms.
   b) a higher product price and a higher equilibrium quantity.
   c) a lower product price and a higher equilibrium quantity.
   d) a higher product price and a lower equilibrium quantity.

6. Which of the following is the best example of a pure public good?
   a) A cigarette
   b) A bus
   c) A lighthouse
   d) An automobile

7. Suppose that an AIDS vaccine is developed. In the absence of government intervention, it is likely that
   a) too few AIDS shots will be administered because individuals will fail to consider the private benefits provided by the shots.
   b) too many AIDS shots will be administered because individuals will consider only the private cost of the shots.
   c) too few AIDS shots will be administered because individuals will consider only the private benefits provided by the shots.
   d) too many AIDS shots will be administered because individuals will ignore the external benefits associated with the shots.

8. If a product creates external benefits, the demand curve that reflects all social benefits

   a) will be to the left of the demand curve that reflects only private benefits.
   b) will be to the right of the demand curve that reflects only private benefits.
   c) will not slope downward.
   d) will be the same as the demand curve that reflects private benefits.

9. Public goods can lead to market failure because they
   a) create external costs.
   b) create social costs.
   c) cannot be sold easily in markets.
   d) cannot be paid for through taxes.

10. Which of the following policies is *not* consistent with this chapter's content?
    a) Imposing excise taxes on beer and other alcoholic beverages
    b) Subsidizing driver's training classes
    c) Imposing excise taxes on smoke detectors
    d) Subsidizing mass transit

11. According to the rational ignorance effect
    a) politicians support special-interest groups because that's where the votes are.
    b) voters choose to remain uninformed because the costs of becoming informed outweigh the benefits.
    c) politicians agree to vote for a proposal they oppose to gain support for a project they support.
    d) bureaucrats restrict all efforts to restrict their agencies' growth or influence.

12. Which of the following best describes the free-rider problem?
    a) Your brother always rides home with you but never pays for the gas.
    b) Some private goods create external benefits for those who have not paid.
    c) Some people think that the environment is a free resource and therefore abuse it.
    d) Some goods cannot be sold in markets because the benefits they confer are available to all—whether they have paid or not.

13. Public-choice economists argue that
    a) majority voting always leads to efficient outcomes.
    b) government bureaucrats tend to act in the public interest.
    c) politicians generally find it in their self-interest to oppose special-interest groups.
    d) self-interest is the motivation of both business executives and politicians.

14. Suppose that a proposed government project would cost $50,000 and convey benefits worth $100 to 1,000 people, and benefits worth $5 to the remaining 9,000 people in the community. If each person were assessed a $50 tax to pay for this project, the theory of public choice predicts that it would be
    a) rejected because the project's total costs exceed its total benefits.
    b) approved because the project's total benefits exceed its total costs.
    c) rejected because voters are unable to reflect the strength of their preferences.
    d) approved because voters recognize that it is an efficient use of society's limited resources.

Use the diagram below in answering questions 15 and 16.

15. Suppose that production of product X creates external costs. In the absence of gov-ernment intervention, this industry would tend to produce
    a) 800 units of output, which is less than the allocatively efficient output of 1,000 units.
    b) 1,000 units of output, which is more than the allocatively efficient output of 800 units.
    c) 800 units, which is the allocatively efficient output.
    d) 1,000 units, which is the allocatively efficient output.

16. At 1,000 units of output, the marginal benefit from consuming the last unit of X is equal to
    a) $6, but the marginal social cost is equal to about $12, and so, from a social point of view, too little output is being produced.
    b) $12, but the marginal social cost is equal to about $6, and so, from a social point of view, too little output is being produced.
    c) $6, but the marginal social cost is equal to about $12, and so, from a social point of view, too much output is being produced.
    d) $12, but the marginal social cost is equal to about $6, and so, from a social point of view, too much output is being produced.

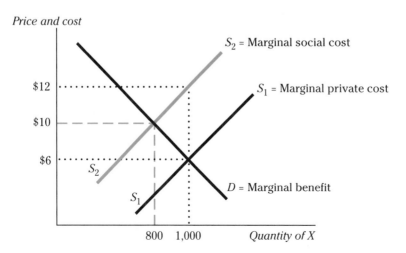

Problems and Questions for Discussion

1. Why should you and I be concerned about whether our society's resources are used optimally?

2. What is market failure, and what are the sources of this problem?

3. How can fines and subsidies be used to correct market failure?

4. Most businesses are concerned about our environment, but they may be reluctant to stop polluting unless all other firms in their industry are also forced to stop. Why?

5. If we force firms to stop polluting, the result will probably be higher product prices. Is that good or bad? Why?

6. Why is it important (from society's viewpoint) to encourage the production and consumption of products that yield external benefits?

7. If we're really concerned about external costs, there would be some logic in fining any spectator who insisted on standing up to cheer at football games. What would be

the logic? What practical considerations make this an impractical solution?

8. Why is a tornado warning system a public good? What about a flood-control dam? Why does it fall into that category?

9. Milton Friedman suggests that although it makes sense to subsidize a general education in the liberal arts, it makes much less sense to subsidize purely vocational training. What do you suppose is the logic behind that distinction?

10. Explain how the free-rider problem leads to market failure.

11. How can the absence of clearly defined property rights lead to the abuse or misuse of a resource?

12. Private bargaining can help to resolve externality problems if the number of parties involved is relatively small. Why is this solution likely to be unworkable when a large number of people are involved, as when a firm's pollution affects thousands of people?

ANSWER KEY

Fill in the Blanks

1. Market failures

2. externalities or spillovers

3. private costs; external costs

4. subsidize

5. Private goods

6. public good

7. internal

8. External benefits

9. private or internal

10. social

11. Public choice

12. logrolling

Multiple Choice

1. a
2. c
3. a
4. d
5. d
6. c
7. c
8. b
9. c
10. c
11. b
12. d
13. d
14. c
15. b
16. c

POVERTY, EQUALITY, AND TRENDS IN THE INCOME DISTRIBUTION

As we've seen, market failure results when a market economy fails to use its scarce resources in an optimal way, that is, when it produces too much or too little of certain products. But even if a market system were able to achieve an optimal allocation of resources, if it distributed income in a way that a majority of the population saw as inequitable or unfair, we might judge that to be a shortcoming of the system.

In a market system, a person's income depends on what he or she has to sell. Those with greater innate abilities and more assets (land and capital) earn higher incomes; those with fewer abilities and fewer assets earn lower incomes. These differences are often compounded by differences in training and education and by differences in the levels of inherited wealth. As a consequence, total reliance on the market mechanism can produce substantial inequality in the income distribution. Some people will have less while others have much more.

THE INCOME DISTRIBUTION IN THE UNITED STATES

How unequal is the income distribution in the United States? The Bureau of the Census tries to answer that question by first determining the amount of total income earned by all the households in our economy together in a given year, and then examining how that aggregate income was divided up among those households—how much went to the richest 20 percent of the population; how much went to the poorest 20 percent, and so on. Column 3 in Exhibit A9.1 represents the income distribution in the United States economy in 2008. As you can see, there is a significant amount of inequality. In 2008, the households in the lowest quintile (the lowest fifth) of the income distribution received less than 4 percent of total money income in the United States, while the households in the upper fifth received 50 percent of total income. As you can see, the households in the upper fifth of the income distribution received as much total income as all the households in the bottom four-fifths of the distribution.

Percent of Aggregate Income Received by Each Fifth of Households in the United States

	1988	1998	2008
Lowest fifth	3.8%	3.6%	3.4%
Second fifth	9.6	9.0	8.6
Third fifth	16.0	15.0	14.7
Fourth fifth	24.3	23.2	23.3
Highest fifth	46.3	49.2	50.0

Source: U.S. Census Bureau reports, *Income, Poverty, and Health Insurance Coverage in the United States: 2008* (September 2009).

TRENDS IN THE INCOME DISTRIBUTION

Although the data in column 3 are revealing, they tell only part of the story. By comparing the figures in column 3 of Exhibit A9.1 to those in columns 1 and 2, we can see that the income distribution is not static; it is growing more unequal. As you can see in the exhibit, the fraction of aggregate income going to the richest fifth of U.S. households increased from 1988 to 2008, while the share going to the remaining four-fifths declined.

The reason for this growing inequality is subject to debate. The most common explanation focuses on "skill-based technological change." According to this explanation, changes in production techniques—the increased use of computers, for example—have increased the demand for highly educated workers. Competition for these more educated workers has driven up their wages, while workers with less skill continue to be paid substantially less. Of course, as this technological change progresses, inequality continues to grow.

Many economists remain dissatisfied with this explanation for our growing inequality. There are several problems, but two of are particularly troubling. First, if inequality is the result of new technologies that are more demanding of skill, why isn't wage inequality also growing rapidly in Western European countries, which have access to essentially the same technology? Second, how do we explain the fact that there is substantial inequality within groups of workers who all seem to possess the same essential skills? As you can see, the skill-based explanation may not be the complete answer. In fact, it

is quite likely that there are several factors that account for the growing inequality we have experienced.[6]

POVERTY IN THE UNITED STATES

The fact that inequality is growing would probably be of much less concern to
Americans if everyone—including households in the bottom fifth of the income distribution—earned enough to live comfortably. What most of us are really concerned about is households that are living in poverty—those with
incomes that are insufficient to provide for their basic needs (according to some
standard established by society).

In the United States, we have adopted income standards by which we
judge the extent of poverty. For example, in 2008 a family of four was classified
as "poor" if it had an annual income of less than $22,025. By that definition
there were 39.8 million poor people in the United States in 2008—13.2 percent
of the population.

Poverty rates differ substantially by race. In 2008, the poverty rate was 24.7
percent for blacks, 23.2 percent for Hispanics, 11.8 percent for Asians, and 8.6
percent for non-Hispanic whites. Poverty rates also differ substantially by family status. For example, the poverty rate among married-couple families was
5.5 percent in 2008, while the rate in female households (without a husband
present) was 28.7 percent and the rate for male households (with no female
present) was 13.8 percent.

Poverty is much more commonplace for children than for adults. In 2008,
the poverty rate for children was 19.0 percent, the rate for adults was 11.7 percent, and the rate for senior adults (65 and older) was 9.7 percent. When young
children live in female households without a husband present, their prospects
look particularly bleak. In 2008, almost 53.3 percent of the children under six
living in these circumstances found themselves in poverty.

POLICIES TO COMBAT POVERTY

The U.S. government has attempted to address the problem of poverty in part
by enacting programs designed to address the source of poverty: the inability
of the family to earn an adequate income. Examples include the earned income

---

[6] Some economists believe that these seeming inconsistencies can be explained in the context of the
skill-based explanation. For a detailed discussion, see "What's Driving Wage Inequality?" by
Aaron Steelman and John A Weinberg (Federal Reserve Bank of Richmond's *Economic Quarterly*,
Summer, 2005.)

tax credit (whereby workers with low incomes receive payments from the federal government rather than being expected to pay income taxes), government-subsidized training program for unemployed workers, and policies designed to reduce discrimination in hiring. In addition, the minimum wage is intended to lift the earnings of unskilled workers.

Other government programs work outside the labor market. Social Security, for example, provides financial assistance to the old, the disabled, the unemployed, and families that are experiencing financial difficulty because of the death of a breadwinner. (Many economists argue that, whatever its limitations, our Social Security system is the primary reason that the poverty rate for senior adults is lower than the overall poverty rate.) Temporary Assistance for Needy Families (TANF) is a federal program that provides money to the states that may be used to aid poor families. In addition to these cash-assistance programs, a variety of in-kind assistance programs provide the poor with some type of good or service. Food stamps, free and reduced-price school lunches, and subsidized housing are three examples. All these programs are designed to improve the status of the poor and in this way moderate the distribution of goods and services dictated by the market.

How effective are these programs in reducing poverty? In 2004, the Bureau of the Census estimated that if we adjust for the impact of these various programs—everything from the earned income tax credit and Social Security to housing subsidies and food stamps—the poverty rate in that year would fall from 12.7 percent to 10.4 percent. That means the overall impact of these programs was to reduce the poverty rate by about 18%.

AMBIVALENCE ABOUT HELPING THE POOR

Why have we not been more successful in reducing poverty? Part of the answer may be the fact that the poor lack lobbyists who can keep their plight in front of politicians (a public-choice observation). But there is more to the answer than that. In truth, although virtually everyone is sympathetic to those who clearly are unable to support themselves—the severely handicapped, for instance, and young children—we, as a society, appear to have some ambivalence about more general help to individuals and families with low incomes. In part this ambivalence appears to stem from stereotypes that characterize the poor as lazy and deserving of their poverty status. Of course, if voters and policymakers believe that the poor deserve to be poor, they will not be motivated to provide assistance. The other source of this ambivalence about helping the poor stems from genuine concerns about the impact of government programs on the incentives of the poor, particularly the incentive to work. Consider unemployment compensation, for example. The more generous the benefits and the longer the period the unemployed are able to receive those benefits, the less urgency they will feel about searching for a job. And while we may not want unemployed workers taking the first job that comes along, we do want the unemployed to have incentive to return to work. As a consequence, even those who feel genuine sympathy toward the poor recognize that it is important to balance compassion and incentives. Unfortunately, balancing compassion and incentives is a value-laden task. Some of us are willing to provide generous benefits and worry less about the impact of those benefits on the incentives of the poor. Others worry more about the incentive effects and less about the adequacy of the benefits.

SUMMARY THOUGHTS ON POVERTY AND INEQUALITY

Any discussion of poverty and inequality unavoidably involves more than economic theory because it has to do with "normative" issues, with what kind of society we want to have. But it is clear that poverty and inequality also have feedback effects on the economic system itself. For example, some inequality may be desirable to provide personal incentives—to motivate us. If we were all paid exactly the same salaries regardless of how hard we worked, most of us would probably choose to work less, and society's output would fall. On the other hand, too much inequality may be demotivating, perhaps even threatening to democratic capitalism itself. The question, then, is how much inequality to tolerate and what to do when you've exceeded that point. Those are the questions that many in the United States are asking today.

3

Macroeconomics: The Economy as a Whole

Macroeconomics is the study of the economy as a whole and the factors that influence the economy's overall performance. (If you have a hard time remembering the difference between microeconomics and macroeconomics, just remember that *micro* means "small"—microcomputer, microfilm, microsurgery—whereas *macro* means "large.") Macroeconomics addresses a number of important questions: What determines the level of total output and total employment in the economy? What causes unemployment? What causes inflation? What can be done to eliminate these problems or at least to reduce their severity? These and many other considerations relating to the economy's overall performance are the domain of macroeconomics.

In Chapter 10 we begin our study of macroeconomics by examining some indicators, or measures, that economists watch to gauge how well the economy is performing. Chapter 11 introduces aggregate demand and aggregate supply and considers how these twin forces interact to determine the overall price level and the levels of output and employment in the economy. The chapter then uses the aggregate demand and supply framework to examine the possibility that the economy is self-correcting in the long run. Chapter 12 deals with fiscal policy—government spending and taxation policy designed to combat unemployment or inflation. It also considers the limitations of fiscal policy and examines the sources and con-sequences of federal budget deficits and the public debt.

Chapter 13 explains how depository institutions, such as commercial banks and savings and loan associations, "create" money and how the Federal Reserve attempts to control the money supply to guide the econ-omy's performance. Chapter 14 explores the debate between "activists," who believe that government should attempt to manage the economy's overall performance, and "nonactivists," who believe that such attempts are ill-advised. Chapter 15 concludes the macroeconomics section of the textbook by considering economic growth. The chapter examines the sources of growth, the impact of growth on our standard of living, and reservations regarding the pursuit of economic growth as an objective.

10

Measuring Aggregate Performance

LEARNING OBJECTIVES

1. Describe how the unemployment rate is calculated.
2. Identify the three basic types of unemployment.
3. Explain why zero unemployment is an unattainable goal.
4. Describe the variation in the unemployment rate among subcategories of the labor force.
5. Explain why changes in the unemployment rate can send misleading signals about the strength of the economy.
6. Discuss the costs of anticipated and unanticipated inflation.
7. Interpret price indexes, and calculate the annual rate of inflation.
8. Describe how U.S. unemployment and inflation rates compare with those of other major industrialized countries.
9. Define gross domestic product (GDP) and real GDP.
10. Describe how GDP is calculated.
11. Discuss the limitations of GDP as a measure of welfare.

What economic problems have the potential to really excite Americans? Do Americans lose sleep over the market power of large corporations? Do they have nightmares about agricultural subsidies, minimum wage laws, or environmental pollution?

Although each of these issues gains the attention of some Americans, national surveys tell us that none of them can hold a candle to two problems that can hit closer to home: unemployment and inflation. In the next few chapters we'll be examining the factors that influence the economy's *aggregate*, or overall, performance and how problems such as unemployment and inflation arise. We will also consider policies to combat unemployment and inflation and the difficulties that may be encountered in applying these policies.

This chapter sets the stage for that discussion by examining some **economic indicators**—signals, or measures, that tell us how well the economy is performing. After all, policymakers can't take actions that lead to better performance unless they know when problems exist. Economic indicators provide that information. The economic indicators we will discuss in this chapter include the unemployment rate, the Consumer Price Index, and the gross domestic product (GDP)—the indicator that many economists believe is the most important single measure of the economy's performance.

MEASURING UNEMPLOYMENT

One dimension of our economy's performance is its ability to provide jobs for those who want to work. For most of us, that's an extremely important aspect of the economy's performance because we value work not only as a source of income but also as a basis for our sense of personal worth. The most highly publicized indicator of performance in this area is the unemployment rate. The **unemployment rate** traditionally reported is the percentage of the civilian labor force that is unemployed. The **civilian labor force** is made up of all persons over the age of 16 who are not in the armed forces and who are either employed or actively seeking employment. The Bureau of Labor Statistics (BLS), the agency responsible for gathering and analyzing labor force and employment data, surveys some 60,000 households throughout the United States monthly to determine the employment status of the residents. It uses the statistics gathered from this sample (which is scientifically designed to be representative of the entire U.S. population) to estimate the total size of the labor force and the rate of unemployment.

Counting the Unemployed

How does the Bureau of Labor Statistics decide whether a person should be classified as unemployed? First, it determines whether the person has a job. As far as the BLS is concerned, you are employed if you did *any* work for pay in the week of the survey. It doesn't matter how long you worked, provided that you worked for pay. You are also counted as employed if you worked 15 hours or more (during the survey week) as an unpaid worker in a family-operated business.

Even if you didn't have a job during the survey week, you are not recognized as unemployed unless you were actively seeking employment. To be "actively seeking employment," you must have done something to try to find a job—filled out applications, responded to want ads, or at least registered at an employment agency. If you did any of those things and failed to find a job, you are officially unemployed. If you didn't look for work, you're considered as "not participating" in the civilian labor force, and consequently you won't be counted as unemployed.

The purpose of the BLS monthly survey is to estimate the size of the civilian labor force (the number employed plus those actively seeking employment) and the number of unemployed. Then the bureau computes the unemployment rate by dividing the total number of unemployed persons by the number of people in the civilian labor force. For example, in June 2009 there were 154.9 million people in the civilian labor force, and 14.7 million of those people were unemployed. That means the **civilian unemployment rate** in June 2009 was 9.5 percent.

$$\text{Unemployment rate} = \frac{\text{Total number of unemployed persons}}{\text{Total number of persons in the civilian labor force}}$$

$$\text{Unemployment rate (June 2009)} = \frac{14.7 \text{ million unemployed persons}}{154.9 \text{ million persons in the civilian labor force}}$$

$$= 9.5 \text{ percent}$$

As you can see from Exhibit 10.1, our unemployment rate does not compare favorably with those of other industrialized nations. In June 2009 the average unemployment rate in the seven nations surveyed was 8.2 percent, 1.3 percent lower than the U.S. rate. When we look at the figures for the last decade, our performance looks much better; the seven-nation average was 6.8 percent,

EXHIBIT 10.1

Unemployment Rates in Major Industrialized Countries

	UNITED STATES	CANADA	JAPAN	FRANCE	GERMANY	ITALY	UNITED KINGDOM	7-NATION AVERAGE
Unemployment rate June 2009	9.5%	7.7%	5.5%	9.7%	8.0%	8.9%	7.9%	8.2%
Average unemployment rate 1999–2008	5.0%	6.2%	4.7%	9.1%	9.0%	8.3%	5.3%	6.8%

Source: The Bureau of Labor Statistics. International statistics are from the Bureau's Division of International Labor Comparisons. The June 2009 figures for Italy and the United Kingdom are estimates based on first-quarter data.

whereas our average unemployment rate was 5.0 percent. We would certainly have settled for 5 percent in 2008! But is 5.0 percent the best the U.S. economy can hope to achieve, or can we do better still? Let's turn to that question.

Types of Unemployment

In general, a high unemployment rate is interpreted as a sign of a weak economy, whereas a low rate is seen as a sign of strength. But to recognize a low rate of unemployment when we see it, we have to know what we are aiming for, what is possible or realistic. That, in turn, requires knowledge of the three basic types of unemployment—frictional, cyclical, and structural—and the extent to which these types of unemployment are unavoidable.

Frictional Unemployment   Even when plenty of jobs are available, there are always some people out of work because they are changing jobs or searching for their first job. Economists call this **frictional unemployment** to distinguish a type of labor-market adjustment involving time lags, or "friction." A certain amount of frictional unemployment is unavoidable and probably even desirable. It is a sign that employers are looking for the most-qualified workers and that workers are searching for the best jobs. Neither party is willing to settle for the first thing that comes along. That's good for the economy because it means that the right people are more likely to be matched to the right jobs. But it takes time for workers and employers to find each other, and meanwhile the job seekers are adding to the nation's unemployment rate.

Cyclical Unemployment   Joblessness caused by a reduction in the economy's total demand for goods and services is termed **cyclical unemployment**. When such a reduction occurs, perhaps because consumers have decided to save more and spend less, businesses that are not able to sell as much output as before usually must cut back on production. This means that some of their workers will become unemployed. We call this unemployment cyclical because we recognize that the economy goes through cycles of economic activity. For a while the economy expands and unemployment declines; then economic activity slows and unemployment rises. These recurring ups and downs in the level of economic activity are known as the **business cycle**. A period of rising output and employment is called an *expansion*; a period of declining output and employment is called a *recession*. The impact of the business cycle on the unemployment rate is evident in Exhibit 10.2.

When people are cyclically unemployed, the economy is losing the output these workers could have produced, and, of course, the workers are losing the income they could have earned. Many economists argue that it is possible to reduce the amount of cyclical unemployment by using government policies to stimulate the total demand for goods and services.

EXHIBIT 10.2

The Unemployment Rate: 1929–2009

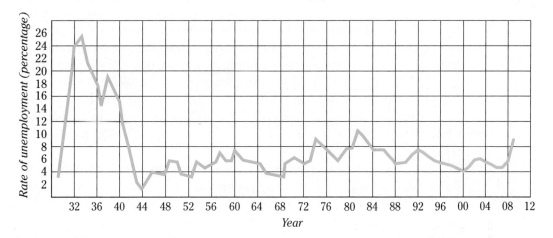

This exhibit shows that the unemployment rate varies significantly from year to year. But even though the unemployment rate is not a constant, there is a pattern to that variation, an up-and-down cycle that keeps repeating itself. For example, we can see that the unemployment rate dropped from a high of about 25 percent in 1933 to approximately 14 percent in 1937. Then the unemployment rate jumped back up to 19 percent in 1938 and started a steady decline that continued until 1944. The same sort of pattern is evident over other time periods, although the magnitude of the changes certainly is not as great.

The rate reported is the civilian unemployment rate. Older data were drawn from *Historical Statistics of the United States*, published by the U.S. Census Bureau. Recent data are from the Bureau of Labor Statistics, U.S. Department of Labor.

Structural Unemployment   Changes in the makeup, or structure, of the economy that render certain skills obsolete or in less demand result in **structural unemployment**. The economy is always changing. New products are introduced and old ones are dropped; businesses continually develop new production methods. These kinds of changes can have a profound effect on the demand for labor. Skills that were once very much in demand may be virtually obsolete today. Consider, for instance, the fate of the blacksmith. Although blacksmiths' skills were once highly regarded, the introduction of the automobile meant that blacksmiths' days were numbered. The same fate has befallen newspaper typesetters. These jobs are gone, eliminated by the introduction of computerized photocomposition machines.

Concerns regarding structural unemployment often focus on the manufacturing sector of our economy. Faced with strong foreign competition, U.S. firms are locked in an ongoing struggle to reduce labor costs. One approach is to automate, to substitute robots and other forms of capital equipment for labor. Another approach is to substitute cheaper foreign workers in place of our own. As a result of these changes, many manufacturing jobs are being eliminated, either because the workers have been replaced by machines or because the work has been shipped overseas to be performed in foreign factories. The jobs that remain are often highly technical jobs, jobs requiring skills quite different from those possessed by the average manufacturing worker. Those lacking the needed skills are often forced to search for work in the service sector of our economy—the sector that has exhibited the fastest growth. But the transition can be difficult. Displaced manufacturing workers may need to be retrained before they can find employment in the service sector. In the interim, they will be structurally unemployed.

The changing skill requirements for the workplace are not the only source of structural unemployment. Some people cannot hold a job in the modern economy because they never received much education or training in the first place. This is the case with many members of inner-city minorities, who often are educated in second-rate school systems that have a high dropout rate. It is also possible for people to be structurally unemployed even though they have marketable skills. For example, unemployed construction workers in Fresno, California, may have skills that are very much in demand. But if the available jobs are on the East Coast, the Fresno workers remain structurally unemployed.

All structurally unemployed workers have one thing in common: If they are to find jobs, they must make drastic changes. They will have to acquire new skills or move to a different part of the country. They may even find it necessary to do both. Because such changes cannot be made overnight, economists see structural unemployment as a more serious and longer-term problem than frictional or cyclical unemployment.

Full Employment versus Zero Unemployment

Because a certain amount of frictional and structural unemployment is unavoidable, economists consider zero unemployment an unattainable goal. Although no one knows precisely how much unemployment is of the frictional and structural varieties, a common estimate is 5 percent. This is considered the **natural rate of unemployment**—the minimum level of unemployment that our economy can achieve in normal times. (Note that this is the rate that would exist in the absence of cyclical unemployment.) When the actual rate of unemployment is equal to the natural rate, the economy has achieved **full employment**.

A Closer Look at Unemployment Rates

Recognizing that full employment doesn't mean zero unemployment is an important step in learning how to interpret unemployment statistics. The next step

Structurally unemployed workers may need to be retrained before they can find jobs.

is learning to look beyond the overall unemployment rate to see how various groups in our society are being affected. Although we all talk about "the" unemployment rate, in reality the rate of unemployment varies substantially among the different subcategories of the American labor force. Historically, blacks have been about twice as likely to be unemployed as whites, in part because, on the whole, they have lower levels of education and training. Teenagers, who are often unskilled and lacking in good work habits, generally have unemployment rates about two and a half to three times the overall rate for their racial group.

Exhibit 10.3 shows the unemployment rates for June 2009. Note that the overall unemployment rate for all civilian workers—that is "the" unemployment rate—was 9.5 percent. During the same period the overall rate for blacks (14.7 percent) was slightly less than twice the rate for white workers (8.7 percent), and this relationship held for each of the subcategories: men, women, and teenagers. The rates for teens were within the expected range: black teens and white teens had unemployment rates about two and a half times the overall rate for their racial group.

As you can see, the overall unemployment rate conceals a great deal of variation across particular groups. Even when the overall rate is low, the unemployment rate among certain subcategories of our population may be unacceptably high. For that reason, those who rely on unemployment statistics for devising policies to combat unemployment or for helping the unemployed in

EXHIBIT 10.3

Unemployment Rates for June 2009

WORKER CATEGORY	RATE	WORKER CATEGORY	RATE	WORKER CATEGORY[*]	RATE
All civilian workers	9.5%	*White*	8.7%	*Black*	14.7%
Men (20 and over)	10.0%	Men (20 and over)	9.2%	Men (20 and over)	16.4%
Women (20 and over)	7.0%	Women (20 and over)	6.8%	Women (20 and over)	11.3%
Teenagers (16–19)	24.0%	Teenagers (16–19)	21.4%	Teenagers (16–19)	37.9%

[*] Detailed statistics are not available for the Hispanic or Latino population. The overall unemployment rate for this group was 12.2 percent.
Source: Bureau of Labor Statistics, U.S. Department of Labor.

other ways must be willing to look beyond the overall rate to gain a clearer picture of the nature and severity of the unemployment problem.

Unemployment Rates: A Word of Caution

Before we leave this section on unemployment statistics, a few words of caution are appropriate. Watching the unemployment rate can help you understand whether the economy is growing weaker or stronger. But changes in the unemployment rate from one month to the next may not be very meaningful and, in fact, can sometimes send misleading signals about the state of the economy.

To illustrate that point, suppose that the economy is in the midst of a deep recession when the Bureau of Labor Statistics reports a small drop in the unemployment rate. Should that drop be taken as a sign that the economy is growing stronger? Not necessarily. When the economy has been in a recession for quite a while, some unemployed workers become discouraged in their search for jobs and stop looking. Because these "discouraged workers" are no longer actively seeking employment, they are no longer counted as unemployed. That makes the unemployment rate look better, but it's not really a sign that the economy has improved. In fact, it may be a sign that labor-market conditions have become even worse.

Of course, we can be misled in the other direction just as easily. Suppose that the economy has begun to recover from a recession and that the unemployment rate is falling. Suddenly the monthly survey shows an increase. Does that mean that the economy is headed back toward recession? It may, but a more likely interpretation is that the economy's improved condition has attracted a lot of additional job seekers who have swelled the labor force and pushed up the unemployment rate. Here the unemployment rate has risen not because the economy is worse but because it is better: People are more confident about their prospects for finding jobs.

Because changes in the unemployment rate can send misleading signals about the strength of the economy, they should be interpreted with caution. But even when the unemployment rate seems to be sending clear signals (for instance, when it has risen for several consecutive months), we must be careful not to base our evaluation of the economy's health solely on this statistic. After all, the unemployment rate looks at only one dimension of the economy's performance—its ability to provide jobs for the growing labor force. Other dimensions are equally important. To obtain an accurate picture of our economy's performance, we must consider each of these dimensions by examining several different economic indicators. (The unemployed were not the only people suffering during the "Great Recession" of 2008–2009. Read "Recession Finds Even Those with Jobs Losing Pay," on page 302, to learn more.)

MEASURING INFLATION

Another important dimension of our economy's performance is its success or failure in avoiding inflation. **Inflation** is defined as a rise in the general level of prices. (The existence of inflation does not necessarily mean that *all* prices are rising but rather that *more* prices are going up than are coming down.) Inflation means that our dollars won't buy as much as they used to. In general, this means that it will take more money to pay the grocery bill, buy clothes, go out for an evening, or do almost anything else.

Unanticipated Inflation and Income Redistribution

Each of us tends to believe that we are being hurt by inflation, but that is not necessarily the case. We forget that at the same time that prices are rising, our money incomes are also likely to be rising, sometimes at a faster rate than the increase in prices. Instead of focusing solely on prices, then, we ought to be concerned about what economists call real income. **Real income** is the purchasing power of your income—the amount of goods and services it will buy. Economists argue that unanticipated inflation is essentially an income redistribution problem: It takes real income away from some people and gives it to others. (As you will see later, when people anticipate inflation, they tend to prepare for it and thereby reduce its redistributive effects.)

Use Your Economic Reasoning

Recession Finds Even Those with Jobs Losing Pay

BY CHRISTOPHER LEONARD

In cubicles, factories and stores these days, anxious workers are trying to ease each other's economic fears with something akin to, "Well, at least we still have a job." Yet for many, that's becoming small comfort as more employers cut hours or hire only part-timers. People paid on commission, meanwhile, are suffering as sales dry up. And state workers around the country have been put on unpaid leaves.

These workers aren't counted in the unemployment rate, which hit 8.1 percent in February [2009]. They're not eligible for federal benefits that provide a safety net for the jobless. Yet their pain is real, and their reduced spending is a drag on the economy. Call them the walking wounded of this deep recession: millions of workers whose incomes have fallen even as they manage to hold onto their jobs. Their shrunken pay has forced many of them to make hurtful sacrifices. "I won't be able to buy the groceries I need to buy to make sure my family can eat until the end of the month," said Rhonda Wagner, a 52-year-old California state employee who has been dealing with less pay due to state-imposed leave. Before her pay cut, Wagner said her paycheck from the Department of Motor Vehicles was barely enough for her to pay her bills. Now, she says she's facing foreclosure and struggling to pay for utilities. . . .

More than 4.5 million workers last year depended at least partly on variable pay, which includes tips and commissions, according to Labor Department figures. Meanwhile, the number of workers forced into part-time instead of full-time work soared 76 percent in the past year. The average number of hours all employees work each week has also dropped. The commission-heavy sectors of retail and auto sales have been especially hammered.

That said, workers whose hours or commissions have dropped still fared better than those who have lost their jobs altogether. Even though workers are being given fewer hours to work, average hourly wages have continued to rise over the past year. Still, many of those who keep their jobs tend to suffer . . . right along with the unemployed, said Edward Lazear, professor of human resources management at Stanford University. . . . As the recession cuts demand for goods and services, companies that don't shed workers outright must squeeze savings from the work force that remains. They typically do so by cutting hours. And as a recession persists, rising competition for jobs tends to shave wages and benefits. Companies lose any incentive to boost pay. "Other guys are now competing with you for that job, and they're willing to take that same job for less money," Lazear said. "While it might not happen in any given month, over the next three years, wage growth will be lower than it would have been had we not had a recession."

When companies cut or freeze wages for salaried or hourly employees, the workers tend to feel the effect gradually. By contrast, for waitresses, car salesmen, retail clerks and others whose variable pay hinges on economic cycles, a pay drop tends to be as steep as it is quick, said Sylvia Allegretto, an economist at the University of California, Berkeley. That's because sales-based compensation is more sensitive to swings in consumer spending. "They're going to be hard hit, because tips, commissions, overtime and all those things, along with hours, are going to be cut," as the economy struggles, Allegretto said. . . .

Until last year, 58-year-old Michael Klein made about $125,000 a year selling Hummer

SUVs at a dealership in Concord, Calif., near San Francisco. With 20 years' experience, Klein was accustomed to moving 15 to 25 vehicles a month. Then gas prices soared and loans dried up. So did his client base. Now Klein works seven days a week, 12 hours a day, just to sell eight cars a month. His income has shrunk by more than half. . . .

While earnings for commission-based workers drop quickly, those paid in wages will endure a somewhat slower pay decline this year, said Ken Abosch, head of the North American practice for Hewitt Associates compensation consultants. A Hewitt survey of 640 companies found they planned to raise wages for salaried employees by 2.5 percent this year. That's the smallest increase since 1976. The companies said executive pay increases would drop from 3.8 percent to 2.2 percent in 2009.

But for millions of workers, the biggest problem is a shortage of hours available. Last month, the average work week fell to 33.3 hours. In January it was an estimated 32.9 hours, the lowest level since the Labor Department began tracking the figure in 1964. More than 8.6 million U.S. employees are working part time because they can't find full-time work, according to department figures, the largest number recorded and a 76 percent increase from 12 months ago.

For workers like Richard Thomas, that means getting by without the health insurance and other benefits afforded to many full-time employees. Thomas worked as a full-time truck driver until last summer, when business slowed. He was paid by the mile. As orders slowed, he sat idle for days at a time. He thought steady work back home in St. Louis would help boost his income. But he could find only a part-time job as a school-bus driver. Thomas, 36, says he usually gets 25 hours a week of work. On good days, he finds odd jobs, like fueling up buses, to boost his pay. . . . Even without a family to support, there's no money left for frills. A typical night of entertainment consists of watching movies on his laptop. He spends much of his spare time hunting for work.

Because they're working, part-time employees like Thomas aren't eligible for unemployment benefits or welfare. But he said he doesn't let that bother him.

"I would rather get one of those good jobs myself," he said.

USE YOUR ECONOMIC REASONING

1. The article says that companies are shedding workers due to "cuts in the demand for goods and services." What label do economists attach to this type of unemployment?

2. The unemployment rate understates the pain felt during an economic downturn because it fails to reflect the pain felt by workers on "variable pay" and part-time workers. Explain. Why are the incomes of workers on variable pay particularly sensitive to swings in consumer spending?

3. High unemployment rates don't just harm those without jobs, they also tend to drag down the starting salaries of those lucky enough to find new jobs and the raises of those still working. How would you explain this impact? Can you use the supply and demand for labor as a starting point?

4. A study by a Yale University economist found that each percentage point increase in the unemployment rate reduces the first-year earnings of new college graduates by about 8 percent (compared with those who graduated in better times). Suppose, then, that the unemployment rate is 7 percent when you graduate. How much lower will your starting salary be compared with someone who graduates when the economy is operating at its natural rate? (Read more about the study in "The Curse of the Class of 2009," by Sara Murray, *Wall Street Journal*, May 9, 2009, p. A1.)

Keeping Pace with Inflation   The people hurt by unanticipated inflation are those whose money incomes (the number of *dollars* they earn) don't keep pace with rising prices. If prices rise by 10 percent but your money income increases by only 5 percent, your real income will have fallen. The amount of goods and services that you can buy with your income will be 5 percent less than before.

Whether your money income keeps pace with inflation depends on a variety of factors. The most important is how flexible your income is, that is, how easily it can be adjusted. Professional people—doctors, lawyers, dentists, and so on—often can adjust the prices they charge their customers and thereby stay abreast (or ahead) of inflation. People who own their own businesses—their own hair salon or apartment house or janitorial service—may be able to adjust their prices similarly. Of course, whether professional people and businesses can successfully increase prices and stay abreast of inflation depends on the degree of the market power they possess. If a seller faces very little competition and therefore has significant market power, it may be able to increase its prices to offset inflation. If it operates in a highly competitive environment, it may not be able to do so.

Workers who are represented by strong unions also may do reasonably well during periods of inflation. Often these unions are able to negotiate cost-of-living adjustment (COLA) clauses, which provide for automatic wage and salary adjustments to compensate for inflation. Other workers may have the forces of demand and supply operating to their advantage. When the demand for workers with a particular skill is strong relative to their supply, those workers often are able to obtain wage or salary increases that more than offset the impact of inflation. Unskilled workers and others in oversupplied fields—those in which there are several prospective employees for each job opening—usually find it more difficult to gain wage increases that match the rate of inflation.

Savers and People on Fixed Incomes   Hardest hit by inflation are people on fixed incomes, whose incomes are by definition inflexible. The classic example is a retired person living on a fixed pension or perhaps on his or her accumulated savings. (Of course, many retired persons are not dependent on fixed pensions. For example, Social Security payments are automatically adjusted for increases in the cost of living.)

Savers can also be hurt by inflation. Whether you are relying on your savings to provide retirement income, to make a down payment on a home someday, or to buy a car next summer, inflation can eat away at the value of your savings account and make your objective more difficult to achieve. For example, if your savings account is paying 6 percent interest and the inflation rate is 10 percent, the purchasing power of your savings is declining by 4 percent a year. After you pay taxes on the interest, you're even further behind.

Creditors versus Debtors   Unanticipated inflation can also hurt banks and other creditors because borrowers will be able to repay their loans with dollars that are worth less than those that were borrowed. As the largest debtor of all, the federal government is probably the biggest gainer from such inflation. Other gainers include families with home mortgages and businesses that borrowed money to purchase factories or equipment.

When Inflation Is Anticipated

The redistributive effects of inflation occur because inflation is unforeseen or unanticipated. To the extent that inflation is anticipated, the redistributive effects will tend to be reduced because individuals and businesses will take actions to protect themselves from inflation.

COLA clauses are one way in which we attempt to insulate ourselves from inflation, but there are others. For example, banks try to protect themselves from anticipated inflation by working the inflation rate into the interest rates they set for loans. If a bank wants to earn 5 percent interest on a loan and expects the inflation rate to be 4 percent, the bank will charge 9 percent interest to get the desired return. If the inflation rate turns out to be 4 percent, neither the bank nor the customer will be harmed by inflation. Of course, the bank's inflation forecast won't always be correct. Forecasting inflation has proved very difficult, and bankers and others will make mistakes. As a consequence, inflation is likely to benefit some and hurt others.

Consequences of inflation extend beyond its effect on the income distribution. When inflation is anticipated, individuals and businesses waste resources in their attempts to protect themselves from its impact. Labor time and energy are expended shopping around and shifting money from one financial institution to another in pursuit of the highest interest rate. Restaurant menus and business price lists must be continually revised, and sales personnel must be kept informed of the most recent price information. In short, efforts to stay ahead of inflation use up resources that could be used to produce other things.

In addition to wasting resources, inflation (whether anticipated or unanticipated) can lead to inefficiency through its tendency to distort the information provided by the price system. To illustrate, suppose that the price of laptop computers increases. Does the higher price indicate greater demand for the product, or does it merely reflect an increase in the overall price level? Because computer manufacturers are uncertain, they may be reluctant to invest in new production capacity. Thus, inflation may slow investment spending and retard the economy's rate of growth.

In summary, inflation, both anticipated and unanticipated, imposes costs on society. Unanticipated inflation causes income redistribution; anticipated inflation causes scarce resources to be wasted and used inefficiently.

Calculating a Price Index

Bankers, union leaders, business executives, and most other people in our society are keenly interested in changes in the general level of prices because they want to try to compensate for those changes; they'd like to build them into the prices they charge their customers and the wages they negotiate with their employers. Government policymakers also want to know what is happening to the price level to know when inflation-fighting policies may be necessary.

Economists attempt to measure inflation by using a **price index**. A price index is really nothing more than a ratio of two prices: the price of an item in a base period that serves as a reference point divided into the price of that item in a period we wish to compare with the base period. For example, if the price of steak was $5.00 a pound in 2000 and $8.00 a pound in 2009, the price index for steak in 2009 would be 160 if 2000 was used as the base year:

$$\text{Price index} = \frac{\text{Price in any given period}}{\text{Price in the base period}}$$

$$= \frac{\$8.00}{\$5.00}$$

$$= 1.60 \text{ or } 160 \text{ percent or } 160$$

(Note that although the price index is in fact a percentage, by convention it is written without the percent sign.)

The price index tells us how much the price of the item in question has increased or decreased since the base period. Because the price index in the base period is always 100, an index of 160 means that a price has increased by 60 percent since the base period.[1] By the same logic, an index of 75 would indicate that a price had decreased by 25 percent since the base period. Although price indexes can be used to determine how much prices have risen or fallen since the base period, their most common use is to determine the annual rate of inflation for a particular product or group of products. The **annual inflation rate** is the percent change in a price index from one year to the next. For example, if the price index for steak increased from 160 in December 2008 to 170 in December 2009, the rate of inflation for steak in 2009 would be 6.3 percent (10/160 = 0.063). Exhibit 10.4 provides another example of how to compute the annual inflation rate.

Three basic price indexes are used in the United States: the Consumer Price Index, the Producer Price Index, and the Implicit Price Deflator. Each index surveys a particular range of goods and services to determine the rate of inflation

---

[1] The price index in the base period is always 100 because the numbers in the numerator and denominator of the price-index formula must be the same. For example, if we want to calculate the price index for steak in 2000 using 2000 as the base period, we would have $5.00/$5.00 = 1.00 or 100 percent.

Computing the Annual Rate of Inflation for College Tuition

The price index for tuition and school fees was 513.7 in June 2008 and 548.7 in June 2009, using 1984 as the base year. What was the rate of inflation in tuition and fees over this time period?

$$\text{Annual rate of inflation} = \frac{\text{Change in the price index from one year to the next}}{\text{Price index in the initial year}}$$

$$= \frac{548.7 - 513.7}{513.7}$$

$$= \frac{35.0}{513.7}$$

$$= .068 \text{ or } 6.8 \text{ percent}$$

among those items. Each computes an overall index showing the average rate of price change for its assortment (or "basket") of commodities and presents individual price indexes for each major class of items in the survey. This makes it possible to determine which products are most responsible for any change in the overall index.

The Consumer Price Index

The best-known index is the Consumer Price Index (CPI). The CPI looks at the prices of some 400 goods and services that have been chosen to represent the kinds of products typically purchased by urban consumers. The CPI measures the purchasing power of consumers' dollars by comparing the current cost of this so-called basket of goods and services to the cost of the same basket at an earlier date.

Exhibit 10.5 shows the kinds of items that are included in the Consumer Price Index survey. You can see how the rate of inflation differs from one class of items to another. The top line—the all-items index—is the CPI usually referred to by economists and the media. It tells us the average rate of price increase for all the items in the market basket. According to the exhibit, the all-items index stood at 214.5 in June 2009. Because the most recent CPI uses the average level of prices between 1982 and 1984 as the base, prices increased about 114 percent between 1982–84 and 2009. More precisely, in June 2009 it cost $214.50 to purchase a basket of goods and services that sold for $100 in the 1982–84 period. As you can see from the exhibit, some items increased even more than that. For instance, tobacco products rose to an index of 746.3, indicating that the cost of cigarettes and other tobacco products increased more than 640 percent between 1982–84 and June 2009. Tuition and school fees (the

EXHIBIT 10.5

Consumer Price Indexes, June 2009 (1982–1984 = 100)

ALL ITEMS	214.5		
Food and beverages	218.1	Apparel	120.2
Housing	217.0	Transportation	178.8
Shelter	249.9	Medical care	375.2
Fuel and utilities	206.3	Tuition and fees	548.7
Household furnishings and operation	129.4	Tobacco products	746.3

Source: Bureau of Labor Statistics, U.S. Department of Labor.

category that includes college tuition) increased by about 450 percent over the same period—to an index of 548.7.

Because consumers spend greater percentages of their incomes on certain index items—more, say, on food and beverages than on apparel and upkeep—merely averaging all the indexes at face value to arrive at the all-items index would be misleading. Therefore, the all-items index is computed as a *weighted average* of the individual indexes. That is, the things for which consumers spend more of their incomes are counted more heavily in determining the all-items index. For example, if consumers spend twice as much on food and beverages as they do on apparel, food and beverage prices will be twice as important in computing the all-items index.

By comparing the 2008 and 2009 consumer price indexes, we can compute the annual inflation rate for consumer goods. Recall that the annual inflation rate is the percent change in the price index from one year to the next. The CPI was 217.4 in June 2008 and 214.5 in June 2009, so prices were actually falling over that period. That's what economists label **deflation**—a reduction in the general level of prices. The rate of deflation over that one-year period was 1.3 percent (2.9/217.4).

How does our economy's performance on the inflation front compare with the experience of other major industrialized nations? As you can see from Exhibit 10.6, most of the nations surveyed were also experiencing deflation in 2008–2009, the result of the worldwide recession. When we look at inflation over the last decade, our average rate is a bit higher than the other nations, but all of the inflation rates are fairly low, so our relative position does not appear troubling.

The rates of inflation reported in this table reflect inflation on consumer goods; the U.S. rates are based on the CPI, and the foreign rates are based on

EXHIBIT 10.6

Inflation Rates in Major Industrialized Countries

	UNITED STATES	CANADA	JAPAN	FRANCE	GERMANY	ITALY	UNITED KINGDOM	7-NATION AVERAGE
Inflation rate June 2008– June 2009	–1.3%	–.3%	–1.8%	–.5%	.1%	.5%	–1.6%	–.7%
Average inflation rate, 1999–2008	2.8%	2.3%	–.2%	1.8%	1.6%	2.4%	2.8%	1.9%

Source: Bureau of Labor Statistics.

similar indexes. But in some instances we may be more interested in inflation at the wholesale level, or the rate of inflation in government services or capital goods (factories and equipment). For these purposes we need to turn to other price indexes.

The Producer Price Index and the Implicit Price Deflator

The Producer Price Index (PPI) and the Implicit Price Deflator (IPD) don't receive as much publicity as the Consumer Price Index, which is closely watched because it is used for cost-of-living adjustments in labor contracts and Social Security payments. Nevertheless, they have their particular uses and advantages. The PPI and the IPD are interpreted in precisely the same way as the CPI; that is, an index of 170 means that prices have risen by 70 percent since the base period.

The Producer Price Index is sometimes called the Wholesale Price Index.[2] It reflects the rate of inflation in the wholesale prices of finished products—both consumer goods and capital goods. Economists pay particular attention to the PPI because they think that it provides an indication of what will happen to consumer prices in the months to come. The logic here is fairly simple. Any increases in wholesale prices are eventually going to be passed on to consumers.

The broadest measure of inflation is the Implicit Price Deflator. This index examines the rate of increase in prices for all the different items included in the

---

[2] Actually, there are three separate Producer Price Indexes: one for finished goods, one for semifinished goods, and one for raw materials. The index for finished goods is the one referred to as the Wholesale Price Index. It's also the one commonly referred to in the news.

gross domestic product (GDP). This includes the prices of consumer goods, but it also includes the prices of items produced for business and government use and for export to foreign buyers. The range of products covered by the Implicit Price Deflator will be more apparent after you have completed the next section.

MEASURING TOTAL OUTPUT

The fundamental purpose of every economic system is to produce output to satisfy human wants. Therefore, many economists argue that gross domestic product (GDP) is the most important single indicator of our economy's performance. **Gross domestic product** is the total monetary value of all final goods and services produced within a nation in one year. In other words, it is a measure of the economy's annual production or output.

Calculating GDP: A Sneak Preview

Because GDP is measured in monetary units rather than units of output, we can add apples and oranges, so to speak; we can sum the economy's output of eggs, stereos, houses, tractors, and other products to produce a meaningful statistic. The procedure is quite simple: The output of each product is valued at its selling price, and these values are added to arrive at a figure for GDP.

Although GDP is a measure of output, you should note that only the output of final goods and services is permitted to enter the GDP calculation. *Final goods* are those that are purchased for final use rather than for further processing or resale. For example, a new pair of jeans is a final good, but the thread, cloth, zippers, and snaps that are used in manufacturing the jeans are *intermediate goods*. Because the value of the jeans already includes the value of the thread and other intermediate goods, only the value of the jeans should count in GDP. If the value of intermediate goods were to be included in the calculation, the result would be double counting, which would overstate the value of the economy's annual production.

GDP and the Circular Flow

There are two ways to measure gross domestic product: the expenditures approach and the income approach. The *expenditures approach* measures how much money is spent in purchasing final goods and services; the *income approach* measures the income that is created in producing these goods and services. Because one person's expenditure becomes another person's income, the two approaches must arrive at the same amount. In dollar terms, total output *must* equal total income.

The equality between total output and total income is reflected in the circular-flow diagram in Exhibit 10.7, which is simplified to show the interaction of only the household and business sectors. The expenditures approach measures GDP by summing the various expenditures that make up the flow depicted at the bottom of the diagram. The income approach computes GDP by adding the various categories of income contained in the flow at the top of the diagram. The circular nature of the diagram indicates that all income spent on final goods and services must be received by someone as income; thus, total output must equal total income.

The Expenditures Approach

As you know, the U.S. economy is much more complex than the system depicted in Exhibit 10.7. In our economy it's not only households that make expenditures for goods and services but also businesses, various levels of government, and foreign consumers. The categories of expenditures made by these groups are as follows:

1. *Personal consumption expenditures*. The total amount spent by consumers for goods and services includes both the purchase of consumer *durables*, such

EXHIBIT 10.7

Total Output = GDP = Total Income

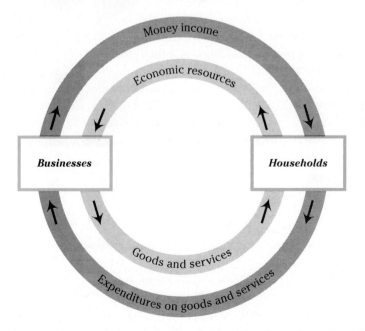

This simplified model of the economy (which ignores government and foreign trade) illustrates that there are two ways to calculate gross domestic product. The total expenditures made by households on final goods and services (the bottom flow) must equal the sum of the income received by the various economic resources (rent + wages + interest + profits)— the uppermost flow in the diagram. Both the total income received by the economic resources and the total household expenditures must equal GDP.

as automobiles, refrigerators, and stereos, and the purchase of *nondurables*, such as food, clothing, and entertainment. This is the largest category of expenditures, accounting for approximately two-thirds of GDP.

2. *Gross private domestic investment.*[3] This category includes all types of expenditures on capital goods, including business expenditures for new factories and equipment and household expenditures for new homes and major home improvements. (For accounting purposes, new homes are classified as an investment.) This category also includes changes in firms' inventories.[4]

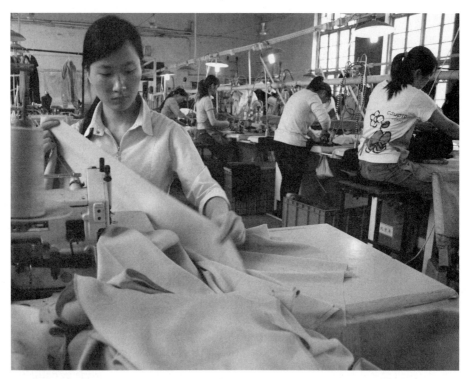

The cloth and thread used in manufacturing clothing are intermediate goods, whereas the finished garment is a final good.

---

[3] The term *domestic* means "limited to our own country"; for example, domestic investment takes place within the boundaries of the United States.

[4] Counting changes in inventories as part of investment also ensures that total expenditures will equal the value of total output. If a business produces something this year but doesn't sell it this year, that production goes into inventory and is not recorded in total expenditures. So if we just add up the various types of expenditures, we'll miss the portion of GDP that was not sold. To adjust for this problem, we add any additions to inventory that occur from one year to the next to make sure that all production is counted. (Decreases in inventories represent the sale of items produced in previous years. Because those items were included in GDP figures for previous years, they must be subtracted from this year's total expenditures if GDP is to reflect current production accurately.)

3. *Government purchases.* This category covers federal, state, and local governments' purchases of all kinds of goods and services—for example, purchases of government vehicles, office supplies, weapons, concrete for roads, and even the consulting services of private firms hired to advise various government departments. This category excludes transfer payments such as Social Security, which do not represent the purchase of newly produced goods and services.

4. *Net exports.* Some of the output of American businesses is sold in foreign countries, so it doesn't show up in our domestic sales. At the same time, some of the final goods and services sold in the United States were produced in foreign countries. To adjust for this situation, we subtract the value of imported goods from the value of our exports. The resulting figure, called *net exports,* is then added to our domestic sales. The formula for net exports is

$$\text{Net exports} = \text{Total exports} - \text{Total imports}$$

The net exports total will be positive when exports exceed imports and negative when imports exceed exports.

To calculate gross domestic product by the expenditure approach, we add these four categories of expenditures. This procedure is illustrated in Exhibit 10.8, which shows the GDP for 2008 as measured by both the expenditures approach and the income approach.

EXHIBIT 10.8

Gross Domestic Product in 2008 (in billions)

EXPENDITURES APPROACH		INCOME APPROACH	
Personal consumption expenditures	$10,057.9	Employee compensation	$8,062.3
		Rental income	64.4
Gross private domestic investment	1,993.5	Net interest	928.8
		Corporate profits	1,090.0
Government purchases of goods and services	2,882.4	Proprietors' income	1,072.4
		Indirect business taxes	1,214.4
Net exports of goods and services	−669.2	Capital consumption allowances	1,832.3
Gross domestic product	**$14,264.6**	**Gross domestic product**	**$14,264.6**

Source: Developed from the May 2009 edition of the *Survey of Current Business,* published by the U.S. Department of Commerce.

— no — ## The Income Approach

Calculating GDP by the income approach is somewhat more complicated than the circular-flow diagram would make it appear. In addition to the various forms of income that are created in the process of producing final goods and services (wages and salaries, rent, interest, and profits), two *nonincome payments* (indirect business taxes and capital consumption allowances) account for a portion of the money received by businesses. The categories of income received by the economic resources and the types of nonincome payments are as follows:

1. *Compensation of employees*. In addition to wages and salaries, this income category includes such things as payroll taxes and employer contributions to health plans.
2. *Rental income*. This is the income earned by households from the rental of property, such as buildings and land.
3. *Net interest*. This category includes the interest earned by households on the money they lend to businesses to finance inventories, build plant additions, and purchase new machinery.
4. *Corporate profits*. The before-tax profit of corporations, this category has three components, representing the three things that corporations can do with their profits: (a) *corporate profits tax liability*—profits used to pay federal and state taxes, (b) *dividends*—profits paid out to stockholders, and (c) *retained earnings*—profits kept by businesses for reinvestment (also called *undistributed corporate profits*).
5. *Proprietors' income*. This category includes the income earned by unincorporated businesses, such as proprietorships, partnerships, and cooperatives.
6. *Indirect business taxes*. Indirect business taxes include sales taxes and excise taxes. The important thing about such taxes is that they are collected *by* businesses *for* government. Therefore, a portion of the money received by businesses must be passed on directly to government; it is not available as a payment to the owners of economic resources. Such taxes are described as *nonincome payments*.
7. *Capital consumption allowances*. Also called *allowances for depreciation*, these are funds set aside for the eventual replacement of worn-out factories and equipment. Like indirect business taxes, they represent a nonincome payment.

To measure gross domestic product by the income approach, we add the five types of income and the two nonincome payments. As you can see in Exhibit 10.8, the answer we get is the same as the one generated earlier by the expenditures approach.[5] Again, that result is necessary because every dollar

---

[5] In fact, the GDP calculated by the income approach never turns out to be exactly the same as the GDP calculated by the expenditures approach. The difference is what the Department of Commerce calls the *statistical discrepancy*. In Exhibit 10.8 the entry for indirect business taxes has been adjusted to incorporate the statistical discrepancy.

spent on output must be received by someone as income or as a nonincome payment. $-$ no $-$

Interpreting GDP Statistics

Now that we know what gross domestic product means and how it is measured, we need to note two facts before interpreting GDP statistics. An increase in GDP does not always mean that we're better off. Similarly, a decrease in GDP is not always a cause for concern and corrective action.

Real GDP versus Money GDP   From 1998 to 2008, gross domestic product in the United States increased from $8,747.0 billion to $14,264.6 billion (from $8.7 trillion to $14.2 trillion), an increase of 63 percent. On the surface that seems like a pretty good performance, particularly when you realize that our population increased only about 10 percent in that period. It looks as though the average American had a lot more goods and services at his or her disposal in 2008 than in 1998.

But numbers can be misleading. Because GDP is the physical output of a given year valued at the prices that prevailed in that year, it can increase from one year to another because of increased output, increased prices, or a combination of the two. (To underscore that GDP can change simply in response to a change in prices, economists often refer to GDP as *money* GDP or *nominal* GDP.) Therefore, if we want to know how much *physical* output has increased, we have to calculate the **real gross domestic product**—that is, the GDP that has been adjusted to eliminate the impact of changes in the price level.

To eliminate the impact of changing prices from our GDP comparison, we need to value the output produced in these two different time periods at some common sets of prices. For example, we could value both the 1998 output and the 2008 output at 1998 prices or at 2008 prices or at the prices that prevailed in some intermediate time period. The Bureau of Economic Analysis (BEA) uses the third approach; it values both years' outputs at the prices that prevailed in some base year, currently 2000. According to the BEA, when 1998 and 2008 outputs are valued at 2000 prices, we find that real GDP increased from $9,006.9 billion in 1998 to $11,652.0 billion in 2008, an increase of 29 percent.

As you can see, the increase in the real GDP (29 percent) was much smaller than the increase in nominal GDP (63 percent); much of the increase in money GDP was due to inflation. This is why economists insist on comparing real GDPs rather than nominal GDPs. Comparison of real GDPs gives us a much better picture of what's actually happening to the economy's output and the population's standard of living.

Use Your Economic Reasoning

Why Beijing Is Trying to Tally the Hidden Costs of Pollution as China's Economy Booms

BY JANE SPENCER

Hong Kong—By conventional measures, China's economy is roaring ahead at a growth rate of more than 10%. But an unusual report by the Chinese government suggests the nation's growth—while swift—may not be quite as dazzling as it seems. Last month, Beijing released the results of a two-year "green accounting" study indicating the nation's rampant pollution problem is quietly undermining long-term economic growth. According to the report, pollution cost the country $64 billion in 2004, the equivalent of three percentage points of economic output. The report suggests China's "true" growth rate in 2004 would have been closer to 7% if the costs of pollution had been factored in.

The so-called green gross-domestic-product figures are part of a long-term Chinese government project aimed at quantifying the economic impact of pollution and may mark a shift in strategy for a regime that has promoted unbridled growth as the key to social stability. The basic idea of green GDP is to subtract the costs associated with environmental degradation from traditional GDP to give a more realistic picture of the health of the economy.

The Chinese report, released jointly by the State Environmental Protection Administration and the State Statistics Bureau, was spearheaded by Pan Yue, SEPA's deputy director. Mr. Pan is in the vanguard of the effort to push environmental issues to the top of the nation's agenda. The "green GDP" concept has been embraced by top political leaders, including President Hu Jintao, who has made "sustainable development" a theme of his speeches this year [2006].

The initiative comes as China confronts the rising costs of the environmental woes linked to its rapid growth, which include widespread air and water pollution and acid rain. This year, China's economy is expected to grow 10.5%—an increase from 10.2% in 2005—and at a 9.5% rate in the first half of 2007, the research office of the country's central bank said Friday.

The Chinese Academy on Environmental Planning estimates that more than 400,000 of China's about 1.3 billion people die from air-pollution-related illness each year. About 300 million Chinese lack access to clean drinking water, partly because of pollution from factories, and the central government pledged to spend $125 billion to address the problem. "China can't go the way of polluting first, and then treating it," said SEPA official Jia Feng, in an interview with local Chinese news media, warning that "the ecological system that shoulders economic development will be crushed."

Green GDP is one part of the budding field of environmental economics, which aims to apply rigorous business-accounting methods to environmental problems. "Green economists" are driven by the notion that typical methods of measuring growth—namely GDP—are too crude a way to measure the overall health of an economy, and their work, though controversial, is attracting increasing interest from such quarters as the World Bank, Columbia Business School and the World Economic Forum in Davos, Switzerland. While GDP looks at the market value of goods and service produced in a country each year, it ignores the fact that a nation might be fueling its expansion by polluting or burning through natural resources in an unsustainable way. In fact, the usual methods of calculating GDP make destroying the environment look good for the economy. If an industry pollutes in the process of manufacturing products, and the government pays to clean up the mess, both activities add to GDP. China's report estimates it would take a one-time direct investment of about $136 billion—nearly 7% of GDP—to clean up all the pollution pumped into the nation's air, water and soil in 2004.

Environmental economists hope solid economic analysis will make the case for protecting the environment harder to dismiss. "This is not some flaky, left-wing offshoot of economics," said Robert Stavins, a professor of business and government at Harvard University and director of the school's growing environmental-economics program. "It is rigorous economics applied to some challenging and important social problems in the environmental domain. . . . If the way a country is growing is by living high on the hog, and spending down its natural capital, you would want that to be reflected in the country's national income accounts—if those accounts are intended to be a long-term measure of welfare.". . .

Many economists dismiss the very notion of tinkering with the GDP formula to incorporate environmental costs. They say GDP was never intended to measure anything but cash flows. There are plenty of other things excluded from GDP, they argue, such as contributions made to the economy by housework or volunteer labor. Instead, some economists favor a system of "satellite accounts," alternative growth indicators that can be considered in conjunction with GDP as a way of adding perspective, but aren't meant to replace the usual GDP data.

Still, it is significant that China is reckoning with its environmental problems in this way. "This kind of analysis is usually done by [nongovernmental organizations] or critics from outside the government," said Daniel C. Esty, a professor of environmental law and policy at Yale Law School. "In this case, the Chinese government is doing it itself, and recognizing that there is a real price paid for economic strategies that disregard environmental protection.". . .

USE YOUR ECONOMIC REASONING

1. What is "green GDP"? How does it differ from conventional GDP?
2. What rationale do supporters provide for focusing on green GDP? How do critics respond to this effort?
3. According to the article, "the usual methods of calculating GDP make destroying the environment look good for the economy." Is that accurate? Explain.
4. In 2007, China suspended efforts to compute green GDP. Local Chinese officials—who are still judged on their ability to foster economic growth—wanted to stop the publication of the data. How would you explain their resistance?

What GDP Does Not Measure   Even real GDP figures should be interpreted with caution. They don't measure all our society's production, and they certainly don't provide a perfect measure of welfare, or well-being. Some of the things that GDP does not consider are as follows:

1. *Nonmarketed goods and services.* GDP does not measure all production or output but only production that is intended to be sold through markets. This means that GDP excludes the production of homemakers and do-it-yourselfers, as well as all barter transactions, in which one person directly exchanges goods or services with another.

2. *Illegal activities.* GDP does not include illegal goods and services, such as illicit drugs, illegal gambling, and prostitution. It also excludes otherwise legal transactions that are unreported to avoid paying taxes—the sale of firewood for cash, for example.

3. *Leisure.* GDP does not measure increases in leisure, but such increases clearly have an impact on our well-being. Even if real gross domestic product didn't increase, if we could produce a constant real GDP with shorter and shorter workweeks, most of us would agree that our lives had improved.

4. *Population.* GDP statistics tell us nothing about the size of the population that must share a given output. A GDP of $2 trillion means one thing in an economy of 100 million people and something completely different in an economy of 500 million people. (It's like the difference between an income of $30,000 for a single person and an income of $30,000 for a family of five.) Economists generally attempt to adjust for this problem by talking about GDP per capita, or per person—that is, GDP divided by the population of the country.

5. *Externalities.* We have a very sophisticated accounting system to keep track of all the goods and services we produce, but we have not established a method of subtracting from GDP when the production process yields negative externalities—air and water pollution, for example. (See Chapter 9 for a review of this concept.)

These are significant limitations. And they have the attention of economists and others. "Green" economists have called for modifications in our GDP accounts to reflect environmental degradation. Others are searching for a better way to measure the quality of life.[6] But these efforts are still in their infancy. For now, we'll have to be satisfied with our imperfect GDP statistics, along with an

---

[6] For an interesting look at some of these efforts, see "A New Measure of Well-Being From a Happy Little Kingdom," by Andrew C. Revkin, *New York Times*, October 4, 2005, p. 1F.

understanding of their limitations. (China is among the first governments to try to adjust GDP to reflect environmental costs. Read about its efforts to compute green GDP in "Why Beijing Is Trying to Tally the Hidden Costs of Pollution," on page 316.)

SUMMARY

To keep track of the economy's performance, people watch *economic indicators—* signals or measures that tell us how well the economy is performing. Three major economic indicators are the *unemployment rate,* price indexes (the Consumer Price Index, the Producer Price Index, and the Implicit Price Deflator), and the gross domestic product. Each of these indicators looks at a different dimension of the economy's performance.

The *civilian unemployment rate* is the percentage of the civilian labor force that is unemployed. (The *civilian labor force* is made up of all persons over the age of 16 who are not in the armed forces and who are either employed or actively seeking employment.) Each month, the Bureau of Labor Statistics surveys some 60,000 households to determine the employment status of the residents. It then uses the results from this sample to estimate the size of the labor force and the rate of unemployment for the nation as a whole.

We attempt to measure inflation with something called a *price index*. A price index is a ratio of two prices: a price in some base period that serves as a reference point divided into the price in whatever period we wish to compare with the base period. For example, if tennis shoes sold for $50 in 1998 and $80 in 2008, the price index for tennis shoes would be 160 if 1998 were used as the base year:

$$\text{Price index} = \frac{\text{Price in any given period}}{\text{Price in the base period}}$$

$$= \frac{\$80.00}{\$50.00}$$

$$= 1.60 \text{ or } 160 \text{ percent}$$

Because the price index in the base period is always 100, an index of 160 means that price has increased by 60 percent since the base period. By the same logic, an index of 75 would indicate that price has decreased by 25 percent since the base period.

The other major indicator, the *gross domestic product* (GDP), is the total monetary value of all final goods and services produced in one year. In other words, it is a measure of the economy's annual production or output. GDP can be estimated by the expenditures approach or by the income approach. The expenditures approach sums the categories of expenditures made for final goods and services. The income approach looks at the forms of income that are created when final goods are produced and adds to those income figures certain nonincome payments.

Because GDP is measured in monetary units (dollars), it is possible to add apples and oranges (that is, to sum the economy's output of eggs, stereos, houses, tractors, and so on) and arrive at a meaningful measure of the economy's total output. GDP figures must be interpreted with caution, however. When we compare the GDPs for two different years, we must be sure to correct for the impact of changing prices—to compare *real GDPs*, not money GDPs. We must also recognize that GDP is not a complete measure of our economy's production because it excludes the work of homemakers and do-it-yourselfers as well as other nonmarket transactions. Nor is it a complete measure of welfare, or well-being; it doesn't take into account the value of leisure, for example, or the negative externalities associated with the production of some goods and services.

KEY TERMS

Annual inflation rate
Business cycle
Civilian labor force
Civilian unemployment rate
Cyclical unemployment
Deflation

Economic indicators
Frictional unemployment
Full employment
Gross domestic product
Inflation
Macroeconomics

Natural rate of unemployment
Price index
Real gross domestic product
Real income
Structural unemployment
Unemployment rate

STUDY QUESTIONS

Fill in the Blanks

1. The study of the economy's overall performance and the factors that influence that performance is called _____ .

2. Clauses that provide for automatic wage and salary adjustments to compensate for inflation are called _____ clauses.

3. _____ are signals, or measures, that tell us how well the economy is performing.

4. The price index that is used to adjust union wage contracts and Social Security payments for inflation is the

   _____ .

5. Unemployment caused by a reduction in the economy's total demand for goods and services is called _____ unemployment.

6. A common estimate for the natural rate of unemployment is _____ percent.

7. People who stop looking for jobs because they are convinced that none are available are called _____ .

8. The two approaches to measuring GDP are the _____ approach and the _____ approach.

9. GDP that has been adjusted to eliminate the impact of changes in the price level is called _____ GDP.

10. The largest component of spending in GDP is _____ spending.

Multiple Choice

1. The civilian labor force is made up of
   a) all persons over the age of 16.
   b) all persons over the age of 18 who are not in the armed forces.
   c) all persons over the age of 16 who are not in the armed forces and who are either employed or actively seeking employment.
   d) all persons over the age of 18 who are not in the armed forces and who are either employed or actively seeking employment.

2. If you are out of work because you are in the process of looking for a better job, economists would say that you are
   a) frictionally unemployed.
   b) cyclically unemployed.
   c) structurally unemployed.
   d) None of the above

3. John recently lost his job because consumers are concerned about the future of the economy and have slowed their purchases of new vehicles. John is
   a) frictionally unemployed.
   b) cyclically unemployed.
   c) seasonally unemployed.
   d) structurally unemployed.

4. The unemployment rate for blacks is about
   a) three times the rate for whites.
   b) twice the rate for whites.
   c) 2 percent higher than the rate for whites.
   d) the same as the rate for whites.

5. Which of the following is false?
   a) Inflation tends to redistribute income.
   b) Inflation is particularly hard on people with fixed incomes.
   c) No one benefits from inflation.
   d) COLA clauses help protect workers from inflation.

6. If the Consumer Price Index is 250, that means that
   a) the average price of a product is $2.50.
   b) prices are two times as high as they were in the base year.
   c) prices have risen 150 percent since the base year.
   d) Both b and c are correct.

7. The natural rate of unemployment is the rate that would exist in the absence of
   a) frictional unemployment.
   b) structural unemployment.
   c) cyclical unemployment.
   d) frictional and structural unemployment.

8. Which of the following items would be counted in GDP?
   a) The work of a homemaker
   b) The sale of a used car
   c) A soda you buy at your local drive-in
   d) The firewood you cut for your home last winter

9. In the 1999–2008 period, the United States experienced
   a) lower than average unemployment and inflation rates when compared with other major industrialized nations.

b) higher than average unemployment and inflation rates when compared with other major industrialized nations.

c) lower than average inflation and higher than average unemployment when compared with other major industrialized nations.

d) higher than average inflation and lower than average unemployment when compared with other major industrialized nations.

10. If both output and prices are higher in year 2 than they were in year 1, which of the following is true?
   a) Real GDP declined from year 1 to year 2.
   b) GDP declined from year 1 to year 2.
   c) GDP increased from year 1 to year 2, but real GDP declined.
   d) Both GDP and real GDP increased from year 1 to year 2.

11. The Consumer Price Index was 126.1 in December 1989 and 133.8 in December 1990. Therefore, the rate of inflation experienced in 1990 was approximately
   a) 26.1 percent.
   b) 7.7 percent.
   c) 6.1 percent.
   d) about 126 percent.

12. Susan's paycheck increased by 5 percent this year. Over the same period, the CPI increased from 180 to 189. What happened to Susan's real income?
   a) It increased.
   b) It decreased.
   c) It did not change.
   d) We can't tell what happened.

13. Which of the following would *not* be considered in computing GDP by the *expenditures approach*?
   a) Personal consumption expenditures
   b) Gross private domestic investment
   c) Compensation of employees
   d) Net exports

14. Which of the following would *not* be considered in computing GDP by the *income approach*?
   a) Rental income
   b) Corporate profits
   c) Indirect business taxes
   d) Government purchases of goods and services

15. If nominal GDP is increasing but real GDP is not, then
   a) the economy must be experiencing inflation.
   b) output must be falling.
   c) the price level must be falling.
   d) population must be increasing.

Problems and Questions for Discussion

1. What is the purpose of economic indicators? Can they be of any value to you?

2. A student could be counted as employed, unemployed, or "not participating" in the labor market. Explain.

3. An increase in the unemployment rate is not always a sign of growing weakness in the economy. Explain.

4. Some frictional and structural unemployment is probably a sign of a healthy economy. Why is that true?

5. How does inflation redistribute income?

6. How can savers be hurt by inflation?

7. Why is it true that "the people who are most hurt by inflation are those who have the least bargaining power in the marketplace"?

8. Some workers are convinced that they are worse off today than they were ten years ago, even though they have received annual raises. Is this possible, or must their perceptions be incorrect?

9. Use the following information to compute GDP by the income approach. (Some figures are not required for solving the problem.)

Employee compensation	$400
Proprietors' income	70
Rental income	25
Indirect business taxes	20
Personal consumption	450
Gross investment	250
Net interest	40
Capital consumption allowance	75
Corporate profits	55

10. Use the following information to compute GDP by the expenditures approach. (Some figures are not required for solving the problem.)

Personal consumption	$500
Exports	10
Gross investment	200
Imports	12
Proprietors' income	450
Government purchases	250
Corporate profits	50

11. Why must total income always equal total output?

ANSWER KEY

Fill in the Blanks

1. macroeconomics
2. cost-of-living adjustment (COLA)
3. Economic indicators
4. Consumer Price Index
5. cyclical
6. 5
7. discouraged workers
8. expenditures; income
9. real
10. consumption

Multiple Choice

1. c
2. a
3. b
4. b
5. c
6. c
7. c
8. c
9. d
10. d
11. c
12. c
13. c
14. d
15. a

CHAPTER

11

Aggregate Demand and Supply: The Model of the Self-Correcting Economy

LEARNING OBJECTIVES

1. Identify three factors that are responsible for the downward slope of the aggregate demand curve.
2. Understand why the short-run aggregate supply curve slopes upward.
3. Explain how the economy's equilibrium output and price level are determined and how this process is represented graphically.
4. Discuss the factors that will shift the aggregate demand and supply curves to new positions.
5. Predict the impact of changes in aggregate demand or supply on the economy's equilibrium output and the price level.
6. Explain how the economy will tend to automatically eliminate unemployment in the long run.
7. Understand why the long-run aggregate supply curve is vertical.

Chapter 10 identified some important dimensions of the economy's overall performance and examined techniques used to measure those aspects of its performance. Now, in this chapter, we will begin to explore why the aggregate economy behaves as it does and how its performance changes. The model most commonly used to examine the economy's overall performance is the model of aggregate demand and aggregate supply. Just as demand and supply are important tools in microeconomics, aggregate demand and aggregate supply are important in macroeconomics. In this chapter we will examine how aggregate demand and supply interact to determine the levels of output, employment, and prices, and how unemployment and inflation arise. We conclude by exploring the possibility that the economy contains a self-correcting mechanism: that it will ultimately return to full employment and potential GDP. We begin our consideration of the aggregate demand–aggregate supply model by introducing the concept of aggregate demand.

AGGREGATE DEMAND

Aggregate demand is the total quantity of output demanded by all sectors in the economy together at various price levels in a given period of time. Thus, aggregate demand (*AD*) is the sum of consumption spending by households (*C*), investment spending by businesses (*I*), government purchases of goods and services (*G*), and net exports (*NX*) to foreign countries. In short, $AD = C + I + G + NX$.

Because the quantity of output demanded by these sectors depends in part on the price level, the *AD* curve slopes downward and to the right (see Exhibit 11.1) like the demand curve for a single product. But the demand curve and the aggregate demand curve are very different concepts. The demand curve shows the relationship between the price of a *particular* product and the quantity of that product demanded. The aggregate demand curve relates the *overall* price level in the economy (as measured by a price index, such as the CPI) to the total quantity of real output that consumers, businesses, governments, and foreigners want to buy.

There are three reasons for the aggregate demand curve's downward slope: the real balance effect, the interest rate effect, and the international trade

---

EXHIBIT 11.1

An Overview of Aggregate Demand and Supply

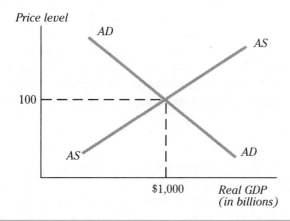

The intersection of the aggregate demand and supply curves determines the equilibrium level of real GDP and the equilibrium price level in the economy.

effect.[1] Let's consider each of these reasons in turn, beginning with the real balance effect.

The Real Balance Effect

When the price level falls, the real value, or purchasing power, of the public's financial assets—savings accounts, retirement funds, and other financial assets with fixed money values—tends to increase. This makes people feel wealthier, and they tend to demand more goods and services—more real output. The **real balance effect** is the increase in the amount of aggregate output demanded that results from the increased real value of the public's financial assets.

As an example, suppose that you work each summer to help pay for college. This summer you managed to save $2,000, your share of the year's anticipated expenses. Now, assume that the overall price level falls to half of what it was when you established your $2,000 objective. In essence, that means that all prices have been cut in half; so your $2,000 will now stretch twice as far as before. How will you react? You will probably start buying things you don't normally purchase because you have $1,000 in your savings account that won't be needed for anticipated college expenses. That's the real balance effect in action; the real value, or purchasing power, of the money balance in your savings account has increased, and this increase in wealth is spurring you to purchase more goods and services. Of course, if the price level increases, everything will work in reverse; your savings will be worth less, so that you feel less wealthy and demand fewer goods and services than before. Either way we describe it, the price level and spending on real output are moving in opposite directions, so the aggregate demand curve must slope downward. Exhibit 11.2 depicts the aggregate demand curve for a hypothetical economy.

The Interest Rate Effect

In addition to its impact on real balances, a change in the price level also has an effect on the prevailing interest rate. The interest rate is determined by the demand and supply of money. When the price level falls, consumers and businesses will require less money for their day-to-day transactions because a given amount of money will buy more goods and services than before. In other

---

[1] The demand curve and the aggregate demand curve slope downward for very different reasons. Recall from Chapter 3 that the demand curve is downward sloping, in part, because of the *substitution effect*. When the price of a product is reduced, consumers respond by substituting more of this relatively cheaper product in the place of other products for which it is deemed a substitute. This substitution effect cannot explain the downward slope of the *AD* curve because a reduction in the price *level* means that the average price of *all* goods and services has fallen. For instance, there is no incentive to substitute tennis shoes for jogging shoes if both have fallen in price.

EXHIBIT 11.2

The Aggregate Demand Curve

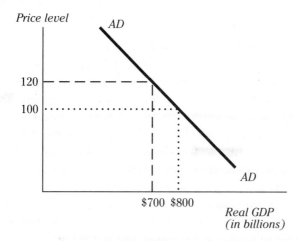

The aggregate demand curve shows an inverse relationship between the overall price level and the quantity of real output demanded. For instance, when the price level decreases from 120 to 100, the quantity of real GDP demanded increases from $700 billion to $800 billion.

words, a reduction in the price level will reduce the demand for money. Because each aggregate demand curve assumes a fixed supply of money in the economy, a reduction in the demand for money will tend to reduce the price of money—the interest rate. When the interest rate falls, the lower cost of borrowing money tends to stimulate investment spending and some types of consumer spending. The **interest rate effect** is the increase in the amount of aggregate output demanded that results when a reduction in the overall price level causes interest rates to fall.[2]

To illustrate, let's suppose that the price level—the average price of goods and services—fell to half of what it is today. Homes that had been selling for $200,000 would cost $100,000; automobiles that had been priced at $20,000 would be available for $10,000. As a consequence, consumers would need to borrow only half as much money as before to finance their new homes and automobiles and other credit purchases. This reduced demand for money would tend to lower interest rates and stimulate spending. Thus, more real output would be

---

[2] The interest rate effect actually has to do with the impact of a price level change on the "real" interest rate—the interest rate after adjustment for inflation. If the nominal interest rate (the interest rate before adjustment) is 15 percent a year and the expected rate of inflation is 5 percent, the real interest rate is 10 percent.

Business investment decisions are influenced by real interest rates, not nominal rates. A higher nominal interest rate (resulting from a higher expected rate of inflation) would not necessarily discourage businesses from borrowing, since they would also anticipate receiving higher prices for their products (and thus a higher nominal rate of return). The proof that a higher price level causes a higher real interest rate is beyond the scope of this text.

demanded at the lower price level. Of course, if the price level increased (which may seem a more realistic possibility), the demand for money would tend to increase, pushing up interest rates and depressing spending on real GDP.

The International Trade Effect

The third way in which price level changes can affect the amount of aggregate output demanded is through international trade. The two basic transactions in international trade are the importing and exporting of products. **Imports** are goods and services that are purchased from foreign producers. Americans' purchases of German automobiles, French wines, and Japanese electronics are examples of U.S. imports. **Exports** are goods and services that are produced domestically and sold to customers in other countries. The Ford automobiles, California wines, and IBM computers that are sold to customers in Germany, France, and elsewhere are examples of U.S. exports.

How would U.S. imports and exports be affected if the overall price level in the United States fell by, say, 10 percent and everything else (including prices in other countries)[3] remained constant? Because U.S. products would become more attractive in price, we'd expect fewer Americans to buy imported products (because they'd buy domestic products instead) and more foreigners to buy U.S. exports. To illustrate, suppose that the prices of U.S. automobiles fell by 10 percent and the prices of comparable foreign cars remained unchanged. Under these conditions, we'd expect to see more Americans buying cars made in the United States (and fewer buying imports) and increased auto exports as well. In short, at the lower U.S. price level, a larger quantity of U.S. automobiles would be demanded. The **international trade effect** is the increase in the amount of aggregate output demanded that results when a reduction in the price level makes domestic products less expensive relative to foreign products. It provides us with a third reason for the downward slope of the aggregate demand curve.

CHANGES IN AGGREGATE DEMAND

As with the demand curve for a single product, we need to distinguish between *movement along* an *AD* curve and a *shift* of the *AD* curve. We've seen that changes in the price level will cause movement up or down along a stationary curve. *Any change in the spending plans of households, businesses, governments, or*

---

[3] Another factor that is assumed constant is the foreign exchange rate, the rate at which one country's currency exchanges for that of another.

foreigners that results from something other than a change in the price level will shift the AD curve. Factors that will shift the aggregate demand curve include changes in the expectations of households and businesses, changes in aggregate wealth, changes in government policies, and changes in foreign income and price levels.

Household and Business Expectations

Suppose that households and businesses become more upbeat about the future, perhaps because the unemployment rate has been dropping and business has been strong. What impact will these optimistic expectations have on aggregate demand? Households may be expected to increase their consumption spending (because they are more confident of continued employment in the future), whereas businesses may increase their investment spending for factories and machinery in anticipation of future business. Because total spending at any price level is greater, the *AD* curve will shift to the right (from AD_1 to AD_2 in Exhibit 11.3), an increase in aggregate demand. More pessimistic expectations have the opposite effect: the *AD* curve will shift to the left, reflecting a reduction in aggregate demand.

Aggregate Wealth

An increase in the overall wealth of the society also tends to shift the aggregate demand curve to the right. Consider, for example, the impact of a stock market

---

EXHIBIT 11.3

Shifts of the Aggregate Demand Curve

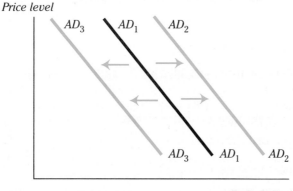

Any change in the spending plans of households, businesses, or government that results from something other than a change in the price level will shift the *AD* curve. A shift to the right is an increase in aggregate demand; a shift to the left is a decrease.

boom that increases the value of households' stock holdings. Because households can finance spending by selling shares of stock and other forms of wealth, this increase in stock values tends to spur consumption spending; households may be expected to demand more real output than before at any price level. A reduction in wealth—due, perhaps, to a decline in the stock market—will shift the *AD* curve to the left. (Many economists believe that the collapse in housing prices, which started in 2006, was a major cause of the recession that officially began in 2007 and lasted into 2009. Read "Homeowners Feel the Pinch of Lost Equity," on page 332, to see the role that housing wealth played in initiating this economic downturn.)

Government Policy

Government can also influence aggregate demand through its policies. For instance, a reduction in government spending for goods and services will cause the *AD* curve to shift to the left, as will an increase in personal income taxes (because consumers have less to spend at each price level). A reduction in the money supply will also cause aggregate demand to fall. The size of the economy's money supply is determined by the Federal Reserve, or Fed. If the Fed decreases the money supply, the interest rate that businesses and others have to pay to borrow money will tend to increase. This, in turn, will tend to depress investment spending by businesses and some forms of consumption spending by households, shifting the aggregate demand curve to the left.

Consider an increase in military spending by the federal government. What impact will that have on aggregate demand? It will increase the amount of real GDP demanded at any price level, and so it will shift the *AD* curve to the right (from AD_1 to AD_2 in Exhibit 11.3). A tax reduction or an increase in the money supply also tends to increase aggregate demand.

Foreign Incomes and Prices

When foreign incomes grow, foreign households increase their consumption spending. Some of this increased spending will be for U.S. products, causing U.S. exports to increase and shifting the aggregate demand curve to the right. Increased foreign prices would also stimulate spending for U.S. products. An increase in foreign price levels would, ceteris paribus, cause U.S. products to appear more attractive and cause foreign consumers to substitute them for those produced domestically. At the same time, Americans would find foreign products less attractive in price, decreasing our imports. Thus, an increase in foreign incomes or price levels would stimulate the demand for U.S.

products and shift the *AD* curve to the right.[4] Reductions in foreign incomes or price levels would shift the aggregate demand curve for U.S. products to the left.

In summary, the aggregate demand curve will shift in response to changes in the expectations of households or businesses, wealth, government policy, foreign incomes, or foreign price levels. These are the major causes of shifts in aggregate demand, but the list is not exhaustive; other changes may have a similar impact. The important point is that any change in spending plans that stems from something other than a change in the price level will shift the *AD* curve; changes in the price level will cause movement *along* a stationary curve. (Instructors wishing to explore the role of aggregate demand in greater detail may want to consider a supplemental chapter, "The Keynesian Total Expenditures Model," which can be accessed from the textbook Web site at www.pearsonhighered.com/rohlf.)

AGGREGATE SUPPLY

Aggregate demand is only half of the model; the other half is aggregate supply. **Aggregate supply** refers to the total quantity of output supplied by all producers in the economy together at various price levels in a given time period.

In the short run, the aggregate supply (*AS*) curve slopes upward, as represented in Exhibit 11.4. This upward slope indicates that businesses tend to supply more aggregate output at higher price levels than at lower price levels. Businesses behave in this manner because increases in the overall price level make it profitable for them to produce more goods and services. This increased profitability results from a fact of life in the business world: Some wages and other resource prices are rigid, or inflexible, in the short run. If aggregate demand increases and pushes up the prices that firms can charge for their *products*, the rigidity of these *resource* prices makes it profitable for those businesses to expand output. The result: higher price levels lead to higher output, so the short-run *AS* curve slopes upward.

As you can see, the rigidity of resource (or input) prices is a critical element in explaining the upward slope of the short-run *AS* curve. But why are some input prices inflexible in the short run? A major reason for such rigidity is long-term contracts. Contracts with labor unions, for example, are commonly

---

[4]This assumes that the foreign exchange rate does not change. Chapter 16 will discuss exchange rates in some detail.

Use Your Economic Reasoning

Homeowners Feel the Pinch of Lost Equity

BY PETER S. GOODMAN

As his wedding day approached last spring [2007], Marshall Whittey found that his money could not keep pace with the grandiosity of his plans. But rather than scale back, he chose instead, like millions of homeowners across the country, to borrow against the soaring value of his home. He and his bride, Holly Whittey, exchanged vows on the grounds of a sumptuous private estate in the Napa Valley. They spent their honeymoon at a resort in Tahiti. But now, in an ominous portent for the national economy, Mr. Whittey has grown tight with his money. His home is worth far less than it was a year ago, and his equity has evaporated. And like many other involuntary adopters of a newly economical lifestyle, he can borrow no more. "It used to be that if I wanted it, I'd just go and buy it and finance it," Mr. Whittey, 33, said. "I'm feeling the crunch, and my spending is down significantly."

The Whitteys and others like them are at the center of deepening worries that the economy is headed for a substantial slowdown, possibly even a recession, as the artery of cash from Americans borrowing against the value of their homes has sharply narrowed. "Everybody was basically using their house as an A.T.M. machine," said Dave Simonsen, a senior vice president for NAI Alliance, an industrial real estate firm in Reno. "Now they are upside down on their house without that piggy bank to go back to."

From 2004 through 2006, Americans pulled about $840 billion a year out of residential real estate, via sales, home equity lines of credit and refinanced mortgages, according to data presented in an updated working paper by James Kennedy, an economist, and Alan Greenspan, the former Federal Reserve chairman. These so-called home equity withdrawals financed as much as $310 billion a year in personal consumption from 2004 to 2006, according to the data. But in the first half of this year, equity withdrawals were down 15 percent nationally compared with the average for the last three years, and consumption supported by such funds plunged nearly one-fourth, according to the Kennedy and Greenspan data. This summer, the size of withdrawals fell even more sharply to about one-third below the level of late last year, according to Mark Zandi, chief economist at Moody's Economy.com. . . .

Much of the attention in the recent collapse of the housing boom has focused on those in danger of losing their home or facing higher monthly payments in their adjustable mortgages. But the broader effect on the economy is likely to come from the much larger group of homeowners who can no longer count on rising home values to bolster their wealth. Consumer spending accounts for about 70 percent of all economic activity in the United States, or about $9.8 trillion, so even a slight dip in home borrowing takes huge amounts of money out of the flow. . . .

Sprawled across desert flats and framed by the rugged peaks of the Sierra, Reno [Nevada] encapsulates, in concentrated form, the forces at work on American consumers. . . . While best known for its gambling, Reno has in recent years diversified, using low taxes to entice major companies like Cisco Systems and Microsoft. With land cheap, the area has been a magnet for Californians who sold homes for spectacular gains, then moved here to buy more space for less money. . . . Ranch land that less than a decade ago was still a moonscape of sun-baked soil dotted with sagebrush has been transformed into golf courses and Spanish-style houses on streets with names like Painted Vista Drive and Rio Wrangler. Free-flowing credit and rampant speculation drove residential sales. From May 2002 to September 2005, home prices in Reno and the adjacent city of Sparks more than doubled, according to First American Loan Performance.

Since then, however, the median house price has slipped 15 percent. Local businesses are already suffering the effects of consumers who are less inclined to buy. A Volkswagen dealership downtown said sales were down two-thirds from a year ago. . . . At Sierra Nevada Spas and Billiards, Ezra O'Connor, the sales manager, complained that not even drastically lower prices were attracting shoppers. "We're way down, 35 percent down from last year," Mr. O'Connor said. "People just aren't wanting to spend."

Mr. Whittey once seemed an unlikely member of that cohort. A sales manager at a flooring and tile company, he exudes the unflappable air of someone raised amid the easy money of the casino world. Until recently, he and his wife regularly embarked on shopping sprees of $1,000 and up. He bought a 21-foot boat and two flat-screen televisions for their home. He sold his old truck and bought a new one, he said, "just 'cause I didn't like the color." Mr. Whittey could live in such fashion because his company was making good money and his house was appreciating.

But today, the value of his own home, which reached $500,000, has fallen and a separate investment property he bought seems likely to fetch far less than the $580,000 he owes the bank. His commissions have diminished, so his income is down. His neighbor recently fell behind on house payments, prompting the bank to foreclose. Anxiety reigns. "We used to go out to eat three or four nights a week," Mr. Whittey said. "Now, we don't go out at all." . . .

USE YOUR ECONOMIC REASONING

A homeowner's "equity" is the difference between what the home is worth and amount owed the bank. If your home is worth $200,000 and you owe $150,000, your equity is $50,000. (If you owe $250,000, you're "upside down" in your loan; you owe more than the home is worth.) For many households, their home equity represents a significant portion of their personal wealth. Historically, banks have been willing make "home equity loans" equal to a portion of that equity. Because banks have the home as collateral (if the borrower fails to repay), these loans have often carried lower interest rates, making them attractive to consumers.

1. Home prices peaked in 2006 and have fallen substantially since then. What impact would falling home prices have on the equity of homeowners? How would this affect their ability to borrow and spend? How would you represent this graphically?
2. Assume the aggregate supply curve remains stable. What impact would you expect a reduction in home equity lending to have on real GDP and the price level? Represent this graphically.
3. It is widely accepted that the housing collapse was one of the initial causes of the economic downturn that was eventually judged a recession (officially said to have begun in December 2007). This article looks at the connection between home equity loans and the slowdown in spending. Can you think of other reasons why a downturn in the housing sector would negatively affect GDP?

EXHIBIT 11.4

The Short-Run Aggregate Supply Curve

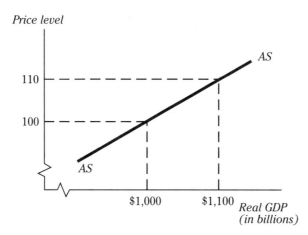

The short-run aggregate supply curve slopes upward because businesses tend to supply more real output at higher price levels than at lower price levels.

renegotiated every three years. During the term of the agreement, wage rates are at least partially fixed. The prices paid for raw materials and manufactured inputs may also be governed by long-term contracts. Because wage rates and other input prices are commonly fixed in the short run, businesses find it profitable to expand output when the selling prices of their products rise. This positive relationship between the overall price level and the economy's real GDP is reflected in the upward slope of the *AS* curve depicted in Exhibit 11.4.

No —

The Short-Run *AS* Curve: A Closer Look

An example from microeconomics may help to illustrate why the short-run *AS* curve slopes upward. Consider the behavior of the competitive firm. Recall that in the model of pure competition, the individual firm is a price taker; it must charge the price dictated by the market. But the firm can sell as much output as it chooses at that price. The firm will continue to expand output so long as the additional (marginal) revenue it will receive from selling an additional unit of output is greater than the additional (marginal) cost of producing that unit. When marginal cost is exactly equal to marginal revenue, the firm will be maximizing its profit (or minimizing its loss). This situation is represented in Exhibit 11.5, which shows a firm that is initially maximizing its profit by producing an output of 1,000 units, the output dictated by the intersection of MR_1 and MC_1.

Now, suppose that the market price of the firm's product increases from $10 to $14. This would be represented by shifting the demand curve upward

EXHIBIT 11.5

Price Level Adjustments and the Individual Firm

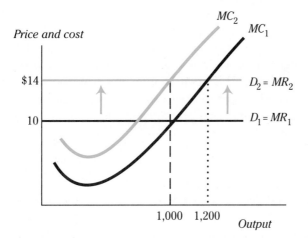

When the price of its product rises and input prices remain unchanged, the competitive firm responds by expanding output. Here output is increased from 1,000 to 1,200 units when the selling price rises from $10 to $14. However, if input prices rise by the same percent as the product price, *MC* will shift up from MC_1 to MC_2, and the profit-maximizing output will be unchanged.

from D_1 to D_2. Note what happens to the firm's profit-maximizing output: It increases from 1,000 units to 1,200 units! The higher price provides incentive for the firm to expand output because the firm can earn a marginal profit on the additional units.

Note that it is not profitable for the firm to expand output indefinitely. Because the marginal cost curve slopes upward, marginal cost will eventually increase enough to match the new price. Of course, production beyond that point will not be profitable. Why does *MC* increase as the firm expands its output? Why does the *MC* curve slope upward? Think back to Chapter 6. In the short run, if the firm wants to produce more output, it has to squeeze that production from its fixed factory. It does this by hiring more labor and using its factory and equipment more intensively. But this leads to more and more crowding of the fixed facility. Workers have to wait to use equipment; machines are subject to more frequent breakdowns; workers begin to get in one another's way; and so on. As a consequence, successive units of output become more costly to produce; that is, marginal cost rises. Eventually the cost of producing another unit will have increased enough to match the new product price. At that point the output expansion will cease; the firm will have achieved its new profit-maximizing level of production.

It is essential to note that the firm would not have expanded output if wage rates and other resource prices had increased along with the price of the firm's product. Proportionally higher wages and other input prices would have shifted the marginal cost curve up from MC_1 to MC_2. Note that MC_2 intersects MR_2 (the new, higher product price) at 1,000 units of output, the original profit-maximizing output. The higher input prices have completely offset the higher product price, eliminating any incentive to expand output. In the long run, this is precisely what we expect to happen because contracts eventually expire, and wage rates and other input prices are able to adjust upward. As a consequence, the long-run aggregate supply curve is vertical, not upward sloping. We'll discuss the long-run AS curve later in the chapter. For now, the important point is that wage contracts and other rigidities provide a gap between product prices and production costs that makes it profitable for firms to expand output in the short run.

No —

CHANGES IN AGGREGATE SUPPLY

The short-run aggregate supply curve slopes upward because there is a positive relationship between the price level and the quantity of aggregate output supplied. This relationship assumes that the other factors influencing the amount of real GDP supplied—the factors other than the price level—remain constant. These nonprice determinants of aggregate supply include resource prices, the level of technology, and the stock of economic resources. Changes in any of these factors will cause a change in the aggregate supply curve; the entire AS curve will shift to a new position. Let's consider each of these factors, beginning with resource prices.

Wage Rates and Other Resource Prices

Suppose that the average wage rate paid by firms in the economy increases. What will that do to the AS curve? If it costs more to produce a given level of output, firms will require higher prices to produce that output; thus, the AS curve must shift upward (to the left). This is represented in Exhibit 11.6 by the movement of the aggregate supply curve from AS_1 to AS_2. Lower wages would have the opposite effect; they would tend to shift the AS curve downward (to the right), from AS_1 to AS_3. Remember that wage rates tend to be fixed by contract in the short term. But when these labor contracts expire, wage rates may be renegotiated up or down, causing the short-run AS curve to shift.

Labor is only one of the resources required to produce output. Businesses also need capital equipment, raw materials, manufactured inputs, and managerial talent. Changes in the price of any of these inputs will tend to shift the position of the short-run AS curve; increases will shift it upward, whereas decreases will shift it downward.

EXHIBIT 11.6

Shifts of the Short-Run *AS* Curve

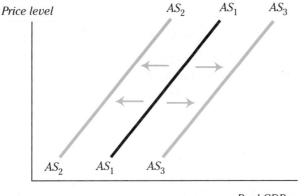

The short-run *AS* curve will shift upward (to the left) if there is a hike in wage rates, an increase in the prices of nonlabor inputs, or a reduction in labor productivity. It will shift downward (to the right) if wages or other input prices fall or if labor productivity rises.

Consider, for instance, what happened in 2005–2006 when a variety of forces—Hurricane Katrina, the war in Iraq, and an expanding global economy—combined to force up the price of gasoline and other petroleum products. When the prices of petroleum-based inputs increased, the cost of producing a given level of output rose; thus, the *AS* curve shifted upward. Bad weather that reduces agricultural output may have a similar impact because it tends to increase the price of wheat, corn, and other agricultural products that are inputs in the production of breakfast cereals and other food items.

Technology and the Productivity of Labor

The cost of producing output is influenced not only by wage rates and other input prices but also by the productivity of labor—by how efficient labor is at transforming inputs into finished products. If the productivity of labor increases, the cost of producing the finished product tends to fall. Suppose that labor is paid $8 per hour and that the average worker is able to produce 10 units of output per hour. The average labor cost of producing each unit of output is $.80 ($8 per hour divided by 10 units per hour). Now, suppose that because of improved training or new technology, the average worker could produce 20 units of output per hour. The labor cost per unit of output would fall to $.40 ($8 per hour divided by 20 units of output per hour). As you can see, an increase in labor productivity reduces the cost of producing a given level of output.

A variety of factors can influence the productivity of labor. For example, if the labor force became more highly educated, we would expect its productivity to rise. A technological change that improved the quality of the capital equipment used by labor could also raise productivity. For instance, a faster computer would allow more work to be done per hour. Regardless of the source of higher productivity, its impact is to reduce the cost of producing the goods and services that make up GDP. We represent this impact by shifting the short-run *AS* curve down and to the right because producers can now offer a given level of output at a lower price than before (or more output than before at the prevailing price).

Supplies of Labor and Capital

Finally, the position of the economy's aggregate supply curve is influenced by the economy's supplies of labor and capital. The larger the labor supply and the stock of capital equipment, the more output the economy is capable of supplying at any price level. Increases in either the labor force or the capital stock will cause the aggregate supply curve to shift to the right. Decreases would have the opposite effect.

Before continuing, let's review. We've seen that the aggregate demand curve shows the quantity of real GDP that will be demanded at each price level, whereas the aggregate supply curve shows the quantity of real GDP that will be supplied at each price level. The aggregate demand curve will shift to a new position if there is a change in the expectations of households or businesses, the level of aggregate wealth, government policy, foreign incomes, or foreign price levels. The short-run aggregate supply curve will shift in response to a change in resource prices, labor productivity, or the supplies of capital or labor.

THE EQUILIBRIUM OUTPUT AND PRICE LEVEL

The interaction of aggregate demand and aggregate supply simultaneously determines the equilibrium price level and real GDP in the economy. This process is illustrated in Exhibit 11.7, which shows the intersection of *AS* and *AD*, resulting in an equilibrium price level of 100 and an equilibrium real GDP of $1,000 billion.

As you can see in the graph, if the price level was initially above equilibrium (120, for example), the amount of real GDP supplied would exceed the amount of real GDP demanded. This would mean unsold merchandise and pressure to cut prices. The price level would decline until the amount of aggregate output

EXHIBIT 11.7

Equilibrium GDP and Price Level

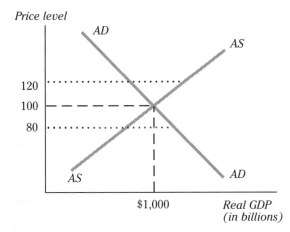

The intersection of the aggregate demand and supply curves determines the price level and the level of output in the economy. Here the equilibrium real GDP is $1,000 billion, and the equilibrium price level is 100.

demanded was equal to the amount supplied. If the price level was initially below equilibrium (80, for instance), the result would be a shortage that would put upward pressure on prices until the equilibrium price level was achieved and the shortage eliminated.

In summary, only at the equilibrium price level is the amount of real GDP demanded equal to the amount supplied. At any other price level, there will be an overall surplus or shortage, which will tend to alter the prevailing price level.

THE IMPACT OF CHANGES IN AGGREGATE DEMAND OR SUPPLY

In a dynamic economy, aggregate demand and supply change frequently. As these changes occur, the equilibrium price and output levels are disturbed, and new levels are established. Suppose, for example, that less optimistic expectations caused businesses to cut back on investment spending. Because this would result in less output being demanded at any given price level, the aggregate demand curve would shift to the left. What impact would this have on the economy? As you can see in Exhibit 11.8, when aggregate demand declines from AD_1 to AD_2, the level of real GDP in the economy contracts from $1,000 billion to $850 billion, and the overall price level falls from 100 to 90. Because the

EXHIBIT 11.8

The Effects of Changes in Aggregate Demand on Real Output and Prices

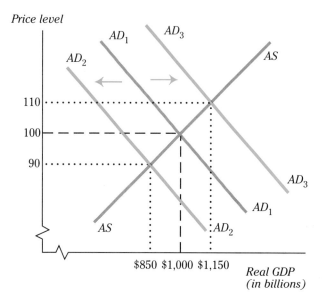

Decreases in aggregate demand will tend to lower the levels of output and employment in the economy while also reducing the overall price level. Increases in aggregate demand will tend to raise output and employment while raising the level of prices.

economy's ability to provide jobs is tied to the level of production, employment in the economy will also tend to fall—which means that, ceteris paribus, unemployment will rise.[5] (In February 2009, the U.S. economy was mired in recession, and unemployment was on the rise. How were Americans reacting to this depressed economy? Did their behavior help to boost the economy or push it deeper into recession? Read "Americans Follow a Basic Instinct—Fear—When Reacting to the Economy," on page 342, and decide for yourself.)

If aggregate demand increased as a result of increased government spending, a tax cut, or some other spur to aggregate demand, the *AD* curve would shift to the right, from AD_1 to AD_3. This would result in higher output and employment but would also push the price level upward; that is, it would generate inflation. Economists describe this as **demand-pull inflation** because it is caused by increased aggregate demand.

The economy's equilibrium can also be disturbed by changes in aggregate supply. Suppose that aggregate supply decreased as a result of a supply shock,

---

[5] The connection between production levels (GDP) and employment is not a rigid one. For instance, as the economy began to recover from the 2001 recession, GDP rose but employment did not. This occurred because employers were reluctant to hire additional workers until they were convinced that the economy was truly on the rebound and because rising productivity made it possible to get by with fewer workers than before.

such as an increase in the price of imported oil or a drought that raised grain prices. Exhibit 11.9 shows that when aggregate supply falls from AS_1 to AS_2, the overall price level is driven up, and the equilibrium level of real GDP is reduced.

In this instance the economy is experiencing supply-side, or **cost-push inflation**; higher production costs are pushing up prices. Although both demand-pull and cost-push inflation mean higher prices for consumers, cost-push inflation is doubly destructive because it is associated with falling real output. As you can see from Exhibit 11.9, when the aggregate supply curve shifts to the left, the level of equilibrium real GDP falls from $1,000 billion to $850 billion. In short, cost-push inflation raises prices while lowering output and employment. This provides us with one possible explanation for the problem of **stagflation**, high unemployment combined with high inflation.

If reductions in aggregate supply are particularly harmful, increases in aggregate supply appear most beneficial. Suppose that aggregate supply expands in response to an increase in labor productivity. As the AS curve shifts to the right (from AS_1 to AS_3 in Exhibit 11.9), the price level is driven down, *and* output and employment are expanded. It is these obviously desirable outcomes that led to a surge of interest in supply-side economics in the 1980s. Supply-siders promoted a variety of policies designed to enhance labor productivity and otherwise lower production costs in an attempt to increase aggregate supply. Chapter 15 will have much more to say about policies to stimulate aggregate supply.

EXHIBIT 11.9

The Effects of Changes in Aggregate Supply on Real Output and Prices

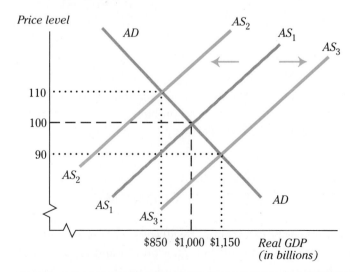

Decreases in aggregate supply will tend to lower the levels of output and employment in the economy while raising the overall price level. Increases in aggregate supply will tend to raise output and employment while lowering the level of prices.

Use Your Economic Reasoning

Americans Follow a Basic Instinct—Fear—When Reacting to the Economy

BY RICK MONTGOMERY

KANSAS CITY, MO.—A new CNN poll confirms what Barbara Hadel has been hearing for months. We're scared. "We'd love to move to another home, but not in this economy!" That's usually the final answer when Hadel, a Reece & Nichols Co. real estate agent, makes courtesy calls to potential clients. "They don't really say what it is, specifically, they're afraid of," Hadel said. "It's just that elusive unknown, 'the economy,' in quotation marks."

Seventy-three percent of Americans who responded to a CNN/Opinion Research Corp. survey released Monday [2009] said they were somewhat or very "scared" about the way things are going in the United States, even though just as many said they were doing fine personally. When Franklin D. Roosevelt famously declared "the only thing we have to fear is fear itself" at his 1933 inauguration, his

audience remained silent. Most likely, they knew they were scared. And, as Americans have shown time and again during crises, they were ready to let government transform itself to help settle their nerves.

Today, fear itself—or something close to it—is flaring here and there, often in puzzling ways. The physiologist Walter Cannon identified the response, in animals, as "fight or flight." Another reflex can take hold in humans. "I see a lot of people just really frozen—they don't know what to do," said Michael Ong, a Leawood, Kan., lawyer who specializes in estate planning. "If you have no clue what the future holds, you stop," agreed Mark Hirschey, a University of Kansas economics professor. Behavioral scientists have a highbrow term for our unease, which isn't strictly rational: We are "loss-averse." That means,

As the preceding discussion indicates, changes in aggregate demand or supply can lead to unemployment, inflation, or even stagflation. The next section examines the economy's response to these problems and considers the possibility that the economy contains a self-correcting mechanism.

THE MODEL OF THE SELF-CORRECTING ECONOMY

As you've seen, the economy is buffeted about by all sorts of demand and supply shocks. Sometimes these shocks result in higher output and employment; sometimes they lead to lower output and unemployment. You learned in

roughly speaking, we are twice as miserable losing something than we are happy gaining the same thing. . . .

Another poll last week by Gallup showed three out of four Americans were cutting back on spending, fearing something. But almost 70 percent of the respondents said they were not worried about losing their jobs or even suffering a cut in wages. "It's a paradox of sorts," Gallup editor Frank Newport said, citing what pollsters call "dissonance reduction." Practically everyone surveyed these days agrees times are bad, and three-quarters of people expect things to worsen. But most people won't cop to being afraid about their own households—especially, the polls say, if they are men. . . .

In uncertain times, you may look around at what other people are doing. "We get herd mentality," said Chris Foote of the Federal Reserve Bank of Boston, where a [research] center studies money and human behavior. Consumer spending fell 3.8 percent in the fourth quarter of 2008. Ho-hum or cause for hysterics? Said Foote: "Even if everyone cuts back just a little —say you go to fewer restaurants— that can have a huge effect on the overall economy, especially on the unemployment rate."

Michael Shellenberger of the California-based Breakthrough Institute, a think tank that predicts future policy trends, said this downturn stirs a sense of helplessness. "There's strong evidence that what we fear most are the things we don't control. We're less afraid driving a car than riding in an airplane, even though air travel is safer, because in a car we're in control. Contrary to the popular notion, Barack Obama was elected on the basis of fear, not hope."

USE YOUR ECONOMIC REASONING

1. The article suggests that the depressed state of the economy in 2009 had many consumers "frozen" with fear. One common reaction was to cut back on spending. What impact would you expect this behavior to have on the economy? How would you represent it graphically?

2. Saving (instead of spending) is one way that consumers can try to prepare themselves for the possibility that they might be tossed into the ranks of the unemployed. For an individual it's a perfectly sensible response to a fragile economy. But if the same behavior becomes widespread, it's self-defeating. Explain.

Chapter 10 that these ups and downs in the level of economic activity are known as the *business cycle*.[6] A period of rising output and employment is called an *expansion*; a period of declining output and employment is called a contraction or *recession*.

Expansions and recessions are short-run phenomena. In the long run, the economy tends to operate at full employment and potential GDP. That's because the economy contains a self-correcting mechanism that tends to ultimately return the economy to potential GDP whenever it is disturbed from

---

[6] Economists disagree about the relative importance of demand and supply shocks in explaining business cycles. Some emphasize demand shocks; others emphasize shocks occurring on the supply side.

that equilibrium.[7] To illustrate that mechanism, let's consider an economy that is currently operating at full employment and potential GDP and examine its short-run and long-run reactions to a change in aggregate demand. We will begin with an increase in aggregate demand and then consider a decrease.

Adjustments to an Increase in Aggregate Demand

Suppose that aggregate demand expands because the federal government reduces personal income taxes. Households now have more to spend, and so they tend to demand more goods and services at each price level—the aggregate demand curve shifts to the right, from AD_1 to AD_2 in Exhibit 11.10.

When aggregate demand increases, the resulting higher price level creates incentive for businesses to expand output. This incentive is provided by the fact that many of a business's costs—particularly wage rates—are fixed by long-term contracts. When product prices rise, these costs do not; thus, firms stand to profit by expanding output. In our example, output will be increased

---

EXHIBIT 11.10

Adjusting to Higher Aggregate Demand

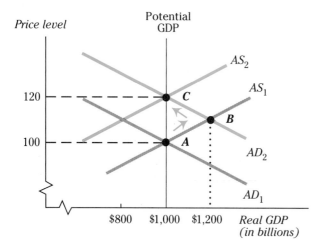

When aggregate demand increases, businesses initially find it profitable to expand output because wage rates and certain other costs are fixed by long-term contracts. Thus, equilibrium real GDP expands beyond potential. But when these contracts expire and costs rise, the short-run AS curve shifts upward and eventually reduces equilibrium output to the level of potential GDP.

---

[7] This self-correcting mechanism is part of the model presented in this chapter, a model that represents reality as many economists see it. Some economists would undoubtedly dispute at least portions of this model.

up to the point at which AS_1 is intersected by AD_2 (point B in Exhibit 11.10), well beyond potential GDP.

It may seem contradictory to suggest that the economy can operate beyond its potential. The term *potential* is commonly interpreted to mean "maximum." But the meaning of potential is somewhat different in this context. Potential GDP is not the maximum output the economy is capable of producing but rather the maximum *sustainable* level of production. Businesses can run factories beyond their designed or intended capacities for some period of time, and workers may be willing to work overtime. However, neither of these practices is sustainable; ultimately equipment breaks down, and employees become disgruntled and unproductive. But in the short run, these actions permit the economy to operate beyond its potential; that is, they allow actual GDP to exceed potential GDP.

As we've seen, businesses expand output beyond potential GDP because higher prices make it profitable for them to do so. But the higher prices that are attractive to businesses are bad news for employees. Workers find that they must pay more for the goods and services they buy, even though their wage rates are unchanged; thus, their *real* wages—the purchasing power of their money wages—have declined.

Eventually firms will have to renegotiate their labor contracts. When that happens, workers will demand higher wages. Other input suppliers, also pressed by higher prices, will demand more for their resources. The result of the higher renegotiated input prices will be an upward shift of the short-run aggregate supply curve. (Remember that a change in input prices will shift the AS curve.) Tight markets for labor and other inputs will put continuing upward pressure on wages and other input prices. The short-run AS curve will continue to shift upward until workers and other input suppliers have regained their original purchasing power. This is represented in Exhibit 11.10 by the shift from AS_1 to AS_2. Note that when contracts have been renegotiated, the incentive that originally motivated businesses to expand real output to $1,200 billion will have evaporated. Equilibrium real GDP will return to $1,000 billion (point C in the exhibit), the level of GDP consistent with the economy's potential output. The self-correcting forces have returned the economy to its potential GDP. As you can see, the long-run impact of the increase in aggregate demand is simply a higher price level since the increase in production cannot be sustained.

Adjustments to a Decrease in Aggregate Demand

The economy's response to a reduction in aggregate demand is similar to its adjustments to an increase, but in the opposite direction. To illustrate, let's

EXHIBIT 11.11

Adjusting to Lower Aggregate Demand

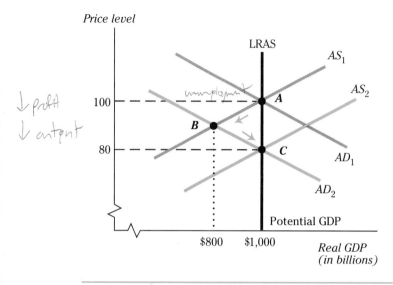

When aggregate demand declines, businesses initially find it necessary to reduce output because certain costs are fixed by long-term contracts. But when those contracts expire and costs fall, the *AS* curve shifts downward, returning the economy to potential GDP.

If we connect the points of long-run equilibrium (*A* and *C*), we find that the long-run aggregate supply (LRAS) curve is a vertical line at potential GDP.

again assume that the economy is operating at its potential GDP (at point *A* in Exhibit 11.11). If aggregate demand fell from AD_1 to AD_2, firms would initially find their prices falling while some of their costs were fixed by long-term contracts. This would cause them to cut back on output (because output levels that had been profitable at a higher price level are no longer profitable) and to reduce equilibrium GDP below potential. This is represented in Exhibit 11.11 by the movement along AS_1 from *A* to *B*. Of course, when actual GDP falls below potential, the rate of unemployment rises above the full employment level.

Eventually labor and other contracts will be renegotiated. At that point, the high unemployment rates and unused productive capacity of input suppliers will cause wages and other resource prices to fall. As that occurs, the short-run *AS* curve will begin shifting to the right, eventually shifting from AS_1 to AS_2 (from *B* to *C*) and returning the economy to potential GDP and full employment. The long-run impact of the reduction in aggregate demand is a lower price level; output and employment have returned to their initial levels.

The preceding examples suggest that although the economy can deviate from potential GDP in the short run, these deviations are ultimately corrected. In the long run, the economy tends to operate at potential GDP and full employment. This implies that in the long run the economy's aggregate supply curve is vertical because the economy ultimately returns to the same level of output, but at a higher or lower price level. If that point is unclear, return to Exhibit 11.11 for a moment. Recall that the economy began at point *A*. The demand shock temporarily pushed it to *B*, but it ultimately came to rest at *C*. If we connect the initial and final equilibrium points, we arrive at a vertical line through points *A* and *C*; the long-run aggregate supply (LRAS) curve is a vertical line at potential GDP. (To test your understanding, review Exhibit 11.10; you will discover that a similar result holds true.)

Shifts in the Long-Run Aggregate Supply Curve

Although the economy tends to return to potential GDP in the long run, potential GDP is not a static concept. The economy's productive capacity can increase over time if the stock of economic resources increases or if those resources become more productive (for instance, if the workforce becomes more skilled or if a technological advance provides workers with better capital equipment). Changes such as these would be represented by shifting the long-run aggregate supply (LRAS) curve to the right, as depicted in Exhibit 11.12.

EXHIBIT 11.12

Shifts in the Long-Run Aggregate Supply Curve

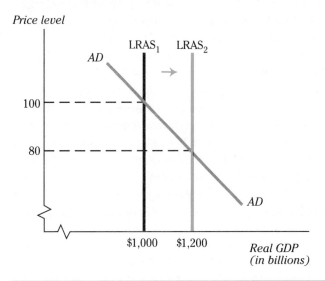

Increases in the stock of economic resources or the productivity of those resources will tend to shift the long-run aggregate supply (LRAS) curve to the right.

Of course, the LRAS curve can also shift to the left, as it would if there was a reduction in the economy's labor supply or in its stock of capital.

As you can see from this chapter, two kinds of changes occur in the macro economy: short-run changes and long-run changes. Short-run changes involve deviations from potential GDP. Long-run changes involve adjustments back to potential GDP, and they may also involve changes in the level of potential GDP itself. Both types of changes are important, and both are explored in this textbook. For instance, the next chapter, "Fiscal Policy," examines the short-run impact of the federal government's tax and spending decisions and considers the possibility that government action may sometimes be needed to speed the economy's return to full employment. Chapter 15, "Economic Growth: The Importance of the Long Run," examines the factors that determine the level of potential GDP and whether government can influence those factors through economic policy.

No

SUMMARY

Economists use the concepts of aggregate demand and aggregate supply to represent the forces that determine the economy's equilibrium GDP and price level. *Aggregate demand* (*AD*) is the total quantity of output demanded by all sectors in the economy together at various price levels in a given period of time. The *aggregate demand curve* slopes downward and to the right, indicating that more real output will be demanded at a lower price level than at a higher price level. There are three reasons for the downward slope of the aggregate demand curve: the *real balance effect*, the *interest rate effect*, and the *international trade effect*. The factors that will shift the aggregate demand curve include changes in the expectations of households and businesses, aggregate wealth, government policy, foreign incomes, and foreign price levels.

Aggregate supply (*AS*) refers to the quantity of output supplied by all producers in the economy together at various price levels in a given period of time. The short-run *aggregate supply curve* slopes upward because higher price levels stimulate businesses to expand output. Because wage rates and some other input prices are commonly fixed by contracts, an increase in the price level provides incentive for firms to expand output. A given short-run *AS* curve assumes the prevailing level of resource prices, the current level of technology and labor productivity, and the existing supplies of labor and capital. If one or more of these factors change, the short-run *AS* curve will shift to a new position.

The intersection of the aggregate demand and supply curves simultaneously determines the level of equilibrium real GDP and the equilibrium price level in the economy. Shifts in aggregate demand or supply will tend to alter these equilibrium values. If aggregate demand increases, both real GDP and the price level will tend to increase. The economy enjoys higher levels of output and employment, but it experiences *demand-pull inflation*. If aggregate demand declines, the levels of output, employment, and prices decline.

Changes in equilibrium can also be caused by changes in aggregate supply. A supply shock, such as an increase in the price of imported oil, will tend to reduce aggregate supply. This will cause *cost-push inflation* because the higher cost of oil pushes up prices. When aggregate supply is reduced, the levels of output and employment in the economy also decline. Supply shocks provide one possible explanation for *stagflation*, high unemployment combined with high inflation. If aggregate supply increases, the results will be doubly beneficial; the levels of output and employment in the economy will tend to increase, whereas the overall price level will decline.

Most modern economists agree that, to some extent, the economy contains a self-correcting mechanism. In the short run, the economy can deviate from potential GDP because certain wages and prices are rigid. In the long run, however, all wages and prices become flexible. As a consequence, reductions in aggregate demand are ultimately met by falling wages and input prices, which cause short-run aggregate supply to expand and return the economy to potential GDP. Increases in aggregate demand eventually lead to higher wages and input prices, which cause short-run aggregate supply to contract and output and employment to fall. Thus, wage and price adjustments ultimately return the economy to potential GDP and full employment. These adjustments imply that the long-run aggregate supply curve is vertical, not upward sloping like the short-run *AS* curve.

KEY TERMS

Aggregate demand
Aggregate supply
Cost-push inflation
Demand-pull inflation

Exports
Imports
Interest rate effect

International trade effect
Real balance effect
Stagflation

STUDY QUESTIONS

Fill in the Blanks

1. The ___Ag. dem.___ curve shows the amount of real output that will be demanded at various price levels.

2. According to the ___real income___ effect, an increase in the price level will reduce the purchasing power of financial assets and cause society to demand less real output.

3. Any change in the spending plans of consumers, businesses, or government that results from something other than a

   change in the ___Price___ will shift the aggregate demand curve.

4. A broad-based technological advance will

   tend to shift the aggregate ___Supply___

   curve to the ___right___.

5. The aggregate supply curve is upward sloping in the short run but

   _____ in the long run.

6. According to the interest rate effect, a reduction in the price level will tend to

   (increase/decrease) _____
   the demand for money, which in turn will

   (increase/decrease) _____
   the rate of interest and lead to (an increase/

   a reduction) _____ in the quantity of real output demanded.

7. Increases in the price level cause businesses to _____ output in

the short-run because some wages and other input prices are fixed by

_____.

8. An increase in government spending will tend to shift the aggregate

   _____D_____ curve to the

   _____R_____.

9. Cost-push inflation is caused by the

   aggregate ___S___ curve
   shifting to the (right/<u>left</u>)

   _____.

10. The term ___Cm___ is used to describe high inflation combined with high unemployment.

11. If the economy is initially in equilibrium at potential GDP, an increase in aggregate demand will tend to raise both output and prices in the short run, but will only raise

   _____ in the long run.

Multiple Choice

1. "The inflation seemed to be the result of optimistic consumers, who were willing to borrow against the escalating value of their homes and use the proceeds to buy furniture, automobiles, and a host of other products." This quote describes
   a) demand-pull inflation.
   b) cost-push inflation.
   c) structural inflation.
   d) expenditure inflation.

2. If a reduction in the price level causes more real output to be demanded,
   a) the aggregate demand curve will shift to the right.

   b) the aggregate demand curve is downward sloping.
   c) the short-run aggregate supply curve will shift to the right.
   d) the short-run aggregate supply curve is downward sloping.

3. Which of the following will shift the aggregate demand curve to the left?
   a) An increase in government spending
   b) A reduction in labor productivity
   c) An increase in personal income taxes
   d) An increase in society's aggregate wealth

4. Which of the following will increase both the price level and real GDP?
   a) A nationwide drought that drives up the prices of agricultural products
   b) A reduction in government spending for goods and services
   c) A reduction in the money supply
   d) Greater optimism among business executives

5. In 1974 disease killed many anchovies and raised anchovy prices. Anchovies are used in cattle feed as a source of protein. The likely short-run impact of this event would be to
   a) raise both the price level and real GDP.
   b) lower both the price level and real GDP.
   c) raise the price level but lower real GDP.
   d) lower the price level but raise real GDP.

6. According to the real balance effect,
   a) a reduction in the price level stimulates spending by lowering interest rates.
   b) an increase in the money supply will shift the aggregate demand curve to the right.
   c) an increase in the price level reduces spending by lowering the real value of society's financial assets.
   d) an increase in society's aggregate wealth will shift the aggregate demand curve to the right.

7. If the U.S. labor force became better educated and therefore more productive, the
   a) aggregate demand curve would shift right, raising both real GDP and the price level.
   b) aggregate supply curve would shift left, lowering real GDP and raising the price level.
   c) aggregate demand curve would shift left, lowering both real GDP and the price level.
   d) aggregate supply curve would shift right, raising real GDP and lowering the price level.

8. A decrease in foreign income levels would, ceteris paribus, tend to shift the aggregate _____ curve for U.S. products to the _____.

   a) demand; right
   b) demand; left
   c) supply; right
   d) supply; left

9. The international trade effect provides a rationale for
   a) shifts in the aggregate demand curve.
   b) shifts in the aggregate supply curve.
   c) the slope of the aggregate demand curve.
   d) the slope of the aggregate supply curve.

10. In the short run, an increase in the money supply will
    a) reduce both real GDP and the price level.
    b) reduce real GDP and increase the price level.
    c) increase both real GDP and the price level.
    d) increase real GDP and reduce the price level.

11. Suppose that the value of the average family home increased dramatically. This change would tend to shift the
    a) aggregate demand curve to the left, lowering real GDP and the price level.
    b) aggregate supply curve to the right, raising real GDP and lowering the price level.
    c) aggregate demand curve to the right, raising real GDP and the price level.
    d) aggregate supply curve to the left, lowering real GDP and raising the price level.

12. Suppose that Congress increased government spending at the same time that the price of imported oil (which is used to manufacture gasoline and heating oil) increased. In the short run, this would
    a) increase both the price level and real GDP.
    b) reduce both the price level and real GDP.
    c) increase the price level, but the impact on real GDP is uncertain.
    d) increase real GDP, but the impact on the price level is uncertain.

13. The short-run aggregate supply curve slopes upward
    a) as a result of the real balance effect and the interest rate effect.
    b) if all wages and input prices are flexible in the short run.
    c) because increases in the overall price level result in enhanced labor productivity and higher real output.
    d) because input price rigidities make it profitable for firms to expand output when product prices rise.

14. Suppose that the economy is operating below potential GDP. According to the self-correcting model, the economy will ultimately return to potential because
    a) the Fed will expand the money supply.
    b) wages and resource prices will fall as contracts expire and are renegotiated.
    c) workers will eventually demand higher wages, and resource suppliers will demand higher input prices.
    d) aggregate demand will automatically increase enough to push the economy back to potential GDP.

15. When the overall price level rises,
    a) businesses tend to reduce output because production becomes less profitable.
    b) wage rates and other input prices tend to increase immediately, forcing businesses to cut back on production.
    c) businesses have incentive to expand output because many costs are fixed by long-term contracts.

    d) businesses may either increase or decrease output, depending on the magnitude of the hike in the price level.

16. According to the self-correcting model, if the economy is producing a level of output in excess of potential GDP,
    a) potential GDP will automatically expand to match the actual level of production.
    b) workers and input suppliers will eventually negotiate higher wages and prices, which will return the economy to potential GDP.
    c) wages and input prices will ultimately fall, which will return the economy to potential GDP.
    d) None of the above; the economy cannot operate beyond potential GDP.

17. According to the self-correcting model,
    a) unemployment can exist indefinitely.
    b) the economy can never operate beyond potential GDP.
    c) unemployment is eventually eliminated by falling wages and prices.
    d) the economy always operates at potential GDP.

18. Which of the following would *not* shift the *long-run AS* curve to the right?
    a) An increase in the stock of capital
    b) A technological advance
    c) A reduction in the average wage rate
    d) An increase in worker training

Problems and Questions for Discussion

1. Explain in detail why the aggregate demand curve slopes downward.

2. Any change that shifts the long-run *AS* curve will also shift the short-run *AS* curve. But the converse is not true. Try to explain why.

3. What role do contracts play in explaining the upward slope of the aggregate supply curve?

4. Suppose that, on average, wage rates increase less than the increase in labor productivity. What will happen to the overall price level and real GDP? Explain how you arrived at your conclusion.

5. Whenever the stock market threatens to tumble (bringing down stock prices), economy watchers worry about its potential impact on the economy. Is there any

justification for this concern—could a large decline in the stock market harm the economy? Defend your answer.

6. Explain the difference between demand-pull and cost-push inflation. Use aggregate demand and supply curves to show how each problem would be represented graphically.

7. Suppose that the economy is in equilibrium at potential GDP and that policymakers increase aggregate demand (perhaps because they do not recognize that the economy is operating at potential). Discuss the short-run and long-run impact of this change. Supplement your answer with graphs.

8. Consider the short-run impact of the changes in the following list. Which changes would cause the economy's price level and real GDP to move in the same direction (both increase, both decrease), and which would cause the price level and real GDP to move in opposite directions (increasing the price level but reducing real output, for example)? After you have worked through the list, see if you can draw any general conclusions.
   a. An increase in government spending
   b. A severe frost that destroys crops
   c. A large decline in the stock market
   d. An increase in labor productivity
   e. An increase in consumer optimism
   f. Higher prices for imported raw materials

9. Suppose that government spending in support of education was increased. Would this action shift the aggregate demand curve, the aggregate supply curve, or both curves? What would happen to the price level and real GDP?

10. Assume that the economy is in short-run equilibrium at less than full employment. Describe the forces that will ultimately return the economy to potential GDP.

ANSWER KEY

Fill in the Blanks

1. aggregate demand
2. real balance
3. price level
4. supply; right
5. vertical
6. decrease; decrease; an increase
7. increase; contracts
8. demand; right
9. supply; left
10. stagflation
11. prices

Multiple Choice

1. a
2. b
3. c
4. d
5. c
6. c
7. d
8. b
9. c
10. c
11. c
12. c
13. d
14. b
15. c
16. b
17. c
18. c

12

Fiscal Policy

1. Describe the content of the federal budget.
2. List the major sources of tax revenue and the major categories of government expenditures.
3. Explain the difference between activist and nonactivist economists.
4. Explain the meaning of recessionary and inflationary gaps.
5. Distinguish between discretionary and automatic fiscal policy.
6. Describe the fiscal measures that activists would take to combat unemployment or inflation.
7. Explain the difference between planned and unplanned budget deficits (or budget surpluses).
8. Describe the factors that limit the effectiveness of discretionary fiscal policy.
9. Discuss the burdens imposed on society by the public debt.

We discovered in the last chapter that the government's spending and taxing decisions affect the level of aggregate demand. In this chapter we will take a closer look at those decisions. What does the federal government do with our tax dollars? What do people mean when they say the federal government is projecting a budget surplus or a budget deficit? Should government deliberately alter its tax and spending plans in an attempt to guide the economy's performance? And what is the public debt? These are some of the questions we will attempt to answer in this chapter. We'll begin with a brief look at the federal budget. Then we'll use the *AD–AS* model from Chapter 11 to examine the cause of unemployment and inflation and to consider the possibility that government might use its tax and spending powers to combat these problems. The chapter will conclude with a look at the public debt and concerns about the debt.

THE FEDERAL BUDGET

The **federal budget** is a statement of the federal government's planned expenditures and anticipated receipts for the coming year. The budget is the result of interaction between the president and Congress. Each February, the president proposes a budget, which is then debated and amended by Congress. Because there are diverse views about the proper functions of government, this process can be protracted. However, it is usually completed before October 1, the start of the federal government's *fiscal* year. (According to Webster, the word *fiscal* means "pertaining to financial matters." So, in essence, a fiscal year is an accounting year. The federal government's fiscal year runs from October 1 to September 30.)

The budgetary process is not over after Congress enacts a budget. If the economy does not perform as expected, the government's expenditures and tax revenues will be different from those anticipated. As a consequence, Congress is commonly required to pass supplemental budgets to accommodate these changes. With this background, we turn now to a consideration of the federal government's budget for the 2010 fiscal year, as represented in Exhibit 12.1.

EXHIBIT 12.1

Federal Budget for 2010 (billions of dollars)

TAX RECEIPTS	$2,333	
Personal income taxes		$1,051
Social insurance taxes		940
Corporate income taxes		179
Excise taxes		75
Estate and gift taxes		20
Customs duties, etc.		68
EXPENDITURE	**$3,591**	
Transfer payments		$2,050
Purchases of goods and services		1,405
Debt interest		136
Deficit	**$1,258**	

Source: Budget of the United States Government, Fiscal Year 2010. (Washington, D.C.: U.S. Government Printing Office, 2009). (Data are from table S-4.)

Tax Revenues

As you can see from Exhibit 12.1, $2,333 billion in tax revenue was projected for fiscal 2010. The major source of federal tax receipts is personal income taxes, which were expected to bring in $1,051 billion in 2010, about 45 percent of the federal government's revenues. Social insurance taxes, such as Social Security taxes and Medicare taxes, were the second most important source of revenue, accounting for an anticipated $940 billion, or about 40 percent of the total. The remaining revenue sources are much less important. In 2010, corporate income taxes were projected to bring in approximately $179 billion (8 percent), while the remaining categories—excise taxes (such as the taxes on alcoholic beverages and tobacco products), estate and gift taxes (taxes on inheritances and gifts), and customs duties (taxes on imported products)—together account for only $163 billion, a little less than 7 percent of total revenue.

Social insurance taxes have become increasingly important as a source of government tax revenue. In the 1960s, social insurance taxes generated about 16 percent of federal tax revenues. By 1980, that figure had expanded to 30 percent. And, as we saw earlier, social insurance taxes are projected to account for about 40 percent of federal revenues in 2010. Over the 1960–2010 period, personal income taxes provided a relatively constant share of federal revenues, but corporate income taxes declined in relative importance (from roughly 23 percent of total revenue in 1960 to about 8 percent in 2010). Excise taxes, estate and gift taxes, and customs duties have also declined significantly in importance (from 17 percent in 1960 to about 7 percent in 2010.)[1]

Government Expenditures

How does the federal government spend our tax dollars? Returning to Exhibit 12.1, you can see that there are three major categories of expenditures: transfer payments, purchases of goods and services, and debt interest.

The largest category of government expenditures is transfer payments. **Transfer payments** are expenditures for which government receives no goods or services in return. Examples of transfer payments include Social Security benefits, Medicare and Medicaid expenditures, unemployment compensation, and farm subsidies. In 2010, the federal government projected expenditures of $2,050 billion for transfer payments, about 57 percent of total federal outlays.

The fraction of the federal budget going to transfer payments has been rising for a number of years. Consider Social Security, for example. In 1970, Social Security accounted for about 15 percent of federal expenditures. By 2010, it is

---

[1] Comparisons are based on statistics drawn from *Historic Tables: Budget of the United States Government, Fiscal Year 2007.*

projected to account for 19 percent of spending. An even more dramatic pattern appears if we look at Medicare and Medicaid. In 1970, these two programs accounted for about 4 percent of federal spending. By 1990, the Medicare and Medicaid programs had grown to more than 10 percent of total expenditures. In 2010, they are expected to absorb almost 21 percent of total spending. As you can see, the growth of transfer payments has been striking. In fact, the persistent growth of transfer payments has become a significant source of concern and heated debate among politicians and others.

The second-largest category of government expenditures is government purchases of goods and services. This category includes government spending for national defense—outlays for submarines, the services of military personnel, and so on—and nondefense purchases—expenditures for roads, parks, schools, the services of legislators and bureaucrats, and so on. In 2010, the federal government anticipated spending $1,405 billion on goods and services. That represents approximately 39 percent of total expenditures, down dramatically from 50 percent in 1970.

The final category of government expenditures is interest on the national debt. As you probably recognize, the federal government sometimes spends more than it earns in tax revenue. This is accomplished by borrowing money, just as you might borrow money to buy a home or finance a vacation. Of course, whenever you borrow money you create a debt. This entry reflects the interest payments that the federal government must make annually to the owners of that debt. In 2010, the federal government projected approximately $136 billion in debt interest, about 4 percent of total expenditures. That percentage is down significantly from 2006–2008, when it was more than 8 percent. (This projected drop was not due to a reduction in the size of the public debt—which continues to grow—rather, it was due to unusually low interest rates and some other special factors.)

If you compare the federal government's projected revenues and expenditures for 2010, you can see that it was anticipating a budget deficit. A **budget deficit** exists if the government spends more than it collects in taxes. According to Exhibit 12.1, the federal government was projecting a deficit of $1,258 billion for the 2010 fiscal year. That's the second largest in history (in both nominal and real terms), following only 2009.

While the projected deficit for 2010 is unusually large—in fact, huge—by historical standards, budget deficits are not a new, or rare, phenomenon for the federal government. Rather, it is **budget surpluses**—when the government collects more in tax revenues than it spends—that are rare. With the exception of a brief period of budget surpluses from 1998–2001, deficits have been the norm since 1960, when the federal government experienced a (nearly) **balanced budget**, with government expenditures equal to tax revenues. We'll have more to say about the causes and consequences of deficits and surpluses later in the chapter.

CLASSICAL ECONOMICS, THE GREAT DEPRESSION, AND JOHN MAYNARD KEYNES

Although the primary objective of the federal budget is to pay for the activities of the federal government, there is a secondary objective as well. The federal budget may also be used as a tool for influencing the performance of the aggregate economy, for helping to combat unemployment or inflation. Before we discuss this function we need to review and expand on some concepts introduced in the previous chapter. Let's begin by revisiting the model of a self-correcting economy.

Chapter 11 concluded that a self-correcting mechanism tends to restore the economy to full employment and potential GDP whenever it deviates from those standards. Prior to the 1930s, economists thought that the economy's self-correcting mechanism not only worked, but worked quickly. The economists of this period are known as **classical economists**, and they believed that any reduction in aggregate demand would quickly be met by falling wages and prices, which would tend to restore full employment. This belief held up reasonably well until the Great Depression, which began in 1929. By 1933, the economy's real GDP had declined by almost one-third, and the unemployment rate had reached 25 percent. Although the economy began to recover after 1933, it was a slow and weak recovery. In 1937, the unemployment rate still hovered around 14 percent.

The Great Depression called into question the classical economists' belief in a quickly adjusting economy. In 1936, John Maynard Keynes, a British economist, offered an alternative view of how market economies work. According to Keynes, if pessimism causes businesses and consumers to reduce their spending, an economy could find itself in an unemployment "equilibrium"—a situation in which output and employment are stuck at low levels for some time. In terms of the *AD–AS* model, Keynes was saying that the self-correcting mechanism may operate slowly. Moreover, Keynes didn't think we should wait for this automatic adjustment to occur. "In the long-run we're all dead" was his comforting way of putting it. Instead, he argued that government should take an active part in trying to stimulate a recovery.

What should governments do? According to Keynes, the federal government should increase its spending or reduce taxes to stimulate private spending. In other words, it should use the federal budget to get the economy moving again. We'll have more to say about these policies in just a moment. For now, the important point is that Keynes saw the federal budget as more than an accounting device; he saw it as a tool for influencing economic performance.

Because of his belief in government intervention, Keynes is regarded as one of the first **activist economists**—economists who see an important role for government in guiding the economy's performance. On the other hand, the classical economists were nonactivists. Because they have faith in the economy's ability to heal itself, **nonactivist economists** do not believe that government intervention is necessary.[2]

Today, most economists appear to believe that there is a self-correcting mechanism operative in the economy. But there is continuing disagreement about how rapidly that mechanism operates and whether government policy can be used to speed the process. Modern nonactivists tend to believe that the economy's self-correcting mechanism works relatively quickly and that government action is either ineffective or counterproductive. Modern activists see the self-correcting mechanism as working slowly and view government intervention—at least in the case of significant deviations from potential GDP— as advisable.

THE EXISTENCE OF UNEMPLOYMENT OR INFLATION

The aggregate demand–aggregate supply model can be used to illustrate the unemployment problem that was the focus of Keynes's analysis of the Great Depression. In Exhibit 12.2(a), we find the economy in equilibrium at an output of $800 billion, an output less than the economy's potential GDP of $1,000 billion. Of course, whenever the economy is operating below its potential, the rate of unemployment in the economy exceeds the natural rate. As we learned in Chapter 10, this situation is commonly described as a recession (the term *depression* is reserved for severe downturns like the Great Depression), and the amount by which the equilibrium GDP falls short of potential GDP is known as the **recessionary gap**. In this example, the recessionary gap is equal to $200 billion, the difference between the potential output of $1,000 billion and the actual output of $800 billion.

Although Keynes was primarily concerned with recessionary gaps, he recognized that economies can also be in equilibrium beyond potential GDP. Exhibit 12.2(b) illustrates that situation. Here we find the economy in equilibrium at an output of $1,250 billion, well beyond the economy's potential GDP. Because the economy is operating beyond potential, the unemployment rate is less than the natural rate, and strong demand for labor puts upward pressure on wages and prices. Because operating beyond potential GDP creates inflationary pressures, we describe the excess in equilibrium GDP as the inflationary gap.

---

[2] Students wishing to explore the debate between Keynes and the classical economists in greater detail can do so by reading "Keynes and the Classical Economists: The Early Debate On Policy Activism," which can be accessed on the textbook Web site at www.pearsonhighered.com/rohlf.

EXHIBIT 12.2

Recessionary and Inflationary Gaps

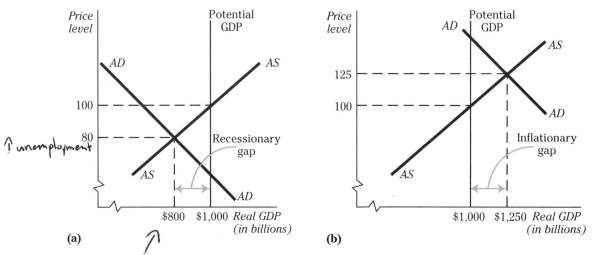

A *recessionary gap* exists whenever equilibrium GDP falls short of potential GDP. Part (a) shows a recessionary gap of $200 billion, the difference between the potential GDP of $1,000 billion and the equilibrium output of $800 billion.

An *inflationary gap* exists whenever the equilibrium GDP exceeds potential GDP. Part (b) shows an inflationary gap of $250 billion, the difference between the potential GDP of $1,000 billion and the equilibrium GDP of $1,250 billion.

More precisely, the **inflationary gap** is the amount by which the equilibrium level of real GDP exceeds potential GDP. In this instance the inflationary gap is equal to $250 billion, the difference between the actual output of $1,250 billion and the potential output of $1,000 billion.

DISCRETIONARY FISCAL POLICY: COMBATING UNEMPLOYMENT OR INFLATION

Since the time of Keynes, activist economists have argued that government policies should be used to eliminate recessionary or inflationary gaps rather than waiting for the economy to self-correct. One form of policy activism involves discretionary fiscal policy. **Discretionary fiscal policy** is the deliberate changing of the level of government spending or taxation to guide the economy's performance. Discretionary fiscal policy attempts to influence an economy's performance by altering the level of spending or aggregate demand.

When a recessionary gap exists and unemployment is above the natural rate, an *expansionary fiscal policy* is called for: increase government spending, reduce taxes, or do both. Increasing government spending for goods and services directly increases aggregate demand because it means more spending at any price level. Tax reductions work indirectly; by reducing taxes, they leave households with more take-home pay, which in turn tends to stimulate the demand for furniture and other consumer items.[3] Either policy would tend to expand the economy to a higher level of equilibrium GDP and lower the unemployment rate.[4] For instance, in Exhibit 12.3(a), we can see that an increase in government

EXHIBIT 12.3

Using Discretionary Fiscal Policy

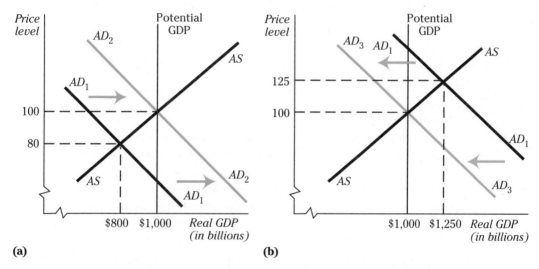

(a)

(b)

According to activist economists, unemployment can be attacked by using an *expansionary fiscal policy:* increasing government spending or reducing taxes. (a) An expansionary fiscal policy shifts the aggregate demand curve from AD_1 to AD_2, thereby eliminating the recessionary gap and the accompanying unemployment.

Inflationary pressures can be eliminated by employing a *contractionary fiscal policy:* reducing government spending or increasing taxes. (b) A contractionary fiscal policy shifts the aggregate demand curve from AD_1 to AD_3, thereby eliminating the inflationary gap and the accompanying inflationary pressures.

---

[3] While increases in government purchases of goods and services directly increase aggregate demand, increases in government spending for transfer payments act indirectly, like a tax reduction. By providing households with additional income, increases in transfer payments tend to increase the demand for goods and services.

[4] An increase in government spending for goods and services would actually shift the *AD* curve farther than an equal-sized increase in transfer payments or an equal-sized reduction in taxes. That's because households would tend to save a portion of the tax reduction or increase in transfer payments.

spending (or a reduction in taxes) has shifted the AD curve from AD_1 to AD_2, raising the economy's equilibrium GDP from $800 billion to $1,000 billion and the price level from 80 to 100. In short, discretionary fiscal policy has eliminated the recessionary gap and lowered unemployment to the natural rate.

The existence of an inflationary gap would call for a *contractionary fiscal policy*: Government spending should be cut or taxes should be increased in order to reduce private spending. By reducing aggregate demand, these policies would tend to contract the level of equilibrium GDP and reduce or eliminate inflationary pressures. For instance, Exhibit 12.3(b) shows that by cutting government spending (or increasing taxes), we can reduce aggregate demand from AD_1 to AD_3. This would reduce the equilibrium level of real GDP from $1,250 billion to $1,000 billion (the economy's potential output) and thereby eliminate the inflationary pressures that had existed.

AUTOMATIC FISCAL POLICY: THE ECONOMY'S AUTOMATIC STABILIZERS

Discretionary fiscal policy, as the term implies, requires Congress to deliberately change the level of government spending and/or taxation. But not all fiscal policy is discretionary; some is automatic. **Automatic stabilizers** are changes in the level of government spending or taxation that occur automatically whenever the level of aggregate income (GDP) changes. This automatic fiscal policy tends to reduce the magnitude of fluctuations in total spending and thereby help prevent wide swings in the level of output and employment.

The federal income tax is one powerful automatic stabilizer. To see how it works, imagine a family earning $50,000 a year and paying $10,000 a year in taxes. (Its average tax rate would be 20 percent because $10,000 is 20 percent of $50,000.) After taxes, our hypothetical family will have $40,000 to spend on food, housing, and whatever else it chooses to purchase.

Now, suppose the economy enters a recession and the family sees its income shrink by $10,000 as a result of reduced hours of work. This will cause the family's tax bill to fall to $8,000, leaving it with $32,000 to spend. The family's ability to purchase goods and services has fallen, but only by $8,000, not by the full $10,000 reduction in income. Other families with falling incomes will have a similar experience; they will receive automatic tax reductions that will cushion the impact of the reductions in income. Because taxes automatically decline with income, the tax system prevents spending from falling as much as it would have if taxes remained constant. This helps to retard the weakening of the economy and prevents unemployment from becoming as severe as it otherwise would.

When the economy strengthens, the tax system operates to dampen inflationary pressures. Increases in income mean higher taxes; consumers are left with less income to spend than they would have if taxes had remained constant. If the higher incomes push families into higher tax brackets (the 30 percent bracket, for example), the increase in after-tax income will be even less.[5] Thus, the income tax helps to dampen spending increases and reduce inflationary pressures.

Federal–state unemployment compensation and state welfare benefits also operate as built-in stabilizers. When the level of economic activity declines and the jobless rate begins to rise, the total amount paid out in the form of unemployment compensation and welfare benefits increases automatically. These transfer payments compensate somewhat for the declining incomes of the unemployed, and in so doing, they prevent a steeper drop in consumption spending by households. This action retards the downward spiral of spending and slows the deterioration of the economy.

When the economy begins to recover and the unemployment rate drops, these transfer payments automatically decrease, which helps prevent inflation by slowing the growth of spending.

Although automatic stabilizers reduce the magnitude of fluctuations in economic activity, they do not ensure full employment and stable prices. They cannot stop a severe inflation once it is underway, and they cannot pull the economy out of a deep recession. In fact, the same fiscal features that tend to stabilize the economy can also retard the economy's recovery from a recession. As the recovery begins, personal income starts to rise, but higher taxes reduce the growth of spending and therefore slow the recovery. For these reasons, activist economists believe that automatic stabilizers must be supplemented by the kinds of discretionary (deliberate) fiscal policies we examined earlier.

FISCAL POLICY AND THE FEDERAL BUDGET

When we resort to fiscal policy to combat unemployment or inflation, we are deliberately tampering with the federal budget. That's what discretionary fiscal policy really is—budget policy.

According to activists, whenever unemployment exists (whenever the unemployment rate is above the natural rate), the federal government should plan a *deficit budget*; that is, it should plan to spend more than it expects to collect in taxes. By taking this action, the government injects the economy with additional spending, or aggregate demand, that should help drive it toward

---

[5] Existing tax law is somewhat progressive; that is, those with higher incomes pay a higher fraction of those incomes in the form of taxes.

full employment. Inflationary times call for the opposite approach, a *surplus budget*, which expresses the government's intention to spend less than it expects to collect in taxes. A surplus budget helps reduce the amount of aggregate demand in the economy and thereby moderates inflationary pressures. According to the activist (or Keynesian) model, a *balanced budget*—a plan to match government expenditures and tax revenues—is appropriate only when the economy is operating at full employment, when it has achieved a satisfactory equilibrium and needs neither stimulus nor restraint.

Planned and Unplanned Deficits and Surpluses

While discretionary fiscal policy calls for deliberate deficits and surpluses, not all federal deficits or surpluses are the result of deliberate action. In fact, even the most carefully planned budget will be inaccurate if the economy performs in unexpected ways. That's true because changes in the level of national income and employment will mean automatic changes in tax revenues and government expenditures. The same automatic stabilizers that help to reduce the magnitude of economic swings lead to deficits when the economy experiences a downturn and to unexpected surpluses during periods of expansion.

To illustrate, consider an experience from the George W. Bush administration. In April 2001, President Bush recommended to Congress a budget with a projected surplus of $231 billion for the 2002 fiscal year. This budget assumed that the economy's real gross domestic product would grow at a rate of 3.3 percent and that the unemployment rate would average 4.6 percent for the year. Both assumptions turned out to be incorrect. Real GDP grew at a rate of only 2.4 percent that year, and the unemployment rate averaged 5.8 percent. As a result of the economy's unexpectedly weak performance, the federal government's outlay for unemployment compensation was higher than anticipated, and tax revenues were lower. These changes were largely responsible for the resulting budget *deficit* of $158 billion, a far cry from the $231 billion surplus that had been projected.

In contrast, sometimes the economy outperforms the projections of planners. When that happens, the automatic stabilizers have the opposite effect on the government's receipts and expenditures. As the economy expands, tax revenues rise, and expenditures for unemployment compensation decline. This tends to decrease the size of the deficit or increase the size of the surplus. The Clinton administration's experience in 1997 illustrates the point. Prior to the start of the year, the administration estimated a budget deficit of $125 billion. But a booming economy lowered the unemployment rate (and the accompanying payments to the unemployed) and ballooned tax receipts. The result was a deficit of only $22 billion, a much lower figure than anyone anticipated.

Unemployment and the Federal Budget

As the foregoing examples show, when the economy performs in unexpected ways, budget planners are likely to miss their target. Moreover, efforts to get the budget back on track can harm the economy. To illustrate, suppose the economy is initially operating at full employment and that the federal government projects a balanced budget. What will happen to the budget if the economy suddenly weakens and unemployment begins to rise? As you know, the fiscal system's automatic stabilizers will work automatically to retard the downturn. But what will this do to the balanced federal budget? It will push it into deficit!

Suppose that Congress insists on restoring a balanced budget. What should be done to accomplish this objective? The logical response would be to increase taxes and reduce government spending. But wait—this response is clearly inconsistent with the activist remedy for unemployment. The reduced level of government spending and concomitant higher taxes will mean less aggregate demand, which will cause the downturn to worsen. Moreover, because this effort to balance the budget prolongs the recession, it may result in a larger cumulative deficit.

According to the activist model, whenever the economy is in recession, the preferred route to a balanced budget entails a deliberate increase in government spending or a reduction in taxes. Obviously, either measure would increase the short-term deficit, but by stimulating output and employment, either action could help pull the economy out of its depressed state. When the economy improves, tax revenues will rise automatically, and government spending for transfer payments will decline automatically. Thus, expansionary fiscal policy may create a larger deficit in the short run. But by restoring the health of the economy, it can lead to a balanced budget.

The classic example of this process occurred in the mid-1960s, when President Johnson pressed for a tax cut to stimulate a depressed economy. In 1964 the federal budget was already in deficit when Congress finally approved an $11 billion tax reduction (originally requested by President Kennedy in 1963) designed to push the economy closer to full employment. The stimulus provided by this tax cut helped increase GDP by some $36 billion and lower the unemployment rate from 6 percent to 4.7 percent. According to Arthur Okun, chairman of the Council of Economic Advisors under President Johnson, the higher tax revenues that resulted from the improved economy brought the federal budget into surplus in the first half of 1965.[6]

---

[6] Arthur N. Okun, *The Political Economy of Prosperity* (New York: W.W. Norton, 1967), pp. 47–48.

ISSUES RELATED TO FISCAL POLICY

The foregoing discussion seems to suggest that discretionary fiscal policy is easily used to combat the problems of unemployment and inflation. It's time to dispel that impression. As we noted earlier, not all economists are activists. And even activists recognize that implementing discretionary fiscal policy is tougher in reality than it is on the chalkboard (or in the textbook). Let's examine why.

Crowding Out

According to activists, unemployment should be combated by increasing government spending (or reducing taxes). This is supposed to increase aggregate demand, pushing the economy back to full employment. But the beneficial impact of higher government spending may be partially offset by a phenomenon known as crowding out.

When the federal government borrows money to finance additional spending, it must compete with private borrowers for funds. Under certain circumstances this increased demand for funds will drive up interest rates, which will discourage private businesses from borrowing for investment purposes. This occurrence is known as **crowding out**: government borrowing pushes aside, or crowds out, private borrowing.

Crowding out has two important consequences that we need to consider. First, crowding out tends to reduce the expansionary impact of any increase in government spending. To illustrate, suppose that a deficit-financed increase in government spending would (in the absence of crowding out) increase the economy's equilibrium GDP by $200 billion. If the higher interest rates associated with government's borrowing reduce investment spending, that reduction will partially offset the expansionary impact of the government's fiscal policy. As a result, the economy's equilibrium output will expand by less than $200 billion, perhaps substantially less.

Second, crowding out can affect the economy's rate of economic growth. Unlike consumption spending, investment spending allows businesses to expand their productive capacity and produce more output in the future. In other words, investment spending permits the economy to grow and, by making more goods and services available, increases the society's standard of living. To the extent that crowding out reduces the level of investment spending, it hinders economic growth and thereby harms future generations. (To the extent that the increased government spending is for roads, schools, and other "investment-like" purchases, this portion of the crowding-out argument is invalidated.)

Crowding out is unlikely to be a significant problem when the economy is in a severely depressed state with substantial excess capacity. Under those conditions, businesses are reluctant to invest, even in the face of low interest rates. Crowding out is more likely to be a problem when the economy is expanding, as it was throughout the late 1990s. Under those conditions, higher interest rates may indeed choke off some private investment spending, potentially slowing future economic growth.

The Expansionary Bias

Activists call for expansionary fiscal policy to combat unemployment and for contractionary fiscal policy to combat inflation. But expansionary policies are more attractive politically than contractionary policies. Incumbent politicians don't want to sacrifice votes, and voters don't want to pay higher taxes—nor do they want to lose government programs that benefit them. The result is a bias in favor of expansionary fiscal policies. It may be relatively easy for Congress to pass measures to stimulate the economy, but it's quite difficult to muster the votes necessary to trim government spending or increase taxes. This bias has led to ongoing deficits in good times and bad and has significantly tarnished the image of discretionary fiscal policy. (Prior to 1998, the last budget surplus experienced by the federal government was in 1969. That's almost 30 years of uninterrupted deficits. Clearly, the expansionary bias was a problem not envisioned by Keynes.)

Time Lags

Many critics argue that the most significant problem associated with the use of discretionary fiscal policy is time lags. Often a substantial interlude passes between the time when a policy change is needed and the time when the economic impact of any change actually takes place. This lag may reduce the effectiveness of the remedial fiscal policy; in some instances, it may even make the change counterproductive.

The time lag associated with fiscal policy has three elements. First, the economy does not always provide clear signals as to what the future will bring. As a consequence, there is commonly a *recognition lag*; that is, some time elapses before policymakers recognize the need for a policy change. Second, even after the need is acknowledged, action is historically slow to take place. It can take a substantial amount of time to draft legislation and get it through Congress. Even if lawmakers are in general agreement that action is needed, there may be heated disagreements about the form that action should take. Many economists argue that this *implementation lag* is unacceptably long and is the real downfall of fiscal policy. The final lag is the *impact lag*. Even after

Currents: The New Old Big Thing in Economics: J. M. Keynes

BY SUDEEP REDDY

The U.S. and dozens of other nations are returning to massive government spending as a recession fighter. It's not because they're sure it'll do the trick. It's because they're running low on options and desperate for tools—even old ones—to fight the global downturn. Around the world, interest rates have been slashed and trillions of dollars have been committed to bailouts. But the global recession is deepening anyway. So policy makers are invoking the ideas of British economist John Maynard Keynes (pronounced "canes"), who argued that governments should fight the Great Depression in the 1930s with heavy spending. With consumer and business spending so weak, he argued, governments had to boost demand directly. . . .

Keynesian policies fell out of favor in the 1970s, as government spending was blamed for helping to spur inflation around the world. But with the global economic turmoil being compared to the 1930s, government spending is once again back in vogue. "The situation is so severe that we're all Keynesians again— Keynesians in the foxhole," says Martin Baily, a former Clinton White House economist at the left-leaning Brookings Institution. "It really is such a difficult time that we're going to need to use whatever ammunition we have." . . .

The International Monetary Fund is urging countries to boost spending by about 2% of their output—more than $1 trillion total—and it's likely they'll exceed that amount. President-elect Barack Obama is planning a stimulus package of as much as $775 billion over two years. China promises to spend almost $600 billion, while the

European Union is pushing a package of more than $250 billion. India and Japan also have announced stimulus plans—although nations often overstate the extent of new spending.

Critics argue that government deficits drive up interest rates and reduce investments in the private sector, which they say is more efficient at deploying capital to improve society. "The U.S. economy has soared highest when the federal government was shrinking, and it has stagnated at times of government expansion," says Brian Riedl of the Heritage Foundation, a right-leaning think tank. Still, with the U.S. economy facing 1930s-style threats, the Obama administration is looking back to that period for guidance. President Franklin Roosevelt's Works Progress Administration provided jobs to millions of Americans during the Great Depression, though it had critics who said the program wasted money on unnecessary projects. The heavy government spending that followed World War II ultimately filled much of the employment gap.

Keynesian fiscal stimulus remained popular globally into the 1960s, particularly in rebuilding Europe and Japan after the war. Latin American nations boosted their economies in the 1960s and 1970s through heavy investment in transportation infrastructure, as governments expanded their budgets thanks to natural-resources income. The efforts often seemed to work. Growth accelerated in the U.S. and Europe, and the big developing markets of the time in Latin America. But limits of Keynes-inspired growth were reached in the following decades. Many countries mistimed their spending, pouring money into their economies just as they were riding out a downturn and leading to economic overheating. Latin America regularly succumbed to hyperinflation, while in the U.S. the "misery index"—the combination of inflation and joblessness—climbed to 20.8% in 1980, from 10.8% a decade earlier. . . .

With the rise of Ronald Reagan and Britain's Margaret Thatcher, critics of stimulus policy came to the fore. The goal became to shrink government. Monetary policy also began to play a bigger role, as central bankers drove up interest rates to bring down inflation. Recessions seemed to grow more distant and less painful. The era from the early 1980s until the recent crisis became known as "the Great Moderation," when economic activity and inflation became less volatile. U.S. Federal Reserve chairmen, especially Alan Greenspan, became economic rock stars for bringing stability to the U.S. economy.

But during this period of financial turmoil, monetary policy has been inadequate. Banks and other creditors remain wary of lending because they're afraid they won't get repaid. The U.S. Federal Reserve lowered its interest-rate target to near zero last month from 5.25% in mid-2007, and is employing other tools to restore growth, but the economy has continued to spiral downward. So, nations are turning again to government stimulus spending to try knocking the economy back on track. . . .

In the U.S., direct government payments to consumers in 2001 and 2008 provided some temporary relief during recessions. But since only a fraction of the funds were spent, while the rest went to savings or debt, the stimulative effect was disappointing.

Now, to ensure money is spent, the U.S. and other nations are focusing on infrastructure investment to create jobs, starting with the battered construction sector. President-elect Barack Obama says he is planning the largest public-works program since the 1950s construction of interstate highways. He also plans to use stimulus funds to repair schools, expand broadband Internet access and put energy-efficient technologies in public buildings. Similarly, in China, the government plans to pour more money into hard infrastructure such as railways and airports. . . .

For any infrastructure investment to succeed as stimulus, nations must ensure people are hired quickly to work to reverse the downturn—and don't become part of a permanent program. U.S. governors say their states have $136 billion in "shovel ready" projects that are fully planned and simply lack funding. But critics doubt those claims. Historically, infrastructure projects have proven to fall behind schedule and over budget. . . .

Inflation has quickly disappeared as a concern around the world. It's likely to reappear once growth perks up. That leaves a big test for the resurgence of fiscal stimulus: Once the economy revives, Mr. Keynes warned, the spending needs to be reversed and deficits cut. That's something nations have had a hard time doing.

USE YOUR ECONOMIC REASONING

1. What policies did Keynes advocate for dealing with a recession? Are those policies evident in the article? Give examples.
2. Why did Keynesian policies "fall out of favor in the 1970s"? Why are they being reconsidered today?
3. "Critics argue that government deficits drive up interest rates and reduce investment. . . ." What is the label attached to this problem? How would activists respond to this criticism of present policy?
4. Policymakers want discretionary spending projects that can be started quickly and that don't become part of a permanent program. Explain the rationale for each of these requirements.

legislation is passed and put into effect, more time is required for policy to have its full effect on aggregate demand.

The existence of these time lags clearly limits the effectiveness of discretionary fiscal policy as a vehicle for guiding the economy's performance. Today, even activists agree that policymakers should not attempt to use discretionary fiscal policy to eliminate every minor increase in unemployment or inflation. Instead, discretionary policies should be reserved for major downturns or inflationary episodes, situations in which the lag will be of less critical importance. (Were lags a concern when the Obama administration was crafting its response to our most recent recession? Read "Currents: The New Old Big Thing in Economics: J. M. Keynes," on page 368, and decide for yourself.)

THE PUBLIC DEBT

No discussion of the federal budget and fiscal policy would be complete without at least some attention to the topic of the **public debt**—the accumulated borrowings of the federal government. Whenever the federal government incurs a deficit—be it planned or unplanned—it must finance that deficit by borrowing. This is accomplished by instructing the U.S. Treasury to sell government bonds to the public—to individuals, businesses, and financial institutions. Each of these transactions increases the public, or national, debt. By the end of 2008, the public debt had increased to $5.8 trillion, a figure so large that it is beyond the comprehension of most of us. That amount represents all the borrowing it took to finance several wars, numerous economic downturns, and a variety of government projects and programs.

Concerns about the Public Debt

The size of the public debt troubles many Americans. Some of their concerns are justified, and some are not. In this section we want to lay to rest some myths and examine the real burden of the debt.

Can We Ever Pay Off the Debt?   A common misconception about the public debt is that it must be paid off at some time in the future. In reality, there is no requirement that the federal government ever pay off the debt. From 1998 to 2001, budget surpluses allowed the federal government to reduce the size of the public debt. But that was not because it was *required* to do so. Instead, government may choose to refinance the debt year after year with new borrowing. As government bonds become due, the Treasury sells new bonds to take their place. So long as there is a market for government bonds, the government can keep issuing them. And because U.S. bonds are probably the most secure investment in the world today, that market is not likely to disappear.

Does the Public Debt Impose a Burden on Future Generations?
Some critics of the debt suggest that it imposes an unfair burden on future generations, who will be forced to pay higher taxes to make the interest payments on the debt.

What this logic overlooks is that one person's debt is another person's asset. Future generations will inherit not only the public debt but also the bonds and other securities that make up the debt. When a future generation pays taxes to service the debt, its members will also be the recipients of the interest payments made by the government. In a sense, this future generation will be paying itself. Of course, some members of the generation will pay more in additional taxes than they receive in interest, while others will receive more in interest than they pay in additional taxes. This will lead to some income redistribution among the members of the generation; some will be better off, and others will be worse off. If this results in greater inequality, we may not like the result. But it's certainly a far cry from the claim that the debt is burdening an entire generation.

Isn't the Foreign-Owned Debt Particularly Burdensome?
It is true that some of our public debt is owed to foreigners, and this portion does threaten to burden future generations. You and your children will pay taxes to provide interest payments to foreign investors, whose dollars thus acquired will permit them to claim a share of the goods and services that might otherwise go to other Americans. Consequently, our standard of living may be lowered somewhat.

The percentage of the debt owned by foreigners has been increasing since 1984, when foreign interests owned about 13 percent of the debt. The rate of increase was gradual until 1995 but became dramatic in the late 1990s. By 2008, foreigners—foreign central banks, corporations, and individuals—owned 48 percent of the debt. This growing percentage is a source of concern because (as noted earlier) it means foreigners can claim a larger share of our GDP. The next section will have more to say about interest payments on the debt.

Can Americans Afford the Interest Payments on the Public Debt?
Even if the federal government never has to pay off the national debt, it must continue to make interest payments on what it owes. After all, that's why people buy securities—to earn interest.

The ease with which Americans can pay the interest on the debt depends on how rapidly their incomes are growing. As long as incomes are growing at the same rate as interest payments, those interest payments will continue to absorb the same fraction of the average taxpayer's paycheck. But if interest payments grow more rapidly than income, they will begin to absorb a larger share.

If we all owned equal shares of the public debt, paying higher taxes would be offset by receiving interest payments on our shares. But whereas most people pay taxes, only some hold bonds and receive interest on the national debt. To the extent that bondholders have higher incomes to begin with, this process tends to produce greater inequality. This effect is at least partially modified by our progressive income-tax system. Those with higher incomes may receive more in interest payments, but they also pay more in taxes.

The higher tax rates needed to service the debt (that is, to make interest payments on it) may also have a negative effect on the incentive to work and earn taxable income. If individuals are allowed to keep less of what they earn, some may choose to work less. Others may attempt to avoid taxation by performing work that is not reported to taxing authorities—work for friends and barter transactions, for example.

Until about 1975, the burden imposed on taxpayers by the interest charges on the public debt was relatively stable. Exhibit 12.4 shows that although the interest payments were growing, so was our GDP—our measure of the economy's income and output. Thus, our ability to make those interest payments was growing also. The last column in Exhibit 12.4 shows that from World War II until 1975, interest payments on the debt represented a relatively constant fraction of GDP—between 1.3 and 1.8 percent. Then, in the late 1970s and early 1980s, the interest cost of the debt began to grow much more rapidly than GDP, primarily as a result of the record budget deficits that characterized this period. (Note that interest payments on the debt climbed to 2.0 percent of GDP in 1980 and to 3.4 percent in 1990.) This trend was a major concern for economists and politicians. Fortunately, in 1993 interest payments began to decline as a percentage of GDP. By 1995 they had dropped to 3.2 percent of GDP, and by 2008 to 1.5 percent of GDP, the lowest fraction since 1975.

Unfortunately, the recent trend is misleading. Debt interest payments in 2008 declined due to unusually low interest rates and other special factors, not because of slow growth in the debt. In fact, very large deficits are projected for 2009 ($1.8 trillion) and 2010 ($1.3 trillion). And substantial budget deficits are projected for the foreseeable future as baby boomers retire and expenditures for Social Security and Medicare increase. Without significant increases in social insurance taxes (or cuts in benefits), these increased expenditures will mean rising budget deficits, dramatically increasing the public debt and interest payments on the debt.

Concluding Comments on the Public Debt

So what can we conclude about the public debt? Given the debt's present size, making interest payments on the debt does not appear to represent a crushing

EXHIBIT 12.4

The Public Debt and Interest Payments in Relation to Gross Domestic Product

YEAR	PUBLIC DEBT (billions)	INTEREST PAYMENT ON DEBT (billions)	GROSS DOMESTIC PRODUCT (billions)	INTEREST AS A PERCENTAGE OF GDP
1930	$ 16.2	$ 0.7	$ 90.7	0.8%
1935	28.7	0.8	68.7	1.2
1940	42.7	0.9	95.4	0.9
1945	235.2	3.1	212.0	1.5
1950	219.0	4.8	265.8	1.8
1955	226.6	4.9	384.7	1.3
1960	236.8	6.9	504.6	1.4
1965	260.8	8.6	671.0	1.3
1970	283.2	14.4	985.4	1.5
1975	394.7	23.2	1,509.8	1.5
1980	711.9	52.5	2,644.1	2.0
1985	1,507.3	129.5	3,967.7	3.3
1990	2,411.6	184.2	5,481.5	3.4
1995	3,604.4	232.2	7,265.4	3.2
2000	3,409.8	222.8	9,962.6	2.2
2005	4,592.2	191.0	12,487.1	1.5
2008	5,803.0	136.0	14,264.6	1.0

Source: Budget of the United States Government, Fiscal Year 2010. (Washington, D.C.: U.S. Government Printing Office, 2009).

burden on American taxpayers. On the other hand, the debt is probably larger than it needs to be. Much of the debt was accumulated due to a lack of political restraint in the last two decades, not in response to automatic stabilizers or the use of discretionary policy. Perhaps more important, huge budgets deficits are projected over the next decade, deficits that would dramatically increase the size of the public debt and could cause the interest on the debt to become burdensome. As this edition goes to press, economists are warning of the need to rein in deficit spending after the current recession passes. That will require political will that has not always been evident in the past.

SUMMARY

The *federal budget* is a statement of the federal government's planned expenditures and anticipated receipts for the coming year. The major source of federal tax revenues is the personal income tax (estimated at 45 percent of total receipts in 2010), followed by social insurance taxes (37 percent). The remaining sources of revenue (customs duties, excise and estate taxes, etc.) are much less important.

The largest category of government expenditures is transfer payments, expenditures for which government receives no goods or services in return. Transfer payments accounted for an estimated 50 percent of 2010 outlays, followed by federal purchases of goods and services (40 percent) and debt interest (4 percent).

Although the primary objective of the federal budget is to pay for the activities of the federal government, there is a secondary objective as well. The federal budget may also be used as a tool for influencing the performance of the aggregate economy.

Prior to the 1930s, economists thought that the economy's self-correcting mechanism worked to quickly restore deviations from full employment. Because these *classical economists* had faith in the economy's ability to heal itself, they can be described as *nonactivist economists*, economists who do not believe that government should play an active role in attempting to guide the economy's performance. The Great Depression called this belief into question. In 1936, John Maynard Keynes, a British economist, contended that an economy could find itself in an unemployment equilibrium—a situation in which output and employment are stuck at low levels for some time. Today, we would say that whenever the economy is in equilibrium below potential, a *recessionary gap* exists. Alternatively, if the level of equilibrium GDP exceeds potential, an *inflationary gap* is present.

Activist economists (like Keynes) argue that government policies should be used to eliminate recessionary or inflationary gaps whenever they exist. One form of policy activism involves the use of *discretionary fiscal policy*. Discretionary fiscal policy is the deliberate changing of the level of government spending or taxation to guide the economy's performance. According to activists, when a recessionary gap exists, the appropriate fiscal policy would involve increasing government spending or reducing taxes. Either of these policies would tend to increase aggregate demand and close the recessionary gap. When an inflationary gap exists, government spending should be reduced or taxes should be increased. These policies would reduce aggregate demand and thereby reduce inflationary pressures.

In addition to discretionary fiscal policy, the economy contains *automatic stabilizers* that help to improve its performance. Automatic stabilizers are the changes in the level of government spending or taxation that occur automatically whenever the level of aggregate income (GDP) changes. The federal income tax and unemployment compensation are examples of automatic stabilizers. These features of the fiscal system help to reduce the magnitude of fluctuations in total spending and thereby help prevent wide swings in the levels of output and employment.

When we resort to fiscal policy to combat unemployment or inflation, we are deliberately tampering with the federal budget. When unemployment exists, the activist model suggests that government should plan a *deficit budget* to stimulate the economy. When inflation is a problem, a *surplus budget* is called for. Only when the economy is operating at full employment is a *balanced budget* appropriate.

Critics of discretionary fiscal policy argue that deficit-financed government spending can be harmful to economic growth because it tends to crowd out private investment spending. *Crowding out* occurs when government borrowing pushes up interest rates and the higher interest rates reduce, or crowd out, investment spending.

The possibility of crowding out is one criticism of discretionary fiscal policy, but there are others. Another major criticism stems from the substantial time lags that occur between the appearance of a problem (a recessionary or inflationary gap) and the economic impact of the remedial policy. As a consequence, by the time the policy is felt, it may no longer be appropriate to the state of the economy.

A final limitation of discretionary fiscal policy is its *expansionary bias*. Expansionary fiscal policy is more attractive politically than contractionary policy. This makes it easy to incur deficits, but difficult to incur surpluses.

When the federal government incurs a deficit, it finances that deficit by borrowing. This results in an increase in the *public debt*—the accumulated borrowing of the federal government. The burden of the debt is perhaps best represented by interest payments (on the debt) as a fraction of GDP. Although this ratio has been declining since 1990, projected budget deficits are likely to add significantly to the public debt and raise its interest burden.

KEY TERMS

Activist economists	Classical economists	Nonactivist economists
Automatic stabilizers	Crowding out	Public debt
Balanced budget	Discretionary fiscal policy	Recessionary gap
Budget deficit	Federal budget	Transfer payments
Budget surplus	Inflationary gap	

STUDY QUESTIONS

Fill in the Blanks

1. Government expenditures for which no goods or services are received in exchange

   are known as _____.

2. In the period from 1960 to 2010, the fraction of government receipts coming from

   _____ taxes increased dramatically.

3. Economists who see a role for government in guiding the economy's performance are

   described as _____.

4. According to the activist (or Keynesian) model, if an economy is experiencing unemployment, the federal government

   should _____ or

   _____ or do both.

5. If the federal government spends more than it takes in from tax revenues, we say that

   it is incurring a(n) _____;
   if it takes in more in taxes than it spends,

   it has a(n) _____.

6. The amount by which the equilibrium GDP falls short of potential GDP is known

   as the _____ gap.

7. The deliberate changing of government spending or taxation in order to guide the economy's performance is referred to as

   _____.

8. _____ tend to reduce the magnitude of fluctuations in total spending without any action by policymakers.

9. According to the activist model, the appropriate fiscal policy to combat inflation

   would be to _____ or

   _____ or do both.

10. If the economy is operating at full employment and Congress decides to engage in deficit spending, the result would proba-

    bly be _____.

11. According to activists, a(n) _____ budget would be appropriate if the economy was operating at full employment.

12. The accumulated borrowings of the federal government are called the

    _____.

13. Examples of automatic stabilizers include unemployment compensation and the

    _____.

14. Political considerations may make it particularly difficult to use fiscal policy in

    combating _____.

15. The time that elapses before policymakers recognize the need for a policy change is

    known as the _____ lag.

Multiple Choice

1. In the period from 1960 to 2010,
   a) personal income taxes have grown as a fraction of federal tax revenue.
   b) corporate income taxes have grown as a fraction of federal tax revenue.
   c) social insurance taxes have grown as a fraction of federal tax revenue.
   d) excise taxes have grown as a fraction of federal tax revenue.

2. The largest category of federal government expenditures is
   a) interest on the national debt.
   b) transfer payments.
   c) purchases of goods and services.
   d) military spending.

3. Suppose the economy is experiencing substantial unemployment and a rising budget deficit. An activist economist would probably recommend
   a) raising taxes to reduce the budget deficit.
   b) waiting for falling wages and prices to restore full employment.
   c) cutting taxes and increasing government spending to combat the unemployment.
   d) reducing unemployment compensation to force unemployed workers to look for jobs.

4. When an inflationary gap exists, activists would recommend a
   a) tax reduction.
   b) surplus budget.
   c) increase in government spending.
   d) deficit budget.

Use the following exhibit in answering questions 5–8.

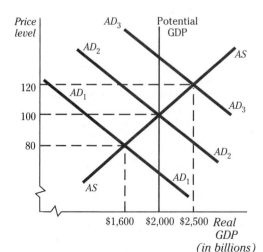

5. If the economy is in equilibrium at the intersection of AD_1 and AS, then
   a) a recessionary gap exists; the gap is equal to $400 billion.
   b) a recessionary gap exists; the gap is equal to $900 billion.
   c) an inflationary gap exists; the gap is equal to $400 billion.
   d) an inflationary gap exists; the gap is equal to $900 billion.

6. If the economy is in equilibrium at the intersection of the AS curve and
   a) AD_1, activists would recommend a surplus budget.
   b) AD_2, activists would recommend a balanced budget.
   c) AD_3, activists would recommend a deficit budget.
   d) AD_2, activists would recommend a deficit budget.

7. **Review Question**: Suppose the economy is in short-run equilibrium at an output of $1,600 billion. If activist policies are not used, the economy will
   a) eventually return to an output of $2,000 billion but at a price level less than 80.
   b) eventually return to an output of $2,000 billion but at a price level of 120.
   c) remain at an output of $1,600 billion indefinitely.
   d) eventually return to an output of $2,000 billion but at a price level of 100.

8. **Review Question**: Suppose the economy is in short-run equilibrium at an output of $2,500 billion. If activist policies are not used, the economy will
   a) return to an output of $2,000 billion when wage contracts expire and the aggregate demand curve shifts to the left.
   b) remain at an output of $2,500 billion indefinitely.
   c) return to an output of $2,000 billion when wage contracts are renegotiated and the aggregate supply curve shifts left.
   d) return to an output of $2,000 billion when the aggregate demand curve automatically shifts back to AD_2.

9. Which of the following is *not* an advantage of automatic stabilizers?
   a) They do not involve the political hassle associated with discretionary fiscal policy.
   b) They help speed recovery from a recession.
   c) They go to work automatically, so lags are minimal.
   d) They help prevent a minor downturn from becoming a major recession.

10. Because of automatic stabilizers, the budget will
    a) tend toward surplus during a recession.
    b) tend toward deficit during an economic expansion.
    c) tend toward deficit during a recession.
    d) always remain in balance.

11. According to the activist model, when the economy is in a recession, the shortest route to a balanced budget may entail
    a) higher taxes.
    b) less government spending.
    c) lower taxes and more government spending.
    d) Both a and b

12. Which of the following statements is true?
    a) Unplanned deficits occur when the economy performs better than expected.
    b) The "expansionary bias" is a source of budget surpluses.
    c) Activists support deficit spending during periods of inflation.
    d) If the economy is operating at full employment, a reduction in taxes may increase inflationary pressures.

13. A legitimate concern regarding the national debt relates to
    a) the higher taxes that are necessary to make the interest payments on the debt.
    b) our inability to pay off such a large sum.

    c) the fraction of the debt owed to foreign factions.
    d) Both a and c

14. "Crowding out" refers to
    a) the unwillingness of politicians to raise taxes or cut government spending to combat inflation.
    b) the reduction in consumption spending that results from an increase in tax rates.
    c) the reduction in investment spending that occurs when government borrowing pushes up interest rates.
    d) the reduced standard of living suffered by U.S. citizens as foreigners purchase a larger share of our public debt.

15. Deficit spending is *least* likely to harm economic growth if it
    a) occurs when the economy is operating at or beyond potential GDP.
    b) is used to finance increases in transfer payments.
    c) crowds out a substantial amount of investment spending.
    d) occurs when there is substantial unemployment.

16. The lags associated with discretionary fiscal policy
    a) make it more effective.
    b) may make it counterproductive.
    c) apply only to changes in government spending, not to changes in tax rates.
    d) apply only to changes in tax rates, not to changes in government spending.

17. The phrase *expansionary bias* refers to the fact that
    a) discretionary fiscal policy works with a lagged effect.
    b) politicians are more willing to lower taxes and increase spending than they are to do the opposite.
    c) policymakers tend to overestimate the size of the recessionary gap.
    d) deficit-financed government spending can lead to crowding out.

Problems and Questions for Discussion

1. When the government increases spending to combat unemployment, why shouldn't it increase taxes to pay for the increased spending? Why run a deficit instead?

2. Deficit spending for education and scientific research may impose less of a tax burden on future generations than deficit-financed increases in transfer payments. Explain.

3. Some experts argue that the ratio of interest payments (on the debt) to GDP is the most reasonable measure of the burden the public debt imposes on society. Explain.

4. Most deficits are not the result of discretionary fiscal policy; they are the result of downturns in the economy. Explain.

5. Why is the fraction of the debt owed to foreigners more troublesome than the fraction we owe to ourselves?

6. What advantages can you see to using tax reductions rather than government spending increases to combat unemployment?

Can your personal values influence which of these approaches you prefer? Explain.

7. George Humphrey, secretary of the treasury during the Eisenhower administration, once declared: "We cannot spend ourselves rich." What do you suppose he meant? Would Keynes agree? Why or why not?

8. List the various types of lags associated with fiscal policy. Why is the existence of lags a serious limitation of such policies?

9. Suppose the federal government decided to pay off the public debt. How would it go about doing it? What do you suppose would be the impact on the economy?

10. Concern over continuing federal deficits once spawned a movement to amend the Constitution of the United States to require the federal government to balance its budget each year. Can you think of any reasons to argue against a balanced budget amendment? Why would it be difficult to carry out such a rule during a recession?

ANSWER KEY

Fill in the Blanks

1. transfer payments
2. social insurance
3. activists
4. increase government spending; reduce taxes
5. deficit; surplus

6. recessionary
7. discretionary fiscal policy
8. Automatic stabilizers
9. reduce government spending; increase taxes
10. inflation

11. balanced
12. public or national debt
13. federal income tax
14. inflation
15. recognition

Multiple Choice

1. c
2. b
3. c
4. b

5. a
6. b
7. a
8. c

9. b
10. c
11. c

12. d
13. d
14. c

15. d
16. b
17. b

13

Money, Banking, and Monetary Policy

LEARNING OBJECTIVES

1. State the three basic functions of money and explain each.
2. Distinguish between money and near money.
3. Distinguish between the M-1 and M-2 money-supply definitions.
4. Explain how depository institutions create money.
5. Calculate the deposit multiplier and explain its purpose.
6. Discuss the functions of the Federal Reserve.
7. Define monetary policy.
8. Describe the three major policy tools the Fed uses to control the money supply.
9. Explain how changes in the money supply lead to changes in output, employment, and prices.
10. Discuss the factors that limit the effectiveness of monetary policy.

Everything you've read thus far in the text has implied a monetary system—the existence of some kind of money. Most of us take the use of money for granted. We pay our bills in money and expect to be paid in money. We compare prices, incomes, and even gross domestic products in terms of money. But exactly what is money, and why is it essential to an economic system? What determines the amount of money in existence, and where does it come from? In this chapter we will provide answers to those questions. We begin by considering the functions performed by money and deciding what constitutes money in the U.S. economy. Next, we examine how banks "create" money and consider why individuals can't do the same. Then we introduce you to the Federal Reserve—the independent government agency responsible for regulating the money supply and performing other duties related to the banking system. You will discover how the Fed attempts to use monetary policy to guide the economy's performance and what the limitations of its policies are. Let's start by examining what is meant by money.

WHAT IS MONEY?

Economists define money in terms of the functions it performs; anything that performs the functions of money *is* money. Money performs three basic functions. First, money serves as a **medium of exchange**: the generally accepted means of payment for goods and services. A medium of exchange enables members of a society to transact their business without resorting to barter. In a barter economy, goods are exchanged for goods. A shoemaker who wants to buy a painting must locate an artist in need of shoes. As you can imagine, this requirement makes trading slow and burdensome. Money facilitates trade by permitting the shoemaker to exchange shoes for money and then use the money to purchase a painting or other goods and services.

The second function of money is to provide a **standard of value**, a unit for expressing the prices of goods and services. In a barter economy, we would need an almost endless list of prices, one for each possible exchange. For example, we might find that one painting equals (exchanges for) one pair of shoes and that one pair of shoes equals four bushels of apples and that four bushels of apples equals two shirts. Which is more expensive: a shirt or a pair of shoes? It may take you a moment to figure out the answer because the absence of a standard of value makes the communication and comparison of prices very difficult. The use of money simplifies this process by enabling us to state all prices in terms of a particular standard of value, such as the dollar. Using the dollar as a standard of value, we can easily determine that if a pair of shoes sells for $50 and a shirt sells for $25, the shoes are twice as expensive as the shirt.

Finally, money is a **store of value**, a vehicle for accumulating or storing wealth to be used at some future date. A tomato farmer would find it difficult to accumulate wealth in the form of tomatoes. They don't keep very well! Money is not a perfect store of value, especially in inflationary times, but clearly it is better than a bushel of perishable tomatoes. By exchanging the tomato crop for money, the farmer can begin to build a nest egg for retirement or to save for some major purchase—a tractor or a new barn, for example. In a sense, the availability of a store of value widens the range of spending choices available to individuals and businesses. Their options are no longer limited to what they can afford to buy (trade for) with a single period's income.

Money and Near Money

What qualifies as money in the U.S. economy? We all know that coins and paper currency are money, and a check is usually as good as cash. Non-interest-bearing checking deposits at commercial banks[1] are known as **demand deposits** because the bank promises to pay at once, or "on demand," the amount specified by the owner of the account. Checks drawn on demand-deposit accounts are an accepted medium of exchange; they are measured in dollars, the standard of value in the United States, and it is certainly possible to accumulate wealth in your checking account. But although it is relatively easy to agree that currency—coins and paper money—and demand deposits are money, some other assets are more difficult to categorize. An **asset** is anything of value owned by an entity—that is, by an individual or an organization, such as a business. Many assets perform some, but not all, of the functions of money. Others perform all the functions of money but do so incompletely.

One debate among economists concerns the proper classification of **savings deposits**—interest-bearing deposits at banks and savings institutions. The traditional household savings account cannot be used directly to purchase goods and services; hence, such deposits do not qualify as a medium of exchange. As a consequence, economists have generally classified savings deposits as **near money**—assets that are not money but that can be converted quickly into money. Not everyone has supported this position, however. Some economists argue that savings deposits should be considered money because they can be converted easily into cash or demand deposits and therefore have essentially the same impact on spending as other financial assets do.

Innovations in banking, moreover, have blurred the distinction between savings deposits and demand deposits. Consider, for example, the negotiable order of withdrawal (NOW) account commonly offered by banks and other financial institutions. The **NOW account** is essentially a savings account on which the depositor is permitted to write checks. Here we seem to have the best of both worlds: the convenience of a checking account plus the earning power of a savings account. Banks have also developed automatic transfer service (ATS) accounts, in which funds from savings can be transferred automatically to a checking account. These types of deposits probably should be considered along with demand deposits as a form of money. But we still face the task of categorizing financial assets that do not function as media of exchange. These include household savings accounts, U.S. government savings

---

[1] Commercial banks are so named because, in their early days, they specialized in loans to businesses. Today, commercial banks engage in a much wider range of lending, including home mortgage loans, automobile loans, and other consumer loans.

bonds, and shares in money-market mutual funds.[2] Are such assets money or not? The answer is not clear, even to the Federal Reserve.

Credit Cards and Debit Cards

If you're accustomed to paying for your books (or your pizza) with a credit card, you probably wonder where that "plastic" fits into this classification system. After all, credit cards seem to work as well as cash, and they are often even more convenient. Actually, credit cards are neither money nor near money; they are simply a means of deferring payment. (Said differently, credit cards are a way of obtaining credit—loans; hence the term *credit card*.) When you pay for something with cash or a check, you have completed the transaction. But when you buy something with a credit card, you are incurring a debt that you ultimately will have to settle by sending the credit card company either cash or a check.

The cousin of the credit card is the *debit card*, a card that allows you to withdraw money automatically from your checking account. When you use a debit card to make a purchase, you are, in effect, telling your bank to withdraw money from your account and transfer it to the store owner's account. Because a debit card is simply a way of accessing your checking balance, it does not constitute a different type of money.

Definitions of the Money Supply

As we noted earlier, the Federal Reserve is responsible for controlling the money supply—the total amount of money in the economy. Before the Fed (as the Federal Reserve is often called) can attempt to control the money supply, it must, of course, decide what money is.

Rather than settling on a single definition of money, the Fed has developed two. The narrowest, **M-1**, is composed of currency in the hands of the public *plus* checkable deposits. **Checkable deposits** are all types of deposits on which customers can write checks: demand deposits at commercial banks; NOW accounts; credit union share draft accounts, which are essentially the same as NOW accounts but are provided by credit unions; and ATS accounts. The primary characteristic of all M-1 money is that it can function easily as a medium of exchange. As you can see from Exhibit 13.1, about 53 percent of this readily

---

[2] A mutual fund is an organization that pools people's money and invests it in stocks or bonds or other financial assets. A money-market mutual fund invests in short-term securities, such as U.S. Treasury bills. If you own shares in a money-market mutual fund, you can write checks against your account, but generally they must exceed some minimum amount (commonly $500). This makes money-market funds less useful for everyday transactions involving smaller amounts of money.

EXHIBIT 13.1

M-1 and M-2 as of June 1, 2009 (billions of dollars)

M-1

Currency (coins and paper money)	$ 851.0
Demand deposits	400.8
Other checkable deposits	345.2
Total M-1	$1,597.0

M-2

M-1 plus small savings accounts and money-market mutual fund balances	$8,349.4

Source: Federal Reserve Statistical Release, "Money Stock Measures," June 11, 2009.

spendable money is in the form of currency. Demand deposits account for another 25 percent of the M-1 money supply. The remaining 22 percent is in other checkable deposits.

The Federal Reserve has also developed a broader definition of the money supply, which it calls M-2. The **M-2** portion of the money supply includes everything in M-1 plus money-market mutual fund balances, money-market deposits at savings institutions, and certain other financial assets that do not function as a medium of exchange but that can be converted easily into currency or checkable deposits—small savings deposits (less than $100,000) at banks and savings institutions, for example.

Throughout this chapter and the remainder of the text, we will use the M-1 definition of money: We assume that money consists of currency plus checkable deposits. These assets function easily as a medium of exchange, the function that many economists regard as the most important characteristic of money.

HOW DEPOSITORY INSTITUTIONS CREATE MONEY

Where does M-1 money come from? The currency component is easy to explain. It comes from the Federal Reserve, which supplies banks with enough coins and paper money to meet the needs of their customers. (Here and throughout the chapter, we use the term *bank* in a general way to refer to all types of depository institutions—commercial banks and savings, or thrift, institutions.[3]) But the checkable-deposits element of M-1 is more of a mystery. Checkable deposits are actually created by the numerous banks that offer such accounts.

A Bank's Balance Sheet

To demonstrate how banks create checkable-deposit money, we can use a simple accounting concept known as a balance sheet. A **balance sheet** is a statement of a business's assets and liabilities. The assets of a business are, as we saw earlier, the things of value that it owns. **Liabilities** are the debts of the business, what it owes. The difference between the business's assets and liabilities is the **owners' equity**, which represents the interest of the owner or owners of a business in its assets. (Owners' equity is also known as **bank capital** or **equity capital**. All banks face minimum requirements for the amount of capital they must maintain. For a closer look at this requirement and the role it played in the recent financial crisis, see the appendix to this chapter.) These accounting statements "balance"; whatever value of the business is not owed to creditors must belong to the owners: assets = liabilities + owners' equity.

We turn now to Exhibit 13.2 to examine the balance sheet of a hypothetical bank, the Gainsville National Bank. The left-hand side of the balance sheet lists the bank's assets. The first entry, *reserves*, includes cash in the bank's vault plus funds on deposit with the Federal Reserve. Banks are required by law to hold a

---

EXHIBIT 13.2

A Hypothetical Balance Sheet: Gainsville National Bank

ASSETS		LIABILITIES AND OWNERS' EQUITY	
Reserves (vault cash plus deposits with the Federal Reserve)	$ 200,000	Checkable deposits	$1,000,000
		Savings deposits	360,000
Securities	450,000	Owners' equity	240,000
Loans	800,000		
Property	150,000	Total liabilities	
Total assets	$1,600,000	+ owners' equity	$1,600,000

---

[3] There are three major types of thrift institutions: savings and loan associations, mutual savings banks, and credit unions.

certain amount of their assets as required reserves. The **reserve requirement** is stated as a percentage of the bank's checkable deposits and can be met only by cash in its vault and deposits with the Fed. Because reserves earn no interest income, banks understandably try to maintain only the minimum legal requirement. Reserves greater than the minimum requirement are called **excess reserves**, and they play an important role in a bank's ability to create checkable-deposit money.

The next two entries on the left-hand side, *securities* and *loans*, are the interest-earning assets of the bank. Banks usually have substantial holdings of U.S. Treasury bills and other securities that are both safe and highly liquid—that is, easily converted into cash. Loans offer less liquidity but generally have the advantage of earning a higher rate of interest.

The final entry on the left-hand side of the balance sheet is *property*, the physical assets of the bank: the bank building, its office equipment, and any other nonfinancial holdings of the organization.

The right-hand side of the balance sheet lists liabilities and owners' equity. In our example the only liabilities entered are *checkable deposits* and *savings deposits*. Although both items are assets for customers, they are debts to the bank. If we write a check on our checking account or ask to withdraw money from our savings account, the bank has to pay. That makes each of those accounts a liability to the bank.

The only remaining entry on the right-hand side of Exhibit 13.2 is *owners' equity*, the owners' claims on the assets of the business. As you know, the two sides of the statement have to balance, because whatever value of the business is not owed to creditors (the bank's liabilities) must belong to the owners (owners' equity).

The Creation of Checkable Deposits

Earlier we noted that all banks must meet a reserve requirement established by the Federal Reserve. Let's assume that the reserve requirement for our hypothetical bank is 20 percent. Our bank has $1,000,000 in checkable deposits; therefore, it is required by law to maintain $200,000 in reserves ($1,000,000 × 0.20 = $200,000). As you can see from the bank's balance sheet, it has precisely $200,000 in reserves.

Even in the absence of regulation, banks would need to maintain some reserves against their deposits. The bank must have the currency to pay a depositor who walks into the Gainsville Bank and writes a check for "cash." However, the bank does not have to maintain $1 in reserve for every $1 of checkable deposits it accepts because it is unlikely that all depositors will request their money simultaneously. In fact, while some depositors are writing checks and drawing down their accounts, others are making deposits and thereby increasing their balances.

The key to a bank's ability to create money is this **fractional reserve principle**, the principle that a bank needs to maintain only a fraction of a dollar in reserve for each dollar of its checkable deposits. Once a bank discovers this principle, it can loan out the idle funds and earn interest. That's the name of the game in banking—earning interest by lending money. In the process of making loans, banks create money: specifically, checkable deposits. We can see how this is true by working through the balance sheet entries of the lending bank. To simplify things somewhat, we will show only the changes in assets and liabilities for each entry, not the entire balance sheet.

Step One: Accepting Deposits   Let's assume that one of the bank's depositors, Adam Swift, deposits $1,000 in cash in his checking account. We would reflect this change by increasing the bank's checkable deposits by $1,000 and increasing its reserves by the same amount.

The bank now has an additional $1,000 in cash reserves (clearly an asset) and the liability of paying out that same amount if Swift writes checks totaling $1,000. Because the bank's deposits have increased by $1,000, it must now maintain an additional $200 in required reserves (20 percent of $1,000). The Gainsville Bank now finds itself with excess reserves of $800:

GAINSVILLE NATIONAL BANK

ASSETS			LIABILITIES	
Reserves		+$1,000	Checkable deposits	+$1,000
required	+$200			
excess	+$800			
		+$1,000		+$1,000

What will the Gainsville Bank do with those excess reserves? If it simply lets them sit in the vault, it would be sacrificing the interest that could be earned on $800. Because the bank wants to show a profit, it will probably use those excess reserves to make loans.

Step Two: Making a Loan   Let's assume that another resident of Gainsville, June Malthus, walks in and asks to borrow $800. How will we record this transaction? On the asset side, we will record a loan for $800. The bank receives this asset in the form of a note, or IOU, agreeing to repay the $800 plus interest. On the liability side of the balance sheet, we increase checkable deposits by $800 (from $1,000 to $1,800):

GAINSVILLE NATIONAL BANK

ASSETS		LIABILITIES		
Reserves	$1,000	Checkable deposits		$1,800
Loans	+$ 800	Adam Swift	$1,000	
		June Malthus	$ 800	
	$1,800			$1,800

This last entry may seem puzzling to you if you have not yet borrowed money. The way you generally receive money borrowed from a bank is in the form of a checking account with your name on it. This is the money-creating transaction of the bank. Malthus has exchanged a piece of paper (an IOU) that is *not* money for something that *is* money, checkable deposits. If you think about this process, you'll see the logic of it: The Gainsville Bank is now using $1,000 in reserves to support $1,800 of checkable deposits. Because of the fractional reserve principle, bank officials can be confident that this support is adequate; they know that not all the original depositors will withdraw their money simultaneously.

Not everyone can create money through lending. When you lend money to a friend, your friend ends up with more money, but you have less. The total money supply has not increased. However, when you borrow money from a bank, you end up with more money, but no one has any less. And the money supply actually increases.

How do we explain the difference? Your IOU does not circulate as money, whereas the IOU of a bank does. What happens when you deposit cash in your checking account? You do not reduce your personal money supply as you would if you had made a loan to your friend. Instead, you merely exchange cash (a form of money) for an IOU known as a checkable deposit (a different form of money). Your currency then serves as reserves for supporting loans that result in the creation of additional deposits. Someone else ends up with more money, but you don't have any less. Once you understand this process, you can see that the bank has really "created" money.

Step Three: Using the Loan   Now that we have seen how banks create money, we can ask what happens to that money when it is used to buy something. Let's assume that Malthus uses her newly acquired checking account to buy furniture in the nearby town of Sellmore—at the Sellmore Furniture Store. Let's also assume that she spends the entire amount of her loan. She will write a check on the Gainsville Bank and give it to the owner of the Sellmore Furniture Store, who will deposit it in the firm's account at the First National Bank of Sellmore. The Sellmore Bank will then send the check to the district Federal

Reserve Bank for collection. (One function of the Federal Reserve is to provide a check collection and clearing service. We'll discuss this and other functions of the Fed later in the chapter.) After the Federal Reserve Bank receives the check, it will reduce the reserve account of the Gainsville Bank by $800 and increase the reserve account of the Sellmore Bank by $800. It will then forward the check to the Gainsville Bank, where changes in assets and liabilities will be recorded. Malthus has spent the $800 in her checking account, so checkable deposits will be reduced by that amount (from $1,800 to $1,000). The bank's reserves have also fallen by $800 (from $1,000 to $200), the amount of reserves lost to the Sellmore Bank.

GAINSVILLE NATIONAL BANK

ASSETS		LIABILITIES	
Reserves		Checkable deposits	
($1,000 − $800)	$ 200	($1,800 − $800)	$1,000
required $200		Adam Swift $1,000	
excess 0		June Malthus 0	
Loans	+$ 800		
	$1,000		$1,000

Note that the Gainsville Bank no longer has any excess reserves. It has reserves of $200, the exact amount required. If the bank had loaned Malthus more than $800 (the initial amount of its excess reserves), it would now be in violation of the reserve requirement. But each bank realizes that when it makes a loan, it will probably lose reserves to other banks as the borrower spends the loan. For that reason, *individual banks must limit their loans to the amount of their excess reserves*. That's one of the most important principles in this chapter, so be sure you understand it before reading any further.

The Multiple Expansion of Loans and Deposits

Recall that the money loaned in the form of checkable deposits circulates. Thus, the money created when the Gainsville Bank made a loan to June Malthus is not destroyed when she uses the loan but rather is simply transferred from one bank to another. The checkable deposits and reserves originally represented on the balance sheet of the Gainsville Bank may now be found on the balance sheet of the Sellmore Bank. This means that the Sellmore Bank will now be able to expand its loans.

We know that each bank can expand its loans to create checkable deposits equal to the amount of its excess reserves. Assuming that the Sellmore Bank also faces a reserve requirement of 20 percent and that it had no excess reserves to begin with, it will now have excess reserves of $640. How did we arrive at that amount? The Sellmore Bank increased its checkable deposits, and thus its reserves, by $800, the amount deposited by the owner of the Sellmore Furniture Store. With a 20 percent reserve requirement, the increase in required reserves is $160 ($800 × .20 = $160). That leaves $640 in excess reserves, which can be used to support new loans and create additional checking deposits.

This expansion of loans and deposits continues as the money created by one bank is deposited in another bank, where it is used to support even more loans. In Exhibit 13.3, we see that the banking system as a whole can eventually create $4,000 in new loans and new money (checkable deposits) from the initial $800 increase in excess reserves received by the Gainsville Bank. We also see the difference between the ability of a single bank and the banking system as a whole to create money. Whereas an individual bank must restrict its loans—and consequently its ability to create money—to the amount of its excess reserves, the banking system as a whole can create loans and deposits equal to some multiple of the excess reserves received by the system. In our example that multiple is 5; the banking system was able to create loans and deposits five times greater than the initial increase in excess reserves ($800 × 5 = $4,000).

EXHIBIT 13.3

The Creation of Money by the Banking System

BANK	NEWLY ACQUIRED DEPOSITS AND RESERVES	REQUIRED RESERVES (20 percent of checkable deposits)	POTENTIAL FOR NEW LOANS (creating money)
Gainsville	$1,000.00	$200.00	$ 800.00
Sellmore	800.00	160.00	640.00
Third bank	640.00	128.00	512.00
Fourth bank	512.00	102.40	409.60
Fifth bank	409.60	81.92	327.68
Sixth bank	327.68	65.54	262.14
Seventh bank	262.14	52.43	209.71
All others	1,048.58	209.71	838.87
Total amount of money created by the banking system			$4,000.00*

*This figure represents the *maximum* amount of money that the banking system could create from an initial $800 increase in excess reserves. The example assumes that all banks face a 20 percent reserve requirement and that they are all "loaned up" (have no excess reserves) initially.

The Deposit Multiplier

Fortunately we need not work through all the individual transactions to predict the maximum amount of money that the banking system will be able to create. As a general rule, the banking system can alter the money supply by an amount equal to the initial change in excess reserves times the reciprocal of the reserve requirement:

$$\text{Changes in excess reserves} \times \frac{1}{\substack{\text{Reserve requirement} \\ \text{(written as a decimal)}}} = \substack{\text{Maximum possible increase in} \\ \text{checkable deposits by the} \\ \text{banking system as a whole}}$$

The reciprocal of the reserve requirement, 1 divided by the reserve requirement, yields a number called the deposit multiplier. The **deposit multiplier** is the multiple by which checkable deposits (in the entire banking system) increase or decrease in response to an initial change in excess reserves.

The reserve ratio in our hypothetical example is .20, so the deposit multiplier must be 1/.20, or 5. Therefore, an $800 increase in excess reserves will permit the banking system to create up to $4,000 of new demand deposits. This $4,000 figure is really the *maximum* possible expansion in checkable deposits, given the stated change in excess reserves and the existing reserve requirement. The actual amount may, for a variety of reasons, be less than the maximum predicted.

An illustration will help. Suppose that the recipient of Malthus's check decides not to redeposit the entire amount in a checking account. This event will reduce the amount of money being passed on to the remaining banks in the system and thus reduce the amount the system can create through lending. The expansion in checkable deposits will also be less than the maximum if bankers maintain some excess reserves. For instance, perhaps some bankers anticipate deposit withdrawals and prepare for them by holding, rather than lending, excess reserves. Or banks may be forced to hold excess reserves simply because they cannot find enough loan customers. For all these reasons, the expansion in the checkable-deposit component of the money supply may be substantially less than the maximum predicted by the deposit multiplier.

The Destruction of Checkable Deposits

The deposit multiplier can also work in reverse. Suppose that Adam Swift, our original depositor, withdrew $1,000 in cash from his account at the Gainsville Bank and kept it in his wallet. What would this transaction do to the money supply? The initial transaction merely changes its composition: Swift is giving up his claim to $1,000 in checkable deposits (a form of money) and is receiving in return $1,000 in cash (another form of money). The size of the money supply remains the same, even though more cash and fewer checkable deposits are in circulation.

What happens next? When Swift withdraws $1,000 from his checking account, the Gainsville Bank loses $1,000 in deposits and reserves:

GAINSVILLE NATIONAL BANK

ASSETS		LIABILITIES	
Reserves	−$1,000	Checkable deposits	−$1,000

Assuming that the bank had no excess reserves to begin with, it now finds itself with a reserve deficiency; that is, it doesn't have sufficient reserves to meet the 20 percent reserve requirement. What is the amount of the deficiency? It is $800—the difference between the amount that Swift has withdrawn from his checking account ($1,000) and the reserve that the bank was required to maintain on that deposit ($200). To correct this deficiency, the bank has two choices. One is to sell $800 worth of securities (remember, banks hold securities, particularly government securities, which earn interest and can be converted easily into cash); another is to allow $800 worth of loans to be repaid without making new loans. In either case, the next bank in the sequence is going to lose $800 worth of deposits and reserves as its depositors buy those securities or repay those loans. That bank will then be faced with a reserve deficiency; it too may need to sell securities or reduce the amount of its loans to build up reserves.

As you may suspect, this contractionary process can spread to other banks in the system and result in a multiple contraction of loans and deposits that is similar to the multiple expansion we observed earlier. Once again, the limit to this process is set by the reserve requirement and the deposit multiplier derived from that requirement. To predict the maximum contraction in checkable deposits, we multiply the initial reserve deficiency times the deposit multiplier. In our example that would mean a reduction of $4,000 ($800 × 5 = $4,000).

THE FEDERAL RESERVE SYSTEM

Now we are ready to examine the role of the Federal Reserve, the central bank of the United States. Virtually every industrialized nation in the world has a **central bank**—a government agency responsible for controlling the national money supply. At one time, the size of a nation's money supply was determined largely by its stock of gold. That's because most of a nation's money supply was currency, and virtually all nations "backed" their currency with gold.[4] But things change. Today, nothing backs the U.S. dollar (or any other major currency) except the faith that the currency can be used to make purchases. Moreover, currency is only a fraction of the money supply in most industrialized nations (about half in the United States, according to the M-1 definition); the rest is checkable deposits. As a consequence, the size of a nation's money supply is no longer tied to its gold stock. Instead, it is determined by its central bank. In the United Kingdom the central bank is the Bank of England, in Japan the Bank of Japan, in the United States the Federal Reserve System.

The Origin of the Federal Reserve

The Federal Reserve was established in 1913. Its original purpose was to act as a "lender of last resort," to make loans to banks only when all other sources had dried up. It was thought that by performing this function the Federal Reserve could prevent or stop the *financial panics* that had characterized this period—situations in which depositors lost confidence in banks and rushed to withdraw their money. In addition to this primary function, the Federal Reserve was also authorized to provide an efficient mechanism for collecting and clearing checks throughout the United States and to help supervise banks to ensure the prudence of their investment and lending practices.

Although the Fed still performs all the functions noted, the contemporary Fed's primary responsibility is to help stabilize the economy by controlling the money supply. We expect the Federal Reserve to manipulate the money supply in an effort to prevent (or combat) unemployment and inflation, a responsibility much broader than the one envisioned by Congress in 1913. Because the responsibility for controlling the money supply grew as the federal government assumed a greater role in managing the economy, the modern Federal Reserve organization is far more powerful than Congress intended it to be.[5] (Some

---

[4] For example, between 1900 and 1933 the United States issued gold certificates that could be redeemed for gold coins. In 1934, the United States stopped *redeeming* currency for gold but continued to maintain 25 percent gold backing for currency. (The Fed could issue $4 of currency for each $1 of gold it held.) Throughout this period, gold continued to be used to pay international debts, and this gradually caused the U.S. gold supply to shrink to low levels. In 1968, the requirement that Fed currency be backed by a gold reserve was eliminated, and in 1971 the United States stopped using gold to settle international debts. That few people noticed either of these events is an indication that the value of our currency stems from what it can buy, not from the backing provided by some scarce commodity.

[5] Unlike central banks in other nations, the Federal Reserve is an independent organization that is not required to take orders from any other agency or branch of government. This gives the Federal Reserve at least the appearance of somewhat greater independence than other central banks. Members of Congress periodically threaten to revoke this independence when the Fed pursues policies they disagree with.

economists argue that it is far too powerful; others believe a powerful Fed is essential for a stable economy. These competing views are examined in Chapter 14.) Moreover, in the wake of the recent financial crisis, the Fed's power is likely to expand even more. In June 2009, President Obama proposed enlarging the Fed's responsibilities to include the regulation of financial risk across the entire system—a dramatic extension of its power. This expansion in the Fed's duties is controversial and may not be approved by Congress. Either way, the Fed will continue to play an important role in guiding our economy—a role that we will examine in detail after taking a closer look at the organization of the modern Federal Reserve System.

The Organization and Functions of the Federal Reserve System

The Federal Reserve System is composed of a board of governors that is located in Washington, D.C., and 12 regional Federal Reserve banks located in major cities throughout the country. The seven members of the board of governors are appointed by the president of the United States to serve 14-year terms. These terms are structured so that one expires every two years, which helps to provide continuity and to insulate board members from political pressure. The president also selects (from among those seven) the chairman of the board of governors, currently Ben Bernanke, who serves a four-year, renewable term.

Ben Bernanke, chairman of the Federal Reserve, has been described as the second-most-powerful person in the world.

Policy decisions are made by the board of governors and by the Federal Open Market Committee (FOMC). The FOMC is composed of the seven members of the board of governors plus the presidents of five regional Federal Reserve banks.[6] While the FOMC's major responsibility is open-market operations (a topic to be discussed in a moment), its meetings have become the forum for most Fed policy discussions. The chairman of the board of governors also serves as the chair of the FOMC, which meets about every six weeks to review the state of the economy and consider changes in monetary policy.

Once policy decisions have been made, they are implemented through the 12 regional, or district, Federal Reserve banks. These banks perform a variety of important functions. First, the 12 Federal Reserve banks hold the reserves (other than vault cash) of all the depository institutions in their districts. Second, they supervise the financial institutions in their districts, a responsibility they share with the Federal Deposit Insurance Corporation (FDIC), the primary agency insuring deposits of financial institutions. (This supervisory function may expand substantially if the Fed is given the responsibility for regulating risk across the entire financial system.) Third, as lenders of last resort, the Federal Reserve banks stand ready to make loans to depository institutions in temporary need of funds. Fourth, the Federal Reserve banks provide the economy with coins and paper money. Fifth, as we have seen, the Fed provides a system for collecting and clearing checks throughout the United States, making it possible for checks drawn on out-of-town banks to be returned to the home institution for collection. But all these functions are secondary to the Fed's primary responsibility: the control of the nation's money supply. That is the topic we will examine next.

MONETARY POLICY AND THE FEDERAL RESERVE

Monetary policy is designed to control the supply of money. More precisely, monetary policy is any action intended to alter the supply of money to influence the level of total spending and thereby combat unemployment or inflation.

Although the objective of monetary policy is the same as that of fiscal policy (to prevent or combat unemployment and inflation), its methodology is somewhat different. In Chapter 12 you saw how policymakers use the government's

---

[6] The presidents of all 12 Federal Reserve banks attend each FOMC meeting but only five are permitted to vote. The voting membership rotates over time, but the president of the New York Federal Reserve always retains a vote. That's because all open-market operations are conducted through the New York Fed.

spending and taxation powers to alter aggregate demand and thereby elimi-nate recessionary or inflationary gaps. Likewise, monetary policy works to influence aggregate demand but through a different mechanism: by increasing or decreasing the money supply.

The Fed does not manipulate the amount of money by printing more currency or by removing existing paper money from circulation. Remember, much of our nation's money supply is balances in checking accounts—demand-deposit accounts, NOW accounts, and other forms of checkable deposits. It is this element of the money supply that the Fed's actions are designed to influence. You have seen how depository institutions create checkable deposits when they make loans. Now you will discover how the Federal Reserve can influence the lending ability of depository institutions and thereby alter the supply of money.

The Federal Reserve uses three major policy tools to control the money supply: (1) the buying and selling of government securities, a process known as **open-market operations**; (2) the ability to alter the reserve requirement of depository institutions; and (3) control over the **discount rate**—the interest rate at which banking institutions can borrow from the Federal Reserve. All three policy tools affect the reserve positions of depository institutions. As you have learned, the more excess reserves a bank has, the more loans it can make and the more money (checkable deposits) it can create. By altering the volume of excess reserves, the Fed is able to influence the banking system's ability to make loans. Because making loans means creating more money, the Fed's actions influence the money supply.

Open-Market Operations

The Federal Reserve controls the money supply primarily through its open-market operations: buying and selling government securities on the open market. Whenever the U.S. government runs a deficit, the Treasury finances that deficit by selling government securities to individuals, businesses, financial institutions, and government agencies. Most are marketable, or *negotiable*, meaning that they can be held until maturity or resold to someone else.[7] Banks find such securities an attractive investment. They not only earn interest but also convert easily into cash in the event that additional reserves are needed. The Federal Reserve uses the market for negotiable securities as a vehicle for controlling the money supply. Let's see how open-market operations work.

---

[7] There are different types of marketable government securities. *Treasury bills* are short-term securities with maturities of ninety-one days to one year. *Government notes* are intermediate-term securities maturing in one to five years. Finally, *government bonds* are long-term securities with maturities of more than five years.

If the Fed wants to increase the money supply by expanding loans, it can offer to buy government securities at attractive prices in the open market. The Fed pays for securities purchased from a commercial bank, for example, by increasing the bank's reserve account at the district Federal Reserve bank. Because this transaction does not increase the bank's deposit liabilities, the additional reserves are all excess and can be used to expand loans and deposits—up to the maximum predicted by the deposit multiplier. As you know, any change in the excess reserves of one bank will lead eventually to a much larger change in the total system's loans and checkable deposits. As commercial banks and other depository institutions make more loans and create more checkable deposits, the money supply will expand.

If the Fed wishes to reduce the money supply, it can shift its open-market operations into reverse and cut the lending ability of banks by selling them government securities. The purchasing banks will experience a reduction in their reserve accounts at district Federal Reserve banks. As their reserves decline, these institutions will have to contract loans or at least limit their expansion. This will cause the money supply to decline or expand at a slower rate.

Changing the Reserve Requirement

The Fed can also influence the reserve position of banks by changing the reserve requirement. Under existing law, the Federal Reserve has the power to specify reserve requirements between 8 and 14 percent for depository institutions above a specified size. (At present, most banks must satisfy a 10 percent reserve requirement.) This flexibility provides the Federal Reserve with a tool for influencing the money supply by changing the lending ability of depository institutions.

Lowering the reserve requirement would convert some required reserves into excess reserves and thereby expand the lending ability of depository institutions. When these institutions increase their loans, they create checkable deposits, and the money supply expands. Increasing the reserve requirement has the opposite effect. As excess reserves are converted into required reserves, lending contracts, and the money supply shrinks.

Modifying the reserve requirement is effective but somewhat dangerous. Even changes as small as one-half of one percent can alter by several billion dollars the banking system's ability to make loans. Changes of this magnitude, particularly when they are sudden, can jolt the economy severely. Therefore, the Federal Reserve uses this tool sparingly, adjusting the reserve requirement only infrequently and relying mainly on other tools to control the money supply.

Changing the Discount Rate

The third policy tool available to the Fed is changing the discount rate. Recall that the *discount rate* is the interest rate charged by the Federal Reserve on loans to depository institutions. In theory, increasing the discount rate should discourage borrowing from the Fed and thus force banks to limit or even contract the number of loans they grant. Of course, if banks contract their loans, the money supply will fall. Lowering the discount rate should have the opposite effect. By encouraging depository institutions to borrow from the Fed and create additional loans and deposits, the lowered rate should increase the money supply.

Note the use of the words "in theory" and "should." In practice, banks generally prefer to borrow through the **federal funds market**, a market that brings together banks that need reserves and banks that temporarily have excess reserves. (The rate charged on such loans is called the **federal funds rate** and usually applies to reserves borrowed on a very short-term basis—often overnight—to meet temporary reserve deficiencies.) That's because the Fed normally keeps the discount rate somewhat above the federal funds rate, making borrowing from the Fed less attractive than this alternative. The "discount window"—the Federal Reserve unit that makes loans to banks—exists largely to provide backstop loans to banks that have exhausted other sources of funds. As a consequence, changes in the discount rate generally have a limited impact and are not viewed as an important policy tool. The Fed's willingness to make these loans—to act as a lender of last resort—remains an important function, however, because it ensures that bankers always have a place to turn to obtain liquidity and maintain the public's confidence in our banking system.[8]

MONEY, INTEREST RATES, AND THE LEVEL OF ECONOMIC ACTIVITY

Now that we've seen how the Federal Reserve can expand or contract the money supply, let's explore how changes in the money supply affect the economy. Economic theory suggests that changes in the money supply affect output and employment primarily by altering interest rates. Because a significant

---

[8] Another purpose of the discount window is to reduce the volatility of the federal funds rate. For technical reasons, the federal funds rate experiences some short-term ups and downs. When the federal funds rate rises significantly, it can rise above the discount rate (if policymakers leave the discount rate unchanged). At that point, bankers can choose to borrow from the Fed instead, helping to keep the federal funds rate from rising further.

amount of consumption and investment spending is financed by borrowing, changes in the interest rate can affect the amount of aggregate demand in the economy and thereby alter the level of equilibrium GDP and the price level. This transmission process can be summarized as follows:

$$\text{Money supply} \longrightarrow \text{Interest rate} \longrightarrow \text{Aggregate demand} \longrightarrow \begin{array}{c}\text{Output,}\\ \text{employment,}\\ \text{and prices}\end{array}$$

Interest Rate Determination

Why would changes in the money supply tend to alter the interest rate? To answer that question, we need to think back to Chapter 3, where we discussed price determination in competitive markets. Like the price of wheat or of cattle, the interest rate—the price of money—is determined by the forces of demand and supply. As a consequence, any change in either the demand for money or its supply will affect the rate of interest.[9]

Federal Reserve policies are not always popular. Here, demonstrators protest policies that raised interest rates to slow the economy and prevent inflation.

---

[9] To simplify matters, we will assume a single rate of interest; in fact, there are several. For example, short-term borrowers generally pay a lower interest rate than those who require the money for a longer period. In addition, borrowers with good credit ratings usually pay lower rates than those with poor ratings.

Consider, first, the demand for money. Like conventional demand curves, the demand curve for money slopes downward. That's because the quantity of money demanded by individuals and businesses is inversely related to the interest rate: the higher the rate of interest, the less money is demanded. To understand that relationship, remember that the money you hold (cash in your wallet or money in your checking account) generally pays little or no interest. But other assets you could hold instead of money—bonds, for instance, or bank certificates of deposit—do pay interest. The higher the prevailing interest rate, the more attractive it becomes to hold these assets instead of money. As a consequence, less money will be demanded when interest rates are *high* than when they are *low*. The demand curve in Exhibit 13.4 shows that $100 billion would be demanded at an interest rate of 10 percent, whereas $300 billion would be demanded at an interest rate of 6 percent.

The supply of money is depicted as a vertical line in Exhibit 13.4 to illustrate that the quantity of money supplied does not respond automatically to changes in the interest rate; instead, it remains constant at the level determined by the Federal Reserve. The intersection of the demand curve and the vertical supply curve determines the equilibrium interest rate: the interest rate at which the amount of money that people want to hold is exactly equal to the amount available. In our hypothetical example the equilibrium interest rate is 8 percent. At that interest rate individuals and businesses are willing to hold $200 billion, exactly the amount being supplied by the Federal Reserve.

EXHIBIT 13.4

The Equilibrium Interest Rate

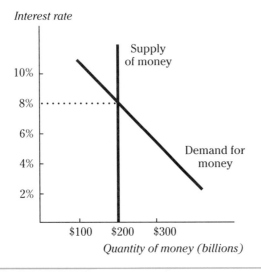

The intersection of the demand curve for money and the supply curve of money determines the equilibrium interest rate—the interest rate at which the amount of money that individuals and businesses want to hold is exactly equal to the amount available. In this example the equilibrium interest rate is 8 percent.

Monetary Policy and the Level of Economic Activity

The Fed attempts to guide the economy's performance by adjusting the money supply and thereby pushing the interest rate up or down. As we've seen, changes in the interest rate alter aggregate demand, and changes in the level of aggregate demand lead to changes in equilibrium GDP and the price level.

To illustrate how monetary policy works, let's assume that the economy is suffering from abnormally high unemployment: A recessionary gap exists. The Fed can attack this unemployment problem by increasing the money supply. This could be accomplished by reducing the reserve requirement, buying government securities, or lowering the discount rate. Any of these changes would shift the money supply curve in Exhibit 13.5(a) from S_1 to S_2, denoting an increase in the money supply from $200 billion to $300 billion. Because the demand for money is unchanged, the equilibrium interest rate will fall from 8 percent to 6 percent. At this lower interest rate, businesses will find it profitable to borrow additional money to invest in plants and equipment; households will be inclined to

EXHIBIT 13.5

Using Monetary Policy to Attack Unemployment

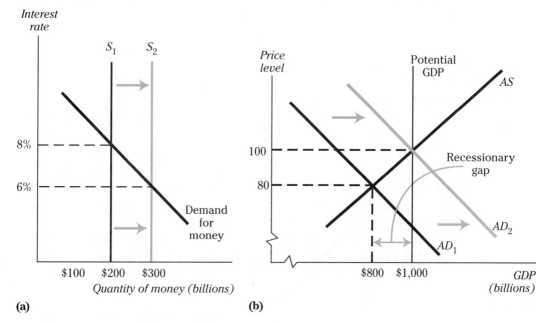

(a)   (b)

By increasing the money supply from S_1 to S_2, as in (a), the Fed can lower the interest rate from 8 to 6 percent. The lower interest rate stimulates consumption and investment spending, shifting the aggregate demand curve from AD_1 to AD_2, as in (b), and eliminating the recessionary gap.

borrow and spend more on new homes, automobiles, and other consumer goods. Thus, by lowering the interest rate, an increase in the money supply raises aggregate demand. This is represented in Exhibit 13.5(b) by a shift of the aggregate demand curve from AD_1 to AD_2. As you can see, this increase in aggregate demand raises the equilibrium level of GDP from \$800 billion to \$1,000 billion, eliminating the recessionary gap and restoring full employment.

To attack inflation, the Federal Reserve must raise interest rates by contracting the money supply. This is accomplished by increasing the reserve requirement, selling government securities, or increasing the discount rate. What is the effect of the higher rate of interest? Businesses will tend to reduce investment spending, and households will be likely to spend less on new homes, boats, camping trailers, and other items that they buy on credit or through borrowing. Reducing the money supply thus raises the interest rate and lowers aggregate demand in the economy, which helps to reduce inflationary pressures.

As you can see, monetary policy works through its impact on the interest rate. By adjusting the cost of money, the Fed is able to influence the level of aggregate demand in the economy and thereby eliminate recessionary or inflationary gaps. (The interest rate that the Fed controls is the federal funds rate. What happens when the Fed has pushed that rate as low as it will go? Read "Fed Reduces Benchmark Rate to as Low as Zero," on page 404, and find out.)

THE LIMITS TO MONETARY POLICY

The Federal Reserve's independent status gives monetary policy some distinct advantages over fiscal policy. When the members of the Federal Open Market Committee decide that action should be taken to combat unemployment or inflation, they do not need to wait for Congress to agree. They can approve the needed changes and have them implemented in a very short time. And the 14-year terms of Federal Reserve Board members help to insulate them from political pressures, although that insulation is not complete in view of periodic threats to bring the Fed under the direct control of Congress.

But monetary policy has limitations as well. (Recall the limitations of fiscal policy that we examined in Chapter 12.) Here we will look at two problems that may be encountered when monetary policy is used in an attempt to guide the economy's performance.

Time Lags

Like fiscal policy, monetary policy is subject to some time lags. Although Federal Reserve authorities don't need the approval of Congress to implement policy changes (thus eliminating the *implementation lag*), they do need time to recognize that a problem exists. As we learned earlier, our economic indicators sometimes send mixed or unclear messages, so some time may elapse before members of the FOMC identify a problem and agree to take action. Of course, this is what we described in Chapter 12 as the *recognition lag*. Once they take action, additional time passes before their policy change exerts its impact on the economy. If committee members decide to stimulate the economy, for example, it will take time for an increase in lending to trigger the associated increase in spending, output, and employment. As before, this is the *impact lag*. If these recognition and impact lags are too long, the added stimulus may hit the economy when it is already on the road to spontaneous recovery. In that event, the Fed's actions may contribute to inflation rather than help to reduce unemployment.

Uneven Effectiveness

Monetary policy may be less effective in combating unemployment than in combating inflation. When the Fed reduces banks' reserves to combat inflation, banks are forced to restrict (or even contract) lending. However, when it implements an easy-money policy to combat unemployment and makes more reserves available to depository institutions, bankers may not choose to use those reserves to support loans. If bankers doubt the ability of customers to repay loans, they refuse to lend; if households and businesses are pessimistic about the future, they may decide not to borrow. Without greater lending and borrowing, spending will not increase; thus, the economy will not receive the stimulus needed to pull it from its depressed state.

How significant are the monetary policy limitations noted here? As recent experience has proven, they can be very significant. In the 2008–2009 recession, the Fed's traditional policies seemed unable to restart the economy. Banks were unwilling to lend despite massive infusions of reserves. And panicky consumers were reluctant to borrow. As this edition goes to press, the economy is finally showing signs of life. But it took some very unconventional Fed policies (see the Use Your Economic Reasoning selection on page 404) and a massive infusion of federal spending; traditional Fed policies were simply not up to the task. Moreover, some economists argue that much of the blame for the recession itself should be laid at the doorstep of the Fed. They argue that the medicine the Fed used to combat the 2001 recession—low interest rates—was continued too long, and that this helped to stoke the "housing bubble" that ultimately burst and produced the recession of 2008–2009. As you might expect, not everyone agrees with that assessment. And even those who do recognize that there is much more to the story. The important point is that Fed policymaking has its critics. Some of these detractors go as far as to suggest that we eliminate the discretion of Fed policymakers—their ability to make the

Use Your Economic Reasoning

Fed Reduces Benchmark Rate to as Low as Zero

The Federal Reserve, urgently rewriting its playbook to fight a deepening recession, cut its benchmark interest rate to as low as zero Tuesday, a surprisingly strong step that should make it cheaper for Americans to borrow on credit cards and pay their mortgages. Wells Fargo, Wachovia and U.S. immediately lowered their prime lending rates from 4 percent to 3.25 percent, and other banks will probably follow suit. Economists cautioned, though, that people frightened by the economy and worried about their own jobs may not feel like taking on more debt.

The Fed's action was unprecedented in the central bank's 95-year history. . . . For the first time, the Fed created a target range for its [federal] funds rate, putting it at zero to 0.25 percent. That was a dramatic reduction from the previous rate, which was an already low 1 percent. The federal funds rate is the interest that banks charge each other for overnight loans. The radical action underscores the breathtaking deterioration in the U.S. economy and the stability of the financial system this fall [2008], and even since Fed policymakers last gathered in late October.

For years, cutting the funds rate had been the Fed's most potent weapon for snapping an economy out of trouble. But the recession, which economists say began a year ago, seems to be worsening despite all the steps taken so far. . . . At the heart of the economic crisis are credit and financial problems that have made worried banks reluctant to lend to customers regardless of how cheap money has become. At the same time, fearful Americans, watching jobs evaporate and their investments crumble, have sharply cut back on spending, including on big-ticket purchases such as homes and cars that typically require financing.

The Fed hopes lower borrowing costs will entice people and businesses to spend more, helping the economy. Citing "weak economic conditions," the Fed said it expected to keep its funds rate at "exceptionally low levels . . . for some time." The bold move on rates surprised not just Wall Street investors but also economists, most of whom were predicting the Fed would cut its funds rate in half, to 0.5 percent.

With the Fed's key rate sinking to near zero, the central bank moved into uncharted territory. Still, Fed Chairman Ben Bernanke and his colleagues insisted the central bank isn't running out of ammunition to fight the crisis. "The Fed will employ all available tools to promote the resumption of sustainable economic growth," the Fed said. It said, for example, that it is weighing the benefits of buying longer-term Treasury securities on the open market in substantial quantities. Doing so might lower rates on those securities and help energize the economy. The Fed also cited a program it announced late last month to buy $600 billion in debt and mortgage-backed securities from mortgage giants Fannie Mae and Freddie Mac. That has already helped push mortgage rates down. And early next year the Fed, in another previously announced program, plans to roll out a $200 billion program to boost the availability of auto loans, student loans, credit card loans and other lending to consumers.

Source: Associated Press Financial Wire, December 16, 2008. Reprinted by permission of the Associated Press. All rights reserved.

The Fed's statement provided a far more gloomy assessment of the economy than the central bank made after its October meeting, citing deterioration in the labor market, consumer spending, business investment and industrial production. "It is a reflection of an utterly desolate economic picture, which will persist for the foreseeable future," said Ian Shepherdson, chief economist at High Frequency Economics. . . . Since the start of the recession, the economy has shed nearly 2 million jobs. Analysts predict 3 million more will be lost between now and the spring of 2010. The recession is shaping up to be the longest since the Great Depression.

President-elect Barack Obama is pushing an economic recovery plan that includes spending on big public works projects to create jobs, in addition to an economic stimulus package aimed at getting people to spend more money. Obama said Tuesday other branches of government should "step up" because the Fed is "running out of the traditional ammunition" in the form of rate reductions.

For consumers, the Fed move essentially means money is now on sale. . . . Still, some economists say there are two problems that lower rates don't address: the reluctance of people worried about their jobs to take on more debt, even at low rates, and the unwillingness of banks to lend to some people who do want to borrow. "When you think about someone giving you a loan, it's not just the rate, it's lenders' expectations of your ability to repay that loan," said John Silvia, chief economist at Wachovia. "This is not the environment to go speculating on making loans to people who may be unemployed in two or three weeks." . . .

USE YOUR ECONOMIC REASONING

1. If the Fed was using open market operations to push down interest rates, would it be buying or selling securities? How would this policy reduce interest rates?

2. According to the article, the Fed has pushed the federal funds rate—the rate at which banks can borrow reserves from one another—close to zero. But the article goes on to say that banks are reluctant to lend. If banks can borrow the reserves they need for next to nothing, why are they unwilling to make loans? Can the Fed force them to use their available reserves to expand their lending?

3. What did President Obama mean when he said that the Fed was "running out of the traditional ammunition that's used in a recession"? Why might economists be particularly supportive of using discretionary fiscal policy in this environment?

4. Traditionally, the Fed combats recession by reducing short-term interest rates. But in this recession, the Fed did that *and* moved into specific markets—the markets for mortgages, auto loans, student loans, and business loans—trying to free up lending. For instance, by buying commercial paper—the short-term IOUs that businesses issue to meet their short-term financing needs—the Fed helped to keep those businesses open when their normal lenders were nervous about extending loans. Why were their normal lenders reluctant to lend? Why didn't the Fed face the same reluctance?

   One reason that bankers were reluctant to lend was the possibility that the borrowers would default—not repay the loans. Banks want to avoid defaults because they reduce profits. They also reduce the bank's "capital," and all banks must meet minimum capital requirements. Concerns about adequate capital thus became an additional reason for restricting loans and a real problem for Fed policymakers. The appendix to this chapter examines this issue.

money supply grow more rapidly at some times and more slowly at others—and make them adhere to strict rules about how fast the money supply will expand. The next chapter takes a closer look at some of these criticisms as it explores the activist–nonactivist debate.

SUMMARY

Economists define *money* as anything that serves as a *medium of exchange*, a *standard of value*, and a *store of value*. Currency (coins and paper money) and *checkable deposits* (checking accounts at banks and savings institutions) clearly perform all the functions of money. Other *assets*—household savings accounts, for example—perform some, but not all, the functions of money or perform those functions incompletely. Assets that are not money but that can be quickly converted into money are termed *near money*.

In its role as controller of the U.S. money supply, the Federal Reserve defines that supply according to two classifications. The narrowest is *M-1*, composed of currency in the hands of the public plus all checkable deposits. A somewhat broader definition of the nation's money supply *M-2*, includes everything in M-1 plus money-market mutual fund balances, money-market deposits at savings or thrift institutions, and small *savings deposits*.

Approximately 53 percent of the M-1 money supply is in the form of currency; the rest is checkable deposits. The Federal Reserve provides depository institutions (commercial banks and thrift institutions) with the coins and paper currency they need to serve their customers. Checkable deposits, on the other hand, are actually created by the depository institutions themselves when they make loans.

According to the *fractional reserve principle*, a bank must maintain only a given fraction of a dollar in required reserves for each dollar in checkable deposits; the balance of those funds can be loaned out to earn interest. In the process of making these loans, banks create checkable deposit money. For example, when a person borrows money from a bank, he or she exchanges something that is not money (an IOU) for something that is money (a checking account balance). This increases the money supply by the amount of the loan.

Each depository institution must limit its loans to the amount of its *excess reserves*—reserves in excess of the sum it is legally required to maintain in the form of vault cash and deposits with the Federal Reserve. This limitation is necessary because as loans are spent, reserves are likely to be lost to other depository institutions. Thus, each institution can expand the money supply by an amount equal to its excess reserves but no more than that.

The banking system (including all depository institutions) does not have to worry about losing reserves. Reserves lost by one depository institution must be deposited in some other bank in the system. The banking system as a whole, then, can create loans and deposits equal to some multiple of its excess reserves. To be precise, it can expand loans and deposits by an amount equal to the initial change in excess reserves times the reciprocal of the reserve requirement (the *deposit multiplier*).

The Federal Reserve, our nation's *central bank*, influences the ability of depository institutions to expand or contract deposits and thereby regulates the size of the nation's money supply. Policy decisions are made by the Fed's board of governors and by the Federal Open Market Committee (FOMC). Once policy decisions have been made, they are implemented by the 12 regional, or district, Federal Reserve banks that oversee the actions of all depository institutions in their districts.

The Federal Reserve has three major tools with which to control the money supply: (1) the buying and selling of government securities, a process known as *open-market operations*; (2) the ability to alter the reserve requirement; and (3) control over the *discount rate*—the interest rate at which commercial banks and other depository institutions can borrow from the Federal Reserve.

All these policy tools affect the reserve position of banks. By influencing the volume of excess reserves, the Fed is able to affect the banking system's ability to make loans and is thereby able to influence the money supply. This control over the money supply enables the Federal Reserve to alter the interest rate, which in turn influences the level of aggregate demand in the economy.

Monetary policy has some distinct advantages over fiscal policy. The lags in monetary policy may be shorter than those in fiscal policy, and because the Fed tends to be somewhat insulated from political pressures, it may have more freedom to pursue long-run goals than Congress does.

Monetary policy is also subject to limitations: (1) the lags in monetary policy have the potential to make Fed action counterproductive; (2) monetary policy may be more effective in combating inflation than in dealing with unemployment.

KEY TERMS

Asset	Excess reserves	Near money
Balance sheet	Federal funds market	NOW account
Bank capital	Federal funds rate	Open-market operations
Central bank	Fractional reserve principle	Owners' equity
Checkable deposits	Liabilities	Reserve requirement
Demand deposits	M-1	Savings deposits
Deposit multiplier	M-2	Standard of value
Discount rate	Medium of exchange	Store of value
Equity capital	Monetary policy	

STUDY QUESTIONS

Fill in the Blanks

1. Money functions as a(n) _____,

   a(n) _____, and a (n)

   _____.

2. Demand deposits, NOW accounts, and ATS accounts are all examples of

   _____.

3. The primary characteristic of all M-1 money is that it can easily function as a(n)

   _____.

4. A bank must maintain reserves equal to a specified fraction of its

   _____.

5. Banks create money when they

   _____; the amount of money that a bank can create is equal to

   its _____.

6. Today, the primary purpose of the Federal Reserve is to regulate or control the

   _____ to combat unemployment and inflation.

7. According to economic theory, an increase in the money supply would tend to (increase/

   decrease) _____ the interest rate, which would tend to (increase/

   decrease) _____ aggregate demand, which, in turn, would (increase/

   decrease) _____ GDP.

8. The primary policy tool used by the Federal Reserve to control the money supply

   is _____.

9. The rate charged by the Federal Reserve on loans to depository institutions is

   called the _____.

10. Monetary policy may be less effective in

    combating _____ than

    _____.

Multiple Choice

1. Which of the following is *not* a component of the M-1 money supply?
   a) Currency
   b) The balances in traditional savings accounts
   c) Demand deposit balances
   d) NOW account balances

2. Which of the following is *not* an example of near money?
   a) A savings account
   b) A government bond
   c) A piece of prime real estate
   d) An account with a money-market fund

3. Which of the following appears as a *liability* on the balance sheet of a depository institution?
   a) Loans
   b) Reserves
   c) Checkable deposits
   d) Securities

4. Assuming that the reserve requirement is 30 percent, how much additional money can the bank represented below create? (All figures are in millions of dollars.)

ASSETS		LIABILITIES	
Reserves	$23	Checkable	$50
Securities	25	deposits	
Loans	17	Owners' equity	40
Property	25		

a) $ 8 million
b) $12 million
c) $15 million
d) $25 million

5. Assuming a reserve requirement of 25 percent, how much additional money can the bank represented below create? (All figures are in millions.)

ASSETS		LIABILITIES	
Reserves	$35	Checkable	$80
Securities	30	deposits	
Loans	25	Owners' equity	20
Property	10		

a) $20 million
b) $15 million
c) $10 million
d) $5 million

6. If the reserve requirement is 25 percent, the deposit multiplier would be equal to
a) 4.
b) 5.
c) 1/4.
d) 10.

7. If the balance sheet represented in question 5 were for the banking *system* rather than for a single bank, the system could expand the money supply by an additional
a) $15 billion.
b) $30 billion.
c) $60 billion.
d) $80 billion.

8. The Federal Open Market Committee is composed of
a) the presidents of the 12 district Federal Reserve banks.

b) the members of the Fed's board of governors and the presidents of five district Federal Reserve banks.
c) the chairman of the Fed's board of governors and the presidents of the 12 district Federal Reserve banks.
d) five members of the Fed's board of governors and the presidents of five district Federal Reserve banks.

9. If banks hold checkable deposits of $300 million and reserves of $80 million and if the reserve requirement is 20 percent, how much additional money can the banking *system* create?
a) $20 million
b) $80 million
c) $100 million
d) $220 million

10. Which of the following is *not* a function of the Federal Reserve?
a) To control the money supply
b) To make loans to depository institutions
c) To insure the deposits of customers
d) To provide a check-collection service

11. If the Federal Reserve wants to reduce the equilibrium interest rate, it should
a) increase the reserve requirement to expand the money supply.
b) sell securities on the open market to expand the money supply.
c) buy government securities to expand the money supply.
d) increase the discount rate to expand the money supply.

12. When the Federal Reserve buys government securities in the open market, the lending ability of banks
a) tends to decline; the money supply shrinks, and the interest rate tends to fall.
b) tends to decline; the money supply expands, and the interest rate tends to rise.
c) increases; the money supply expands, and the interest rate tends to fall.
d) tends to decline; the money supply shrinks, and the interest rate tends to rise.

13. Let's assume that all banks in the system are "loaned up" (have no excess reserves) and that they all face a reserve requirement of 20 percent. If the Federal Reserve buys a $100,000 security from Bank A, how much new money can the banking *system* create? (*Hint:* Remember that the Fed will pay for the security by increasing the reserve account of Bank A.)
    a) $100,000
    b) $1,000,000
    c) $400,000
    d) $500,000

14. If the Federal Reserve wanted to reduce inflationary pressures, what would be the proper combination of policies?
    a) Increase the reserve requirement, decrease the discount rate, and sell securities
    b) Increase the reserve requirement, increase the discount rate, and sell securities
    c) Increase the reserve requirement, increase the discount rate, and buy securities
    d) Decrease the reserve requirement, decrease the discount rate, and buy securities

15. To combat unemployment, the Federal Reserve should
    a) reduce the money supply by selling government securities.
    b) reduce the money supply by lowering the reserve requirement.
    c) increase the money supply by raising the discount rate.
    d) increase the money supply by buying government securities.

Problems and Questions for Discussion`

1. Explain each of the functions of money. Which of these functions does a traditional savings account perform? A NOW account?

2. Explain what is meant by the fractional reserve principle. How is it related to a bank's ability to create money?

3. Why must individual banks limit their loans to the amount of their excess reserves?

4. If a bank can create money, why can't you?

5. What is the deposit multiplier, and how is it calculated?

6. If you asked for your loan in cash rather than accepting a checking account, what impact would this action have on the money-creating ability of your bank? What about the banking system as a whole?

7. Suppose that you have a credit card with a $1,000 limit (you cannot charge more than $1,000). Should that $1,000 be considered part of the money supply? Why or why not?

8. Why might monetary policy be less effective in combating unemployment than in combating inflation?

9. Why might activists prefer discretionary monetary policy to discretionary fiscal policy as a tool for guiding the economy?

10. According to Keynesians, monetary policy works through the rate of interest. Explain.

11. Suppose that the Federal Reserve increases the reserve requirement. Explain the step-by-step impact of that change on the economy.

12. Why is the discount rate often described as a weak policy tool?

13. What are the advantages of open-market operations over changes in the reserve requirement?

14. Suppose that the housing industry is depressed. What monetary policy actions would you recommend to help the housing industry? Why do you think they would help?

15. If the Fed buys a government security from a private individual, the money supply will immediately be increased. If the Fed buys a government security from a bank, this action will not affect the money supply until a loan is made. Explain the difference. That is, why does one transaction have an immediate impact while the other does not?

ANSWER KEY

Fill in the Blanks

1. medium of exchange; standard of value; store of value

2. checkable deposits

3. medium of exchange

4. checkable deposits

5. make loans; excess reserves

6. money supply

7. decrease; increase; increase

8. open-market operations

9. discount rate

10. unemployment; inflation

Multiple Choice

1. b	4. a	7. c	10. c	13. d
2. c	5. b	8. b	11. c	14. b
3. c	6. a	9. c	12. c	15. d

THE GREAT RECESSION, CAPITAL REQUIREMENTS, AND FED POLICY

The Great Recession, the Financial Crisis, the Subprime Mortgage Meltdown—all these descriptions have been used to characterize what happened to our economy in 2008–2009. If these terms seem to describe separate events, they don't. All these events were connected to one another and to an esoteric regulation—the bank capital requirement. This appendix examines those connections and why Fed policymaking was particularly difficult during this period.

Let's begin with the housing market. Prior to 2006, the housing market seemed to be on fire. Demand was skyrocketing, and housing prices were shooting up—particularly in some really hot markets like Las Vegas. Lenders were grabbing for the gold ring and trying to wring everything they could out of the upturn. In chasing profits, many resorted to exotic loans that they probably should not have extended (and borrowers should not have accepted). For instance, some lenders offered variable interest rate loans with low introductory rates (called "teaser rates") that were low for the first couple years and then jumped to a higher rate. Others offered "no documentation" loans, where the home buyers were not asked to verify their incomes, a key factor in their ability to repay the loans. Why would anyone borrow money this way? Probably because they expected to refinance the loan into a more conventional fixed-rate loan before the rate jumped or sell the home (for a profit) before the loan payments became a problem. Why would banks make these loans? First, because these exotic loans had the potential to be very profitable; many banks earned substantial profits from the "origination fees" they charged for making the loans. Second, the banks often did not plan to keep the loans as an asset on their balance sheet. Rather, they intended to sell the loans to a third party, who would "securitize" the loans—in effect, selling pieces of the loans to investors. Consequently, the creditworthiness of borrowers—normally a major concern for a lender—became much less important. Furthermore, if the buyers couldn't make the payments, the bank could always take the house (which was expected to increase in value) to recover its money.

For most borrowers (and banks) everything would probably have worked out as planned if home prices had continued to rise. But they didn't. They peaked in July 2006 and started to drop. That meant home buyers couldn't refinance their homes to get out of their mortgages before the interest rate jumped or sell the homes at a profit. The drop in home prices also meant that billions and billions of dollars of wealth were destroyed—eliminating the ability to obtain home equity loans and making it harder for consumers to support their old spending habits. That drop in spending, coupled with the loss of construction and related jobs in housing, helped to push the economy into recession—a recession that ultimately spread throughout the economy.

When recession rears its head, the first line of defense is normally the Fed. Fed policy is less effective in combating recession than unemployment, but it usually works—it just takes longer than we would like. But in this recession, traditional Fed policy seemed remarkably ineffective. To understand why, we need to look at how this recession was affecting bank balance sheets.

As you learned earlier, a loan is recorded as an asset on the balance sheet of a bank. If a borrower fails to repay a loan—defaults on the loan—that asset is destroyed or reduced in value. (The bank will get the home, but if the home is worth less than the loan, the bank will lose the difference between the amount of the loan and the amount that can be recovered from the sale of the home.) Of course, there has to be a corresponding entry on the right side of the balance sheet, and that is of critical importance in understanding the problems facing Fed policymakers. When a borrower defaults on a loan, the adjustment on the right-hand side of the balance sheet is an adjustment in owners' equity, which is also called *bank capital* or *equity capital.*

All deposit-taking financial institutions are subject to minimum regulatory capital requirements. The purpose of these requirement is to protect depositors from a loss. If borrowers default on a loan, the owners (stockholders) of the bank will lose money rather than the depositors or the FDIC (the agency that insures deposits), so long as adequate bank capital is maintained. As this recession dragged on, banks found that far too many of their home mortgage borrowers were defaulting. This started with borrowers who received the more exotic, higher-risk, loans. But as the recession deepened and unemployment grew, defaults spread to other borrowers. As defaults became increasingly widespread, they depleted bank capital—pushing banks closer and closer to the minimum levels required by regulators. To protect themselves from further defaults, banks became increasingly cautious about making new loans. Of course, that helped protect the banks, but it meant that less lending (and spending) was going on, deepening the recession. And traditional Fed policy—which alters reserves but not bank capital—didn't seem to motivate them to make more loans.

In an attempt to get lending started, in October 2009 the Treasury Department took the extraordinary step of injecting capital directly into many of the nation's largest financial institutions (in return for stock in the banks). Citigroup, JP Morgan Chase, Bank of America, and Wells Fargo received $25 billion each, and lesser amounts went to smaller banks. In all, $250 billion was appropriated for this purpose. Clearly, the impact of defaults on bank capital had forced policymakers well beyond their normal range of policies.

STUDY QUESTIONS ON THE APPENDIX MATERIAL

To help solidify your understanding of the events described, let's work though a series of questions using the balance sheet of a hypothetical bank. In this example, assume that the bank is required to maintain $200,000 in capital and that the reserve requirement is 15 percent.

ASSETS		LIABILITIES AND OWNERS' EQUITY	
Reserves	$200,000	Checkable deposits	$1,000,000
Securities	$450,000	Savings deposits	360,000
Loans	$800,000	Owners' equity (capital)	240,000
Property	$150,000		
		Total liabilities	
Total assets	$1,600,000	and bank capital	$1,600,000

1. Suppose borrowers fail to repay $40,000 of loans. The asset "loans" would decline in value by $40,000 (to $760,000). What entry should be recorded on the right-hand side of the balance sheet?
2. Next, assume that a new customer walks into the bank and asks to borrow $25,000. Why might the bank be reluctant to lend to her? If she defaulted, would the bank still have adequate capital?
3. Traditionally, the Fed tries to stimulate the economy by using open market operations to expand lending. Suppose the Fed buys $50,000 of securities from the bank (expanding bank reserves by $50,000 and reducing its securities holdings by $50,000). Would you expect the bank to expand loans in this environment? Why or why not?
4. One novel policy the Fed used to get lending going in this environment was "capital infusion." Under this policy, the Fed provided the banks with new capital (generally in return for stock in the bank). To illustrate, suppose this bank received $50,000 in capital (that's the entry on the right side) and this went into reserves (left side). Why might the bank be more willing to expand loans now than it was under the scenario outlined in question 3?

The Activist-Nonactivist Debate

1. Discuss the views held by monetarist economists.
2. Explain the monetary rule and why monetarists support it.
3. Discuss the views of the new classical economists.
4. Explain the theory of rational expectations.
5. Discuss the policy ineffectiveness theorem.
6. Discuss the views held by supply-side economists.
7. Describe the policies that supply-side economists advocate.

In theory, monetary and fiscal policies can be used to maintain full employment and stable prices. But each of these demand-management policies is subject to limitations. Activists argue that despite their limitations, these policies can still play an important role in guiding the economy's performance. Nonactivists find the limitations so severe as to make the policies ineffective or counterproductive. This is the controversy that concerns us in this chapter.

As you can see, we have returned to the activist–nonactivist debate that we first encountered in Chapter 12. Just as Keynes and the classical economists disagreed about the advisability of government intervention to guide our economy, modern Keynesians disagree with monetarists and new classical economists (also known as rational-expectations theorists). This chapter introduces you to the views of these competing schools of thought and examines the debate about demand-management policies. It also takes a brief look at supply-side economics. We turn first to a short review of the Keynesian, or activist, position.

THE ACTIVIST POSITION: KEYNES REVISITED

As you learned in Chapter 12, Keynes did not believe that capitalist economies necessarily tend to full employment. Rather, he argued that because of the volatility of spending, particularly investment spending, they could be in equilibrium at a level of output either less or greater than potential GDP. If business executives were pessimistic, they might choose to cut back on investment spending, sending the economy into a tailspin and causing unemployment. If they were optimistic about the future, they might choose to expand investment spending, pushing GDP above potential and causing inflation.

Keynes was an activist economist in the sense that he advocated government action to prevent outbreaks of unemployment or inflation and to combat these problems when they occur. According to Keynes, the central government should use fiscal and monetary policies to ensure sufficient aggregate demand to achieve full employment without inflation.

Fiscal policy, you will recall, is the manipulation of government spending or taxation in order to guide the economy's performance. The appropriate Keynesian fiscal policy for a period of unemployment would be to increase government spending for goods and services or to reduce taxes. These policies would expand aggregate demand, raise the equilibrium GDP, and lower unemployment. Inflation calls for reductions in government spending or higher taxes. By reducing aggregate demand, these policies will reduce inflationary pressures.

Monetary policy—deliberately changing the money supply to influence the level of economic activity—can also be used to combat unemployment or inflation. If unemployment exists, the Federal Reserve can increase the money supply to drive down the market rate of interest. The lower interest rate will tend to stimulate investment spending and certain forms of consumption spending. By stimulating aggregate demand in this manner, monetary policy can raise equilibrium GDP and lower unemployment. Inflation can be attacked by reducing the money supply and thereby raising the prevailing rate of interest. A higher interest rate will cause businesses and consumers to cut back on their borrowing (and spending) and reduce inflationary pressures.

Even if fiscal and monetary policies work in the manner Keynesians suggest, why would anyone consider using them? If the economy is self-correcting in the long run, why not let it take care of itself? According to Keynesians, waiting for the self-correcting mechanism to work may be too painful. The adjustment process described in Chapter 11 takes time, perhaps a substantial period of time. If the economy is experiencing a recession, society loses output that will never be regained, individuals suffer the humiliation of being without work, and families deplete their savings or are forced to rely on charity or government assistance. In short, unemployment is costly, and the losses incurred as we wait for self-correction may be unacceptable.

Production above potential also imposes costs on society. As we saw in Chapter 11, when equilibrium GDP exceeds potential, the price level is pushed up, generating inflation. Although society benefits from the additional output and employment, unanticipated inflation tends to redistribute income in an arbitrary way. Moreover, the long-run adjustment process will ultimately eliminate the short-term gain in output and leave the economy with a still higher price level.

In summary, Keynesians believe that capitalist economies are inherently unstable, so that they are always in danger of operating either above or below potential GDP. Although the economy will ultimately return to potential GDP, waiting for this long-run adjustment to occur is needlessly costly to society. Instead, fiscal and monetary policies should be used to prevent deviations from potential GDP or to minimize their duration if they occur.

THE NONACTIVIST POSITION: THE MONETARISTS

Not all economists agree with the activist, or Keynesian, position. The two major groups, or schools, of nonactivist economists are the monetarists and the new classical economists (rational-expectations theorists). We will begin by examining the monetarist position.

Monetarism is the belief that changes in the money supply play the primary role in determining the level of aggregate output and prices in the economy. Economists who hold this belief are called *monetarists*.

According to monetarists, an increase in the money supply will tend to stimulate consumption and investment spending, raising equilibrium output and the price level; a reduction in the money supply will have the opposite effect. Keynesians agree that changes in the money supply can alter output and prices, but they emphasize that other factors—changes in investment or government spending, for instance—can also influence the economy. Monetarists tend to see these other factors as decidedly secondary; changes in the money supply are what really matter.

Fiscal Policy and Crowding Out

The paramount importance that monetarists attach to the money supply is illustrated by their criticism of Keynesian fiscal policy. According to monetarists, fiscal policy is ineffective unless it is accompanied by monetary policy. To illustrate this view, let's suppose that the economy is suffering from unemployment and that Congress decides to increase government spending to combat the problem. What will happen? The monetarists believe that if the money supply is not increased, government borrowing to finance the larger deficit will drive up the interest rate and discourage, or crowd out, investment spending. In an economy with more government spending but less investment spending, the net effect will be no stimulus to the economy. However, if the Federal Reserve allowed the money supply to expand while the government borrowed, it *would* be possible to provide some net stimulus to the economy. The interest rate would not be bid up, and so investment spending would not be discouraged; thus, total spending would actually expand. Monetarists are quick to point out that the stimulus in this situation results from the increase in the money supply, not from the added government spending.

Monetary Policy and the Monetary Rule

Because monetarism focuses attention on the money supply, eager students sometimes conclude that monetarists must favor the use of discretionary monetary policy to guide the economy's performance. But that's not the case. Monetarists believe that changes in the money supply are too important to be left to the discretion of policymakers. Instead, they support a **monetary rule** that would require the Federal Reserve to expand the money supply at a constant rate, something like 3 percent a year.[1]

If the Fed were required to increase the money supply at a constant annual rate, it would no longer be free to use changes in the money supply as a policy tool; it could not increase the money supply more rapidly to combat unemployment or slow the growth of the money supply to combat inflation. In other words, a monetary rule would eliminate the possibility of the activist monetary policies described in Chapter 13. In a sense, the Fed would be put on autopilot. Monetarists favor this approach because they are convinced that the Fed's attempts to combat unemployment or inflation have often made things worse rather than better.

---

[1] Monetarists believe that the money supply should be expanded at 3 percent a year because they think that potential GDP expands at about that rate. If sustainable output is growing at 3 percent a year, a 3 percent larger money supply is needed to facilitate this greater volume of transactions. But whether we choose to increase the money supply at 3 percent or 4 percent or 6 percent is not too important, so long as we pick *some* rate and stick with it. If the money supply is growing more rapidly than the economy's ability to produce output, inflation will result. But because it will be a reasonably constant rate of inflation, we will know what to expect and will be able to build it into our wage agreements and other contracts. Thus, it will not tend to redistribute income the way unanticipated inflation does.

Milton Friedman, shown here accepting his Nobel Prize in economics in 1976, would like to see the Federal Reserve adhere to a monetary rule.

Policy Lags and the Self-Correcting Economy

According to the monetarists, it is time lags that tend to make discretionary monetary policies counterproductive. Obviously, Fed policymakers cannot take action until they recognize that a problem exists. Unfortunately, the economy commonly sends mixed signals about its performance. As we learned in the previous chapter, this results in a *recognition lag* before agreement is reached that a problem exists. Even after the problem is recognized and policymakers take action, there will be an *impact lag* before the economy feels the effect of the policy.

The existence of lags would not be a major argument against discretionary monetary policy if the economy tended to remain in an unemployment or inflationary equilibrium indefinitely. But that's not what happens. As our discussion of the self-correcting mechanism indicates, the economy ultimately begins to solve its own problems. When we recognize this self-correcting tendency, lags can mean trouble for policymakers. To illustrate, suppose that the economy gradually weakens and begins to experience a recession. Fed policymakers eventually recognize the problem and take action to expand the money supply. But if the recognition and impact lags are long enough, the economy may begin to recover on its own before these policies start to take effect. Thus, monetary policy may begin to stimulate spending when such stimulus is no longer welcome. Of course, too much spending can lead to inflation, which is precisely what monetarists believe has happened on several occasions.

In summary, monetarists shun discretionary monetary policy because they believe that it often has a destabilizing effect on the economy—creates additional problems—rather than the stabilizing effect that Keynesians predict. In fact, monetarists believe that government tinkering with the money supply may be the major destabilizing force in the economy. For example, Milton Friedman—who is sometimes referred to as the father of monetarist economics—argues that it was inept monetary policy that caused the Great Depression. According to Friedman, the Fed turned what could have been a serious downturn into a major catastrophe by allowing the money supply to fall substantially in the early 1930s. He contends that a policy of stable money growth would have been vastly superior.[2]

Monetarism: Concluding Points

Perhaps the major source of disagreement between Keynesians and monetarists is about the nature of the economy. Keynesians tend to see the economy as inherently unstable and relatively slow to recover from demand and supply shocks. Monetarists, on the other hand, believe that the economy is fundamentally stable and returns fairly rapidly to potential GDP whenever deviations occur. If it persists in deviating from potential GDP, it is due to government tinkering, not to the nature of the economy.

Monetarists emphasize that eliminating the Fed's ability to tinker with the money supply would not completely eliminate unemployment or inflation. Fluctuations in spending would still occur, and some unemployment or inflation would result. But the adoption of a monetary rule would eliminate the major source of fluctuations in spending—fluctuations in the growth of the money supply—and would therefore tend to minimize any unemployment or inflation.

Criticisms of Monetarism

Keynesian economists disagree with monetarists on several basic points. First, they believe that monetarists attach too much importance to the money supply. Keynesians agree that changes in the money supply can alter GDP, but they argue that other factors are also important—perhaps even more important. These factors include changes in the level of investment or government spending. Keynesians believe that such autonomous changes can lead to inflation or unemployment, even if the money supply expands at a constant rate. For instance, Keynesians argue that pessimism about the future might cause

---

[2] Milton Friedman, "The Case for a Monetary Rule," *Newsweek,* February 7, 1972. Reprinted in Milton Friedman, *Bright Promises, Dismal Performance: An Economist's Protest* (Sun Lakes, Az.: Thomas Horton and Daughters, 1983).

businesses to cut back on investment and that this might lead to unemployment, even if the money supply continues to expand at a steady rate.

Second, although virtually all Keynesians agree with monetarists that crowding out reduces the effectiveness of fiscal policy, Keynesians believe that only a small amount of investment spending will normally be crowded out, so that expansionary fiscal policy can still have a significant impact on equilibrium GDP.

But many modern Keynesians are quite critical of the long lags involved in implementing changes in taxation and government spending. Because the lags in implementing monetary policy are generally shorter than the lags in implementing fiscal policy (though pro-rule monetarists argue that they are still too long), monetary policy is seen as the primary technique for stabilizing the economy.

Third, Keynesians are critical of the monetary rule because they believe that it could contribute to greater, rather than less, unemployment and inflation. Because Keynesians believe that the economy is *inherently* unstable (due to the volatility of investment spending), they argue that Fed policymakers need discretion to be able to offset fluctuations in spending and thereby maintain full employment without inflation.

THE NONACTIVIST POSITION: THE NEW CLASSICAL ECONOMISTS

As you probably noted, monetarists have much in common with the classical economists we discussed briefly in Chapter 12. Both groups see the economy as fundamentally stable and believe in laissez-faire policies. But another school of modern economists has even more in common with the original classical theorists, so much so that this school has been dubbed the "new" classical school of economics.

The new classical economics is based on two fundamental beliefs: (1) wages and prices are highly flexible, and (2) expectations about the future are formed "rationally." The remainder of this section investigates the implications of those beliefs.

Wage/Price Flexibility and Full Employment

Like the classical theorists of old, the economists of the new classical school (of which the most prominent members are Robert Lucas of Chicago, Thomas Sargent of Stanford, and Robert Barro of Harvard) believe that wages and prices are highly flexible. This flexibility permits markets to adjust quickly to changes in supply or demand so that shortages or surpluses are prevented. In short, highly flexible prices ensure that the quantity of the good or service demanded will equal the quantity supplied; markets will "clear."

New classical economists believe that the market-clearing principle applies not only to individual markets—the markets for shoes or cars or accountants, for instance—but also to the aggregate economy. Its implications for the overall labor market are particularly important. To illustrate, let's suppose that the economy experiences a decline in aggregate demand. Of course, when the overall demand for products declines, the demand for labor must also fall. But the new classical economists do not believe that this reduction in labor demand will result in unemployment. Because wages are highly flexible, the reduced level of labor demand will cause wages to drop. Lower wage rates will both encourage employers to hire more workers and reduce the amount of labor supplied (at the lower wage, some workers will prefer leisure to work). The reduction in wages will thus restore equilibrium in the labor market; everyone who is willing to work at the new, lower wage will find employment, and every employer who is willing to pay that wage will find workers.[3] Any unemployment must be voluntary.

The Importance of Expectations   The belief in highly flexible wages and prices and the voluntary nature of unemployment is not new; this view was held by the original classical economists. But the new classical economists are not clones of the originals; they have made their own distinctive contribution to economic thinking. The distinctive feature of the new classical economics is its focus on expectations and the way that expectations influence people's behavior.

These economists remind us that different expectations about the future can lead to different decisions today. For instance, if consumers expect new-car prices to be lower in a few months, they will probably wait to buy; if they expect prices to be higher, they will buy now. These are commonsense observations that few of us would challenge. But the new classical economists go well beyond these observations. They are interested in how expectations are formed; in other words, they want to know how individuals come to expect whatever they expect—higher car prices, lower interest rates, or more rapid inflation, for instance.

Keynesians and monetarists disagree about many things, but both groups have assumed that individuals base their expectations only on experience—by looking backward at past events. The new classical economists argue that this assumption implies that individuals are irrational because it presumes that they ignore current events that they know will influence the

---

[3] The new classical economists do not believe that labor contracts make wages so inflexible as to prevent these adjustments.

future. As an alternative, the new classical economists have proposed the theory of rational expectations.

The **theory of rational expectations** suggests that people use all available information to develop realistic (rational) expectations about the future. According to this theory, the public is quite perceptive in forming its expectations. Households and businesses do not merely project past trends into the future; they also take current economic developments quickly into account.

For instance, when forecasting inflation, people will consider the inflation of recent years, but they will also consider the potential impact of upcoming labor negotiations, the rate of productivity growth, the anticipated quality of agricultural harvests (and their impact on food prices), developments in the Middle East (and their impact on oil prices), and—perhaps most important of all—the expected government response to inflation.

Rational Expectations and Discretionary Policy

The belief that wages and prices are highly flexible and that expectations are formed "rationally" leads the members of the new classical school to some interesting policy conclusions. According to the new classical economists, *systematic* monetary and fiscal policies cannot alter the level of output or employment in the economy; they can change only the price level. This belief is known as the **policy ineffectiveness theorem**. The implications of the policy ineffectiveness theorem are clear: government attempts to reduce unemployment are doomed to failure; they will result only in inflation.

The problem, according to the new classical theorists, is that systematic policies whereby the government always responds to a particular set of economic conditions in a given way are *predictable*. But if discretionary policies are predictable, individuals will anticipate those policies and alter their behavior in ways that make the policies ineffective. Thus, individuals, *acting on rational expectations*, make government stabilization policies ineffective.

To illustrate, let's suppose that historically the Fed has expanded the money supply whenever the measured unemployment rate reached 6 percent.[4]

---

[4] How can the unemployment rate reach 6 percent if wages and prices are highly flexible? According to the new classical economists, this can occur as a result of *unexpected* shocks in aggregate demand or supply—reductions in planned investment, the outbreak of war, or significant crop failures, for instance. Because these events are unexpected, they may be misperceived by workers. For instance, if the economy experiences a reduction in aggregate demand, some workers may mistakenly assume that the downturn has affected only their industry. Equally important, they may fail to recognize that the overall price level has also fallen, so that the real wage—the purchasing power of their money wage—is unchanged. Suffering from these misperceptions, they are unhappy with their lower money wage. Thus, workers quit their jobs and set out in search of positions that pay as much as they are accustomed to earning. In this way an unexpected shock may lead to unemployment.

Now, let's assume that the unemployment rate reaches that magic number and the Fed feels compelled to take action. Of course, when the money supply is expanded, the aggregate demand curve will shift to the right, as depicted in Exhibit 14.1 by the movement from AD_1 to AD_2. This increase in aggregate demand would, ceteris paribus, tend to raise the level of output in the economy. In our example, output would be expanded from the original equilibrium of $900 billion to $1,000 billion (the intersection of AS_1 and AD_2). Because increased output normally means additional jobs, employment would also tend to expand.

But supporters of the theory of rational expectations believe that the assumption of ceteris paribus is unreasonable in this situation. They argue that workers and businesses have learned to anticipate the Fed's policy response to unemployment. Moreover, they have discovered that when the money supply is increased, inflation inevitably follows. (Note that the increase in aggregate demand pushes up the price level along with the level of output.) So when the public perceives that the Fed is likely to increase the money supply, it takes actions to protect itself from the anticipated inflation. Workers ask for higher wages, suppliers raise their input prices, and businesses push up product prices. Because prices and wages are assumed to be highly flexible, these adjustments occur immediately, the moment the public anticipates higher prices.

EXHIBIT 14.1

Rational Expectations and Economic Policy

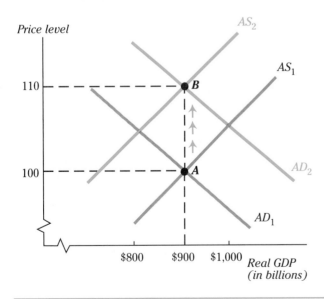

According to the theory of rational expectations, anticipated changes in monetary or fiscal policies cannot alter the level of output or employment; they can change only prices. In this example the expansionary monetary policy that shifts the aggregate demand curve from AD_1 to AD_2 is anticipated, causing workers to ask for higher wages and suppliers to ask for higher input prices. These changes cause the AS curve to shift upward from AS_1 to AS_2, neutralizing the output effect of the monetary expansion and raising the overall price level.

Of course, if wage rates and other costs rise, the aggregate supply curve will tend to shift upward (from AS_1 to AS_2 in Exhibit 14.1), and so less real output will be supplied at any given price level. Because the government-mandated increase in aggregate demand has been immediately offset by a *reduction* in aggregate supply, the net effect is to leave output and employment unchanged. The only impact of the expansionary monetary policy has been an increase in the price level from 100 to 110.

The preceding example focused on efforts to combat unemployment, but the theory of rational expectations has equally interesting implications for the the battle against inflation. To illustrate, let's suppose that the inflation rate rises to some level that Fed policymakers have openly designated as unacceptable. According to the theory of rational expectations, if the public is convinced of the Fed's commitment to reducing inflation, it will expect lower inflation; workers will therefore immediately accept wage cuts, and input suppliers will accept lower prices. As a consequence, the AS curve will quickly shift downward, lowering the price level but preserving the same level of output and employment. Once again, discretionary policy alters only the price level; it has no impact on real output or the level of employment. (Note that this result is quite different from the effect predicted by Keynesians. Keynesians would argue that because *some* wages and prices are rigid due to contracts, a reduction in aggregate demand would lower *both* the overall price level and the levels of output and employment. In fact, a major concern of Keynesians has been the unemployment "cost" of combating inflation.) Although these examples have dealt with monetary policy, the same conclusions would hold for systematic applications of fiscal policy.

The Need for Policy Rules

What conclusions can we reach from the preceding examples? The primary conclusion is that systematic monetary and fiscal policies affect only the price level; they do not alter either the level of output or employment. Of course, for discretionary policies to have the effect intended by Keynesians, they must be systematic; it wouldn't make sense to expand the money supply or to cut taxes at random time intervals. So, in effect, the new classical economists are arguing that discretionary monetary and fiscal policies cannot be used to reduce unemployment.

Because the new classical economists are convinced that government policies cannot be used to alter employment, they believe that policymakers should concentrate on achieving and maintaining a low rate of inflation. This, they suggest, can be best accomplished by permitting a slow, steady growth of the money supply and avoiding large budget deficits. Thus, the new classical economists favor rules much like the monetarists': Increase the money supply at a constant rate, and balance the federal budget over some agreed-on period (not necessarily on an annual basis but over some predictable time frame). These rules will prevent government policymakers from aggravating inflation in their well-intentioned but futile attempts to lower unemployment. (Were President Franklin D. Roosevelt's attempts to lower unemployment "well-intentioned but futile"? Did the New Deal teach us anything about the effectiveness or ineffectiveness of discretionary fiscal policy? Read "For Insight on Stimulus Battle, Look to the '30s," on page 430, to learn how economists view these policy efforts.)

Criticisms of the New Classical Economics

The new classical economics is quite controversial. Both the assumption of wage/price flexibility and the assumption of rational expectations have been criticized. Few economists seem willing to accept the assertion that wages are sufficiently flexible to ensure that labor markets are continually in equilibrium. These economists point to the prolonged unemployment of the Great Depression and periods in the 1970s and 1980s as evidence that wages adjust slowly, not rapidly as the new classical model implies.

The belief that expectations are formed rationally has also been met with skepticism, both by Keynesians and by many monetarists. Critics argue that the public does not gather and analyze information as intelligently as the theory suggests; nor does it always make fully rational decisions based on that information. Studies of the theory of rational expectations have produced mixed results. Although some early evidence supported the theory, its performance on more recent tests has not upheld its initial promise.

If either of the basic assumptions is incorrect, the policy ineffectiveness theorem of the new classical economists is invalidated. In other words, monetary and fiscal policies would be capable of generating short-run changes in the levels of output and employment. This seems to be the view held by most economists. Of course, whether such policies should be used to change output and employment still depends on the length of the lags involved in policy implementation—the issue raised by the monetarists.

A DIFFERENT FORM OF ACTIVISM: MANAGING AGGREGATE SUPPLY

The debate about the desirability of government efforts to manage aggregate demand has been with us for a long time. Given that it is very difficult to prove statistically which of the schools of thought has the most accurate model of the economy, the debate is likely to continue. We'll indicate a few areas of consensus among macroeconomists after we take a brief look at supply-side economics.

Even if monetary and fiscal policies work as Keynesians suggest (which is certainly not the conclusion of the monetarists or the new classical economists), they produce mixed results. As we saw in Chapter 12, efforts to reduce unemployment tend to aggravate inflation, whereas policies to reduce inflation lead to greater unemployment. In addition, demand-management policies are incapable of offsetting supply shocks—unexpected reductions in aggregate supply. Because supply shocks lead to stagflation, they put pressure on policymakers to combat the two problems instead of one. But once again policymakers are confronted by trade-offs. If they choose to combat inflation, they make the unemployment problem even worse; if they decide to attack unemployment, the inflation rate escalates. In the late 1970s these limitations led to an intense interest in policies to increase aggregate supply.

Supply-Side Economics

The attraction of increasing aggregate supply is probably obvious. Anything that causes the AS curve to shift to the right will raise output and employment, while also lowering the overall price level. As you consider Exhibit 14.2, suppose that the economy is operating at point A, at the intersection of AD and AS_1. If policymakers can increase aggregate supply from AS_1 to AS_2, they can move the economy to point B; they will have increased equilibrium output (and employment) in the economy while also reducing the overall price level. Policymakers will have succeeded in simultaneously reducing unemployment and inflation.[5]

Theory suggests a variety of policies for increasing aggregate supply. The phrase **supply-side economics** is commonly used to refer to a branch of economics that focuses on stimulating aggregate supply through policies that involve minimal government intervention. Supply-side economists advocate policies such as the following:

1. *Encourage saving and investment through tax policies.* By encouraging saving through a reduction in taxes on interest income, for example, the government can make more funds available for investment purposes. Various techniques can then be used to encourage businesses to borrow this money and invest it. *Investment tax credits* would allow firms to deduct a certain

---

[5] Policymakers are aiming to increase both short-run and long-run aggregate supply. For continuity, this chapter focuses on the short-run AS curve. The next chapter, which explores policies to increase aggregate supply in greater depth, will focus on the long-run AS curve.

EXHIBIT 14.2

The Impact of Supply-Side Remedies

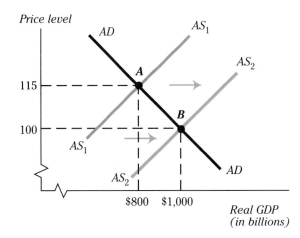

The purpose of supply-side remedies is to shift the aggregate supply curve to the right, thereby reducing the overall price level while increasing output and employment.

percentage of their investment outlays from their tax liabilities. To the extent that such policies encourage businesses to borrow and invest in new factories and equipment, they help to increase the economy's productive capacity so that more output is supplied at any given price level. Of course, if more output is produced at each price level, the aggregate supply curve shifts to the right, as depicted in Exhibit 14.2.

2. *Reduce government regulations that drive up the cost of doing business.* We all recognize that government regulations are necessary to protect consumers, the environment, and the health and safety of workers. In some instances, however, regulations may add substantially to the cost of producing goods and services yet may provide little real benefit for the society. For example, the Food and Drug Administration has been accused of driving up the cost of developing new drugs by needlessly prolonging the testing that is required to gain FDA approval. Reducing such costs should free resources to produce other goods and services; thus, more output can be supplied at each price level.

3. *Encourage individuals to work harder and longer by reducing marginal tax rates.* Marginal tax rates are the tax rates paid on the last increment of income. For example, under a progressive income tax system, an individual earning $35,000 might be required to pay a tax of 15 percent on the first $30,000 and 20 percent on the remaining $5,000. Supply-siders insist that high marginal tax rates discourage work. The way to get people to work more (and

thereby increase aggregate supply) is to reduce marginal tax rates and let them keep more of what they earn.

Unlike monetary and fiscal policies, supply-side remedies have the very desirable feature of being able to combat unemployment and inflation at the same time. To confirm this conclusion, consider once again the situation represented in Exhibit 14.2. If the economy is initially in equilibrium at point A, policies that are successful in increasing aggregate supply from AS_1 to AS_2 will move the economy to point B, increasing the economy's equilibrium output and raising employment, while simultaneously reducing the overall price level. Policymakers will have succeeded in simultaneously reducing employment and inflation.

The Reagan Supply-Side Experiment

When President Reagan took office, he presented several supply-side features in his Program for Economic Recovery (announced in February 1981). The cornerstone of Reagan's program was the Economic Recovery Tax Act (ERTA) of 1981. ERTA called for a 5 percent reduction in tax rates in 1981 and a 10 percent reduction in 1982 and 1983. ERTA also contained provisions to encourage saving and to stimulate business investment. According to its supporters, the reduction in tax rates would cause the economy to grow rapidly as the lower tax rates stimulated saving and investment and convinced Americans to work harder.

What actually happened? Initially, the effects of the Reagan administration's tax cuts were more than offset by a restrictive monetary policy engineered by the Federal Reserve to combat inflation (which was running at more than 12 percent a year in 1980). While these policies helped to quell inflation, they also pushed the economy into the deepest recession since the Great Depression.

The recession ended in December 1982, and output and employment expanded rapidly through 1984. For the remainder of the 1980s, however, economic growth was unspectacular (President Reagan's term ended on January 20, 1989). Overall, the rate of economic growth experienced in the decade of the 1980s was identical to the experience of the previous decade; in both decades the average annual growth rate of real GDP was 2.7 percent. Clearly, the supply-side measures did not lead to the spectacular economic growth that some supporters expected.

Judged by what some supply-siders initially promised—an explosion in work effort, investment, and saving—the Economic Recovery Tax Act was clearly a disappointment. Moreover, Keynesian economists attributed most of the economic expansion of the Reagan years not to the supply-side policies but to the demand-side stimulus provided by the substantial budget deficits.

Use Your Economic Reasoning

For Insight on Stimulus Battle, Look to the '30s; For Left and Right, Issue Rekindles New Deal Debate

BY STEVEN MUFSON

Underlying the partisan division over President Obama's stimulus bill is a dispute over history—a decades-old debate between liberals and conservatives over the impact the New Deal had in bringing the country out of the Great Depression. Senate Minority Leader Mitch McConnell (R-Ky.) said flatly last week that "the big-spending programs of the New Deal did not work." Sen. Richard Shelby (R-Ala.) said, "If we look back, even to the New Deal, it's not going to help employment." And two economists argued in the *Wall Street Journal* that "there was even less work on average during the New Deal than before FDR took office."

But most mainstream economists say the lessons of the Depression, which didn't end until World War II spending kicked in, are different. They say New Deal spending programs instituted by President Franklin D. Roosevelt—combined with moves to bolster the banking system, loosen monetary policy and end the gold standard—did help put millions of people back to work. . . .

Like most disputes about the past, the wrestling match over the lessons of the Depression has everything to do with the present. If Roosevelt's New Deal programs—such as the Civilian Conservation Corps, the Works Progress Administration and Social Security—didn't revive the economy in the 1930s, Republicans in Congress have a powerful argument justifying their opposition to President Obama's stimulus program. And if the Roosevelt programs worked, Democrats can justify the huge stimulus package as following a successful precedent. . . .

Many economists say that fiscal stimulus did not end the Depression because fiscal stimulus was not really tried; the spending increases were too small. . . . "The standard view among economic historians . . . is that the most important thing FDR did to get us out of the Depression was abandoning the gold standard, which freed the Federal Reserve to follow a more expansionary monetary policy," said N. Gregory Mankiw, a Harvard University economics professor who served as President Bush's chairman of the Council of Economic Advisers.

In an essay for the *Encyclopedia Britannica*, Christina Romer, now chairman of the Council of Economic Advisers, argued that the 42 percent increase in the money supply from 1933 to 1937 was the main driver of recovery. A tightening of money supply after the Fed ordered an increase in bank reserves in 1936–37, not just the cut in spending, explains the slowdown of the economy at the outset of Roosevelt's second term. "The actual increases in government spending and the government budget deficit were small relative to the size of the economy," Romer wrote. "This is especially apparent when state government budget deficits are included, because those deficits actually declined at the same time that the federal deficit rose. As a result, the new spending programs initiated by the New Deal had little direct expansionary effect on the economy. . . .

Asked how she squares that with her current support for the stimulus bill, Romer yesterday said: "Normally economists like me would say that when faced with recession, let monetary policy be the first tool. It is something you can change quickly." But, she added, "The thing that is striking about this time is that it is not an ordinary recession. Here we had one caused . . . by a financial meltdown. And even when the Fed tried to be fairly aggressive, it wasn't enough. That's why the usual rules would not apply." Moreover, she said, the current stimulus is much bigger than anything Roosevelt tried. "It's a completely different animal in terms of size," she said. Mankiw said that because New Deal spending was relatively tepid, "spending as stimulus is really betting on a theory rather than on empirical evidence. That's why economists are so divided on this."

Recently, economists have focused on the impact of regulatory actions during the New Deal. Lee E. Ohanian of the University of California at Los Angeles argues that the National Labor Relations Act and the National Industrial Recovery Act dampened competition and kept prices artificially high, thus reducing demand rather than stimulating it. "If you're GM and I'm Ford, the government said, 'Keep prices high and don't undercut each other, and we'll let you do that as long as you help workers with higher salaries,'" Ohanian said. "It sounded good, and it was good for the workers who had those jobs, but . . . you're not going to hire many workers. And if you raise the prices of industrial goods above competitive circumstances, people aren't going to be able to buy many of them."

The debate over the New Deal and the Depression is often a matter of massaging numbers. Ohanian has helped fuel the conservative critique of the New Deal, in part by writing in a *Wall Street Journal* op-ed that "comparing hours worked at the end of the 1930s to those at the beginning of FDR's presidency doesn't paint a picture of recovery. Total hours worked per adult in 1939 remained about 21 percent below their 1929 level, compared to a decline of 27 percent in 1933." But the same statistics can be used to say something quite different: Despite a growing population, the hours worked per adult rose 8 percent from 1933 to 1939—hardly a smashing success but at least a step toward recovery.

McConnell said last week that "in 1940, unemployment was still 15 percent. What got us out of the doldrums that we were in during the Depression was the beginning of World War II." But is that an argument for or against stimulus? During the war, government spending soared sixfold and federal government debt more than doubled. It was only in 1936 that John Maynard Keynes published his *The General Theory of Employment, Interest and Money,* the book that provided the intellectual underpinning for deficit spending in economic downturns. . . .

USE YOUR ECONOMIC REASONING

1. Why would a monetarist expect the additional government spending associated with the New Deal to be ineffective in stimulating the economy?
2. The new classical economists argue that discretionary fiscal policy will be ineffective because it is predictable, and individuals will take actions that offset its intended impact. Would that viewpoint have been valid in the 1930s when discretionary policies were untried? Why or why not?
3. There is general agreement that the New Deal spending was not responsible for pulling the economy out of the Great Depression. Why, then, is there significant support for President Obama's stimulus package? What does Professor Mankiw mean when he says, that "spending as stimulus is really betting on a theory rather than on empirical evidence"?
4. When the U.S. economy recovers from the 2008–2009 recession, economists will be interested in determining the role of the stimulus package in spurring that recovery. Why will that be a difficult task?

President Reagan's Program for Economic Recovery contained several supply-side features.

These economists argue that tax cuts shift both the aggregate demand curve (the traditional Keynesian impact) and the aggregate supply curve (the supply-side impact). However, they believe that in the short run, the supply-side impact tends to be minor in comparison with the demand-side effect.

Even if Keynesians are correct about the short-run impact of supply-side policies, we should not conclude that measures to enhance aggregate supply are to be ignored. On the contrary, virtually all economists agree that expanding aggregate supply is crucial to the long-run well-being of Americans. The next chapter, "Economic Growth: The Importance of the Long Run," examines this issue in much more detail.

SUMMING UP: FINAL THOUGHTS ON POLICY ACTIVISM

Economists obviously disagree about the role of government in attempting to maintain full employment and about the possible benefits of supply-side remedies. This section is the author's interpretation of current thinking.

1. Virtually all economists agree that the economy contains, to one degree or another, a self-correcting mechanism. The economy tends to return to potential GDP and full employment in the long run. Economists disagree about how long this adjustment process takes.

2. Economists disagree about the ability of demand-management policies to speed up the adjustment to potential GDP and full employment. Keynesians support such measures; monetarists and new classical economists do not.

   The differences between activists and nonactivists may not, however, be quite as great as they first appear. Even Keynesians recognize that discretionary policies are subject to lags. Thus, modern Keynesians believe that it is undesirable to attempt to fine-tune the economy—to try to correct every minor increase in unemployment or in the overall price level. Instead, they believe that policymakers should confine their efforts to combating major downturns or inflationary threats.

3. The new classical economics has clearly shaken up macroeconomic thinking but hasn't gained very many converts. Most economists do not appear to believe that expectations are formed in a totally "rational" manner. Even fewer economists are willing to accept the classical contention that wages are highly flexible and that markets are continuously in equilibrium. If economists reject these arguments, they must reject the policy ineffectiveness theorem that grows from them.

   Although few economists seem willing to embrace the entire new classical model, most tend to agree that the theory of rational expectations is an improvement on the expectations models previously applied by Keynesians and monetarists. Moreover, there appears to be support for a weaker version of the policy ineffectiveness theory: Fully anticipated policy changes have *smaller* effects than unanticipated changes.

4. Virtually all economists support measures to stimulate aggregate supply. But evidence suggests that supply-side measures do little in the short run to stimulate GDP or to lower the price level. The major impact of supply-side policies comes in the long run, when their benefits can be substantial.

SUMMARY

Although economists generally agree about the existence of a self-correcting mechanism, they disagree about the speed with which this adjustment process occurs and about the desirability of government efforts to enhance these naturally occurring forces.

Keynesians believe that the economy's self-correcting mechanism works quite slowly. Thus, they support an active role for government in speeding the adjustment process through discretionary monetary and fiscal policies.

Monetarists believe that the economy's self-adjustment mechanism works reasonably quickly and that government efforts to aid this process are either ineffective or counterproductive.

According to monetarists, changes in the money supply play the primary role in determining the level of aggregate output and prices in the economy. Government efforts to stimulate the economy through fiscal policy are futile because they lead to the crowding out of investment spending.

The monetarists also argue against the use of discretionary monetary policy. Because of the recognition lag and the impact lag, the effect of a monetary policy change may be felt when it is no longer appropriate. Thus, discretionary monetary policy has a destabilizing effect on the economy: it contributes to greater unemployment and inflation.

Because monetarists believe that discretionary monetary policy tends to intensify the economy's problems rather than to lessen them, they support a *monetary rule* that would require the Fed to expand the money supply at a constant annual rate.

Monetarists are not alone in opposing the use of discretionary policies to guide the economy's performance; *new classical economists* also argue against such intervention. The new classical economics is founded on two basic tenets: (1) wages and prices are highly flexible, and (2) expectations about the future are formed rationally.

Because new classical economists believe that wages and prices are highly flexible, they believe that the economy quickly tends toward full employment. Reductions in aggregate demand are met by falling wages and prices, which quickly restore equilibrium. Any unemployment is voluntary.

New classical economists emphasize the impact of expectations on behavior; different expectations about the future can lead to different decisions today. The *theory of rational expectations* suggests that people use all available information to develop realistic expectations about the future.

The new classical economists' belief in highly flexible wages and prices and rational expectations led to the *policy ineffectiveness theorem.* According to this theorem, systematic monetary and fiscal policies cannot alter the level of output or employment in the economy; they can change only the price level.

Because the new classical economists are convinced that government policies cannot be used to alter output or employment, they believe that policymakers should concentrate on achieving and maintaining a low rate of inflation. The new classical economists, like the monetarists, favor rules to achieve this objective.

The activist–nonactivist debate has focused on the desirability of demand-management policies. But in the late 1970s, supply-side remedies—policies to increase aggregate supply—attracted a great deal of attention. The desirable feature of such policies is that they can reduce unemployment and inflation at the same time. Available evidence suggests that supply-side measures have a relatively modest impact on aggregate supply in the short run; most of the impact comes in the long run.

KEY TERMS

Monetarism

Monetary rule

Policy ineffectiveness theorem

Supply-side economics

Theory of rational expectations

STUDY QUESTIONS

Fill in the Blanks

1. Keynesian economists who advocate government intervention to guide the economy's performance are also known as

   _____ .

2. The two modern schools of thought that oppose the use of demand-management

   techniques are the _____

   and the _____ .

3. The primary reason that monetarists oppose the use of discretionary monetary policy is because such policy is subject to

   _____ .

4. According to the _____

   and the _____ , the Fed should be required to expand the money supply at a constant rate.

5. _____ is often called the father of monetarism.

6. According to the _____ , expectations are formed rationally.

7. The belief that systematic monetary and fiscal policies cannot alter the level of output or employment is known as the

   _____ theorem.

8. The requirement that the Fed expand the money supply at a constant rate is known

   as the _____ .

9. The use of monetary or fiscal policy in an attempt to eliminate even minor increases in unemployment or inflation is known

   as _____ the economy and is opposed by virtually all modern economists.

10. Unlike monetary and fiscal policies,

    _____ remedies can be used to reduce unemployment and inflation at the same time.

Multiple Choice

1. Which of the following schools of economists would be described as "activists"?
    a) Classical economists
    b) Keynesian economists
    c) Monetarist economists
    d) New classical economists

2. Which of the following statements about the activist–nonactivist debate is true?
    a) Monetarists advocate the use of discretionary monetary policy to manage aggregate demand and to ensure full employment.
    b) New classical economists support the use of fiscal policy to guide the economy but believe that monetary policy is ineffective.
    c) Keynesians advocate government intervention because they believe that the self-correcting mechanism works too slowly.
    d) All of the above

3. According to the monetarists,
    a) fiscal policy is ineffective because of crowding out.
    b) fiscal policy is more effective than monetary policy.
    c) increases in government spending tend to lower interest rates, thus stimulating investment spending.
    d) increases in government spending tend to stimulate investment spending by making business leaders more optimistic.

4. Which of the following is a true statement about the monetarists?
    a) They favor the use of discretionary monetary policy to guide the economy's performance.
    b) They believe that the money supply should be increased at a constant rate.
    c) They favor legislation to provide Fed policymakers with more power to guide the economy's performance.
    d) Both a and c

5. The "monetary rule" is advocated by
    a) Keynesians and calls for greater reliance on monetary policy and less reliance on discretionary fiscal policy.

    b) monetarists and calls for exclusive reliance on discretionary monetary policy in guiding the economy's performance.
    c) Keynesian economists and calls for the Fed to regularly pursue lower interest rates to stimulate investment spending.
    d) monetarists and calls for the Fed to increase the money supply at a constant annual rate.

6. Both the monetarists and the new classical economists
    a) advocate the use of policy "rules" rather than discretion in guiding the economy.
    b) oppose the use of discretionary fiscal policy but support the use of discretionary monetary policy.
    c) oppose the use of discretionary monetary policy but support the use of discretionary fiscal policy.
    d) believe that the economy is inherently unstable and requires periodic intervention to maintain acceptable performance.

7. The major reason monetarists oppose the use of discretionary monetary policy to guide the economy's performance is that they
    a) do not believe that changes in the money supply have any impact on output or employment.
    b) believe that lags cause monetary policy to have a destabilizing effect on the economy.
    c) believe that monetary policy is not as effective as fiscal policy.
    d) believe that rational expectations make monetary policy changes ineffective.

8. Keynesians believe that the economy is inherently unstable because of
    a) the instability created by government fiscal policy.
    b) fluctuations in the level of government spending.
    c) the volatility of investment spending.
    d) Federal Reserve monetary policies.

9. Which of the following is *not* a belief of the new classical economists?
   a) Wages and prices are highly flexible.
   b) Expectations are formed rationally.
   c) Unemployment is voluntary.
   d) Labor markets adjust very slowly to changes in demand.

10. According to the theory of rational expectations,
    a) households and businesses base their expectations only on past experience.
    b) people use all available information in developing their expectations about the future.
    c) it is reasonable for households and businesses to ignore the actions of policymakers.
    d) only policymakers have sufficient knowledge to develop accurate estimates of future price levels.

11. According to the policy ineffectiveness theorem,
    a) anticipated changes in monetary or fiscal policy will alter only the price level.
    b) fiscal policy is ineffective unless it is accompanied by monetary policy.
    c) monetary policy is ineffective unless it is accompanied by fiscal policy.
    d) unanticipated changes in monetary or fiscal policy will alter only the price level.

12. The new classical economists believe that any increase in the money supply that is anticipated by the public will
    a) drive down interest rates and expand output and employment.
    b) increase investment spending and potential GDP.
    c) result in a higher price level with no change in output or employment.

    d) immediately result in an increase in aggregate supply.

13. According to Keynesians, which of the following is true?
    a) When unemployment is caused by inadequate aggregate demand, expanding the money supply will reduce unemployment but intensify inflation.
    b) When inflation is caused by a supply shock, reducing the money supply will lower the rate of inflation but aggravate unemployment.
    c) When unemployment is caused by a reduction in aggregate supply, increasing the money supply will reduce unemployment but aggravate inflation.
    d) All of the above
    e) None of the above

14. Which of the following is *not* a supply-side policy?
    a) Use tax credits to encourage investment.
    b) Reduce marginal tax rates to encourage people to work longer and harder.
    c) Increase tax rates on interest income in order to discourage saving and stimulate consumption spending.
    d) Eliminate government regulations that do not serve a valid purpose.

15. In the short run, reductions in marginal tax rates probably increase
    a) only aggregate demand.
    b) only aggregate supply.
    c) both aggregate demand and aggregate supply but have a greater impact on demand.
    d) both aggregate demand and aggregate supply but have a greater impact on supply.

Problems and Questions for Discussion

1. Given that the economy has a self-correcting mechanism, what is the essence of the Keynesian argument for government intervention to combat unemployment?

2. Why do the monetarists believe that fiscal policy cannot be used to stimulate the economy?

3. Discuss the lags involved in the implementation of monetary policy.

4. Keynesians blame the inherent instability of capitalist economies on the volatility of investment spending. Why do you suppose investment spending by businesses is more volatile than consumption spending by households?

5. What is the nature of the *monetarist* argument for a monetary rule?

6. The new classical economists sometimes argue that only random monetary policy can alter output and employment. Use their model to explain this conclusion. Does this mean that policymakers should replace Keynesian demand-management policies with random policies?

7. Explain the logic behind the policy ineffectiveness theorem of the new classical economists. Supplement your explanation with a graph.

8. Discuss the similarities and differences between the monetarists and the new classical economists with regard to the issue of demand-management policy.

9. List as many supply-side remedies as you can remember, and discuss the rationale for each.

10. Critics of the Reagan experiment with supply-side economics often argue that it was "oversold." What do they mean? What evidence might they summon to support their position?

ANSWER KEY

Fill in the Blanks

1. activists

2. monetarists; new classical economists

3. lags

4. monetarists; new classical economists

5. Milton Friedman

6. new classical economists

7. policy ineffectiveness

8. monetary rule

9. fine-tuning

10. supply-side

Multiple Choice

1. b	4. b	7. b	10. b	13. d
2. c	5. d	8. c	11. a	14. c
3. a	6. a	9. d	12. c	15. c

15

Economic Growth: The Importance of the Long Run

LEARNING OBJECTIVES

1. Explain what is meant by economic growth.
2. Measure changes in the standard of living.
3. Recognize the impact of economic growth on material well-being.
4. Identify the sources of economic growth.
5. Describe the policies that may be employed to stimulate economic growth.
6. Discuss reservations regarding the pursuit of economic growth.

Will you live as well as your parents? Will you be able to buy your dream house, send your kids to college, and retire while you're still young enough to enjoy it? These are important questions! The answers depend in part on individual decisions—on how hard you work and the career choices you make, for instance. But they also depend on something largely beyond your personal control; they depend on the long-run performance of the economy—on how rapidly it grows. In this chapter we explain what is meant by economic growth and examine how it affects our material standard of living. Then we explore the determinants of economic growth and the policies that promote growth. We conclude by examining some debates and concerns about economic growth.

ECONOMIC GROWTH AND WHY IT MATTERS

Thus far, we've spent very little time discussing economic growth. Instead we've focused on the short run and the factors that cause the economy's output to deviate from potential GDP. You've discovered that actual GDP sometimes falls short of potential, creating a "recessionary gap," and that the economy's GDP sometimes surges ahead of potential, creating an "inflationary gap." You've also learned that activists and nonactivists disagree about whether discretionary policy can speed the return to potential. What may not have been evident in the preceding chapters, however, is that potential GDP can change; it is not a static concept. **Economic growth** is defined as an increase in an economy's production capacity or potential GDP. As we will see in a moment, it is this expansion in potential GDP that is responsible for long-run increases in a society's standard of living.

Economic Growth and the Standard of Living

How do we know when we're better off, when our standard of living has increased? The most common measure of a society's standard of living is GDP per capita—output per person. This measure of well-being is relatively easy to calculate. We simply divide an economy's GDP in a given year by its population in that year. For example, the United States' GDP was $14,264.6 billion in 2008, while the U.S. population was 304.2 million. We can conclude that GDP per capita was

$$2008 \text{ GDP per capita} = \frac{\$14,264.6 \text{ billion in GDP}}{304.2 \text{ million people}} = \$46,892$$

This figure compares favorably with other developed nations of the world. For example, 2008 per capita GDP was $34,800 in Germany, $32,700 in France, and $34,200 in Japan. These figures dwarf those for less-developed nations such as Bangladesh ($1,500) and Ethiopia ($800).[1] Exhibit 15.1 displays figures for additional nations.

Of course, if we want to make comparisons over time—for instance, if we want to determine whether we in the United States are better off today than we were in 1990—we have to base those comparisons on real GDP rather than nominal GDP. As you learned in Chapter 10, GDP can increase either because of rising output or because of rising prices. We need to eliminate the impact of rising prices to find out if we really are better off. If real GDP per capita is increasing, we can conclude that our material standard of living has increased because we have more goods and services per person. Of course, that doesn't ensure happiness, and it doesn't indicate that *everyone* in our society is sharing in the increased output. But it does suggest that the average person's standard of *material* well-being has increased.

---

[1] Data are from Central Intelligence Agency, *The World Factbook, 2009*, Washington, D.C.

EXHIBIT 15.1

Per Capita Gross Domestic Product, 2008

COUNTRY	GDP PER CAPITA	COUNTRY	GDP PER CAPITA
Afghanistan	$800	Japan	$34,200
Argentina	$14,200	Malaysia	$15,300
Australia	$38,100	Mexico	$14,200
Bangladesh	$1,500	Nicaragua	$2,900
Botswana	$13,300	Pakistan	$2,600
Brazil	$10,100	Puerto Rico	$17,800
Canada	$39,300	Russia	$15,800
China	$6,000	Saudi Arabia	$20,700
Cuba	$9,500	Singapore	$52,000
Denmark	$37,400	South Africa	$10,000
Egypt	$5,400	South Korea	$26,000
Ethiopia	$800	Sweden	$38,500
France	$32,700	Switzerland	$40,900
Germany	$34,800	Taiwan	$31,900
Ghana	$1,500	Turkey	$12,000
Haiti	$1,300	United Arab Emirates	$40,000
Hong Kong	$43,800	United Kingdom	$36,600
India	$2,800	United States	$47,000
Iran	$12,800	Vietnam	$2,800

Projections from the Central Intelligence Agency, *The World Factbook, 2009.*

Per Capita GDP: The United States' Experience

Americans have enjoyed a rising standard of living for about as long as they have kept records. Consider the progress that has been made in the last 40 years (about the length of a person's working life). Per capita real GDP was $18,200 in 1968 (measured in 2000 dollars). By 1988 it had climbed to $27,521, and by 2008 it had risen to $38,304. In a little more than a generation, output per person increased about 110 percent, an impressive increase in the standard of living.

How do we explain this increase in the standard of living? Let's begin with the basics. For a nation's standard of living to rise, real GDP must increase more rapidly than population. That may be obvious, but let's take a moment to consider the logic behind that statement. Suppose a nation's population increases by 1 percent a year. Under those circumstances, real GDP (output) must increase by 1 percent a year to provide the population with the same amount of goods and services, the same standard of living. If real GDP increases more rapidly than population, the standard of living (per capita GDP) increases; if population increases more rapidly than GDP, the standard of living declines. In recent decades, the U.S. population has been increasing at a rate of about 1 percent a year, so, for example, when real GDP increases by 3 percent, per capita GDP increases by 2 percent. Many less-developed nations are not as fortunate. For instance, the population of Ethiopia is increasing at a rate in excess of 2 percent, so a 3 percent increase in Ethiopia's real GDP would increase the standard of living by less than 1 percent.

Exhibit 15.2 plots the growth of real GDP in the United States since 1970. As you can see from the exhibit, the trend in real GDP (the green wavy line in the exhibit) clearly has been upward. But while real GDP has grown over time, the expansion has not been steady or regular. Sometimes, output has grown rapidly. At other times, output has grown slowly or even declined. As you discovered in Chapter 10, we call these recurring ups and downs in the level of economic activity the *business cycle*. A period of rising output is called an *expansion*; a period of declining real output is called a *recession*. In the short run, the business cycle can have a significant impact on real GDP, lowering it during recessions and raising it rapidly during expansions. But over the long run, it is the behavior of *potential* GDP that really matters, because actual GDP tends toward potential GDP.

The smooth black curve in Exhibit 15.2 represents potential GDP. This curve shows potential GDP increasing at a rate of 3 percent a year, about the average rate at which real GDP has increased over the last 30-year period. As you can see, actual GDP was sometimes above potential, sometimes below. But the self-correcting model tells us that in the long run, actual GDP returns to potential. That's why it is the growth rate of potential GDP that is important in determining our standard of living: because it is the behavior of potential GDP that dictates the path that actual GDP will *ultimately* follow.

The Rule of Seventy-Two: Why the Growth Rate Matters

There's no reason to believe that potential GDP must always increase at the 3 percent rate we've experienced over the last 30 years. In fact, there is substantial

The Trend of Real GDP in the United States

Billions of (2000) Dollars

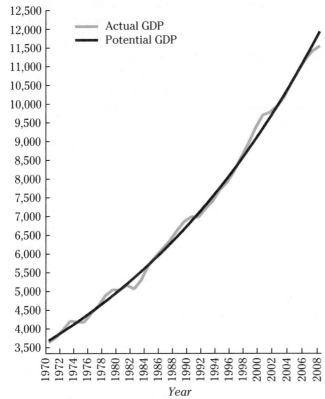

In the period from 1970 to 2008, potential GDP (represented by the smooth black curve) increased by approximately 3 percent a year. Actual GDP (the green wavy line) diverged from potential, sometimes growing more rapidly, sometimes more slowly.

evidence that potential GDP increased at something like 4.5 percent a year in the 1960s, and many economists believe that the growth rate of potential GDP accelerated in the last half of the 1990s. But why should we care about the growth rate of potential GDP? For example, suppose that the growth path of potential GDP was steeper; suppose, for instance, that potential GDP was growing at 4 percent a year instead of 3 percent. What impact would this have on our lives?

Small differences in the growth rate don't matter very much in the short run, but they matter a great deal in the long run. To illustrate, let's look at something you have a personal stake in—your income. Suppose you graduate from college at 22 and take a job paying $30,000 a year. How long will it take for your income to double—to increase to $60,000 a year? Obviously, it depends on how big your raises are! If your raises average 2 percent a year, it will take 36 years for your salary to reach $60,000. (You'll be 58 years old!) If your raises average 3 percent, the time drops to 24 years (so you'll make it by the time you're 46). If you're fortunate enough to receive 4 percent raises, your income will double in only 18 years. You'll be earning $60,000 by the time you turn 40, and your income will be $120,000 at 58. A percentage point or two may not seem like much, but in the long run it matters a great deal.

We base the preceding predictions on the **rule of seventy-two**, which states that a variable's doubling time equals 72 divided by the growth rate. (So, for instance, at a 4 percent growth rate, income would double in $72/4 = 18$ years.) The mathematics behind the rule of seventy-two need not concern us here. The important point is that seemingly small changes in the growth rate make a big difference in the long run. The rule of seventy-two applies to any numeric value, including potential GDP—the source of rising living standards. If potential GDP is expanding at a rate of 3 percent a year, then potential GDP doubles every 24 years. At a 4 percent rate, GDP will take 18 years to double. That one percentage point difference in the rate of growth has a substantial impact on our standard of living. It gives us more of the "fun stuff" like sports cars, vacations, and computer games. It also provides more of the important things like housing, education, and health care. In summary, the rate of economic growth can have a significant impact on our lives. But what determines the rate of economic growth? We now turn to that question.

SOURCES OF ECONOMIC GROWTH

We've defined economic growth as an increase in potential GDP. Because the long-run aggregate supply (LRAS) curve is a vertical line at potential GDP, we can represent economic growth by shifting the long-run aggregate supply curve to the right, as represented in Exhibit 15.3.[2] The question, then, is what factors can cause the LRAS curve to shift to the right? These factors are the sources of economic growth.

There are basically two sets of factors that can shift the LRAS curve to the right: increases in the stock of economic resources (land, labor, or capital) and increases in technology; that is, technological advance. Let's explore these possibilities.

_____

[2] Recall from Chapter 1 that economic growth can also be represented by shifting the economy's production possibilities curve to the right. A rightward shift in the production possibilities curve indicates that the economy's production capabilities have increased. This is simply another way of saying that potential output has expanded.

EXHIBIT 15.3

Graphing Economic Growth

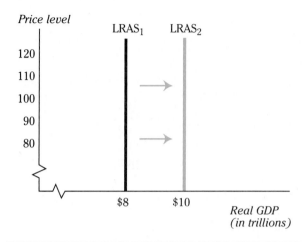

We define economic growth as an increase in an economy's productive capacity, or potential GDP. It is represented graphically by a rightward shift in the economy's long-run aggregate supply curve.

Growth in the Stock of Natural Resources

We discovered in Chapter 1 that economists use the term "land" to refer to society's stock of natural resources. The term encompasses surface land, but it also includes timber, mineral deposits, oil, water, and so on.

The discovery of additional supplies of natural resources does not appear to play a major role in the economic growth of modern economies. On the one hand, Japan developed into a major world power with very little in the way of a natural-resource base. And the Asian tigers—South Korea, Taiwan, and Singapore—appear to be on a similar path. On the other hand, some resource-rich nations—Brazil and Argentina, for instance—have experienced relatively slow rates of economic growth.

While at this time the availability of natural resources does not appear to be a make-or-break factor for a nation's economic growth, that could someday change. Land is the only economic resource on the planet that is truly in fixed supply. Because greater output requires more natural resources, the earth's fixed supply of natural resources may eventually mean an end to rising per capita incomes. Many economists argue that with technological advances (which we will discuss later) we can postpone that day for centuries—perhaps indefinitely. Others argue that, one way or another, natural-resource constraints—including those imposed by the ozone layer and available supplies of clean air and water—will eventually bring an end to rising living standards. We'll have more to say about this issue in the last section of this chapter.

Growth in the Labor Supply

Another possible source of increases in potential GDP is increases in the labor force—the supply of labor. Recall from Chapter 10 that we define the U.S. labor force to include all persons over the age of 16 who are working or actively seeking work. The labor force can increase for two reasons: because of more rapid growth in the (working-age) population or because a larger fraction of that population chooses to work.

By itself, population increase does not appear to be a very promising avenue for increasing living standards. Think about our definition of the standard of living—GDP per capita. While an increase in population can help to raise potential GDP—the size of the pie we have to divide—it also raises the number of people who want shares of that output—the number of slices of pie. This dual effect limits the benefit to be derived from an increase in population. In fact, less-developed countries like China and India devote their efforts to limiting population, not to stimulating its growth.

An increase in the labor-force participation rate—the fraction of the population that chooses to enter the labor force—is more promising. In 1950, only about one-third of women 16 and over were in the labor force. Today, the fraction is approaching two-thirds.[3] This increase allows the economy to increase potential GDP without adding to the number of mouths to be fed. Of course, this avenue of growth is not free. Working moms or dads are not home raising kids, doing their own home repairs, or learning to play tennis. As you already know, every choice involves an opportunity cost.

Growth in the Capital Stock

An increase in the labor supply may have little impact on the rate of economic growth unless the additional workers are provided with capital to supplement their efforts. As we discovered in Chapter 1, the term *capital* is most commonly used to refer to **physical capital**—physical aids to production such as machines, tools, and factories. Computers are an example of physical capital, as are delivery trucks, robots, and hand tools (hammers, saws, etc.). Imagine a business hiring an additional secretary without providing the employee with a computer. That worker would be required to share someone's existing computer, using it only when it was vacant. Although this new employee would probably make a contribution to the firm, the contribution would clearly be less than if the business had been willing to provide additional capital to enhance the new worker's productivity.

---

[3] As the labor-force participation rate for women has risen, the rate for men has fallen (from about 86 percent in 1950 to roughly 75 percent today). The overall rate (the rate for men plus women) has continued to rise.

The addition of **human capital**—the knowledge and skills that are embodied in labor—can also enhance worker productivity. Human capital is acquired through education and training. You're acquiring human capital right now, as you work on your college degree! A person with a college degree generally has more human capital than a person with only a high-school education. And a person with a graduate degree generally has more human capital than a person with an undergraduate degree. The more education and training, the more human capital you possess.

Consider our secretary again. Once we have provided this secretary with a computer, we will need to provide training programs on how to use particular types of software, how to troubleshoot for computer problems, and so on. The more knowledgeable this secretary becomes—the more human capital he or she acquires—the more productive this person will be. Of course, as workers become more productive, the economy's ability to produce output increases, so the economy's long-run aggregate supply curve shifts to the right.

The acquisition of additional capital—either physical capital or human capital—requires an investment on the part of society. There are basically two ways that a nation can acquire the money needed to finance investment expenditures: saving and borrowing. Neither option is painless. A decision to increase saving requires that we consume less now, lowering our current enjoyment. Borrowing requires that we eventually repay what we have borrowed, lowering future pleasure.

The pain associated with investment helps to explain why many less-developed countries have remained so. Because incomes in these nations are often extremely low, savings rates tend to be low—in some instances, virtually zero. The average citizen simply cannot forgo current consumption in order to save. That's why these nations try to attract foreign investment as a way of breaking out of this cycle.

Technological Advances

Technology is our state of knowledge about how to produce products. It dictates the ease with which the economy can convert resources into goods and services. **Technological advances** are discoveries that make it possible to produce more or better products from the same resources. For instance, technological breakthroughs in the area of genetics have provided farmers with hybrid seeds that allow them to obtain much higher corn and wheat yields from their fields. Advances in information technology, in turn, have made it possible to use the Internet and e-mail to communicate instantaneously, avoiding the need for more costly (and slower) forms of communication.

Technological change is generally regarded as the most important source of economic growth. It is also the least understood. Why does technological change occur more rapidly in some countries than in others? And why does it occur more rapidly at some times than at others? Unfortunately, we cannot answer these questions conclusively. The following factors may, however, provide some clues.

One factor that appears to influence the rate at which technological advances are made is the level of education. The more educated the workforce, the greater its ability to make technological breakthroughs. The rate of technological change also seems to depend on the availability of funding for research and development. Developing new products and new ways of doing things is not free, so success depends in part on how much money is spent in the search.

The profit potential associated with new technologies is also important. Private enterprises exist to make profits, so businesses are more interested in advancing technology when they can see its impact on their profit–loss statements. Consider, for example, genome research—the attempt to map human DNA. An important factor driving this research is the immense profit potential that better medicines might bring. According to George Scanos, president and CEO of Exelixis, Inc., a genetic-information company in San Francisco, California, "In a few years all the genes that are useful for treating diabetes, Alzheimer's and cancer will be known. . . . Whoever gets them first will get significant intellectual property rights and a significant competitive advantage."[4]

Finally, competition plays a role in promoting technological advance. When competitive pressures are present, firms have incentive to innovate to avoid being outperformed by their rivals. For example, many of the advances in U.S. automobiles—both in design and reliability—have been made in response to competitive pressures from foreign carmakers, particularly the Japanese carmakers.

As you can see, a variety of factors appear to influence the rate of technological advance, including everything from the education level of workers to the degree of competitive pressure felt by producers. Given this complexity, is there anything that government policymakers can do to promote technological change? We turn now to a discussion of policies to promote economic growth.

POLICIES TO PROMOTE GROWTH

Until recently, economists questioned whether a government's economic policy could influence an economy's long-run growth rate. Today, both economic theory and empirical evidence suggest that government policy does affect long-term growth, though not always in a positive way.[5] In this section, we explore

---

[4] Scott Hensley, "New Race Heats Up to Turn Gene Information into Drug Discoveries," *Wall Street Journal,* June 26, 2000, p. B1. Mr. Scanos's comment was made in 2000, so he may have been overly optimistic about the rate of discovery. Still, his observation about the motivation to be first remains valid.
[5] Federal Reserve Bank of Kansas City, *Policies for Long-Run Growth,* 1992. See the "Symposium Summary," by George A. Kahn.

the role of government policy in promoting economic growth. We will concentrate our attention on policies designed to increase the capital stock (including both physical and human capital) and the rate of technological advance. These policies are all intended to enhance the **productivity of labor**: the amount of output the average worker can produce. For instance, if we provide workers with more or better capital equipment, we enable them to produce more output. Enhancing their skill level through education or training has a similar impact. We begin by examining policies designed to increase the capital stock. Then we turn to policies to promote technological advance.

Promoting Capital Investment

If we want workers to become more productive, one approach is to provide them with more capital, either more physical capital (tools, machinery, etc.) or more human capital (education and skill). As we've already seen, increasing the capital stock requires investment spending.

To understand investment decisions, we need to become familiar with the **loanable funds market**, the market in which businesses and households borrow funds to make investments. The price that borrowers must pay to obtain funds is the interest rate. As you can see from Exhibit 15.4, the demand curve for loanable funds slopes downward. This indicates that businesses and others are willing to borrow more funds at lower interest rates than at higher interest

---

EXHIBIT 15.4

The Loanable Funds Market

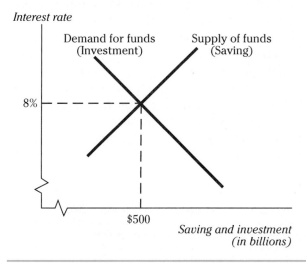

In the long run, the interest rate is determined by the demand and supply of loanable funds. The demand for loanable funds comes from borrowers seeking to finance investment projects. The supply of loanable funds comes from saving. The equilibrium interest rate balances demand and supply.

rates. The supply of loanable funds comes from saving. The upward-sloping supply curve indicates that more will be saved at higher interest rates than at lower interest rates. In our hypothetical example, the interaction of demand and supply results in an equilibrium interest rate of 8 percent. At that rate, $500 billion is saved and invested.[6]

Policies to Encourage Saving

If a nation wants to increase its investment spending, it must consume less to provide the saving necessary to finance that investment. In short, increased investment requires increased saving.

There are two sources of saving, private saving and public saving. **Private saving** is done by households. It is the amount of income that households have left over after subtracting taxes and consumption spending for goods and services. **Public saving** is done by government. It is the amount of tax revenue that is left over after government pays for its spending. The sum of private saving and public saving is called **national saving** (private saving + public saving = national saving); it represents the total amount of saving occurring in the economy. If policymakers want to increase national saving, they can target private saving, public saving, or both. Let's consider these possibilities.

Spurring Private Saving

How do we encourage households to save more? Some economists are convinced that private saving can be increased by providing tax incentives to households. For instance, the federal government could eliminate the tax on interest income—the income earned from savings accounts. Or it might allow households to make larger tax-deductible contributions to Individual Retirement Accounts (IRAs), accounts intended to promote saving for retirement. A more far-reaching proposal would replace the federal income tax with a **consumption tax**, also called an **expenditure tax**. A consumption tax is like a national sales tax; individuals are taxed on what they spend (consume) rather than on what they earn. Because spending is taxed and saving is not, this proposal should encourage saving.

Each of these proposed changes would cause households to save more at any given interest rate, shifting the supply curve of saving to the right, as illustrated in Exhibit 15.5. The rightward shift in the supply curve would, in turn, reduce the equilibrium interest rate. This would encourage businesses to borrow and invest in physical capital, and it would encourage workers to increase their investment in human capital. (Is it possible for economic

---

[6] If you think we've discussed interest-rate determination before, you're right! Chapter 13 examined how interest rates are determined in the *short run*, by the supply and demand for money. The loanable funds model shown here looks instead at how interest rates are determined in the *long run*, by the supply and demand for saving.

EXHIBIT 15.5

Tax Incentives to Increase Saving

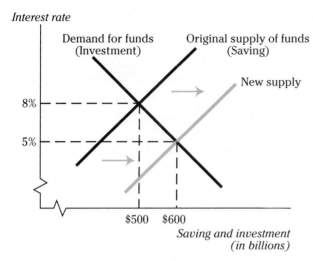

Tax incentives can be used to increase saving. These policies, by lowering the interest rate, can increase the amount of investment spending.

conditions to alter households' willingness to save? Read "Shift from Spending to Saving May Be Slump's Lasting Impact," on page 452, to learn how Americans behaved during the recent economic downturn.)

Increasing Public Saving   We discovered earlier that public saving is the amount of government tax revenue that is *not* spent. Alternatively, we could say that whenever government runs a budget surplus (takes in more tax revenue than it spends), it is engaging in "public" saving.

To clarify why economists call budget surpluses *public saving*, consider what happens when the federal government runs a surplus. What does it do with the surplus? It can't spend it; if it did there would be no surplus. Instead, it must somehow save the surplus. One approach is to use the surplus to buy back some of the government bonds that make up the national debt. This provides the former bondholders with funds that they can make available to investors. Alternatively, the government could use its surplus to purchase the stocks and bonds of private companies, providing them with the funds they need to make investments. Either way, the federal government is supplying additional funds to the loanable funds market. Of course, this shifts the supply curve of loanable funds to the right, lowering the interest rate and thereby

Use Your Economic Reasoning

Shift from Spending to Saving May Be Slump's Lasting Impact

BY CATHERINE RAMPELL

The economic downturn is forcing a return to a culture of thrift that many economists say could last well beyond the inevitable recovery. This is not because Americans have suddenly become more financially virtuous or have learned the error of their free-spending ways. Instead, these experts say, Americans may have no choice but to continue pinching pennies.

This shift back to thrift may seem to be a healthy change for a consumer class known for spending more than it earns, but there is a downside: American businesses have become so dependent on consumer spending that any pullback sends ripples through the economy. Fearful of job losses and anxious over housing and stock declines, Americans are squirreling away more of their paychecks than they were before the recession. In the last year, the savings rate—the percentage of after-tax income that people do not spend—has risen to above 4 percent, from virtually zero.

This happens in nearly every recession, and the effect is usually fleeting. Once the economy recovers, Americans revert to more spending and less saving. Over the last 30 years, the savings rate has fluctuated from over 14 percent in the 1970s to negative 2.7 percent in 2005, meaning Americans were spending more than they made. This time is expected to be different, because the forces that enabled and even egged on consumers to save less and spend more—easy credit and skyrocketing asset values—could be permanently altered by the financial crisis that spun the economy into recession. . . .

Sustained increases in household saving would cause a difficult period of restructuring for the American economy, which has become increasingly driven by consumer spending. . . . Add the decline in consumer spending to the planned expiration of government stimulus spending, and a painful readjustment in demand for goods and services could occur, economists say. The effect would be felt here and abroad, as many developing economies also depend on America's big-spending ways. "If Americans cut back, as they almost have to do, what will replace that source of demand?" asked William G. Gale, director of the economic studies program at the Brookings Institution, a liberal-centrist policy research group. "The easy answer is the Chinese consumer," he said, but unlike their more prodigal American counterparts, the Chinese save about a quarter of what they earn. "We may cut back faster than they expand into that space, so there might be a lull."

Why might the higher savings rate outlast the recession? Social critics like David Blankenhorn, president of the Institute for American Values, hope that introspection about America's "culture of consumption" will awaken Americans to the virtues of thrift, just as the Great Depression reset American financial values for a generation. But many economists believe consumers will change their habits for more pragmatic reasons. Consumers have lost a huge chunk of their net worth, in the housing bust and the stock market, and to resuscitate their retirement accounts or children's college funds they will have to channel more of their paychecks toward saving—unless those asset markets soar again. Forms of easy credit that were once prevalent, like mortgages with no down payments, also may not return, either because the government regulates them out of existence or because banks dare not venture back into such risky lending. That means if Americans want to buy a house, they will have to save more and borrow less.

Whether for reasons moral or otherwise, consumers are already thinking a bit differently about their long-term budgets. A recent Pew Research Center survey found that many more Americans had begun regarding products like microwave ovens as luxuries rather than necessities. Such attitudes suggest that retailers will have to change their marketing strategies, said J. Walker Smith, executive vice chairman of the Futures Company, a marketing and research consultancy. "People are realizing they can't accumulate everything they want anymore, and they'll have to prioritize more," he said. "That may be hard for a lot of brands—figuring out not only how to get considered by consumers, but put at the top of their list."

Consumers planning big purchases are also anticipating that their borrowing options will remain limited. Last year [2008], Aryn Kennedy and her husband, Brian Ewing, who live in Los Angeles, spent "every dollar" they earned on debt repayment and living expenses. When local housing prices began to fall, Mr. Ewing toyed with the idea of a low-down-payment mortgage. "By the time we really started looking at buying, I knew from reading blogs that most loans like that were not really available anymore, since lenders didn't want to take risks," said Ms. Kennedy. . . . Since then, through "windfalls" like a salary increase for Mr. Ewing, and by cutting expenses for clothing, entertainment and other items, Ms. Kennedy says the couple has begun saving about 25 percent of their take-home pay in anticipation of making a traditional down payment of 20 percent on a house. Even after they buy, Ms. Kennedy said, the couple plans to keep saving 25 percent of their pay. A recent Gallup poll found that most Americans who have recently increased their savings believe their budget adjustments represent a "new, normal pattern for years ahead."

Despite the immediate jolt to the economy, more personal saving would be a positive step in the long run, analysts say. More saving leads to more investment, which promotes economic growth, which leads to better living standards. At the family level, social critics, economists and even many consumers seem to agree that a forced financial conservatism may be for the better. . . .

USE YOUR ECONOMIC REASONING

1. Why are Americans saving a higher fraction of their incomes? Does this represent an increase in private or public saving? What is the downside of this behavior in the current economy?
2. Why do some analysts believe that this change in saving behavior will last "long beyond the inevitable recovery" from the recession? Do you agree with their assessment?
3. As households were trying to ramp up their saving, the federal government was incurring massive budget deficits to combat the recession. What impact will these deficits have on national saving and long-run interest rates?
4. The article suggests that more saving will spur economic growth. What is the connection between saving and growth? Try to explain it step by step.
5. Substantial budget deficits are forecast for several years to come. Would it be possible for national saving to decline despite the increase in private saving described in this article? How would that outcome impact long-run interest rates and economic growth?

EXHIBIT 15.6

Budget Policy and Saving

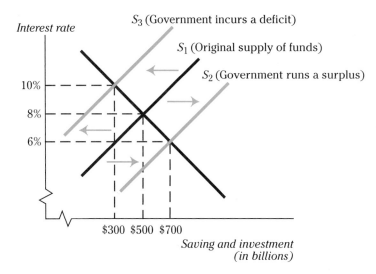

Budget deficits tend to reduce the supply of saving, driving up interest rates and reducing investment spending. Budget surpluses have the opposite effect; they increase the supply of saving, lowering interest rates and increasing investment spending.

encouraging investment. This process is depicted in Exhibit 15.6 by the rightward shift of the supply curve from S_1 to S_2.

Budget surpluses have been a relative rarity for our federal government. Rather, budget deficits have been the norm. In fact, with the exception of a brief period of budget surpluses from 1998–2001 (and a tiny surplus in 1969), we've had uninterrupted budget deficits since 1960—with enormous deficits projected from 2009–2011 and sizable deficits stretching well beyond that period. Budget deficits mean that the federal government is spending more than its tax revenue, so public saving must be negative. In effect, government is borrowing money rather than saving money. As a consequence, budget deficits represent a reduction in national saving; they shift the supply curve of saving back to the left, as represented by the shift from S_1 to S_3 in Exhibit 15.6.

Why do deficits have this impact—why do they reduce national saving? When the federal government incurs a deficit, it must borrow the money to finance that deficit. This government borrowing reduces the supply of funds available to finance private investment spending by businesses and households. Of course, this drives up the interest rate, reducing the willingness to borrow and invest. Note that by using the loanable funds model we arrive at the same answer we obtained in Chapter 14; budget deficits *crowd out* private investment spending.

The foregoing analysis suggests that budget deficits are always undesirable because, by crowding out investment spending, they slow economic

EXHIBIT 15.7

Tax Incentives to Stimulate Investment

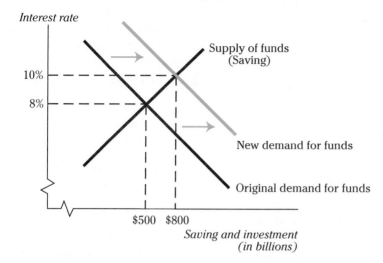

By increasing profit potential, tax incentives (such as an investment tax credit) can increase investment spending.

growth. But long-run growth is not our only performance objective. We're also interested in short-run goals, including full employment and stable prices. As we learned earlier in the text, activists regard budget deficits as a tool for combating short-term unemployment. This conflict points out the necessity of evaluating policies in terms of both their short-run and long-run effects. There's no free lunch, not even for policymakers![7]

Policies to Encourage Investment The preceding proposals attempt to stimulate investment indirectly, by lowering the prevailing interest rate. Other policies attempt to stimulate investment more directly. For example, **investment tax credits** reduce taxes for firms that invest in eligible equipment. By increasing the potential profitability of investments, this policy encourages businesses to undertake additional investment, shifting the demand curve for loanable funds to the right, as represented in Exhibit 15.7.

Tax incentives for education and training have the same impact. For instance, the **Lifetime Learning Tax Credit** targets adults who want to go back to

---

[7] The conflict in objectives may be more apparent than real. Keynesians argue that crowding out is less likely to be a problem during periods of unemployment because business borrowing tends to be depressed under these conditions anyway. Rather than replacing or crowding out business borrowing, government borrowing tends to absorb funds that would otherwise have been unused.

school to prepare for new careers or upgrade their skills. It provides a tax deduction equal to 20 percent of the cost of qualified educational expenses.

Note that the impact of investment incentives is different from that of saving incentives. Because these policies tend to increase the *demand* for loanable funds rather than the supply, they result in higher interest rates. These higher interest rates help to ensure that funds are available to finance the expanded level of investment spending. As interest rates rise, households move along their supply curve of saving, supplying the higher quantity of loanable funds now being demanded.

Promoting Technological Progress

Growth in the capital stock, both in the stock of physical and human capital, is an important source of economic growth. The other major source of growth is technological progress—discoveries that make it possible to produce more or better products from the same resources.

To make sense out of technology policy—policy to promote technological development—we need to recognize that technological progress proceeds in stages. The initial stage generally involves **research**, the process of gaining new knowledge. Research is sometimes categorized as *basic research* (research conducted to gain knowledge for its own sake) and *applied research* (research conducted with a commercial purpose in mind). The distinction is far from clear-cut, however, because even basic-research agendas tend to be influenced by the practical concerns of the day.

Research can lead to **invention**—the discovery of new products or processes that might have practical applications. Inventions are ideas in their formative stages, before we really know if they have practical value. The final stage is **innovation**, the process of converting an invention into something marketable. This is the stage where firms try to get the kinks out of new products and processes so that they will gain commercial value.

Taken together, the three stages that lead to technological advances are often referred to as **research and development**. To illustrate these stages, consider research and development efforts in the drug industry. As AIDS research has provided insights into how the AIDS disease progresses, researchers have invented drugs that they believe might be successful in combating the disease. But there is still much that is not known about AIDS, so the researchers' models are incomplete. It takes additional research and clinical trials to discover which of these drugs have real medical value. This is the innovation stage. Unfortunately, many of these drugs have not turned out to have practical benefits, so relatively few have made it to the market. The same is true of many other inventions; they can't be converted into marketable products.

Policymakers generally attempt to promote technological progress by trying to stimulate one or more of the stages in the research and development process. Consider, for example, the following policies.

Direct Support for Basic Research   Most of the basic research conducted in the United States is supported by the federal government and is carried out either in federal laboratories or by universities receiving government grants. The justification for government support of basic research is similar to that for public goods.[8] Basic research seldom produces discoveries of direct economic benefit to the researchers. Hence, private firms will tend to ignore such research. But even though they do not benefit the researchers, such projects may have a significant payoff to the economy as a whole. In fact, economist Edwin Mansfield estimates that some basic research discoveries represent returns on investment in the neighborhood of 30 percent.[9]

Tax Policies to Promote Research and Development   Private firms tend to concentrate on applied research and innovation, projects that are more likely to return a profit. Like investment, these activities can be encouraged through tax policy. For instance, government can increase the incentive to invest by providing tax credits for research and development. Likewise, policies that increase the supply of saving (through tax incentives or increasing the federal budget surplus) can stimulate research and development by driving down the interest rate and thereby reducing the cost of financing research and development projects.

Policies to Protect Intellectual Property   One area where technological progress may require unique forms of government policy is in the protection of intellectual property rights—the ownership rights to new ideas. The development of new products and processes is an expensive proposition, and success is never assured. In many instances, firms invest millions of dollars in research and development without producing commercially viable products. Firms are unlikely to invest in these inherently risky projects unless they believe that successful products will allow them to recoup their investment, including their investment in unsuccessful projects. But if rivals can easily copy successful new products or processes, any profits will be quickly competed away, destroying the incentive to invest in the research and development necessary to make them possible.

---

[8] Recall from Chapter 9 that public goods convey their benefits equally to payers and nonpayers. This creates a *free-rider problem*, which makes it difficult for private businesses to earn a profit by providing such products.
[9] Martin Baily, Gary Burtless, and Robert Litan, *Growth with Equity* (Washington, D.C.: Brookings Institution, 1993), p. 89.

To encourage research and development, economists support the granting of patents—exclusive rights to control a new product or process—to temporarily shield innovating firms from competition. It can be argued that technological progress would be enhanced by lengthening the period for which patents are granted (currently, 20 years) or by increasing the variety of discoveries that may be patented. Of course, the growth-enhancing benefits of these changes must be weighed against the resulting reduction in competition. This cost-benefit comparison will be increasingly difficult in the New Economy, where patents are requested for more and more intangible innovations. For instance, Amazon.com Inc. was able to patent its "1-Click" purchasing method. And CyberGold was granted a patent on using incentives to reward customers for reading Internet ads. Do these patents protect legitimate innovations, or do they merely stifle competition in electronic commerce? And what about the patents on human genes? While some argue that it is wrong to issue patents for elements of nature, advocates counter that drug research is expensive and that without patents firms would be unwilling to engage in such research. These questions illustrate the complexity of the patent question and why patent policy is the subject of much current debate.[10]

Antitrust Policy to Foster Innovation   The nature of competition is changing, particularly for firms in the information-intensive sector of our economy. Rather than competing on price, these firms tend to compete on innovation, developing new products and new processes. It is important that our antitrust laws keep pace with this trend. For example, some economists argue that firms should have greater leeway to engage in **joint research ventures**—research projects in which firms pool their resources and share the costs of research and development—rather than having those joint ventures blocked by antitrust policy. Joint ventures can potentially cut the cost of developing new products while also reducing each firm's risk of failure.

Some critics of antitrust support more far-reaching changes. They argue that antitrust is poorly suited to the fast-paced world of the Internet and e-commerce. In their view, antitrust enforcers are always behind; they are looking at markets as they once were and at rivalries that no longer exist. By the time they spot a potential problem, the situation has changed and their proposed remedies are unnecessary or counterproductive. In short, these critics view antitrust

---

[10]Another interesting area of debate is the granting of patents for "pure" medical procedures. For instance, a patent was granted for a particular type of incision that is used in cataract surgery. Critics of such medical method patents argue that, unlike new drugs, new medical methods are often discovered during the normal course of medical practice and do not require substantial capital investment. Therefore, these patents do little to encourage new procedures. Instead, they allow patent owners to charge monopoly prices without providing any offsetting gain to society. In fact, by hindering doctors from sharing information, they may actually slow the use of such new procedures.

as an antiquated doctrine that needs to be scrapped or enforced very sparingly. Not surprisingly, Joel Klein, assistant attorney general for antitrust during the Clinton administration, disagrees. According to Klein, "While technology changes, human nature does not." The anticompetitive techniques "used to protect and extend monopoly power in the New Economy are essentially no different from those used throughout history." It remains to be seen how this controversy will be resolved.

Industrial Policy: Can Government Pick the Winners?   A minority of economists argue that government should do more than provide general incentives and support for research and development. They believe that policymakers should single out specific industries and technologies for targeted support (either through grants or tax incentives). For instance, if genetic engineering is deemed to be a particularly promising avenue for stimulating economic growth, the federal government could make tax credits available for research in this area, or it could provide grants to firms with expertise in genetic engineering. Note that this is a variation of the *industrial policy* used by Japan and South Korea to guide the growth of their economies.

As you can see, promoting technological progress is a complex task. It involves everything from providing government grants for basic research to carefully designing the patent system. As you might expect, these policies have varying degrees of support. In fact, not everyone agrees that economic growth is an objective worth pursuing. The last section considers these issues.

DEBATES ABOUT GROWTH POLICY

Before closing this chapter, we need to explore two ongoing debates about growth policy. The first debate is about details, about the specific policies that should be pursued to promote growth. The second debate is more fundamental; it voices concerns about the impact of economic growth on the earth's environment and questions the wisdom of economic growth as an objective. This final section examines the basic elements of these two debates.

The Devil Is in the Details: Debates about How to Stimulate Growth

Economists *generally* support the goal of economic growth. They disagree, however, about the role that government should play in this process and about the specific policies that should be employed to promote growth. In part, this disagreement stems from philosophical differences regarding the proper role of government in the economy. As we learned in Chapter 14, *supply-side economics* refers to a branch of economics that focuses on stimulating aggregate supply through policies that involve minimal government intervention. Supply-side economists were first visible and vocal during the Reagan administration, when they advocated cuts in marginal tax rates to stimulate work effort (and increase the labor supply), tax incentives to increase saving and investment, and reductions in government regulation to reduce the cost of doing business. Supply-siders in George W. Bush's administration promoted similar policies. But while supply-siders deserve credit for calling attention to the importance of aggregate supply, they are not the only economists interested in stimulating economic growth. Keynesians also support policies to stimulate long-run growth, but they are often willing to accept more direct government involvement than supply-siders would find palatable.

While the disagreement between these groups is partly philosophical, it also stems from different interpretations of empirical evidence. The different policies these groups propose to stimulate saving illustrate their disagreement. Keynesians see little evidence that tax policy has been effective in stimulating saving, and they therefore prefer deliberate budget surpluses as a more promising route. Supply-side economists disagree. They believe that tax policy has proved effective in stimulating saving. Moreover, supply-side economists are philosophically opposed to government surpluses, preferring to cut taxes (and tax revenues) as a method of limiting the size of government. As you can see, even economists who agree on the need to stimulate growth often disagree about the policies used to pursue that goal.

Will Economic Growth Harm the Environment?

As we mentioned earlier, not everyone supports economic growth as a goal. Although economists see economic growth as largely beneficial, environmentalists do not. They tend to see economic growth exhausting our nonrenewable resources and generating ever-increasing amounts of pollution. There are basically two sources of this problem: rising population and rising GDP per capita. People use resources, so as population expands there are increased demands placed on the earth, both as a source of resources and as a waste receptor. Rising incomes intensify these demands because increased affluence causes people to consume more resources per person.

Environmentalists see a limit to this process. Eventually, we either run out of resources or we generate enough pollution to destroy life as we know it. A study published in 1972 (and updated in 1992) under the title *The Limits to*

Growth illustrates these concerns. Researchers, using a computer model to simulate likely future outcomes, reached the following conclusion:

> If present growth trends in world population, industrialization, pollution, food production, and resource depletion continue unchanged, the limits to growth on this planet will be reached sometime within the next one hundred years. The most probable result will be a rather sudden and uncontrollable decline in both population and industrial capacity.[11]

Although this computer model raises very serious concerns, most economists would be quick to criticize its assumptions—that present trends in population, food production, resource depletion, and so on will continue. As we've seen throughout this textbook, market participants respond to economic incentives. When incentives change, their behavior changes. As nonrenewable resources become scarcer and therefore more expensive, one response is to switch to other resources—including renewable resources. Another response is to develop technologies that use less of that resource (and to develop completely new alternatives to that resource). The point is that markets are not static, so the assumption that the future holds more of the same is almost certainly incorrect.

To illustrate, consider the way that the lumber and construction industries have responded to the rising price of timber—the result of cutting down much of our "old-growth" timber. Sawmills now use the thinnest blades imaginable to cut logs into lumber; they want to salvage as much lumber as possible while turning as little as possible into sawdust. The sawdust and wood particles that might once have been discarded are combined with resins to produce particleboard and waferboard. And small pieces of lumber are joined using superstrong glues to produce larger support beams, reducing the need for the longer logs usually associated with old-growth timber. Of course, builders must adjust to the higher lumber prices as well. They respond by using the less-expensive categories whenever possible, reserving the higher-grade lumber for fewer, more critical applications. In this way rising timber prices help to conserve our use of lumber while providing the incentive to search for alternatives.

Economists anticipate similar changes in other areas. For instance, we know from past experience that as incomes and education levels rise, population growth rates tend to fall and concern for the environment tends to increase in importance. Of course, slowing population growth would reduce one source of pollution and resource depletion. And increased concern for the environment

---

[11] Donella Meadows, Dennis Meadows, Jorgen Randers, and William Behrens III, *The Limits to Growth* (New York: Universe Books, 1972), p. 23.

would magnify those adjustments. In short, the process of economic growth unleashes all sorts of changes—changes that tend to modify the trends in population, food production, and so on that are incorporated in the *Limits to Growth* forecast.

While the preceding explanation provides some reason for optimism, too much optimism could be a mistake. One element that we have left out of this debate is the timing of these adjustments. We can be confident that population growth will slow, that we will develop less-polluting technologies, and so forth. The critical issue is when, on what timetable. We need to make these adjustments before we destroy our ozone layer, before global warming makes parts of the world uninhabitable, and before biological diversity decreases in ways that critically damage the ecosystem. Can we count on market forces and the invisible hand to do this? Robert Solow, Nobel laureate in economics, believes that the answer is no! He argues that markets do not adequately consider the future, at least not the distant future. So policies to stimulate growth must be combined with policies to direct that growth toward less-polluting technologies.

Solow's position is a controversial one. It takes us to another form of the activist–nonactivist debate. Some economists agree with Solow that, by themselves, markets are not up to the task. Others are convinced that government "help" will only make matters worse. These are legitimate issues for debate. It is a debate we can't afford to postpone; it is a debate we need to have now.

SUMMARY

Economic growth is defined as an increase in an economy's production capacity or potential GDP. The rate of economic growth is the key determinant of changes in a society's standard of living, which is commonly measured by GDP per capita. When potential GDP is growing more rapidly than population, a society's standard of living is increasing. When potential GDP is growing more slowly than population, the standard of living is decreasing.

Relatively small differences in the growth rate of potential GDP ultimately translate into large differences in the standard of living. According to the *rule of seventy-two*, a variable's doubling time roughly equals 72 divided by the growth rate. So, for example, if potential GDP is growing at 4 percent a year, it will double in approximately 18 years. But if potential GDP is growing at only 2 percent a year, it will require 36 years to double.

There are two sources of economic growth: increases in the stock of economic resources (land, labor, and capital) and increases in technology. The most important of these are increases in the capital stock and *technological advances*.

The capital stock includes both *physical capital*—physical aids to production such as machines, tools, and factories—and *human capital*—the knowledge and skills embodied in labor.

Policymakers can influence the rate of capital investment in a variety of ways. For instance, *investment tax credits* can be used to increase the potential profitability of investments and to encourage businesses to undertake additional investment. Alternatively, policymakers can drive down the interest rate as a way of encouraging investment. This can be accomplished through tax policies that encourage households to save more (by eliminating the tax on interest income, for instance, or replacing the federal income tax with a *consumption tax*), or by deliberately incurring a budget surplus.

Policymakers can also attempt to stimulate economic growth by spurring the rate of technological progress. Technological progress generally proceeds in stages. The first stage, *research*, is the process of gaining new knowledge. The second stage, *invention*, is the discovery of new products or processes that have practical applications. The final stage, *innovation*, is the process of converting inventions into something marketable.

Attempts to promote technological progress generally do so by stimulating one or more stages in the *research and development* process. For instance, basic research can be promoted by increasing the size of government grants to universities. And applied research and innovation can be encouraged through tax policy—for instance, by providing tax credits for research and development. Some economists believe that government policymakers should single out critical industries or technologies to be the recipients of this support, though this *industrial policy* approach is controversial.

Technological progress may also require government policies to protect intellectual property. Firms are unlikely to invest in risky research and development projects unless they can protect their results through patents and copyrights. In addition, government may need to modify antitrust laws to promote research and development.

Although economists generally endorse the goal of economic growth, they disagree about the role that government should play in that process and about the specific policies that should be employed to promote growth. Supply-side economists generally prefer policies that will stimulate aggregate supply with minimal government intervention. Keynesians are often willing to accept more direct government involvement.

Environmentalists generally oppose economic growth because they see it exhausting our nonrenewable resources and generating ever-increasing amounts of pollution. While some economists are confident that market forces will provide the incentives necessary to avoid these catastrophic outcomes, others believe that government intervention will be needed.

KEY TERMS

Consumption tax	Joint research venture	Public saving
Economic growth	Lifetime Learning Tax Credit	Research
Expenditure tax	Loanable funds market	Research and development
Human capital	National saving	Rule of seventy-two
Innovation	Physical capital	Technological advances
Invention	Private saving	
Investment tax credit	Productivity of labor	

STUDY QUESTIONS

Fill in the Blanks

1. A common measure of a society's standard of living is _____ .

2. The term _____ refers to the knowledge and skills embodied in labor.

3. The market where businesses and households borrow funds to make investments is called the _____ market.

4. One policy for encouraging saving would be to replace the federal income tax with a(n) _____ tax.

5. National saving is the sum of _____ saving (by households) and _____ saving (by government).

6. The process of converting an invention into something marketable is referred to as _____ .

7. To encourage research and development, economists support the granting of _____ to temporarily shield innovating firms from competition.

8. Investment _____ reduce taxes for firms that invest in eligible equipment.

9. The term _____ is used to describe a program of targeted government support for research and development in specific industries or technologies.

10. The discovery of new products or processes that *might* have practical application is known as _____ .

Multiple Choice

1. Economic growth is defined as
   a) an increase in GDP per capita.
   b) an increase in real GDP.
   c) an increase in potential GDP.
   d) an increase in GDP.

2. According to the *rule of seventy-two*, if potential GDP is expanding at a rate of 3 percent a year, then potential GDP doubles in approximately
   a) 72 years.
   b) 18 years.
   c) 24 years.
   d) 36 years.

3. The most common measure of an economy's standard of living is
   a) median family income.
   b) per capita income.
   c) GDP per capita.
   d) average household income.

4. In 2008, the United States' GDP per capita was approximately
   a) $24,000.
   b) $47,000.
   c) $56,000.
   d) $17,000.

5. The country with the standard of living most closely approximating the United States is
   a) Germany.
   b) France.
   c) South Korea.
   d) United Arab Emirates.

6. If a country's population is increasing at 2 percent a year and its real GDP is increasing at 5 percent a year, then per capita real GDP will be
   a) rising at a rate of 7 percent a year.
   b) falling at a rate of 2 percent a year.
   c) rising at a rate of 3 percent a year.
   d) falling.

7. Population growth, by itself, may do little to raise the standard of living because
   a) any increase in real GDP must be divided among a larger population.
   b) without additional capital, there can be no increase in real GDP.
   c) people are not an economic resource.
   d) population growth inevitably leads to inflation.

8. The term *human capital* refers to
   a) machines, tools, and factories.
   b) money.
   c) the knowledge and skills of workers.
   d) None of the above

9. Which of the following would tend to increase *private* saving?
   a) Providing investment tax credits to firms that invest in eligible equipment
   b) Reducing the size of the federal budget deficit

   c) Reducing the size of the tax-deductible contributions that households are allowed to make to individual retirement accounts
   d) Replacing the federal income tax with a consumption tax

10. Policies that increase the supply of loanable funds lead to more investment spending because they
    a) reduce the taxes of firms that increase their investment spending.
    b) lower the interest rate and thereby encourage borrowing.
    c) make firms more optimistic about the future.
    d) lower the price level in the economy.

11. Suppose that a change in tax policies causes households to save more but increases the size of the budget deficit. In that case the policy would
    a) increase both private and public saving.
    b) decrease both private and public saving.
    c) increase private saving but reduce public saving.
    d) increase public saving but reduce private saving.

12. Investment tax credits tend to
    a) increase the supply of loanable funds and reduce interest rates.
    b) increase the supply of loanable funds and raise interest rates.
    c) increase the demand for loanable funds and reduce interest rates.
    d) increase the demand for loanable funds and raise interest rates.

13. Which of the following policies would a supply-side economist be *least* likely to support?
    a) Cuts in marginal tax rates designed to spur work effort
    b) Investment tax credits designed to stimulate investment spending
    c) An industrial policy intended to promote technological advances
    d) Tax incentives to spur saving by households

14. Suppose households are saving $500 billion a year, all state and local governments together have a budget surplus of $300 billion, and the federal government has a $150 billion deficit. How much is national saving?
    a) $350 billion
    b) $500 billion
    c) $650 billion
    d) $950 billion

15. Deficit spending may slow the rate of economic growth by
    a) raising interest rates and lowering investment spending.
    b) increasing the level of national saving.
    c) reducing aggregate demand.
    d) lowering consumption spending by households.

16. Patents are most likely to encourage research and development when
    a) the new product or process is discovered by accident.
    b) the cost of developing the new product or process was minimal.
    c) a major investment was required to develop the new product or process.
    d) Both a and b are true.

17. Under an industrial policy,
    a) all businesses would receive substantial tax breaks to encourage research and development.
    b) corporate income taxes would be reduced to provide additional funds for research and development.
    c) government policymakers would select critical industries to receive tax incentives and other support for research and development.
    d) tax incentives would be used to encourage saving, lower interest rates, and spending for research and development.

18. Rising incomes may pose a threat to the environment because
    a) this trend generally leads to less-rapid population growth.
    b) this trend generally leads to more-rapid population growth.
    c) rich people tend to care less about the environment.
    d) rich people consume more resources per capita.

19. Economists argue that present trends in population, food production, and resource depletion will probably not continue because
    a) as resources become scarcer, prices will rise, and this increase will lead to conservation.
    b) new technologies will be developed to conserve scarce resources and augment food supplies.
    c) as incomes rise, population growth rates tend to slow.
    d) All of the above

20. Robert Solow argues that government may need to supplement market forces to avoid the eventual destruction of the environment. He bases this recommendation on the fact that
    a) resource scarcity does not appear to alter the behavior of consumers or businesses.
    b) government policymakers always have better foresight than markets.
    c) markets do not adequately consider the distant future.
    d) population growth rates appear to be independent of economic variables such as income.

Problems and Questions for Discussion

1. When we compare the per capita GDP of a less-developed country like Ethiopia with that of a more-developed country like the United States, the differential may somewhat exaggerate the true difference in the standards of living. Can you think of any reasons why this comparison may be unfair to the less-developed country? (*Hint:* What is included in a nation's GDP?)

2. Why is an increase in the labor-force participation rate a more promising avenue for increasing the standard of living than is population growth?

3. Less-developed countries tend to have much lower rates of capital investment than more-developed countries. Why?

4. Technological progress and increases in the labor-force participation rate are both avenues to a higher standard of living. Which would you prefer and why?

5. Explain in step-by-step fashion how an increase in the supply of loanable funds leads to an increase in capital investment.

6. Why do budget surpluses represent increases in national saving? How do they promote investment spending?

7. Suppose that households are saving $600 billion a year and that the federal government is running a surplus of $200 billion. Ignoring the budgets of state and local governments, how much is national saving?

8. Starting from the information provided in question 7, suppose that the federal government reduces personal income taxes by $100 billion. If households consume (spend) 75 percent of each additional dollar they receive—including dollars from tax cuts—what will be the new levels of public, private, and national saving?

9. Economists argue that increases in per capita GDP indicate a rising standard of living. Environmentalists view rising per capita GDP as a source of pollution. Discuss.

10. Keynesians see deliberate budget deficits as desirable during periods of unemployment. But budget deficits can soak up savings, reducing the pool of funds available for private investment and slowing growth. Can these two outcomes be reconciled?

11. Robert Solow argues that markets and the invisible hand may not be capable of avoiding irreparable and catastrophic environmental damage. What does Solow see as the critical shortcoming in the market mechanism?

ANSWER KEY

Fill in the Blanks

1. per capita GDP

2. human capital

3. loanable funds

4. consumption or expenditure

5. private; public

6. innovation

7. patents

8. tax credits

9. industrial policy

10. invention

Multiple Choice

1. c
2. c
3. c
4. b

5. d
6. c
7. a
8. c

9. d
10. b
11. c
12. d

13. c
14. c
15. a
16. c

17. c
18. d
19. d
20. c

PART

4

International Economics: Trade, Exchange Rates, and the Role of Trade Agreements

Chapter 16 begins by introducing the economic rationale for international trade and considering the consequences of barriers to trade. You will learn the meaning of such concepts as "absolute advantage" and "comparative advantage" and see why these concepts are used to summon support for free trade. The benefits of more open trade will be explored, and the role of regional and global trade agreements will be examined.

The second half of the chapter will consider the financial dimension of international transactions. You will see how exchange rates are determined and learn how changes in exchange rates influence international trade. Finally, the chapter will explore government attempts to "manage" exchange rates and the motivation for such management.

16

International Economics

1. Explain the difference between open and closed economies.
2. Define imports and exports.
3. Explain the principle of comparative advantage.
4. Describe the sources of comparative advantage.
5. Discuss the benefits of trade based on comparative advantage.
6. Explain why the benefits of trade are diffused while the costs are concentrated.
7. Describe the different types of trade barriers.
8. Describe the role of the World Trade Organization and the various trade agreements.
9. Explain how exchange rates are determined and why they matter.
10. Explain the meaning of currency appreciation and depreciation.

The first 15 chapters of the text have included numerous examples involving our economic relationships with other nations. We've previewed the benefits of international trade, and we've considered the impact of trade on our GDP. We've seen how international influences can dominate the process of price determination in competitive markets and how a recession in Europe or some other part of the world can affect the U.S. economy. We've included these examples because, like it or not, the U.S. economy is increasingly an **open economy**—an economy that exchanges goods and services with other nations. (A **closed economy**, by contrast, does not exchange goods and services with other nations.)

The increased openness of the U.S. economy is a matter of some controversy. Many Americans see foreign competition as a destructive force that threatens their jobs and their way of life. Others view foreign competition as a blessing that provides quality products at prices lower than domestic producers charge. Economic policymakers must weigh these costs and benefits as they develop policies to promote or retard international trade. In this chapter we'll explore the theoretical basis for free, or unrestricted, international trade, and we'll take a closer look at the costs and benefits associated with it. We'll also examine how the *exchange rate* between currencies is determined and discuss why changes in exchange rates can have a significant impact on consumers and businesses.

INTERDEPENDENT ECONOMIES AND U.S. TRADE

Statistics show that the economies of the world are becoming more interdependent. Consumers in the United States are buying more foreign products, and foreign consumers are buying more U.S. goods. Producers around the world are using more imported parts and raw materials in the products they manufacture. In short, foreign trade is already more important than most Americans realize, and current signs indicate that it will gain even more importance in the future.

Import and Export Trends

The Sony television sets, Nike tennis shoes, and Raleigh bicycles we see in U.S. stores are all **imports**—goods or services purchased from foreign producers.[1] In the last 40 years, trade between the United States and other nations has expanded significantly. More Americans are driving Toyotas, Hondas, BMWs, and Saabs; are listening to CD players made in Japan and Singapore; are drinking wine from France and Italy and Australia; and are wearing clothes made in China, Mexico, Taiwan, Romania, and other countries. These products are but a few examples. As you can see from Exhibit 16.1, imports more than tripled as a fraction of GDP between 1968 and 2008.

U.S. exports are expanding as well. **Exports** are goods and services produced domestically and sold to customers in other countries. For example, U.S. farmers export wheat and rice and a variety of other agricultural products, while U.S. manufacturing firms export products such as earthmoving equipment, computer programs, pharmaceuticals, and jet airplanes. Exports of goods and services accounted for 5 percent of our gross domestic product in 1968; by 2008 that figure had climbed to more than 17 percent of GDP. That is

---

[1] The services component of imports includes such items as transportation charges for moving goods and passengers between nations and expenditures made by tourists while traveling in foreign countries.

EXHIBIT 16.1

Trends in U.S. Imports and Exports

	1968	1988	2008
Exports of goods and services	$45.5 billion (5% of GDP)	$431.1 billion (8.4% of GDP)	$1,826.6 billion (12.8% of GDP)
Imports of goods and services	$45.3 billion (5% of GDP)	$545.7 billion (10.7% of GDP)	$2,522.5 billion (17.7% of GDP)

Source: Bureau of Economic Analysis, U.S. Department of Commerce.

low compared with the percentage of GDP in Canada (35 percent), Germany (47 percent), and Ireland (83 percent), but it is a significant fraction of GDP and one that will undoubtedly increase in the future.[2]

As you can see from Exhibit 16.1, the value of our imports of goods and services exceeded the value of our exports by roughly $700 billion in 2008. That means the United States had a **trade deficit** in that year. If our exports had exceeded our imports, we would have enjoyed a **trade surplus**—something we haven't experienced for several years. Of course, when other countries send us goods and services, they expect to receive something in return. So, if we are not sending them enough goods and services to offset what we are buying from them, we must be sending them something else of value. For the most part, that "something else" is stocks and bonds and bank account balances. In effect, we get to enjoy the goods and services now; our trading partners receive financial assets that they can use to buy our goods and services later.

THE RATIONALE FOR INTERNATIONAL TRADE

Why do countries trade? How do we explain the flow of goods and services captured by the foregoing statistics? One obvious reason for trade is to obtain products or resources that countries are simply incapable of producing themselves. If a nation lacks oil reserves or iron ore deposits, it has little choice but to trade if it wants to acquire these resources or the products produced from them. Here, a nation's stock of natural resources is truly a limiting factor. But resource limitations are not the sole—or even the most important—reason for

[2] The percentage figures for foreign nations are based on information from Statistics Canada, Germany's Federal Statistical Office, and Ireland's Central Statistics Office. All figures are for 2008.

trade. Most countries are capable of producing almost any product its citizens desire—if they are willing to expend the necessary resources. For example, while Britain's climate is ill-suited to growing citrus fruits, Britain could certainly grow hothouse oranges and grapefruit if it chose to. And Saudi Arabia could probably raise lobster if it were so inclined. The important point is that neither country chooses to expend its resources this way because other countries can produce these items at much lower cost.

Absolute and Comparative Advantage

To Adam Smith, the founding father of economics, it seemed obvious that a nation should import those items that other countries could produce at lower cost. For him, lower cost meant lower *resource* cost. Smith believed that the basis for trade was **absolute advantage**—the ability to produce a product more efficiently—with fewer resources—than another country. To illustrate, suppose Spain can produce a shirt using only four hours of labor while France requires six hours. And suppose France can produce a bushel of wheat using four hours of labor while Spain requires six. Smith's conclusion: Spain should produce shirts and import wheat; France should produce wheat and import shirts. Both countries will benefit by specializing in the product in which they have an absolute advantage and trading for the products that others can produce more efficiently.

While Smith's observation lent support to international trade, it also suggested that trade would only occur when the potential trading partners had offsetting efficiencies. If one country had an absolute advantage in everything—for instance, if Spain could produce both shirts and wheat at a lower resource cost than France—trade would not occur.

The principle of absolute advantage governed thinking about trade until the early 1800s when British economist David Ricardo had an important insight. Ricardo pointed out that the relevant cost of producing something is the opportunity cost, not the resource cost. The real cost to Britain of producing hothouse oranges is not the resources that this consumes. Rather, it is the other products that Britain could have produced with those same resources. The same is true of Spain and France; the true cost of producing shirts or wheat is the other products that must be sacrificed to obtain these products. Ricardo argued that trade should be based on **comparative advantage**—the ability to produce a product at a lower opportunity cost than another country. Ricardo noted that even if a country was more efficient than its potential trading partner in everything, it could still benefit by focusing on the product in which it was most efficient and allowing its trading partner to specialize in the product in which it was least inefficient. An example should help to clarify Ricardo's observation.

The classic example of comparative advantage doesn't involve foreign countries; it has to do with a lawyer and the lawyer's secretary. The lawyer, Ms. Legal Wizard, not only is the best legal mind in the country but also types better than anyone else around. We could say that she has an absolute advantage over her secretary (and everyone else in the community) in both jobs because she can accomplish more work in a given amount of time. Why, then, does the lawyer have her secretary, Mr. Average Typist, do the typing? The answer is probably obvious to you! By having the secretary do the typing, the lawyer frees her own time to do more legal work—-the more valuable use of her time.

Consider the high opportunity cost of having the lawyer do her own typing. It would mean the loss of the additional income she could have generated by handling more cases. The secretary, who has almost no talent for legal work, has a comparative advantage in typing because the amount of legal work he gives up to perform the typing duties is insignificant. The secretary does the typing not because he is a better typist than the lawyer (absolute advantage) but because he is better at typing than at legal work (comparative advantage). By allowing individuals to concentrate on the jobs they do best—the jobs in which their absolute advantage is the greatest or their disadvantage the least—the firm is able to handle more clients, earn more money, and thereby raise the standard of living of all its staff members.

Imagining Life without International Trade

Countries can benefit from specialization and trade in much the same way that the lawyer and the secretary benefit from their relationship. But if we want to demonstrate the benefits of trade we need to first consider what life would be like without it. To do that, imagine a world composed of only two nations, the United States and Britain. Imagine also that these nations produce only two products, computers and motorbikes. We can represent the production abilities of these two countries by using a tool we introduced in Chapter 1, the production possibilities curve. As you will recall, a production possibilities curve (PPC) shows the combinations of two products that a country is capable of producing with its stock of economic resources and the existing techniques of production. To simplify the analysis, we'll assume that the resources within each country are equally well suited to the production of both computers and motorbikes. That simplification will allow us to utilize a linear production possibilities curve rather than the bowed-out curves we encountered in Chapter 1.

According to Exhibit 16.2, the United States can produce 10,000 computers if it devotes all its resources to computer production, or 10,000 motorbikes if it concentrates its resources on motorbike production. Britain, on the other hand, can produce either 3,000 computers or 9,000 motorbikes. Without trade, these production possibilities curves outline the maximum amounts of the two

EXHIBIT 16.2

Production Possibilities for the United States and Britain

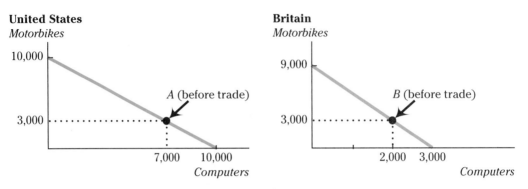

Before trade, the United States is capable of producing either 10,000 motorbikes or 10,000 computers, or any combination of motorbikes and computers on its production possibilities curve. Britain can produce either 9,000 motorbikes or 3,000 computers, or any combination on its production possibilities curve.

goods that each country can produce and consume.[3] Of course, the United States can choose to operate anywhere along (or inside) its production possibilities curve; Britain can do the same.

In the absence of trade, both Britain and the United States would produce some combination of computers and motorbikes with the exact amounts of each depending on the strength of demand for the two products. To have a starting point for later comparison, let's assume that the United States opts to produce 7,000 computers and 3,000 motorbikes (point *A* on the U.S. production possibilities curve) while Britain produces 2,000 computers and 3,000 motorbikes (point *B* on the British production possibilities curve). We'll return to these points in just a moment.

The Gains from International Trade

The production possibilities curves in Exhibit 16.2 do more than outline the production and consumption possibilities prior to trade; they also allow us to determine each country's comparative advantage. Remember, a country has a comparative advantage in producing a product if it can produce that product at a lower opportunity cost than another country! For the United States, the

---

[3] If our two hypothetical economies are of the same size—have the same quantity of resources (though not necessarily the same quality)—we can say that the United States has an absolute advantage in the production of both computers and motorbikes because it can produce more of each with the same quantity of resources.

opportunity cost of producing 10,000 computers is 10,000 motorbikes forgone; the opportunity cost of each computer is one motorbike. For Britain, the opportunity cost of producing 3,000 computers is 9,000 motorbikes; the opportunity cost of each additional computer is three motorbikes. As you can see, the United States has the comparative advantage in computer production because it can produce computers at the lower opportunity cost (1 motorbike versus 3 motorbikes).

Which country has the comparative advantage in motorbike production? If the United States has to sacrifice one motorbike to gain each computer, the converse is also true; the opportunity cost of each motorbike is one forgone computer. For Britain, the opportunity cost of producing 9,000 motorbikes is 3,000 computers, so the opportunity cost of each motorbike is one-third of a computer. That means Britain is the low-cost producer of motorbikes (1/3 computer versus 1 computer) and has the comparative advantage in that area.

Suppose that the United States decides to specialize in the production of computers (where it has a comparative advantage) and offers to trade one computer to Britain for two motorbikes. Would the British agree? Of course they would agree! Through trade they can acquire a computer for two motorbikes, whereas they would have to sacrifice three motorbikes to produce one domestically. As U.S. citizens, would we be better off with this arrangement? We certainly would be. We would be getting two motorbikes for each computer we traded, whereas we would be able to manufacture only one motorbike from the resources we used to produce each computer. The actual rate at which computers are traded for motorbikes—what economists call the **terms of trade**—might differ from the rate assumed here. However, for trade to be attractive the rate must lie between 1 computer = 1 motorbike and 1 computer = 3 motorbikes, the exchange possibilities established by the opportunity costs within each nation.[4]

We can see the gains from trade more clearly by returning to the production possibilities curves, reproduced in Exhibit 16.3. Let's assume that the United States specializes in computer production, producing 10,000 computers, and Britain specializes in motorbike production, producing 9,000 motorbikes. Now, suppose that the United States trades 3,000 computers for some motorbikes. With an exchange ratio of one computer to two motorbikes, the United States will receive 6,000 motorbikes in return for its 3,000 computers and will still have 7,000 computers left over (point A' in Exhibit 16.3). Britain will have 3,000 motorbikes left over plus 3,000 computers (point B' in Exhibit 16.3). The United States will have 3,000 more motorbikes than it had prior to trade, and Britain will have 1,000 more computers.

---

[4] The actual terms of trade are established by supply and demand conditions in the two nations and will influence how the gains from trade are divided between the two trading partners. The closer the rate is to 1 computer = 3 motorbikes, the more of the gain flowing to the United States. The closer the rate is to 1 computer = 1 motorbike, the more of the gain flowing to Britain.

EXHIBIT 16.3

Comparative Advantage and the Gains from Trade

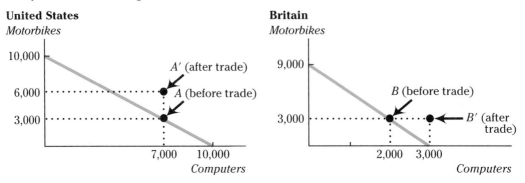

Through specialization and trade based on comparative advantage, both the United States and Britain can enjoy a higher standard of living. Before trade, each country was forced to consume a combination of products on or inside its production possibilities curve. Trade allows each country to enjoy consumption possibilities beyond its own production capabilities.

Trade and specialization along the lines of comparative advantage have made it possible for each country to move beyond its PPC and to consume a combination of products that it could not obtain on its own. Moreover, total world production increased from 6,000 to 9,000 motorbikes, and from 9,000 to 10,000 computers. The principle of comparative advantage has allowed each of the trading partners to obtain more goods from its resources and to enjoy a higher standard of living.

Sources of Comparative Advantage

We've seen that trade based on comparative advantage can increase the living standards of the trading partners. But what determines a country's comparative advantage? The primary source of a nation's comparative advantage appears to be its stock of economic resources—the amount and quality of the natural resources, labor, and capital it has at its disposal.

Different products require different resource endowments. A country tends to have a comparative advantage in the production of a product if it has a relative abundance of the input most needed to produce that product. For instance, a country with an abundance of fertile land and a long growing season is likely to have a comparative advantage in agriculture. A country with a large supply of highly educated workers is likely to have a comparative advantage in producing highly technical products.

Consider China, for instance. With its enormous supply of low-skilled workers, it has a well-recognized comparative advantage in producing apparel and other items that can easily be produced by workers with limited skill. The United States, on the other hand, has a much greater supply of skilled workers and relatively abundant capital. It has a comparative advantage in products requiring relatively large amounts of these inputs—developing new pharmaceuticals and computer programs, for example, and the production of commercial aircraft. Australia's abundant land gives it a comparative advantage in raising cattle, while Canada's forests make it a net exporter of timber. This list is just beginning, but you probably have the idea. Comparative advantage stems from a nation's resource endowment.

Comparative advantage is not a static concept. After World War II, Japan's comparative advantage was in low-tech products requiring relatively little capital and unskilled labor. Today, Japan has lost its comparative advantage in those products to China and India and other countries with more abundant supplies of low-skilled workers. But as Japan has developed the quality of its labor force and enlarged its capital stock, it has moved on to more sophisticated products—developing a comparative advantage in cutting-edge electronics and quality motor vehicles, for example. Changes in technology can also produce new comparative advantages. For instance, advances in communications technology have opened up new opportunities for India's relatively large supply of English-speaking workers. Indian doctors are reading X-rays for U.S. patients, and workers in Indian "call centers" are taking orders for U.S. products. What's certain, then, is that the future will be different, probably in some ways we can't now predict. If the model of comparative advantage is correct, the future should also hold higher living standards for the world's trading partners. Change is never painless, however, and, as we will see in a moment, there will be winners and losers.

Additional Benefits from Trade

As you have seen, trade based on comparative advantage results in increased world output. By itself, that would be a substantial benefit. But there are others: increased competition and greater product variety, chief among them. For a variety of reasons, product specialization is often incomplete, even when countries pursue trade based on comparative advantage.[5] As a result, consumers find themselves able to choose between domestic and foreign product offerings. This

---

[5] Even in the absence of trade barriers, specialization may be less than complete. That is, the United States might continue to produce some motorbikes and Britain might continue to produce some computers. To conclude that foreign trade along the lines of comparative advantage will lead to complete specialization, we must make a number of assumptions. For example, we must assume that (1) the products offered by British and U.S. manufacturers are identical—that U.S. computers are the same as British computers, for instance, and (2) that transportation costs are not large enough to outweigh the differences in production costs in the two nations. To the extent that these assumptions are not met, specialization will be less than complete.

Competition from foreign automobile manufacturers has helped to hold down new-car prices in the United States.

greater product variety does more than add spice to our lives; it also limits the pricing discretion of domestic producers and forces them to be more responsive to consumer demands. Consider the U.S. automobile market, for example. Foreign competition has not only given U.S. consumers more brands to choose from, it has also helped to hold down automobile prices and spurred domestic manufacturers to improve the quality and reliability of their offerings. Perhaps more important, the presence of foreign competition helps to keep domestic producers on their toes and looking for ways to improve their products. When we consider the benefits of trade in permitting greater specialization along the lines of comparative advantage and fostering greater competition, we can understand why economists generally support free trade and oppose trade barriers of any type.

BARRIERS TO TRADE

As we've seen, there are substantial benefits to trade. But while trade clearly benefits a nation as a whole, it can impose significant costs on some within that nation. Our model assumes that the economic resources—the workers, factories, and equipment—no longer needed by the U.S. motorbike industry will flow to the U.S. computer industry, and the resources released by the British computer industry will flow to the British motorbike industry. But this transition is never painless. Unemployed workers need time to find jobs, and factories must be put to other uses. Some of these resources will never be reemployed because firms are reluctant to investment money to retrain a 55-year-old motorbike mechanic, for example, or remodel a 30-year-old computer plant. So even though the total output of both countries will be greater than before trade, not every individual or group will be better off. Thus, specialization has costs as well as benefits.

Economists are in general agreement that the benefits of free trade outweigh the costs by a substantial margin. But the benefits of free trade tend to be widely diffused across a large number of people, each of whom is made a little better off. (For instance, more open trade may allow each of us to save 10 or 20 dollars on each pair of shoes we buy, or perhaps a few hundred dollars on each automobile we purchase.) The losses, however, tend to be concentrated on a relatively small segment of society—the workers who are forced out of jobs and the firm owners who are forced to shut down. Not surprisingly, the segment that is significantly harmed by foreign competition is likely to be more vocal than the group whose welfare is slightly improved. That's why politicians in the United States and elsewhere hear more often about the costs of free trade than about its benefits. And, as the public-choice economists have warned, these complaints are likely to be heeded by vote-maximizing politicians.

Virtually all the nations of the world impose trade barriers of one sort or another, largely in response to political pressure from those who fear they will be harmed. These trade barriers are designed primarily to limit competition from imports, although export restrictions are sometimes established. The most common devices for limiting import competition are import quotas and protective tariffs.

Quotas

An **import quota** specifies the maximum amount of a particular product that can be imported. The volume of imported wine, for example, might be limited to 50 million gallons per year, or the quantity of imported steel could be limited to 100,000 tons each year.

Import quotas can be either global or selective. A *global quota* limits the amount of a product that can be imported from the rest of the world. When the limit is reached, all further imports of that item are prohibited. A *selective quota* specifies the maximum amount of a product that can be imported from a particular country. For example, the United States might set a global quota of 500,000 imported automobiles per year and further specify selective quotas: 250,000 cars from Japan and 50,000 from Germany, perhaps, and the remaining 200,000 from other countries.

The impact of quotas can be substantial. For example, the Government Accountability Office estimated that sugar quotas cost American consumers $1.9 billion in higher prices in 1998. (Because of import quotas, sugar sold for

22 cents a pound in the United States but only 11 cents a pound in the world market. That meant higher U.S. prices for soft drinks, candy, and numerous other products.)[6] And when Congress flirted with the idea of using import quotas to protect our steel industry, economist Gary Hufbauer estimated that each of the jobs saved would cost American consumers $800,000 a year.[7]

Tariffs

The other major tool for limiting import competition is tariffs. A **tariff** is a tax on imported goods. Its purpose is either to generate revenue for the taxing country through a revenue tariff or to protect domestic producers from foreign competition by means of a protective tariff. Historically, revenue tariffs were the major tool for financing government expenditures. Such tariffs served as the principal source of revenue for the U.S. government through the nineteenth century and remain the principal source in some less-developed countries.

Today, most developed countries rely on other forms of taxation for revenue—income and sales taxes, for example. When developed countries, such as the United States, employ tariffs, their main purpose is to protect domestic producers. A tariff on a foreign product increases its price and makes it less competitive in the marketplace, thereby encouraging consumers to buy domestic products instead. For instance, the United States imposes tariffs of up to 20 percent on imported luggage and almost 40 percent on some imported footwear. Of course, these tariffs make the imported items less attractive relative to domestic products, thereby helping to insulate U.S. producers from foreign competition.

While tariffs are harmful to consumer welfare, economists generally view them as less damaging than quotas. When increased demand causes the prices of domestic products to rise, comparable tariff-bearing foreign products become more competitive because the price differential between the foreign and domestic products is reduced. Because foreign products are now a more viable alternative for consumers, domestic producers may be restrained from raising prices further, lest they lose sales to foreign rivals. This is not the case with import quotas. When domestic producers are protected by quotas rather than tariffs, rising domestic prices cannot call forth additional units from foreign suppliers once the quotas have been met. As a consequence, domestic producers have more freedom under a quota system to increase prices without fear of losing their market share to foreign firms.

---

[6] Robert E. Robertson, *Sugar Program: Supporting Sugar Prices Has Increased Users' Costs While Benefiting Producers* (Government Accountability Office, Report Number RCED-00-126, June 9, 2000).
[7] Gary Clyde Hufbauer, *Steel Quotas: A Rigged Lottery* (Policy Brief 99-5, Institute for International Economics, June 1999).

Other Restrictions

Trade agreements (which are discussed later in the chapter) have helped to discourage the use of quotas and have reduced tariff rates significantly. But other forms of trade protection are more subtle and more difficult to legislate against. For example, health and safety laws are sometimes invoked to prevent or complicate the importation of certain products. The acquisition of import licenses can be made difficult or expensive, perhaps under the guise of ensuring the quality or reliability of the imported products. These practices are difficult to outlaw, in part because it is difficult to prove that the intent is the protection of domestic industry rather than, say, the health and safety of consumers. As a consequence, protectionism can exist, even in the absence of tariffs or quotas. (The recession of 2008–2009 led to an increase in "legal" protectionist measures. Read "Big Slide in Global Trade Looms over G-20 Meeting," on page 484, for a look at the measures being pursued and how they threaten our trading system.)

In addition to these subtle forms of protectionism, entirely new forms of trade interference have emerged, largely to bypass, or take advantage of, the rules in existing trade agreements. One troubling method of discouraging imports is to accuse foreign firms of dumping. **Dumping** occurs when a product is sold to foreign consumers at a price that is less than the cost of producing that good or service. The United States has long held that dumping is an unfair form of competition, perhaps because (in *rare* circumstances) it might be used to drive a competitor out of business. As a consequence, U.S. laws prohibit dumping and call for additional tariffs to be imposed on products dumped in the U.S. market. Existing trade laws permit such "antidumping duties," in large part due to the insistence of the United States.

Because it is difficult for trade courts to determine the true cost of producing a product, the mere fact that a firm is selling its product in foreign markets for less than it charges in its own domestic market is often taken as evidence of dumping. Economists find this logic flawed. As you discovered in Chapter 7, selling to different markets at different prices may make perfect economic sense. In fact, profit maximization requires that firms charge higher prices in markets where consumers are less price-sensitive (where demand is less elastic) and lower prices in markets where consumers are more price-sensitive (where demand is more elastic). Economic logic notwithstanding, dumping remains illegal in the United States. The U.S. Department of Commerce judges cases involving dumping in the United States and generally finds in favor of American companies. As a consequence, the mere threat of a dumping case is often enough to convince foreign firms to raise their prices. Of course, the real loser is the consumer.

Big Slide in Global Trade Looms over G-20 Meeting

BY BRADLEY S. KLAPPER

With global trade sliding, analysts say some of the world's most powerful leaders may need to offer more than ritual support for open markets when they meet this week [March 2009] if they are to steady a teetering economy and avoid a damaging retreat to protectionism.

The presidents, prime ministers and chancellors of the Group of 20 nations have halfheartedly respected their pledge of four months ago to avoid turning inwards in fighting the economic crisis. Since then, world commerce has plummeted in a way unseen since the Great Depression. With no concerted strategy for a revival, some economists say a rash of go-it-alone stimulus packages and industry bailouts could lead to trade wars causing havoc in one of the key driving forces to the world's economic growth since World War II. "We're playing with fire," said Jagdish Bhagwati, an economist at Columbia University. "The system was designed to avoid the free-for-all wrestling of the 1930s. If the U.S. and France start saying, 'This is legal so I am going to do it,' everyone else will start to play that game."

The World Bank says 17 of the 20 countries whose leaders are meeting in London on Thursday have resorted to protectionist measures since declaring their opposition to such action during a November conference in Washington.

The World Trade Organization says most of the major powers from the United States and European Union to China and India have erected new barriers to imports in the form of tariffs, subsidies or other measures designed to protect domestic industries.

Part of the problem is that the financial collapse shattered confidence in the world's economic order, which includes as a major tenet the free flow of goods and services. With the recession deepening, pressure has ramped up on governments to come up with more ways to protect farmers, manufacturers and service providers from competitors overseas. "The case for trade needs to be made more effectively, including by us," said Keith Rockwell, spokesman for WTO chief Pascal Lamy, who will attend the London summit. "It behooves all of us to explain the benefits of trade, and what it means to economic growth and development."

For 60 years, international trade has been a major driver of the global economy, outpacing GDP growth and spurring gains in both rich and poor countries. But trade is being hit hard by the crisis, with the WTO recently predicting that global commercial activity will shrink 9 percent in 2009 after 27 years of uninterrupted expansion. The main cause is the sharp drop in demand for goods, both domestic and foreign, but

---

Source: Associated Press, March 31, 2009. Reprinted by permission of the Associated Press.

REDUCING BARRIERS: THE ROLE OF TRADE AGREEMENTS

Trade barriers are not new. Protectionist sentiments ran particularly high during the Great Depression. The job losses and business failures of that period led to pleas for protection from foreign competition. In 1930, Congress responded

analysts warn that protectionist sentiment threatens to make recovery far more difficult. And slower, said Ed Gresser, trade director at the Progressive Policy Institute in Washington. He said merchandise imports in the United States, the world's biggest market for foreign goods, has fallen about a third to $210 billion a month from $310 billion only a half-year ago. That's slightly worse than the 30 percent fall in trade in the first six months after the 1929 market crash. "We're in bad shape and I wouldn't say we've seen the bottom yet," Gresser said. "Governments haven't really been working together. But they aren't really working at odds with each other. If they did, we could be in for a very hard time."

From footwear to steel to automaking, the G-20 countries have contributed to a protectionist swing, and there may be little the leaders can do in London to immediately reverse that trend, beyond broader attempts to stimulate the economy and fire up demand.

There are a host of smaller spats among the participants. China is fuming over a U.S. ban on its poultry over safety concerns; Washington is looking to move against subsidies it accuses Beijing of paying manufacturers. Farm exporters are upset with the 27-nation European Union's reintroduction of dairy subsidies; and European nations are bickering among themselves over auto bailout packages and which members will have to shoulder job cuts.

The danger is best highlighted in a dispute between the U.S. and Mexico over trucking. Mexico has raised tariffs on 89 American products worth $2.4 billion in annual trade in retaliation for a U.S. decision to cancel a program that gave Mexican truckers access to U.S. highways. American fruit, wine and washing machines will be among the goods affected. "If anyone doubted the danger of tit-for-tat, the Mexican response was a pretty clear indication that things can spiral out of control pretty easily," said Rockwell at the WTO. "That helps nobody. Everybody knows this intellectually, but each and every one of the leaders is facing protectionist pressures from domestic constituents."

USE YOUR ECONOMIC REASONING

1. Why are nations turning to protectionist measures now, after years of reducing trade barriers?
2. Jagdish Bhagwati is concerned about nations taking actions that are "legal" (not explicitly banned by trade agreements) but have the effect of restraining trade. For example, most nations have some leeway to raise their tariffs because they have established them below the legal maximums. What other actions are noted in the article?
3. "Governments haven't really been working together. But they aren't really working at odds with each other. If they did, we could be in for a very hard time." Explain this comment.
4. What danger is highlighted by the dispute between the United States and Mexico over trucking?

by passing the Smoot-Hawley Act, which raised import tariffs to an average of 50 percent. Other countries retaliated, and the result was a lessening of trade, which may have contributed to a deepening of the Depression. Fortunately, the remainder of the twentieth century saw significant, though halting, progress toward eliminating trade barriers.

The Reciprocal Trade Agreements Act of 1934 began the work of undoing Smoot-Hawley. The act permitted the president to engage in negotiations with individual trading partners of the United States to reduce tariffs. Because negotiations were on an item-by-item basis, progress was slow. But by the end of World War II, substantial progress had been made: U.S. tariff rates had been reduced from the 50 percent range to about half that.

International Trade Agreements: GATT and the WTO

Following World War II, the United States led efforts to reduce trade barriers still further. In 1947, twenty-three countries signed the General Agreement on Tariffs and Trade (GATT), which established some basic rules for trade and created an organization to oversee trade negotiations. Under GATT rules, countries are discouraged from using import quotas. Instead, they are expected to use tariffs as their means of import protection. Although tariffs are viewed as the preferable form of import protection, the primary objective of GATT has been to reduce tariff rates. This has been accomplished through periodic negotiations known as "rounds."

The most recent round of GATT negotiations, the Uruguay Round (so named because it was held in Punta del Este, Uruguay), concluded in 1993. The Uruguay Round succeeded in reducing tariffs by about one-third. As a consequence, the average tariff applied by industrial nations fell to less than 3 percent, a far cry from the 50 percent rates of the Depression era. These talks also resulted in the formation of the World Trade Organization (WTO) to replace GATT and to arbitrate trade disputes between nations.

In its relatively short existence, the WTO has had both successes and failures. The WTO's dispute settlement body, which is like a court for resolving trade disputes, seems to work reasonably well. Unlike those of its predecessor, the WTO's decisions are binding on members; if members fail to comply, they may face trade sanctions. This puts some teeth, something that was lacking under GATT, into efforts to solve trade disputes. But the organization has had little success in moving trade negotiation forward to tackle the tough issues that continue to impede free trade. How do we eliminate agricultural subsidies—subsidies that may unfairly advantage a country's producers? Can the United States and the other major powers be convinced to curtail their use of antidumping laws as a tool for discouraging imports? What can be done to eliminate subtle forms of protectionism, such as the use of health and safety laws to discourage imports? As Laura D'Andrea Tyson, chief economic advisor under President Clinton, noted, "The easy issues in multilateral trade negotiation have largely been resolved. Tariffs have been slashed and quotas eliminated for most manufactured goods. Further negotiations will focus on . . . politically sensitive sectors."

Domestic workers often protest against imported products.

With 148 member countries—-some rich, some poor, some in-between—-several critics argue that the WTO is simply too large and too diverse a body to make any headway on the complex issues that remain to be resolved. As a consequence, some observers believe that the future may lie in bilateral trade agreements—agreements between two countries—-and regional trade accords that generally involve only a handful (or a few handfuls) of nations. As you'll see in a moment, economists have a mixed reaction to these bilateral and regional trading agreements. But if the WTO remains in a state of gridlock, these bilateral and regional agreements may be the best we can hope for.

Regional Trade Agreements

The GATT agreements and the WTO have as their objective the reduction of trade barriers worldwide. But in the last decade or so we've seen the emergence of regional trade agreements that attempt to eliminate or reduce trade barriers only among countries in a particular region or *trading block*. Trading barriers are removed or reduced for members of the trading block but not for nonmembers. For example, the European Union (a trading block currently composed of 27 European countries, with more on the way) has eliminated most tariff barriers among member nations while continuing to impose tariffs on imports from nonmembers. A portion of the trading block has also chosen to adopt a common currency—the *euro*—to further facilitate trade between members. At present, 16 countries have chosen to join the *euro zone*, including Germany, France, Spain, and Italy.

The North American Free Trade Agreement (NAFTA) created a similar trading block involving the United States, Canada, and Mexico. This agreement, which was signed by the United States and Canada in 1989 and joined by Mexico in 1993, eliminated tariffs between the countries over a ten-year period. While the European Union and NAFTA are perhaps the most visible examples of trading blocks, there are many more examples: the Caribbean Community (CARICOM), the South American Community of Nations (CSN), the Association of Southeast Asian Nations (ASEAN), the Central American Common Market (CACM)—the list goes on and on. And there are numerous bilateral agreements as well. For instance, the United States has agreements with Bahrain, Chile, Morocco, Singapore, and Oman, among others.

Are these bilateral and regional trade agreements a good thing? Economists aren't so sure. Although both the GATT and NAFTA agreements appear to be steps in the direction of more-open, or less-restricted, trade, economists are generally more supportive of GATT (and now of the WTO) than of NAFTA. If the world moves toward trading blocks rather than open trade among all nations, the principle of comparative advantage may be compromised. For example, the United States may find itself buying shoes from Mexico (because Mexico can produce shoes at a lower opportunity cost than the United States) but forgoing shoe imports from Taiwan (which may be able to produce shoes at a lower opportunity cost than Mexico) because Taiwan is outside our trading block and thus faces higher U.S. tariffs. If this occurs, the U.S standard of living will be somewhat lower than it would have been under a system that provided equal access to all producers—the kind of system the WTO is designed to promote. On the other hand, if membership in regional trading blocks like NAFTA increases the willingness of nations to negotiate in a larger forum like the WTO, then NAFTA will ultimately lead to a more efficient trading system. At this point, it is too early to determine the impact that these bilateral and regional trading agreements are likely to have.

Building Support: The Case for Trade Adjustment Assistance

As the United States continues to sign trade agreements, some Americans are optimistic while others are fearful. This mixed reaction is easy to understand. As we've seen, reductions in trade barriers will help most of us, but will significantly harm a minority. To help these individuals—and to build support for more open trade—many economists believe that efforts to reduce trade barriers should be accompanied by programs to retrain workers and otherwise assist those harmed by foreign competition.

The Trade Adjustment Assistance Reform Act of 2002 (which builds on earlier legislation) attempts to provide such assistance. Under the act, workers who lose their jobs due to import competition or the shifting of production overseas qualify for financial assistance while they search for a job, undergo retraining, or engage in remedial education. (Displaced workers now qualify for 78 weeks of TAA income support beyond the normal 26 weeks of unemployment compensation.) The act also provides a relocation allowance for workers who are forced to move to find reemployment, as well as assistance in maintaining health insurance. For impacted workers 50 and older, the act also provides a two-year wage subsidy equal to 50 percent of the difference between their new salary and their old salary, up to a maximum of $10,000.

While the benefits outlined above clearly ease the impact of losing one's job, the Trade Adjustment Act is not without its critics. Some argue that these benefits are still inadequate—particularly for those workers with poor educational backgrounds who may require substantial remedial education and/or retraining. Others question the logic in singling out these workers for special treatment. Why is it that workers who lose their jobs due to domestic competition normally qualify for 26 weeks of unemployment compensation while those harmed by foreign competition qualify for 104 weeks? The answer appears to be a political one. To garner support for more open trade, politicians have opted to provide greater benefits to those harmed in its pursuit.

EXCHANGE RATES

As we've focused on the benefits of trade and efforts to promote more open trade, we've ignored one important element of international transactions—the fact that they almost always involve money. In fact, one of the distinguishing features of

Because manufacturers desire payment in their domestic currency, U.S. importers must convert dollars into Japanese yen, South Korean won, and other currencies to purchase foreign products.

trade between nations is that they typically involve two different types of money—the currencies of the two nations participating in the transaction.

If you want to buy a Japanese radio, you can pay for your purchase with cash, check, or credit card. Ultimately, however, Japanese producers want to receive payment in yen, their domestic currency, because their workers and domestic suppliers expect to be paid in yen. That's why Mexican avocado growers seek payment in pesos and Swiss watchmakers expect payment in Swiss francs. The need to convert dollars into foreign currency (or foreign currency into dollars) is the distinguishing feature of our trade with other nations.

The rate at which one currency can be exchanged for another currency is called the **exchange rate**; it is simply the price of one nation's currency stated in terms of another nation's currency. If you have traveled abroad, you know that the exchange rate is of more than passing interest. Suppose that you are having dinner at a quaint London restaurant where steak and kidney pie costs ten pounds (£10). How much is that in U.S. money? If the exchange rate is £1 to $3, you'll be spending $30; if it's £1 to $1.50, the same meal will cost you only $15.

U.S. importers also want to know the dollar cost of British goods. A wool sweater that sells for £25 will cost the importer $75 if the exchange rate is £1 to $3, but it will cost $100 if the exchange rate is £1 to $4. Whenever the pound is cheaper (whenever it takes fewer dollars to purchase each pound), U.S. tourists and importers will find British goods more attractive. If the pound becomes more expensive, fewer tourists will opt for British vacations, and fewer British products will be imported into the United States.

Determining Exchange Rates

Today, exchange rates are determined primarily by market forces, by the interaction of the demand and supply of the various currencies. This is described as a system of **flexible**, or **floating**, **exchange rates**, since rates are free to move up or down with market forces.

To illustrate how the system works, assume that the United States and Britain are the only two countries in the world, so that we need to determine only one exchange rate, that between the U.S. dollar and the British pound. As you can see from Exhibit 16.4, the demand curve for pounds slopes downward because, ceteris paribus, as the price of the pound falls, Americans will tend to buy more British products. For example, if the dollar price of the pound fell from $2.00 per pound ($2.00 = £1) to $1.50 per pound ($1.50 = £1), U.S. consumers would tend to buy more wool fashions, Scotch whiskey, and London vacations. Of course, to buy these products, they would demand more British pounds. This assumes that the other factors affecting the demand for British pounds remain unchanged. The factors that are assumed to be constant include the tastes and preferences of U.S. consumers, interest rates in the United States and Britain, and the overall price levels in the two countries. If any of these factors changes, the entire demand curve will shift to a new position.

The British supply pounds when they want to purchase dollars. If British residents want to buy U.S. products or to visit Disneyland or to invest in California real estate, they exchange their pounds to buy dollars. The supply curve of pounds slopes upward because, other things being constant, as the value of the pound increases (which means that the dollar becomes less expensive), the British want to buy more U.S. products and will therefore supply more pounds. This assumes that the tastes and incomes of British consumers remain unchanged, that British and U.S. interest rates remain constant, and that the price levels in the United States and Britain are unchanged.

The Equilibrium Exchange Rate

The intersection of the supply and demand curves for British pounds determines the **equilibrium exchange rate**—the exchange rate at which the quantity of pounds demanded is exactly equal to the quantity supplied. In our example these market forces will lead to an equilibrium exchange rate of $1.50 = £1. At that rate 10 billion pounds are demanded and supplied.

If the exchange rate in our example were temporarily above or below the equilibrium level, pressures would exist to push it toward the equilibrium rate. For

EXHIBIT 16.4

The Equilibrium Exchange Rate

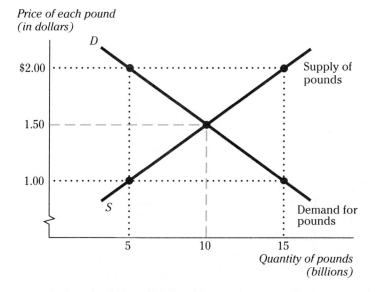

At the equilibrium exchange rate ($1.50 = £1), the quantity of pounds demanded is exactly equal to the quantity supplied. If the dollar price of the pound is too high for equilibrium, the resulting surplus will tend to reduce the price of the pound. If the price is too low for equilibrium, the shortage of pounds will tend to increase its price.

instance, if the exchange rate were $2.00 = £1, 15 billion pounds would be supplied, but only 5 billion would be demanded. This surplus of pounds would drive down the dollar price of the pound, just as a surplus drives down the price of wheat or cattle or anything else sold in a competitive market. At an exchange rate of $1.00 = £1, 15 billion pounds would be demanded but only 5 billion supplied, and the resulting shortage would tend to push the price of the pound upward. These pressures would exist until the equilibrium exchange rate had been established.

Changes in the Equilibrium Exchange Rate

Exchange rates can change frequently and sometimes quite dramatically. Any change that results in a shift of either the demand or the supply curve for a currency will cause the exchange rate to change. The factors that can shift the demand and supply curves include changes in tastes or income levels, changes in relative interest rates, and changes in price levels.

Changes in Tastes or Income Levels   Suppose that the average income in the United States increased. This would cause U.S. consumers to demand more goods and services, including British goods and services. The result would be an increase in the demand for British pounds: The demand curve for pounds would shift to the right, as depicted in Exhibit 16.5. The same thing would happen if Americans suddenly found British fashions more appealing or decided to switch from American beers to those imported from Britain.

When the demand curve for pounds shifts to the right, the dollar price of the pound is driven up. For example, in Exhibit 16.5 you can see that the dollar price

---

EXHIBIT 16.5

An Increase in the Demand for Pounds

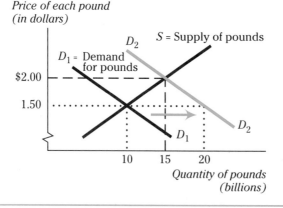

An increase in U.S. incomes or an increased preference for British products would tend to increase the demand for pounds. This would cause the pound to appreciate in value; each pound would buy more U.S. dollars than before. When the pound appreciates, the dollar depreciates; it takes more dollars to buy each pound.

EXHIBIT 16.6

An Increase in the Supply of Pounds

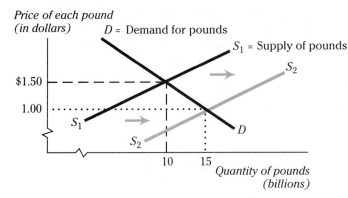

Price of each pound (in dollars)

An increase in British incomes or an increased preference for U.S. products would lead to an increase in the supply of pounds. This would cause the pound to depreciate and the dollar to appreciate.

of the pound has risen from $1.50 per pound to $2.00 per pound. The dollar has **depreciated** (lost value against the pound) because it now takes more dollars to buy each pound. Conversely, the pound has **appreciated** (gained value) against the dollar because each pound now buys more dollars than before.

How would we represent the impact of an increase in British incomes or an increased desire to buy American fashions—Levi's blue jeans, for example? Either of these changes would increase the demand for U.S. products and consequently would increase the demand for U.S. dollars. And the British acquire more dollars by supplying more pounds. Remember that! To acquire more dollars, the British must supply more pounds! As a consequence, the supply curve of pounds will shift to the right, as depicted in Exhibit 16.6. Would these changes cause the dollar to appreciate or to depreciate? What about the pound? Take a moment and try to answer these questions before reading further.

The correct answer is that an increase in the supply of pounds would cause the dollar to appreciate in value. As you can see from Exhibit 16.6, the dollar price of the pound has declined from $1.50 to only $1.00. The dollar must be more valuable—must have appreciated—because it now takes fewer dollars to buy a pound. Conversely, the pound has depreciated in value because each pound now buys fewer dollars than before.

Changes in Relative Interest Rates   In the short run, one of the most important sources of changes in exchange rates is changes in relative interest rates. If British interest rates increased relative to those in the United States, we could expect U.S. households and businesses to buy more British securities to earn the higher interest rates. This would shift the demand curve for pounds to the right (much like the situation in Exhibit 16.5) and cause the pound to appreciate relative

Use Your Economic Reasoning

UK Pound Drops to Record Low against Euro

BY EMILY FLYNN VENCAT

LONDON—The British pound fell to a record low against the euro on Monday, flirting with one pound per euro as two gloomy economic forecasts stoked expectations that the Bank of England will make further interest rate cuts next year. The pound fell to just euro1.022 [€1.022] Monday, its lowest since the euro's 1999 launch, after reports predicting unemployment will rise and house prices will fall in 2009. Those downbeat reports led currency traders to bet that the Bank of England will cut interest rates further early next year.

The rapid decline in the value of the pound, which has now fallen by around 13 percent against the common European currency this month alone, is making life tougher for British tourists, many of whom are already getting just

one euro for each pound. For instance, the Travelex foreign exchange company was on Monday selling euro1 for exactly 1 pound at its online store, where tourists can order foreign currencies for pickup in the company's outlets at tourist locations like airports.

The pound is being driven down by expectations that the Bank of England will cut interest rates to stimulate the economy, which shrank by 0.6 percent in the third quarter, and looks like it is heading into a serious recession. Interest rate cuts can weaken demand for a country's currency by reducing the yield on interest-bearing investments.

On Monday, Hometrack housing researchers said house prices fell by nearly 9 percent in 2008 and predicted that they would fall

to the dollar.[8] Of course, if U.S. interest rates rose relative to British rates, this situation would be reversed. British investors would want to purchase more U.S. securities. To accomplish this, they would demand dollars by supplying pounds (as in Exhibit 16.6). The result would be an appreciation of the dollar relative to the pound. (For a Brit's look at the impact of a change in relative interest rates, read "UK Pound Drops to Record Low against Euro," above.)

Changes in Relative Price Levels   Changes in relative price levels also influence exchange rates. To illustrate, imagine a U.S.-made automobile that sells for $30,000 in the United States and a comparable British auto that sells for

[8] The change in relative interest rates can also affect the *supply* of pounds. When British interest rates rise relative to U.S. rates, the British will tend to purchase fewer U.S. securities. This means they will supply fewer pounds than before—the supply curve of pounds will shift left. This also tends to appreciate the pound.

further next year. At the same time, the Chartered Institute of Personnel and Development predicted that employers will lay off at least 600,000 people in Britain next year, making 2009 the worst year for job cuts since 1991. "We all know that the economy is full of bad news for 2009—jobs are going to be scarce, GDP is going to fall, and inflation could drop below 1 percent," said James Hughes, a currency analyst with CMC Markets. "And so, we're expecting an interest rate cut of 50 to 100 basis points in January or February." In financial terminology 100 basis points is one percentage point.

The pound has fallen by more than 25 percent against the euro this year as the Bank of England has lowered interest rates from a peak of 5.75 percent to a more than 50-year low of 2 percent. Interest rates in the euro zone remain higher at 2.5 percent, despite a 0.75 percent cut by the European Central Bank earlier this month.

The lower pound raises costs for Britons when they travel to the 15 countries that use the euro, and raises the price of imported goods. Exporters, who usually benefit from a lower currency, are not getting much help from the pound's decline because the global economic slowdown is leading to weaker consumer demand in Britain's major export markets of the United States and Europe. The pound was little changed against the U.S. dollar on Monday at $1.4598. At this time last year, 1 pound would buy more than $2.

USE YOUR ECONOMIC REASONING

1. According to the article, the British pound is now buying 25 percent fewer euros than a year ago. Does that mean the pound has appreciated or depreciated in value?
2. Why will lower interest rates in Great Britain tend to drive down the value of the pound? Represent this situation graphically using demand and supply curves for the British pound.
3. The article states that exporters generally benefit from a lower currency (a cheaper pound). Explain. Why aren't they seeing that benefit in this case?

£20,000 in Britain. At an exchange rate of $1.50 = £1, these vehicles will have the same sticker prices; the U.S. auto will sell for £20,000 in Britain and the British auto for $30,000 in the United States. Consumers in each country will choose between these vehicles on the basis of design features, available options, and other nonprice characteristics.

Now, suppose that Britain experiences 20 percent inflation while inflation in the United States is only 10 percent. On average, prices in Britain will increase by 20 percent, so the price of the British auto will be pushed up to £24,000. U.S. prices, including automobile prices, will rise by only 10 percent, and so the U.S.-made automobile will now sell for $33,000. At an exchange rate of $1.50 = £1, U.S. automobiles now cost British consumers £22,000, whereas British automobiles will be available for $36,000 in the United States. The same thing will happen to the prices of the other products traded by the two countries. Because U.S. products have become more attractive in price, the result will be an increase in the supply of pounds (as British consumers demand more U.S. products) and a

EXHIBIT 16.7

The Effect of a Rise in the British Price Level

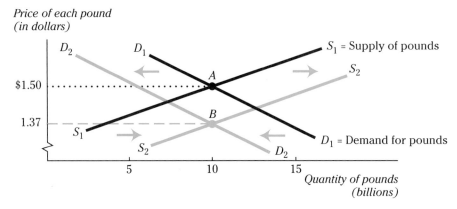

If prices in Britain rise in relation to those in the United States, U.S. products will become more attractive. British consumers will supply more pounds as they demand more U.S. products, and U.S. consumers will demand fewer pounds as they demand fewer British products. The dollar price of the pound will fall from $1.50 to $1.37 (we move from equilibrium point *A* to point *B*).

reduction in the demand for pounds (as U.S. consumers demand fewer British products). As you can see from Exhibit 16.7, these changes will cause the dollar price of the pound to fall from $1.50 to $1.37. The pound has depreciated in value, whereas the dollar has appreciated.

The Impact of Changes in Exchange Rates

How will Americans react when the dollar appreciates relative to the pound? Will they be happy about the stronger dollar or unhappy? (When the dollar appreciates relative to another currency, it is described as getting stronger, whereas the other currency has weakened.) In truth, it depends on which Americans we are talking about. Consider U.S. exporting firms, for example. If the dollar appreciates as it did in Exhibit 16.7, U.S. products will become more expensive for British consumers and thus less attractive. To illustrate, consider a computer that is selling for $1,500 in the United States. When the exchange rate is $1.50 = £1, that computer will cost British consumers £1,000. But if the dollar appreciates so that it takes only $1.00 to buy each pound, that same computer will cost British consumers £1,500. Predictably, fewer British consumers will buy U.S. computers at the higher price, and U.S. exporters will find their sales suffering as a result of the appreciation of the dollar. And if U.S. exports suffer, some U.S. workers lose their jobs.

The other side of the story has to do with U.S. importers of British products. A stronger dollar means a weaker pound. And a weaker pound means that British products will be cheaper for Americans. Consider a bottle of premium Scotch whiskey that sells for £40 in Britain. When the exchange rate is $2.00 = £1, that bottle of whiskey will cost a U.S. importer $80. But if the pound depreciates so that the exchange rate is $1.50 = £1, that same bottle of whiskey will cost a U.S. importer only $60. So the strong dollar will be welcomed by U.S. businesses that import foreign products and by U.S. consumers who buy those products. The point is that whenever the exchange rate changes, there are winners and losers; some individuals and businesses will like the change, and others will not.

MANAGING EXCHANGE RATES

Although changes in exchange rates are always unpopular with some groups, wide swings in exchange rates—whereby the currency appreciates or depreciates substantially in a relatively short period of time—are particularly disruptive. For example, in 1997 Indonesia, Malaysia, and South Korea saw the value of their currencies fall more than 50 percent against the dollar in a period of less than six months. This much volatility creates a great deal of risk for firms trading internationally because they cannot know how much imports will cost (in their own country's currency) or how much they will receive for their exports.[9] In addition, wide swings in exchange rates can have a major impact on the competitiveness of exporting firms and firms facing import competition. This, in turn, can translate into undesirable volatility in the level of employment. Because of these problems, many countries attempt to "manage" exchange rates—they attempt to influence exchange rates by altering the supply or demand for their currency.

The task of managing exchange rates is carried out by the world's central banks, the Federal Reserve and the Bank of England, for example. To illustrate how central bank intervention might occur, let's assume that the exchange rate between the dollar and the pound is initially $2 = £1. This is represented in Exhibit 16.8 by the intersection of demand curve D_1 and supply curve S_1. Now, suppose that the demand for British pounds increases, perhaps because rising U.S. incomes cause our citizens to demand more British products. As you can see, this will cause the dollar price of the pound to rise; the pound will appreciate and the dollar will depreciate.

---

[9] Many exporters and importers protect themselves against exchange rate changes by buying and selling foreign exchange in the "futures market." For example, if an importer wanted to protect itself against a change in the exchange rate, it would buy forward foreign exchange of the country whose products it was importing. This means that the importer buys foreign currency to be received in the future at an exchange rate agreed on now. This service is not free, so it increases the cost of trade. Because most futures contracts cover only a few months, long-term importing and exporting agreements remain risky.

EXHIBIT 16.8

Managing the Exchange Rate of the British Pound

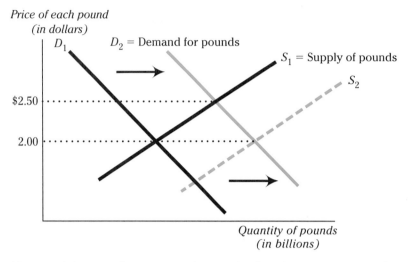

If the demand for pounds increases from D_1 to D_1, the pound will tend to appreciate. But if central banks are willing to supply additional pounds to the foreign exchange market—shifting the supply curve from S_1 to S_2, they can (at least temporarily) prevent this appreciation from occurring. This intervention is termed "managing the exchange rate."

If the Fed wants to prevent or slow this outcome, it could intervene in the foreign exchange market by using its reserve of pounds (the Fed has a reserve, or stockpile, of all major currencies) to buy dollars. By supplying pounds, the Fed would shift the supply curve of pounds to the right (to S_2 in Exhibit 16.8), maintaining the exchange rate at $2 = £1 and preventing the depreciation of the dollar. Because the Fed's reserves of pounds are limited, it won't be able to maintain this exchange rate indefinitely. It may, however, be successful in slowing the adjustment process and smoothing the transition to a weaker dollar.

Of course, the United States is not the only party with a stake in the prevailing exchange rate. Suppose it's the British central bank, the Bank of England, that wants to prevent the pound from appreciating, perhaps to protect its export sector. As before, the central bank will need to increase the supply of pounds to S_2 to maintain the exchange rate. (So, the bank would supply pounds and buy dollars.) As before, this process would make it possible to maintain the exchange rate at $2 = £1.[10]

---

[10] Because each country's central bank has an essentially unlimited supply of its own currency (but strictly limited reserves of foreign currencies), it is always easier for a central bank to weaken its currency—or prevent it from getting stronger—than to strengthen it.

Many economists are skeptical about a government's ability to manage exchange rates. As we've already noted, central banks have limited reserves of foreign currencies, so they can't prop up a nation's currency for very long. In addition, there has to be a degree of cooperation between the central banks of the currencies involved or any attempt at intervention is doomed to failure. For instance, if the Fed wants to prevent the dollar from appreciating and the Bank of England wants to hasten its appreciation, their efforts are likely to be offsetting. And, because sovereign governments commonly have different interests, it is unlikely that the needed cooperation will always be forthcoming. For these reasons and others, many economists are skeptical about the ability of central banks to manage exchange rates. Like it or not, businesses and consumers will have to learn to live with significant exchange rate volatility.

SUMMARY

The economies of the world are becoming more interdependent. Americans are buying more *imports*—goods or services purchased from foreigners—and foreign consumers are buying more of our *exports*—products produced domestically and sold in other countries. Although most countries can produce any product their citizens desire, trade may permit countries to import products much more cheaply—at a lower opportunity cost—than they can produce them domestically.

According to the theory of *comparative advantage*, each country should specialize in the products it can produce at a relatively low opportunity cost and trade for the items that other countries can produce efficiently. This principle will permit each nation to achieve a higher standard of living than it could possibly attain if it remained self-sufficient. Even when specialization is incomplete, trade can benefit consumers by providing them with a wider variety of products, limiting the pricing discretion of domestic producers, and forcing domestic producers to be more responsive to consumer demands.

Although free, or unrestricted, trade generally benefits consumers, it often imposes substantial costs on particular groups in any society—workers who are forced out of jobs by foreign competition, for instance. At least partly in response to pressure from these groups, countries erect *trade barriers*—legal restrictions on trade—to protect their domestic industries. The most common devices for restricting imports are protective tariffs and import quotas. A *tariff* is a tax on imported products. A tariff on a foreign product increases its price and makes it less competitive in the marketplace, thereby encouraging consumers to buy domestic products instead. An *import quota* specifies the maximum amount of a particular product that can be imported.

Economists tend to condemn all forms of trade barriers. Such barriers allow domestic producers to charge higher prices and to be less responsive to consumers. They also prevent countries from concentrating on the things they do best and trading for the best products produced by other countries. In the period following the Great Depression, the world's governments cooperated to reduce trade barriers. The General Agreement on Tariffs and Trade (GATT) produced seven rounds of negotiations, which substantially reduced the average tariff applied by industrial countries. The most recent round, completed in 1993, led to the formation of the World Trade Organization (WTO), a body intended to replace the GATT organization and extend its trade liberalization efforts. In addition to the GATT agreements, a number of regional trade agreements have been negotiated between particular countries or trading blocks. The North American Free Trade Agreement (NAFTA) and the European Union (EU) are example of regional trade agreements. Because these agreements reduce trade barriers within the trading block only, economists view them as less desirable than worldwide trade agreements such as GATT.

Although consumers benefit from more open trade, removal of trade barriers often imposes substantial costs on particular groups in society. When businesses are subjected to foreign competition, they may be forced to close their doors and lay off workers, who may have a difficult time finding employment elsewhere. Therefore, efforts to reduce trade barriers should be accompanied by programs to retrain workers and otherwise assist those harmed by foreign competition.

The feature that distinguishes international trade from trade within a nation is the need to convert the currency of one nation to the currency of some other nation. The rate at which one currency is exchanged for some other currency is called the *exchange rate*. Under a system of *flexible*, or *floating, exchange rates*, exchange rates are determined by market forces, by the interaction of demand and supply. At the equilibrium exchange rate, the quantity demanded of a currency is equal to the quantity supplied, and there is neither a shortage nor a surplus of the currency. The equilibrium exchange rate will change in response to the changes in the demand or supply of the currency being exchanged. When the exchange value of a nation's currency increases relative to other currencies, the currency has *appreciated* in value; when its exchange value declines, it has *depreciated* in value. Factors that will shift the demand and supply curves of currencies include changes in tastes and income levels in the trading countries, changes in relative interest in trading countries, and changes in relative prices in the trading countries. Central banks sometimes attempt to counteract these changes in demand or supply to *manage* a country's exchange rate.

KEY TERMS

Absolute advantage
Appreciated
Closed economy
Comparative advantage
Depreciated
Dumping

Equilibrium exchange rate
Exchange rate
Exports
Flexible (floating) exchange
  rate
Import quota

Imports
Open economy
Tariff
Terms of trade
Trade deficit
Trade surplus

STUDY QUESTIONS

Fill in the Blanks

1. If country A can produce all products more efficiently than country B, country A is said to have a(n)

   _____ in the production of that product.

2. If country A can produce a given product at a lower opportunity cost than country B, country A is said to have a(n)

   _____ in the production of that product.

3. A(n) _____ is a tax on imported products.

4. A(n) _____ specifies the maximum amount of a particular product that can be imported.

5. Aid to workers who have been harmed by foreign competition is called

   _____.

6. In most situations the (benefits/costs)

   _____ of free trade are widely diffused, whereas the

   (benefits/costs) _____ tend to be concentrated.

7. Most economists would like to see trade barriers eliminated. However, if they are forced to choose between tariffs and quotas, they would probably agree that

   _____ are less damaging to consumer welfare.

8. The _____ replaced GATT as the organization for settling international trade disputes.

9. Under a system of flexible exchange rates, if it takes more British pounds than before to buy a U.S. dollar, we can say that the

   dollar has _____ and that

   the pound has _____.

10. If interest rates are higher in the United States than they are abroad, foreign investors will tend to invest more money in the United States, and the dollar will tend to (appreciate/depreciate)

    _____ in value.

11. If the dollar appreciates in value, it will be

    (harder/easier) _____ for U.S. producers to sell their products abroad.

Multiple Choice

Use the following information in answering questions 1–4. All figures in millions.

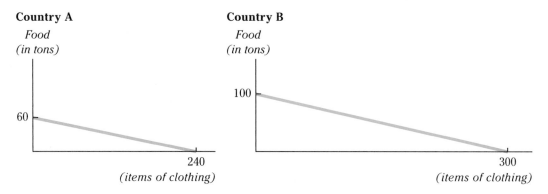

Country A

Food
(in tons)

60

240
(items of clothing)

Country B

Food
(in tons)

100

300
(items of clothing)

1. In country A, the opportunity cost of a ton of food is
   a) 4 units of clothing.
   b) 60 units of clothing.
   c) 240 units of clothing.
   d) 1 unit of clothing.

2. According to the table,
   a) country A has a comparative advantage in food.
   b) country B has a comparative advantage in clothing.
   c) country A has a comparative advantage in clothing.
   d) country B has a comparative advantage in both food and clothing.

3. According to the principle of comparative advantage,
   a) country A should specialize in food, and country B should specialize in clothing.
   b) countries A and B should each continue to produce both food and clothing.
   c) country A should specialize in clothing, and country B should specialize in food.
   d) country B should specialize in clothing, and country A should specialize in food.

4. Which of the following is most likely to represent terms of trade that both countries would agree to accept?
   a) 1 ton of food exchanges for 4 units of clothing
   b) 1 ton of food exchanges for 3 units of clothing
   c) 1 ton of food exchanges for 5 units of clothing
   d) 1 ton of food exchanges for 3.5 units of clothing

5. Which of the following is *not* a correct statement about trade barriers?
   a) Import tariffs are taxes on imports.
   b) Tariffs encourage consumers to buy domestic products.
   c) Quotas specify the maximum amount of a product that can be imported.
   d) Tariffs are probably more harmful to consumer welfare than quotas.

6. Which of the following is an accurate description of the impact of tariffs?
   a) They tend to raise the prices of imported products that are subject to the tariff.
   b) They tend to raise the prices of domestically produced products that are comparable to those being taxed.

c) They permit inefficient industries to continue to exist.

d) All of the above

7. Suppose that Italy can produce a maximum or either 20 million bicycles or 100 million calculators while Taiwan can produce either 10 million bicycles or 80 million calculators. Which of the following statement is true?

a) Taiwan has a comparative advantage in bicycles.

b) Italy has a comparative advantage in calculators.

c) Taiwan has a comparative advantage in calculators.

d) Taiwan has a comparative advantage in both calculators and bicycles.

8. Why do economists prefer tariffs to quotas?

a) Consumers may continue to buy imported products despite the tariff.

b) Tariffs do not really hinder trade; in fact, they may enhance trade.

c) As domestic products increase in price, foreign products become more competitive.

d) Both a and c

9. Dumping occurs whenever a firm

a) charges a lower price in foreign markets than it charges in its home market.

b) sells a lower-quality product in foreign markets than it sells in its home market.

c) earns economic profits on its sales to foreign markets.

d) disposes of wastes by shipping them to disposal sites in foreign countries.

10. Which of the following is not a source of foreign exchange for the United States?

a) Foreign tourists visiting the United States

b) U.S. exports to France

c) U.S. imports from Japan

d) German investments in the United States

11. If Americans decide to buy more Japanese automobiles,

a) the demand curve for Japanese yen will shift to the left.

b) the demand curve for American dollars will shift to the right.

c) the demand curve for Japanese yen will shift to the right.

d) the supply curve of Japanese yen will shift to the right.

12. If interest rates in the euro zone increased relative to those in the United States,

a) Americans would tend to demand fewer euros.

b) Europeans would tend to supply more euros.

c) the euro would tend to appreciate relative to the dollar.

d) the dollar would tend to appreciate relative to the euro.

13. If the price level in Japan increases more rapidly than the price level in the United States,

a) the Japanese will tend to supply more yen, appreciating the dollar relative to the yen.

b) the Japanese will tend to supply fewer yen, appreciating the dollar relative to the yen.

c) U.S. consumers will tend to demand more yen, depreciating the dollar relative to the yen.

d) U.S. consumers will tend to demand more yen, appreciating the dollar relative to the yen.

14. If the European central bank intervenes in the foreign exchange market by buying dollars for euros, the intervention would tend to

a) depreciate the dollar relative to the euro.

b) appreciate the euro relative to the dollar.

c) depreciate both the euro and the dollar.

d) appreciate the dollar.

15. If the British decide to purchase more U.S. products,

a) the demand curve for the British pound will shift to the right

b) the supply curve of the British pound will shift to the right.

c) the supply curve of the American dollar will shift to the right.

d) the supply curve of the American dollar will shift to the left.

16. If the yen price of the dollar (the price of a dollar stated in terms of Japanese yen) declined,

a) Japanese cars would cost Americans fewer dollars.

b) Japanese tourists would find American meals less expensive.

c) American cars would cost Japanese consumers more yen.

d) American tourists would be encouraged to tour Japan.

Problems and Questions for Discussion

1. Suppose that your roommate can make a bed in three minutes, whereas it takes you six minutes. Suppose also that your roommate can polish a pair of shoes in ten minutes, whereas it takes you 15 minutes to do the same chore. What can we say about comparative advantage and absolute advantage in this example? How could the principle of comparative advantage be used to make you both better off? Does it make any difference how often each of these tasks must be performed?

2. Explain the difference between comparative advantage and absolute advantage. Why do economists emphasize the concept of comparative advantage (rather than absolute advantage) as the basis for trade?

3. The chapter mentions that politicians in the United States and elsewhere often hear more about the costs of free trade than the benefits. Why is that the case?

4. How do trade barriers contribute to the inefficient use of a society's scarce resources?

5. Some economists have suggested that interference with free trade may be legitimate if it is used as a bargaining chip to convince another country to lower its trade barriers. Economist Robert Lawrence has criticized this approach, likening it to a nuclear deterrent—something that is effective only if it isn't used. Explain Lawrence's position.

6. If resources (including labor) could move freely from one industry to the next, there would be less opposition to the removal of trade barriers. Explain.

7. As University of Wisconsin economist John Culbertson once suggested, "There is little comparative advantage in today's manufacturing industries, since they produce the same goods in the same ways in all parts of the world." ("'Free Trade' Is Impoverishing the West," *New York Times*, July 28, 1985, p. F3.) How could less-developed countries gain access to the same type of capital equipment employed by the United States? Could they operate it if they could obtain it? What are the implications of Culbertson's statement?

8. Why are regional trade agreements, such as NAFTA, sometimes viewed as inferior to international agreements, such as GATT?

9. How can domestic firms use antidumping laws to stifle foreign competition?

10. If you were visiting London, which exchange rate would you prefer: $4 to £1 or $3 to £1? Why?

11. Suppose that we are operating under a system of flexible exchange rates. If Americans demand more British automobiles, will the dollar tend to appreciate or depreciate? Show this result graphically. What about the pound? Will it appreciate or depreciate?

12. Japan's central bank has often intervened to buy dollars and prevent the dollar from depreciating relative to the yen. What is the rationale for such intervention?

13. Japan's central bank is in a better position to keep the dollar from deprecating than is the U.S. central bank (the Fed). Why? (*Hint:* How would the Fed go about trying to appreciate the dollar?)

14. Suppose that the Fed pursues a restrictive monetary policy to combat inflation in the United States. What impact would this policy have on the exchange value of the dollar relative to other currencies?

15. If Europe's economy entered a recession, what impact would this have on the exchange rate between the euro and the U.S. dollar? Why would it have this impact?

ANSWER KEY

Fill in the Blanks

1. absolute advantage
2. comparative advantage
3. tariff
4. quota
5. trade adjustment assistance
6. benefits; cost
7. tariffs
8. WTO
9. appreciated; depreciated
10. appreciate
11. harder

Multiple Choice

1. a
2. c
3. c
4. d
5. d
6. d
7. c
8. d
9. a
10. c
11. c
12. c
13. a
14. d
15. b
16. b

GLOSSARY

Absolute advantage. One nation's ability to produce a product more efficiently—with fewer resources—than another nation.

Activist economists. Economists who see an important role for government in guiding the economy's performance.

Aggregate demand. The total quantity of output demanded by all sectors in the economy together at various price levels in a given time period.

Aggregate supply. The total quantity of output supplied by all producers in the economy together at various price levels in a given time period.

Allocative efficiency. Using society's scarce resources to produce in the proper quantities the products that consumers value most.

Annual inflation rate. The percent change in a price index from one year to the next.

Antitrust laws. Laws that have as their objective the maintenance and promotion of competition.

Applied research. Research conducted with a commercial purpose in mind.

Appreciation of currency. An increase in the exchange value of a currency relative to other currencies.

Asset. Anything of value owned by an entity.

Automatic stabilizers. Changes in the level of government spending or taxation that occur automatically whenever the level of aggregate income (GDP) changes.

Average fixed cost (AFC). Total fixed cost divided by the number of units being produced.

Average total cost (ATC). Total cost divided by the number of units being produced.

Average variable cost (AVC). Total variable cost divided by the number of units being produced.

Balanced budget. A situation in which government tax revenue is exactly equal to government expenditures.

Balance sheet. A statement of a business's assets and liabilities.

Bank capital. The owners' claims on the assets of the business; it is equal to assets minus liabilities. Also known as *equity capital* and *owners' equity.*

Barriers to entry. Obstacles that discourage or prevent firms from entering an industry; examples include patent restrictions, large investment requirements, and restrictive licensing regulations.

Basic research. Research conducted to gain knowledge for its own sake.

Budget deficit. The situation that exists when government expenditures exceed tax revenues.

Budget surplus. The situation that exists when government tax receipts exceed government expenditures.

Business cycle. The recurring ups and downs in the level of economic activity.

Capital. Physical aids to the production process; for example, factories, machinery, and tools.

Capitalism. An economic system in which the means of production are privately owned and fundamental economic choices are made by individual buyers and sellers interacting in markets.

Cartel. A group of producers acting together to control output and the price of their product.

Central bank. A government agency responsible for controlling a nation's money supply.

Ceteris paribus. "Other things being equal"; the assumption that other variables remain constant.

Change in demand. An increase or decrease in the quantity demanded at each possible price, caused by a change in the determinants of demand; represented graphically by a shift of the entire demand curve to a new position.

Change in quantity demanded. An increase or decrease in the amount of a product demanded as a result of a change in its price, with factors other than price held constant; represented graphically by movement along a stationary demand curve.

Change in quantity supplied. An increase or decrease in the amount of a product supplied as a result of a change in its price, with factors other than price held constant; represented graphically by movement along a stationary supply curve.

Change in supply. An increase or decrease in the amount of a product supplied at each and every price, caused by a change in the determinants of supply; represented graphically by a shift of the entire supply curve.

Checkable deposits. All types of deposits on which customers can write checks.

Civilian labor force. All persons over the age of sixteen who are not in the armed forces and who are either employed or actively seeking employment.

Civilian unemployment rate. The percentage of the civilian labor force that is unemployed.

Classical economists. A school of eighteenth- and nineteenth-century economists who believed that market economies automatically tend toward full employment.

Closed economy. An economy that does not exchange goods and services with other nations.

Coefficient of demand elasticity. A value that indicates the degree to which quantity demanded will change in response to a price change.

Coefficient of supply elasticity. A value that indicates the degree to which the quantity supplied will change in response to a price change.

Collusion. Agreement among sellers to fix prices or in some other way restrict competition.

Command socialism. An economic system in which the means of production are publicly owned and the fundamental economic choices are made by a central authority.

Common-property resources. Resources that belong to society as a whole rather than to particular individuals.

Comparative advantage. One nation's ability to produce a product at a lower opportunity cost than other nations.

Complement. A product that is normally purchased along with another good or in conjunction with another good.

Conscious parallelism. A situation in which firms adopt similar policies even though they have had no communication whatsoever.

Consumer sovereignty. An economic condition in which consumers dictate which goods and services will be produced by businesses.

Consumption tax. A tax assessed on the amount spent. Also called an *expenditure tax*.

Cost-benefit analysis. A systematic comparison of costs and benefits.

Cost-push inflation. Inflation caused by rising costs of production.

Crowding out. The phenomenon that occurs when increased government borrowing drives up interest rates and thereby reduces the level of investment spending.

Cyclical unemployment. Joblessness caused by a reduction in the economy's total demand for goods and services.

Deficiency payment. A payment made to farmers on a price-support program; equal to the difference between the market price and the support price times the number of bushels sold.

Demand. A schedule showing the quantities of a good or service that consumers are willing and able to purchase at various prices during a given time period, when all factors other than the product's price remain unchanged.

Demand curve. A graphical representation of demand, showing the quantities of a good or service that consumers are willing and able to purchase at various prices during a given time period, ceteris paribus.

Demand deposits. Non-interest-bearing checking accounts at commercial banks.

Demand-pull inflation. Inflation caused by increases in aggregate demand.

Deposit multiplier. The multiple by which checkable deposits (in the entire banking system) increase or decrease in response to an initial change in excess reserves.

Depreciation of currency. A decrease in the exchange value of a currency relative to other currencies.

Determinants of demand. The factors that underlie the demand schedule and determine the precise position of the demand curve: income, tastes and preferences, expectations regarding prices, the prices of related goods, and the number of consumers in the market.

Determinants of supply. The factors that underlie the supply schedule and determine the precise position of the supply curve: technology, resource prices, and number of producers in the market.

Discount rate. The rate of interest charged by the Federal Reserve on loans to depository institutions.

Discretionary fiscal policy. The deliberate changing of the level of government spending or taxation in order to guide the economy's performance.

Diseconomies of scale. Increases in the average cost of production caused by larger plant size and scale of output.

Dominant strategy. A strategy that should be pursued regardless of the strategy selected by a firm's rivals.

Dumping. The sale of a product to foreign consumers at a price that is less than the cost of producing that good or service.

Economic growth. An increase in an economy's production capacity or potential GDP.

Economic indicators. Signals or measures that tell us how well the economy is performing.

Economic loss. The amount by which total cost, including all opportunity costs, exceeds total revenue.

Economic profit. The amount by which total revenue exceeds total cost, including the opportunity cost of owner-supplied resources; also called an *above-normal profit.*

Economic resources. The scarce inputs used in the process of creating a good or providing a service; specifically, land, labor, capital, and entrepreneurship.

Economics. The study of how to use our limited resources to satisfy our unlimited wants as fully as possible.

Economic system. The set of institutions and mechanisms by which a society provides answers to the three fundamental questions.

Economic theories. Generalizations about causal relationships between economic facts, or variables.

Economies of scale. Reductions in the average cost of production caused by larger plant size and scale of output.

Entrepreneurship. The managerial function that combines land, labor, and capital in a cost-effective way and uncovers new opportunities to earn profit; includes willingness to take the risks associated with a business venture.

Equilibrium exchange rate. The exchange rate at which the quantity of a currency demanded is equal to the quantity supplied.

Equilibrium price. The price that brings about an equality between the quantity demanded and the quantity supplied.

Equilibrium quantity. The quantity demanded and supplied at the equilibrium price.

Equity capital. The owners' claims on the assets of the business; it is equal to assets minus liabilities. Also known as *bank capital* and *owners' equity.*

Excess reserves. Bank reserves in excess of the amount required by law.

Exchange rate. The price of one nation's currency stated in terms of another nation's currency.

Exchange rate risk. The risk of losing income or wealth when the exchange rate changes unexpectedly.

Excise tax. A tax levied on the sale of specific products.

Expenditure tax. A tax assessed on the amount spent. Also called a *consumption tax.*

Explicit cost. A cost that is easily recognized because it involves a monetary payment.

Exports. Goods and services produced domestically and sold to customers in other countries.

External benefits. Benefits paid for by one party or group that spill over to other parties or groups; also referred to as *spillover benefits.*

External costs. Costs created by one party or group and imposed on other (unconsenting) parties or groups; also referred to as *spillover costs.*

Externalities. Costs or benefits that are not borne by either buyers or sellers but that spill over onto third parties.

Federal budget. A statement of the federal government's planned expenditures and anticipated receipts for the upcoming year.

Federal funds market. A market that brings together banks in need of reserves and banks that temporarily have excess reserves.

Federal funds rate. The rate of interest charged by banks for lending reserves to other banks.

Financial capital. Money.

Firm. The basic producing unit in a market economy. Firms buy economic resources and combine them to produce goods and services.

Fixed costs. Costs that do not vary with the level of the activity in which the individual or business is engaged and that cannot be avoided; for businesses, costs that do not change with the level of output.

Flexible exchange rate. An exchange rate that is determined by market forces, by the supply and demand for the currency. Also described as a *floating exchange rate*.

Floating exchange rate. See *flexible exchange rate*.

Fractional reserve principle. The principle that a bank needs to maintain only a fraction of a dollar in reserve for each dollar of its demand deposits.

Free trade. Trade that is not hindered by artificial restrictions or trade barriers of any type.

Frictional unemployment. People who are out of work because they are in the process of changing jobs or are searching for their first job.

Full employment. When the actual rate of unemployment is equal to the natural rate of unemployment.

Game theory. The study of the strategies employed by interdependent firms.

Government failure. The enactment of government policies that produce inefficient and/or inequitable results.

Government franchise. An exclusive license to provide some product or service.

Gross domestic product. The total monetary value of all final goods and services produced within a nation in one year.

Gross national product. The total monetary value of all final goods and services produced by domestically owned factors of production in one year.

Household. A living unit that also functions as an economic unit. Whether it consists of a single person or a large family, each household has a source of income and responsibility for spending that income.

Human capital. The knowledge and skills that are embodied in labor. Human capital is acquired through education and training.

Implicit cost. A nonmonetary cost associated with using your own resources.

Import quota. A law that specifies the maximum amount of a particular product that can be imported.

Imports. Goods and services that are purchased from foreign producers.

Income effect. Consumer ability to purchase greater quantities of a product that has declined in price.

Industry. A group of firms that produce identical or similar products.

Industry structure. The makeup of an industry: its number of sellers and their size distribution, the nature of the product, and the extent of barriers to entry.

Inferior good. A product for which demand decreases as income increases and increases as income decreases.

Inflation. A rise in the general level of prices.

Inflationary gap. The amount by which the equilibrium level of real GDP exceeds potential GDP.

Innovation. The process of converting an invention into something marketable.

Interest rate effect. The increase in the amount of aggregate output demanded that results from the lower interest rates that accompany a reduction in the overall price level.

Internal benefits. The benefits accruing to the person or persons purchasing a good or service; also referred to as *private benefits*.

Internal costs. The costs borne by the firm that produces the good or service; also referred to as *private costs*.

Internalize costs. Consider external costs as if they were private costs.

International economics. The study of international trade and finance: why nations trade and how their transactions are financed.

International trade effect. The increase in the amount of aggregate output demanded that results when a reduction in the price level makes domestic products less expensive in relation to foreign products.

Invention. The discovery of new products or processes that might have practical applications.

Investment tax credit. A tax reduction available to firms that invest in eligible equipment.

Invisible hand. A doctrine introduced by Adam Smith in 1776 holding that individuals pursuing their self-interest will be guided (as if by an invisible hand) to achieve objectives that are also in the best interest of society as a whole.

Joint research venture. Research projects in which firms pool their resources and share the costs of research and development.

Labor. The mental and physical work of those employed in the production process.

Laissez-faire economy. An economy in which the degree of government intervention is minimal.

Land. All the natural resources or raw materials used in production; for example, acreage, timber, water, iron ore.

Law of demand. The quantity demanded of a product is negatively, or inversely, related to its price. Consumers will purchase more of a product at lower prices than at higher prices.

Law of increasing costs. As more of a particular product is produced, the opportunity cost per unit will increase.

Law of supply. The quantity supplied of a product is positively, or directly, related to its price. Producers will supply a larger quantity at higher prices than at lower prices.

Liabilities. The debts of an entity, or what it owes.

Lifetime Learning Tax Credit. A federal program that provides a tax deduction equal to 20 percent of the cost of qualified educational expenses.

Loanable funds market. The market in which businesses and households borrow funds to make investments.

Logrolling. The trading of votes to gain support for a proposal.

Long run. The period of time during which all a business's inputs, including plant and equipment, can be changed.

Long-run equilibrium. A situation in which the size of an industry is stable: there is no incentive for additional firms to enter the industry and no pressure for established firms to leave it.

Loss. The excess of total cost over total revenue.

M-1. Federal Reserve definition of the money supply that includes currency in the hands of the public plus all checkable deposits; the narrowest definition of the money supply.

M-2. Federal Reserve definition of the money supply that includes all of M-1 plus money-market mutual fund balances, money-market deposits at savings institutions, and small savings deposits.

Macroeconomics. The study of the economy as a whole and the factors that influence the economy's overall performance.

Managed exchange rates. Exchange rates that are determined by market forces with some intervention by central banks. Also described as a *managed float.*

Managed float. See *managed exchange rates.*

Marginal. Additional or extra.

Marginal cost (MC). The additional cost of producing one more unit of output.

Marginal revenue (MR). The additional revenue to be gained by selling one more unit of output.

Marginal social benefit. The benefit that the consumption of another unit of output conveys to society.

Marginal social cost. The cost that the production of another unit of output imposes on society.

Market. All actual or potential buyers and sellers of a particular item. Markets can be international, national, regional, or local.

Market failure. Situations in which a market economy produces too much or too little of certain products and thus does not make the most efficient use of society's limited resources.

Market power. Pricing discretion; the ability of a firm to influence the market price of its product.

Means of production. The raw materials, factories, farms, and other economic resources used to produce goods and services.

Medium of exchange. A generally accepted means of payment for goods and services; one of the three basic functions of money.

Merger. The union of two or more companies into a single firm.

Microeconomics. The study of the behavior of individual economic units.

Mixed economies. Economies that represent a blending of capitalism and socialism. All real-world economies are mixed economies.

Monetarism. The belief that changes in the money supply play the primary role in determining the level of aggregate output and prices in the economy.

Monetary policy. Any action intended to alter the supply of money to influence the level of total spending and thereby combat unemployment or inflation.

Monetary rule. A rule that would require the Federal Reserve to increase the money supply at a constant rate.

Monopolistic competition. An industry structure characterized by a large number of small sellers of slightly differentiated products and by modest barriers to entry.

Monopoly. An industry structure characterized by a single firm selling a product for which there are no close substitutes and by substantial barriers to entry.

Motivating. The function of providing incentives to supply the proper quantities of demanded products.

Nash equilibrium. A situation in which each firm's strategy is the best it can choose, given the strategies chosen by the other firms in the industry.

National saving. The sum of private saving and public saving; the total amount of saving taking place in an economy.

Natural monopoly. A situation in which a single firm can supply the entire market at a lower average cost than two or more firms could.

Natural rate of unemployment. The minimum level of unemployment that an economy can achieve in normal times. The rate of unemployment that would exist in the absence of cyclical unemployment.

Near money. Assets that are not money but that can be converted quickly to money.

Nonactivist economists. Economists who do not believe that government should play an active role in attempting to guide the economy's performance.

Normal good. A product for which demand increases as income increases and decreases as income decreases.

Normal profit. An amount equal to what the owners of a business could have earned if their resources had been employed elsewhere; the opportunity cost of owner-supplied resources.

Normative judgments. Value judgments about what should be, rather than what is.

NOW account. A savings account on which the depositor can write checks; NOW stands for negotiable order of withdrawal.

Official reserve transactions. The purchase and sale of reserve assets by central banks.

Oligopoly. An industry structure characterized by a few relatively large sellers and substantial barriers to entry.

Open economy. An economy that exchanges goods and services with other nations.

Open-market operations. The buying and selling of government securities by the Federal Reserve as a means of influencing the money supply.

Opportunity cost. The best, or most valued, alternative that is sacrificed when a particular action is taken.

Owners' equity. The owners' claims on the assets of the business; it is equal to assets minus liabilities.

Physical capital. Physical aids to production. Examples include machines, tools, and factories.

Policy ineffectiveness theorem. The theory that systematic monetary and fiscal policies cannot alter the level of output or employment in the economy; they can change only the price level.

Price ceiling. A legally established maximum price below the equilibrium price.

Price discrimination. The practice of charging different consumers different prices for the same product.

Price elasticity of demand. A measure of the responsiveness of the quantity demanded of a product to a change in its price.

Price elasticity of supply. A measure of the responsiveness of the quantity supplied of a product to a change in its price.

Price index. A measure of changes in the general level of prices. Three basic price indexes are used in the United States: the Consumer Price Index, the Producer Price Index, and the Implicit Price Deflator.

Price leadership. An informal arrangement whereby a single firm takes the lead in all price changes in the industry.

Price searcher. A firm that possesses pricing discretion.

Price support. A legally established minimum price above the equilibrium price.

Price taker. A firm that must accept price as a given that is beyond its control.

Private benefits. The benefits accruing to the person or persons purchasing a good or service; also referred to as *internal benefits.*

Private costs. The costs borne by the firm that produces the good or service; also referred to as *internal costs.*

Private goods that yield significant external benefits. Products that convey most of their benefits to the person making the purchase but also create substantial external benefits for other individuals or groups.

Private saving. The amount of income that households have left over after subtracting taxes and consumption spending.

Product differentiation. Distinguishing a product from similar products offered by other sellers in the industry through advertising, packaging, or physical product differences.

Production efficiency. Producing a product at the lowest possible average total cost. The essence of production efficiency is that each product is produced with the fewest possible scarce resources.

Production possibilities curve. A curve that shows the combinations of goods that an economy is capable of producing with its present stock of economic resources and existing techniques of production.

Productivity of labor. The amount of output the average worker is able to produce. A common measure of the productivity of labor is output per hour.

Profit. The excess of a business's total revenue over its total cost.

Profit maximizer. A business that attempts to earn as much profit as possible.

Property rights. The legal rights to use goods, services, or resources.

Public choice. The study of how government makes economic decisions.

Public debt. The accumulated borrowings of the federal government; also known as the *national debt.*

Public goods. Products that convey their benefits equally to paying and nonpaying members of society.

Public saving. The amount of tax revenue that is left over after the government pays for its spending.

Pure competition. A situation in which a large number of relatively small buyers and sellers interact.

Pure private goods. Products that convey their benefits only to the purchaser.

Rationing. The function of dividing up or allocating a society's scarce items among those who want them.

Real balance effect. The increase in the amount of aggregate output demanded that results from an increase in the real value of the public's financial assets.

Real gross domestic product. Gross domestic product that has been adjusted to eliminate the impact of changes in the price level.

Real income. The purchasing power of your income; the amount of goods and services it will buy.

Recessionary gap. The amount by which the equilibrium level of real GDP falls short of potential GDP.

Rent ceiling. A legally established maximum rent below the equilibrium rent.

Research. The process of gaining new knowledge. Research is sometimes characterized as *basic research* or *applied research.*

Research and development. The term used to describe the three stages leading to technological advances: research, invention, and innovation.

Reserve requirement. The fraction of a bank's checkable deposits that must be held as required reserves. These reserves must be in the form of vault cash or deposits with the Federal Reserve.

Rule of seventy-two. The mathematical principle that a variable's doubling time roughly equals seventy-two divided by the growth rate.

Savings deposits. Interest-bearing deposits at commercial banks and savings institutions.

Secondary rationing device. A nonprice condition that supplements the primary rationing device, which is price.

Shortage. An excess of quantity demanded over quantity supplied.

Short run. The period of time during which at least one of a business's inputs (usually plant and equipment) is fixed—that is, incapable of being changed.

Shut down. To temporarily stop producing output.

Social benefit. The full benefit received by all the members of society; the sum of private benefits and external benefits.

Social cost. The full cost to a society of the production and/or consumption of a product; the sum of private, or internal, costs and external costs.

Stagflation. High unemployment combined with high inflation.

Standard of value. A unit in which the prices of goods and services can be expressed; one of the three basic functions of money.

Store of value. A vehicle for accumulating or storing wealth to be used at a future date; one of the three basic functions of money.

Structural unemployment. Unemployment caused by changes in the makeup, or structure, of the economy, whereby some skills become obsolete or in less demand.

Subsidy. A payment that government makes to private producers or consumers for each unit of output that they produce or purchase.

Substitute. A product that can be used in place of some other product because, to a greater or lesser extent, it satisfies the same consumer wants.

Substitution effect. Consumers' willingness to substitute for other products the product that has declined in price.

Sunk cost. Costs that cannot be avoided.

Supply. A schedule showing the quantities of a good or service that producers are willing and able to offer for sale at various prices during a given time period, when all factors other than the product's price remain unchanged.

Supply curve. A graphical representation of supply.

Supply-side economics. The branch of economics that focuses on stimulating aggregate supply through policies that involve minimal government intervention.

Surplus. An excess of quantity supplied over quantity demanded.

Tariff. A tax on imported goods.

Technological advance. Discovery that makes it possible to produce more or better products from the same resources.

Technology. The state of knowledge about how to produce products.

Terms of trade. The price a country receives for its exported product(s) relative to the price the country must pay for its imported product(s).

Theories. Generalizations about causal relationships between facts, or variables.

Theory of rational expectations. The theory that people use all available information to develop realistic expectations about the future.

Total cost (TC). Total fixed cost plus total variable cost.

Total revenue (TR). The total receipts of a business from the sale of its product. Total revenue is calculated by multiplying the selling price of the product times the number of units sold.

Trade adjustment assistance. Aid to workers and firms that have been harmed by import competition.

Trade barriers. Legal restrictions on trade.

Trade deficit. Imports of goods and services exceed exports of goods and services for an unfavorable balance of trade.

Trade surplus. Exports of goods and services exceed imports of goods and services for an unfavorable balance of trade.

Transfer payments. Expenditures for which no goods and services are received in exchange.

Trusts. Combinations of firms organized for the purpose of restraining competition and thereby gaining economic profit.

Tying contract. An agreement specifying that the purchaser will, as a condition of sale for some product, also buy some other product offered by the seller.

Unemployment rate. See *civilian unemployment rate*.

Utility. Personal satisfaction.

Variable costs. Costs that change with the level of output, tending to increase when output increases and to decrease when output declines.

INDEX

Page numbers followed by *f* indicate figures.
Page numbers followed by *n* indicate footnotes.